Marketing Communications

Marketing Communications

A Brand Narrative Approach

Micael Dahlén

Fredrik Lange

Terry Smith

A John Wiley and Sons, Ltd, Publication

Library of Congress Cataloging-in-Publication Data

Dahlén, Micael.
  Marketing communications : a brand narrative approach / Micael Dahlén,
Fredrik Lange, Terry Smith.
      p. cm.
  Includes bibliographical references and index.
  ISBN 978-0-470-31992-5 (pbk.)
    1. Communication in marketing.   2. Branding (Marketing)   I. Lange, Fredrik.
  II. Smith, Terry, 1955-   III. Title.
  HF5415.123.D34 2010
  658.8'02—dc22

                                                                    2009025220

A catalogue record for this book is available from the British Library.

Set in 9/11pt ITC Garamond by Thomson Digital, India
Printed in Spain by Grafos, SA

Brief Contents

Contents

List of Cases

Chapter 7: Tactics and Techniques of Positioning

Chapter 8: Building Brand Equity

Chapter 9 : Brand Narrative and Relational Management

Chapter 10: The Marketing Communications Mix

Chapter 11: Advertising Strategy

Chapter 12: Advertising Creativity

Chapter 13: Media Concepts and Media Planning

Chapter 14: Public Relations and Hybrid Marketing Communications

Chapter 15: Sales and Sales Promotion

Chapter 16: Beyond Traditional Marketing Communications

Chapter 17: Evaluating Marketing Communications

Preface

The cornerstones of good marketing communications are target audience, message and media, with integration and interactivity being crucial requirements. The context within which these are set is dynamic and all have been exposed to change: consumers live in an information-obsessed, media-saturated world with an incredible choice of brands; the impact of technology has altered the way we see, read and process communication messages; and the need to engage audiences with a compelling message is absolutely critical to successful marketing communications. In this text we examine fully integrated '360° campaign planning' and the implementation of idea-driven, and media-neutral marketing communications. We therefore look closely at:

1. The traditional tools of communications: advertising, public relations, direct marketing, personal selling and promotional activities.
2. The 'hybrid' communications tools such as the 'captured content' of product placement.
3. The new emerging developments which have taken marketing communications beyond the traditional mix of tools and media.
4. Various contexts (such as not for profit and business to business) which provide unique challenges to marketing communications.
5. The rise of consumer-generated content.

Students will be introduced to the mechanics and magic of marketing communications in its modern environment, with a comprehensive discussion of the conceptual frameworks of successful campaign planning and implementation.

UNIQUE CHARACTER OF THE BOOK

This text offers an innovative approach with a coherent 'brand narrative' thread that interweaves the concepts and contexts of both marketing communications and branding. It has a practical, entertaining texture underpinned with current real-world dynamics and academic research. It features the following differentiating elements:

- **Marketing communications orientation:** books on marketing communications generally espouse an 'integrated' approach, quite rightly putting the focus on coherent planning and implementation of communications activities, so much so that 'integrated' is not just a prerequisite but has now become a truism: all communications have to be part of a coherent, consistent representation of brand positioning and differentiation. The emphasis in this text is clearly focused on organic planned (and often unplanned) brand development as the primary integrating factor of marketing communications. It is the market which drives the brand and the brand which drives message and media.
- **Brand narrative approach:** whilst being in line with current brand management developments evident in recent changes in brand campaigns, the examination of the 'story arc' of brand development makes the discussion of various brand developments much more engaging. This is key to the understanding of the role and purpose of marketing communications since it engages both the consumer and indeed the student. For example, two cars share a similar ABS braking system:

Volvo and *BMW*. Their communications have created a narrative around their respective brands: *Volvo* has been synonymous with 'safety' and ABS *protects*; in contrast, BMW symbolises the 'ultimate driving machine' and ABS allows you to *drive faster safely*. We will be examining why this association has become restrictive and how Volvo has shifted gear and *'used the Net to escape the cage'* (see Chapter 16).

What this demonstrates is that although the underlying form and structure has to be analysed and evaluated in order to understand the *mechanics* of marketing communications (planning, strategy, tactics, communications mix etc.), it is also important to examine how the brand organically adapts to its environment and responds in its relationship with the target audience. For example, see the *Stella Artois* case in Chapter 1 for an explication of the changing narrative of a brand.

- **Media-neutral planning approach:** reflecting the latest thinking of multimedia, multi-message communications, this book supports the belief that all messages and media should be fully integrated but recognises the need for target audience requirements to dictate schedules. The primary objective is for the message to find the market; the secondary objective is to use the appropriate media to carry the message. Examples are sprinkled throughout the book of organisations using so-called 'non-traditional' media to reach groups: for example, the election of *Barack Obama* and the repositioning of *M&S*, who both had a *YouTube* presence in order to hit a younger market; *Cadbury's* creating a viral marketing campaign to instil word-of-mouth 'buzz' into a repositioning campaign; *Mercedes Benz* using video pod-casting to ensure impact and message delivery.

- **Reflecting the changes which have happened and are continuing to develop:** the rise in consumer-generated content; the impact of social media; media neutral planning; as well as the trend towards captured content as opposed to captured audiences.
- **Student and lecturer orientation:** the text has been written from a teaching perspective with structure, content and pedagogical logic which reinforces teaching. Guidance on how current branding practice links to theory in modern marketing and social sciences is done in an entertaining manner which makes this a very student-friendly book.
- **Academic and practical underpinning:** the application of theory and context will inform case studies and analysis of practical campaigns, whilst encouraging students to engage in research-based theory.
- **Cross-discipline and inter-textual nature:** elements of philosophy, psychology, anthropology and sociology, combined with a wide range of cultural references give the text a unique energy and will encourage student appreciation of the wider context within which marketing communications is set.

Studies of branding have more often than not focused on it being a rational reaction to marketing communications. A more helpful approach is to examine the subjective lived experience of brands that consumers have. Research by Levy (2003), McCracken (1999) and Aaker (1991) has identified **meaning** as being the key driver of consumer behaviour and it is brands where meaning resides. Brands not only reflect people's lives but also form an integral part of an ongoing personal narrative which 'braids the filaments of everyday empirical and eternal truth into a common strand' (Sherry 2005). Successful brands have emerged from a 'culturally constituted' world (McCracken 1999) where the purpose of marketing communications is to co-create customer experience rather than merely build brand image through personality associations. Brands should not be seen as the residual end to a process but as a means to meaning for consumers.

In the current financial climate, even global brands have been forced to rethink strategy. According to the Kellogg Management School, for today's brands to survive, they must meet the challenges of: **cash** (the balance of short-term costs against long-term investment); **consistency** (remaining loyal to the brand promise by maintaining message and positioning); and **clutter** (being heard amongst the noise from communication overload). In avoiding what Sherry (2005) refers to as the 'branding doom loop'–losing long-term brand trajectory through repositioning by price reduction–there must be a 'singular cultural logic which is coherent' (Grant 2006), and marketing communications must be a holistic, co-produced collaboration of marketers' intentions and consumers' interpretations through the conduit of social media.

The orientation of *Marketing Communications: A Brand Narrative Approach* is to view marketing communications as the servant of branding: its purpose, application and measure being brand longevity by creating and sustaining consumer meaning not merely selling product. Schultz and Schultz (2005) highlight a key transformation of marketing's focus shifting from the traditional 'four Ps' (product, price, place and promotion) with a new emphasis on the 'five Rs' (customer relevance, receptivity, response, recognition and relationship). This underpins the key arguments in this book. At the same time, acknowledgement of the changing media environment requires a thorough understanding of how 'increasing spheres of influence', more often than not facilitated by the phenomenon of social networking, has altered the way communication is now negotiated rather than passively received.

STYLE, APPROACH AND PEDAGOGICAL LOGIC OF THE BOOK

The three key threads of this book–target audience, message content and media channels–are embedded in the overall structure of analysis, planning, implementation and control. We will present well-researched theory in practical contexts and show throughout the application of marketing communications. The analysis and evaluation of a variety of successful (and some unsuccessful) communication campaigns is given a very practical flavour and is encapsulated in the book's integrated planning model.

The constituent parts of the CAMPAIGN planning framework are:

- *Current brand evaluation*: research into market share, brand and company history, brand health, strategic role within brand portfolio, market meaning.
- *Analysis*: market assessment, environmental influences, target market and customer dynamics, and other contextual considerations.
- *Marketing communication effects and objectives*: corporate (or SBU), marketing, brand and communication effects and objectives.
- *Planning*: strategic framework, segmentation, targeting and positioning, tactics, techniques and budgets.
- *Application*: all message (communications mix, branding, reputation management, relationship management) and media (channels and media, intermediaries, communication industry).
- *Implementation*: creative, media and production implementation.
- *Goal evaluation*: budgeted resources, share of voice, awareness, purchase, referrals, market share, customer retention.
- *Next stage of development*: the future of the brand narrative, direction of brand development, feedback from the marketplace into the start of the next cycle of planning.

The CAMPAIGN model is intended to be a useful learning tool for students and tutors when analysing marketing communications campaigns. It is purposely designed to be meaningful in as much as the student is encouraged to evaluate the campaign objectivity of brands in terms of achieving both short- and long-term objectives and analysing how marketing communications have been (or should be) applied. It also forms a framework for delivery of the modules associated with marketing communications and the book's layout is consistent with this structure. Finally it is incorporated into some of the case analyses in the online learning resources available with this book.

Other pedagogical features include:

- **Chapter outlines.** Each chapter outline sets the scene for the topics to be discussed within the chapter providing a précis of the subject matter, the debates, concepts and marketplace dynamics.
- **Learning objectives.** Highlighted at the start of each chapter to give directed guidance to students and act as a chapter 'agenda'.
- **Chapter opening and closing case studies.** Each chapter has an extended mini case introducing and summarising the specific chapter topic, showing how marketing communications has been used but with specific reference to a student-friendly topical subject. For example, Chapter 6 features a case study on the *Nintendo Wii* showing how the brand, through the use of marketing communications, was so successfully repositioned that it effectively recreated its brand category. These case studies are designed to reinforce the learning objectives of each specific chapter and act as a review of conceptual learning and contextual relevance. Each is two to three pages long and, together with suggested topic questions, is ideal for use in one-hour seminar group work and as a stimulant for further independent research.
- **Matter of Fact boxes.** These are academic reports from the marketplace showing research on relevant market findings within the context of the chapter's discussion. They encourage the integration of theory and practice, demonstrating how research into consumer behaviour underpins the successful application of marketing communications and conversely how changes in consumer attitudes, motivation, perceptions and so on are achieved by well-targeted and executed marketing communications campaigns.
- **In Focus boxes.** These put the spotlight on a particular aspect of the marketing communications mix as applied in the marketplace. Showing figures, tables and full-colour illustrations, together with industry opinions, they act as 'bite-size' case studies which can be used to illustrate concepts in lectures or as materials for seminars.
- **Conceptual models.** The full range of marketing communications and buyer behaviour concepts is fully illustrated with detailed student-friendly tables and figures referencing the 'received wisdom' of

CLOSING CASE STUDY

Microsoft Windows: Life Without Walls: Microsoft's Multimedia Fight Back Goes Right to the Core of Apple's Story

When Steve Ballmer, *Microsoft* CEO, delivered his first post-Gates keynote with a promise to bring the 'three screens' – mobile, PC and TV – together in a seamless experience, he spoke of the one billion *Windows* users as 'a vibrant community of individuals'. *Microsoft* has outgrown the limits of the personal computer and has progressed to 'Cloud' with *Windows Live* and *Windows mobile*.

'We're at the start of transforming what Windows is from a PC operating system to a connected experience. When I think of the future of Windows, I think of a life without walls'. The 'Life Without Walls' tagline reaffirms the mission of the *Windows* brand to put fewer walls between people, their passions and the global community.

Windows packs a punch in its fight-back campaign

MATTER OF FACT

The Importance of Brand Name across Industries
In order to understand the importance of different variables in brand choice, researchers use a technique called **conjoint analysis**. Consumers are asked to rank options with various product attributes (e.g. price, brand name and service). Each attribute is assigned different category or range levels (e.g. low price–high price, weak brand name–strong brand name). The table below shows how important the attribute brand name is for different product categories (e.g. services, consumer products and industrial products).

Hotel chains		Cleansers		Electric equipment in factories	
Attribute	Attribute importance	Attribute	Attribute importance	Attribute	Attribute importance
Price	27.4%	Price	18.7%	Price	24%
Bed size	25.4%	Abrasive-ness	21.4%	Delivery time	27%
Pool (Y/N)	19.4%	Versatility	12.6%	Technology	19%
Cleaning	11.6%	Type	20.1%	Brand name	16%
Brand name	16.2%	Brand name	27.2%	Spare parts	14%

Brand choice across different industries

Sources: Cobb-Walgren, Ruble and Donthu (1995); Bendixen, Bukasa and Abratt (2004).

PROMOTION IN FOCUS

Nikon. **Push and Pull Promotion**

Nikon is favourably placed in the intensely competitive Compact Digital Camera category of the 'Culture, Leisure and Travel sector'. However, in order to achieve significant relative positioning amongst the 5–6 rival major manufacturers, the *Coolpix* camera was launched to help differentiate in a category which offered very similar products in terms of quality, features, range and benefits.

In order to raise awareness and interest in the *Nikon* range of *Coolpix* digital cameras within the trade, incentivise and motivate counter staff to push product through demonstration and recommendation, and to pull traffic through the stores, a *Nikon Coolpix Adventure* sales promotion was launched. This involved a clever hands-on practical promotion established and contemporary academic writers and industry commentators. Popular theories and models are fully explained and in some cases developed beyond the standard application.

- **Chapter reflective questions.** Highlighted at the end of each chapter to encourage students to recall and relate the concepts and contexts discussed. These provide a check and balance for each chapter's learning objectives.
- **Research projects.** Offer encouragement to pursue personal research – either on brand or concept – and are provided at the end of each chapter.
- **Illustrative marketing communications glossary.** A glossary is included to help student learning and offer descriptions and applications as further examples to illuminate the definition of specific topics. Direct links to company and brand websites continue the discussion and the glossary is an excellent accompaniment to in-class discussion.

	Description	Application
Advertising spend	Usually referred to as *adspend* equating to the total spent on media, creativity, design and evaluation of campaign	*'Red Bull'*'s total advertising spend for 2007 in the UK was £21 million covering...' *www.redbull.com*

WEB RESOURCES AND ACCOMPANYING WEBSITE

Online supplementary learning materials, designed to extend the learning experience for students and lecturers, are available on the accompanying website. The website features an interactive glossary with links to videos of real advertisements, PowerPoint slides, a lecturers' test bank, student self-test quizzes and an overview of the CAMPAIGN model which guides students through all stages of planning a successful campaign.

The accompanying website also includes a fully updated instructor resource manual to help lecturers plan their courses and make teaching even easier. The instructor resource manual includes session specifications, additional formative assessments for set reading, as well as additional case study and research question guidance for lecturers.

Connect to the website now at **www.marketing-comms.com.**

BOOK CONTENTS AND LAYOUT

This book is divided into the following sections:

Part 1: Introduction to Marketing Communications

The key talking points of today's marketing communications landscape – brand narratives, media-neutral planning, social media, consumer-generated content, viral marketing, the need for multi-step conversational communications, negotiated brand meaning – are explained and offered as a framework for helping our understanding of how marketing communications works in today's cluttered marketplace.

Chapter 1   Introduction to Marketing Communications
Chapter 2   How Marketing Communications Works

Part 2: Analysis and Planning for Marketing Communications

Preparation for marketing communications strategies requires a comprehensive understanding of target audience characteristics and needs before an estimation of communication effects (e.g. changes in perception, attitude formation) can be agreed. Strategic and tactical positioning provide a creative platform for the location of the brand in the market and in the mind of the consumer.

Chapter 3   Analysis of Target Audiences
Chapter 4   Effects and Objectives
Chapter 5   Strategy and Planning
Chapter 6   Strategic Positioning
Chapter 7   Tactics and Techniques of Positioning

Part 3: Implementation and Control of Marketing Communications

As branding and development of brand narratives is a central unique thread of this text, two chapters are devoted to a comprehensive discussion and explication of key concepts and applications. Whilst the primacy of advertising is acknowledged in two chapters devoted to strategy and creativity, newer alternate media approaches such as online marketing communications and content-captured product placement are included.

Chapter 8   Building Brand Equity
Chapter 9   Brand Narrative and Relational Management
Chapter 10   The Marketing Communications Mix
Chapter 11   Advertising Strategy
Chapter 12   Advertising Creativity
Chapter 13   Media Concepts and Media Planning
Chapter 14   Public Relations and Hybrid Marketing Communications
Chapter 15   Sales and Sales Promotion
Chapter 16   Beyond Traditional Marketing Communications
Chapter 17   Evaluating Marketing Communications

PART 1

INTRODUCTION
TO MARKETING COMMUNICATIONS

CHAPTER

INTRODUCTION TO MARKETING COMMUNICATIONS

"The days of mass media advertising are over. Any single ad, commercial or promotion is not a summary of our strategy. It's not representative of the brand message. We don't need one big execution of a big idea. We need one big idea that can be used in a multidimensional, multilayered and multifaceted way.
Larry Light (2004)

This chapter is an introduction to marketing communications and gives a brief outline of why it is now vital for overarching, ongoing brand narratives to be built and maintained in order to involve consumers and reinforce the brand's 'story'. It promotes the idea of meaning generated by two-way dialogues and examines the dynamics of implementing well-integrated, cross-media campaigns to achieve this.

Good brand communications is based on an orientation around a dominant, coherent 'big brand idea' as a platform for creating, involving and sustaining customer engagement. It's about communicating with a single 'voice' where the strands of the communication message must be coordinated and consistent.

Meaning through consumption is a common thread throughout the book, and in this opening chapter we take a look – whether it be individual (B2C) or organisational (B2B) buyer behaviour – at how marketing communications helps in this process, and conversely how understanding customer dynamics informs marketing communications.

There is a good range of evidence discussed here to show how the combined value-added effect of the 'whole being greater than the sum of the parts' has helped top brands to achieve long-term marketing goals through marketing communications.

LEARNING OBJECTIVES

After reading this chapter, you'll be able to:

- Understand what marketing communications is and how it can be analysed.
- Appreciate how marketing communications can help create 'meaning' for consumers.
- Understand the need to create an ongoing brand narrative in order to engage with target audiences.
- Describe the advantages of media-neutral planning in scheduling brand communications.
- Appreciate the media need for extended narratives due to the effect of technology on viewing patterns and behaviour.

Larry Light's comment on the nature and dynamics of marketing communications is both alarming and illuminating. With only 25% of budgets spent on traditional 'above-the-line' advertising (Kitchen 2003), the move away from mass and traditional communications and media, and with the consumer much more in control of receiving and interpreting brand messages, the communication landscape has changed dramatically. As a result, today's marketing communications has to be integrated, must move away from a tactics orientation (Holm 2006) and must be able to grow with the target audience. Marketing is moving away from managing customer transactions to managing internal and external relationships (Vargo and Lusch 2004) and from passive to interactive multi-channel marketing communications strategies.

Marketing communications is concerned with engagement: the planned, integrated and controlled interactive dialogues with key target audiences to help achieve mutually beneficial objectives. Coherence of message, not replication, is now much more important. Jaffe (2007) describes communication morphing into 'conversational marketing' where consumers are not passive, empty vessels but connectors. Whilst an organisation may have growth, profit and investment goals, an individual who fully connects with a brand will enter into an interdependent relationship of functional and symbolic meaning. Where technological innovation quickly spreads and now limits the possibilities of sustainable tangible competitive advantage, meaningful brands offer intangible benefits and create relationships with consumers.

Whilst this book will examine the managerial processes of communication transmission, the transfer of messages and sequential behavioural models, it will have at its heart the meaning generated by two-way dialogues of marketing communications.

OPENING CASE STUDY

Stella Artois: Reassuringly Expensive Wife Beater?

When *Stella Artois* was introduced into the UK in the early 1970s, the brand grew very slowly. The 1980s saw it positioned as an aspirational 'premium' lager, becoming a top brand with one of the best communication campaigns of all time and, by the end of 1995, it was the top take-home brand. However, in 2006, with supermarkets offering it as a loss-leading, high-strength beer, *Stella*'s market position was looking decidedly precarious. *The Brighton Recorder* reports

(Continued)

John Hardy giving judgement in a domestic violence case: 'There are key words which recur all too frequently in cases involving young men and alcohol. They are "*Stella*" and "binge drinking".' This was categorical proof that, in the minds of the target audience, the positioning of *Stella Artois* as being 'reassuringly expensive' was at odds with its public reputation as a 'wife beater' brand. This demonstrated that transmitted communications had been hijacked by the negotiated meaning of word of mouth. InBev, the brewer, had to go back to basics: when things went off message it decided to go online.

Since May 2007, the company's emphasis has been on distancing the brand from its 'lager lout' image and shifting people's perceptions of premium quality. The first move was to relaunch the brand as part of the *Artois* heritage – 'la famille Artois' – featuring the 4% ABV *Peetermans Artois* along with the bottled premium *Artois Bock*, a 6.2% version. It dropped the 'Reassuringly Expensive' slogan in favour of 'Pass on Something Good' and focused on the unrivalled 600 years of Belgian brewing heritage behind the *Artois* beers. The extension of this story can be seen in the new 'in-pub' image highlighted with the introduction of Artois-branded, 'feminine' stemmed chalice glasses, ornate fixtures and classy point-of-sale materials, all designed to discourage heavy-drinking young men and undermine the macho image of the brand.

To help build up this brand narrative of communicating the *Artois* mother brand, the values of *Artois* as a brewery (dating back to 1366 in Leuven in Belgium) the craftsmanship, knowledge and dedication of the master brewers all feature prominently in the 'Pass on Something Good' campaign. InBev, with the help of its London agency Lowe Worldwide, has launched a global, through-the-line campaign driving traffic to a new international website. The brewing giant said that this is the first time it has put a site at the centre of marketing communications. The campaign, which also includes TV, outdoor and print, has been in development for over two years and includes over an hour and a half of video footage put together exclusively for the site.

At the heart of the *Stella Artois* online experience is the movie, *La Bouteille*, a short film featuring a bar man who must navigate his way through the streets with a perfect bottle of *Stella* to a lady (also seen in edited form on TV and cinema). The movie acts as the navigation bar for the site, at any point allowing the visitor to enter an interactive site or to resume the screening. At various stages of the film, visitors to the site are invited to interact with the mythical world of 1366 in *Le Courage*, a section of the site combining film and game. Beer lovers are called upon to keep the flat world level, fight good and evil, and even prevent the sun from setting into the sea! 'We believe it is truly revolutionary. A cinematic experience that brings the brand to life,' says Neil Gannon, Global Brand Manager at *Stella Artois*. 'We are well aware of the quality of *Stella Artois* commercials, and wanted to bring that to life online and avoid the flat structure of a corporate website'.

Stella's social networking communication

Source: www.facebook.com.

In the run up to the launch, *Stella* targeted key opinion leaders (a group of 100 key bloggers) who were given snippets of information and access to content. This has had great viral word of mouth and the medium lends itself to the interaction of pseudo-game communications. *La Publicité* takes visitors into an old-fashioned theatre in which *Stella Artois* TV advertisements are shown. The selection includes 'Last Orders', 'Master Work', 'Destiny', 'Jacques', 'Ice Skating Priests', 'Returning Hero', 'Train' and 'Swag'. In the 3D animated *Le Défi*, players challenge their friends to rescue a fresh-poured goblet of *Stella Artois* by engaging in a number of complex puzzles.

Visitors are introduced to the origins of *Stella Artois* in *L'Origine*, exploring the role of the horn in the naming of Den Horen House. In *L'étranger* visitors can enter an old-fashioned saloon filled with old-world, accordion-fed music and challenge the bartender to pour a *Stella* properly or watch him show how it's done with the nine-stage pouring ritual. The communication narrative has been extended into the social media site *Facebook*, with a page called 'L'Academie Artois Ambassador' which is designed to encourage 'Artois tipplers' to feedback information and follow the social life of 'L'Academie Artois Ambassador'. This is actually a very creative excuse to show outdoor events like the Bistro St Michael and the O2 arena but also engages people in another aspect of the story.

The creation of a mythical brand narrative has allowed *Stella* to reposition the brand and started to help erase the negative associations. The core brand essence has been restated and re-imagined whilst at the same time emphasising brand quality and heritage. It has provided an ongoing story arc with maximum audience participation and engagement with the benefits of the accelerated word of mouth of online and viral marketing, truly 'multidimensional, multilayered and multifaceted'.

QUESTIONS

1. What are the communication benefits of building a 'brand narrative' in the way *Stella Artois* has?

2. Do you think this is the best way to improve dialogue with the target audience?

3. Another alcoholic brand, *Jack Daniels*, has a similar narrative emphasising the Mississippi master brewers' art and the brand's heritage. Is this irrelevant to the 'rock 'n roll' image it has?

It is now vital for overarching, ongoing brand narratives to be built and maintained in order to involve consumers and reinforce the brand's 'story' in all brand encounters.

The cornerstones of good marketing communications as seen in Figure 1.1 are target audience, message and media, which have integrated and interactive dimensions. All three have been exposed to change: consumers live in an information-obsessed, media-saturated world with an incredible choice of brands; the impact of technology has altered the way we see, read and process communication messages; and the need to engage audiences with a compelling message is absolutely critical to

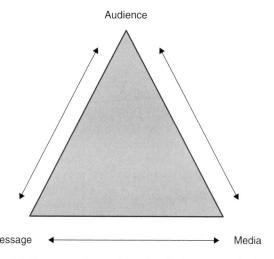

Figure 1.1: The cornerstones of good marketing communications

successful brand communications. In this book, we'll be examining fully integrated '360° campaign planning', the implementation of idea-driven and media-neutral marketing communications.

Most effective integrated marketing communications are driven through a core brand narrative, will coordinate all elements of the communications mix and have a presence across all media: traditional, non-traditional and a whole range of new user-generated content. A well-integrated, cross-media campaign therefore needs to have:

- an orientation around a dominant, coherent big brand idea (the **brand narrative** is a platform for creating, involving and sustaining customer engagement);
- a **single communication voice** (the strands of the communication message must be coordinated and consistent);
- a consistent appeal and appearance in all **brand encounters** (the replication of the brand image whenever the consumer touches the brand such as in advertisements, brochures, call centres, shop layouts, websites, vehicle livery etc. must be the same);
- a **combined value-added effect** of the 'whole being greater than the sum of the parts' (the brand narrative is the cumulative effect of all brand encounters and multimedia channels); and
- a **cross-media presence** which is dictated by users more than the strength of the medium (a 'media-neutral' approach where the message finds the target rather than fits into the medium).

This holistic approach requires a persuasive narrative to be created in a literal way (common symbols, characters, values and a persistent and consistent story arc) and laterally (driven across different offline and online media channels). Figure 1.2 illustrates the components of the brand narrative: the aims and objectives, image and relational brand management, market and 'mind' positioning, the construction of the messages for intended audiences, the mediascape space that messages will be carried in, and the integrated applied brand communications mix.

We can see from Figure 1.2 that all of the key elements of the marketing communications strategy and process are both separate but also interdependent and feed out from, and into, the all-pervasive brand narrative.

Image, brand and relational management describe how brands can evoke positive perceptions, differentiate and gain competitive advantage, enable faster introduction of new products, reinforce brand awareness and improve overall company and brand image and enhance trust. Although brands may have identities, images and personalities, they also have quasi-human qualities which are a psychologically deeper part of the brand's values. Brands have **intrinsic product qualities** like ABS braking systems and

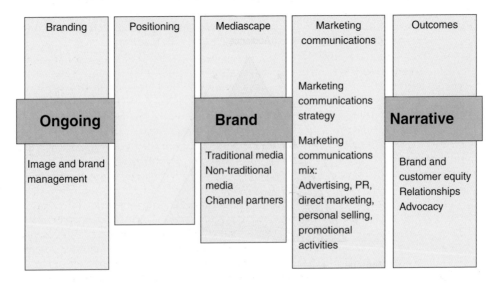

Figure 1.2: Brand narrative components

high-performing engines, but they also have **extrinsic representational qualities**: they fulfil emotional and psychological needs such as status, recognition, self-esteem, nostalgia, affiliation, spiritual satisfaction and companionship. Brands help us identify real and symbolic function and meaning, help consumers to recognise quality and consistency, provide information and reduce time in seeking out product suitability and perceived risk in purchasing. But brands also allow us to engage in a relationship with the product. Research has identified 'branding as a semiotic venture which helps shape the experience of engaged stakeholders into transactions' (Sherry 2005). See Chapters 7 and 8 for a fuller discussion.

Positioning is more in the mind than the market and describes the actual and perceived position of the brand: the product/market and mind space in terms of customer expectations and the consumer's perceptions of other competing brands (see Chapter 6 for a fuller discussion).

The **mediascape** is the array of channels available which will carry the message. A communications medium can be anything which carries a message: TV, radio, posters and other forms of traditional media; the newly emergent interactive online media as well as ambient marketing techniques; and even things we wouldn't necessarily regard as media like promotional artefacts, literature, even face-to-face selling (see Chapter 13 for a fuller discussion).

The **marketing communications mix** covers all the forms of message creation such as advertising, promotions, public relations and personal selling as well as 'hybrid communications' such as direct-response advertising, sales/PR exhibitions, online exhibitions and so on (see Part 3 for a fuller discussion).

MEANING IN COMMUNICATIONS

One of the characteristics of what is often referred to as 'post-modernism' is the significance placed on the symbolic nature of consumer purchasing behaviour. To a certain extent, individuals express who they are, which group they belong to or aspire to join, and project status, role and achievement through the brands they purchase.

Kjedgaard (2009) explores the 'meaning of style in consumption discourse' and echoes the view that the meaning of consumption is essentially the consumption of meaning: we are what we wear, eat, watch, drive, play and so on. Brand concepts, as vessels of meaning, are managed by appealing to 'customer's functional, symbolic and experiential needs through effective communications' (Shimp 1993, p. 11).

Whilst consumers use marketing communications to actively seek out personal meaning (McCracken 2005) through the consumption of brands, meaning is of course dependent upon the cultural context within which consumption occurs. McCracken (1988) refers to this as 'culture and consumption being mutually constituted'. This is key to understanding how meaning is defined in marketing communications: **individual identity construction** takes place where the 'individual is a consumer of symbols as much as products' (Ventkatesh 1999, p. 3).

Brand positioning (see Chapter 6) balances the integration of both deliberately transmitted messages as well as the subjective inferences of meaning (Smith 2007, p. 325). Figure 1.3 shows how marketing communications contributes to mediated transmitted meaning construction by explicit projected marketing meaning (the intrinsic attributes of product and packaging, distribution) and implicitly symbolic meaning projected through endorsement, semiotics and word of mouth.

However, the marketing environment meaning may not always reflect the explicitly projected intended marketing meaning. When meaning is 'transferred', celebrity-endorsed brands act as 'way-stations of meaning' in the 'culturally constituted world' (McCracken 1986). The implicitly symbolic meaning of brand loyalty is implicated in what the user assumes the brand 'stands for' and, by association, what the user is.

The debate about what true representation is has seen a developing movement away from the owner-dominated media to a more democratic user-generated space of online 'virtual communities' like *MySpace*, *Facebook* and *YouTube* which affords individuals a growing sense of cyber-identity. This emerging 'word of mouse' (Blackwell, Miniard and Engel 2006) communication represents a recent consumer-to-consumer (C2C) development which may undermine intended brand communications. This current discussion of technology-assisted user-generated brand conversations is the central theme of Chapter 16.

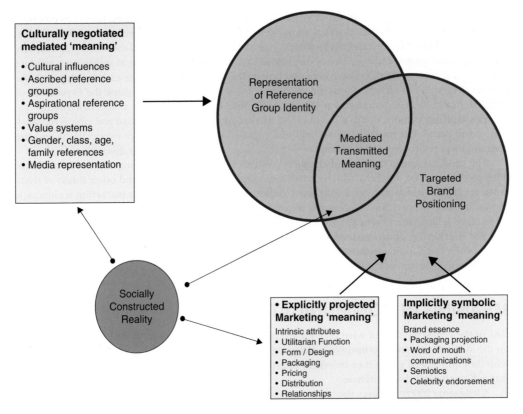

Figure 1.3: Meaning construction: socially constructed reality

BRAND MEANING IN FOCUS

According to Kapferer (2000, p. 56), 'Products are mute; the brand is what gives them meaning and purpose, telling us how a product should be read'. Brands project identity and guide our perceptions of products. Kapferer illustrated this with reference to the *Volkswagen Eurovan Transporter* MPV vehicle (made by *Sevel-Nord* in a joint venture between *PSA* and *Fiat*) developed to compete with the *Renault Espace* 'people carrier'. This MPV product was virtually the

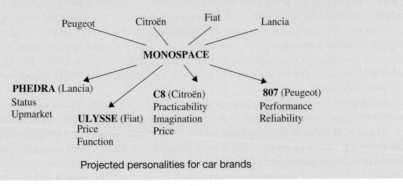

Projected personalities for car brands

same under the shell of the car but was communicated as having different brand personalities (or meaning) in different markets. Therefore, *Fiat* became associated with practicability; *Lancia* with flair and class; *Peugeot* with quality driving and reliability; and *Citroën* with imagination and escape. The products were practically the same, but differentiation was created which gave the brand its meaning.

Source: Kapferer (2000, p. 56).

HOW MARKETING COMMUNICATIONS LINKS TO BUYER BEHAVIOUR

Whether the target audience is individuals (business-to-consumer or B2C) or organisations (business-to-business or B2B), understanding customer dynamics informs marketing communications. Equally, good marketing communications can help consumers make purchase decisions. Consumer behaviour has changed from a **behaviourist** to a **cognitive orientation**, which attempts to analyse how consumers use both internal processes (e.g. memory, perception and learning) and external stimuli (i.e. marketing communications).

Marketing communications can be used to achieve a number of cognitive and behavioural changes including:

- repositioning the brand (due to a change in the physical product or service) as being new, reformulated or revised;
- changing misunderstanding;
- building credibility;
- changing performance beliefs;
- changing attribute priorities;
- introducing a new attribute;
- changing perception of competitor's product;
- changing or introducing new brand associations;
- using corporate branding to extend credibility;
- changing the number of attributes used.

Different types of decision making require different types of communications, dependent upon the level of personal low or high involvement in the decision. Sometimes a consumer may require a lot of information when purchase involves a complex decision-making process (**extended problem solving**) or less if the decision is simple (**limited problem solving**).

The more important a brand is in fulfilling a consumer's self-concept and adding value to a person's life, the more motivated will be the individual to search out information and be involved in the decision. The application of marketing communications to help this depends on:

- **personal factors** such as self-image, health, beauty;
- **product factors** such as the physical, financial, social and psychological perceived risk of use; and
- **situational (or instrumental) factors** such as the rituals attached to gift giving, consumption involving a shared experience or hedonistic, individual indulgence.

Of course consumption decisions depend on:

- the individual differences (demographics, psychographics, values and personality);
- consumer resources;
- motivation (knowledge and attitudes); and
- environmental influences (culture, social class, family, personal and situational influences).

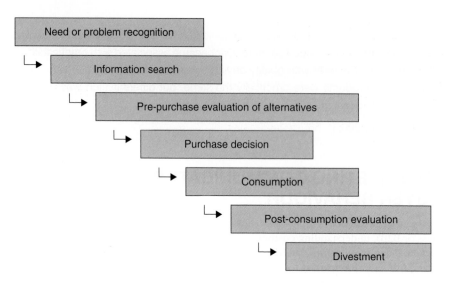

Figure 1.4: The Consumer Decision-Making Process Framework

Source: Blackwell, Miniard and Engel (2006).

The use of water in a bottle has been sold to us over the last couple of decades to the point where consumers feel that they not only need water but want (i.e. must have) a certain brand of water. Paying more for water than petrol is a dramatic example of symbolic consumption which is a 'sign of health and wealth' (Greve 1998).

Blackwell, Miniard and Engel (2006) devised the Consumer Decision-Making Process Framework (Figure 1.4), which they referred to as representing 'a roadmap of consumers' minds that marketers and managers can use to help guide product mix, sales strategies and marketing communications'. This shows the stages that a consumer may go through when purchasing and consuming a product or service.

Consumer motivation 'represents the drive to satisfy both physiological and psychological needs through product purchase and consumption' (Berkman, Lindquist and Sirgy 1997). Needs are activated when there is a perceived difference between a consumer's actual state and desired state. Marketing communications focuses on tapping into existing, latent or potential motivation by appealing to a need or identifying a problem. Some consumer needs take precedence over other needs (Maslow 1970), dependent upon the individual's personal and contextual disposition, and fall into one of the following categories:

- **Utilitarian-functional needs:** basic product benefits like quenching one's thirst, related to the basic principles of reward and punishment.
- **Hedonistic-experiential needs:** based on pleasure.
- **Value expressive:** expressing consumer's central values or self-concept and highly relevant to lifestyle analyses, where consumers cultivate a cluster of activities, interests and opinions to express a particular social identity.
- **Ego-defensive function:** attitudes that are formed to protect the person, either from external threats or internal feelings of insecurity. Studies of housewives in the 1950s showed how they resisted the use of instant coffee because it threatened their conception of themselves as capable homemakers. Deodorant campaigns stress the embarrassing social consequences. The 'macho' image of *Marlboro* cigarettes appeals to insecurities about masculinity.

Indeed, Maslow offered a 'hierarchy of needs' (safety and health; love and companionship; financial resources and security; social and affiliation; as well as the need to possess, to give and be 'self-actualised'), which describes a classification of needs. Eating is a basic physiological need but dining in an expensive restaurant is a want. The respective communications for two similar products position *Wall's* ice cream as a family product projecting basic family values and *Häagen-Dazs* as a luxury, indulgent brand personifying hedonistic consumption. Some needs may be in conflict with others. **Approach–approach motivational conflict** (Miller 1959) requires consumers to choose between desirable alternatives; **avoidance–avoidance** is between two undesirable alternatives; and an **approach–avoidance** dilemma is where consumption has to be a balance between desirable and undesirable consequences. An example of this last motivational conflict is the 'ego–eco contradiction' (Smith 2007) of the purchase of a car which fulfils the need for performance and social status but has to deal with the conscience consumption element of damaging the environment. Look at how many car brands, boldly positioned as high-powered, status machines in the 1980s and 1990s, are now communicated as being in some way environmentally friendly. Some car brands, however, deliberately take the purely hedonistic stance of focusing on pleasure rather than conscience. The advertisement shown in Figure 1.5 for *Jeep* is a good example of this.

Information search in this case becomes even more complicated as the consumer becomes highly involved in this complex decision and the element of conscience consumption is added to the need for functional and symbolic consumption. Ethical sourcing and divestment of product have become increasingly important aspects of consumption. This is evident in the appeals of 'fair trade' and environmental initiatives communicated by retailers for example.

In today's competitive marketplace, distinction between products can be minimal: 'me-too' products, copy-cat pricing and share-of-voice advertising spend sometimes negate differentiation (for a full discussion on share-of-voice advertising tactics, see Chapter 11). **Evaluation of alternatives** is

The Häagen-Daz pleasure principle

© Häagen-Dazs. Reproduced with permission.

Figure 1.5: *Jeep*'s lack of conscience?

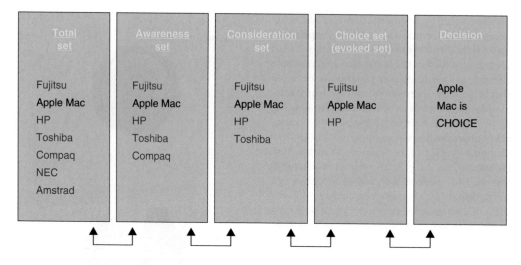

Total set	Awareness set	Consideration set	Choice set (evoked set)	Decision
Fujitsu	Fujitsu	Fujitsu	Fujitsu	Apple
Apple Mac	Apple Mac	Apple Mac	Apple Mac	Mac is
HP	HP	HP	HP	CHOICE
Toshiba	Toshiba	Toshiba		
Compaq	Compaq			
NEC				
Amstrad				

Figure 1.6: Evaluation of alternatives

the point in the decision-making process where brand comparisons are made once all information is gathered and the competitive value propositions can be assessed. These value propositions may include functional and symbolic comparisons and rely on the strength of marketing communications to convey actual as well as perceived differences. Good communications will make sure that a brand is in a consumer's **evoked set**, composed of all possible brands remembered from previous campaigns' knowledge, memory or previous use (known as **awareness** and **consideration sets**). The presentation of attributes can be both objective and subjective since a purchase decision can be both rational and irrational. We can see this in the example illustrated in Figure 1.6, which shows how an *Apple Mac* is selected from a range of possible choices. The way that this proposition was represented by *Apple* can be seen in the extract from the 'Hello, I'm Mac!' campaign featured in Figure 1.7 where the iconic, alternative, trendy, sociable image is projected through the *Mac* brand persona.

In order to maintain satisfaction and reinforce brand loyalty, a vital part of any marketing campaign has to be what is communicated after the product is bought and even after the brand is consumed. Examples of communications aimed at post-purchase evaluation are evident in the mailings, follow-up satisfaction emails, and even advertisements using testimonials to alleviate **cognitive dissonance** (post-sales regret).

Figure 1.7: *Apple Mac* make Microsoft the odd one out

BRAND NARRATIVE IN MARKETING COMMUNICATIONS

The primacy of dialogues over monologues is at the heart of marketing communications. Conversation and engaging storylines are now a prerequisite. Jensen and Jepsen (2006) declare that: 'the brand with the best story wins', and this is true of all successful brands both in terms of achieving marketing objectives and brand longevity.

All advertising provokes some sort of story through the use of framing, characterisation, cultural codes and the evocation of cultural expectations and stereotypes. They present a frozen moment, a snapshot of life and are sort of broken narratives. Against a backdrop of advertisement-avoidance devices such as *TiVo*, PVRs, *Sky+*, and alternative methods of individualised viewing, it is ever more important for companies to be innovative in order to grab attention and to create a brand story arc which connects and retains audience involvement.

Individual brand congruity (Smith 2007) occurs when the essence and core value of the brand resonate with the memories and emotional connections of the audience. A brand narrative encourages the consumer to engage with the story arc of the brand both cognitively and affectively. Escalas (2004) claims that 'narrative processing creates or enhances self/brand connections (SBC) because people generally interpret the meaning of their experiences by fitting them into a story'.

The more an advertisement encourages narrative processing and therefore becomes linked to the consumer's self-concept, the more meaningful a brand becomes. Narrative-driven marketing communications triggers memory by personalising company products; consumers feel that these products are integral to the expression of their individuality, their lifestyle, their notion of self. Escalas (2007) draws a distinction between narrative self-referencing ('Imagine yourself.....') and analytical self-referencing ('Let us introduce you to the brand.....'). According to Vincent (2002, p. 9) 'consumers in the post-modern world seek a narrative (or narratives) upon which to base their identity'. He describes how legendary brands such as *American Express*, *Apple* and *Harley-Davidson* forge bonds with consumers through narratives and myths rooted in emotion, identity and personal philosophy.

Marketing has been called the 'commercialisation of emotions' (Jensen and Fischer 2004). But how does the *Nike* 'swoosh' come to signify success and heroic victory? How does a *Harley-Davidson* motorbike personify grit and determination and feed into the Kerouac open road mythology? Why is *Ben & Jerry's* ice cream still seen as hippy with a counter-culture persona? Why does the *Virgin* brand, fronted by a multi-millionaire Knight of the Realm, still retain an anti-establishment ethos? Hopefully, we'll be able to answer these questions as we go along.

However, brand narratives have to create worlds which reflect the times. In the 1980s, we wanted brands to conspicuously consume, but in the 1990s brand experiences became central to marketing communications. We have seen a transfer of meaning-making activity away from civic life, family life and faith communities to the private sector and the emphasis changing from not just what we consume but how we live. Today's consumers are bombarded by information and now, with many reasons to have a 'conscience', want truer relationships with brands. Successful brands, to a large extent, have facilitated this process, by producing not just economic capital but replacement cultural capital (i.e. intangible benefits from the relationships of family and friends, beliefs in government and religion, guidance from schools and so on) and creating meaningful brand experiences. Let's look at some examples to illustrate this.

MARKETING COMMUNICATIONS IN FOCUS

Dove Real Beauty Campaign

The first step for many brands towards standing for something true is being socially responsible. *Dove* created its own 'truth' narrative with the creation of the 'Campaign for Real Beauty'

(Continued)

Dove spread the word about real beauty

and the 'Dove Self-Esteem Fund'. This not only positioned *Dove* against the 'because you're worth it' ethos of the competition but against the dominant Western culture's damaging and unrealistic expectations of notions of 'beauty' inculcated in women's minds. Audience engagement has been achieved not just through heavy TV and press exposure but through website interactive dialogue aimed at spreading very strong word-of-mouth advocacy. The *Dove* narrative is really about the effects and experiences of ageing and this was directly aimed at women over 45. A good example was when they invited women to write about their lives with winners able to work with a professional playwright, paid for by *Dove*, to create and act in a drama about their 'experiences of ageing'. The genius of this is not just tying cosmetics into the narrative of 'real women's experience', but distancing the brand from the manufacturer *Unilever*, who own and manufacture many of the products that contribute to the concept of false beauty opposed by *Dove*.

This narrative has had an effect not only on *Dove*'s audience, but also *Dove*'s competitors. *L'Oréal*, with the inclusion of mature women (albeit exceptionally 'beautiful' ones such as Jane Fonda), have started the extension of the 'because you're worth it' self-image ethos of *L'Oréal* in much the same way as the parallel men's 'because we're also worth it' platform.

One way companies can gain an advantage in how their brand is perceived is tapping into the *zeitgeist* of the moment. Consumers now demand to know the ethical origins of where the product is sourced as well as being concerned with the functional and symbolic use of the brand. Brands like *Innocent Smoothies* have created a narrative of honest marketing communication by making a feature of provenance and have undoubtedly been one of the success stories of the decade in terms of meeting consumer need to drive brand development. *Innocent* appear to be meeting the challenge of a machine age by adding a human conscience to mass production, telling us what is in the product, what health benefits the product gives us, and what element of 'fair trading' is involved in sourcing the product. It uses the semiotics of smiley faces, self-deprecating on-pack humour, the semi-mythical 'Fruit Towers', and the promise of caring, earth-loving friendly folk to signpost chapters in the *Innocent* story and integrate communication story threads. In the soft-drinks sector, it has succeeded in not just creating a different narrative but a new product category. Again, this is an example of how a brand narrative – civic-minded, sharing responsibility – can be constructed even if it sits at odds with the selling and making profits mantra of capitalism.

how do you make a smoothie innocent?

innocent by nature

Innocent's 'natural' ingredients

As with the *Innocent* story, some brands rely on the narrative of their founders (Bill Gates' *Microsoft*; Richard Branson's *Virgin*) whilst other brands use fictitious family constructs to develop a 'slice of life' narrative such as the *Oxo* family, now superseded by the *BT Technology* family.

Apple iMac is a brand which evokes cool and non-conformity, innovation and individualism. Like *Virgin*, *Apple* is synonymous with being the *Avis* 'we try harder', outside-of-the-box underdog, and has a name for dedication to fresh and non-conventional thinking. 'Liberty regained,' was how BDDP Agency Chairman Jean-Marie Dru described *Apple*'s brand narrative. The agenda was set when the *Apple Macintosh* narrative was introduced to the world in a prime-time shocker of an advertisement in which the brand was personified by a female runner hurling a sledgehammer at the huge Orwellian screen depicting the industry monolith, *IBM*. A long-time critic of the power of branding, *No Logo* author Naomi Klein claimed that *Apple* and certain other brands were selling the consumers' own ideas back to them. 'They are selling the most powerful ideas that we have in our culture,' she said, 'such as transcendence and community, even democracy. These are all brand meanings now'. And yet, *Apple* conferences are attended with a sort of quasi-religious zeal and enjoy evangelical brand loyalty that other brands envy.

Calvin Klein has used an ambiguous, sexually ambivalent narrative very effectively, telling a story unrelated to its products, but which consumers identify as a 'Calvin Klein story'. The characters, behaviours and responses to events are all suggestions of associations layered into the brand and in the mind of consumers. Use of implied celebrity endorsement featuring Kate Moss and more recently Garrett Neff, some in a variety of suggested sexual situations, has created an aura about this brand of mythical proportions. The *CK* brand has not only been at the forefront of the latest youthful trends, but also at the centre of much controversy: using teenage models – some as young as 15 – in provocative poses with much nudity; life-size posters of male models wearing only *CK* underwear. Many critics questioned whether the advertisements were fashion or pornography and this could have been counter-productive. The edgy, ambiguous nature of the *Calvin Klein* brand narrative, with sexually ambivalent imagery meant that this didn't happen.

The imaginary world of *Calvin Klein*

Stella Artois constructed an intriguing brand narrative which won a prestigious Gold Award in the 2007 Digital Marketing Awards. The integrated campaign 'Traps' imagines a set of fabled 'traps' built by the local people in Leuven, Belgium to protect their treasured brew, reported initially in spectacular print advertisements leading consumers to investigate the ledefi-stellaartios.com website. Huge 'traps' were constructed and toured around various countries and visitors to the site were asked to investigate the secret of the mythical contraptions. Engagement and interaction were unprecedented, resulting in fantastic interest and the creation of a story arc with long-term potential.

The creation of a brand narrative, therefore, provides an ongoing framework within which marketing communications can engage audiences and build long-term relationships.

The Media Need for Extended Narratives

One aspect which is changing the media paradigm is the effect of technology on viewing patterns. TV-focused leisure time is fundamentally different; families no longer sit around the TV set and thus are not a captive audience. We have entered what some people refer to as TV's 'third age' where control of viewing is increasingly in the hands of the viewer not the sender of communication:

- *BBC iPlayer*, *ITV.com*, *Sky+*, *V+*, PVRs and DVD HDD recorders allow time flexibility of viewing and 'zapping' of advertising slots in content.
- Cable, *Sky*, *Virgin* and *Freeview* boxes broaden the available content but also dilute the concentration of audiences.
- Hi-Definition/cinema style equipment allows dedicated viewing which may eliminate viewing of advertising or limit content (e.g. movies only).
- Social network websites like 'Room Mates' on *MySpace TV* and 'Kate Modern' on *Bebo* are examples of people viewing TV content as part of multimedia/multi-tasking.

- New equipment such as *Slingbox* (allows remote call up for viewing), PSP, consoles and TV/laptops allows flexibility of viewing by location; and
- *Sky Sports* has been responsible for increasing multiple viewing (e.g. live football) which has increased an element of captive audience but in a shared social setting.

The impact on the communication of brands means that there has to be an even greater emphasis on cohesive integrated campaigns, expanded use of other media and the creation of long-term brand narratives to sustain audience engagement.

TRANS-MEDIA AND MEDIA-NEUTRAL PLANNING IN COMMUNICATIONS

The traditional means of communicating marketing messages has been based on the transmission of messages through the conduit of single channels and not a consistent message through different media. The modern consumer has many more opportunities to receive the brand messages, as well as the ability to ignore them. In order to cut through the message clutter and media saturation, there is a need for the placement of messages to be where the consumer would be willing to receive it, and not in 'silo-based' scheduling. **Media-neutral planning** recognises how customers consume media in a multi-channel fragmented media world. The new 'intermediaries' of long-form media like websites, podcasts and consumer-generated content, alongside changing behavioural patterns like multimedia multi-tasking, and the use of viral marketing campaigns to create pre-campaign 'buzz', are all contributing to what Saunders (2004) calls the 'joined-up thinking' of media-neutral planning. He cites the likes of *Tesco, Absolut Vodka* and *Stella Artois* as having a 'strong, differentiated promise [...] vividly and memorably expressed in a consistent way across all media'. Similarly, **trans-media planning** refers to the development of a single nonlinear brand narrative replicated across all brand touch-points, designed to generate brand communities with built-in accelerated word of mouth (i.e. viral marketing). A full examination of media neutral-planning is given in Chapter 5.

Philips' 'Sense and Simplicity' 2006 US campaign is a great example of a well-integrated, cross-media campaign. *Philips* wanted to position its products as solutions to consumers' overly complicated lives. The spread of multimedia scheduling was a key feature of this campaign. TV featured 'seamless editions' of *NBC Nightly News* and *The Today Show*, allowing for fewer interruptions and more actual news stories. *Philips* also sponsored college football games without TV time-outs, reducing the run length of games by half an hour. Print publications saw the removal of irritating business reply cards (BRCs) that always fall out of the magazine (sponsored by *Philips*). In cinemas, *Philips* removed all local advertisements/promotions from the screen prior to trailers. There was a strong online presence to the campaign which also featured *Philips*-sponsored free access to *NYTimes.com*. This was cross-referenced in all printed publications and also announced by the *New York Times*. As well as the use of conventional media, *Philips* used the 'guerrilla' tactics of uniformed agents present throughout key cities enabling people to relax in street-side lounges and helping people out of taxis with their packages, luggage and other belongings. This not only helped create a 'simplicity' narrative that was extremely salient (see Chapter 12 for a full discussion of salience in advertising) to the target audience, it also helped achieve awareness and recall goals: 25% unaided awareness of simplicity initiatives; 50% higher brand recall versus *Philips*' norm for new efforts; *Philips*' aided brand awareness was 95%+ in key markets; and extended unpaid-for editorials and PR 'pick-ups', including the *Wall Street Journal*, the *New York Times* and *USA Today*.

Multimedia, multi-message neutral scheduling allows brand creation and storytelling to be complemented by reinforcing the linear brand narrative with interactive 'My Narrative' hooks which are in sync with the 'create, customize and share' user-generated consumer experiences of *Facebook* and *YouTube*, which can help to shape the brand narrative in a nonlinear manner. *Nike* tapped into the 'new religion of brand consciousness' and fitness craze with its 'Just Do It' ideal and managed the impossible feat of being anti-establishment and big business. *Nike* is credited with embracing not only resolve and purpose, but also the 'beauty, drama and moral uplift of sport'. This isn't just reinforced with a linear story in its legendary TV spots, but *NIKE ID*'s 'Create your own shoe' application provides a nonlinear online complement that actually allows consumers an interactive opportunity to participate in the story. This engages, creates and extends the brand's ethos of the 'Just Do It' tagline to a two-way interactive experience. Sometimes the narrative can go 'off message' as with the jingoistic use of a bloodied Wayne Rooney in the build up to a major tournament. Whilst this advertisement got fantastic press coverage (the UK tabloid *The Sun* even reprinted it as a poster), it alienated a lot *of Nike's* target audience.

JUST DO IT

Rooney doesn't do it for *Nike*

Pantene is another example of recreating a brand narrative across media and with completely integrated marketing communications. All aspects of the *Pantene* brand experience were redesigned across the full range of consumer touch-points: brand identity, package design, product mix including the addition of *Pantene* combs, brushes, hair accessories, in-store communications, merchandising, branded environments, sampling systems, brochures, as well as a fully interactive website.

MATTER OF FACT

The Role of Emotion in Advertising

The role of emotion in advertising means that narratives can be constructed to build dialogues since humans are hardwired to respond to narrative. Jackson *et al.* (2004) suggested, 'Advertising that resonates emotionally stands more chance of inducing a change in beliefs and values than are based on logic or expertise alone'. This has been reinforced by research recently conducted by the Advertising Research Foundation (ARF) and the American Association of Advertising Agencies (AAAA) who concluded that communicating a branding story – engaging the consumer through narrative – is more effective than focusing on mere product positioning. Their White Paper showed clear evidence that narrative-based advertising provides dyadic conversations with target audiences whereas traditional positioning strategies are based on one-way communications.

Source: Brandweek (29 October 2007)

CLOSING CASE STUDY

Cadbury's: The Joy of the Gorilla and the Chocolate Factory

In the UK, our love affair with chocolate is ingrained in our psyche. We celebrate, show our appreciation, reward and even apologise with chocolate. We spend over £7 million a day on it and a seventh of that is on one product alone: *Cadbury's Dairy Milk*.

In early 2000, our affectation reached theatrical proportions with the opening of *Cadbury's World of Chocolate*, a real-world chocolate factory. Then, disaster struck in June 2006 when a series of salmonella outbreaks in *Cadbury* factories resulted in a recall of over one million bars of chocolate from all retailers across the country. This was exacerbated by *Cadbury's* decision to delay

(Continued)

telling the authorities for a further five months. The year before, a £10 million UK launch of the US chewing-gum *Trident* had been mired in controversy after an advertisement featuring an Afro-Caribbean poet was deemed by the Advertising Standards Authority as racially offensive. Further PR disasters like the recall of thousands of Easter eggs, which were distributed without nut allergy warnings, placed *Cadbury* on the edge of calamity. In a climate of general concern about child obesity, poor diet and the statement from the ACMSF (the Food Standards Agency's independent Advisory Committee on the Microbiological Safety of Food) that *Cadbury*'s method of salmonella risk assessment could not be relied on for foods such as chocolate, a miracle was needed and a hero was desperately required. That miracle was marketing communications and the hero turned out to be a gorilla!

With *Cadbury*'s position as the world's biggest confectioner under threat, and the negative concentration on the safety of the product, it was of critical importance to re-establish the *Cadbury's Dairy Milk* brand – with sales of over £350 million, a key part of *Cadbury's* brand portfolio – in the hearts of consumers. A new campaign had to build long-term brand values, but it also had to quickly affect short-term sales. *Cadbury* started this process with the creation of a new brand narrative underpinned by the biggest ever UK integrated marketing communications budget for chocolate. However, the ideas for the new story and approach faced three key problems:

1. No chocolate was to be shown in the advertisements.
2. Any media schedule could only take place in the spring.
3. The proposed creative platform went against the grain of traditional TV advertising.

For years, the semiotic and even iconic symbol of 'one and a half pints of milk' on every element of *Cadbury* communication had persuaded us of the goodness of the product. The new creative proposals for the commercial did not show chocolate or people eating chocolate; it didn't make any mention of the word 'chocolate'. Now, Creative Director Juan Cabral was claiming: 'Chocolate is about joy and pleasure. For years *Cadbury* has told us that it was generous, through the glass and a half strap line. We thought, don't tell us how generous you are; show us. Don't tell us about joy; show us joy'. And so the metaphor for the whole campaign was to be JOY.

Initially, this caused as much panic as the salmonella scares. 'Without chocolate' said one veteran *Cadbury* executive, '*Cadbury* ads lose their sensual appeal and along with that go sales'. Would a campaign far removed from conventional chocolate advertising be effective? Cabral didn't want to whet our appetite for gorgeous tasting chocolate, he simply wanted to entertain. The second problem was the timing of the campaign. The peculiarities of the UK chocolate market meant that the only chance to build brand momentum was in the spring; Easter and Christmas were separate, seasonal markets and audience engagement and long-term development of brand message would be lost in the clutter of an overcrowded advertising period.

Lastly, Fallon (the advertising agency responsible for the creation and implementation of the campaign) recognised that the way we view and react to TV advertising has changed dramatically. The phenomenon of what Laurence Green, Planning Director of Fallon, calls 'interruption advertising' was no longer appropriate to building a far-reaching story arc. '*Cadbury* traditionally did well. Built ads for the interruption age when consumers had an implicit media deal with advertisers. In exchange for free TV they would allow us to interrupt their programmes with commercials', says Green. 'For a brand that is so well known, it's arguable whether the old style interruption advertising model is the best model for the future. So we are trying to engage more genuinely with our audience'. So, in June 2007, *Cadbury* ended its long sponsorship association with ITV's soap opera *Coronation Street* and began a campaign that was to re-engage an audience, re-establish a brand and probably rescue a company.

Drumming out the joy of *Cadburys*

Prime-time TV advertising was the second phase of the £6.2 million marketing campaign which launched with outdoor poster activity. When the initial advertisement was aired on 31 August 2007, right in the middle of the populist *Big Brother*, it was a deliberate cross between a short film and a music video and opened with a title, 'A Glass and a Half Full Productions presents.....'. The advertisement begins with Phil Collins's 'In the Air Tonight', playing in the background with an intriguing close-up of the new face of *Cadbury's Dairy Milk*: a gorilla. As the chorus begins, the gorilla breaks into a passionate and entertaining drum solo. It is not until the final still that it is revealed that the advertisement is brought to you by *Cadbury's Dairy Milk*, 'A glass and a half of full joy'.

Not many people had a clue what it was about, but when it was tested by Millward Brown, it was ranked in the top fifth of all advertisements ever tested for enjoyment. The campaign ran until the end of the year and was seen an average of 10 times by 84% of the adult population. The dramatic departure from pushing product through traditional advertising means, and instead producing 'entertainment pieces', appealed to a broader range of consumers. A second burst of exposure costing £700,000 coincided with England's appearance in the Rugby Union World Cup Final against South Africa in October 2007.

A crucial element was the recognition of the power of viral marketing to help consumer engagement and rapidly spread word of mouth. Together Fallon and Hyper had created an advertisement in the style of a viral which could be replicated and distributed across video-sharing websites like *Facebook, Digg, Delicious, StumbleUpon and YouTube*. Indeed, it was viewed almost 500,000 times on *YouTube* the week after it was released and many sites sprung up including 70 on *Facebook* like the 'We love the *Cadbury*'s drumming gorilla' group. By the end of 2007, it was the most popular advertisement on TV and on the web, scoring an incredible 10 million hits. A number of spoof advertisements were created by individuals and tacitly approved by *Cadbury* although one 'official' one for *Wonderbra* (Two cups full of joy) fell foul of copyright.

The campaign ran on billboards, newspapers, magazines, cinema, event sponsorship and an extended online presence contracted out to specialists Hyperhappen. In conjunction with this,

(Continued)

Two cups of joy for *Wonderbra*

an on-pack barcode promotion, 'Win a Prize and a Half', to drive incremental sales of *Cadbury's Dairy Milk* ran from 31 August to 8 March 2008, offering consumers a chance to win more than 50,000 exclusive prizes such as a trip to *New York Fashion Week*, or a shopping trip in Marrakesh. There were many other linked promotions and PR events such as sponsoring the 'Great Gorilla Run' charity race through London on 23 September 2007.

To push product out through the trade and help boost retail sales, dealer support featured special point-of-sale materials including dump bins and counter-top merchandising units carrying the banner 'Prize and a Half'. The campaign continued from 30 March 2008 with a more obscure Glass and a Half Production called 'Airport Trucks', this time featuring *Queen's* 'Don't Stop Me Now'. Both can be viewed through an extended online experience featuring a special 'Chocolate Factory' that hosts the gorilla, the studio it was filmed in, an alternative reality game (ARG-lite) that opens up a password-protected vault holding downloadable clips of Trucks and the domain of *Dairy Milk*. It even features some of the top gorilla remixes!

Despite initial worries about the non-conventional and ambivalent aspects of the campaign, sales of *Cadbury's Dairy Milk* had increased by 9% from the same period the year before, *YouGov* showed that 20% more people viewed the brand favourably and it picked up a number of prestigious accolades including the D&AD 'Black Pencil' Award and *Campaign Magazine*'s 'Campaign of the Year' Award. More importantly perhaps is the changing emphasis on the pleasure of eating chocolate achieved by the creation of a story framework which can run and run. As Green has said 'We've created a branded space in which *Cadbury's* can be generous in bringing joy'.

QUESTIONS

1. The agency responsible for this award-winning campaign claimed that 'Advertising can be effective without a traditional "message", "proposition" or "benefits". Indeed, some of the latest advertising thinking suggests that attempts to impose them can actually reduce effectiveness. We are trading our traditional focus on proposition and persuasion in favour of deepening a relationship'. Do you think this represents a philosophical shift from selling to entertaining? Do you think this reinforces the idea of a brand narrative?

2. Advertisers have often used the expression 'sell the sizzle not the steak'. Do you think this is an appropriate way to communicate all brands or is it only appropriate to hedonistic consumption like eating chocolate?

3. What message is being communicated here? Is it the joy of 'guilty pleasures' being secretly indulged or is it just the agencies (and us) having a laugh?

CHAPTER SUMMARY

In this chapter we discussed marketing communications and gave a brief outline of why it is now vital for overarching, ongoing brand narratives to be built and maintained in order to involve consumers and reinforce the brand's story. We examined the idea of meaning generated by two-way dialogues and the dynamics of implementing well-integrated, cross-media campaigns to achieve this.

We saw how good marketing communications is based on an orientation around a dominant, coherent 'big brand idea' as a platform for creating, involving and sustaining customer engagement.

Meaning through consumption is a common thread throughout the book, and in this opening chapter we looked at how marketing communications helps in this process, and conversely how understanding customer dynamics informs marketing communications.

REFLECTIVE QUESTIONS

a. What are the cornerstones of good marketing communications? Look for examples of how these key elements are combined to good effect in a successful brand.

b. The brand narrative is a platform for creating, involving and sustaining customer engagement, with an orientation around a dominant, coherent 'big brand idea'. Research your own examples for brands which have engaged audiences in a storyline.

c. It is necessary to have a consistent appeal and appearance in all brand encounters (the replication of the brand image whenever the consumer touches the brand such as advertisements, brochures, call centres, shop layouts, websites, vehicle livery etc. must be the same). Think of one of your favourite brands and trace all the 'brand encounters' you experience in your relationship with it.

d. An example of 'hybrid' communications – elements of communication tools which overlap – is a sales person's attendance at an exhibition. It's public relations but it's also selling. Before you get to the discussion on 'hybrid' communications' (Chapter 15), can you think of any two communication tools which overlap?

e. *Snapple*, *Green & Blacks* and now *Innocent* have sold all or part of their businesses to bigger organisations. Do you think they have 'sold out'? Will it affect their appeal as the smaller, credible brand?

RESEARCH PROJECTS

Using McCracken's 1986 paper 'Culture and Consumption: A Theoretical Account of the Structure and Movement of the Cultural Meaning of Consumer Goods' published in the *Journal of Consumer Research*, summarise the key arguments by the author in relation to meaning in consumer behaviour.

Visit the *Nike* and *Adidas* websites and compare their different approaches to projecting 'meaning' through great marketing communications.

CHAPTER  2

HOW MARKETING COMMUNICATIONS WORKS

"Apple is consistent. You know what it means, what it stands for and what it will always stand for. Namely: Microsoft sucks!"
Garfield (2006)

This chapter is about the 'mechanics' of the communication process: all the underlying conceptual models and frameworks that are used to explain how marketing communications works and, in some cases, doesn't work! There is a full examination of the links between marketing communications and branding. We argue that the driving force is the brand, dictating the use and application of the communications mix. It covers all the influences which help or hinder the successful reception of organisational/audience dialogues and discusses the growing impact of peer-to-peer communications. It also places the debate between managerial and individual 'meaning' interpretation perspectives into a contemporary setting.

LEARNING OBJECTIVES

After reading this chapter, you'll be able to:

- Understand how and why marketing communications is both an appropriate and integrative practice.
- Evaluate the links between branding and the power of marketing communications.
- Appreciate how the building of a brand narrative can provide an overarching, ongoing framework to ensure brand longevity and effectiveness.
- Consider the need for the management of all brand encounters and brand conversations.
- Examine the dynamics of the marketing communications process.
- Evaluate conventional approaches to how marketing communications works.
- Examine the influence of communication intermediaries in the dissemination of information in the marketing communications process.
- Consider the evidence for different marketing communications process perspectives.
- Discuss the application of sequential models of marketing communications.

The skill with which different consumer needs are met with different communication methods and how this is synchronised is the essence of marketing communications: one message, multimedia planning and implementation. In this chapter we examine components of this: the relationship between marketing communications and brand building; the mechanics of how marketing communications works; as well as the 'transmission' and 'interpretivist' communication process debate. We'll be evaluating how organisations sustain competitive advantage and create meaningful dialogue through interactive communications. We'll also be looking at how marketing communications can be purposively planned to achieve brand image and initiate action, how it can be unplanned through word of mouth and negotiated meaning within the target audience and the factors which affect communications in today's mediated environment.

The notion of exchange relationships is at the heart of successful marketing and Bob Garfield's comment above helps us to locate marketing communications in the two most important areas: the strategic positioning of the organisation's value proposition in relation to the competition; and its perceptual positioning in the minds of the target audience. At its best, marketing communications helps create brands which provide functional and symbolic meaning to consumers and help engender long-term customer loyalty. It tries to do this by informing, reassuring and persuading consumers of the appropriateness of an organisation's product or services in matching their needs and wants.

OPENING CASE STUDY

Apple Macintosh: 'Hello, I'm a Mac'

Apple has been referred to as the 'people's champion', taking on the mighty *IBM* corporation. This proved to be an excellent creative platform on which to build brand differentiation, positioning *Apple* as the 'David' against the IBM 'Goliath'. This strategy had echoes of the now

(Continued)

famous brand battle between *Avis* and *Hertz* car rental companies in the 1970s. As Number 2, *Avis* created a self-deprecating tagline of 'We Try Harder' which not only won the hearts and minds of consumers but also market share from the competition. However, at the end of 2005, despite *iPod*'s staggering success, *Apple Macintosh* still remained a niche player in the computer market. At that time, the *Apple Mac* did not enjoy a significant product advantage over the competition and lacked the cultural capital of the iconic *iPod*. It just did not translate into the PC world; it did not have the same meaning in the minds of its target audience.

All this changed with the introduction of new Intel-based *Macs* in 2006, presenting an opportunity to tap back into the *Apple* story arc and making the *Mac* as culturally relevant as the *iPod*. The 'Get a Mac' campaign created a simple metaphor of using personifications of 'Mac' and 'PC' comparing the easy, fun, creative *Mac* experience with PC's frustrating complications. In the original US version, 'Mac' was played by actor Justin Long and 'PC' by John Hodgman of *Daily News* fame. The resemblance to the two founding members – youthful Steve Jobs and nerdy Bill Gates – was not an accident. This helped compare both the category and brand alternatives (see below and Chapter 1 for a discussion on evaluation of alternatives in the decision-making process) demonstrating all the reasons to purchase a *Mac*: not exposed to viruses; restarting isn't a problem; multimedia applications are better. These reflected the 'top-of-mind concerns' expressed by PC users. Market share grew by 42%, and the campaign was seen as 'culturally influential' and achieved a prestigious American Marketing Association 2007 'Effie Award' in the process.

The Effie Awards are the pre-eminent award in the industry, honouring marketing communications 'ideas that work – the great ideas that achieve real results and the strategy that goes into creating them'. Judges are asked to evaluate a campaign's effectiveness, allocating 70% of the marks for: (i) the strategic challenge presented in the brand's market sector, (ii) the creative idea or story to help achieve marketing communication objectives, and (iii) the manner in which the idea is 'brought to life'; and 30% based on the results of the campaign. The strategic challenge for *Apple* was to compete with other PCs in a very competitive sector. It did this by effectively positioning the *Mac* not just as an alternative brand but almost as a separate product category. The personifications of 'Mac' and 'PC' allowed for indefinite brand comparisons and provided an ideal, continuing framework to communicate the functional and symbolic aspects of the brand. What this also illustrated is that there has been a definite move away from demanding authoritative respect to creating genuine brand affection between organisation and audience.

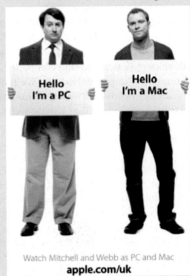

Watch Mitchell and Webb as PC and Mac
apple.com/uk

Mitchell or Webb? Mac or PC?

To be eligible to enter the Global Effies, a campaign must have a single brand idea running across at least four countries in two or more regions worldwide. The success of this narrative was replicated in various countries with the two characters of 'Mac' and 'PC' being played by popular comedians with individual national celebrity currency. The UK version used David Mitchell and Robert Webb, two 'cult' celebrities with considerable cultural capital, which fed perfectly into the extended *Mac* storyline. Other adaptations have translated this personality comparison into other cultures.

Apple's success, according to the judges, was that 'they managed to do it with humour, class, and honesty without falling into the trap of overtly negative competitive advertising', using non-aggressive, carefully camouflaged product comparisons. The Effies recognise any and all forms of consumer engagement that contribute to a brand's success: print, tv, radio, outdoor, Internet, guerrilla, digital, package design, events, street teams, PR, paid or unpaid media. Other examples of brands creating effective global campaigns are *Vaseline, Kellogg's* and *Dove*. The repositioning of *Vaseline* as the skin authority with its 'Keeping Skin Amazing' campaign, running across 15 countries around the world, arrested a 30-year share decline. Similarly, *Kellogg's Special K* 'Drop a Jean Size Challenge' rallied hundreds of thousands of women across 15 nations of the world, resulting in the brand's relevance growing beyond the breakfast and summer mindset. *Dove*'s Pro-Age campaign sparked worldwide debate by challenging the concept of age and beauty and made it a force in the fiercely competitive anti-ageing category.

QUESTIONS

1. How can *Apple* continue to use marketing communications to make the *Mac* as culturally relevant as the *iPod* brand?

2. What elements would be required to produce a campaign which had the ability to run across 'at least four countries in two or more regions worldwide' as required by the Effie judges?

3. What do you think is meant by 'ideas that work'?

BRANDING AND THE POWER OF MARKETING COMMUNICATIONS

As a means of differentiating an organisation's offer or communicating to a consumer, branding applies to most organisations in almost all contexts: the public sector, the voluntary or 'third' sector services, industrial and financial sectors as well as the ever-growing dominance of retailer brands. The purpose of marketing communications is to develop a continuing dialogue with target audiences to build **brand equity** – brand associations (awareness and image), brand dominance and brand prospects. Although branding is 'not the product [...] it gives the product meaning and defines its identity in space and time' (Kapferer 2000, p. 17). A full discussion of brand management is undertaken in Chapter 9. Let's first take a look at how important branding is in the marketing communications process.

In a way, a brand is like a capsule of meaning. How could a mother consider white powder to sprinkle on her child's sensitive skin without having the confidence of a trusted brand? The brand's meaning is wrapped up in the security and safety of huge organisational research and development, generations of word-of-mouth recommendations and in all the exposure to marketing communications messages. But its meaning also resides in the symbolic use of the brand: being a good parent. The original 'washes whiter' soap powder advertisements touched implicitly on the

Thou shalt never be the same girl twice.

Different girl or just different product features?

nerve of being a 'proper mother'. Types of packed goods can therefore be more about the projection of the brand than the protection of the product. Now, imagine purchasing shampoo in transparent, unlabelled bottles. How would you distinguish between *Pantene, L'Oréal, The Body Shop, Head & Shoulders, Fructis* or *Clinique*? Alternative products with different benefits must be distinguished from each other by brand names, logos and packaging, all crucial to consumers when making product choices. *GHD*'s 'Thou shalt never be the same girl twice' campaign is a clever way of showing a product's features (in this case hair straighteners) but at the same time appealing to the notion of individual identity. It plays on an idealised construct of feminine sexuality but uses the device of 'self-construction' to appeal to its audience.

Brand elements are not by themselves sufficient to convince consumers of brand superiority. Imagine (if you can), buying a soft drink only based on packaging and brand name. How would you know if *Sprite, Dr. Pepper, Coca-Cola, Evian, Tropicana, Fanta* or *Pepsi* was your best option? Would you even know the differences between some of the brands? You would have to try each brand several times before you could judge which one was best. In order to help with purchase decisions and simplify choice, marketing communications tries to create a distinct image for the brand.

Brand associations are made explicitly and implicitly in order to encourage linkages with places, personalities or even emotions. Years ago (younger readers should Google this!) when the 'Juice Man from Del Monte' said: 'Yes!' a brand was being differentiated from a generic product. *Del Monte*'s use of the best oranges was implied. Nowadays, orange juice is positioned using other associations: against a backdrop of an iconic Manhattan skyline, the brilliant New York sunshine pouring over an inviting breakfast, with a sexy duet playing in the background, sits a carton of *Tropicana* orange juice. This creates a sophisticated brand personality more to do with what the pack projects than the quality of the juice. This shows how brand communication adds value to the product. Research undertaken by Cobb-Walgren, Ruble and Donthu (1995) and Bendixen, Bukasa and Abratt (2004) highlighting the power of branding in different contexts is featured in the Matter of Fact box below.

MATTER OF FACT

The Importance of Brand Name across Industries

In order to understand the importance of different variables in brand choice, researchers use a technique called **conjoint analysis.** Consumers are asked to rank options with various product attributes (e.g. price, brand name and service). Each attribute is assigned different category or range levels (e.g. low price–high price, weak brand name–strong brand name). The table below shows how important the attribute brand name is for different product categories (e.g. services, consumer products and industrial products).

Hotel chains		Cleansers		Electric equipment in factories	
Attribute	Attribute importance	Attribute	Attribute importance	Attribute	Attribute importance
Price	27.4%	Price	18.7%	Price	24%
Bed size	25.4%	Abrasiveness	21.4%	Delivery time	27%
Pool (Y/N)	19.4%	Versatility	12.6%	Technology	19%
Cleaning	11.6%	Type	20.1%	Brand name	16%
Brand name	16.2%	Brand name	27.2%	Spare parts	14%

Brand choice across different industries

Sources: Cobb-Walgren, Ruble and Donthu (1995); Bendixen, Bukasa and Abratt (2004).

We can clearly see that brand names add value in all three industries. A strong brand name works as a sort of **halo effect**, a spill-over phenomenon which offers a perceived enhanced solution to the overall product. That is, it is the most important factor in the FMCG (fast moving consumer goods) category but it is relevant also for hotel chains and in the industrial market.

In the industrial (B2B) market, the importance of brand name varied across groups in the workplace (i.e. B2B decision-making unit). For buyers, the importance of brand names was the same as the overall results show (16%). For users (28%), technical specialists (24%) and decision makers (19%), the brand name was relatively more important. For gatekeepers the brand name importance was only 7%.

Meanings that are projected through consumption of brands can be highlighted, nurtured and even created by marketing communications. The 'exchange relationships' referred to in the chapter opener illustrate the key linkage between branding and communications. The market exchanges espoused by Bagozzi (1978, cited in Lott and Maluso 1995) are now enhanced by relationship exchanges (Dwyer *et al.* 1987, cited in Sheth and Shah 2003) and emotional exchange. This mutually beneficial arrangement can be both symbolic and symbiotic. Now, let's examine the importance of branding in this process.

Advertising and other information sources affect how the psychological and physical aspects of a brand are perceived; perceptions are the foundation of brand value and marketing effectiveness. The so-called 'cola wars' between *Coca-Cola* and *Pepsi* demonstrate both the power of marketing communications as well as the cognitive and emotional relationship that consumers have with brands. In 1985, following 'blind taste tests', consumers expressed a preference for *Pepsi* (51%) over *Coca-Cola*. In response, and in an act of now infamous rashness, *Coca-Cola* withdrew the classic formula *Coke* for a 'New Coke' to take on the taste of *Pepsi*. Public reaction was overwhelmingly negative: the Coca-Cola Company totally underestimated the intangible, symbolic value to the target audience of the original product. Consumers felt that iconic *Coke* epitomised the spirit of America and rejected the 'new' brand. Some people even likened the change in *Coke* to trampling the American flag! On 11 July, *Coca-Cola* had to quickly retreat, taking *New Coke* from store shelves and reintroducing *Coke Classic*. With the help of extensive marketing communications, *Coca-Cola* succeeded in clawing back lost business but it has learnt a bitter lesson: 'We did not understand the deep emotions of our customers', admitted company President Donald R. Keough.

Latterly, PepsiCo has invested enormously in product development and marketing communications in an effort to gain market share in this category, but *Coca-Cola* remains the leading brand, outselling *Pepsi* in more or less every geographical market (de Chernatony and McDonald, 1998). According to Interbrand's annual ranking of the best global brands, *Coca-Cola* still has a brand value (financially) that is more than five times higher than *Pepsi*. How has *Coca-Cola* achieved such a strong relative position compared to *Pepsi*?

Pepsi tastes at least as well as *Coca-Cola* but can't translate this into brand sales and market share. That's because there is a difference between 'actual' and 'communicated' product; the difference is **perceptual**: what consumers think and feel about the brand is critical. And marketing communications helps consumers link certain associations to a brand, to position a brand in the mind as well as the market. Figure 2.1 shows the results of similar 'blind tests' for a number of beer brands. Figure 2.1(a) shows where brands have been tested blind and Figure 2.1(b) where they have been labelled. Differences between test groups were dramatic. One can clearly see how different beer brands have taken distinctive positions in the market and how these positions affect taste perceptions.

Even when customers objectively realise physical differences, they can have different subjective opinions about brands. This can be seen in some recent academic research (Cobb-Walgren, Ruble and Donthu 1995) which looked at brands with similar offers but differentiated by advertising and other marketing communications. Tables 2.1 and 2.2 show results from the hotel category. In Table 2.1, Consumer Reports (an independent organisation that has high credibility in consumer product tests and surveys) ratings are depicted. The two hotel chains *Holiday Inn* and *Howard Johnson* were at the time of the study very similarly evaluated. The customer satisfaction index (on a 100-point scale) is almost identical and the Consumer Reports ratings on hotel attributes are identical with one exception – locations.

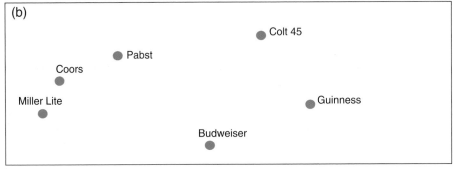

Figure 2.1: Positioning maps that show how different beer brands are perceived in blind taste tests (a), and when the brand names are disclosed in taste tests (b)

Source: Keller (1998).

Criterion	Brand	
	Holiday Inn	Howard Johnson
Customer satisfaction	73	74
Cleanliness	3	3
Size of room	3	3
Bed comfort	3	3
Climate control	3	3
Noise	3	3
Amenities (linen & toiletries)	3	3
Staff (helpful & efficient)	3	3
Food quality	2	2
Swimming pool	3	3
Locations	East Midwest South West	East Midwest South
Typical locales	Central City Highway Resort	Central City Highway Resort

Consumer Reports ratings (1–5 scale, except 'Customer satisfaction' 100-point scale) of hotels

Table 2.1: Consumer Reports hotel ratings

Source: Cobb-Walgren, Ruble and Donthu (1995).

Brand	Unaided brand awareness	Advertising awareness	Perceived quality (1–7)	Brand associations (numbers)			
				Total	Positive	Neutral	Negative
Holiday Inn	85%	87%	5.4	4.0	1.9	1.8	0.3
Howard Johnson	10%	56%	3.6	3.5	0.4	2.0	1.1

Table 2.2: Customer-based brand equity for hotels

Source: Cobb-Walgren, Ruble and Donthu (1995).

This data is expanded upon in Table 2.2 with research into usage experience. When the researchers investigated the two hotel chains' advertising spends, interesting differences surfaced. They identified that *Holiday Inn* used marketing communications much more than *Howard Johnson*: from two to five times more in terms of advertising. How did this impact on consumer evaluations?

Here, typical advertising effectiveness measures are presented. Unaided brand awareness (brand recall), advertising awareness, perceived quality and brand associations (positive, neutral, and negative) were measured (see Aaker 1991). The results are striking. The difference between unaided brand awareness and the effects of advertising is marked: awareness is higher; perceived quality is enhanced; and brand associations are more favourable. Barnard and Ehrenberg (1997) referred to the ability of marketing communications to 'nudge' quality evaluations.

The relationship between positive and negative associations is also dependent on marketing communications. On average, each person in the study had almost two (1.9) good things to say about *Holiday Inn*. For *Howard Johnson*, only two out of five persons (on average) had something positive to say about the *Howard Johnson* brand. Negative associations show the opposite result (more negative thoughts about *Howard Johnson*).

Comparisons were also made on purchase intentions and preferences and the importance of brand name as a feature in a choice situation was also measured. The purchase intentions were clearly higher for *Holiday Inn* than for *Howard Johnson*. The same results were found for preferences where *Holiday Inn* had 9.75 times greater utility than *Howard Johnson*.

Whilst brand building is dependent on marketing communications, there is also an interesting reverse relationship in how the brand affects how marketing communications are received and perceived. For example, initial brand knowledge preconditions advertisement perceptions (Lange and Dahlén 2003) with marketing communications for a familiar brand being interpreted differently than for an unfamiliar brand. Similarly, marketing communications for a strong brand are evaluated differently than marketing communications for a weak brand (Broniarczyk and Gershoff 2003; Dahlén and Lange 2005). There are also qualitative differences between brands that are equally familiar and strong which may affect how marketing communications are perceived, based on the brands' positioning in the market. The Matter of Fact box below features research conducted by Aaker, Fournier and Brasel (2004) into brand perceptions.

MATTER OF FACT

The Effect of Branding on Consumer Evaluations

Consumers relate to brands in different ways and marketing communications are perceived differently. How can the brand relationship be affected? In a controlled experiment over a two-month period in 2004 for an online film-processing company, two online brand images – a 'sincere' brand and an 'exciting' brand – were created and communicated in different ways:

(Continued)

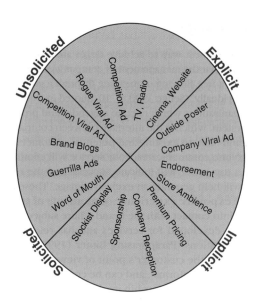

Figure 2.3: Brand encounters

audiences and stakeholders. *Levi Jeans* priced deliberately above the competition communicates the perceived distance between them and other denims.

Implicitly Planned Brand Encounters

Other elements of the marketing mix may implicitly communicate: the store ambience and cleanliness of a retailer (physical evidence) will convey a message of quality and service. The illustration on the right shows a typical *Halifax Bank* 'front of house' layout. The queue lines and graphics which may convey specific one-off brand messages will also help to position the brand 'in use'. This type of layout and appearance is entirely consistent with a financial services brand which needs to convey an image of credibility and efficiency and project a feeling of organisation.

Halifax front of house physical evidence

The opposite may be true of other stores which may need to communicate a different image dependent upon their market, their product and their value proposition. *Topshop* is a 'fast fashion' retailer which mainly competes on price. Similarly, H&M competes by being able to get the key trends from the catwalk to the store, before the next issue of *Vogue* has arrived on the shelves. Their stores are laid out in a way that evokes excitement, style and fashion.

Packaging can convey sophisticated luxury (*Ferrero Rocher*) or corporate and social responsibility (supermarket plastic bags policy). The absence of communication (Calonius 1989, cited in Grönroos 2004) can say more about a company or brand and have a negative effect on consumer perceptions. *Coca-Cola's* attempt at repeating in the UK their US success with *Dasani* bottled water was a PR disaster with the lack of immediate official explanation to a contamination problem sealing its fate. The use of celebrities to endorse brands can be either explicit (e.g. when the celebrity makes a statement of endorsement) or implicit (e.g. when a celebrity appears alongside a brand without making obvious reference to its qualities). Whereas Lewis

Fast fashion Topshop

Hamilton wearing his sponsors' corporate colours is considered **explicit sponsorship**, consumers who wear this sort of team uniform are like **implicit brand ambassadors**. This can sometimes undermine the brand: *Burberry* has been adopted by a group who has given the brand a 'Chav' image; the original *Fred Perry* sportswear has been appropriated as a youth uniform.

Solicited Planned Brand Encounters

Communications can be solicited (planned, semi-planned and authorised) through intermediaries which have a degree of uncontrollability. An organisation that depends on third parties to achieve, for example, a retail presence, may not have total control over the way the product is displayed or merchandised. Some companies recognise this and attempt to use some kind of leverage to standardise the way product is seen. For example, *Coca-Cola*, *Pepsi*, *Lucozade* and other soft drinks companies operate a 'free fridge tied distribution' policy which allows them to dictate what products are stocked and how they are displayed. This gives them a degree of control over how they introduce new products and the messages they need to put across to a mass audience at point of sale.

Unsolicited Unplanned Brand Encounters

Unsolicited communications may include: 'blogs' which discuss brands and do not represent the company's message or image; rogue viral advertisements which distort and ruin planned campaigns; competition viral advertisements which aggressively compare brands without recourse. This will impact on any positive word of mouth generated. Social network sites like *Facebook* and user-generated sites like *YouTube* have presented opportunities for extended dialogue. This can present problems with message or image. Organisations try to combat this by putting out their own materials (the Labour Party reacted to Gordon Brown's 'fortnight horribilis' in May 2007 by releasing official material onto *YouTube*) or encouraging replications of advertisements (see the case study on *Cadbury's* 'JOY' campaign in Chapter 1). The *Stella Artois* case study featured in Chapter 1 demonstrates how a brand's intended brand image and positioning was subverted by the brand's users.

Grönroos and Lindberg-Repo (1998, p.10) describe planned and unplanned communications as 'What the firm SAYS', 'What the firm DOES' and 'What others SAY and DO'. The degree to which these three types of communication are trusted is in direct variance to the degree of planning and control. That is, the least trustworthy is the company's planned campaign, and the most trusted source is peers in the brand experience. Figure 2.4 shows this range of explicit and implicit brand messages.

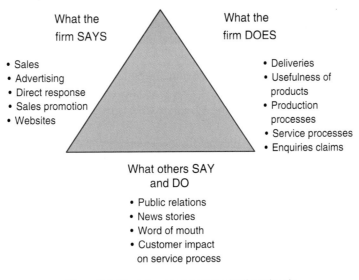

What the firm SAYS
- Sales
- Advertising
- Direct response
- Sales promotion
- Websites

What the firm DOES
- Deliveries
- Usefulness of products
- Production processes
- Service processes
- Enquiries claims

What others SAY and DO
- Public relations
- News stories
- Word of mouth
- Customer impact on service process

Figure 2.4: The integrated communication triangle

Source: Grönroos and Lindberg-Repo (1998, p. 10).

MARKETING COMMUNICATIONS IN FOCUS

How Marketing Communications Works

Take the trends for fruit smoothies, hectic lifestyles, health supplements, energy-inducing drinks, and the adoption of 'shots' as the trendy consumption method of choice. Put them together in a small bottle with a big kick and you have *Big Shotz*, the first nutrient-fortified fruit juice shot with levels of vitamins and minerals to match multivitamin supplements.

Recently launched into the chilled impulse sector, developed by *Shotz Health*, *Big Shotz* is effectively a new brand in a new category and is aimed at emulating the success of other start-up brands such as *Innocent Smoothies*. This brand is a good example of how all elements of marketing communications can be combined cohesively to present a consistent narrative:

Big Shotz moments of truth

- **Targeting and positioning:** aimed at 'time-poor', convenience-minded consumers in the chilled impulse category as a hybrid between energy drinks and vitamin supplements.
- **Product:** Mango and passion fruit flavour containing 17 vitamins and minerals, omega 3, pre-biotic fibre and ginseng all crammed into a 120ml bottle, providing an easy solution to diet supplementation.
- **Packaging:** Unique liquid food-form vitamin drink packaged in small bottles styled on potion bottles, to enhance the bold message graphic (designed by *a.m.associates*).
- **Brand name and identity:** chosen as being descriptive of product benefit and synonymous with target market use, the name has helped to position the brand in the marketplace within the 'chilled impulse category' as well as alongside products in the 'vitamin supplements' sector. The use of the noun 'shotz' is resonant of the target market practice of drinking 'shots' of trendy brands.
- **Offline press and online website advertising:** the continuation of the 'It's a nutrition revolution' tagline across all media platforms (as well as packaging and point-of-sale materials) conveys a strong brand message. The *Big Shotz* story is present in all media and the back history is extended online.
- **Promotion:** in-store sampling of product has been helped by the convenient 120ml bottles which provided evidence of drink potency and taste.
- **Distribution:** initially launched exclusively to *Selfridges*, but now with wider distribution through leading multiples such as *Waitrose* and *AMT Coffee*. Details of how new distribution can be set up is available on its website.

For a campaign which demonstrates total integration of marketing communications, it is quite apt that the agency who has largely conceived, designed and implemented the *Big Shotz* story is called *Branded Moments of Truth*.

BRAND CONVERSATIONS

The move to more relational communications characterises a change from a 'telling and selling' managerial perspective to one of brand community sharing. The impact of technology-assisted peer-to-peer communications has made the need to have continuous conversations even more acute. Most organisations will now extend the brand's narrative on websites. This represents an opportunity to engage in some form of dialogue or **brand conversation** in which interactivity is critical. Because of the interactive nature of the Internet the communication process has become a 'real-time dialogue' (Grönroos 2004).

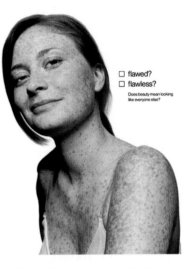

Dove's flawless communications

Brands like *Dove* have not only sold lots of product, but engaged the target audience in a dialogue which is continued and expanded on the company website. The 'What is Beauty?' agenda may have been instigated in the advertisements or in the marketplace, but the *Dove* brand is now perceived as an authentic, authoritative company with integrity and meaning.

According to Ballantyne and Varey (2006), 'marketing's unused potential is in the dialogical mode'; this requires participation, shared meaning and the motivation to build and maintain ongoing communication. Hoffman and Novak (1999) describe this interactivity as being not just between people but mediation of machines also. These types of **brand conversations** that can occur directly or indirectly between company and customer are illustrated in Table 2.3.

Description	Type	Direction	Characteristics	Source	Recipient	Example
Primary B2C	Mass	One-way outbound	Monologue OUT TO target audience	Company initiated	Stakeholders and selected target market	Campaign to raise brand awareness
Secondary B2C	Mass	One-way outbound	Monologue OUT TO target audience	Company initiated	Customer	
B2B	Inter	One-way outbound	Monologue OUT TO target audience	Company initiated	Transaction intermediaries	
B2B	Inter	Two-way outbound	Monologue OUT TO/IN target audience	Company initiated	Transaction intermediaries	
C2C	Inter	Two-way across	Monologue OUT TO target audience	Company initiated	Customer	
C2C	Intra	Two-way across	Monologue OUT TO target audience	Company initiated	Customer	
B2E	Intra	One-way internal	Monologue OUT TO target audience	Company initiated	Employee	

(Continued)

Description	Type	Direction	Characteristics	Source	Recipient	Example
E2B	Intra	One-way internal	Monologue OUT TO target audience	Company initiated	Company	
E2B	Intra	One-way internal	Monologue OUT TO target audience	Company initiated	Company	
E2B	Intra	Two-way internal	Monologue OUT TO target audience	Company initiated	Company/ Employee	

Abbreviations: B2C – business to consumer; B2B – business to business; C2B – consumer to business; C2C – consumer to consumer; B2E – business to employees; E2B – employees to business

Table 2.3: Brand conversations

THE MECHANICS OF THE MARKETING COMMUNICATIONS PROCESS

In order to begin to understand how organisations create and maintain ongoing dialogues with target audiences, and equally, how individuals interpret brand meaning, we need to examine the mechanics of the communication process. All successful marketing communications has to be underpinned with a sound knowledge of buyer behaviour, so there needs to be a discussion on how we process information from marketing communications stimuli. But we also need to examine the nuts and bolts of the process and consider both the endogenous (within the process) and extraneous (outside environmental influences) factors which condition the way communication is received. What are the sequential processes that consumers have to go through to make product choices? According to Rossiter and Bellman (2005, p. 24), there are three simultaneous levels of marketing communications effects: the processing of the actual communication itself (e.g. a press advertisement); the stage in the decision-making process (e.g. searching for information); and the overall stage in the brand communication effects (e.g. selection of brand preference). There are a number of views on how communication is transmitted, mediated or individually negotiated, and the following section provides an introduction to this debate.

CONVENTIONAL APPROACHES TO HOW MARKETING COMMUNICATIONS WORKS

Most of the conventional communication 'process models' derive from Schramm's original 1954 Linear Communication Model and the subsequent versions refined by Weaver and Shannon (1963). The basic premise of these communication frameworks is that marketing messages are transmitted from a source to a receiver through some sort of media conduit. Indeed, linear-developed and sender-controlled marketing campaigns have for some time been the main paradigm for marketing communications: inject a message through media as a stimulus to a target audience and evoke a response. This transmission effect process has grown out of cybernetics, underpinned by behaviourist psychology, and may not be entirely appropriate to today's media and consumer. In this section, we will analyse how the process works and doesn't work, but let's firstly look at the components which make up the transmission model:

• **Source or sender** can be an individual or organisation responsible for identifying a need (e.g. a new hybrid car being introduced to provide an answer to ecologically friendly motoring) as a market opportunity who wants to convey this message to a target audience. Effectiveness of communication, according to Kelman (1961), will be a result of whether we feel the source is: **credible** (the claim of an advertisement appears to come from an 'expert'); **attractive** (we like the person making the claim); or the source has **power** to affect behaviour because of perceived reward or punishment (e.g. Inland Revenue self-assessment advertisements which frighten the self-employed to comply). *Gillette's* campaign featuring the Holy Trinity of Tiger Woods, Roger Federer and Thierry Henry is a powerful use of celebrities who have credibility and are attractive. When companies use celebrities to endorse brands because they are perceived as credible or attractive sources, meaning may be transferred. The *Halifax Bank* in the UK has used actual employees as spokespersons for its brand, such as Howard Brown from the Sheldon Branch of the *Halifax* who personifies the honesty and integrity of the company and reinforces this by being an authentic source of communication.

Gillette gets the best endorsers

- **Encoding** is the representative element of the brand message or idea used to convey meaning: words, colour, pictures, signs, symbols or even music (e.g. the sound of a brass band being redolent of simpler times or heritage). This can often be the semiotic arrangement of 'cues' (e.g. the *Nike* 'swoosh' indicates success).
- **Media** refers to all the communication channels which carry the message from sender to receiver and can affect the meaning of the brand to the target audience. This may be positive (e.g. exposure of a product at a prestigious event) or negative (e.g. brands scheduled on Channel 4 during the *Big Brother* race scandal). For a full discussion on media, see Chapter 13.
- **Decoding** is the process of interpreting messages and relies on correct encoding and the ability of the receiver to deconstruct transmitted meaning.
- **Feedback** is crucial since dialogues are two-way and depend on reaction to intended communications. This feeds back into the communication process and future messages may be changed and made more appropriate.

Figure 2.5 shows how all the elements are integrated located within a linear flow model or communication loop which may start with the sender (brand owner) but meaning may be negotiated and altered by the audience(s) who receive the message.

As we can see, there are a number of factors which may prevent intended messages being correctly received and interpreted:

- **Source or sender's 'frame of reference'** refers to the fact that the sender is both the originator of the communication and also part of the process. The sender's analysis of the market dynamics and audience is critical to successful communications. Whether or not a message will be understood by an audience is dependent upon the sender's judgement in the management of emotion, information or ideas which make up message formation.
- **Receiver's 'frame of reference'** can be influenced by attitudes, values and perceptions stemming from knowledge, experience or the influence of other people. Successful communication is predicated on both the sender's and receiver's frames of reference coinciding and the receiver's ability to interpret and understand the message sent. If the language, images or symbols used by the sender are not understood by the receiver, communication of the message will not take place. *Carling* used the theme of affiliation to communicate an association of brand and social situation in its

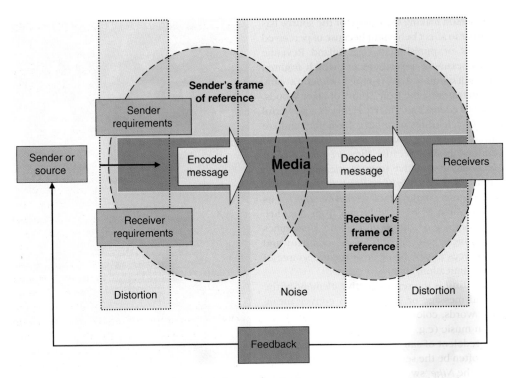

Figure 2.5: The communication process

Source: after Schramm (1954) and Shannon and Weaver (1963).

The Carling gang sells affinity

'Belong' TV and cinema campaign. Initially, the use of migrating birds to illustrate the natural 'flocking together' of kindred spirits proved to be a little too ambiguous to its target audience. Later incarnations showing a 'gang of lads out for the night' had a much bigger impact as the images were within the 'frame of reference' of those receiving the communications. The juxtaposition of 'the lads together' set in unusual places (in a tent atop Mount Everest or boarding the Shuttle for the moon) only added to the obvious common associations of not being allowed into clubs or celebrating a birthday even when circumstances may prevent it.

- **Noise** is the physical or psychological elements either from inside or outside of the process which may block or interfere with communications. Physical noise is often badly produced images or messages (e.g. poor print quality) or elements of distraction (e.g. competitive messages or consumer 'zapping' of TV advertisements). Psychological noise could be mixed meanings, poor credibility of source or the irrelevance of the message to consumer requirements.
- **Distortion** can occur when a message is badly coded or decoded. The salesperson who is badly briefed or misses the point of a new product launch may distort the organisation's intended launch pitch. Word of mouth is a powerful agent in marketing communications but can sometimes distort the intended sender's message. Remember the *Stella Artois* case study in Chapter 1? The basic

problem there was the distortion of the sender's intended message: 'Reassuringly Expensive' by the target audience who perceived the brand as 'Wife Beater'.

There are extraneous factors which may influence either positively or negatively the message sent. There may be informal media conduits – or communication intermediaries – who help spread the brand message.

THE INFLUENCE OF INTERMEDIARIES IN THE DISSEMINATION OF INFORMATION

As far back as 1948, Laszerfeld, Berelson and Gaudet, in an analysis of the 1940 US Presidential election campaign, identified a significant factor in the dynamics of how communication works between sender and receiver. Their 'two-step' intermediary model of communication was later developed within a marketing context where it was noted that people tend to be more affected by influential **homophilous groups** (family and friends) and also **heterophilous groups** (outside an individual's personal network) rather than by the mass media (Laszerfeld and Menzel 1963).

This process, known as **social mediation**, introduced the notion of opinion leaders (sometimes called gatekeepers or parasocials). Opinion formers (sometimes known as change agents) having a formal expertise occupy a professional position of formal influence over groups: doctors, lawyers, journalists and so on. Opinion leaders and opinion formers are influential in shaping the opinions of others (Flynn, Goldsmith and Eastman 1996); opinion formers are considered to be official specialists in the product area (Egan 2007; Smith and Taylor 2004). Opinion leaders are regularly perceived by their immediate peer group to embody the characteristics of an innovator, a socialite and to be of a higher social status (Smith and Taylor 2004). Opinion leaders do not have the same standing in terms of offering expert recommendation, but they have higher social standing and are very influential within a peer group. Figure 2.6 illustrates the role opinion leaders have in the process, adding another link in the communication chain and acting as a 'meaning filter' for the targeted audience.

Whereas **non-personal communications** (such as the traditional media of mass-media advertising) are characterised by a 'delayed feedback', and **personal communications** (such as face-to-face

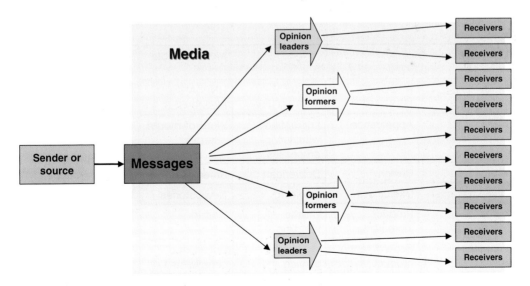

Figure 2.6: Two-step flow communication process

Source: after Katz and Laszerfeld (1955).

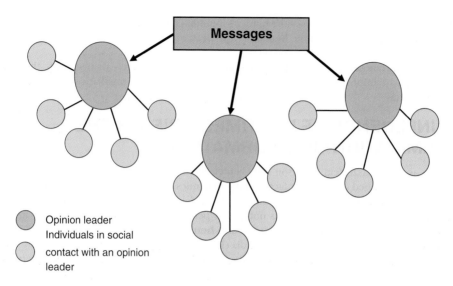

Figure 2.7: Two-step flow communication process showing OL influence

selling) may be undermined by the credibility of the source, **interpersonal communications** are seen as having a major influence on consumer decision making. As targets for direct communications, opinion leaders become surrogate media experts and filter messages from sender to receiver, occupying a position of informal influence over the attitude of others through trust and credibility. These types of communication are often described as 'trickle-down' (mass communications), or even 'trickle-up' (feedback 'up' from the marketplace), but more often in evidence is **'trickle-across'** **communications** from group to group. This phenomenon is one of the key factors in successful marketing: oral communications or word of mouth. Figure 2.7 shows how opinion leaders can be targeted to filter information to groups of like-minded consumers. Sources of communication range from the least trusted (company planned campaigns) to most trusted (peer referrals). Table 2.4 shows a continuum of credibility.

Least credible			**Most credible**	**ABSENCE of COMMUNICATION**
PLANNED MESSAGES	PRODUCT MESSAGES	SERVICE MESSAGES	UNPLANNED MESSAGES	**No information or feedback when an**
Mass communications	Appearance	Interaction with service processes	Word-of-mouth referrals	**unexpected delay or service failure has occurred, or in**
Brochures	Design	Deliveries	References	**any situation when the customer feels**
Direct response	Usefulness	Invoicing	News stories	**he is out of control**
Sales	Product ingredients	Claims handling	Gossip	**of the situation**
Websites	Eco-content of product	After sales service	Unreported complaints	

Table 2.4: Sources of communication by type

Source: After Duncan and Moriarty (1997).

WORD OF MOUTH AND PEER-TO-PEER COMMUNICATIONS

The impact of word of mouth is very often greater than planned communications since the source is not seen as being from the company but from other customers. Key to this is the neutrality of the source, but so is the nature of marketing communications which is based on the relationships engendered by long-term experiences and behavioural commitment. Lindberg-Repo and Grönroos (1999, p. 115) refer to this as 'psychological comfort or discomfort' which underpins the advocacy bonds that brand loyalty breeds. The person who has positive personal experience will be seen as an objective source of information. The word of mouth generated for Nintendo's *Wii* has proved to be much more positive than that of the competing brands. For the first 60 days after launch, Windows *Xbox* sales followed *Wii*, but, together with the rest of the competition, just couldn't keep up, as illustrated in Figure 2.8.

Word-of-mouth communication is particularly relevant to the introduction of new product or services where 'connected marketing' can help ignite conversations in target markets which result in positive word of mouth and ultimately add value to the brand. Rogers (1962) referred to opinion leaders as 'innovators' who are first to adopt brands before helping to diffuse them throughout the rest of the market. Innovators are people who consume product information and media content, interpreting and disseminating it to opinion followers. A campaign aimed at opinion leaders will be different to the communications aimed at the rest of the marketplace. Specialist magazines, conferences and other forms of specifically targeted communications and small, restricted opinion leader media will be used.

Digital technology provides not just an opportunity for more immediate and direct (and in some instances more personalised) communications, but provides a much more mediated context which enables the influence of opinion formers and leaders within the media and the target audience peer group. Far more consumer conversations happen in the 'digital world' where, as Rowley (2004, p. 25) states: 'marketing communication is concerned with creating presence, relationships and mutual value'. She draws the distinction between 'one-to-many' linear communications like TV, press, radio, newsletters, direct mail and so on which have a 'push' approach, and the nonlinear, free-flow 'many-to-many' and 'one-to-one' online communications. Hagel (1999) referred to 'community, commerce, content and communication as essential components for successful web presence', engaging consumers in online virtual communities being key to understanding and developing ongoing relationships. These B2B, B2C and C2C communities are personal interest-oriented and extended transaction-oriented media and therefore have more relevance in disseminating communication.

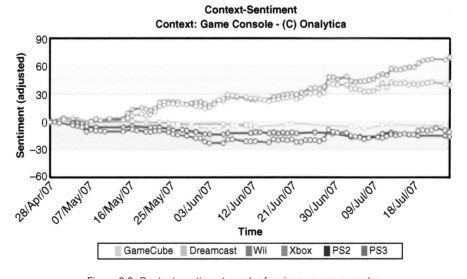

Figure 2.8: Context-sentiment graph of various games consoles

With the growing availability of broadband, expansion of Web 2.0, and augmented consumer empowerment, the power of spreading information by word of mouth becomes more powerful on the Internet (or Blogsphere) where the proliferation of online communities and social network sites (such as *Facebook*, *MySpace* and *LinkedIn*) facilitates conversations that can hyper-accelerate the spread of information. People may filter out advertisements, but they do listen to people they know and trust. Social network theory and the ever-increasing emotional connection with brands allow for the element of advocacy and referral to create a 'buzz' around a brand.

An increasingly influential marketing communications phenomenon is **viral marketing**, a sort of interactive advertising. Hotmail was reputedly the first example of this online 'accelerated word of mouth' (or 'word of mouse' if you prefer!), encouraging people to redistribute messages in a rapid fashion. In 2005, a blogger heard a rumour about a new project starring Samuel L. Jackson (*Snakes on a Plane*). This soon had a life of its own resulting in incredible word of mouth.

This type of B2C network-enhanced word of mouth is dependent upon the 'pass-along rate' from person to person (C2C) and has the advantage of peer credibility and source authenticity. It takes advantage of social networking where 'market mavens' (Childers 1986) act as 'social hubs' (Feick and Price 1987). Social scientists tell us that each person has a network of 8–12 people in their close network of friends, family and associates. A person's broader network may consist of scores, hundreds or thousands of people.

Gladwell (2000) described a 'tipping point' in the adoption process where trends are ushered into popularity by small groups of individuals that he classified as mavens, connectors and salesmen. 'Mavens' are knowledgeable about product and have a strong compulsion to help other consumers to make informed decisions; 'connectors' are individuals who have acquaintances in many different social spheres and act as cultural conduits (informal channels of communication), helping to engender connections, relationships and cross-fertilization of information; and 'salesmen' are charismatic people who can be extremely persuasive in inducing others' buyer behaviour.

Research has been done into the informal internal marketing activities and subsequent learning processes that occur through informal information sharing between employees. As a result of using this approach, insights have been made into how the sharing of work experiences can create successful service encounters and help employees find their roles as part-time marketers within their organization.

One example of message and media being channelled direct to the user was the *Flickr* viral 'It's Flicky' campaign (designed and executed by *The Viral Factory*, info@theviralfactory.com) devised for *Samsung UK's X830* mobile phone which resulted in close to three million views with over 55% expressing positive purchase intentions. This was a good example of how to demonstrate product (the unique easy-to-use 'flick' feature) within the context of the target audience. Another example, which the *Sunday Telegraph* described as 'the most imaginative car ad yet', was the viral advertisement for *Ford's SportKa*. Positioned as 'the evil twin to the *Ford Ka*', this advertisement featured a pigeon being catapulted across the road and was listed on 200 separate sites according to *Google*.

Viral marketing has sometimes been pejoratively referred to as 'stealth marketing' because it allows a pre-launch buzz to be generated for a brand and is often done without traditional media influence. The movie *The Blair Witch Project* was screened in 1999 after months of mythical misinformation on the Internet; *Cadbury's* created their *Gorilla* advertisement in the style of a *YouTube* viral and won the best advertisement award for 2007; and latterly the movie *Cloverfield* evoked post 9/11 paranoia in America with its slow-burn, mysterious Manhattan attack imagery of its ambiguous trailers.

However, in today's world of online 'create, customize and share' consumer experiences, it's the new form of nonlinear communications that allow consumers to participate in and shape the brand narrative. *GE*'s *Ecoimaginaton* story – with its engaging nonlinear 'Plant a seed and watch it grow' online application – extends its *Ecoimagination* ideal from a linear television narrative to an interactive opportunity for consumers to participate in the brand story. *Nike*'s 'Just Do It' ideal is reinforced with a linear story in its TV schedulings, but *Nike ID*'s 'Create your own shoe' application provides a nonlinear online complement that actually allows you to Just Do It . . . online. These examples demonstrate how the traditional linear, one-directional, transmitted communication process is being supplanted by interactive, two-way, nonlinear dialogues.

DIFFERENT MARKETING COMMUNICATIONS PROCESS PERSPECTIVES

The tradition of studying marketing communications draws heavily on communications 'science' (Buttle 1995) emphasising meaning as explicitly uni-directional, transmitted through a channel. This is essentially what is called a 'formalist/objectivist' approach where meaning is contained within a 'conduit' (Reddy 1979) of an active sender and the receiver takes a passive role in a single-step process. Marketing communication has been described as being a one-way, one-dimensional, linear process from sender to receiver. This has been referred to as the 'hypodermic needle' approach (Klapper 1960), or latterly 'bullet theory of communication' (Schramm 1971) where a message is injected into a mass media channel, implying that the intended message remains intact and is not changed throughout the process. It derives from the US business transmission models of communication. However, there are other perspectives which supplement this linear model: one where meaning is negotiated or constructed in a dialogical, socially interactive way which is referred to as 'constructionist'; and another 'subjectivist' view. These last two are more symmetrical models and espouse individual interpretation and re-creation.

Gorgeous Weightwatchers

Hackley and Kitchen (1998, p. 232) posit that a social constructionist perspective legitimises the notion of marketing communications as it becomes more difficult to 'see consumer behaviour in terms of an elicited response to a targeted message' as meanings are socially constructed or 'culturally constituted' as McCracken (1988) originally claimed. Put simply, the appeal has to have relevance to the audience. The *WeightWatchers* 'Top up your gorgeousness' campaign featured a series of post-feminist (à la *Sex and the City*) appeals espousing both female achievement and indulgence.

In today's mediated environment (Borcher 2000) this is no longer the case, as the mass media is seen often as being used as an information source with messages filtered through other intermediaries who act as surrogate conduits in the dissemination of information. Also, communications can be both **overt** (advertising, TV, word of mouth, writing or signalling to each other) and **covert** (viral marketing, loyalty expressed by wearing clothes and using brands) and may be recreated by users of the brand and the brand communications. What this implies is that marketing communications does not operate in a vacuum and cannot rely on one-way communications: it is subject to external influences and internal interpretations. It also considers the fact that models based on rational appeals linked to product features are not the only method of communicating to (or more importantly with) an audience. But what are the cognitive and behavioural stages that the target audience must be taken through to effect behaviour change? Let's have a look at some of the traditional 'sequential models' which help explain this.

APPROACHES TO HOW CONSUMERS PROCESS MARKETING COMMUNICATIONS IN MAKING PURCHASE DECISIONS

As has been previously stated, the purpose of marketing communications is to:

- differentiate a brand against its competitors;
- provide information about product features or the brand's value proposition;

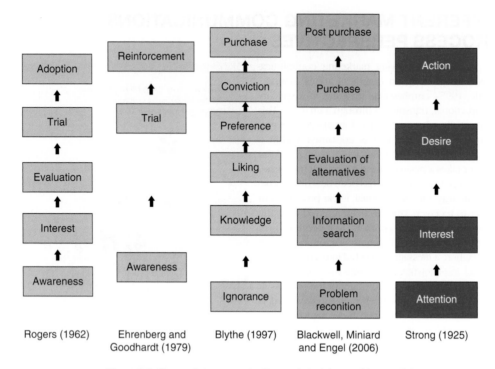

Figure 2.9: Sequential communication and decision-making models

Source: Rogers (1962), Ehrenberg and Goodhardt (1979), Blythe (1997), Blackwell, Miniard and Engel (2006), Strong (1925).

- reassure or remind consumers that the brand is still available, and will still do all the things that have previously been claimed; and
- persuade the target audience to change attitude, select product from possible choices and alternatives and continue to stay loyal to the brand when future purchase decisions are made.

What approach to communicating should we take to achieve these objectives? How do consumers process information from marketing communications to make decisions of product purchase? Dependent upon the stage in the sequence, the communication objective may be **cognitive** (awareness, knowledge, information gathering), **affective** (liking, preference, conviction) or **conative** (purchase, action). This often gets translated into 'think, feel, do' or 'head, heart and hands'. These may be linked and this is referred to as a **communication objective chain**, implying a sequential process or hierarchy of effects. Figure 2.9 shows some of the sequence of decision-making models which have been the mainstay of discussions on 'how marketing communications works'.

There are varying views of whether marketing communications has a cause and effect impact on audiences. Some suggest a direct link to action; others argue that marketing communications only support decision making and do not induce it.

There are basically two perspectives on information processing and how consumers respond to marketing stimuli: **cognitive (logical reasoning)** and **hedonistic (sensory-emotive)**. Figure 2.10 shows these two opposites on a continuum of the 'highly cognitive, systematic and reasoned' (Shimp 1997) CPM (consumer processing model) and the 'fantasies, feelings and fun' HEM (hedonistic, experiential model) suggested by Holbrook and Hirschman (1982).

The CPM perspective has its roots in psychological research: exposure to communication stimuli; paying selective attention to messages which are relevant and of interest; interpreting or making sense of messages by comprehending perceptual encoding; retaining information in memory; and through to action and then brand loyalty. This process describes a thoughtful, considered selection of

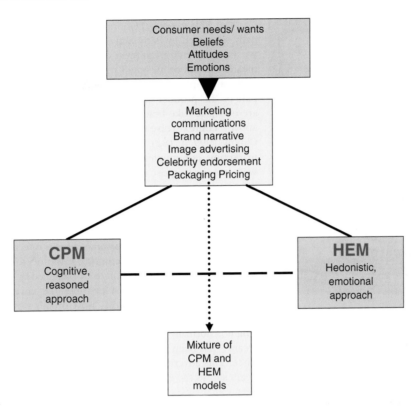

Figure 2.10: Approaches to consumer processing of marketing communications stimuli

Source: after Holbrook and Hirschman (1982) and Shimp (1997).

messages and progression to purchase: utility, value for money, best bargain, and what the functional attributes of the product are (for a full discussion on consumer decision making, see Chapter 3).

There is considerable debate as to whether consumers actively or passively process information, whether these extended process models are applicable to low-involvement as well as high-involvement products, and whether consumers are information processors or cognitive problem solvers.

In the 1980s, the 'cognitive paradigm' was challenged by researchers who took an experiential approach to consumption 'as a primarily subjective state of consciousness with a variety of subjective meanings, hedonic response and aesthetic criteria' (Holbrook and Hirschman 1982, p. 132). They placed HEM in a purely subjective perspective which sees products as more than objects: 'fun, fantasy and feelings'.

One approach outlines the facts; the other evokes feelings. Look at this advertisement for *Range Rover*. Would you say it appeals to CPM or HEM processing? The advertisement claims both functional benefits (the *Rover* is capable of standing up to enormous physical demands – and particularly against the domestic competition – *Volvo*) but it also uses very evocative and emotive imagery to make its point. Is the consumer being asked to act as analytical, logical, rational decision maker or as a result of feelings or even fantasy?

The truth is probably somewhere between the two (as suggested in Figure 2.10). Schramm (1997, p. 59) sums this up perfectly: 'you should think of these models as bipolar perspectives that anchor a continuum of possible consumer behaviours [...] pure reason – cold, logical, and rational; [...] pure passion – hot, spontaneous and perhaps irrational'.

Rugged Range Rover

Ben & Jerry's ice cream conscience.

Reproduced by permission of Unilever.

The ELM model (Elaboration Likelihood Model), originally suggested by Petty and Cacioppo (1986), suggests that we are motivated to process or respond directly to communication media or messages through one of two routes: centrally or peripherally. Stimuli which are intrinsic are a central part of the product or the brand's message; stimuli which are extrinsic (like brand image, price, location as discussed above) 'contextualise the [brand] experience' (Gabbott and Clulow 1999, p. 182). The degree to which we engage with marketing communications is called **elaboration**. Either way, it is the purpose of brand communications to reinforce links to help consumers make associations: *Nature Valley Crunchy Granola* positioned as 'natural'; the *Pentax K200D* and *Sony Handycam TG3* 'reflecting your dreams' and capturing 'special moments'.

A footnote on this discussion is what is referred to as the 'eco/ego contradiction' (Smith 2007): the need for pleasurable, self-centred consumption to be balanced by conscience consumption. We now must consider the environment as well as individual gratification. Most brands now feature a 'green' element in their communications. Even a product which is normally associated with pure pleasure – eating ice cream – has been positioned to appeal not just to hedonistic and rational needs and wants but conscience. This advertisement for *Ben & Jerry's* (a brand with a semi-hippy narrative) *Baked Alaska* ice cream shows the extended eco-friendly positioning.

CLOSING CASE STUDY

Microsoft Windows: Life Without Walls: Microsoft's Multimedia Fight Back Goes Right to the Core of Apple's Story

When Steve Ballmer, *Microsoft* CEO, delivered his first post-Gates keynote with a promise to bring the 'three screens' – mobile, PC and TV – together in a seamless experience, he spoke of the one billion *Windows* users as 'a vibrant community of individuals'. *Microsoft* has outgrown the limits of the personal computer and has progressed to 'Cloud' with *Windows Live* and *Windows mobile*.

'We're at the start of transforming what Windows is from a PC operating system to a connected experience. When I think of the future of Windows, I think of a life without walls'. The 'Life Without Walls' tagline reaffirms the mission of the *Windows* brand to put fewer walls between people, their passions and the global community.

Windows packs a punch in its fight-back campaign

After the derisive 'I'm a Mac' campaign, it was important to reflect the vast and varied human community in telling the story of the *Windows* brand. 'Windows versus Walls' clearly states *Microsoft*'s positioning: emphasise the connected, communal world by breaking down technological and psychological barriers between people; and attack *Apple*'s PC stereotypes.

Apple, as Number 2 'challenger brand' has been repeatedly attacking *Microsoft* since 2006 in much the same way as *Pepsi* and *Avis* have had to do against *Coca-Cola* and *Hertz*. With its monopoly dominance and ubiquity, *Microsoft* doesn't need to convince people to buy *Windows*, it needs to connect emotionally, experientially. It won't improve *Windows*'

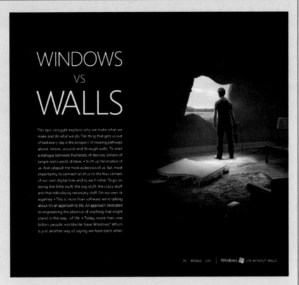

Windows vs Walls means Microsoft vs Apple

market share, but it may win 'mind share' and reassure its users. Its objective is to turn *Windows* users into advocates of PCs. The $300 million spend on advertising has brought the debate full circle. This time the strategy is simple: let the people defend us, by using real people in their advertisements to tell our individual stories. Users are encouraged to upload a 15-second or 30-second video to *MSN Video* and anyone can vote on them. *Microsoft* will pick the best and incorporate them into TV and web advertisements. Although there is prize money for those selected, the real benefit is ownership by the consumer, with user-generated content made in the style of TV advertisements and therefore reinforcing the message in a uniform but seemingly user-authored way. This turns the 'Windows is everywhere' ubiquity into the replication of many similar user testimonies.

The 'Windows Without Walls' and 'I'm a PC' campaigns are extended beyond TV and Press advertising (which feature normal people from all walks of life) as well as celebrities like Eva Longoria and astronaut Bernie Harris) via billboards, digital display units in airports and public buildings, and a parallel online story in websites, links and *YouTube* platforms. The common thread is community and engagement leading to signed-up advocacy. This campaign had antecedents in *Microsoft*'s internal communications in which an internal

Users pledge their allegiance to the brand

Microsoft marketing video was posted to *YouTube* which was so popular because it succinctly contrasted *Microsoft*'s approach to product marketing with *Apple*'s approach: humanity versus smugness.

QUESTIONS

1. How do you think *Apple* reacted to this counter campaign?

2. Why was online and offline synergy so important to the *Microsoft* campaign?

3. Why do you think that *Microsoft* has extended the creation of this storyline to its customers?

CHAPTER SUMMARY

In this chapter, we looked at: the 'mechanics' of the communication process; the purpose of applied brand communications; the links between integrated marketing communications and branding; and all the influences which help or hinder the successful reception of organisational/audience dialogues. We discussed the growing impact of peer-to-peer communications and we also examined the managerial versus interpretivist debate between traditional transmission models and a number of different perspectives including individual meaning interpretation.

Research into the importance of brand name across industries was discussed, providing an insight into the impact of branding on marketing communications. We saw how everything and everyone communicates and examined brand encounters which equate to exposure experiences or 'moments of truth' when a consumer comes into contact with the brand and where subjective evaluation takes place. The brand encounter frequently is the organisation from the customer's point of view, and we examined this in explicit and implicit brand communications in the marketing mix. This was extended to include those that were solicited (sanctioned by the company) and those that were not.

Overall, the importance of understanding target audience requirements and the need to create long-term meaningful dialogues was seen as the key to successful marketing communications.

REFLECTIVE QUESTIONS

a. How can a brand be described as being 'like a capsule of meaning'?

b. How can marketing communications affect how the psychological and physical aspects of a brand are perceived?

c. Brand encounters are 'moments of truth' (Normann 1991, p. 16) when a consumer comes into contact with the brand and where subjective evaluation takes place. Can you think of examples for a brand which you have purchased and consumed recently?

d. Differentiate between linear-developed and sender-controlled marketing campaigns and one which involves social mediation.

e. What were Lindberg-Repo and Grönroos (1999, p. 115) referring to in describing 'psychological comfort or discomfort' as underpinning the advocacy bonds that brand loyalty breeds?

RESEARCH PROJECTS

Look at the paper on 'Advertising Weak and Strong Brands: Who Gains?' written by Micael Dahlén and Frederick Lange published in 2005 in *Psychology and Marketing* (22(6), 473–88) and evaluate the arguments presented on advertising strong and weak brands.

Obtain a copy of Buttle's paper published in 1995 in the *International Journal of Advertising* ('Marketing Communications Theory: What Do the Texts Teach Our Students?' 14, 297–313). Compare the arguments described for 'positivist' and 'interpretivist' approaches to marketing communications.

Prepare for a debate on the different approaches.

PART 2

ANALYSIS AND PLANNING

FOR MARKETING COMMUNICATIONS

CHAPTER  3

ANALYSIS OF TARGET AUDIENCES

"Marketing fragmentation is a response to disconnected post-modern lifestyles, behaviours, moods, whims and vagaries of contemporary consumers. A product of profusion in a profusion of products, the post-modern consumer performs a host of roles, each with its requisite brand name array: wife and mother, career woman, sports enthusiast, fashion victim, culture vulture, hapless holiday-maker, Internet avatar and many, many more."
Brown (2000)

"The meaning in consumer goods is one of the ways in which we give our lives a consistency in the face of the overwhelming change to which it is subjected."
McCracken (1999)

This chapter makes the link between marketing communications and the dynamics of buyer behaviour. Individual motivation, attitude formation, perceptions, beliefs and so on are conditioned by the cultural and social environment within which they are constituted and stimulated by the elements of the marketing communications mix.

Therefore, in order to present a coherent, resonant proposition to target audiences, a thorough understanding of customer dynamics must be undertaken. We will be discussing a comprehensive range of buyer behaviour techniques and concepts in order to fully appreciate the role that an understanding of buyer behaviour has on marketing communications.

LEARNING OBJECTIVES

After reading this chapter, you'll be able to:

- Understand what the issues are in marketing communications and buyer behaviour.
- Examine the nature of consumer decisions.
- Compare the difference between informational and transformational motivations.
- Describe the internal and external influences on the buying decision process.
- Appreciate the role of marketing communications in consumer decision making.

There is an inextricable relationship between marketing communications and consumer behaviour:

- Knowledge of target markets informs marketing communications.
- Marketing communications is instrumental in affecting behaviour change, assisting and influencing consumer decision making.
- Equally, knowledge of how and why consumers purchase brands informs good marketing communications.

The formation and alteration of brand beliefs is assumed to influence, and therefore precede, brand buying behaviour (Winchester, Romaniuk and Bogonolova 2008). Consumers can be conditioned to develop favourable or unfavourable attitudes towards images (stimuli), including products and brands (Shimp 1991). When making purchase decisions, the credibility of the source of information, and the association with the benefits of the brand are important. Brand belief will depend on how complex the decision is and how involved the consumer is with the brand.

Therefore, a thorough understanding of what motivates individuals and how this can help to successfully position brands to mutually benefit company and consumer is required.

OPENING CASE STUDY

Ugg Boots: From Farm Footwear to Fashion Icon, How We Have Learned to Love the 'Uggly' Booty

The 200-year-old journey of the humble Australian sheep shearer's furry footwear to become the iconic choice of celebrities is a fascinating story. In 1978 when an enthusiastic young Australian surfer, Brian Smith, transported a piece of 'Down Under' magic to California, the *Ugg* boot fashion legend was born. Originally called 'Ug' or 'Ugh' (short for 'ugly'), it wasn't until it gained some form of cultural currency through celebrity exposure that consumers learned to love the ugly duckling *Ugg* boot. Now a high-fashion staple, an entirely new category of fashion footwear has been created. This is an unusual organic brand success story, and it is through imitative consumer behaviour that the brand has grown in both sales and appeal.

Uggly fashion

Source: Ugg® Australia.

(Continued)

Following the acquisition by *Deckers* in 1995, the *Ugg* brand was repositioned at the top end of the US retail market and received high-profile media attention. In fact, it could be argued that *Ugg* boots have enjoyed more celebrity endorsement than any other small fashion brand. In 2000, *Nordstrom*, the US chain of department stores, sold the boots in its branches all across America. The following year, the hugely influential Oprah Winfrey was sent a pair, which resulted in her declaring *Uggs* as one of her 'favorite discoveries of 2000'. She then spent more than $50,000 buying pairs for her 350 staff. As with so many brands, once Oprah's approval was secured, acceptance escalated and other endorsements by key influential celebrities soon followed.

By the time the first pair of *Uggs* arrived on British shores in 2003, the brand was an instant cult success. In 2004, the popular culture phenomenon *Sex and the City* featured Sarah Jessica Parker wearing custom-made red *Ugg* boots. Limited-edition remakes in key retailers instantly sold out. The affection for the boots has gathered apace with the likes of Kate Hudson, Cameron Diaz, Gwen Steffani, Liv Tyler, Carmen Electra, Sadie Frost, Jennifer Aniston, Kate Moss and a whole host of other high-profile female celebrities regularly photographed wearing theirs. *Ugg* President Connie Rishwain says, 'I pinch myself every time I see a pair on someone famous'. *Ugg* has arguably enjoyed more free celebrity endorsement than any other small fashion brand. 'It helps that they're such a recognisable item, too – it's so obviously an *Ugg* boot in those pictures'.

Recently, men have started wearing *Uggs* too. Justin Timberlake, Brad Pitt, Rolling Stones' Ronnie Wood, Leonardo DiCaprio and Jude Law are already fans and have helped to give the boot fashionable credentials whilst retaining the original masculine heritage of the brand. The launch of *Ugg* in Covent Garden featuring fashion-conscious Chelsea footballers mean this trend is set to continue.

The effect that celebrities have on buyer behaviour is in influencing consumer attitudes towards brands. Observing role models with cultural currency allows vicarious trial of the product and at the same time 'meaning is transferred' (McCracken 1986) from celebrity to consumer.

Ugg boots have grown organically by celebrities embracing the product. The issue of free product to key influential celebrities who act as surrogate consumers and unofficial brand ambassadors is a great example of the power of how 'free (gratis) product placement' can work.

QUESTIONS

1. What are the communication benefits of 'free (gratis) product placement' for a product like *Ugg* boots?

2. How do celebrities put 'meaning' into basic products like footwear?

3. How does marketing communications help this process?

MARKETING COMMUNICATIONS AND BUYER BEHAVIOUR

As we have seen, a thorough understanding of individuals' motivation and how this can help to position brands successfully to mutually benefit company and consumer is a prerequisite for successful communication. Solomon, Bambossy and Askegaard (2002, p. 6) explain this well by interpreting the consumer and marketer perspectives of three of the stages of the decision-making process: pre-purchase, purchase and post-purchase (Figure 3.1).

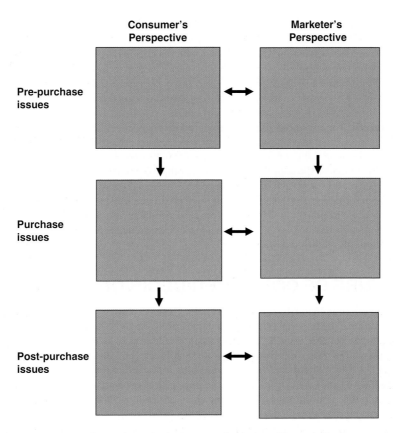

Figure 3.1: Issues in marketing communications and buyer behaviour

Source: Solomon, Bambossy and Askegard (2002, p. 6). Reproduced by permission of Pearson Education Ltd.

Pre-purchase: the difference between what a consumer **needs** to purchase and wants to purchase depends on the type of product, how it will be used and the context within which it will be consumed. Some products which are functionally or technically superior to other products may still suffer in comparison because they do not have the same cultural currency as other brands, and do not offer any value over and above the mere function of the product. *Apple* uses emotional branding and the symbolic meaning of consumption to position the *iPod* as not just another MP3 player but as a fashion item which helps consumers relate to other users. For other companies to compete, they have to match the emotional or 'affective' attachment that consumers have with this brand. At the heart of this is the notion of exchange relationships: that which is being exchanged when a consumer purchases a brand. If marketing communications directs purchases by offering signs, information and associations, the consumer needs to know where to get information from, and the brand owner needs to know how attitudes are formed and what communication cues will be effective in affecting attitude. In the *iPod* example, whilst *Apple* makes associations between its product and artefacts of cultural significance – be they celebrities or social settings – it also sends email information to previous users and potential customers (online enquirers) with full product details.

Purchase: the meanings that are ascribed to brands are negotiable. It is absolutely imperative that marketing communications presents the brand in the social context of how the brand will be consumed. The symbolic content of a brand in relation to consumer needs and the competition and how situational factors such as where and when the product is sold affect opportunities to purchase, is fundamentally important to successful marketing communications. What the brand says about the user is perhaps the most important aspect for some consumers, and products or services purchased for purely functional or economic reasons may require a less emotive message, as with the 'distress' purchase of car insurance – nobody wants to but we all have to! The rational comparison of alternatives is illustrated with the *Tesco Compare* website for example. Yet even these brands can be presented with an injection of brand personality, as with the friendly bulldog *Churchill*.

   Post-purchase: the meanings that are projected through marketing communications partly reflect consumers' individual perceptions, and partly the desired organisational position for the brand. As the life-time customer value of repeat purchase is vital to companies, and the further spread of word of mouth essential to the adoption of product, companies have to build in this element of social intercourse to the brand's narrative. The post-purchase regret (cognitive dissonance) which consumers experience may be functional, social, psychological or even ethical. For example, fair trade 'ethical' sourcing and environmentally friendly disposal of products add another layer of consideration to the consumer's purchase decision, and the stamp of conscience is becoming ubiquitous for many retail organisations and individual brands.

THE NATURE OF CONSUMER DECISIONS

In terms of sources of individual value in society, we have recently witnessed the diminishing influence of the traditional institutional pillars of the family, religion and education. Families have become cellular; society has become secular; education as a moulder of values has been supplanted by other information sources (see Blackwell, Miniard and Engel 2001 for a discussion on the diminishing influence of the culturally transfusive triad). As a result of this, the purchase of products, or more to the point, consumption of meaning through the purchase of brands, has taken on a completely different aspect. More and more consumers look to the marketplace for meaning and direction, which has as much to do with the impact of marketing communications as it has with the erosion of influence of the three institutional pillars of family, education and religion. The extreme of the rational/emotional continuum sees 'brand-obsessed shoppers [who] have adopted an almost fetishist approach to consumption in which the brand name acquires a talismanic power' Klein (2000). In making purchase decisions, consumers are influenced by the actual and perceived utility that is transferred with use: in other words, the consumption values of the brand. Sheth,

Choose Churchill? Oh yes!

© RBS Insurance. Reproduced with permission.

Newman and Gross (1991, p. 161) list five 'consumption values' that are acquired when individually or collectively choosing a brand:

- **Functional value:** the capacity of the brand to fulfil 'utilitarian' or practical requirements. Soap powder brands are communicated as 'washing whiter' than alternatives and focus on very basic functional ingredients.
- **Social value:** some brands are perceived as offering value because of their ability to enable affiliation with other groups (e.g. age, social class, country).
- **Emotional value:** this is acquired when a brand precipitates or perpetuates specific feelings. The trend for 'retro' brands feeds into our nostalgic associations which transfer us to a different place or time in our lives through memories of family, youth or formative years.
- **Epistemic value:** the 'curiosity' factor in a purchase – new adventures, different places and expanding one's experience. Holiday companies tap into this need for 'travel to broaden the mind'.
- **Conditional value:** certain situational factors such as celebration of events (birthdays, marriage, gift giving) carry another level of significance above the functional, social and emotional levels.

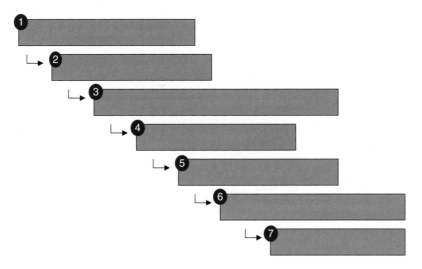

Figure 3.2: The Consumer Decision-Making Process Framework
Source: Blackwell, Miniard and Engel (2006).

The application of these consumption values is contingent on circumstance. What is important for marketing communications is that the company understands which values are important and why they are significant to the individual, and to design marketing communications programmes which position brands to resonate with consumers. How consumers process information and respond to marketing communications is the most important aspect of marketing communications. The two alternative cognitive/rational and emotional/experiential perspectives are discussed in Chapter 2.

Whether purchases are habitual, limited or require an extensive, involved thought process, consumers use a lot of marketing communications to help process information about product purchase. It is the responsibility of brand owners to present that information, in amongst the clutter of competing images and perceptions, in order to facilitate consumer choice. If marketing communications does this effectively, the more that brand loyalty will be maintained. So how do consumers process, interpret and integrate information? Blackwell, Miniard and Engel (2006) devised the Consumer Decision-Making Process Framework (Figure 3.2), which they referred to as representing 'a roadmap of consumers' minds that marketers and managers can use to help guide product mix, sales strategies and marketing communications'. This shows the more rational information-processing stages that a consumer may go through when purchasing and consuming a product or service.

1 Need or Problem Recognition

For companies, 'strategy isn't about beating the competition; it's serving customer's real needs' (Ohmae 1988). For consumers, needs are the initiators of the decision-making process; they may be physiological (e.g. hunger) or psychological (e.g. pleasure) and are activated when consumers perceive sufficiently large differences between their **actual** state and their **desired** state (Bruner and Pomazal, 1988). Marketing communications works at stimulating demand – often latent – or **thresholds** that activate needs or help solve 'problems' (see Figure 3.3 for stimulating thirst).

As long as the difference between actual and desired states is below the threshold, the consumer will not feel a need; as soon as the discrepancy increases and exceeds the threshold level, the need is recognised. The thresholds vary from one consumer to the next and also between product categories for the same individual consumer.

Consumers can also be motivated to varying degrees by different mind states: some consumers are more motivated by changes to their actual state (i.e. moving away from their current situation), whereas others are more inclined to change their desired state (i.e. motivated by the opportunity to get to a new

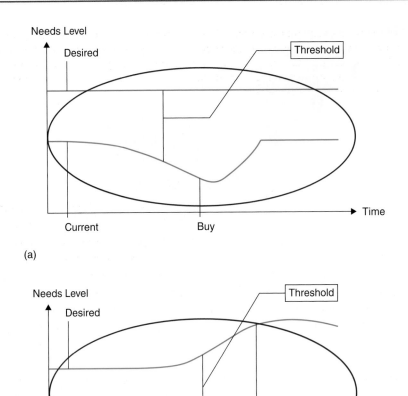

Figure 3.3: Consumers may purchase a product to (a) move away from the actual state;
(b) get to the desired state

Source: Dahlen and Lange (2003). *Optimal marknadskommunikation*, Liber Ekonomi. Reproduced with permission.

situation). Advertisements for a slimming product showing 'the new you' or a thirst-quenching drink will appeal to consumers wishing to change their actual state; one showing a 'last-minute travel deal' to the Mediterranean in November will be aimed at consumers wishing to change their desired state.

When a need is activated by an actual state discrepancy and then satisfied, the consumer is likely to 'return' to the original actual state. For instance, when thirst has been quenched the need is deactivated until the consumer gets thirsty again (see Figure 3.3a). Desired state purchases can sometimes result in an upward move in both the actual and desired states (see Figure 3.3b). Research has shown that when consumers replace an existing product with a new and better product, they sometimes raise their expectations in the category. Afterwards, the original product will be less attractive than before. For instance, if a new car is an upgrade in quality compared to the previous one, consumers will be unlikely to return to the previous quality level in future purchases. Some desired state purchases are short sighted and are not likely to induce systematic changes in future actual and desired states.

Another factor that may influence when, how and what kind of needs are recognised is time. Time is naturally important in everyday consumer needs (e.g. different seasons, weekdays versus weekends, day time versus night time), but changes over longer time periods also have a strong effect on need recognition (especially over the family life cycle with big changes following employment, marriage, salary increases, having children).

CONSUMER BEHAVIOUR IN FOCUS

Nice Coffee Cola. **Not Knowing the Customer**

In the 1990s a new energy drink was launched, *Nice Coffee Cola*. With the message 'Nice Coffee Cola – the Best from Two Worlds . . . For all Coffee and Cola Lovers' communicating its positioning on all its packaging, the brand tried to create a new category: a carbonated coffee drink with cola flavour. This offered the benefit of combined associations between caffeine-based beverages (coffee and cola) and the growing category of energy drinks. The benefits to company and consumer were obvious and the potential was tremendous since the market for a strong caffeine product aimed at cola lovers was enormous. However, it failed and *Nice Coffee Cola* did not last long on the market. Consumers did not really have a desire to drink the products simultaneously and the three categories of 'coffee', 'cola' and 'energy' represented distinctly different consumer needs.

Another example of not fully understanding consumer needs is what *PG tips* (tea) tried to do in the late 1990s. It had noticed the trend for soft drinks companies to supply refrigerated drinks cabinets to retailers in order to provide ready-to-serve cold drinks at the point of purchase. Shops, supermarkets, garages, sandwich bars and retail outlets could then provide an immediate way to satisfy consumer thirst in the most refreshing way. This was a great way for companies like *SmithKline Beecham*, *PepsiCo* and of course *Coca-Cola* to have 'tied distribution', forcing guaranteed stocking of their drinks. Consumers could also buy hot drinks in some of these places, so why not offer hot tea in a can in the same way? After all, companies like *Klix* and *Flavia* were offering hot drinks vending machines. So, the principle was reversed: offer a cabinet free of charge which could *heat* a range of favourite tea and coffee brands. It failed miserably. The taste of the tea produced and the fact that drinks were 'straight from the can' did not meet consumers' perceptions of what 'the need for a hot cup of tea' was and these cabinets went the same way as another classic misinterpretation of consumer needs: Clive Sinclair's now infamous *C5*, a 15-inch-high electric road vehicle!

The marketing examples above illustrate that companies often think of product benefits instead of consumer needs when they launch new products, and the two are different. If a consumer does not see the benefit or how the brand is different to others in the category, the impact of communicated messages will be negated. New products that are launched following a need analysis have a much better chance of success. Microwave ovens and sugar-free chewing gum are two examples of new products that were successful because they satisfied needs that consumers actually had. Microwave ovens were launched against a backdrop of 'time-poor' consumption needs and capitalised on growing consumer needs for quickly prepared meals. The chewing gum category grew significantly as consumers enjoyed chewing sugar-free gum without jeopardising the health of their teeth. Academically speaking, this satisfies what is referred to as **approach–avoidance** motivation: the attraction of chewing gum is offset by health concerns which are in turn dissipated by the new 'sugar-free'

Motivation	Description
Problem removal	Activated when consumers perceive that a problem needs solving or regular tasks have to be satisfied. Communications focus on problem solving like cravings for coffee or sweets or everyday chores like having to do the laundry to trigger the need for purchase
Problem avoidance	Sometimes consumers perceive that problems may happen and are motivated to make sure that they avoid a future problem. Distress purchases like insurance, toothpaste and deodorant all have communication appeals based on problem avoidance needs
Mixed approach avoidance	This motivation describes where consumers like some parts but dislike other parts of a product. Crisps may satisfy hunger but also make us put on weight. Communications which appear to provide a solution, for instance low-fat crisps and low-alcoholic beer, provide a good and reassuring solution to the problem
Incomplete satisfaction	Where existing brands do not fully answer needs, new brands may capitalise by offering a 'new and improved formula' or improved functionality
Normal depletion	Regular replenishment of purchase (particularly staple diet products like coffee, pasta, milk and batteries) are advertised for the convenience of stocking up

Table 3.1: Informational motivations

ingredient. Needs are not only utilitarian but also driven by emotions (Johar and Sirgy, 1991), and we can see this illustrated in Table 3.1. Rossiter and Percy (1998) list the different types of needs activated in purchase motivations, describing them as informational motivations (activated when a consumer recognises a need in the actual state) and transformational motivations (activated when consumers feel a need to move to a desired state).

All the five informational motivations require marketing communications messages which are based on emphasising functional solutions to problems; the three transformational motivations (Table 3.2) must highlight 'altered states' of some sort in communications.

Motivation	Description
Sensory gratification	This purchase motivation is about sensory experience (sight, hearing, taste, smell and touch). Consumers go to good restaurants to enjoy a nice meal, use aftershave and perfume to smell good, travel to beautiful places to see spectacular views and famous places to experience history. Appeals to sensory gratification are very common in transformational advertising where different pleasurable experiences are conveyed
Social approval	Consumers reduce their uncertainty by comparing behaviours of others to make sure that they fit in socially. Consumers have a strong social need to be affiliated to ascribed or aspirational reference groups. These groups indicate to the consumer what the 'right' product is as in famous social approval campaigns like 'Pepsi, the choice of a new generation'
Intellectual stimulation or mastery	Consumers want to learn more, get intellectual challenges and master new challenges. Educational products (like the *Nintendo DS*), adventure travel agencies, computer game companies, book publishers, universities and so on use this appeal for these sort of needs

Table 3.2: Transformational motivations

Source: based on Rossiter and Percy (1998, p. 56). Reproduced by permission of John Rossiter and Larry Percy.

Transformational messages must connect to consumer emotions to be effective. The functional solutions that may be used in informational marketing communications are not at all effective. The dual types of needs/motivations have many different names in marketing. Informational motivations are often referred to as rational, functional and utilitarian needs. Transformational motivations are expressive, experiential, emotional, symbolic and hedonistic needs.

MATTER OF FACT

Alternative Model of Needs and Message Strategies

The six-segment 'message strategy wheel' model is divided into both rational and hedonistic types of needs, which may form platforms for communication appeals.

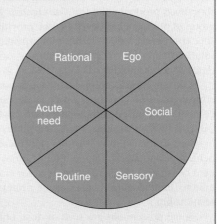

Message strategy wheel

Hedonistic needs

Ego: emotionally important purchases, allowing consumers to make an identity statement. Advertisements in categories like clothing and jewellery often execute image-based messages acknowledging an 'I am me' individual positioning.

Social: appeals for brands which make a statement to others focus on getting noticed, gaining social approval, engaging in socially correct behaviour and reliving social experiences through consumption of the product.

Sensory: in the case of product categories like music, fragrances, and clothing, the role of marketing communications is to convey sensory transformation.

Utilitarian needs

Routine: consumer decisions that are made on the basis of rational buying motives but where consumers do not spend a lot of time deliberating and buy according to habit. Advertisement appeals would be subsequently on the basis of convenience, ease of use, and product efficacy where appropriate. Claims of superiority are often not seen as relevant in categories such as groceries and personal-care products.

Acute need: here, a consumer's need is fairly urgent. Lack of time limits the amount of information that can be gathered. In this type of situation, where consumers are likely to choose only what is available, the role of marketing communications is to provide brand familiarity and brand recognition so that the brand is known and trusted at the right time. Examples of categories are car replacement parts and cleaning supplies.

Rational: relevant in situations where consumers are rational, conscious, calculating and deliberate individuals. The desire for information is high and consumers have the motivation and ability to evaluate different alternatives. Advertising may focus on comparisons and uniqueness. The role of marketing communications is to inform and persuade. Cars, computers and household appliances are all examples of relevant product categories.

Source: Tayor (1999).

Needs and Product Categories

In some categories, one type of need is prevalent or characteristic: shoe laces, batteries are rational/ informational appeals; beer and computer games rely on hedonic/transformational associations. However, utilitarian and hedonic needs are not mutually exclusive, consumers can perceive both types of needs simultaneously (Voss, Spangenberg and Grohmann 2003). For instance, cars are purchased on appearance, design, image and status; purchase criteria for insurance tends to be on policies, safety, corrosion protection and resale value. In Figure 3.4, some product categories are listed using the axes of 'hedonistic' and 'utilitarian'.

We can see that consumers associate some categories with both types of needs: some categories score high mainly on one dimension; other products score low on both dimensions (these are often short-lived products like the *Tamagotchi* Japanese toy popular in the UK in the 1990s). The first group of products has developed by providing solutions to new types of needs (e.g. jeans and sports shoes becoming fashion items, cars providing driving pleasure and status but also safety and new fuel solutions). It is difficult for marketers to compete in these product categories if they do not fulfil both types of needs and this has to be evident in marketing communications.

Consumption is an integral part of consumers' identity construction. Belk (1988) argued that consumption may also be a way of defining people's sense of who they are and possessions become the **extended self.** Some products get their meaning in a 'person–thing–person relationship' (Ahuvia 2005). Consumers seek out others with the same desires and construct even stronger connections to the product together. For these types of products, it is useful to think about consumer behaviour and marketing communications in new ways. The decision-making process is a permanent consumption activity (the need for more is always there) and consumer involvement may seem infinite. Individual purchases of the product are manifestations of a strong, enduring and complex relationship.

Some possessions are seen as 'love objects' that people become emotionally attached to. Emotional attachment is normally attributed to 'parent–child' relationships and between spouses and partners, but it has been shown to affect consumer–object relationships as well (Thomson, Macinnis and Park 2005). Emotional attachment is driven by affection to, and passion for, connection to the partner or the product. Sustained ownership of products with emotional attachment is of paramount importance for these types of consumer. Moreover, emotional attachment is associated with

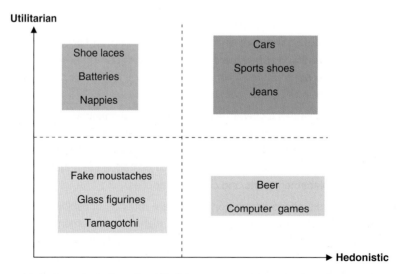

Figure 3.4: Rational and hedonistic needs for product categories

Source: Voss, Spangenberg and Grohmann (2003). Reproduced with permission.

specific behaviours. Strong emotional attachment is revealed by proximity maintenance (people want to spend time with the object), emotional security (people feel secure when close to the product), separation distress (people do not like to be far away from the product) and safe haven (people turn to the product when in need of comfort).

2 Information Search

When a need has been recognised, consumers begin searching for information to help them locate product categories and brands that can fulfil that need. According to Blackwell, Miniard and Engel (2001, p. 106), this information search is defined as 'the motivated activation of knowledge stored in memory, or acquisition of information from the environment, concerning potential need satisfiers'. Information search can be divided into **memory-based** (internal) and **action-based** (external) searches, with every purchase involving some degree of **internal search**, and consumers generally do this by 'scanning' their long-term memory. This can be described as an associative network where knowledge about product features, suitable usage situations, price levels, retail stores and also subjective evaluations (i.e. attitudes, opinions) are stored.

The total amount, or degree, of search depends on the level of involvement and the risks we perceive in making the purchase. Perceived risk can be: functional ('Will the product work as well as I want it to?'); financial ('Can I afford it?'); social ('What will my friends think?'); and ego ('Will I feel good when using the product?'). The higher the level of involvement (i.e. the purchase decision is complex and/or important) and the greater the perceived risk, the more information is sought. This more complex decision making is referred to as **extended problem solving** (EPS). When information stored in memory is not sufficient to make a purchase with confidence, consumers may utilise an external search. External information search is frequently purchase specific, but some may want to learn more about the product in-between purchases, and engage in ongoing search (e.g. for lifestyle products such as fashion, wines, cars, travel, furniture, interior design, music and outdoor living – see Figure 3.5 for examples). Here, consumers use several sources of information such as other consumers, friends, web pages and store personnel before they make a purchase. The depth of external search prior to a purchase will therefore decrease if consumers spend time and effort in ongoing and purchase-specific searches as increased knowledge (about alternative brands, lifestyles, possible purchase behaviour etc.) will be stored in long-term memory.

Reproduced by permission of *IKEA*   Reproduced by permission of *Decanter*

Figure 3.5: The *IKEA* catalogue and the *Decanter* wine magazine are used in ongoing search

On the other hand, where purchases are low involvement and low risk (**limited problem solving – LPS**), or are routine, frequently purchased, low-involvement brands (**routinised response behaviour – RRB**), we are more likely to rely on information from marketing communications and memory. If information and knowledge (acquired by first-hand product experience and communication messages) stored in long-term memory is sufficient, no external information search may be necessary. When consumers have been previously satisfied, internal information search is enough. In other words, the degree of information search is often small. Think about how many purchases you make of products you have bought before and where the purchase need was activated because of normal depletion (e.g. renewal of subscriptions, food supplies and underwear). Brand loyalty is born out of the LPS consumption; consumers may limit themselves to visit one store only and they buy one brand that they have decided on before entering the store.

MATTER OF FACT

Information Search

Information search before purchase is often very insignificant. According to one well-known academic study, consumers spend on average 12 seconds on a purchase decision in grocery stores. More than 50% of shoppers spent less than five seconds when purchasing coffee, cereal, margarine or toothpaste (these product categories were tested in the study). Also, consumers search for very little information when making larger purchases – 26% searched for minimum information before making a car purchase; 19% were satisfied with talking to a good friend who was knowledgeable about cars; 17% searched for a lot of information; the rest, approximately 35%, conducted an average-level information search.

Sources: Dickson and Sawyer (1990), Furse, Punj and Stewart (1984).

The direction of search refers to the specific content of an external search. Consumers may use different sources of information: (i) personal and non-personal contact points and (ii) commercial/non-commercial messages. In Table 3.3, we see how message format and type of contact point interact to create different communication channels which consumers use in the external information search.

Consumers use a combination of contact points and message formats to gain knowledge about products. With company-generated messages, there is a degree of control over what kind of information consumers may receive; communication which is not company generated, which is increasingly influential with peers, is much more difficult to control. For example, in 2006, *Business Week* magazine featured stories about *McDonald's* ranging from trans-fat issues in restaurants, challenges on

Non-commercial/Non-personal	Non-commercial/personal
Mass media	Friends and family 'word of mouth'
Giving consumer advice	Visual consumption
Consumer testing	Reference groups
Commercial/Non-personal	**Commercial/personal**
Advertising on TV, radio, newspapers, etc.	Seller, personal bank manager, surveyor
Store information and promotion	Shop personnel
Sponsorship	Loyalty programmes
	Direct advertising

Table 3.3: Type of contact point and message format can be divided into personal/non-personal and commercial/non-commercial

the Japanese market, success with shrimp burgers in Japan (!), improved dividends to shareholders, to news about a product launch of premium roast coffee to compete with *Starbucks* and *Dunkin' Donuts*. In the whole of the year, there were only 26 articles specifically about *McDonald's*. A couple of years earlier when the movie *Super Size Me* was released, *McDonald's* was all over the news. A *Google* search for 'Super Size Me' gives more than 1 million hits. Of course, these are just a small selection from everything that has been written about the *McDonald's* brand. Since the brand is well known and well regarded, it is very likely that the news stories have been the start of discussions between people (and recently a topic on Internet blogs).

The links between personal and non-personal communications have generated much positive and negative word of mouth, since news and scandals about brands are topics of conversation. Internet blogs have dramatically increased the possibilities for consumer interaction, giving advice and recommendations to others. This type of peer word-of-mouth communication is essentially 'free' advertising (East *et al.*, 2005). When consumers are searching for information, listener motivation can be high, whether word of mouth is positive or negative.

Many purchase decisions affect more than one consumer (e.g. the decision-making unit of the family) and information search can occur from one consumer to another within the circle of family, or between friends and acquaintances. When social acceptance is a main purchase motivation, consumers use **reference groups** or endorsers as guidance in understanding what a brand and product category is all about, registering what other consumers in their environment are using. Englis and Solomon (1995) describe that consumers have reference groups (e.g. adolescents, sports fans, lifestyles, professional careers) where they aspire to membership. Their purchase decisions are highly influenced by what other, relevant consumers are buying and using. For instance, consumers' perception of the fashion retailer *Zara* is to a large extent dependent on the direct and indirect information they get from existing *Zara* customers.

Internet search engines are fast becoming the information source of choice. Traditional travel agencies have been challenged by online travel marketing companies who offer not just depth of information, but a rich search experience, sometimes featuring '360° room and resort' search facilities. Beldona (in press) identifies four underlying travel information search modes within the context of online pleasure travel planning: deliberative and deterministic (when a goal-oriented information search is undertaken); and affective and innovative (when an experiential-oriented information search is undertaken).

3 Evaluation of Alternatives

Looking for information and evaluating alternatives, although separate parts of the decision-making process, are often linked: we find information, compare it to existing products and category uses (simultaneously and alternately) and then retain or reject it. Evaluation of alternatives takes place when consumers consider the relative merits of different brands to fulfil the needs identified. Consumers use **evaluative criteria** to make a purchase decision. This will be different for different categories and brands: from strictly functional dimensions of the product to hedonistic and emotional aspects. Buying a house might involve functional criteria such as size of the house, number of rooms, price, quality standard, comfort, practical solutions, distance to work and important infrastructure in the neighbourhood. But consumers will also take emotional aspects into account like aesthetic value of the house, design solutions, views, neighbourhood reputation and how they would feel as owners of the house (see Figure 3.4 which shows rational and hedonistic purchases).

Evaluative criteria can be product, price or brand specific: in some instances, a product type might only suffice (price is an attribute that consumers always consider (Mitra 1995)); and the branding of the product works as a surrogate indicator of quality in consumer purchase decisions (Maheswaran, Mackie and Chaiken 1992). Of course, these criteria are contingent on category context and depend on what consumers perceive as being 'salient'. **Salience** is where one aspect is more prominent or apparent in a category than others (Alba and Chattopadhyay 1986, Biehal and Chakravarthi 1983) and is the strongest influence on the purchase decision. If, for example, consumers perceive little quality difference between brands in a category, price will be highly influential in the choice making; where brands are perceived as being different from one another, the brand will be the salient attribute. This applies of course to other attributes (e.g. country of origin, taste, environmentally friendly, simple, store atmosphere, technical capacity).

Goal fulfilment is another significant evaluative criterion (Johnson 1984) where a need (e.g. 'I do need to get away from my hectic job') is formulated as a problem that has to be solved. The solution is a **consumption goal** (e.g. 'My goal is to take a well-deserved holiday next month'). For a low-involvement decision like choosing an afternoon snack, several product categories may be considered (e.g. chocolate bars, fruit, sweets, ice cream, Danish pastries or biscuits), but they would be perceived as one attribute. Consumers may evaluate within and across product categories. Within product categories, research studies have shown that complete loyalty is a relatively rare phenomenon, with most consumers being **variety-seekers**, accepting and switching between alternatives in a product category (Menon and Kahn 1995, Ratner, Kahn and Kahneman 1999), with a 'choice set' of brands that they select from (Alba and Chattopadhyay 1985, Negundi 1990). It is the role of marketing communications to either provoke or prevent brand switching.

MATTER OF FACT

Brand Switching

A research study shows brand switching between different brands in the grocery category, which shows a high level of 'brand promiscuity'.

Category	Number of brands
Soft drinks	5.0
Coffee	4.0
Beer	6.9
Detergent	4.8
Yoghurt	3.6
Shampoo	6.1
Deodorant	3.9
Butter	4.1

Brand promiscuity in the grocery category

Source: Hauser and Wernerfelt (1990).

Consumers know and choose among a subset of the total amount of brands that exist in the market. If we take the individual consumer's perspective, we can categorise brands into three groups (see Figure 3.6).

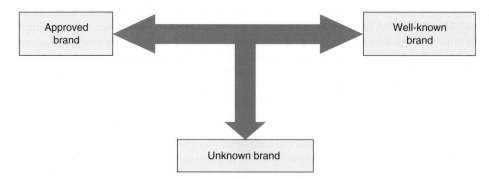

Figure 3.6: Brands can be categorised into three product groups

Source: Dahlen and Lange (2003). *Optimal marknadskommunikation*, Liber Ekonomi. Reproduced with permission.

A product category can be split into three groups or sets: consideration set, inept set and inert set.

- The **consideration set** is the list of brands that the consumer chooses between in the category, comprising brands that have been established as good choices in long-term memory and brands that the consumer identifies as good choices during external information search. Consideration set membership comes from previous consumption experience, exposure to the brand in advertising or in stores.
- The **inept set** is the known set of alternatives that have been rejected, due to previous consumption experiences, ethical concerns, price, or even aversion to the brand's marketing communications.
- The **inert set** is the set of brands that exists in the market of which the consumer is not aware.

These classifications are made from the consumer's individual perspective. Empirical studies have shown that the three sets are relatively stable over time, and great efforts are needed from marketing communications to alter the consumer's opinions.

Relatively often when consumers fulfil consumption goals, they consider brands from distinct categories (Ratneshwar, Pechmann and Shocker 1996). Across-category consideration is frequent especially when the consumer either has a goal conflict (i.e. when one product category cannot single-handedly fulfil the consumption goals) or there is goal ambivalence (i.e. when salient goals are missing or when the consumer wants to satisfy non-specific goals/needs (i.e. the goal conflict of eating tasty but not nutritious food). Generally speaking, however, consumers do not evaluate brands completely rationally and meticulously; it is difficult for consumers to absorb all market information. Instead, they have to rely on **heuristics** (i.e. rule of thumb, commonsense intuitive judgements used to guide evaluation of alternatives). Hoyer (1984) and Maheswaran, Mackie and Chaiken (1992) researched this area well. In summary, this covers:

- **Cut-off points:** such as price threshold, minimum technical or functional level ingredients.
- **Warranties as risk reduction:** quality indicators and an insurance against perceived risk.
- **Price:** the price of a product is also a marketing signal, high prices indicating high quality and diminishing the risk of buying inferior products (e.g. as in the purchase of cosmetics and clothes or in gift giving).
- **Decision rules:** consumers may use different decision rules when they make a choice of one alternative within the consideration set – either simplistic, non-compensatory/compensatory, or sequential (see Table 3.4).

Decision rule	Description
Simplistic, habitual	'I buy the same brand as usual'
Simplistic, by attribute	'I buy the least expensive/most expensive'
Simplistic, by attitude	'I buy the one my family likes'
	'I buy the brand I like the most'
Non-compensatory, attribute focus	Compare brands on the most important attribute
Non-compensatory, brand focus	If several are equally good, go on to the second most important attribute
	Continue until one brand stands out as better
	Evaluate one brand at a time against cut-off points on all attributes
	Brands that do not pass all cut-off points are taken away
	The first brand that passes all cut-off points is chosen

(Continued)

Decision rule	Description
Compensatory, simple Compensatory, weighted (see also Matter of Fact later in this section)	Count positive evaluations for all attributes for each brand The brand with most positive evaluations is chosen Each attribute gets a relative weight depending on its importance Each brand is evaluated on all attributes. The brand that scores highest is chosen
Sequential	One choice rule is used to limit the number of alternatives further (e.g. cut-off points). Another choice rule is used for the final choice (e.g. compensatory, weighted)

Table 3.4: Different decision rules used in a purchase situation

Use of decision rules when evaluating alternatives is connected to the levels of involvement and risk: 'simplistic' and 'simple compensatory' choice rules are common for habitual purchases where consumers perceive low risk (Hoyer 1984); 'sequential' decision rules are often used in evaluation of alternatives from different product categories (Gensch 1987); 'non-compensatory' and 'weighted compensatory' decision rules are normally used in high-involvement purchases (Eagly and Chaiken 1993, Ginter 1974).

4 Purchase

The fourth step of the decision-making process, purchase, is the least complex part of the process. The decision to make a purchase of one specific brand can be regarded as nothing more than a manifestation of the information search and the evaluation of alternatives. The mere transaction when product and money are traded is very much standardised.

Three aspects are worth looking at in more detail in the purchase step of the model: (i) Where is the purchase made? (ii) What degree of planning is made before purchase? (iii) What is the consumer's attitude towards shopping?

Point of Purchase

Consumers can make purchases of products at many different places. They can purchase things over the phone, write a letter, click on links on the Internet, use mail order services or send an SMS with a mobile phone and so forth. Still, the absolute most important point of purchase is retail stores. Many retailers have built strong chains of stores (*H&M, The Gap, Wal-Mart, Aldi, Carrefour, Sainsbury's* etc.) and they should be regarded as important consumer-oriented brands. The strong position of store chains and also of competing individual stores implies that store choice is to a greater extent about evaluation of alternatives. Consumers have consideration sets for retail stores and use decision rules to choose stores to visit. To treat retail stores just as a means of making a purchase is misleading.

Planning

The degree of planning affects how much consumers use stores in the decision-making process (Cobb and Hoyer 1986). Planned purchases may be **totally planned purchases** where the consumer has decided on the exact product category, the exact brand and the exact branded article (e.g. one specific *Whirlpool* microwave oven) to purchase.

The other extreme is when the consumer has only planned the purchase on an overall, goal-related level (e.g. something to eat for dinner). In this case, the product choice and the brand choice are unplanned and not decided upon before visiting the store.

Three other types of (un)planned purchases are possible. **Category planning** means that the consumer has decided on a product category but will decide on the brand in the store. **Unplanned**

Figure 3.7: Sales often tempt consumers to make impulse purchases

purchases occur when the consumer is reminded of a purchase need or purchase motivation in the store ('Oh, that's right, I need new batteries to the remote control'). These unplanned purchases are driven by rational needs and motives. Unplanned purchases may also be emotionally motivated, so-called **impulse purchases**. Here, emotional desires for a product influence the purchases. Impulse purchases have been described as spontaneous, intensive, powerful, compulsive, exciting and stimulating with no regard for the consequences (Rook 1987) – see Figure 3.7.

The degree of planning is associated with consumer involvement and attitude towards shopping. At low involvement, consumers often make totally planned purchases because they have a strong heuristic that guides the purchase behaviour. But low-involvement consumers may also make many unplanned purchases as they choose to use the store environment as inspiration.

High involvement leads to a willingness to let store environments influence decisions and also to ask sales people for help in making a choice. Here, product planning is frequent and the shopping trip is a great part of the information search and evaluation of alternatives.

MATTER OF FACT

Temporary Judgements

People have limited cognitive capacity. Moreover, people face an abundance of information and are unable to memorise everything they hear and read. As a result, consumers memorise fractions of messages (e.g. a brand name, information about a product attribute) and attitudes are likely to be heavily influenced by the salience of whatever relevant information comes to mind. People's judgements are not fixed. They are temporary and often constructed in real time.

This has been empirically demonstrated for various consumer variables: similarity judgements, attitudes and choice (more on choice in Chapter 10). The table shows empirical results for similarity judgements. The situational goal for the apple pairs (–orange, –donut) was 'things people might eat as snacks when in a hurry' and the situational goal for the granola bar pairs (–candy bar, –fruit yoghurt) was 'things people may carry along to eat in their cars'. When no situational goal was probed, people tended to judge similarity based on product category membership but when the situational goal was salient they made similarity judgements on convenience in the usage situation.

(Continued)

Product pair	Low situational goal salience	High situational goal salience
Apple–Orange	8.34	6.74
Apple–Donut	1.72	6.21
Granola bar–Candy bar	5.34	7.62
Granola bar–Fruit yoghurt	5.34	3.56

Goal salience and brand selection

Sources: Reed, Wooten and Bolton (2002), Ratneshwar *et al.* (2001).

Shopping

Consumers' attitude towards shopping has received a lot of attention. Shopping is indeed a phenomenon that affects consumers in their daily life. Many consumers happily shop in their free time. Big shopping malls, city centres and large retail chains are very successful in attracting consumers and are a large part of the tourism industry. At the same time there are also shopping trips that consumers perceive as boring chores that must be done. It is safe to say that shopping trips have become polarised. Consumers want simple problem solving for the everyday shopping (groceries, ticket reservations and so forth) but they are actively seeking hedonistic experiences in stores that sell products which they are interested in or curious about.

Both personal motives and social motives might be the cause of shopping proneness. Consumers may see a store visit to purchase something as a reward or the shopping trip itself as recreation/pleasure (Chandon, Wansink and Laurent 2000). It can also be a social activity to spend time with friends or family or to meet other consumers with similar interests.

The role of marketing communications at point of purchase is to secure brand recognition and to create favourable purchase intentions. Consumers are influenced by packaging design (for brand recognition), recommendations from sales personnel and special price deals. Moreover, the store atmosphere may be used to influence consumers. Some brands focus all their marketing communications on in-store activities. They enter into people's consideration set by being accessible on the store shelves.

5 Consumption and Post-Purchase Evaluation

The decision-making process is not over when a purchase has been made. Two post-purchase behaviours are important. Firstly, there is of course consumption of the product and, secondly, it is likely that the consumer does some kind of evaluation of the product. The post-purchase evaluation is about satisfaction/dissatisfaction of the need that initiated the process. This evaluation is what marketers are very interested in because it might be a prediction of future purchases.

Thus, the evaluation after purchase is critical for the marketer as the consumers may come to the conclusion that future purchase decisions will be more effective if the consumers purchase the same brand again. A purchase where the brand has 'delivered' what the consumer wants is naturally an ideal purchase, both for the consumer and the marketer.

The Influence of Consumption

As in previous steps, it is constructive to separate low- and high-involvement consumption. When the involvement is high, the consumption may be associated with religious metaphors, so-called **sacred consumption**. In these situations, the consumption is important and extraordinary for the consumer. It is planned carefully and well in advance. The consumer is proactively seeking consumption opportunities. Long journeys, anniversaries, interior decoration, pets, events (concerts, sports) and collections are often mentioned among the examples of sacred consumption.

However, the majority of consumers' consumption is 'profane' (used as a contrast to sacred) where the consumption is not at all important. In **profane consumption** the consumers are more price sensitive, less impulsive and more inclined to react to marketing stimuli that simplify the choice compared to sacred consumption.

Another important dimension of consumption is **conspicuous consumption**. Many consumers use consumption to show others who they are and what kind of lifestyle they have (Englis and Solomon 1995). Product categories where the consumption of brands is visible to others are suitable for signalling identity to other consumers. Cars, clothes, restaurants, watches, mobile phones, places to live and hotels are only a few examples of categories with strong signalling value. The choice of brand is often made carefully because other people will later be able to recognise which brand was chosen. In conspicuous consumption, brand names are a very important part of the consumption. The usage situation may interact with brand names as well. It has been empirically demonstrated that the usage situation affects how important brand names might be. For instance, brand name is a more critical attribute when buying a beverage in a restaurant than when buying a beverage in retail stores.

Satisfaction and Retention

In general, customer satisfaction is the most significant aspect of evaluation after purchase for the marketer (Blackwell, Miniard and Engel 2001). At this stage the consumers decide if they are happy with their purchase or not. Satisfied or dissatisfied customers are likely to act differently in future purchases. The evaluation after a purchase is not always a conscious, analytical process where the pros and cons of a purchase are weighed against each other.

In low-involvement situations, the evaluation is often simply a confirmation that the brand satisfied the need or not. The evaluation process is especially short when consumers are purchasing known brands. Consumers, who are not completely satisfied with existing alternatives and those who are variety-seekers, may do a more extensive evaluation after purchase, especially when they are trying a new product variant.

The evaluation after purchase is affected by the **frame of reference** (i.e. expectations). Framing is a comparison process that begins with what consumers believe they will get from the purchase and ends with the outcome. Was it better or worse than expected? The most-used definition of customer satisfaction is that the product exceeds – or confirms – the expectations before purchase. The objective for the marketer is to make sure that the product is better than customer expectations, or at least that the product lives up to the expectations. If expectations are not fulfilled, the consumption experience will not be what the customer desired and the end result is customer dissatisfaction.

There is an interesting psychological principle that makes consumers in general more satisfied than dissatisfied with a purchase. This principle is called **cognitive consistency** and its basis is that people would like to be perceived by other people as consistent individuals that make well-motivated decisions (Cialdini 2003). The aspiration for cognitive consistency will make consumers rationalise their decisions afterwards so that the decisions look even better than they actually are. A consumer who just bought a new TV set will point out its advantages even more intensely after the purchase. The same consumer is also likely to downgrade competing TV sets.

The consistency principle is especially strong in situations where some aspect of a product is not perfect, or when a competing alternative may have one or two advantages. Consumers do try to reduce the **cognitive dissonance** they feel by identifying arguments that work in the favour of their previous actions (Cialdini 1993). It is important to note that cognitive dissonance does not work for really strong negative experiences, for instance in the case of a broken product due to defects.

If the customer is satisfied with the purchase, there is reason to believe that the customer will consider purchasing the same product the next time the same need is recognised. Empirical studies in consumer behaviour research have shown that the correlation between customer satisfaction and customer retention is positive (Gustafsson, Johnson and Roos 2005). However, the correlation is far from perfect (one-to-one relationship). There are factors that 'disturb' the relationship between customer satisfaction and repeat purchases.

Variety seeking is one factor that can explain the disturbance. When consumers like variation they will search for another product just for the sake of variety. Naturally, previous satisfaction with a product has little effect in that kind of situation. Other factors are salience of the brand at the next purchase occasion, price decreases of competing brands, marketing communications of other brands and customer inertia (forgetting what was purchased before). All these factors affect consumers in their information search and evaluation of alternatives and affect customer retention negatively.

Thus, there is a combination of consumer behaviour characteristics and marketing communication activities that affect the relationship between customer satisfaction and customer loyalty. Throughout the book, we will discuss marketing communication tools that help marketers to gain relative advantage over competitors and to achieve marketing objectives.

MATTER OF FACT

Consumer–Brand Relationships

Susan Fournier is the researcher behind the most influential consumer–brand relationship studies. Her research shows that consumers may have strong emotional bonds with brands just like we may have strong emotional bonds with other people. Consumer–brand relationships are mainly built in usage and consumption and may be accentuated by marketing communications. Examples of strong relationships are brand combinations at specific consumption occasions (as in food recipes), brands that are strongly linked to certain states of mind (as celebrations, holiday traditions), and brands that have a long individual history for a consumer (for instance from childhood).

Certain emotions have been especially linked to consumer–brand relationships. The consumers experience strong feelings of love and passion towards a particular brand. Consumers feel that something important is missing when they cannot use the brand. In addition, the brand helps consumers to get a positive self-image, for instance by associating with happy memories and life situations where the consumer felt good or was successful. Moreover, the brand is tightly connected to consumption rituals where other brands are unacceptable.

In strong consumer–brand relationships, consumers make a conscious commitment to avoid other brands. They also feel that the relationship with the focal brand is complex and multifaceted. Consumers have rich associations with the brand and they are evoked during consumption. The brand is also seen as a reliable partner that would never betray the consumer by changing the contents of the product or changing the marketing communications.

Source: Fournier (1998).

A large part of marketing communications should be focused on post-purchase processes. It is important to convince customers that they have made the right choice. This may be achieved by marketing communications that strengthen consumer evaluation of the company. The mobile phone operator *Vodafone* has used this in its marketing. A few days after a purchase, the customer gets a welcome letter with some additional information about the product. There is no practical reason for the delayed information and it could have been given to the customer at the purchase transaction. However, *Vodafone* gets another opportunity to build the relationship with its customers by having additional contact.

THE ROLE OF MARKETING COMMUNICATIONS IN CONSUMER DECISION MAKING

The overall objective for all marketing is to get customers to purchase the company's products. To accomplish that, the marketer needs to work with marketing activities in each and every step of the consumer decision-making process (see Figure 3.8). An understanding of how consumers think in each step is also necessary to develop the right marketing communications. An example is the development of the Internet and how it has impacted on the consumer decision-making process. When the Internet grew dramatically in the 1990s, people believed it would change consumer behaviour fundamentally. Great investments in e-tailing were made and many web stores were launched. Initially, many of them

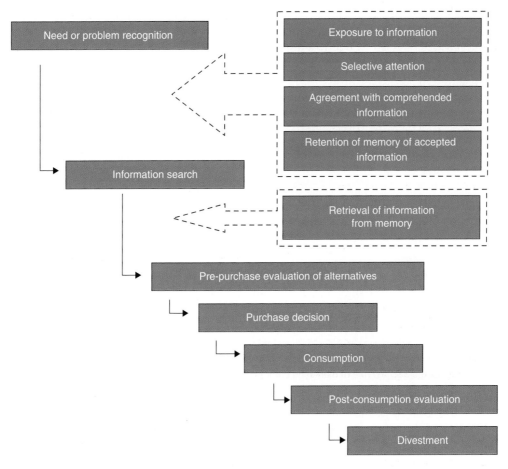

Figure 3.8: The role of marketing communications in consumer decision making 1
Source: combining Blackwell, Miniard and Engel (2001) and Shimp (1993).

failed and played a great part in the collapse of the Internet 'bubble', underestimating the complexity of the consumer decision-making process. They focused too much on the purchase aspect and too little on pre-purchase processes. For instance, they did not realise that people needed to be convinced about security issues before they would transfer purchase decisions from traditional stores to e-stores.

Now, marketers have realised that the Internet may have a different role in marketing than originally expected. For instance, the Internet may be part of the need recognition and information search even though people still make purchases in traditional stores. It can also be the other way around as when people talk to traditional store personnel about a product and make (often a less expensive) purchase of the product on the web. When the Internet and traditional marketing environments are truly integrated, understanding of the decision-making process is a great help in the design of marketing activities. See Figure 3.9.

PRODUCTS, CONSUMERS AND SITUATIONS

The consumer decision-making model is generic. All purchases, from a family vacation to toilet paper, have in common that the consumer must go through the five steps of the model. However, it is important to modify the nature of the model based on certain factors because different purchases certainly have different characteristics.

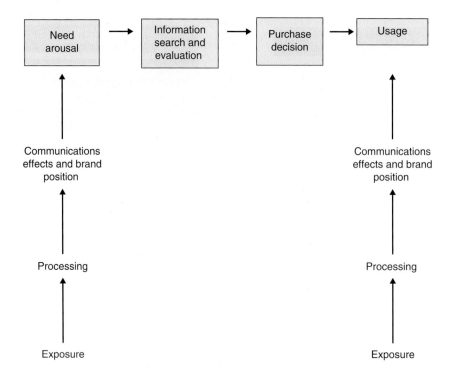

Figure 3.9: The role of marketing communications in consumer decision making 2

Source: Rossiter and Percy (1998, p. 85). Reproduced by permission of John Rossiter and Larry Percy.

One central factor that influences decision making is the **product factor**. For some products, the purchase process may be very short and last for only a few seconds. This occurs frequently when consumers are purchasing groceries. Sometimes the purchase process can take several months as in, for instance, a car purchase. Different products have different levels of consumer involvement. Involvement may vary from low to high, or at times be close to non-existent as in a routine purchase. For low-involvement products, consumers try to simplify the decision-making process. For high-involvement products, consumers carefully evaluate several aspects and consequences of the purchase. Product complexity and product costs are two other factors that affect the nature of the decision-making process. See Figure 3.10.

In addition, the marketer should consider the **consumer factor**. Examples of individual differences are consumer experience (based on previous purchases and previous use of the product), consumer interest, consumer motivation and consumer expertise (high level of knowledge of the product). Also, the marketer should realise that there is a **situational factor** (Belk 1975, Fennell 1978). Situations may be related to usage and purpose (e.g. a gift, everyday consumption, or holiday) or may be related to other consumers affected by the purchase (e.g. family members, friends, guests). There is a large body of research on these factors which you will find in textbooks on consumer behaviour (for example Blackwell, Miniard and Engel 2006, Evans, Jamal and Foxall 2006, Howard 1989, Solomon, Bambossy and Askegaard 2005).

New or Established Products

Market factors are also generally relevant. One market factor is how far the product has come in the **product life cycle** (introduction–growth–maturity–decline; Figure 3.11). The different phases of the product life cycle affect consumer perception of uncertainty and consumer need for external information search. Moreover, the product life cycle influences the number of customers that are aware of the company's brands and how many customers may consider purchasing them.

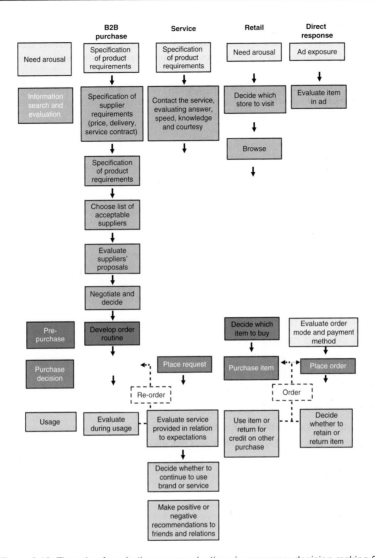

Figure 3.10: The role of marketing communications in consumer decision making 3

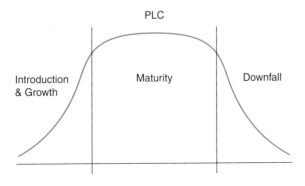

Figure 3.11: The stages of the product life cycle

Source: Dahlen and Lange (2003). *Optimal marknadskommunikation*, Liber Ekonomi. Reproduced with permission.

During the introduction and growth stages, many customers will make their first purchase in the product category. At that point, the decision-making process is normally extensive and a lot of effort is put into external information search. Employees' recommendations, advertising awareness and brand awareness are important factors of influence.

On a mature market, consumers are generally more confident and trust internal information search processes (recall of information from memory). They make routine purchases to a much larger extent. Brand image is relatively more important.

Competing Products

Another market factor to consider is **competitor intensity**. On markets where there are many alternatives to choose between and where brands are perceived as different, consumers are stimulated to increase their level of information search and alternative evaluation. On markets where alternatives are perceived as more similar, the decision-making process is generally less extensive.

MATTER OF FACT

Business Buyer Behaviour and Marketing Communications

The customer decision-making process in business buying behaviour is similar to a large extent to consumer decision-making processes. There are three different kinds of business purchases: new task, modified re-buy and straight re-buy. They may be compared to extended problem solving, limited problem solving and routine purchases in consumer behaviour (see information search earlier in this chapter).

Two aspects that need special attention in business buying behaviour and that are important to highlight are the buying centre and the stages in the buying process. In business buying behaviour several groups of people are involved in the decision. All groups need to be convinced by the marketing communications. The buying centre consists of

- users;
- influencers (e.g. technical personnel);
- buyers (people with formal authority to select suppliers);
- deciders (people with formal and informal power to approve decisions);
- gatekeepers (people that control the flow of information like agents, information managers and assistants).

There are a few more stages in the buying process in business buyer behaviour compared to consumer buyer behaviour but the overall idea is about the same. In buyer behaviour the stages are (for new task and modified re-buy): problem recognition, need description, product specification, supplier search, proposal solicitation, supplier selection, order-routine specification and performance review. The main difference lies in the proposal solicitation phase where the customer is very active. Moreover, the marketing communications is more often a result of direct demands by customers in business markets compared to in consumer markets.

Source: Kotler and Keller (2006, Chapter 7).

As we have seen in Chapter 1, marketing communications can be used to affect a number of cognitive and behavioural changes including: repositioning the brand; changing misunderstanding; changing performance beliefs and attribute priorities and so on. At the same time, properly researched knowledge of target market behaviour is vital to underpin successful marketing communications. In Chapter 4 we examine the desired communication outcomes informed by this consumer research.

CLOSING CASE STUDY

Australian Tourist Board: Destination Australia: Culture's up in the Air Down Under

The notion of 'place branding' refers to the promotion of a nation's economy, countries, cities and regions to try to create and maintain a strong brand positioning strategy. As an island

continent, Australia has made a name for itself since the 1960s as a strong 'destination brand'. In 2006, Australian tourism had faced the unique problem of interest shown in visiting the country not being translated into actual tourist inflows. *Tourism Australia* is a statutory authority of the government of Australia set up to promote the country as a tourist destination, and in 2006 commissioned *Saatchi & Saatchi* to promote Australia as a destination brand. The firm had previously helped promote tourism in New Zealand with the successful '100% Pure New Zealand' campaign.

The desired communication effects were to promote Australia as a rough and wild but friendly place for tourists. It was launched by Fran Bailey (then Australian Tourism Minister), on 27 February 2006. The advertisements in the 'So Where the Bloody Hell are You?' campaign featured a total of 11 scenes and 13 still images depicting a diverse range of experiences on offer in Australia. It was launched through multiple media channels and fronted by Australian model Lara Bingle, the aim being to invite people to visit Australia and enjoy the diverse range of experiences available there. However, whilst the campaign acknowledged the impact of opinion leaders and influential consumers, it did not take into account the impact it would have on other cultures.

Specific campaign objectives were aimed at capitalising on the awareness created through previous advertising campaigns and converting the huge interest shown by those who had responded positively to marketing communications efforts into actual travel bookings. After extensive marketing research, a conscious decision was made to target 'Experience Seekers', those early adopters who play a major role in influencing the

Tourism Australia appeal tarnished

purchasing behaviour of other people. The view was that successful communications to this group would result in emulative behaviour in others and create strong word-of-mouth referrals. The TV and magazine advertising campaign received wide media coverage and was also accessed online by many people. Initial response was very positive, encouraging many additional tourists to visit the country.

However, the campaign became controversial right from the start in some of the target markets; it was not only the effect of marketing communications on consumer behaviour, but also the effect on different cultures which undermined its success. *Tourism Australia* was criticised

(Continued)

for not taking into account specific cultural issues in target markets while developing a global marketing communication. The campaign attracted the wrath of many visitor country regulators because of the use of swear words such as 'bloody' and 'hell'. These words were part of the Australian slang but their use in the advertising campaign was perceived as offensive in some of the target markets. It was initially banned in some countries such as the UK and Canada. While the UK banned it for the use of the word 'bloody', Canada banned it for the opening line in the advertisement of the campaign, 'We've bought you a beer' which, it said, implied the consumption of unbranded alcohol.

Tourism Australia defended the use of the words, saying they were part of Australian slang and were intended to portray Australia as 'warm, friendly, and inviting'. In 2007, Singapore insisted that *Tourism Australia* remove the words 'bloody' and 'hell' before releasing the campaign in that country. Asian countries were particularly distraught, Tourism Minister Desley Boyle claiming that 'they didn't get the joke at all, it wasn't funny to them to have this word bloody which can be a serious word in their culture. It came across as a demand for people to visit Australia, not an invitation and that's not at all culturally appropriate in many of the countries in which we are working to encourage people to come and see us'. In a storm of cultural indignation, *Tourism Australia* withdrew the campaign in February 2008.

Because of the alienation of different cultures, the $180 million campaign may have generated tremendous publicity around the world (as well as several damning spoofs on video website *YouTube*), but did not generate any major increase in visitor numbers. Indeed, in the first year of its launch, tourist arrivals actually fell: the number of UK tourists fell by 2.3%; Japanese tourists by 5.7%; and the number of German tourists dropped by 4.7%.

QUESTIONS

1. What did *Tourism Australia* get fundamentally wrong in the understanding of its target audience which affected the success of marketing communications?

2. How could a more culturally tailored approach benefit future campaigns?

3. Why does this case underline the importance of understanding target audience against campaign creativeness?

CHAPTER SUMMARY

In this chapter we have presented a discussion of consumer decision making. Understanding this is critical for effective marketing communications. By now, you should be familiar with the complicated ways in which consumers select products: functional and rational attributes, but also based on emotional and hedonistic values. Consumers are then motivated to search for information (internal and/or external search) and evaluate alternatives before making the purchase. The decision-making process also entails evaluation after purchase.

The decision-making process model is complemented in two important ways. We have argued that in some instances there is no deliberate decision-making process. Consumers merely construct their judgements and choices based on external stimuli. We have seen that consumers may have temporary attitudes and that the choice process may be constructed in real time. Another criticism comes from researchers who study the cultural significance of consumption. They argue that consumption of some products is so important that they cannot be fully captured by the relatively simplistic decision-making processes. To fully understand consumer behaviour, marketers need to also focus on the intimate relationships between products and consumers and the creation of identity by way of certain possessions of products.

REFLECTIVE QUESTIONS

a. How can marketing communications make products 'culturally relevant'?

b. Think about two recent purchases you have made. One should be limited problem solving and the other should be extended problem solving. Describe the purchases by using the consumer decision-making process model presented in this chapter.

c. In the model of rational and hedonistic product categories (see Figure 3.4) there are some categories that are both rational and hedonistic. Try to identify ways that add hedonistic benefits to the shoe laces category and ways that add rational benefits to the beer category.

d. Identify a product that is so important to you that you identify strongly with it. Describe your relationship with the product.

e. Make a list of the brands in a product category (select one yourself) and divide the brands into your individual consideration set and inept set. Compare the two groups and discuss the main differences between them. Evaluate what your evaluative criteria and choice rules may be when you look at these two groups.

RESEARCH PROJECTS

Look at Terence Shimp's discussion of 'Neo-Pavlovian Conditioning and its Implications for Consumer Theory and Research', published in 1991 in the *Handbook of Consumer Behaviour*, and evaluate how marketing communications can be used to condition consumers in purchasing brands.

Visit the www.tourism.australia.com website and see whether the debacle over underestimating different cultural interpretations of advertising messages has impacted on the current approaches to marketing communications.

CHAPTER  4

EFFECTS AND OBJECTIVES

"The findings indicate that brand positioning is perhaps the most misguided marketing idea in the last 30 years."
Advertising Research Foundation (2007)

This chapter examines the reasons why marketing communications objectives are central to the planning process and instrumental in developing the brand's story arc and subsequent deployment of media and messages to reach target audiences. Objectives provide the framework and direction for marketing communications, allow us to compare and contrast with different campaigns and use of resources and provide a focus for communication between agencies, employees and customer.

LEARNING OBJECTIVES

After reading this chapter, you'll be able to:

■ Understand why target audience segmentation is fundamentally important to determining marketing communications objectives.

■ Appreciate the different 'effects' of category need, brand awareness, brand attitude, brand purchase intention and purchase facilitation.

■ Examine why they are required in order to affect customer purchase.

■ Understand how these desired effects and objectives can help create 'meaning' for consumers.

■ Discuss the different types of communication objectives at different stages of adoption and life cycle.

Marketing communications articulates the company and brand story, and is therefore concerned with all communications aimed at all stakeholders in order to elicit a positive image and gain a competitive brand position. The overriding purpose is to locate the brand in the target market category and consumers' minds in order to create distinction: to determine that primary brand choice and competitive differential are achieved and maintained in the category. To achieve this, brand awareness and brand preference are therefore fundamental to all marketing communications. What we will be discussing in this chapter is communication effects and communication objectives. Rossiter and Percy (1998, p. 129) describe communication effects as 'mental associations or responses, connected to the brand that are left "in the buyer's head" through marketing communications'. Brand positioning is the result of this process and can be modified through consumer experience, word of mouth and changes to the marketing mix (price policy, availability, store layout and so on), as well as the components of the communication mix.

We must first direct our attention to the recipients of marketing communications: the target audiences. The narrower 'target audience' perspective is focused on here since we will be examining objectives that are actionable and therefore specifically category and brand oriented. Rossiter and Bellman (2005, p. 81) define target audiences as 'the group or groups from whom most of the action attributable to the campaign will come'. This provides a good framework within which to examine the communication effects, although the parameters need to be extended to include media targets (who are influential on the dissemination of information and development of brand image), and 'creative targets' (the decision role-players in the purchase).

OPENING CASE STUDY

Kellogg's Special K: *Kellogg's* on the Ball for Slimmer Summer Self-Confidence and Soaring Sales

Reproduced by permission of Kellogg's Europe Trading Ltd.

In 2001, faced with a dramatic level of falling sales, *Kellogg's* had two specific marketing communications objectives: immediately effect an increase in sales and engage its target audience as part of a long-term strategy to reposition the company. One of *Kellogg's* stable of breakfast cereal products – *Kellogg's Special K* – fitted the bill perfectly. A series of campaigns was designed with

(Continued)

Special K special promotion pack
Reproduced by permission of Kellogg's Europe
Trading Ltd.

changing her shape by incorporating the cereal into
her regular diet .The campaign featured strong 'red'

Stay Special leaflet
Reproduced by permission of Kellogg's
Europe Trading Ltd.

the objective of tapping into the health-conscious
concerns of its target audience ABC1 20–44-year-old
'shape-conscious' women. The results were an increase in sales of over 22% and the development of
an engaging brand storyline.

Initially the 'Kick Start' campaign, aimed at
weight-conscious females, sought to raise awareness
about the health benefits of consuming the brand.
This was developed further with the incorporation
of a 'diet-plan campaign' element and *Kellogg's*
knew it had tapped into a relevant and resonant narrative: maintaining a healthy lifestyle.

To build a long-term sustainable brand platform
for *Special K*, *Kellogg's* strategy was to effect a shift
in positioning from 'health and beauty' and lock into
the trend in 'shape management' (see Chapter 6).
This was achieved by a series of promotional campaigns, all linked into the overall strategy. Key ingredients were the inclusion of resonant elements such
as 'Slimmer Waist for Summer Challenge', which
featured many images of a 'normal' woman in various stages of preparing for her summer holiday by

Special K summer challenge

imagery of the
woman's biki-
ni, dress and
other clothing
items which
we see her fit
into by gradu-
ally changing her shape and growing in self-confidence. This
is emphasised by the brand's 'K' logo echoing the curves of
the reshaped lady. The tactical objectives here were to use
associations of colour, sign, shape and situation to reinforce
the strategic positioning of transformation from 'health' to
'shape management'. The use of signs in marketing communications is referred to as semiotics, a topic which is explored
fully in Chapter 12.

One of the overriding strategic objectives for *Kellogg's* was to identify and link with the latest trend in shape
management before it became mainstream. This was, in
effect, to aim at owning the category of 'shape management', to seize the market and 'mind share' (Ries and Trout
1980) before the other cereal manufacturers. So, to drive
sales against fierce price competition was imperative, but

Kellogg's wanted to do this by adding value to the product rather than debasing the price. This was perfectly demonstrated in the '*Kellogg's Special K* Red Ball' self-liquidising promotion which included a specially designed *Kellogg's Special K* Red Ball, a fitness instruction video produced by Lucy Knight (together worth £25) which customers could redeem for £9.99 and two vouchers. This was communicated on 6.5 million packs, via 27,000 personal emails, supported by national TV and press coverage, website conversations and 'shape management' advice lines, point-of-sale merchandising in 500 stores, together with fitness demonstrations and videos in key retailers such as *ASDA*. By the end of 2003, redemptions for the promotion were at three times the industry average and fitness balls had become a trend in the UK and the Republic of Ireland and have now become a fixture in fitness centres. The key marketing communications objectives of repositioning, sales uplift and target audience engagement and 'ownership of the brand' had been achieved and continue to be part of *Kellogg's* sustainable 'shape management' and lifestyle brand narrative.

QUESTIONS

1. What were the key marketing communications objectives of the *Kellogg's Special K* Red Ball campaign and how did they tie in with the desired communication effects?

2. Tactically, *Kellogg's* used associations of femininity and the self-concept to reinforce its strategic positioning of extolling the virtues of 'shape management'. Do you think this will alienate some people who don't buy into this social element of branding?

3. What do you think is meant by aiming at 'owning the category', to seize the market and 'mind share' (Ries and Trout 1980) before the other cereal manufacturers?

There is still some debate as to whether marketing communications should be focused on sales-oriented promotional activity or assume a wider holistic role. As Smith, Berry and Pulford (1999, p. 26) point out, the emphasis has changed from concentrating on communications as 'a set of tools... to adjust objectives and strategies to changing communication realities'. Overall marketing objectives are hard-nosed sales, market share and profit-oriented goals, and any long-term brand building has to be underpinned by sales. But as Fill (2005) rightly suggests, some managers default to sales-related promotional objective setting; tactical orientation inevitably conditions a pragmatic, short-term fixation. Plus, how can we evaluate the impact of a tactical sales promotion purely in isolation from any other communications objective? What part has 'brand building' or 'image management' played in creating the right conditions to precipitate the sale? Marketing communications has been elevated above a mere 'promotional' role, driven by often changing tactical communications (Joachimsthaler and Aaker 1997), and taken on a more holistic perspective to effect the achievement of management and brand strategic objectives (Kitchen *et al.* 2004) integrated into the 'vertical structure of corporate, marketing and communication objectives' (Smith, Berry and Pulford 1999). And even this perspective has broadened to embrace a 'societal marketing orientation where firms are still required to create exchanges that satisfy individual and organisational objectives, but in a way that preserves or enhances public interest or consumer and societal well-being' (Kitchen 1994, p. 20).

TARGET AUDIENCE SEGMENTATION

In marketing, market 'potential' can often be segmented by using various demarcation criteria: demographics, socio-geographics, psychographics and so on. However, as far as marketing communications is concerned, the state of purchase readiness towards a brand in a particular category may be a much more appropriate approach. In this context, segmenting by the degree of actual or likely purchase behaviour – in other words **brand awareness** and **brand preference** – may offer a more meaningful method than by age, gender, class and so on. Rossiter and Bellman (2005) propose that, in order to achieve the successful positioning of communications with target audiences, this must be

Brand loyals (BLs)			
1	Single-brand loyals	⎫	OUR CURRENT BRAND'S CUSTOMERS
2	Multi-brand loyals		
Favourable brand switchers (FBSs)			
3	Experimental favourable brand switchers		
4	Routinised favourable brand switchers		
		⎬	
Other-brand switchers (OBSs)			
5	Favourable other-brand switchers	⎫	OTHER BRANDS – WHO COULD TRY OR RETRY OUR BRAND
6	Neutral other-brand switchers		
7	Unfavourable other-brand switchers		
Other-brand loyals (OBLs)			
8	Favourable other-brand loyals	⎬	
9	Neutral other-brand loyals		
10	Unfavourable other-brand loyals		
New category users (NCUs)			
11	Positive new category users	⎫	NON-USERS OF THE CATEGORY – WHO COULD TRY OR RETRY CATEGORY VIA OUR BRAND
12	Unaware new category users		
13	Negative new category users	⎬	

Table 4.1: Brand loyalty segmentation

Source: Rossiter and Bellman (2005, p. 83). Reproduced with permission.

done by segmenting by brand loyalty. Table 4.1 shows five major segments (subdivided into 13 loyalty types) that are essentially measures of customer equity.

Table 4.1 describes three major groups of customers based on category orientation: (i) our current brand customers; (ii) other brands' customers who might be persuaded to convert to our brand; and (iii) those who have stopped or have never used the category but might be converted using marketing communications.

- **Our current brand customers:** Brand loyalty may be as a result of inertia or apathy, high switching costs, or because of a deep relationship with the brand. 'Single' or 'multi-brand loyals' (BLs) are the bedrock of the customer base. Communications must concentrate on building relationships and rewarding loyalty and can be used to facilitate new product introductions and accelerate purchase levels. Incentive schemes like *Tesco Clubcard* and *Sainsbury's Nectar* card are examples of strategic/ tactical promotional activities with the action objective of reinforcing brand preference strength and growth from within. On the other hand, some regular customers may have weak brand preference and might experiment with various brands in a category. This may become 'routinised' where one brand is preferred but consumers remain indifferent to these types of products (e.g. bread, frozen peas). These two groups of 'favourable brand switchers (FBSs) need promotions aimed at 'buying' loyalty, keeping aware and reinforcing preference.

- **Other brands' customers who might be persuaded to convert to our brand:** The two categories of 'other brand switchers' (OBSs) do not currently (or have ceased to) use our brand and they range in degree from: 'favourable' OBSs (who might consider switching to our brand) to 'unfavourable' OBSs (who would not consider switching to our brand because of negative associations with our company or product or even through to an aversion to our communications).

Tesco online promotion

Source: www.tesco.co.uk.

These groups may respond to the brand being repositioned or some alteration to the elements of the communications mix being changed. When chocolate is repackaged in different forms, the brand may be more acceptable to OBSs. *Kit Kat Chunky, Mars Delight* and *Celebrations* are examples of brands repackaged and communicated to different audiences of OBSs. 'Other brand loyals' (OBLs) are similar to OBSs but they exhibit strong brand allegiance to at least *one other* brand. Communications must try to break loyalty by undermining the brand to which OBLs are loyal.

- **New category users:** The three remaining categories of 'new category users' (NCUs) are either positive, or negative or unaware of the category. Positive NCUs can be categorised as *new* users since they have the potential due to some other use. Take *Heinz WeightWatchers* range of soups. This could be attractive to customers who use *Weight-Watchers'* products and like soup or *Heinz* soup customers who are interested in losing weight. NCUs who

Directing Next customers to online promotion

Source: www.next.co.uk.

are unaware of *Next's* online shopping facility may respond to an email or magazine insert to open an online clothes shopping account.

What selection criteria do we use to ascertain which messages are appropriate for which target group? This depends on the short-term bottom-line sales objective and the long-term brand equity objective. Sales objectives (in this broad context of generating actual sales directly or indirectly) are either

sales maintenance objectives, where the emphasis is on retention and development of customers, or sales growth objectives, where the acquisition of new customers is of paramount importance (see Chapter 9 for a comprehensive look at this). *Red Bull* has recently targeted customers outside its target market of 14–28 year olds; *Saga* (travel and insurance) has lowered the target age group to 45+ rather than 60 year olds; *Baileys* repositioned its brand by appealing to a much younger age group; *Apple* launched the *iPod* with an inclusive advertising campaign targeted at all age groups. Therefore, in order to properly direct communications, we must be able to assess the target audience's leverage potential. For example, for an FMCG brand, groups 5 to 13 in Table 4.1 should be targeted to encourage trial of the product, whereas groups 1 to 4 should receive communications aimed at repeat purchase.

These are **action goals** and action is all about affecting the behaviour of end customers. These can be categorised as: **pre**-purchase, **purchase** and **post**-purchase. In the preamble to sales, direct sales and marketing organisations (e.g. those involved in the home improvement market for fitted kitchens, bathrooms and bedrooms) will use marketing communications to generate sales leads, entice a visit to the showroom, appeal to enquirers to visit the company website and so on. Car dealers will try and get potential buyers to engage in showroom visits or test the car on the road in order to get the customer to simulate use after purchase. Purchase of the product will be different in different contexts and different stages of the product's life cycle. For new products, which are not only new to the category but may even be new to the market, first purchase is essentially a 'trial' purchase. Brand loyalty may accrue from a satisfactory experience of the brand in use. The same is true of FMCG brands, making the action objective trial through free samples, reduced size samples, introductory offers or bundled promotional offers with well-established compatible brands.

Selling into intermediaries such as distributors and retailers will have an element of post-sale impact which is part of the 'push' element' of strategy (see Chapter 5 for a comprehensive look at trade promotions strategy). Although the 'initial purchase order' may be the primary objective, future stocking, displays, merchandising, sales representation and referrals – which lead on from the initial 'opening stock order' – will accelerate the acceptance of new products and insulate the company against the competition to some degree. With consumers, promotional activity in post-purchase situations is becoming the most important aspect of marketing communications and the messages to assuage fears about the purchase decision or product in use are critical. Equally, the recommendations, which can come from word-of-mouth communications, are particularly relevant to new products and can act as a credible source of positive advertising which may not cost the company anything. The 'conspicuous consumption' of proudly displaying brands generates a sort of **visual** word of mouth ('word of eye' if you will!). These are either pre-established (e.g. a user will know that a car will satisfy the need for transportation) or built by cumulative communications (e.g. consumers will know that 'Beanz Meanz Heinz'). If these effects do not already exist in the mind of the target market, marketing can be used to communicate these goals.

MATTER OF FACT

'Advertising has no effect on me'

In 2003, a large poll of US consumers revealed that 82% were not affected by advertising in making the decision of what car to buy. Could this really mean that 82% of all car advertising (amounting to extensive amounts of resources) was wasted? Purchase of high-risk, expensive brands such as new cars is a high-involvement process where consumers tend to seek out a lot of information for their decision making and will therefore probably pay more attention to marketing communications. So could this mean that maybe even more than 82% of advertising in general (considering that consumers tend to seek out less information for most other products) is wasted? UK researchers Robert Heath and Agnes Nairn set out to answer this question.

Using tracking data for a brand of dog food, they compared consumers' claimed exposure to advertising ('Have you seen any advertising for this brand?') with their actual recognitions of the advertising. Overall, only 25% claimed they had seen the advertising, and yet 70% of all consumers did in fact recognise the advertising when it was shown to them! Most interestingly, the majority of those recognising the advertising (two-thirds) had previously reported that they had not seen it, meaning that the more convinced consumers were that they had not seen the advertising, the more likely it was that they had seen it! When comparing those consumers who recognised the advertising (remember, two-thirds of this group consisted of consumers who claimed they had not seen the advertising) with those who did not recognise the advertising, the former group rated the brand of dog food much more favourably. This means that most people had seen the advertising but forgotten about it, and formed a much more favourable impression of the brand thinking it had nothing to do with the advertising (when, in fact, it did). They just hadn't made the association of the image in the memory being derived from advertising.

In a follow-up test, the authors used tracking data for a life insurance company (where consumers would be more likely to seek out and process information). The results were even more pronounced. Whereas only 27% claimed to have seen the advertising, almost 80% of those who thought they had not seen the advertising did in fact recognise it, and consequently evaluated the insurance company much more favourably.

Source: Heath and Nairn (2005).

COMMUNICATION EFFECTS

Communication effects are the buyer states that are required (e.g. being aware of the brand) in order to affect customer purchase; objectives are the specific targets (e.g. unprompted recall from an advertising campaign of a brand's message) to be achieved by marketing communications (see Figure 4.1). In determining desired effects and objectives for marketing communications, the sequential information processing models – for example Blackwell, Miniard and Engel (2001) – and the traditional communication 'hierarchy of effects' models – for example 'Attention Interest Desire Action' – are often quite rightly linked together to demonstrate the relationship between buyer behaviour and marketing communications. Sometimes these are referred to as communication

COGNITIVE STAGE	AWARENESS ↓
	INTEREST ↓
AFFECTIVE STAGE	DESIRE ↓
BEHAVIOUR STAGE	ACTION

Figure 4.1: Objective stages

Source: Rowley (2001, p. 385).

objectives 'micro chains' and are the different intermediate objectives to be achieved by marketing communications. Colley (1961, cited by Yeshin 2006) instilled in advertising agencies and brand managers the need to think 'DAGMAR' – **D**efine **A**dvertising **G**oals for **M**easuring **A**dvertising **R**esults – in order to plan moving consumers through the states of awareness, comprehension, conviction and action. Kotler (2000) used a similar chain or hierarchy: Awareness – Knowledge – Liking – Preference – Conviction – Purchase. Ehrenberg (2000) offered an even shorter version of the chain – the Attention–Trial–Response (ATR) model.

These essentially rational frameworks match the internal mental processing of 'exposure, attention, comprehension, acceptance and retention' with the communication goals of moving consumers through the stages: grabbing attention, gaining interest, instilling desire and, hopefully, precipitating action. If we combine the various models from Belch and Belch (2001), Blackwell, Miniard and Engel (2006) and Rossiter and Percy (1998) we can illustrate this by sitting the AIDA factors against the three elements of attitude change: cognitive, affective and conative or behavioural stages (Figure 4.2). The

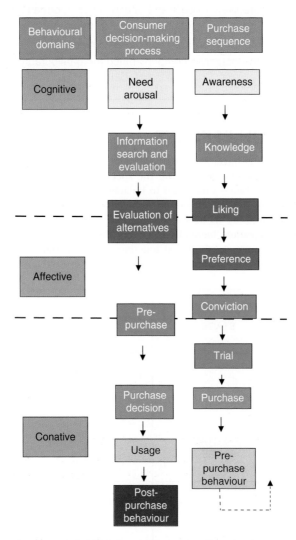

Figure 4.2: Objectives, effects and communications

Source: Belch and Belch (2001); Blackwell, Miniard and Engel (2006); Rossiter and Percy (1998).

Communication effect	Definition
Category need	Buyer's acceptance that the category (a product or service) is necessary to remove or satisfy a perceived discrepancy between the *current* motivational state and the *desired* motivational state
Brand awareness	Buyer's ability to identify (recognise or recall) the brand, within the category, in sufficient detail to make a purchase
Brand preference (formerly attitude)	Buyer's evaluation of the brand with respect to its perceived ability to meet a currently relevant motivation (the evaluation is based on brand benefit beliefs and the motivation-related emotional weights of the benefits and of possible freestanding emotions)
Brand purchase intention	Buyer's self-instruction to purchase the brand or to take purchase-related action
Purchase facilitation	Buyer's assurance that other marketing factors (marketing mix) will not hinder purchase

Note: Rossiter and Percy's approach is in fact an amalgam of the 'hierarchy of effects' models and the Hull–Spence theory.

Table 4.2: Communication effects defined

Source: Rossiter and Percy (1998, p. 110).

communications models all require a sequential approach to tell the target audience that 'we compete in this category', or to help change attitudes, reinforce positioning against the competition and so on.

Featured in Table 4.2 are the five 'communication effects' (Rossiter and Percy 1998) which describe the buyer states:

- category need;
- brand awareness;
- brand attitude;*
- brand purchase intention;
- purchase facilitation.

OBJECTIVES IN FOCUS

Owning the Category

Dominance in a category can be a vital ingredient in the battle against competition. Marketing communications objectives will be focused on two essential customer measures: brand loyalty and category satisfaction. Successful brands will 'own the category' and become synonymous

(Continued)

---

*In Rossiter's later collaboration with Bellman in 2005, this communication effect has been altered from 'attitude' to 'preference', a more meaningful descriptive of the required buyer state. It is this latter significant modification which has been adopted here and incorporated retrospectively into some of the tables and figures referenced.

with the need being fulfilled. These brands become exemplars and are yardsticks for consumers to evaluate alternatives and for competitors to emulate.

Some brands are 'category makers' and see an opportunity to reinvent the category need because the market is not being served well or a new innovative product or approach gives them advantageous relative positioning. These brands build new 'market spaces' by communicating different value propositions:

- *Starbucks* reinvented the concept of coffee shops with a fun, social appeal.
- *Amazon.com* provided an online book service with a customer profiling facility.
- *Fedex* provided an overnight delivery service for small packages.

Category appeals stay in customers' minds and this is fundamental to brands which need to maximise share of voice and subsequently dominate categories in order to maximise market share.

Two brands which attempt to do this compete in two completely different sectors: *Nestlé's Kit Kat* and the UK TV channel *Sky News*. The chief reason for *Nestlé's Kit Kat* advertising expenditure is not only to make *Kit Kat* synonymous with the category need 'break-time nourishment', but also to make it first choice for that category. Similarly, *Sky News* highlights all bulletins with the claim that it is 'First for Breaking News'. This is the most salient feature for news services such as *Sky* and its marketing communications objective is to be 'first in category'.

Primary Level Buyer Motivation

We can see that objectives are instrumental in affecting communications, but communication effects must remain constant, irrespective of what communications tools are used or what objectives are desired. Of the five effects, 'category need' is the primary need, since positioning a brand in relation to competition and within the minds of the consumer is the platform upon which strategy is built: everything is conditional on category entry.

The 'buyer state' describes the perspective of the consumer in relation to the targeted category. If the category need is already established, there is no need to include any message about the category characteristics in the objectives set. Latent category needs (e.g. irregular purchase and lapsed demand) are included in communication objectives only to remind consumers of a previously established need. Where there is no real recognition of a need in a particular category, a key communication objective has to be to educate audiences about the characteristics and potential need satisfaction of a category. Motivation for category need effect can be negatively originated where there is dissonance with a problem or current solution to the problem:

- **Problem removal:** a broken car exhaust or punctured tyre can be remedied by the expertise and utility of a *Kwik-Fit* fitter.
- **Problem avoidance:** the fear of burglary may cause a customer to anticipate a future problem and seek out alarms or insurance companies.
- **Incomplete satisfaction:** a campaign for the *Nationwide Building Society* plays on the dissatisfaction with other high-street finance companies who may not be meeting the requirements of existing customers.
- **Mixed approach-avoidance:** customers may like the rates for *Barclays* savings products but be put off because of the organisation's involvement in South Africa.
- **Normal depletion:** appeals to stock up on product are normally aimed at brand loyals (BLs).

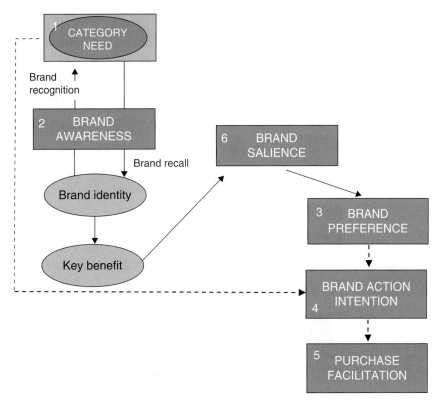

Figure 4.3: Desired communication effects

Source: adapted from Rossiter and Bellman (2005, p. 103).

Motivation can also be positively originated where there is a value-added element to the category need:

- **Sensory satisfaction:** the user seeks extra physiological stimulation in using a brand like a German *Bang & Olufsen* CD player.
- **Intellectual stimulation:** the user seeks extra psychological stimulation in using the brand as in the *Booker* of the *Booker Prize* collection of novels.
- **Social approval:** the user gains an added social credibility from displaying use of the product to friends as in an HD-ready TV.

This is a dynamic model which demonstrates the necessity of communication effects being at full strength in the buyer's mind before purchase takes place (Figure 4.3).

Secondary Level Buyer Effects

The prerequisite effects to any major communications campaign or individual promotion must be the establishment of brand awareness and brand preference within a category: consumers must know the value proposition of your brand and select it as their first choice in a particular category. Brand awareness and preference precede the creation of attitude, reputation or any long-term narrative development of the brand, and are the anchors for purchase intention and brand loyalty. Indeed, in the absence of any other communication objectives, these two must always be aimed at.

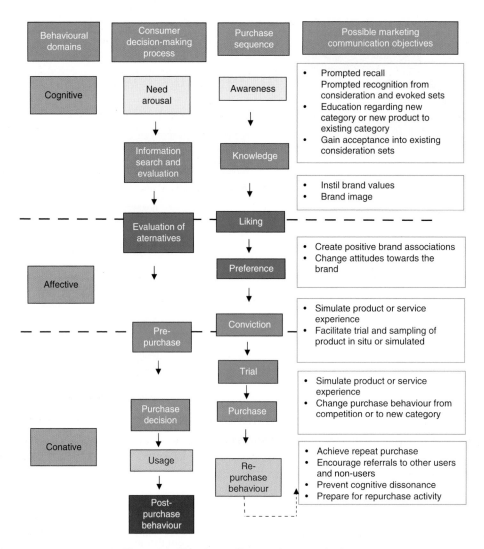

Figure 4.4: Objectives, effects and communications

Source: Belch and Belch (2001), Blackwell, Miniard and Engel (2006), Pickton and Broderick (2005).

1. Category Need; 2. Brand Awareness

There are two components to brand awareness: brand recognition and brand recall. Figure 4.4 shows how they work in conjunction to associate brand identity (i.e. logo, name, pack design) with the category. With brand recognition, the consumer associates the brand (identity) with the category. It is the opposite with brand recall as the brand (identity) is prompted AFTER a category need arises.

Recognition is important when customers select the product themselves (e.g. packaged food from a supermarket shelf). If they don't recognise the product, they won't be able to buy it. Researchers check prompted and unprompted recognition in order to measure how well marketing communications works. Communications have to emphasise what the brand looks like. This is referred to as 'visual iconic recognition learning'. Whilst shelf-talkers, gondola aisle displays and wobblers can assist recognition in store, consumers must learn to recognise the *Kellogg's* cockerel, or the *Jolly Green Giant* on the tin of sweetcorn. The semiotics of package design mean that whilst a pack may protect the contents, its primary function is to project the brand. Encoding the associate to the category is therefore vital for recognition. Recognition

of logos, colours and names is significant in brand awareness. There are no prizes for guessing whose image is shown here – it is one of the most recognisable signs on TV, on the road and inside our heads.

Recall measures the ability of the target audience to remember the brand from memory. This is important if customers don't visually select the product themselves (e.g. searching on the web, ordering a product over the phone, making a choice from a menu at a restaurant). In these situations, customers cannot see the product and must make a choice from memory. Brand recall could be measured with a direct focus on the brand (so-called 'aided recall'). The aim for this is for the brand to be the first one that the target audience comes to think of among all products in the category, which is often called 'top-of-mind' recall (Holden and Lutz 1992). Brand awareness can also be measured in terms of so-called **response latencies** (e.g., Pullig, Simmons and Neteemyer 2006), which are the exact amounts of time it takes for consumers to recognise or recall a brand.

3. Brand Preference

Rossiter and Bellman (2005, p. 110) quite rightly state that **brand preference** is the correct term for brand attitude since that is exactly the communication effect – preference over the competition in a category – which is required. The choices in terms of communication objectives are summarised in Table 4.3.

NHS becomes unhooked from targets

© Department of Health. Reproduced with permission.

In social marketing, where unselling category need occurs (with attempts at kicking addiction to cigarettes, drugs and alcohol), the objective is to encourage moderate preference to change the state from smoker to non-smoker. Carbon footprints, water conservation, using public transport are all examples of anti-selling a category in order to change preference. The controversial NHS campaign encouraging people to 'become unhooked' in order to quit smoking was hard-hitting and criticised for going too far.

4. Brand Purchase Intention

Conscious action intention is a key objective for purchasing high-involvement products (e.g. I *will* buy that brand. I will *stop* using Brand X). It's a sort of self-instruction. So the communication objective is to generate brand action intention. Omitting brand action intention is a key objective for purchasing low-involvement products.

Target customer's prior state of preference	Communication objective	Target audience
Negative preference	Change to moderate preference	Negative NCUs, unfavourable OBSs and unfavourable OBLs In social marketing, where unselling category need occurs
Unaware	Create strong preference	Unaware NCUs, neutral OBSs and neutral OBLs
Moderate preference	Increase strong preference	Favourable OBSs and favourable OBLs
Strong preference	Reinforce strong preference	Our own BLs

Table 4.3: Brand preference options for objectives

Source: based on Rossiter and Bellman (2005, p. 111).

5. Brand Purchase Facilitation

For frequently purchased products, where the consumer knows where and how to buy the brand, brand purchase facilitation should be omitted.

6. Brand Salience

One vital addition to the Rossiter and Bellman model is brand salience which breaks into the stages between brand awareness and brand preference. It is an amalgam of attributes, awareness, image and attitude to the brand. Salience is the ability of a brand to stand out from all other brands in a category over and above the competition as 'important, prominent, noticeable' (Egan 2007, p. 84). In a crowded marketplace, the ability to be heard above the crowd and cut through the clutter of advertising gives brands like *McDonald's* and *Coca-Cola* a head start in being accepted into consumer's consideration sets (Barnard and Ehrenberg 1997) because of their brand salience. Salience has to do with 'customer/consumer relevance' (Pickton and Broderick 2005, p. 603). Gordon (1991) claims that 'salience is a far more valuable tool for understanding what a brand means than brand awareness' and this is echoed in Holt's (2004, p. 125) analysis of *Budweiser* as 'a brand with cultural and political authority'. The salience of this sort of iconic brand is based on 'the nation's collective expectations that the brand can and should author a particular type of story' (how men find respect and camaraderie). Salience will vary between customers and between categories. As Ehrenberg and Goodhart (2000) say, 'it is not so much how well your brand is regarded, but how many consumers regard your brand well'.

MATTER OF FACT

'Expressway to Liking'

In two studies measuring consumers' awareness of different coffee brands and jeans brands, people were asked what brand they could think of in those categories (Öhman and Dahlén 2007). They listed the brands in the order they could recall them. One week later (after they had forgotten about their responses in the first questionnaire), consumers were given a list with all the brands in the categories and were asked to evaluate them in terms of attitude (absolute and relative). Results showed that the brands listed high (i.e. easily recalled) in the first questionnaire received higher attitude ratings and the brands listed low (less easily recalled) received lower attitude ratings. Thus, recall and liking seemed to go hand in hand. To see if this was due to the fact that people tend to easily recall brands that they like or the fact that people tend to like brands that they recall easily, the studies were repeated in reverse order: the first week, consumers rated brands in terms of absolute and relative attitude; the second week (having forgotten about the ratings), they were asked to list brands in the categories in the order they recalled them. When comparing results between the first and second sets of studies, it was found that the effect was stronger from recall on attitude (first studies) than the other way around (second studies). The tests proved that quick and easy recall could be an expressway to liking. The tests were repeated with recognition (consumers were shown groups of packages and logos in the product categories and asked to mark them in the order they were recognised). The conclusions, and the expressway, were the same.

Source: Öhman and Dahlén (2007).

To accomplish desired effects, communication objectives (e.g. assisting brand recall) need to be set, targeted and achieved. These communication objectives (the communications effects that are desired as outcomes from the campaign) must state what the response objectives are. Table 4.4 shows some examples of how communication effects link to communication objectives.

Communication effects	Communication objective options
Category need	*Omit* if assumed to be present
	Remind if latent
	Sell if new category users are targeted
Brand awareness	*Brand recognition* if choice made at point of purchase
	Brand recall if choice made prior to purchase
	Both if justified
Brand attitude	*Create* if unaware
	Increase if moderately favourable
	Maintain if maximally favourable
	Modify if moderate with no increase possible
	Change if negative
Brand purchase intention	*Assume* in advertising for low-risk brand
	Generate in all other advertising and in promotion
Purchase facilitation	*Omit* if no problems with other marketing elements
	Incorporate in campaign

Table 4.4: Effects options when setting communication objectives

Source: Rossiter and Percy (1998, p. 129). Reproduced by permission of John Rossiter and Larry Percy.

COMMUNICATION OBJECTIVES

Setting marketing communications objectives is important because: it acts as a means of assessing how best to build ongoing dialogues with audiences in order to maintain the brand narrative and sustain competitive advantage; it provides a check on the use of marketing resources in the process of communicating; and it provides some arbitrary mechanism for evaluating the progress and cost of deploying these resources against budgets, previous campaigns and the competition. As Yeshin (2007, p. 329) states: 'The underlying imperative is the need for an identification of clear, concise and measurable communications objectives that will enable the selection of the appropriate communications tools to achieve the tasks set'. According to Egan (2007, p. 108), objectives fall into three broad categories:

- **Knowledge-based objectives:** aimed at gaining attention, stimulating awareness and encouraging interest.
- **Feeling-based objectives:** changing attitudes through the development of brand identity and image, creation of shared values and associations with the brand and company.
- **Action-based objectives:** mainly sales oriented, the generation of information and the building of customer relationships.

The sales school/communications school dichotomy is well expressed by Fill (2005, p. 364), and he makes the point that both are not mutually exclusive in objective setting. Short-term sales goals need not necessarily be seen as unjustified in the context of overall company and brand communications, as long as they are a support not a substitute and they don't constitute ad hoc, unlinked promotions. Equally, it is not sensible to have a general communications objective which is nebulous and does not recognise the integrated and cumulative effects of marketing communications. Nonetheless, the long-term development of the brand consists of many incremental steps, often tactical diversions, which contribute and form the story arc of the brand. Figure 4.5 illustrates this by plotting the different types of marketing objectives which might be required to assist consumers in their individual brand journeys and accumulate brand equity in building both sales and brand image.

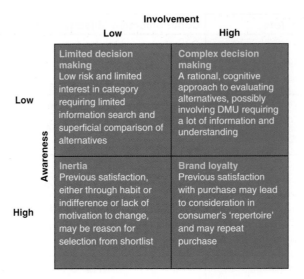

Figure 4.5: Awareness grid

Source: Assael (1992).

The general approach to setting objectives is the now clichéd 'SMARTT Objectives framework'. Nonetheless, this well-used acronym does help to focus realism on what has to be achieved, what can be achieved and within what time frame:

- **Specific**: the actual marketing communications effect which is to be achieved – awareness levels, perception.
- **Measurable**: the qualitative and quantitative metrics to evaluate.
- **Achievable**: are the objectives attainable within the market context?
- **Realistic**: given the time, resources and competitive situation, is the achievement of communication objectives feasible?
- **Targeted**: are the target audiences accurately identified?
- **Timed**: how long will it take to achieve the communication objectives?

Communication Objectives at Different Stages of Adoption and Life Cycle

Two models which should not be new to students of marketing are the ubiquitous Product Life Cycle and the Diffusion of Innovation models developed by Rogers back in 1962. Whilst they are fairly basic concepts they are very useful in campaign planning as they can help us evaluate buyer 'readiness states' and category needs and suggest marketing communications objectives to match with the communication effects required.

The **product life cycle** is really the timeline for the life of the product, plotting the stages in the product's journey, and is used to gauge customer communication needs at each point in time: if the audience is confused, we need to explain; if they are being tempted away by competitive promotions, we need to react with a sales promotion; if the image of the brand is outmoded, we need to reposition the brand or consider repackaging.

Rogers' (1962) **Diffusion of Innovation** model plots the stages in the audience's adoption of the product and can also be used to gauge customer communication needs at each point in time: if the product is brand new to a category, the 'Innovators' and 'Early Adopters' will be prime targets for communication; if the product has sufficient critical mass (i.e. it has diffused in the marketplace by achieving penetration of a market), communications may be geared towards distribution and anti-competitive appeals; if there is a newer version of the product, the 'Laggards' can be promoted to in order to make way for the new product. The notion of an 'innovation' does not mean 'invention'. Something which is new to a market or category can be seen as innovative if it represents a new value proposition to the market. Consider the trend for recycling. In Japan, the *Book Off* chain of bookstores has spotted the category need for second-hand books at cheaper prices, which provides an ethical flavour to book purchase (think *Waterstone's* meets *Oxfam*!). This retailer chemically cleans old books and resells them as new. This may catch on in Europe and we will see these stores (obviously with a suitable name change) introduced in an innovative way to sell books similar to how *Amazon* provided an innovative alternative to *Borders* or *WH Smith* or even *Tesco*. The characteristics of adoption are:

- **Relative advantage:** does the innovation offer a reason to change from the current brand? The *Sinclair C5* electric car didn't; the *Toyota Hybrid* does.
- **Compatibility:** does it fit in with the way a consumer is currently satisfied by a category need? Fitted home office furniture bombed in the 1970s but has now achieved rapid growth due to changing social trends and home working.
- **Complexity:** do the potential users understand it and can they use it?
- **Visibility:** does the innovation have the visibility of conspicuous consumption? Will it help spread 'word of eye' and provoke emulative behaviour?
- **Communicabilty:** can the benefits and brand values be communicated to an audience in a coherent and effective manner?

If we look at the different stages in the product life cycle and match these with the types of adopters who may be targeted with different communication messages, we get a fairly good picture of the marketing communications effects we need to bring about and the marketing communication objectives which will help us achieve this. Figure 4.6 juxtaposes product life cycle stages with target audience adoption types and suggests possible marketing communications objectives to achieve these stages and encourage adoption.

A product which is new to a category has to be introduced and explained to a target audience. Alternatively, a group of customers new to a category need educating about the concept, the features and benefits which buying into the category will bring. The emphasis may inevitably be on achieving the objectives of awareness and comprehension and may require an advertising campaign, for example the introduction of the *Nintendo Wii* game console in 2007 (see the *Wii* case study featured in Chapter 6). Trial of the product as *Skoda* did with the launch of the *Fabia* may be involved. The conventional method of achieving awareness has been dominated by the power of mass-market advertising to achieve rapid, huge exposure.

That is not to say that this method is inappropriate, but its power has been diminished of late and other approaches may be more suitable to the particular category. A recent development has been the slow-burn word-of-mouth 'buzz marketing' which is the subject matter for later chapters. Nonetheless, recall and recognition objectives are critical in the early stages of the life cycle. Recognition, and therefore association with a category need, is a fundamental entry to a market. Acceptance into the consumer's consideration set will be dependent upon how the target becomes familiar with the brand and understands what it stands for and what value it can offer. An objective in the introductory phase might be brand attribute education by the brand owner. On the other hand, if the brand and category are both new, emphasis cannot just be on brand attributes; it must involve the objectives of category need education as well as matching brand to category.

When the must-have gadget of Christmas 1979 was an exciting new machine called a VCR, nobody would have guessed dominance of *JVC*'s VHS format in home entertainment for more than 20 years. The victory of *JVC* over its rivals was partly down to communications and partly attributable to distribution: as video rental shops were persuaded to take on the less cumbersome VHS format, consumers (at that time faced with up to £50 to buy a video cassette film) became educated about the category. But, despite holding off rival *Sony's Betamax* alternative, who conceded defeat in 1987, *Toshiba* already had its *Digital Versatile Disc* (DVD) ready and waiting. This category has expanded beyond expectations due to the way the product was introduced and the close promotional efforts with the likes of the supermarkets and cheap distribution of machines. The recent *HD-DVD* versus *Blu-Ray* new format battle is an interesting parallel. *Sony* are the winners this time with *Toshiba* having now withdrawn the *HD-DVD* format.

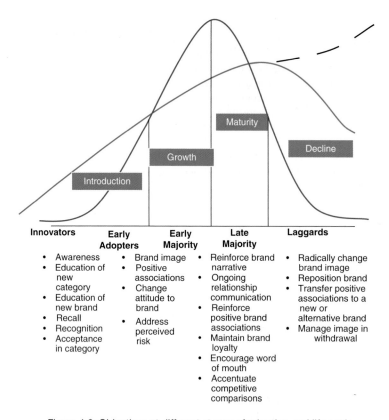

Figure 4.6: Objectives at different stages of adoption and life cycle

Source: adapted from Rogers (1983) and from Egan (2007, p. 110).

We should not assume that brands with a long history and appreciable brand equity do not have to create awareness. Even the mighty *Coca-Cola*, the most recognised brand on the planet, is only recognised by 40% of the people in China. *Coca-Cola*'s sponsorship of the 2008 Beijing Olympic Games provided not just a parity amongst other companies but gave a massive opportunity ahead of its rival, *Pepsi*. *Pepsi* was not one of the 12 'Top Olympic Partners' who were official sponsors and therefore was restricted over the four-year sponsorship to link with this event.

Once a product gets into the growth stage of its life cycle, objectives switch from awareness and recognition as the key focus, and the building of brand image, the creation of positive associations,

OBJECTIVES IN FOCUS

Kindle. Introducing an Innovation

The introduction of a new product can sometimes not just involve clever marketing communications to create awareness and brand positioning, but also education of an audience in terms of what the actual concept is. 2007 saw the introduction of something that could revolutionise the way that people read. Students and academics alike have long seen the advantage of reading books electronically through PDF documents, email attachments, scanned-in book chapters accessed online and the increasing availability of electronic books. Now the *Kindle* from *Amazon*

could become the *iPod* of textbooks, with *Amazon* the equivalent of *Apple iTunes Store*.

Introduced in November 2007, the *Kindle* is an e-reader developed by *Amazon* to allow easy access to a vast library of electronic books. With over 90,000 books which can be downloaded and read on the device available at launch, this hybrid product is a natural progression from laptops, MP3 players and even games consoles. Sales are expected to be in the region of 500,000 units by mid-2009 with sales likely to be over two million by 2010. With 'book' downloads estimated to be well over 10 times that amount initially, *Amazon* may be starting to bite the hand that has fed it. For an organisation built on books, the introduction of an electronic alternative could precipitate its death. With a student-friendly version just launched this year, *Amazon* sees the educational market as one which will itself help educate the market in this introductory stage of its life cycle.

Visit www.amazon.co.uk and see the product for yourself (unless you already have one!). What are the campaign objectives for introduction? What else does Amazon.com have to do to communicate this to its target audience in the introductory stage? How will the launch of rivals *iLiad* and *iBook* affect its successful introduction?

	2008E	2009E	2010E
Kindle Unit Sales			
Units Sold	189,000	467,000	2,208,000
Price	$399	$339	$288
Revenue	$75,411,000	$158,383,050	$636,516,720
Annual Revenue Recognition Rate	50%		
Recognized Unit Revenue	$37,705,500	$116,897,025	$397,449,885
Kindle Book Sales			
Units In Circulation	189,000	656,000	2,864,000
Attach Rate (Books Per Month)	1.0		
Price Per Book	$9.99		
Year 1 Book Sale Revenue	$22,657,320	$78,641,280	$343,336,320
Year 1 Total Revenue ($MM)	$60	$196	$741
Current Est. AMZN Revenue	$19,626	$24,051	$28,464
Kindle As % of Est. AMZN Revenue	0.3%	0.8%	2.6%

Source: Citi Investment Research

Crunching Kindle's numbers

changing attitudes and addressing perceived risk in purchase and achieving wider distribution of the product become central. Sponsorship, cause-related marketing (e.g. *Tesco*'s 'Computers for Schools') and the efforts put into trade promotions to 'push' the brand through retailer and merchants may help. In the maturity stage, the brand narrative has to be reinforced by maintaining ongoing relationships and perpetuating the myths surrounding the brand.

This is where the notion of brand salience helps communications, as some brands will have an extraordinary element to their brand essence which helps to give an element of competitive immunity. *Marks & Spencer* had this relevance to its target audience which helped it tread water in the late 1990s until it could regroup and relaunch.

The encouragement of word of mouth is appropriate at any stage of the life cycle, but mature products now engage in activities which help foster referrals and feed into the social aspect of the product. Promoting a new aspect of the brand's story can also extend the equity in an organisation's brand. Again with *Marks & Spencer*, the '100 Point Plan' for ethical trading has attempted to demonstrate this new positioning, with point-of-sale materials, shop fronts, advertisements, PR and other elements of the mix being used to demonstrate this. Also, sales promotions can give a brand a boost if the objective is to maintain market share as this helps sales and counters competitive activities.

Once a product goes into decline, for example changing tastes or new superior alternatives may kill the brand off. Sometimes, however, excellent promotion will give the brand a new lease of life. This was the case with *Heinz Salad Cream* which was becoming the *Betamax* dressing against the likes of *Hellmann's Mayonnaise*. Well-judged PR and some clever new packs and advertising secured the return of the family favourite.

OBJECTIVES IN FOCUS

Retail PR Objectives

A study of UK retailers revealed significant differences between the type and emphasis of the public relations objectives set by various organisations. Strong marketing orientation was reflected in the declared identification of existing and new customers as being key to achieving marketing communications objectives. *Russell & Bromley*, at the top end of the sector, had PR objectives focused on achieving publicity for product in order to increase footfall, support the marketing of merchandise and emphasise the quality aspect of the store's offer. And whilst *Harrods'* luxury department store also had a strong emphasis on product publicity, there was a broader set of other objectives relating to employee communications and external corporate communications. At both *Marks & Spencer* and *CWS*, the emphasis appeared to be on longer-term image building. Whilst the generation of product publicity remained an important PR objective for both of these retailers, there was an equally strong emphasis on achieving a more strategically oriented range of objectives relating to each company's relationships with both external and internal corporate stakeholders.

The achievement of the product PR objectives by each of the four retailers was clear to see, but it proved more difficult to assess the degree to which any broader corporate communications objectives had been achieved. The emphasis on achieving short-term product objectives seemed to take precedence over the longer-term corporate communications objectives of image/reputation-related issues.

Source: Moss, Warnaby, and Thame (1996).

Different Perspectives of Organisational and Customer Objectives

It is interesting to compare the different perspectives of the objectives to be achieved from a customer and a company point of view (see Table 4.5).

Company objectives	Customer objectives
Increase sales	Affect trial or purchase behaviour
Maintain or improve market share	Encourage repeat purchase
Create or improve brand recognition	Create significant associations between use and brand
Create a favourable climate for future sales	Engage target audience in ongoing dialogues and engagement
Inform and educate	Build associations with brand and cultural usage
Create a competitive advantage	Highlight functional, emotional or symbolic differentiation between others in category
Improve promotional efficiency	Design logical connections between messages

Table 4.5: Different perspectives of objectives

Source: based on Belch and Belch (2001) and Shimp (2000).

CLOSING CASE STUDY

Sky TV: The Sky's the Limit for Top Set-Top Box

On 5 February 1989, the *British Sky Broadcasting Group plc (BSkyB)* launched *Sky Television*, a direct-to-home service offering four channels. By the end of 1990, the one-millionth subscriber had signed up. With key sponsorship deals like the English Premier League, and more channels becoming available, by 1995 the level of paying customers had reached five million. 1998 saw the introduction of the UK's first digital TV, and *Sky* quickly grew its customer base by offering free boxes and mini dishes to regular customers. In 1999, innovation continued with interactive facilities being made available for 'upgrade' to the existing client base.

Sky operates in a highly dynamic marketplace where the 'convergence' of the means of delivery has blurred the conventional competitive demarcation lines. Suppliers including cable television providers, digital and analogue terrestrial television providers, telecommunications providers, betting and gaming companies, developing new technologies and other suppliers of news, information, sports and entertainment, as well as other providers of interactive services, have been encouraged to participate in this category. The rate of development also means that any competitive advantage is quickly copied and neutralised.

Then, in 2001, came the launch of *Sky+*, a fully integrated personal recording facility launched on the back of the success of products like *TiVo* and *ReplayTV* in the US. By 2002 *Sky Digital* had signed up 5.7 million customers, growing to 7 million in 2003 and 8.1 million in 2005. What communication objectives were set and what campaign strategy was employed to help achieve such high penetration of a market

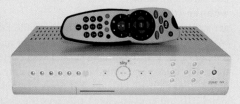

Sky+ TV recorder

which had been used to only paying the *BBC* Licence Fee for the privilege of watching TV?

The *Sky+* case is a good example of marketing communications being used to introduce an innovation into a market by careful segmentation of target audiences, the principle of Rogers' theory of Diffusion of Innovation and the setting of communications objectives linked to key communications effects.

At the start of 2000, *Sky* was faced with the communication task of educating an audience about a new category (namely PVRs), a technology which was still seen as more 'pie in the sky than sky on the box', and awareness levels which were restricted to its relatively small customer base. Because of the problems with this type of technology in the past, *Sky* had to be very cautious that the opportunity was not blown as had happened with cable. In order to trial the product prior to launch, 6000 customer advisors – the door-to-door installers – were allowed either free equipment or boxes that were heavily discounted. This was aimed at ironing out any technical problems before a full release of the product, but had the added bonus of creating the vast majority of these 'silent salesmen' as brand ambassadors who could advocate the product in situ and as the ultimate credible source – the neutral expert. In turn, existing *Sky* and cable customers were targeted with mailings, emails and messages attached to monthly statements.

Once trialling was complete, and *Sky* was happy that there was sufficient confidence in the product, it still kept tight reins on the potential of the product in order to control the 'buzz' about the brand. Despite very positive feedback from carefully selected media experts (opinion formers) who had boxes installed, initial release in 2001 was at a prohibitively high price of £399. This was a deliberate tactic to ensure that initial uptake was aimed at 'innovators' (representing only 1% of *Sky's* customer base) who then would act as privileged 'mavens' (opinion leaders), spreading positive

(Continued)

word of mouth. *Sky* knew that this type of highly desirable prestigious innovation carries a lot of cultural currency in social networks and communities, and the social media of the Internet helped accelerate online word of mouth.

By 2003, *Sky* installed sets in the homes of key celebrity opinion formers like Chris Moyles and Chris Evans whose shows had sufficient clout with the wider tar-

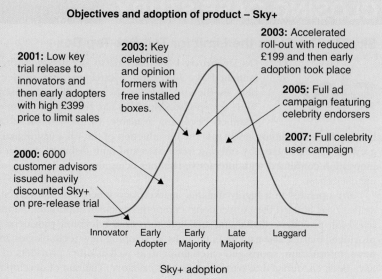

Objectives and adoption of product – Sky+

2001: Low key trial release to innovators and then early adopters with high £399 price to limit sales

2003: Key celebrities and opinion formers with free installed boxes.

2003: Accelerated roll-out with reduced £199 and then early adoption took place

2005: Full ad campaign featuring celebrity endorsers

2007: Full celebrity user campaign

2000: 6000 customer advisors issued heavily discounted Sky+ on pre-release trial

Innovator   Early Adopter   Early Majority   Late Majority   Laggard

Sky+ adoption

Source: adapted from Rogers (1983).

get audience and who became high-profile advocates. Sponsorship of influential radio stations like *Virgin* helped create positive word of mouth and acted as oblique referrals. Then, in September, a new £199 pricing model was targeted at the competition of HD-DVD recorders in the marketplace and rolled out to the next tranche of customers – the 'Early Majority'. Backed by a £20 million advertising and press campaign focusing on the product attributes of 'control, simplicity and convenience', this was the first time *BSkyB* had promoted the benefits of *Sky+* outside its customer base (*Sky* Press Release 2003). The campaign comprised both push and pull components of strategy and consisted of TV advertising, posters, radio sponsorship, direct mail, the *Sky* customer magazine, in-store retailer marketing (including product trialling and salesperson advice), and a dedicated website www.skyplus.com. The campaign featured a number of 'odd' celebrity couples (Noddy Holder/Simon Callow, Ronnie Corbett/Alice Cooper, Kelly Brook/Bruce Forsyth) and demonstrated the key category need of flexibility and choice with the message '*Sky+* – create your own TV channel'. With two million customers signed up by 2007, the campaign was a huge success and the verb 'to *Sky+* it' entered the lexicon of viewers from here on in. Further extensions to new markets included, for example, a tie-up with www.Bounty.com explaining the advantages of *Sky+* recording to new parents. The 2008 campaign used celebrities like Michael Parkinson, appealing to a broader market – the 'Late Majority'.

QUESTIONS

1. What were the key communication objectives of the *Sky* campaign and how did they tie-in with the desired communication effects?

2. Rogers' Diffusion of Innovation model is featured in the case to illustrate the key target audiences in *Sky*'s campaign. Research this and show how the key 'requirements of adoption' (relative advantage, compatibility, complexity, visibility and communicability) helped *Sky* achieve its marketing communications objectives.

3. Look at Table 4.1 and show how Rossiter and Bellman's categories of customer can be applied to the customer groups referred to in the *Sky* case.

CHAPTER SUMMARY

This chapter looked at the reasons why marketing communications objectives are central to the planning process and instrumental in developing the brand's story arc and subsequent deployment of media and messages to reach target audiences. We saw how objectives provide the framework and direction for marketing communications, allow us to compare and contrast with different campaigns and use of resources and provide a focus for communication between agencies, employees and customers. It was established that understanding the importance of target audience segmentation is fundamentally important to determining marketing communications objectives.

We examined the different effects of category need, brand awareness, brand attitude and brand purchase intention and purchase facilitation, and discussed why they are required in order to affect customer purchase and can help create meaning for consumers. A full discussion of the reasons why there is a need for different types of communications objectives at different stages of adoption and life cycle was provided.

It was established that brand awareness and brand preference are therefore fundamental to all brand communications in order to locate the brand in the target market category and consumers' minds to create distinction: to determine that primary brand choice and competitive differential is achieved and maintained in the category.

REFLECTIVE QUESTIONS

a. Why would segmenting by the degree of actual or likely purchase behaviour – in other words brand awareness and brand preference – offer a more meaningful method than by age, gender, class and so on?

b. What selection criteria can be used to ascertain which messages are appropriate for different target groups?

c. What is the difference between communication effects and communication objectives?

d. What are the five communication effects as discussed by Rossiter and Percy (1998) which describe buyer states?

e. Egan (2007, p. 108) claims that objectives fall into three broad categories: (i) knowledge-based objectives; (ii) feelings-based objectives; and (iii) action-based objectives. What does he mean?

RESEARCH PROJECTS

Ehrenberg's (2000) ATR model offered a shorter version of the 'effects chain' minimising marketing communications objectives to just three required effects: Attention-Trial-Response. Seek out the paper that this comes from – Ehrenberg, A.S.C. (2000). Repetitive advertising and the consumer. *Journal of Advertising Research*, **40**(6), 39–48 – and critically analyse this framework.

Objectives of social marketing are often described as unselling where the aim is to change antisocial behaviour (e.g. kicking addiction to cigarettes, drugs and alcohol). Investigate the NHS Change 4 Life Campaign and the Department of Health's F.A.S.T. and compare the different campaign objectives.

CHAPTER  5

STRATEGY AND PLANNING

"Forget product. Study consumer wants and needs. Forget price. Understand the cost to satisfy that want or need. Forget place. Think convenience to buy. Forget promotion. The word now is COMMUNICATION."
Schultz, Tenenbaum and Lauterborn (1992)

This chapter discusses why marketing communications has changed because of the explosion of media, power of the consumer, access to technology and the need to have dialogues with audiences, and how this has caused a shift in the way in which organisations now approach marketing communications strategy. It covers the chief components needed to plan and implement successful marketing communications campaigns and describes the dynamic contexts within which marketing communications is set.

LEARNING OBJECTIVES

After reading this chapter, you'll be able to:

■ Appreciate the 'promoting to–communicating with' dichotomy.

■ Understand the difference between 'strategic' and 'tactical' positioning and demonstrate how they support one another.

■ Visualise the contexts within which marketing communications strategy is set in order to provide a realistic impression of which audiences must be targeted, and what objectives and strategy are required to bring about effective communications.

■ Analyse and compare the key components of marketing communications planning.

■ Appreciate why target audience, message and media must be integrated, and work cohesively together.

■ Describe and examine the constituent parts of the CAMPAIGN planning framework.

Research shows that over 20 years ago, 75% of marketing budgets were heavily biased towards a mass communication advertising model. The emergence of the Internet has radically overturned this paradigm, and today, with only 25% given to above-line activity (Kitchen 2003), the landscape has changed from a company-dominated communication environment towards a more democratically user-generated one. There is now a wider range of communication tools which can be deployed to target rapidly fragmenting audiences, but this is counter-balanced by a saturation of direct and newly emerging indirect competition. Against this backdrop, the need for a more strategic and integrated approach to marketing communications is more vital than ever. And whilst 'integrated marketing communications' is not a new concept or philosophy, the primacy of communication in the interface a company has with its customers is now unquestioned.

Indeed the transition from promoting to audiences to communicating with customers has changed marketing communications from both an organisational and consumer perspective. As marketing mantras go, 'getting close to the customer' is as self-evidently obvious as it is fundamentally important. If marketing communications is the pathway through to the customer, any approach to communications strategy should start by looking there: why is integrated marketing communications so important from a customer's perspective? Schembri's (2006, p. 388) comment that 'a genuine understanding of the customer and their views begins with a direct understanding of their world' is exactly right. Key to this, as Fill (2002) points out, is the fact that consumers do not see elements of the communication mix as separate and divisible components. Yeshin (2007, p. 327) puts this well by stating that 'although they may be unaware of the concept, they recognise integration and see it as making it easier for them to build an overall brand picture'. Integrated marketing communications helps make the links between messages coherent and understandable, providing a holistic environment within which the brand narrative exists.

This is important because, whilst it is necessary to achieve marketing and communication objectives as effectively and efficiently as possible, there is no purpose to it if the consumer is confused or does not perceive a relationship with the brand that has meaning and value. As Grant (2006) suggests 'consistency should come from strategy and values, not executional similarity'. The coordination and management of resources is not the main purpose of integrated marketing communications, but it is necessary in order to create coherent, meaningful dialogue with the customer.

OPENING CASE STUDY

LEGO: Rebuilding the LEGO Legend Brick by Brick

LEGO was named the 'Toy of the Century' in 2000 by the British Association of Toy Retailers and *Fortune* magazine. By 2004, over €1 billion of classic plastic bricks and online games had been sold and the brand was the fourth-largest toy manufacturer in the world. With over 75% of its sales coming from new products, *LEGO* seemed to have it all: a heritage brand which had adapted well to the digital age. However, despite having an extraordinary grip on children's imagination, financially it had lost a grip on reality.

Estimated to be losing €250,000 a day, the company had made losses in four out of the seven years between 1998 and 2004. Sales had dropped by 30% in 2003, a further 10% in 2004, and profit margins were −30% in 2004. The story of how the *LEGO* legend was rebuilt – brick by brick – is one of organisational restructuring and alterations to the supply chain, but it is

Boys build the Lego legend

also one of recapturing its audience's imagination and how the application of integrated marketing communications helped to rebuild the *LEGO* brand narrative.

How could it have gone so wrong? Some say it was pressure from low-cost producers in China and a chaotic supply chain which caused poor customer service; others say it was over diversification with ventures into clothing and theme parks. In the digital era, the lost childhood (what child psychologists call 'age compression') is a major concern for toy manufacturers; *LEGO*, as a toy with links to another age, was particularly vulnerable.

Although the fabled Danish *LEGO* Group's story begins in 1932, with Ole Kirk Christiansen's original children's wooden toy, the famous *LEGO* building interlocking brick system wasn't launched until 1958. As then, the magic formula of the brand was a product which fired children's imagination and prepared them for the world of adults (*LEGO* bricks promote motor, cognitive and creative skills). This has been one of the many reasons that the brand equity of *LEGO* has been sustained. *LEGO DUPLO* was launched in the late 1960s for younger children, and the first of four billion *LEGO* figures was introduced in 1974, encouraging role-play and letting children inject their own personalities into their *LEGO* creations. Whilst it may seem too low-tech for today's youth, *LEGO factory.com* and *LEGO Digital Designer* – digital design facilities introduced in 2004 – have given a more online face to the company and demonstrated that *LEGO* can keep up with trends. This allows the ultimate in mass-customisation of consumer designs. Their move into the digital toy territory was extended with a licensing deal with Lucas Arts for creating video games (the *LEGO Star Wars II: the Original Trilogy* video game has been a top-selling game since its release) and the high-tech *LEGO Mindstorms NXT*, motorised robotic construction kits for older children (in collaboration with MIT Media Lab).

LEGO has two enormous competitive advantages: the brand enjoys worldwide recognition – ranked fifth in the global toy market behind *Mattel, Hasbro, Sega* and *Nintendo* – and *LEGO. com* is amongst the 10 most visited children's websites. And yet, ironically the strength of the brand's history was being undermined by the history of its distribution strategy. The supply chain had always been geared for custom delivery to smaller retailers who had owned the toy market in the 1950s but were now choking potential. Two-thirds of the 1500-item stock levels were no longer manufactured, and 80% of sales were represented by just 30 products. Retailers, in effect, owned the brand and yet had little experience in direct consumer sales.

LEGO did involve key customers in new product development and promotional activities, and worked hard to improve its relationships with toy retailers by creating better in-store displays and filling a higher percentage of orders. But following ventures into online gaming and movies, the brand became diluted. President Søren Torp Laursen claimed that LEGO had 'been going down the wrong path and had to get back to its roots'. This was to be achieved by marketing 'business units' driving a comprehensive campaign of integrated marketing communications through a retailer promotional platform and an advertising campaign that retold the 'brand that builds' legend. This took the form of 'living point-of-purchase' road-shows using specially designated marketing teams.

LEGO's marketing is organised under vertical channels (or 'product portals') which are segmented by product or specific strategic knowledge unit (SKU) genre: *Explore* focusing on pre-school; *Stores and Action* concentrating on play themes; and an *Endorsed* portal with new products such as *Bionicle*. The business units are marketing teams made up of sales, advertising, PR, event management, in-store merchandising and finance which use the 'targeted 'laser gun' platform of 'mobile tours' (e.g. 'Bionicle Unleashed' and 'What Will You Make?'), focusing on specific products or target-defined age groups. The company takes a customer-related or 'back-to-front' approach to events: starting with the consumer and understanding who they are, what their passions are, where they go and what they do, and constructing events around them. Following the new marketing mantra, activation must be hands on. Whilst event management of this sort was taking the *LEGO* story 'to the people' as it were, it couldn't reach 100% of the target audience. It had to be geared towards one-to-one 'experiential programmes' aimed specifically at innovators and early adopters, who in turn would spread word of mouth and influence others. *LEGO* road-shows try to influence consumer behaviour by creating awareness and influencing brand preference with what the company refers to as 'targeted touches': the number of consumers the brand actually has physical contact and verbal dialogues with (e.g. *Bionicle's* initial mobile tour produced 355,000 'TTs' with children who understood the story, had a hands-on experience with the product and interacted with the vehicle). These brand road-shows are referred to within the company as staged 'retailtainment' programmes, and took the initiative in store, provided excitement and drove purchase. *LEGO* will be opening branded retail stores (á la *Disney*) in Cologne and Milton Keynes this year, which will further extend the story.

LEGO had used a holistic approach to create a true *LEGO* experience, with the integrated marketing communications programme using a comprehensive campaign aimed at retailers, parents and children. The 'living point-of-purchase' campaign that was moved from store to store, elicited the type of responses that static, cardboard signs could not. The

Capturing a child's view of the Lego brand

(Continued)

delivery of consistent 'content' of the *LEGO* brand narrative to customers in the form of a print magazine provides dialogue and gives practical tips on how consumers can extend their use of *LEGO* products; promoting user-generated content in the *LEGO* magazine and website and having links between the two media. An element of the customer base is made up of heavy spenders and they are communicated to with more advanced content: *BrickMaster* and a discussion forum for other advanced builders which enhance the *LEGO* experience called *Brickjournal.com*.

Capturing an adult's view of the Lego brand

The end-user (children) and key decision-making unit (DMU) influencers (parents) were promoted through family events, online parent-specific content and advertising which attempts to get parents to 'see the world through a child's eyes'. This simply, but brilliantly, evoked memories in parents and clearly showed the essence of the brand: a child's imagination. The advertisement pictured[TJH4] is from the 'Build it' campaign which won a Gold Lion at the Cannes International Advertising Festival in 2007.

In its attempts to build a brand community around the product, *LEGO* used a PR agency (360PR) who created an online platform to bring back the thrill of *LEGO* toys amidst the digital world of game consoles and *iPods*. This approach to social networking consists of thousands of individual stories born in true user experiences which make up the total *LEGO* brand narrative. The '*LEGO* Builders of Tomorrow' campaign, targeted parents reminding them that children grow into successful adults through cultivating creativity and imagination. It emerged that parents were also techno-savvy, using the Internet regularly. Three devices were established to promote discourse with parents about the importance of imaginative play: a website with parents' stories about 'Builders of Tomorrow', a scholarship contest and play tips for parents; a '*LEGO* Playtime' podcast; and a regular interactive blog. This boosted sales, spread a positive brand message to young children and their parents and attracted 5000 unique monthly visitors, and achieved fantastic press coverage including a 'Dawn of the Dad' feature which extended the idea of brand narrative.

The *LEGO* vision 'Idea, Exuberance and Values' requires that all *LEGO* products stimulate children's imagination and creativity and this has been done through a 360-degree multimedia approach. In other words, building a tapestry of individual stories has been achieved through communications and content, using actual and metaphorical building bricks to create an engaging, ongoing brand narrative and marks the return of the *LEGO* legend, a brand name that literally means 'play well'. *LEGO* and the *LEGO* logo are trademarks of the *LEGO* group, here used with special permission. © 2009 The *LEGO* group.

QUESTIONS

1. Throughout the book, we will examine the underlying mechanics of how integrated marketing communications works in a coherent, cohesive manner. Why do you think *LEGO* has been successful in recreating the *LEGO* legend?

2. Do you think this sort of approach is sustainable given the short attention span, instant gratification of young consumers today?

3. Do you think the scope for developing the *LEGO* narrative is in brand image-building campaigns that evoke memory and imagination or in engaging users in online dialogues which are essentially user generated?

WHY DOES MARKETING COMMUNICATIONS HAVE TO BE INTEGRATED?

Mooij (1994, p. 374) described **integrated** marketing communications as tuning 'groups, goals, messages and means of communication in such a way that they complement and reinforce each other so that the overall effect yields more than the sum of the parts'. According to Lee and Park (2007), it is a concept 'under which a company systematically coordinates its multiple messages and many communication channels and integrates them into a cohesive and consistent marketing communications mix'. Tynan (1994) emphasised the belief that 'the most successful communications are those in which the consumer receives one message from various sources'. Therefore, integration of media and messages to harness the synergy of all brand communications and customer contact points creates brand value and uses customer preferences as a starting point for dialogue, not the end result. Consumers are searching for more than a single element; they buy into the array of relevant experiences which surround the brand. Iddiols (2000) lists the consumer advantages of these 'links' as: providing short cuts to understanding what a brand stands for; adding depth or 'amplifying' a particular message or set of brand values; and demonstrating professionalism on the part of the brand owner.

According to Shimp (2000) this integration should be characterised by a marketing communications mix so tightly coordinated that 'you can look from medium to medium, from programme event to programme event, and instantly see that the brand is speaking with one voice'. It is what Holm (2006) describes as 'the art of uniting a sender's purposes and goals with the carefully selected receiver's prerequisites of interpretation and pre-understanding'.

However, we must remember that there are many elements which must be integrated but together they must present one clear, coherent message. Christensen, Firat and Torp, (2008, p. 424) suggest that 'in order to integrate its communications, an organisation needs to embrace diversity and variety and to balance the wisdom of its many voices with the effort to secure clarity and consistency in its overall expression'.

IS IT PROMOTIONAL STRATEGY OR MARKETING COMMUNICATIONS STRATEGY?

Within the 'promoting to–communicating with' dichotomy, the debate about whether promotion should be segregated as an instrument of the marketing mix or whether communication is an all-pervasive, cross-discipline, integrating force has been polarised both in theory and in practice. Sometimes, short-term sales or promotional tactics take precedence over long-term brand-building strategy. There may be a desperate requirement, especially in tight economic conditions, to concentrate on 'getting sales through the factory gate' if the main objective of a firm is short-term survival, and of course everything in an organisation has to be built on sales.

Ultimately, however, a business depends on people coming back on a regular basis, and this can only be done by mutual understanding and customer focus. Indeed, early definitions of marketing communications still featured the word 'promotion' in its broadest sense of 'broadcasting' messages: 'Promotional strategy refers to a controlled, integrated programme of communication methods designed to present an organisation and its products or services to prospective customers; to communicate need-satisfying attributes to facilitate sales; and thus to contribute to long-run profit performance' (Engel, Warshaw and Kinnear 1994).

Fill (2001, p. 19) traces the 'incremental development of integrated marketing communications' (Figure 5.1) which an organisation needs to go through to effect a change in orientation to integrated marketing communications: customer care, attitude and cultural change are built on cross-functional cohesion and bringing together the total external and internal communications effort. But whilst short-term tactics and long-term strategy can be uncomfortable bedfellows, they *have* to be integrated. Van Raaij (1998) provided a useful comparison of the differences between the traditional, classic approach to marketing communications and its more 'post-modern' integrated incarnation (see Table 5.1).

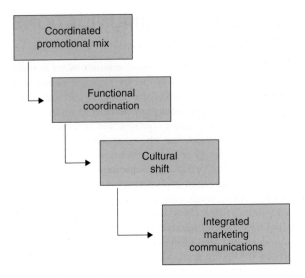

Figure 5.1: Incremental development of integrated marketing communications

Source: Fill (2001, p. 19). Reproduced with permission.

Classic communications	Integrated marketing communications
Aimed at acquisition	Aimed at retention and relationship
Mass communications	Selective communications
Monologue	Dialogue
Information is sent	Information is requested
Information provision	Information self-service
Sender takes initiative	Receiver takes initiative
Persuasive 'hold-up'	Provide information
Effect through repetition	Effect through relevance
Offensive	Defensive
Hard sell	Soft sell
Salience of brand	Confidence in brand
Transaction	Relationship oriented
Attitude change	Satisfaction
Modern, linear, massive	Post-modern, cyclical, fragmented

Table 5.1: Comparison of classic and integrated marketing communications

Source: Van Raaij (1998), Yeshin (2007).

STRATEGY IN FOCUS

Dove Real Beauty Campaign

Marketing communications strategy must be cohesive and sustainable, achieving objectives which include competitive positioning and customer satisfaction. 'Consistency is the responsibility of the marketer . . . [to] keep all disciplines – people, messages, and tactics – performing in unison, and must constantly guard against tactics straying from the overarching brand strategy' (Liodice 2008). In 2002, the soap brand *Dove* was to be repositioned to become a *Unilever* master brand. Nothing in the *Unilever* heritage could aid this process (Aaker and McLoughlin 2007).

When *Dove* stated that the aim of its strategy was to both launch a range of new 'firming' products and 'strike a blow for women's self-esteem', the goals were clear: differentiate its offer against competitors in its category and create a brand narrative which had to be engaging and sustainable. *Dove* became the epitome of the 'experiential' approach to branding: it made strategy a cause.

To tie the marketing communications into the overall function, purpose and future direction of the organisation, and construct a framework for continuing customer dialogue, required careful planning and execution. The central fulcrum for all strategy and tactics was to be *Dove's* 'Real Beauty' campaign which focused both customer and company attention on capitalising on the alienation of 'real women' to the stereotypical perceptions of beauty prevalent amongst other cosmetics brands such as *L'Oréal* and *Garnier*. Whilst this strategy is not new (*Marks & Spencer* disastrously attempted this approach in the UK in the 1980s), the reinforcement of the narrative was provided with the *Dove Self-Esteem Fund*, an ongoing Internet conversation which locks consumers and employees internally into a cultural mission.

Traditional media – TV, press, point of sale and various promotional activities – reinforced the overall strategy, but it was the use of viral marketing which breathed most life into the campaign. The development of three interactive videos – 'Onslaught', 'Amy' and 'Evolution' – featured on the *Dove* website and released into social networking sites, encouraged ownership, conversation and the accelerated word of mouth of digital media. The debate about 'how the "effortless" beauty we see on billboards is actually created' has challenged other competitors but has also put approaches to marketing communications strategy and transparency in creating projected brand images up for discussion.

THE 5Rs OF MARKETING COMMUNICATIONS PLANNING

A radical approach to marketing communications planning, but set in the context of a 'converging marketplace' in terms of user-generated, media-neutral, cross-discipline communications is what Schultz (2001) refers to as the '5Rs'. Control is ultimately with customers not companies and therefore the following customer-oriented approach may be more apposite:

- **Responsiveness:** asymmetrical communication is geared towards talking not listening, monologue not dialogue. The reverse should be the case if companies are to understand buyer behaviour and respond to the informational needs of the consumer.
- **Relevance:** this is the interruption versus value issue. Interruption marketing (e.g. TV 30-second spot advertising, print advertising) is not as effective and in some cases not relevant. It's essential that added-value communications enrich the information search experience, entertain and educate, as well as addressing consumer not company needs.
- **Receptivity:** information of value must be communicated when and how consumers need it.
- **Recognition:** brands which build affiliation can differentiate from the competition. Ongoing communications and brand encounters are the source of unique relationships between company and customer.

- **Relationships:** retention marketing and the customer–company interface are vital elements of the relationships that are built up and a customer service-oriented organisation is of paramount importance.

Smith, Berry and Pulford (1999) define integrated marketing communications as:

- the management and control of all marketing communications;
- ensuring that the brand positioning, personality and messages are delivered synergistically across every element of communication from a single consistent strategy; and
- the strategic analysis, choice, implementation and control of all elements of marketing which efficiently (best use of resources), economically (minimum costs) and effectively (maximum results) influence transactions between an organisation and its existing and potential customers, consumers and clients.

This is shown diagrammatically in Figure 5.2. The left-hand side shows the elements of marketing strategy which have to be achieved by positioning, branding, the management of relationships and the mix of media and messages which have to be constructed for the communications tools available.

It was actually the American Association of Advertising Agencies (1998) which very early on gave us a real insight into what integrated marketing communications should be. It was described as 'a concept of marketing communications planning that recognizes the added value of a comprehensive plan that evaluates the strategic roles of a variety of communications disciplines and combines them to provide clarity, consistency and maximum communication impact through the seamless integration of discrete messages'. The essence of this is that the process is comprehensive, and it combines various communication elements to achieve a coherent, cohesive 'added value' to the customer. Yeshin (2007) draws in some consistent themes in the descriptions of integrated marketing communications which demonstrate its all-pervasive nature:

- A sound knowledge of the organisation's stakeholders, acquired through two-way interaction with these parties.
- The selection of communication tools which promote the achievement of communications objectives; are reasonable in regard to the organisation's resources; and are favourable to the intended recipient.

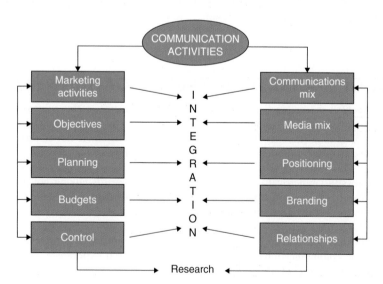

Figure 5.2: An integrative approach to marketing communications

Source: Hughes (1999, p. 255). Reproduced with permission.

- The strategic coordination of various communication tools in a manner consistent with the organisation's brand positioning, and which maximises their synergistic effect so as to build strong brands and stakeholder relationships.
- The use of appropriate, timely and data-driven evaluation and planning to determine the effectiveness of this process.
- Strong inter-functional and inter-organisational relationships with those responsible for implementing marketing communications campaigns.
- Impact on customer relationships, brand equity and sales.

The benefits of integrated marketing communications are summarised in Table 5.2, derived from previous research by Linton and Morley (1995), Kitchen and Schultz (1999) and Yeshin (2007).

Characteristics	Benefits
Increased impact of communications dialogue	All programmes deliver the same message
	All communications speak with the same 'voice'
	Overall strategy for the brand rather than individual tactical use of communication tools
	Reinforcement of message helps recall and recognition
	Reduces confusion in the minds of the consumer
	Cumulative effect adds to brand equity
	Consistency of message delivery
	More control over unplanned communications
	Helps eliminate misconceptions
Corporate cohesion	Used as a strategic tool in communicating its corporate and brand image for both external and internal cohesion
	Aids operational efficiency
Interaction	Better flow of communications between company, intermediaries and end-user consumer
	Better flow of communications between creative agencies and media
	Easier working relationships
Participation	Two-way dialogues encourage co-authorship of brand narrative
	Communication complicity with employees and intermediaries
Resource efficiencies	Greater control over communications budget
	Measurability
	Reduces cost because of cohesion of communication mix components
	Maximises strengths of individual components
	Unbiased marketing recommendations
	Media schedules not agency-led
	Greater marketing precision
	More effective creative ideas

Table 5.2: Benefits of integrated marketing communications

Source: derived from Linton and Morley (1995), Kitchen and Schultz (1999) and Yeshin (2007).

Fill (2002) encapsulates the ongoing strategic need for permanency of narratives by claiming integrated marketing communications to be 'the management process associated with the strategic development, delivery and dialogue of consistent, coordinated messages that stakeholders perceive as reinforcing brand propositions'. It should create meaningful customer benefits and exchange, but the customer *has* to be the driver.

STRATEGIC MARKETING COMMUNICATIONS

The key components of marketing communications strategy are listed in Table 5.3. The strengths of sustainable competitive advantage (USP in 'mind space' positioning) should be articulated to an audience to reinforce category positioning. Strategy will provide direction and a framework from which marketing objectives can be achieved through the effective and efficient application of the marketing communications mix.

Before we look at planning marketing communications, let's look at the environment within which marketing communications is set.

Communication components	Strategic purpose
Positioning	Should restate and consolidate the positioning
Benefits	Should reinforce benefits wanted by customers (and unfulfilled by the competition)
Strengths	Draws on sustainable competitive advantage
Competition	Competitive dimension
Customers	Segments and targets the market plus considers all the stages in the buying process from generating awareness and enquiries through to maintaining repeat sales
Direction	Gives clear direction (in terms of positioning, strengths, etc.)
Tools	Defines the range of communications tools
Integration	Ensures the communications tools are integrated
Sequence of tools	Does the advertising need to build brand awareness before converting to sales and direct mail? Does the PR break before the sales launch etc?
Timescale	Longer term than tactics and operational activities
Resources	Indicates the emphasis and size of spend on certain tools (whether the communications are going to be advertising-led or sales-driven etc.)
Objectives	Can make reference to the overall objectives of the strategy
Marketing strategy	Should be consistent with and draw from the overall marketing strategy

Table 5.3: Key components of marketing communications strategy

Source: Smith, Berry and Pulford (1999). Reproduced with permission.

THE CONTEXTS OF MARKETING COMMUNICATIONS

It is important to visualise the contexts within which marketing communications strategy is set in order to provide a realistic impression of which audiences must be targeted, and what objectives and strategy are required to bring about effective communications. In order to correctly align any communication, the customer context is central to this – our researched understanding of the elements which affect consumer decision making (motivations, attitudes, perceptions and behaviour). The immediate impact of a customer's perceptions of a brand and organisation will be affected by the brand encounters experienced in the customer–company interface. The degree of customer orientation (as manifest in values, culture and company attitudes) will all affect this. In the same way that customer service can often be the only differentiating factor between companies, marketing communication often presents the only differentiating feature offered to potential consumers (Shultz, Tenenbaum and Lauterborn 1992). Therefore the internal context – employees, management and staff – are a key target audience for communications and have to deliver the brand promise expressed in any marketing communications campaigns. Ownership of the brand can be a difficulty; any organisation that has to channel communications through the conduit of intermediaries, and rely on messages being disseminated in part by the media, must recognise and plan for the influence of mediated messages. Also, the societal impact of green issues, ethical behaviour and so on conditions the content and context of communications, as do the wider global environment factors. All these factors inform the view that marketing communications isn't just tactical, it is strategic. When strategy is planned, cognisance has to be given to the four contexts shown in Figure 5.3.

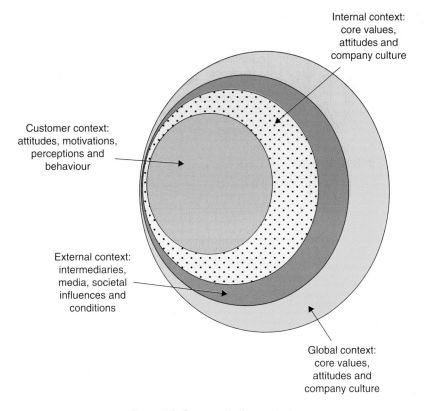

Figure 5.3: Communication contexts

Source: adapted from Fill (2001, p. 23).

MATTER OF FACT

Online Integrated Marketing Communications

Research by Gurău (2008) into the need for a new framework of integrated marketing communications has helped develop an appropriate online model. The three factors which differentiate online communications from other channels are interactivity, transparency and memory (in terms of storing information). These factors are transforming the profile and behaviour of online audiences in the following ways:

- the audience is connected to the organisation via a network not a pipeline;
- the audience is connected to one another;
- the audience has access to other information;
- the audience 'pulls' information.

Internet technologies allow organisations different approaches to marketing communications:

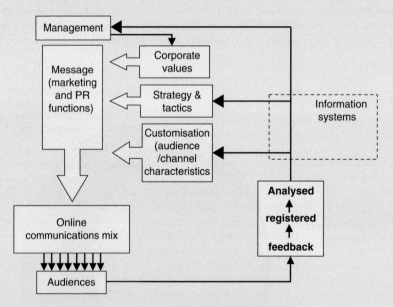

Online approaches to marketing communications

- the integration and coordination of communication modes (includes one to one (emails), one to many (web pages) and many to many (discussion forums));
- the integration and coordination of various types of communication (text, sounds and images, static or dynamic);
- the integration and coordination of complex information flows between organisational intranet and Internet (includes one to one (emails), one to many (web pages) and many to many (discussion forums));
- capacity to capture and register customer data and feedback;
- to analyse and use data for one-to-one segmentation;
- the ability to utilise existing databases to launch highly coordinated communication campaigns.

> Messages have to respect and reflect corporate values, adapt to strategy and tactics, and should consider the target audience in terms of how communication can be customised.
>
> *Source:* Gurău (2008).

PLANNING MARKETING COMMUNICATIONS

As we have seen from Chapter 1, the cornerstones of good marketing communications are target audience, message and media which must be integrated, working cohesively together. The interface between company, customer and media are all points of contact within which the brand 'talks' to existing and potential customers and help constitute brand meaning. As we have previously stated: everything and everyone communicates through brand encounters – the exposure experience or 'moments of truth' (Normann 1991, p. 16) that were discussed in Chapter 2. Although this has service industry antecedents, it has relevance for the 360° planning and control of integrated marketing communications. Direct or remote interaction can be planned or unplanned, formal or informal, and can be company, competitor or even customer generated.

These brand encounters take place in a partly controlled environment where not all communication can be managed. As illustrated in Figure 5.4, there are four different types: (i) explicit planned brand encounters; (ii) implicit planned brand encounters; (iii) solicited planned brand encounters; and (iv) unsolicited unplanned brand encounters.

Explicit planned brand encounters are campaigns which are objectively researched with communication mix elements such as advertising and direct marketing applied. The company has the most control over these factors since the way messages are transmitted can be tested beforehand and adjusted with feedback from the market to ensure planned messages get through. **Implicit planned brand encounters**, like the physical evidence of a reception or the ambience of a retail store, have a degree of subjective interpretation and so are more difficult to control. How consumers interpret associations and inferences in communications is always an area which needs constant monitoring. **Solicited planned brand encounters** are third-party sanctioned expressions of the organisation's brand by intermediaries. How products are displayed and merchandised, how the brand story is projected second-hand through stockists, retailers and other intermediaries can be semi-controlled by organisations. Manufacturers attempt to control their image and brand messages by offering free-of-charge displays and merchandising

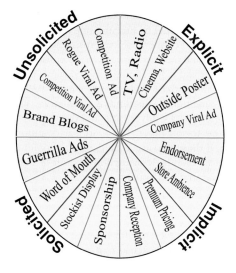

Figure 5.4: Brand encounters

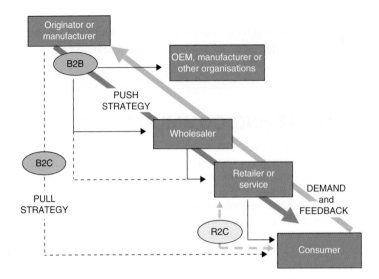

Figure 5.5: Flow of communication

Source: adapted from Fill (2002, p. 334).

units, discounts on products displayed, merchandising teams to dress shops in a uniform fashion, staff training and so on. And finally, **unsolicited unplanned brand encounters** include word of mouth, miscommunications by competitors or uninformed parties presenting a distorted impression of the brand such as competitor's misrepresentation, viral advertisements and so on.

Therefore, it is important to coordinate message, media and audience in marketing communications strategy. The flow of communication is dependent upon the routes to market, and this can be seen in Figure 5.5.

- **B2B push strategies:** some manufacturers will deal through intermediaries who provide bulk-breaking and cost advantages as well as access to markets for the company. They offer time, choice, location and added-value utilities to end users. So, for example, computer manufacturer *Hewlett-Packard* (*HP*) sells its computer products via computer retailer *PC World*; this is business-to-business (B2B). *HP* employs a trade 'push' strategy to assist the flow of communication from the company as manufacturer/brand owner through to end-user consumers. The manufacturer objectives will be to prepare and service the consumer market by incentivising the trade through displays, staff training, point-of-sale promotional materials, cooperative advertising, and dedicated promotional activities aimed at providing a coherent brand message through to the consumer. The retailer provides 'opportunities to see' for the consumer and helps communicate positive messages at point of sale, particularly to counter perceived risk in purchase. This is really a linear B2B2C communication flow.
- **B2C pull strategies:** at the same time as distributing through *PC World*, *HP* is busy creating consumer demand for the *HP* brand by TV advertising and direct marketing campaigns aimed at the consumer, which is a business-to-consumer (B2C) circular communication flow, since feedback allows for two-way dialogue. If these two are in tandem, and communication messages are coordinated and consistent, product which is demanded as a result of consumer advertising campaigns will be in stock and ready to be sold and bought.
- **B2C push/pull strategies:** some companies (e.g. *Dell Computers*) do not deal through intermediaries and have a direct link with their end customers with a direct business-to-customer (B2C) circular flow of both transaction and communication. This strategy is dependent upon B2C communications, such as websites, catalogues, mailings, online sales and after sales, having consistency. Even with a direct communication model such as *Dell*, some intermediaries such as delivery service and warranty collection agents can enhance or destroy reputation in brand encounters.

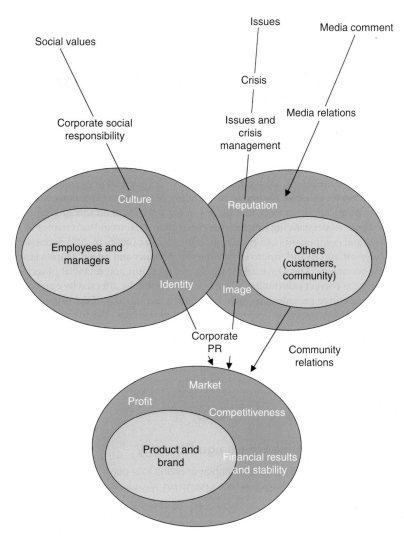

Figure 5.6: Profile strategy

Source: Pieczka (2006, p. 291). Reproduced by permission of Taylor & Francis Group LLC.

- **R2C push/pull strategies:** retailers have a dual role in the communications flow: they act as intermediaries for manufacturers (80% of food goes through the supermarkets; 67% of UK retail goes through *Tesco, ASDA, Sainsbury's* and *Morrisons*); they also have strong corporate brand images and sell their own branded product ranges. In fact, the power has switched to retailers so much in the last 20 years that consumers often communicate primarily with the retailer not the manufacturers' brands. This has had such an impact on the way we buy and sell brands that it warrants a category on its own. The switch of power to retailers has made the business-to-customer (B2C) relationship much more meaningful and retailers invest heavily in sustaining this retailer-to-customer (R2C) flow of communication.
- **B2B push/pull strategies:** some companies supply direct to other businesses and organisations on a contract basis (e.g. *Dell* has a B2B division) or sell components to other manufacturers or OEM organisations (e.g. *Michelin* tyres to *Ford*).

Push and pull strategies need to be in harmony for them to work. These also have to be integrated with the third part of marketing communications strategy, usually referred to as a **profile strategy** (Fill 2002, p. 339), which considers the dialogues required with various commercial and non-commercial stakeholders. Often there is a blurring of the demarcation lines between public relations activities, corporate branding and image and reputation management, but they all amount to the same thing strategically: the management of internal and external stakeholder perceptions in order to maintain corporate reputation and brand equity. The days when retail organisations present only a store persona or when manufacturers have anonymity in a consumer context are nearly over. Organisations such as *Marks & Spencer* have realised that corporate and social responsibility and an ethical supply chain are important to end-user consumers. Even *P&G* has started to see the selling of the *P&G* image cannot only be B2B and is communicating a more direct route to the market.

Relations with the media, the community and the wider societal perspective have put corporate image and reputation on an equal footing with branding of products. This is such an important issue in marketing communications strategy that there is a full discussion on this in Chapter 14. However, for the sake of easier understanding here, Figure 5.6 is extracted from that chapter in order for us to consider the role and components of a profile strategy. Pieckza (2006, p. 290) delineates the three domains of the *internal*, *micro* and *macro* environments: product and brand; employees and managers; and the wider community. The key market, profit, competition and financial objectives need to be achieved through the correct positioning of the brand. This will be affected by corporate and community as well as competitive pressures. In turn, the culture and identity of the organisation is projected through (and affected by) the values expressed through employees. The broader societal context has taken on a greater corporate and individual significance, with ecological and ethical considerations now inextricably bound to profit. The days of Milton Freidman's mantra of 'The business of business is business' are now long gone.

STRATEGY IN FOCUS

World of Warcraft Online Campaign Strategy

World of Warcraft (WOW) is a massive multiplayer online role-play (MMORPG, MMOG or MMO) game released in 2004 and dominates the MMORPG market (62% according to mmogchart .com 2008). Creative approaches to marketing communications strategy have built this virtual world community into one of the biggest customer bases in the real world, recruiting and retaining over 11 million subscribers.

World of Warcraft game

Positioned as a product for the 'Hard Core Neo Tribe' gamer, WOW's B2C communications (company to audience) were restricted to advertising on specialist gaming websites and forums and reserved advertisements on mainstream sites such as *play.com*. The advantage of this was that messages were targeted to serious gamers (with time, commitment and hardware to play); the disadvantage is those gamers were averse to website banner advertising; click-through rates were worryingly high.

New category recruitment required an increase in uptake and this was done by encouraging peer-to-peer communications and a series of value-added initiatives. The implementation of a rewards scheme was designed to stimulate sales, engender better relationships and enhance the gaming experience. A 'Free 10 Day Trial', a 'Recommend a Friend' scheme and 'WOW Trading Cards' encouraged peer-to-peer recruitment, positive word of mouth and offline attendance at WOW conventions.

The use of existing customers/players as brand ambassadors was a very effective way of encouraging C2C marketing as the source credibility of friends is exceptionally high in this context. The tactic of allowing user-generated content had two massive benefits:

- Games were 'beta tested' by willing opinion leaders and information on new launches disseminated rapidly and positively.
- Online bloggers were encouraged to spread word of mouth.

WOW used this resource to profile customers and this facilitated better games and better communications:

- Release of 'patches' to selected gamers encouraged ownership and word of mouth.
- Viral marketing was encouraged through sites such as *YouTube* most notably an entertainment video about team playing called 'Leeroy Jenkins' which spread word of mouth on TV shows such as *My Name is Earl*.

Communications has recently moved more into the mainstream with TV advertising and celebrity endorsement. Offline buzz has been generated and sustained by massive PR stunts such as the 'midnight release' of games extensions into high-street stores. Over 1000 people queued outside the London Oxford Street *HMV* store. The online and press campaign encouraged game innovators to: 'Be the First' and 'Don't Get Left Behind'.

CAMPAIGN PLANNING FRAMEWORK

Whilst there are plenty of planning structures to describe the different approaches to researching, creating and managing a marketing communications plan, Kotler's failsafe summary of analysis, planning, implementation and control (APIC) still provides a backbone to most academic and practitioner marketing or communication plans. The one we feature here, the **CAMPAIGN marketing communications planning framework©**, is a summative structure designed to illustrate the following elements of marketing communications strategy:

- Outline the various planning and implementation stages in the development of marketing communications.
- Visually demonstrate the integrated and coherent aspect of campaign planning as a continuing process.
- Underline the core components consistent with marketing plans (i.e. analysis, planning, implementation and control).
- Emphasise the fact that running throughout is the overarching brand narrative which all communication strategies, tactics, mix elements and resources create and contribute to.
- Provide a useful *aide memoire* using the acronym CAMPAIGN which will help students and managers understand and apply this strategic structure.

Therefore, the constituent parts of the CAMPAIGN planning framework (as shown in Figure 5.7) are:

- *Current brand evaluation*: research into market share, brand and company history, brand health, strategic role within brand portfolio, market meaning.
- *Analysis*: market assessment, environmental influences, target market and customer dynamics, and other contextual considerations.

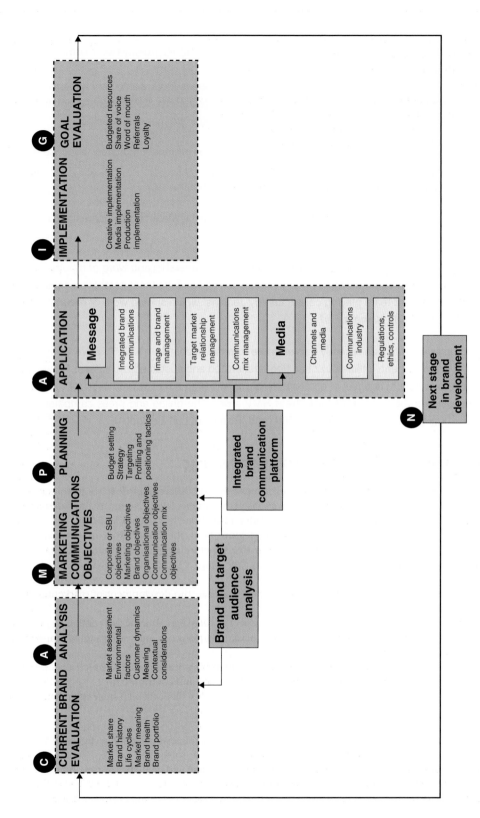

Figure 5.7: CAMPAIGN planning framework

C CURRENT BRAND EVALUATION

Market share
Brand history
Life cycles
Market meaning
Brand health
Brand portfolio

A ANALYSIS

Market assessment
Environmental factors
Customer dynamics
Meaning
Contextual considerations

M MARKETING COMMUNICATIONS OBJECTIVES

Corporate or SBU objectives
Marketing objectives
Brand objectives
Organisational objectives
Communication objectives
Communication mix objectives

P PLANNING

Budget setting
Strategy
Targeting
Profiling and positioning tactics

A APPLICATION

Message
Integrated brand communications
Image and brand management
Target market relationship management
Communications mix management

Media
Channels and media
Communications industry
Regulations, ethics, controls

I IMPLEMENTATION

Creative implementation
Media implementation
Production implementation

G GOAL EVALUATION

Budgeted resources
Share of voice
Word of mouth
Referrals
Loyalty

N Next stage in brand development

Integrated brand communication platform

Brand and target audience analysis

- *Marketing communication effects and objectives*: corporate (or SBU), marketing, brand and communication effects and objectives.
- *Planning*: strategic framework, segmentation, targeting and positioning, tactics, techniques and budgets.
- *Application*: all message (communications mix, branding, reputation management, relationship management) and media (channels and media, intermediaries, communication industry).
- *Implementation*: creative, media and production implementation.
- *Goal evaluation*: budgeted resources, share of voice, awareness, purchase, referrals, market share, customer retention.
- *Next stage of development*: the future of the brand narrative, direction of brand development, feedback from the marketplace into the start of the next cycle of planning.

SETTING BUDGETS FOR MARKETING COMMUNICATIONS

The setting of marketing communications budgets is always a source of debate in organisations, and exposes differing perspectives on whether marketing communications is a cost or an investment, and on whether there is cause-and-effect input/output scientific objectivity to its deployment. Some of the tried-and-trusted methods are listed below:

- **Arbitrary:** there is no pre-determined set amount for expected marketing communications expenditures. Ad hoc decisions are made on the basis of market conditions, competitive activities and changing brand requirements. This method may well be flexible in that management responds to environmental factors, spend is not fixed and possibly not appropriate, but it is not really budgeting in the proper sense of the word.
- **All that you can afford:** expediency may well be the order of the day and greater priorities such as management of cash flow and even survival might condition how much the organisation can afford. Again, this is not really a scientific method or approach, and misses the point that marketing communications is an investment to help recruit customers and achieve sales targets. However, in times of severe competitive or economic pressure to exist and maintain existing sales levels, this may be the most appropriate in the short term irrespective of whether this has long-term impacts.
- **Historic basis:** the assumption that previous levels of expenditure, cause-and-effect results and the appropriateness of the message, media and mix have been successfully deployed may well be a good basis to retrospectively examine the impacts of marketing communications, but it is not an appropriate way to plan future campaigns. There may be contextual differences and changes in market dynamics which require proper analysis before judgements are made as to how, where and when funds are spent.
- **Competitive parity:** matching spend with competitors to achieve relative positioning, 'share of voice' or even psychological equity can often be an appropriate method of budget setting, especially for challenger brands which seek category comparison or competitive parity. This gives the initiative to others and may or may not be appropriate. A new entrant to a category might have to spend more to achieve the same impact and level of penetration.
- **Percentage of sales:** some organisations have a fixed proportionate amount based on expected level of sales. This amounts to a formulaic approach of sorts and is often based on past experience or competitive or industry reference points. Whilst this assumes a correlation between input and output, it underplays the role of marketing communications to affect sales and limits the potential for greater impact. It is also dangerous because the tendency to over-estimate expected sales can be irresponsible.
- **Experiment and test:** controlled experiments may prove the efficacy of campaign components within a sample market, amongst a range of communication mix elements or the space purchased in the various media. This may restrict immediate impacts but could prove beneficial in terms of reducing wasteful deployment by aiding accurate prediction of the implementation of the campaign.

- **Modelling and simulation:** based on industry norms, competitive parity, previous campaigns, test markets and use of proprietary software, a sophisticated model can be used to simulate possible budgeting scenarios. This can be updated with feedback from the campaign both in terms of 'formative' (pre-test assessment) and summative evaluation (post-test assessment). See Chapter 17 for a fuller discussion on evaluation.
- **Objectives and task:** by far the best method of setting budgets is to assess what changes or reinforcement in target market behaviour and purchase intentions have to be effected in order to achieve marketing objectives. This is the most scientific approach as it starts from a zero budget standpoint: how much will a specific input cost to achieve a specific outcome and how appropriate is that expenditure likely to be?

CLOSING CASE STUDY

Zara: Fast Fashion Formula Finds Gap in the Market

One of the most consumer-driven sectors is the global retail apparel market. According to Stuart Green of Interbrand, the ultimate yardstick for brand effectiveness in this sector 'lies in the end-user experience'. Equally, marketing communications strategy is dependent upon the type of value proposition a brand offers and how it is to be positioned in the marketplace. Valued at over €4469 million in 2009 (Interbrand valuation), *Zara*, the Spanish-based chain owned by Inditex, is the largest fashion retailer (by sales) in Europe and has now taken over the mantle of the American *Gap* brand to become the world's biggest

Zara makes a big impression on the high street

fashion retailer. And they've achieved this by having a sustainable formula and a brand concept which has been consistently communicated. What is fascinating is the fact that *Zara* is a follower in fashion but an innovator in the way the product is marketed and communicated.

In the 1960s, consumers were introduced to the mass marketing discount concept facilitated by the supermarket and hypermarket. In the 1990s, with the arrival of a new generation of brands like *Sephora* and *Grand Optical* in France, and *H&M* in Sweden, retailing was transformed. *Sephora* is still the only beauty cosmetics chain structured like a supermarket; the French *Grand Optical* is a high-end optician; the Swedish helped change fashion with *H&M* in the retail/apparel sector. They all offered a completely new approach to retailing. Whereas retail chains such as French hypermarket *Carrefour*, Germany's *Aldi* or the UK's *Marks & Spencer* sell products and services that are comparable with those of other competitive hypermarkets, the new type of 'formula' retailers deliver a retail brand concept. Right at the front of this new breed is Spain's *Zara*.

The distinction between formula and chain is essential in order to define communication strategies. *Zara*, along with *H&M* in Sweden, *C&A* in Germany, *Gap* in the USA, and the UK's *Topshop* and *Next*, have been influential in 'democratising fashion'. Once positioned as 'haute couture', a luxury only for the elite, fashion is now accessible to all. High-street brands such as *Zara*, *Topshop* and *H&M* have put fashion within the reach of anyone, whilst massive media attention has turned designers such as Tom Ford, Alexander McQueen and Stella McCartney into brands in their own right.

Zara is vertically integrated, designing, producing and distributing product through self-owned retail outlets. Significantly, communication and integration are critical success factors.

An astonishing turn-around design and distribution cycle of just two weeks from drawing board to store has been hugely instrumental in reinventing this category: popularising 'fast fashion'. *Zara* is particularly innovative in response to customer requirements and providing an excellent in-store experience. All 'brand touch-points' from space, merchandise assortment, style right the way through to customised service project brand image.

There are five key elements to marketing strategy: store location; store window merchandising; interior design and store image; assort-

Zara's in-store communications

ment display; and customer service. This is replicated across all markets. However, there is an unusual approach to marketing communications. One distinguishing feature of *Zara's* marketing communications strategy is the lack of image advertising and promotion compared to competitors in the same category. Whereas *Gap* advertise extensively (4% of turnover), and *H&M* use advertising and celebrity-endorsed annual events (3.5% of annual turnover), *Zara* schedules advertising campaigns only for the opening of a store, with buzz marketing having built word of mouth. As CEO Echevarria puts it: 'Our marketing strategy tends to be humble. We don't use a mass-market approach or big campaigns. Instead, we focus on the customer and the store label. Our store is the most effective marketing communications tool.'

Zara's image and positioning strategy are global but adapted for each country since consumers perceive fashion brands as fashion-bound (Fabrega 2004). In other words, 'country-of-origin' branding effect (i.e. 'Made in Spain') is not considered a contributory factor to its positioning (Keegan and Green 2005), something which is increasing because of *Zara's* global expansion. There is a dualithic brand-name strategy (Riezebos 2003), unique brand names for the same product group: 'Zara Woman', 'Zara Basic' and 'Zara Trafaluc'. In fact, perceptions reinforce *Zara's* 'global but local' perception. For example, recent research by *Vogue* magazine in France (Blanco and Salgado 2004) found that French consumers perceived the brand as being 'French'. This strength of brand loyalty has transformed *Zara* from a local to a global brand in 20 years.

QUESTIONS

1. How do you think *Zara's* image and positioning strategy achieve the unique individual country brand image rather than 'country of origin'?

2. What is the retail brand concept *Zara* offers and how is it achieved?

3. Do you think *Zara's* marketing communications strategy of a lack of image advertising and promotion compared to competitors in the same category is a sensible one?

CHAPTER SUMMARY

This chapter discussed why integrated marketing communications has changed because of the explosion of media, power of the consumer, access to technology and the need to have dialogues with audiences. We saw how this has caused a shift in the ways in which organisations now approach marketing communications strategy and examined the chief components needed to plan and implement successful marketing communications campaigns.

We examined the difference between 'promoting to' and 'communicating with' audiences. The difference between 'strategic' and 'tactical' positioning was explained and it was demonstrated how they support one another. The key components of marketing communications planning were discussed. We saw why target audience, message and media must be integrated. The constituent parts of the CAMPAIGN planning framework were analysed and a wide range of communication tools were discussed. We critically analysed the need for a more strategic and integrated approach to marketing communications, so important from a customer's perspective. The need coordination and management of resources was seen as critical to achieving successful integrated marketing communications in order to create coherent, meaningful dialogue with the customer.

REFLECTIVE QUESTIONS

a. Schultz (2001) refers to the '5Rs' as a radical approach to marketing communications planning. Describe what these are and why they have importance in the context of a 'converging marketplace' in terms of user-generated, media-neutral, cross-discipline communications.

b. Describe the component parts of the CAMPAIGN planning framework.

c. List the key components of marketing communications strategy.

d. Van Raaij (1998) suggests a useful comparison between the traditional, classic approach to marketing communications and its more 'post-modern' integrated incarnation. How do these perspectives fundamentally differ?

e. Explain the statement: 'We are witnessing the transition from asymmetrical communications to an era of two-way dialogues'.

RESEARCH PROJECTS

Visit the websites for organisations from three different sectors (e.g. B2B, the public sector and the financial services sector), and gather information on their differing approaches to marketing communications strategy. Using the CAMPAIGN planning framework, compare the content and execution of strategic and tactical positioning, marketing communications mix, and overall structure of the individual strategies.

Christensen, Firat and Torp (2008) discuss the importance of strategically and tactically integrating marketing communications organisations. This involves tight control over messages, symbols, procedures and organisational behaviours across organisational boundaries. They suggest that rigidity makes strategy too inflexible to react to changing market dynamics. Critique the argument in the context of what has been discussed so far.

CHAPTER  6

STRATEGIC POSITIONING

"Positioning is not what you do to a product. Positioning is what you do to the mind of the prospect. That is, you position the product in the mind of the prospect."
Ries and Trout (1980)

This chapter discusses the concept of positioning. Positioning plays a pivotal role in marketing strategy because 'it links market analysis and competitive analysis to internal corporate analysis' (Lovelock 1996, p. 169). Positioning is about a brand's territorial rights: claiming, establishing and maintaining a product/market space in the target market segment and a mind space in the consciousness of the target audience. Two factors are particularly important in creating and developing a long-term brand value proposition: the capacity to build strong, favourable and unique associations with the brand; and the budget to develop an ongoing brand narrative. In an overcrowded market-place, positioning can be considered as being a systematic approach to finding a space for dialogue with an audience. And yet some marketers are doing the wrong thing by thinking 'the answer to clutter is more clutter'. It isn't; it is clarity that is required more than anything in communications, and positioning is at the very heart of establishing the clarity of a brand.

tests. Other elements included email competitions, SMS, events and a viral video featuring 'CCTV footage' which found further and wider exposure on *YouTube*. These internal communications elements have helped employee complicity and engagement, generating real momentum and buzz ready to deliver the external brand promise.

QUESTIONS

1. What are the key integrated communication elements which reinforce *BT*'s positioning as the primary supplier of SME IT services?

2. Why has the medium of TV been selected to carry the bulk of what is essentially a B2B message?

3. What other positions could be adopted by *BT*'s competitors in this category?

PLANNING FOR BRAND POSITIONING

Sengupta (2004, p. 16) echoes the paramount importance of positioning as 'a fountainhead decision and an integrating concept'. Jobber (2004) claims that the key to successful brand positioning is 'clarity, consistency, competitiveness and credibility'. There must be a coherent idea of the market/product space to be targeted; there has to be integration of all brand messages; the value proposition should be comparable if not better than the main competitors; and the offer and claims should stand up against scrutiny. Consistency refers to 'one-voice' communications, but it does not mean that the position has to remain fixed – it has to be flexible and organic, responding to a dynamic competitive environment and changing customer needs. The crux of achieving strategy objectives is segmentation, targeting and positioning. In the succinct prose of Tybout and Calkins (2005), brand positioning answers three fundamental questions:

- Who should we target for brand use?
- What goal does the brand allow the target market to achieve?
- Why should they choose our brand over brands that achieve the same goal?

As far back as 1956, Wendell Smith made the distinction between segmentation being about market size and customer wants, and positioning being about accentuating the differences in our offer compared to competitive brands. As we have seen in Chapter 3, segmentation is about dividing the market into groups of existing or potential customers with similar needs, product preferences and buying behaviour. Once the most attractive segments or parts of segments are selected to target, and marketing communications objectives have been agreed, the brand's offering and image must be established. Smith and Taylor (2004, p. 316) refer to spending time 'interrogating the brand' before an estimation of where and how to position is arrived at. Segmentation identifies a product category; positioning highlights attributes and benefits of a specific offering. In other words the strategic task of positioning is selecting the subset of needs and wants of a selected target audience and developing a positioning proposition so that the brand occupies 'a meaningful and distinctive competitive position in the target customers' minds' (Kotler 1997).

From an organisation's perspective, it is also a reflection of the organisation's strategic vision (Saren 2006, p. 175) and we therefore need to analyse the context within which the brand is to be positioned. Tybout and Sternthal (2005) suggest a useful checklist:

- Which market or markets do we want to target?
- What is the customer profile and behaviour of the target market? What are their identifying characteristics such as psychographics (lifestyle attitudes, opinions and interests)? These are selected on the basis of category and brand usage.

- Who are or will be our main competitors?
- What is the 'frame of reference' of the target audience? What needs will be served by brand consumption? Usually goal-derived motivations and so on.
- What do we want our brand(s) to stand for? What is the 'point of difference' to select amongst alternatives?
- What are the reasons to believe the claims (abstract credence or concrete verifiable)?
- How do we ensure that our target audience (or audiences) perceives our brand as the superior alternative?
- Can we ensure that we have a better position than our competitors?
- Do we use one brand or several brands to achieve effective market coverage?

Although the positioning of a brand is formulated in marketing plans, it has to be grounded in the perceptions of the target audience. From a consumer's perspective, positioning should answer the questions:

- What is it?
- What's it for?
- What does it do?
- What will it do for me?
- What are the benefits for me?
- Why is it different to my regular brand?
- Will it be worth using this brand long-term?

Therefore, in order for us to appreciate how an organisation achieves market space and mind space, we need to fully examine the theoretical and practical applications of positioning.

Porter (1996) said that when we select a market space to target, there are two conditioning factors: the type of customers that we might have to service and the competition we are likely to meet in doing this. Baker and Hart (2007, p. 64) describe this as 'spatial competition'. How the market is being or may be served is key to how we might position our brand. Figure 6.1 illustrates three coordinates in plotting brand positioning.

An assessment of company capability and capacity is essential as the balance has to achieve compatibility with corporate objectives and overall equity. Any strategic positioning decision must add to

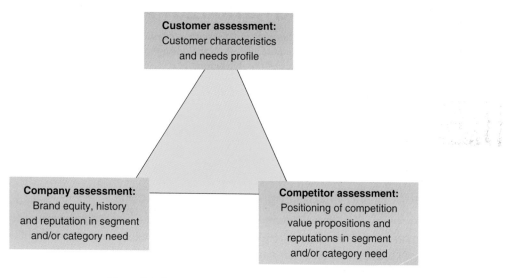

Figure 6.1: The triad of competitive positioning

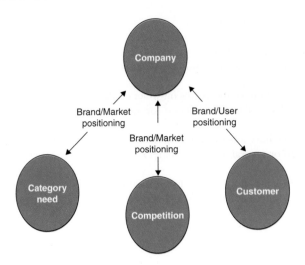

Figure 6.2: Possible positioning orientations

Source: Adapted from Rossiter and Percy (1998).

the totality of organisational commitments. Whether matching or exceeding competitive propositions, a full assessment of actual and perceived competitive positioning(s) should be undertaken. Are we capable of competing, and is association with the competition desirable? Of course, the most important ingredient to positioning, and in some ways the starting point, is evaluating customer requirements. The market may be mature and the parameters of operating too well established, thus necessitating adherence to existing category needs. On the other hand, there may be potential to change the way the target market is served and brand/market positioning may involve more customer orientation. However, brand/market positioning strategy may be conditioned by a company's status in market entry and level of influence in the sector. New entrants to an existing market may have to follow a 'challenger' brand strategy (Morgan 2009) and adopt a 'me-too' position. It follows that a company may take a number of possible positioning orientations. Figure 6.2 (developed from Rossiter and Percy 1998) illustrates this.

BRAND POSITIONING – STRATEGY AND TACTICS

To achieve this 'competitive positioning' entails both strategic and tactical considerations: there must be a strategy to achieve sustainable and profitable long-term market location; and this must be tactically achieved by the techniques of the marketing mix.

    This balance is important as we saw with the *BT* case study above, which demonstrated how a clear understanding of the dynamics of the B2B market required consideration of both strategic and tactical positioning. However, there is evidence that some B2B organisations see competitive position-

POSITIONING IN FOCUS

Smirnoff. Brand Positioning – Strategy and Tactics

Consider the case of *Smirnoff Vodka* – the best-selling vodka brand in the world. *Smirnoff*, a Russian brand introduced in the 1860s, was launched into the American market but was not successful until purchased by an American company, *Heublein Inc.*, in 1938. The Russian-sounding name (known as 'country of origin positioning') was integral to its successful dominant actual and perceived quality positioning. In the 1960s, a fiercely competitive brand, *Wolfschmidt*, entered the same 'strategic group' (Hooley, Saunders and Piercy 1998, p. 8) using the tactics of lower pricing and heavy advertising. How would *Heublein* respond? Instead of matching a lower price, a different strategy was chosen. It actually raised the price to reinforce its position as a quality brand and invested the extra revenue in promoting this main point of difference. These tactics cemented *Smirnoff*'s dominance and further distanced it from *Wolfschmidt*. What *Smirnoff* also

The Smirnoff brand portfolio
Source: www.smirnoff.com.

did strategically was introduce two new brands – *Relska* (same price as *Wolfschmidt*) and *Popov* (lower price than *Wolfschmidt*) – which strategically blocked off *Wolfschmidt* above and below the *Smirnoff* brand. This strengthened *Smirnoff*'s position which reinforced the Russian connections and allowed *Heublein* to use the two new brands as a contrasting frame of reference (Riezebos 2003). A good balance of strategic and tactical positioning protected the brand and underpinned market share.

ing as tactical rather than strategic. Research done by Kalafatis, Tsogas and Blankston (2000, p. 432) suggests that some organisations are still sales-oriented and a broader perspective is often ignored. As we will see below, there is a growing recognition in B2B markets (and other contexts as well) that competitive positioning is only one part of the positioning triad of company, competition and customer.

POSITIONING FROM A CUSTOMER'S PERSPECTIVE

In markets which are characterised by competitive clutter and consumer confusion, positioning helps to reinforce brands in consideration sets (see Chapter 3) in a sort of mental 'product ladder' in the mind of the consumer (Ries and Trout 1980). Lautman (1993) suggested the basics of positioning as: **attributes** like store location or 100% pure orange; **benefits** which may be actual or perceived; and the **claims** made by marketing communications like 'Probably the Best Lager in the World'. This can be done either physically (e.g. our product gives you fresh breath when you brush with our toothpaste) or psychologically (e.g. show others how you take care of yourself). The essence of actual and perceived differentiation is perfectly captured by Arnott's (1994) comment that 'positioning is concerned with the attempt to modify the tangible characteristics and the intangible perceptions of a marketable offering in relation to the competition'. Ries and Trout (1980) put this well by stating that it is the 'degree to which brands own values and have meaning in consumers' lives which determines differentiation'.

According to Keller (2007, p. 30), 'Brand positioning is about establishing a core promise within the marketplace and relevant to a target constituency which enables a brand to function on both a rational and emotional level'. From a customer's perspective, it is, at its core, about creating and managing brand meaning. We can see that the link between market segmentation and competitive positioning is customer needs, a point which Hooley, Saunders and Piercy (1998, p. 202) make, as illustrated in Figure 6.3.

This common overlap where customer needs are located is where brands succeed or fail. If brand loyalty is to be achieved, it has to be secured by correct interpretation of customer needs and carefully applied communications. It is very much an organic, iterative process of assessing changing want satisfaction and competitive offerings.

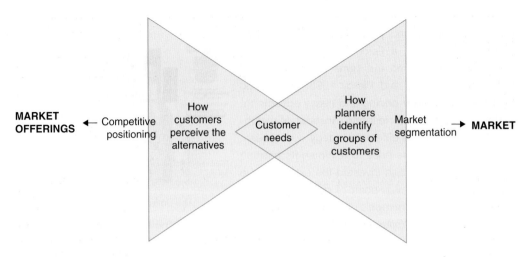

Figure 6.3: Competitive positioning and market segmentation

Source: Hooley, Saunders and Piercy (1998). Reproduced with permission.

Quite often, the definition of customer needs is crystallised down into 'benefits sought'. Is it 'fresh breath', 'social confidence' or 'fighting tooth decay' which is the benefit sought in the toothpaste category? Holt's (2004, p. 15) view that 'mind share branding' is a 'focused position in the prospect's mind, usually a benefit associated with the product category' has antecedents in the unique selling proposition (USP) concept, which has been a mainstay of marketing communications. Ries and Trout (1980) were the main exponents of the idea of 'mind space' positioning which led on from the USP approach and this started to broaden positioning away from a one-dimensional reiterative benefit appeal to something akin to a relationship with the brand. Kotler *et al.* (2004, p. 443) draw the distinction between the two positioning strategies of USP and ESP (emotional selling proposition). Whilst the former advocates the emphasis of attribute as distinction in a category, the latter position sees brands which have unique associations for consumers. Again, the assessment of category needs has to be done from a consumer's point of view. Plenty of mistakes have been made by underestimating or misinterpreting customer needs. *Bic*, a brand synonymous with disposability, had unprecedented success with razors, pens, cigarette lighters and other throwaway items. When a pocket-sized disposable perfume spray was launched, it failed because the target audience see 'perfume' and 'disposable' as incompatible.

Research by Yang, Allenby and Fennell (2002) into the motivations of 'demand-creating conditions' shows the starting point to be the motivations behind the interests and concerns which influence brand preference. If we look, for example, at the array of appeals for new motor cars, the main reason for purchase may differ between customers, but not many would say only 'to get me from A to B'. The conscious or unconscious need would be 'freedom', or 'status' or 'fitting in with my friends' or 'because I'm worth it'. (No sorry that's *L'Oréal* but you get the idea!) So, we often focus on 'selling the sizzle, not the steak'. And yet even hedonistic drives (excuse the pun) are being tempered with a 'need' to placate our conscience about the environment, so what constitutes a category need in the mind of the consumer is not always obvious. Try it yourself. Have a look at Table 6.1 and see what might be the category need from a consumer's perspective. They are all food examples, so you can't cheat and just put 'satisfy hunger'.

What we can start to see from this is that category need is very much about individual perceptions. If we remember the discussion on segmentation variables, the category for motor cars can be apportioned by 'benefits sought' such as 'need for speed', 'family', 'status', 'conspicuous consumption' or even projection of 'eco credentials'. Brands are infused with social and psychological symbolic meaning which may resonate with a consumer's self-concept (Grubb and Hupp 1968). There has to be individual brand/congruity (Smith 2007) as consumers will be drawn to a brand which reflects how they see themselves or would like to be seen. So when we select a brand, we are knowingly or unknowingly purchasing meaning through either private consumption (e.g. personal hygiene products

Brand	Product category	Consumer need
McDonald's	Fillet-o-Fish and fries	
Harry Ramsden	Fish and chips	
McCain	Frozen fish and chips	
Local restaurant	Dover sole and chips	
Top-class London restaurant	Poisson et pommes frites	

Table 6.1: Category need from a consumer's perspective

like soap, deodorant, shampoo) or group consumption (e.g. alcohol and sportswear). The success of the *Nintendo Wii* (featured in the closing case study) demonstrates the repositioning of this brand from 'gamers only' to 'fun for all the family'. This is vital to positioning as the brand's value proposition is both explicitly and implicitly contained within a **positioning statement**: what the brand is, what values are associated with it, and what it means to the target audience. It's a focusing device to put the overall marketing strategy into a clear vision which is the brand's promise to deliver. The positioning statement is the heart and soul of the brand which embraces the representations and imagery which the brand must build associations with, and the 'voice' the brand should have to communicate with its audience. It's about the value of building brand identity and allowing a solid narrative to grow from a clear positioning statement. It is also a link between the brand strategy approach to be taken and the tactics and techniques needed to accomplish it. It will form the basis of the creative brief from which strategic positioning is to be achieved. Rossiter and Percy (1998, p. 141) refer to this as the 'macro' or general format, stating that this echoes advertising agency practice with a typical positioning statement of: 'To (the target audience), _____ is the brand of (category need) that offers (brand benefit or benefits)'. Tybout and Sternthal (2005) identify framed reference (customer's expectations) and point of difference (the brand's superiority over the competition).

If positioning is a sort of mental framework that consumers have about a brand in relation to the competition as well as perceived attributes and benefits, it makes sense to try and map this out. Perceptual maps are used to profile the relationship against competition, requirement of category and customer needs, and the value proposition of brand benefits offered. Even if a brand is technically competing within a market sector, it does not necessarily follow that all competing brands in a category will necessarily be part of a customer's consideration set. Negative experience in previous brand encounters may cause a brand to be excluded as a possible choice. Or it may be that the perception of a brand is not seen as similar or dissimilar in a particular category. In other words, it may not offer sufficient similarity or difference to existing brands. In this sense, projected categories can shape perception.

Consumers automatically use existing knowledge or **schemas** about categories when they encounter new information (e.g. a new product). The existing knowledge is used to categorise products into mental positions of quality, value, price, strength, weakness and so on. The category schema affects consumer expectations (e.g. performance, point of purchase, design) about the product and also consumer preferences towards it. It will condition acceptance of new entrants and new product concepts. For example, the introduction of *Mars Ice Cream Bars* in the UK in 1998 relied on consumers' knowledge of both ice cream and chocolate bars. The new hybrid product was readily accepted and indeed created a brand new category. When digital cameras were first introduced, consumers perceived them either as a new type of camera or as a new type of product for digital images that replaced scanners. The two original categories shaped expectations and preferences in different ways. However, when comparisons were made to cameras rather than to scanners, consumers had far higher performance expectations and preferences.

When new products are adopted, they are either assimilated into existing categories or accommodated when a new category is constructed. People have a preference for assimilation and will try hard to assimilate new information into existing categories as the learning phase is shorter

The iconic iPod

and does not require much effort. The acceptance of *Apple iPods* by consumers was largely due to the path paved by *Sony Walkmans* — not transistor radios or 'ghetto blasters'. *Apple* used established customer knowledge about categorisation to influence how the *iPod* would be perceived by potential customers.

One way that consumers can visualise comparisons of competitive brands is to describe a mental picture of how the category is made up. This is referred to as a **perceptual map**. This is not just limited to an advertising agency's creative interpretation. Every consumer will have a perceptual map as a frame of reference in which new and existing brands occupy a space with denotations and connotations.

The idea of a perceptual 'brand ladder' where competing brands are seen as located in a hierarchy is a useful concept to help us understand this perceptual process. Some years ago, in the car rental market, *Avis* classically supplanted *Hertz* as Number 1 in the category by associating connotations of complacency with being in first position. By adopting the now-famous 'Avis – We Try Harder' tagline, the perception of a challenger brand having to 'empty more ash trays, clean cars more closely etc.' presented *Avis* as offering much more value for money. This is why Ries and Trout emphasised the importance of communications aimed at achieving a space in the mind of the target audience.

In the banking sector, the definition of 'product' can be varied, so mapping this can be useful. Consider the example of financial services company *Intelligent Finance*. When weighing up the options for banking, a consumer has to consider a number of factors: cost, level of service, convenience, type of financial products and so on. What is required by the consumer and how the market can be served is critical. Different customers may require different elements of product/service from an organisation. Perceptual mapping allows comparisons of potential positions and may suggest new positions or confirm location in the marketplace. Figure 6.4 shows the range of possible choices available to the consumer in a simple illustration of a perceptual map showing how the company found a gap in the market showing the vector spaces of 'High Quality Service/Quick Standard Service' and the cost of using these different services.

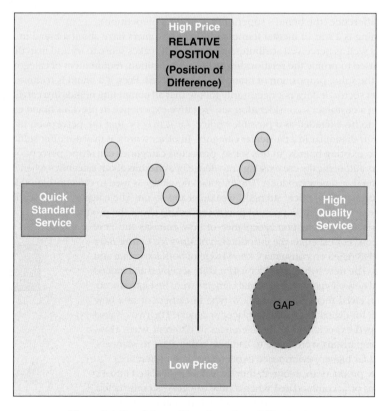

Figure 6.4: Possible positions for a financial institution

POSITIONING AND CATEGORISATION

Although frames of reference can be represented by product attributes, often this can be done by reference to 'abstract consumer goals' (Tybout and Sternthal 2005). An abstract consumer goal can be a need like status, affiliation, self-fulfilment and self-esteem. Therefore, we need to understand firstly what category need has to be served. This can be done on a macro level (e.g. total health and beauty market) or a micro level (e.g. within a specific category). If we look at *Nivea*'s product categories (Figure 6.5), there is a 'Sun Care' category (worth £173 million in 2005) of which *Nivea* had 17% (IRA; HBA outlets, 24 December 2005). When a target customer engages with marketing stimuli relating to our brand and our competitors' brands, they may or may not already have a need or desire for the type of product we are offering. In other words, there may be a 'latent' category need which we must fulfil. The emerging 'metrosexual' market for men's care products is the fastest-growing sector, reflecting changing social trends and consumer needs. It is vital that we evaluate category needs from a customer's not the organisation's perspective. This is because there is a difference between market space and mind space and between a manufactured product and a carefully positioned brand, and this has to be projected through the integrated application of communications in all brand encounters. If the delivery and manifestation of the positioning messages are inconsistent, then consumers will be confused. This will affect long-term strategy and development of the brand. So if, for example, a brand is aimed at a particular market segment and all communications support this, dialogue between organisation and audience will reinforce this positioning. In the case of the German supermarket chain *Aldi*, its original UK entry strategy was to target the gap in the lower segment of the market to compete with the likes of *Kwik Save*. Now, having developed a solid UK presence, trying to match its homeland positioning (in Germany they are similar to *Sainsbury*'s in the UK) is proving difficult because positional cues like location, stock and store ambience may have created a positioning straightjacket for them.

Similarity and Typicality

Once a category need is established in the marketplace, brand preferences occur 'within-category' using similarity and typicality reference points:

- **Similarity** describes brand-to-brand comparisons (i.e. how similar two brands are). *Dell, Compaq, Fujitsu, Toshiba, Samsung* and *Apple* have a similarity when alternative brands are being evaluated for the 'laptop' category. Every time a new design of car is launched, there soon appears a similar shape

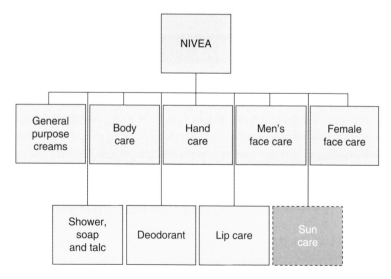

Figure 6.5: *Nivea* product categories

Same shape, different brands

on the market until the *Ford Focus* and *Vauxhall (Opel) Astra* have an almost generic look for that category. Competing brands must conform to this tacit specification and be similar to competitors.

- **Typicality** is the degree to which a brand is characteristic of its product category; some brands are seen as more typical than others. Some are so typical that they are more or less synonymous with (or seen as the prototype brand for) the product category. *Kellogg's* and *Gillette* have the heritage, image and equity in their specific categories. *Hoover* was seen as such a closely associated name with vacuum cleaners that the word 'hoover' became generic for 'vacuuming'. Some brands in effect create a category: *Nokia* had an early focus on design and became a prototype brand in

Red Bull dominates energy drink category

the mobile phone category. *Coca-Cola* is the proto-typical cola brand; *Red Bull* is fast becoming the proto-typical energy drink brand. The new hybrid 'energy/cola' drink from *Red Bull* is fast creating a new category. Other brands may be less typical in their respective categories, and this may provide competitive advantage. *Egg* provided the market with financial services in a less typical way than how the market was being served. Similarity is about how alike two brands are, whereas typicality relates to the strength of the link between the individual brand and the product category.

MATTER OF FACT

Similarity

Similarity is a contextual thing. Brands might be perceived as similar or dissimilar, dependent on the market and brand context. An example from a psychological research study of countries illustrates this. People were asked to group countries in pairs based on perceived similarity. The conditions differed between experimental groups, the first test group being asked to 'pair' Austria with Norway, Sweden or Hungary; the second pairing Austria with Poland, Sweden or Hungary.

In the first test group, 60% thought that Austria was most similar to Hungary (they are neighbouring countries and were also a united nation historically, and both these conditions apply to Sweden and Norway as well); 14% thought that Austria was most similar to Sweden.

In the second test group, 49% perceived that Austria was most similar to Sweden; 36% thought that Austria and Hungary was the most similar pair. Austria and Sweden belong to Western Europe in contrast to Hungary and Poland which were Eastern European countries (and at the time of this study, 1977, part of the communist bloc in Europe). When Norway was used as a comparison to Poland, similarity fell from 60% to 36% and increased for Austria–Sweden from 14% to 49%. This shows that other comparisons and contexts affect similarity perception.

Source: Tversky (1977).

Perceptions about brands can be affected in the same way. In other words, the similarity between brands depends on other brands in the context. Remember Porter telling us that when we select a target market, we select customers to aim for and competitors to compete with? Companies may choose their competitors by placing the brand in the right category. So, for example, *Walkers Crisps* and *Mars Bars* are dissimilar when positioned in a confectionery segment but similar when positioned in a meal replacement category. *Coca-Cola* and *Pepsi* are in the same strategic group and are directly similar, but *Coca-Cola* could also be seen as similar when positioned with *Seven Up* against *Tropicana*. Even products which are definitely not the same can be positioned as similar brands in a category.

To develop this idea of category similarity, consider the positioning strategy required in a retail context. With over 10,000 line items to sort and display for maximum effect, your average supermarket needs to be very careful when positioning brands. Indeed, category management is a key tool in facilitating this. Typicality, a slight variation of similarity, is a frame of reference that consumers use when mentally placing possible brands for selection. Let's look at how this applies below.

MATTER OF FACT

Typicality

The idea of typicality is generic and applies to all kinds of categories. A product or brand may be seen as more or less typical dependent upon how consumers perceive a category. An American study demonstrated this effect for snacks. Firstly, people stated on a nine-point scale how typical different snack products were in the snacks product category. Later, they judged how typical the snack brands were in certain usage situations. This is referred to as goal-derived categories because they describe what motivates purchase.

As we can see in the table below, potato chips, popcorn, chocolate bars, granola bars and apples are among the most generally typical snack products. When we introduce a specific usage situation, the typicality picture is very different. At parties on a Friday night, pizza slices are just as typical as potato chips and popcorn whereas apples and chocolate bars are atypical. In the usage situation 'snacks instead of a regular breakfast' the typicality structure of the snacks category is again different. Here, bagels, apples and granola bars are the most typical products whereas popcorn and potato chips are atypical and no longer associated with the category.

It is important to notice that atypical snack products (overall) such as pizza slices and bagels may become typical as goal-derived snack products.

(Continued)

Product	Overall typicality	Friday night party	Instead of breakfast
Potato chips	8.0	8.2	2.2
Pizza slice	3.3	8.1	4.4
Popcorn	7.0	7.9	2.4
Chocolate bar	6.9	1.6	3.7
Granola bar	6.8	2.7	7.5
Bagel	4.6	2.6	8.4
Apple	6.2	3.0	8.3

Typicality in the snack category for two goal-derived categories

Source: Ratneshwar and Shocker (1991), Reisberg (2001).

When a brand is solidly associated with a category, this is a tremendous asset in positioning that brand in the minds of consumers. However, it can also be restrictive. *Kellogg's Corn Flakes*, with their age-old claim to be the breakfast cereal of choice – 'The Best to You Each morning!' – had prominence in the cereal category. When the *Kellogg's* brand began to be severely undermined by supermarket own brands, it had to reposition the brand away from breakfast-only associations.

Absolute and Relative Position

Key to a brand's positioning, therefore, is the creation of both category association and brand differentiation – referred to as 'absolute' and 'relative' positioning:

- **Absolute position** requires that a brand must ensure that it shares enough of the characteristics and associations with other brands in the targeted category. It must be positioned to target a market space within the category. In terms of the semiotics of elements such as product design, packaging design, pricing and distribution channels, there becomes a sort of brand protocol in which all elements of competing brands are similar; they communicate what the category stands for, quickly and easily. However, a brand's identity can be lost in amongst the competition. It may not be sufficient to be 'associated' with a category; differentiation from the rest of the category propositions may be essential. *Häagen-Daz* owns an occasion, 'DVD at Home Night'. Other examples are *Gillette*'s 'Best a Man Can Get', *Kit Kat*'s 'Have a Break, Have a Kit Kat' and *Carlsberg*'s 'Probably the Best Lager in the World'. *Marks & Spencer* has tried to emulate this with its 'Not Just Food, M&S Food' campaign.

  Within the consumer's frame of reference, the points of difference help to position the brand as superior in category.

- **Relative position** gives the brand a unique and special label in the category. A brand's relative position should give the target audience explicit and/or implicit reasons to differentiate from the competition. When the brand successfully communicates its relative position in the category it will own a relevant category attribute. It becomes an exemplar for the category. When a brand is highly associated with an attribute or a benefit, it is more difficult for competitors to position themselves against identical attributes or benefits and the brand becomes the most typical brand for that particular attribute.

  It is essential to build strong brand awareness in a category in order to achieve top-of-mind awareness. In other words, in a consumer's consideration set, we must aim for our brand to be considered in the targeted category. It is critical to get premier position in some markets; first position is remembered. For example, the precedence of *VHS* over *Betamax* video formats because of the better positioning of

	Points of parity	**Points of difference**
Mercedes-Benz	Customer service	Superiority in product
Sony	Customer service	Superiority in product
Harley-Davidson	Product performance	Compelling user and usage imagery
Calvin Klein	Product performance	Compelling user and usage imagery

Table 6.2: Points of parity and points of difference

marketing communications is echoed with the recent *Blue Ray/HDD DVD* struggle for market dominance. The winner is the brand which articulates relative positioning most persuasively to the target audience. In the UK supermarket market, *Sainsbury's*, gave up its pursuit of *Tesco* as an all-round retailer to concentrate on being 'first for food', attempting to become the most typical brand for that particular attribute. The *Sainsbury's* narrative has reinforced this with an agenda of eating correctly, recipe advice, focus on health and the endless celebrity endorsement of someone seen as an expert source for excellent food: Jamie Oliver. Relative positioning which purports to claim primacy in a category sees brand's claiming: 'The Choice of a New Generation' (*Pepsi*); 'Maybe she's born with it. Maybe it's *Maybelline*'; 'Technical fabrics are always the best-in-class' (*GORE-TEX*); and 'First in class' (*Mercedes*).

Keller (2000, p. 6) refers to absolute and relative positioning as 'points of parity' and 'points of difference'. In order to 'occupy particular niches in consumers' minds', brands must strive to be similar to but different from competing brands to be properly positioned. Following his examples, Table 6.2 illustrates this:

If we look at all the different approaches to positioning shown in Figure 6.6, we can see the whole topic in context. All the alternative strategic positionings are 'within category' and show brands aiming at competitive parity (i.e. the same value proposition of the chief competitors), or offering the market an alternative product or service in order to achieve a differentiated position. This illustrates the market strength (or weakness) of the brands in the category. Category space is the market/product segment in the marketplace. More and more categories are becoming commoditised. According to Ries and Trout (1980), fewer categories are differentiated as 'they don't own a meaningful idea that makes them unique; they don't have a story'.

POSITIONING IN FOCUS

Volvo. Category Positioning

To 'own' a category can be the ultimate objective in positioning the brand. In the same way that the name *Kellogg's* is synonymous with breakfast cereal, *Hoover* stood for vacuuming and *Volvo* stood for safety. Decades of great advertising campaigns like the 'Cages Save Lives' used 'operant conditioning' which was mainly responsible for building up associations with the main brand salience – safety. Equally, the customer base for *Volvo* was limited and comprised a loyal but older demographic. The target 25–40 year olds were not attracted by the 'safe' but boring *Volvo* brand heritage. The Volvo strength soon became a weakness and a major repositioning exercise was needed (see Chapter 16).

Firstly, a strategy was required to take the brand out of the 'safety only' category to focus on a younger market. All marketing communications were to be aimed at changing brand perceptions and recruiting younger, more influential consumers. Recently, the brand has softened its masculine 'iron' mark with a more curved, thicker bevel-edged logo with a softer matt shade of silver to create a more luxurious feel. In addition, positioning has been

(Continued)

broadened to embrace a number of different approaches with the objective of moving the brand into a more '*Volvo* for Life' emotional area:

- The 'Feel Pleasure' campaign was designed to inspire people to enjoy life and feel more connected to the environment.
- The 'Who would you give a Volvo to?' campaign was an attempt to sell 'affiliation'.
- Togetherness: the 'Life is Better Together' campaign tried to distance the brand away from the status symbol competitors and emphasise a new affiliation theme.
- A recent move in 2008 was to take an ecological approach with the 'The new eco friendly cars from *Volvo*' positioning laced with humour and extending the safety narrative to an environmentally-conscious approach.

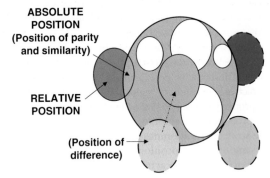

	Position	Description and approach to market
	Category space	Total segment for a particular category need
	Central dominant position	A pioneer or an innovative late entrant that has the leading position in the category
		Actual or perceived image as 'first in', 'best in class' or radically different approach to how the market is served
	Competing parity brands achieving 'similarity' with other brands	Brands sharing the same category fulfilment with similar attributes that copy the market leader's position
		'Me-too central' positioning with more or less like-for-like brands offering very similar attributes. Creative plagiarism the main strategy
	Competing differentiated brands achieving 'absolute position' by being associated with the category but differentiated by having competitive advantage	Several brands in the category each having specialised on a certain attribute
		'Me-too differentiated' positioning with points of parity but differentiated by perceptual differences like service or ethical stance
	Competing peripheral brands achieving 'typicality' whilst not directly competing	Brands sharing some aspect of main brand's value proposition
		Diluted 'me-too' positioning
	Innovative late entrant achieving 'relative position' but differentiation distinguishes the brand in a significant way	Late entrant to a mature market
		Radically different approach to how the market is served but appealing to central positioning value proposition
	Niche	Brands that have created a subcategory of their own based on a distinctive attribute but still serve a very similar category need
		Radically different approach to how the market is served (e.g. luxury, environment)

Figure 6.6: Different positioning approaches

POSITIONING THE PRODUCT CATEGORY

As well as individual brands, categories themselves can be positioned. In Chapter 3, we looked at consumer decision-making processes and saw that tapping into 'goal-derived' motives is useful in marketing communications. Goal-derived motivations can be separate categories: planning a holiday may require categorising possibilities into choosing between visiting cities, holiday resorts, historically significant places, national parks and having wildlife experiences. A family-oriented, outdoor-centred, water-activity holiday is very specific and very much a category on its own. In this age of micro-marketing with more and more specific targeting of segments, it is vital to achieve accurate projections of categories if they are to be communicated correctly.

The days of cheap foreign holidays for Europeans may soon be over because of the impact of the 'credit crunch', growing safety fears and concern about damage to the environment. As a result, the old-fashioned 'stay-at-home' holiday may become the default for this category. Often, the market leader is in the best position to promote the category, but an entirely new brand may also be launched with the purpose of changing and developing the category. A new innovation can dramatically redefine a category. For example, the impact of music downloading has totally obliterated the 'singles' market which has impacted on producers, radio stations, retailers and consumers. However, incremental changes can also transform product categories. Supermarket retailing has been transformed from stockist of manufacturers' food brands to general retailers covering a wider range of many category types but this has been done organically. Although *Tesco* has an overall market positioning, there is also 'in-store' positioning as well: *Tesco's 'Finest'*, *Tesco's Own Brand* and *Tesco's Value* ranges all hit different positions and present the customer with three alternative solutions to these category needs.

CHANGING CATEGORY PERCEPTIONS

There are a number of ways in which category perceptions can be changed:

- new products;
- new attributes;
- new communications;
- new distribution channels.

New products being introduced to categories may render all competitive parameters irrelevant. *Dyson* completely changed the vacuum cleaner category when its 'bag-less vacuum' was introduced against brands which had parity but little differentiation other than brand perceptions created by marketing communications. Just think about how the sport of mountain biking has changed consumer perception and purchase of bicycles nowadays (Figure 6.7). Bicycles look differently today compared to 25 years ago, they are manufactured in other materials, they have a more sporty design, they have

Figure 6.7: Two images of bicycles. (a) The unsuccessful launch of the 'plastic bike' and (b) how mountain bikes affect the design of all bikes today.

many more gears, and there is an aftermarket (e.g. annual service packages are included in the price). Of course, the price of a bicycle may be much higher today (considering inflation) and the price span between normal bikes and the most expensive ones is very wide. More importantly, bicycles have more cultural significance these days.

Another product that has been changed to a large extent is sports drinks/energy drinks. Originally, these products were sold mainly in connection with sports activities (e.g. *Gatorade, Lucozade*) but when energy drinks such as *Red Bull* entered the market, new consumption patterns emerged. Compared to when there were only sports drinks in this category, there have been dramatic changes in usage occasions, packaging design, marketing communications and pricing (energy drinks are more expensive than sports drinks). The emergence of the Internet has changed the newspaper category. A newspaper does not have to be in paper format any longer as web versions are often just as comprehensive and can be instantly updated.

New attributes or innovations can radically alter both consumers' perceptions and the competitive nature of the category. Consider products like the sports bra, sugar-free chewing gum, portable music (*iPod*) and microwave ovens. These solutions have changed the product category perceptions because they have a focus on a unique attribute that they link to the sponsor brand. These attribute changes develop the category because competitors quickly respond to them and broaden their assortment with an own alternative. For instance, sugar-free chewing gum expanded the market for chewing gum by 30% in the introduction phase, mainly due to increased consumption by adults. Similarly, *Vidal Sassoon* in-

Toyota displays green credentials

troduced a hybrid shampoo/conditioner product – *Wash & Go* – in an unoccupied position. Hybrid cars have been responsible for redefining the car category in terms of having a conscience element, after Standard Utility Vehicles (SUVs) and 'people carriers' had previously repositioned the van/family traveller category. *Toyota Prius*, a revolutionary hybrid car, has paved the way in this category and gained both market leadership and the imagination of the target audience. The green credentials of the product exactly match the mood of the moment and this has helped *Toyota* 'own the category' even under severe competition. In its marketing communications campaigns, *Toyota* has used some very innovative approaches, none more so than the poster sites which have real trees growing through the billboards to accentuate the brand's 'relative' position of differentiation against the competition.

Absolut creativity

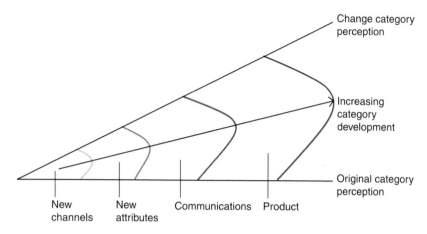

Figure 6.8: Category development and changed category perceptions in four steps: new distribution, new attribute, new communications, and new product

Source: Dahlen and Lange (2003). *Optimal marknadskommunikation,* Liber Ekonomi. Reproduced with permission.

New or innovative approaches to communications can help differentiate a brand against competitors when there are no real changes to the product proposition or how the brand is distributed. Market development rather than product development may be the preferred strategy, with brand communications to achieve repositioning being the most appropriate. *Lucozade, Baileys* (even *Marlboro* from an original female positioning) are all examples of how marketing communications helped change category perceptions. Another example is the Swedish *Absolut Vodka,* the third largest alcoholic spirits brand in the world (after *Bacardi* and *Smirnoff*). It created a sophisticated brand personality with highly creative marketing communications projecting the brand through the distinctive bottle shape. In its now famous 'In An *Absolut* World' campaign, the impression of the bottle is seen in many guises, countries and cultures and cleverly broadens the cultural appeal of the brand. *Absolut* is a major sponsor of gay events and is influential in the art world.

The brand positioning of sports clothes and sports shoes has changed dramatically over the last few years with brands like *Nike, Reebok* and *Adidas* being the frontrunners. Sports products have become fashion products as well. The *Adidas* sub-brand *Y-3* is a strong example of this trend.

New distribution channels can alter category perceptions, often the case in mature markets. For instance, when cosmetics and hygiene product companies sell products into hairdressers and speciality stores because there is less price sensitivity than in the traditional supermarket and pharmacy sectors. And of course the brand can be communicated differently in different contexts (either as a result of seasonality, or special circumstances like big sport events and concerts where the captive audience has a totally different willingness to pay). In Figure 6.8 we see that the degree of change in category perceptions is linked to what type of value proposition the brand has and how this is to be positioned.

POSITIONING IN NEW AND EMERGING MARKETS

Positioning strategies are dependent upon when the brand is introduced and how marketing communications are managed. Research shows that the first entrant in a category usually outrivals the later entrants and is a pioneer in a new or emerging market sector. The pioneering advantage may be based on a specific technological factor: new and improved versions like 'more is better' (e.g. technologically advanced product categories) or 'new is better' (e.g. seasonal product categories like fashion).

However, advantage could be gained from the first-entry establishment of 'attribute frame of reference'. That is to say that pioneers set the ground rules and parameters of parity on which all competitors will be judged. Category perceptions will therefore be based on the pioneer brand's decision to highlight specific attributes in the trial period before product adoption. In terms of consumer purchasing, perceived risk is reduced by a pioneer brand's initial marketing communications and consumers will use the stated communication of attribute importance as frame of reference for purchase. It becomes a benchmark for considering a brand's suitability to fulfil category needs.

So if a brand, first into the laptop segment or as an innovative late entrant, emphasises a key attribute as being important (e.g. the 'Intel Inside' co-branding campaign highlighting the inclusion of a key processor), then this will guide consumer preference and establish the inclusion of *Intel Pentium Processors* as a benchmark for PCs. Similarly, auxiliary ports to accommodate the use of *iPods* in cars are fast becoming the norm due to changing buyer behaviour and the need to maintain competitive parity. The rate of technological change does not allow many companies to retain a product or functional edge for very long, and so often advantage is perceptual. Pioneers try to establish the 'first in category' position. Some classic examples are:

- '*Coca-Cola* – this is it'
- '*IBM* **is** computers'
- '*Levi's* – the original'
- '*Kellogg's* – the original and best'
- *Toshiba* has extended its 'Leading Innovation' approach to new and mature markets, achieving both individual category development and overall brand image enhancement.

Late entrants into the market can use the following positions: 'me-too central', 'me- too differentiated' or pioneering or innovative late entrants. Often, 'me-too' brands position on price and attempt to transfer the pioneer's brand image to themselves. In the PC market, the *IBM* PC standard was copied by cheaper versions. Other late entrants may take a differentiated position, by emphasising advantage in attribute comparisons or by the introduction of a new attribute (e.g. diet versions of food and drink). This may cause category fragmentation which might be intentional or inadvertent. Pioneers may be challenged and the assumed or established value proposition may be changed. Examples of this phenomenon are:

- Razor blades: *Gillette* usurped the pioneer – *Star* – by powerful communications and innovative product attributes.
- Disposable nappies: *Chux* lost ground very quickly to *P&G's Pampers* brand.
- Video format: *JVC's VHS* beat *Sony's Betamax* format through marketing communications rather than technological superiority.
- Search engines: *Google* is a massive global brand leader even though *Alta Vista* was first to market.
- Web browsers: *Netscape* lost considerable early advantage against *Internet Explorer*.

Motorola's mobile fashion

These examples demonstrate the power of marketing communications to position a brand as a superior choice when consumers are making purchase decisions. A late entrant may identify an attribute as being key to purchase and put a lot of expenditure into stressing this to gain share of voice in a category (for a full discussion on share of voice, see Chapter 14). Even in high technological markets, sometimes the focus on another attribute can gain advantage. In the saturated mobile phone sector, *Nokia* realised the value of superficial 'fashion' design (e.g. new colour combinations, sizes and changeable covers) and edged *Sony Ericsson* out of pole position. This type of realignment tactic may actually change category perceptions and has been copied by other competitors (see *Motorola*'s advertisement). *Dell's* entry into the PC market was so successful that it displaced *Compaq* as the PC of choice and its direct model of B2C communications has been copied by many organisations within and outside the PC sector. *AXE* deodorant (*LYNX* in many countries) has been hugely successful in re-orienting consumer perceptions by focusing on transformational motivations (i.e. 'The *LYNX* effect' and 'Because you never know when' concentrate on helping males in the mating game) rather than informational motivations (i.e. the problem solving of removing unwelcome smells).

Therefore, as market leadership is to a large extent perceptual, it is crucial to be first in consumers' minds rather than first in the market. Brands in mature markets with well-established brand storylines can dominate market categories. Having a brand story about being unique is crucial, even if brands are not first in. Companies that grab market share first often grab the glory, but they aren't always the last one standing. At one time, *P&G* was second to *Union Carbide* in marketing disposable nappies/diapers. *Dell* unseated *Compaq* by marketing to the upcoming college generation.

POSITIONING IN MATURE MARKETS

Mature markets have characteristically stable product categories. By their very nature, these segments have demand patterns and usage behaviour which are more settled. Consumers have entrenched knowledge about the category and firmly rooted attribute requirements. At this stage in the product life cycle of the segment, it is not so much about differentiating but creating distinct brand image and loyalty. Any innovations are quickly copied and neutralised. Price changes often result in like-for-like changes although EDLP (every day low pricing) has now become a sort of strategic tactic in that it is a permanent feature.

Global manufacturers and retailers like *P&G* and *Wal-Mart* have been hugely instrumental in neutralising the effect of irritating late entrants by having semi-fixed pricing. When new products are introduced into a mature category, this often is in the form of an established brand extending product life cycles with line extensions or new brands replacing old. Ehrenberg (2000) argued that there are bigger differences within brands than across brands. Mature brands concentrate on strong category-to-brand associations: hi-tech brands push technology designed for the way we live (*Bosch* – 'Invented for life'; *Panasonic* – 'Ideas for life'); food brands emphasise health associations (*Flora* – 'Love your heart'). A classic case of repositioning is that of *Lucozade*. Figure 6.9 shows the long-term 'broadening' of positioning (Davidson 1997, p. 400) from a convalescent drink for children to an energy and sports drink.

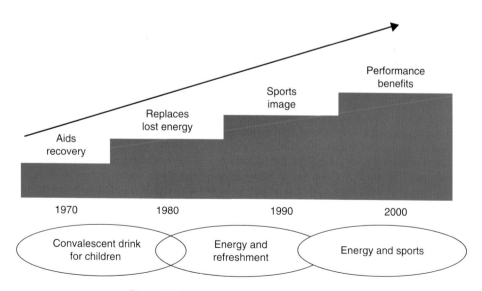

Figure 6.9: *Lucozade* – brand extension staircase

Source: Davidson (1997, p. 400). Reproduced with permission.

POSITIONING IN DIFFERENT CONTEXTS

Retailing

The phenomenal change in power from manufacturers' brands to retailers' has seen the evolution of 'retailer image' as the primary source of store patronage. Positioning is a vital element for retailers, influenced by both strategic and tactical considerations, 'affected by an amalgam of the physical environment; apparent atmosphere; convenience; types of shoppers using the store; merchandise available; service levels; and many other dimensions real and perceived' (Sullivan and Adcock 2002, p. 78). A retailer brand 'builds loyalty by developing a clear, distinctive image of its retail offering and consistently reinforcing that image through its merchandise and service' (Levy and Weitz 2007, p. 132).

As with product brands, positioning for retailer brands 'involves the design and implementation of a retail mix to create an image of the retailer in the customer's mind relative to its competitors' (Morgan, Strong and McGuinness 2003, p. 1409). Retail brands differ in two important aspects: positioning has to be achieved through **selection** of store and **loyalty** to that store. An integrated policy comprises decisions about four specific areas: merchandise; store format/environment; customer service; and customer communications (Devlin, Birtwistle and Macedo 2003). Although there is plenty of evidence showing that companies promoting a product-plus approach (Styles and Ambler 1995) have achieved short-term differentiation, a sustainable position requires a totally different strategic and tactical approach. This may involve a full review of customer store experience, and in some cases rebranding.

This is particularly marked in the fashion sector. The repositioning, and indeed rebirth, of *Lewis's* department store fashion 'separates' is a case in point. Set in the spirit of the 'swinging '60s', *Lewis's*

Retail re-branding

repositioned their youth fashion offer as *Chelsea Girl* (Lea-Greenwood 1993). However, by the late 1980s, this proved to be incompatible with its partner chain (*Concept Man*) and it was rebranded as *River Island*. This was successful and placed the brand as direct competitor to *Next for Men* and *Burton Menswear* in the 'fashion-led younger customer category' (Birtwistle and Freathy 1998).

The phenomenal rise in the power of grocery retailers from mere brand intermediaries to becoming the brand has effected a fundamental shift in positioning strategies in this sector. Even though there is evidence of stores altering positioning tactically between localities by adjusting various elements of their individual marketing mixes, supermarkets display a wide range of positioning strategies. One way we can get a visual impression of the spread in the grocery sector is to locate different positions on a perceptual map. It helps us to determine actual, perceived and possible market positioning. If we look at UK retail positioning estimated by the *Nielsen Research* group in Figure 6.10, the various positions are mapped on just two dimensions: age and socioeconomic group of their customer base.

In terms of market positioning, the full spectrum is evident in the grocery sector. *Tesco* holds a position similar to *M&S* in terms of the penetration of the ABC1 social groups but has a much younger customer profile. *Somerfield* has achieved some success in repositioning *Kwik Save* under the *Somerfield* brand but has been hampered by a largely incompatible customer profile. *Aldi*'s positioning strategy, when it first entered the UK market, was to dominate the lower-priced 'no frills' sector between *Netto* and *Kwik Save* which it has succeeded in achieving. However, this has proved to be very restrictive as the attempts to move away from this lower position have been conditioned by customer perceptions of *Aldi* as a cheap discounter.

Research done by *Neilsen* identifies supermarkets *Aldi* and *Sainsbury's* as 'holistic brands' offering different marketing mixes and serving two distinctly different customer profiles: *Sainsbury's* to an ABC1 customer profile; *Aldi* ostensibly to the lower C2Ds. On the surface, the difference appears

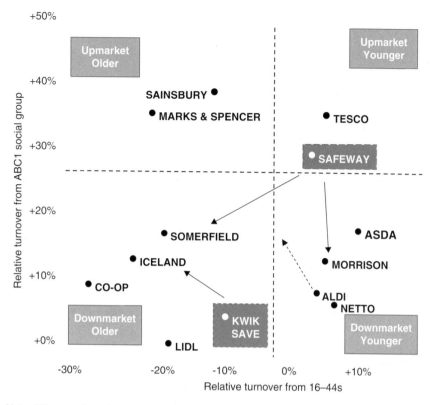

Note: 0% on each scale represents the national average penetration in those age/social bands

Figure 6.10: Perceptual map for retailers showing position
by age and socioeconomic group

Source: Based on Neilsen (2000).

to be *Sainsbury's* as quality-positioned and *Aldi* as price-positioned, and yet their findings show an actual price differential based on a perceived different value-added positioning. Whereas *Sainsbury's* manages its positioning through promotion, *Aldi* does this by tight control of product, store format and price positioning (Brandes 2004). We can redraw this map by looking at two other key retail positioning factors: store location and retail format. Figure 6.11 shows a different arrangement of positions which highlights another peculiar aspect of retail market product positioning: location and retail format are key strategic choices in positioning.

The phenomenon of 'multi-positioning' is not new to retailing; fashion retailers like *Arcadia* have a whole range of different faces in the high-street shop portfolio (see Table 6.3); *Boots* operates under eight different store types.

Sullivan and Adcock (2002, p. 79) refer to this as 'a multi fascia strategy that utilises a store portfolio with several different retail approaches'. With the supermarket end of the grocery market at saturation point and restriction of growth possibilities due to the limiting of planning permission, the top brands operate in different formats 'drawing upon and reinforcing the power of the main brand, while signalling different positions and purposes' (McGoldrick 2002, p. 172). Not including online formats, the following illustrates the different location/format positions. *Tesco*'s UK stores operate different formats aimed at capturing different customer requirements: 'Extra' are larger, mainly out-of-town hypermarkets; 'Superstores' are standard large supermarkets; 'Metro' are mainly located in city centres, the inner city and in small towns; 'Express' stores are neighbourhood convenience shops; 'One Stop' is the only category which does not include the word *Tesco* in its name; and 'Homeplus' offer all types

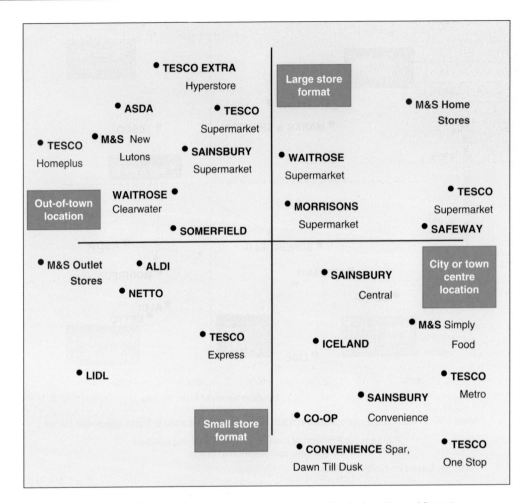

Figure 6.11: Perceptual map for retailers showing position by location and format

Store fascia	Target customers	Assortment characteristics
Burton Menswear	Men	Mainstream/value clothing
Dorothy Perkins	Women	Mainstream/value clothing
Evans	Women	Size 16 and above
Miss Selfridge	Young women	Clubwear, accessories and cosmetics
Outfit	Women, men and children	Out-of-town retailer of Arcadia brands
Topman	Young men	Fun, fast-moving fashion
Topshop	Young women	Fun, fast-moving fashion
Wallis	Women	Higher-quality clothing

Table 6.3: Arcadia Group

Source: Arcadia website (2008).

Dimension	Barnes & Noble	Independent stores	Mall bookstores
Price	1.0	3.0	2.0
Knowledgeable staff	6.2	5.1	1.8
Selection of books	8.0	2.1	0.9
Store ambience	8.5	2.9	1.2
Store hours	7.2	1.7	2.8
Café and lounge	8.1	n/a	n/a

Table 6.4: Value innovation positioning in US book retailing

Source: adapted from Kim and Mauborgne (1999) with permission.

of non-food in warehouse-style units in retail parks. *Sainsbury's* operates three main store formats: regular *Sainsbury's* stores; a 'convenience store' format *Sainsbury's* Local and *Sainsbury's* Central which are smaller supermarkets in urban locations. *Waitrose* has a standard supermarket format and a larger retail park 'Clearwater' format.

Retailers need not be restricted by 'the convention of a two-dimensional matrix' (McGoldrick 2002, p. 172). Quite often customer expectations are based on what is supplied by retailers. 'Creation of new market space' (Kim and Mauborgne 1999, p. 83) requires looking at what customers' needs are. Table 6.4 illustrates innovation in the US book market and shows how the main retailer, *Barnes & Noble,* communicated different positions by offering a multidimensional position.

In the UK, the extension of leisure and lifestyle into the bookstore category has seen the likes of *Borders* and *Waterstones* incorporating coffee franchises like *Costa Coffee.* This both differentiates these outlets from the direct and online competition (e.g. *Tesco, WH Smith* and *amazon.com*), but enhances the customer experience, making the positioning less commodity oriented.

Business to Business

In the same way that product and service brands 'occupy a space in the mind of a consumer' (Ries and Trout 1980), industrial organisational brands (i.e. B2B) have to try and communicate a positioning in the mind of the buying company and in relation to competing organisations' offers organisational buyers 'perceive products as bundles of attributes (for example, quality, service)' (Hutt and Speh 1998, p. 305). At the peak of their dominance in the computer market, decisions to buy *IBM* equipment were based on the 'total offering of hardware, software and services giving buyers a set of benefits that no competitor could match' (Randall 2000, p. 1). The legend bears testimony to the power of branding: 'No-one ever got fired for buying *IBM*'. Its positioning was as a full service/total cover proposition offering 'business solutions'. For *Dell Computers,* competing with this huge corporate monolith, its success was achieved by a customised, low-price positioning. As Brennan, Canning and McDowell (2007, p. 166) claim: 'the position becomes a short-hand that evokes the supplier and establishes the supplier in an idealised position that most closely matches the customer need'. Marketing communications is a vital ingredient in B2B positioning and companies must ensure that all brand encounters reflect this. When *Avis* classically positioned themselves as 'No 2' against *Hertz* by indirectly associating with the category leader, it became a mission statement born out of an advertising strategy.

At the core of B2B positioning is 'understanding what targeted market segments and firms regard as superior value' (Anders and Narus 1999, p. 127) and how this is communicated to prospect organisations in the target sector. There are a few different approaches to positioning used by organisations: product leadership, customer intimacy or operational excellence. For example, *Microsoft* communicates 'innovation' to B2B audiences by allowing users to automatically update changes across multiple applications with *Microsoft Office.* This innovation positioning is echoed in *Intel's* CEO mandate to 'double machine performance at every price point every year'. *Intel* also communicates customer intimacy to both B2B and consumer markets through its 'Intel Inside' campaign, educating end-use customers about new product performance capabilities. *Dell* communicates extraordinary service and choice for extremely competitive prices. Returning to the opening *BT* B2B case at the start of the chapter, we can see that *BT Business* is trying to position itself as an exemplar brand in the SME category by a combination of product leadership and operational excellence.

Service Marketing

In service industries, competitive posture can only be achieved by an understanding of the role strategic positioning has in communicating a vast array of corporate image, service product and individual attributes and benefits. Quite often service is the only differentiator between one organisation's offer and a competitor's. However, the peculiar characteristics of intangibility and the experiential nature of many services makes 'an explicit positioning strategy invaluable in helping prospective customers to get a mental "fix" on a product that might otherwise be rather amorphous' (Lovelock 1996, p. 171). Consider the relative positions of tourist destinations such as *Disney World* or *SeaWorld*. Each has a 'significant share of mind developed over many years of marketing communication efforts [...] which strongly influence such customer behaviours as word-of-mouth communications, repeat purchasing and brand loyalty' (Fisk, Brown and Bitner 1993, p.33). The challenge is not just to focus on the crucial element of the service (and how it differs from competitors) but to try and suggest what the service product might be like in use. Because experiencing a service involves an act of production and consumption, and is therefore intensely personal, how can we be sure we are correctly interpreting customers' needs?

Education

Take the case of education. Sargeant (2005, p. 120) imagines a university (Bloomsville) wanting to identify how prospective undergraduate students perceive its offer. Using a perceptual map (Figure 6.12), an estimation of possible positioning will be somewhere on the academic/social life spectrum. Competition for a European university in supplying 'education' as a service may come from similar institutions in Europe. The positioning may be tactical (e.g. matching modules offered

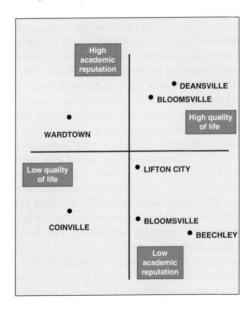

Figure 6.12: Perceptual map for a university

Source: Sargeant (2005).

at similar fee costs over the same time scale) and may be aimed at direct competitors. However, other generic competition may come from local colleges, private training organisations, distance learning or self-study options like books, DVDs and so on.

A strategic positioning might be seen as a hybrid university/college and position the institution as 'the University in the Community'. The same campus, even the same course, may represent different value propositions to different markets. The local business community and the local residents may represent other market segments to position the offer as well as national undergraduate recruitment. In the UK, the 'educational category' (specifically the higher education undergraduate sector) has expanded dramatically as a result of government directives (the Labour manifesto expresses the wish to have at least 50% of school leavers in higher education) and the newly acquired status of some of the old polytechnics. It is now more of a consumer market and this has led to the acute need for correct positioning. We now see institutions positioned as offering a better 'social environment', 'wide exposure to ideas', 'career skills'. A university's positioning, therefore, is a product of governmental directive, user benefit and consequences – material success, meaningful career or forming lasting relationships – as well as in relation to other competing institutions. The reality is that product, process and outcome and positioning of a university may be under an umbrella platform of 'opportunities' (Gutman and Mioulis 2003, p. 109).

CLOSING CASE STUDY

(Nintendo) Nintendo Wii: Wii are Family: Gaming for Non-Gamers is the Name of the Game

By 2006, *Nintendo* had become a third-party developer, known mainly for products like *Mario* and *Game Boy* and failing to compete against the dominant *Sony PlayStation* and *Microsoft Xbox*. *Nintendo*'s customer base was mainly made up of children and teens with all its products aimed at these markets, segments of diminishing importance and fast becoming oversaturated and dangerously competitive. The problem, and therefore the challenge, was to reposition the brand both in the marketplace and in the minds of a new target audience. Within a year, the relaunch had started, now positioned to a wider market and with a highly innovative seventh-generation product which practically reinvented the gaming category in an industry worth over £15 billion annually.

The revolutionary *Nintendo Wii* gaming system, launched in a bid to become market leader, had first to consider the crucial elements of repositioning: the competition; the target customer; the category need; and the essential benefits of the brand to be offered (see Figure 6.1). Firstly, the key to strategy had to start with an assessment of the competition (in terms of customer characteristics and needs profile). As we have seen above, the creation of both category association and brand differentiation is vital: the brand should have a unique and special label in the category. In other words, it should be positioned relatively to the competitors in its category, giving the target audience explicit and/or implicit reasons to differentiate from the competition and yet be distinctive. *Nintendo*'s CEO, Satoru Iwata, made this very clear when he stated that: 'We're not thinking about fighting *Sony*. The thing we're thinking about most is not portable systems, consoles, and so forth, but that we want to get new people playing games'. The marketing research that preceded the launch of the *Wii* also reflected the change in targeting. Whereas competitors recruited A-listers and influential opinion leaders in the world of predominantly male gaming, *Nintendo* approached working women and mothers, allowing them to test and see the benefits of this product for their families, as well as for other forms of social interaction. This was the stroke of genius: gaming for non-gamers. Either by chance or choice, *Nintendo* had not only reinvented a product category but also had tapped into a set of emerging social concerns: the break-up of the nuclear family into cellular disconnected units

(Continued)

and even the nation's health. Targeting a broader demographic beyond the remit of *Microsoft's Xbox 360* and *Sony's PlayStation3* (Wii: The Total Story, IGN, retrieved 29 June 2008), *Wii* now had a completely different positioning focused on the core value proposition of a family-oriented, interactive social experience. Indeed, the alignment of the brand with 'lifestyle and health' redefined the category.

Nintendo has concentrated on a new segment with these products, in order to reposition the *Nintendo* brand in the mind of the consumer (Simms and Trott 2007). Nuttall (2006, p. 2) noted that *Nintendo* targeted women and more middle-aged consumers, within 'multi generational families'. Szmigin and Carrigan (2000. p. 128) found in the 'UK 45–55 year olds account for 23 % of all household expenditure', this market therefore offers huge potential and at the centre of this was the acknowledged role of mothers in the family decision-making unit. The use of family has been researched in relation to building brand equity and repositioning by Gil, Andres and Salinas (2007). They found the family to be very influential in brand choice and loyalty, they also found that a strong bond with the brand can be created by family memories being linked to the products.

The re-creation of the product category is undoubtedly facilitated by the innovative motion-sensitive, wireless technology which allows easy use but encourages multi-user participation and physical activity. The *Wii* Remote is a wireless controller which is used as a hand-held pointing device (or Nunchucks as *Wii* players have come to know them) and detects movement in three dimensions. It is this ability for users to control the game using physical gestures as well as traditional button presses which makes the product unique in the category and emphasises differentiation against the competition. *WiiConnect24* enables messages to be received and updates via the Internet (whilst in 'standby' mode) which creates customer lock-in and encourages brand loyalty and brand relationship building. Online connectivity through *WiiConnect24* also includes: Internet Channel, Virtual Console, Forecast Channel, Everybody Votes Channel, a News Channel and a Check Mii Out Channel. An added UK feature is the BBC announcement that the *BBC iplayer* would be available through the *Wii* Internet Channel.

Nintendo connects the family and the world

The predominant feature of the massive $300 million communications programme has been to target new users, people who would never normally be interested in gaming of this sort. The name *Wii* is meant to signify two players and suggests a plurality which will be invaluable in terms of brand extension. The justification for the name explains the usage possibilities: '*Wii* can be easily remembered by people around the world, no matter what language they speak. No confusion. No need to abbreviate. Just *Wii*' (Wii Get It Now, Amy McDonough, www.1up.com. Retrieved 29 June 2008).

Launched with the inclusive appeal of '*Wii* would like to play' and 'Experience a new way to play', this was the most broad-based advertising campaign *Nintendo* had ever engaged in. Featuring a wide assortment of users enjoying the *Wii* system, the *Wii* has really captured a cultural moment across a broad spectrum with reports of pensioners, surgeons, even the Queen using the product. The launch also used the 'alpha Mum', who would spread the message at school gates, work, as well as to friends, family and neighbours to create word of mouth. Women are three times as likely to tell someone else about a good or bad experience (Miller 2005), and this makes them perfect 'mavens' in generating word of mouth. The *Nintendo* website also reflects a new strong brand identity, using the colours synonymous with the new consoles, and opening with a line of characters from many different cultures and nationalities holding hands, this again reflecting that family and social roots are important to the new *Nintendo* brand.

The launch of the exercise-simulation software – *WiiFit* – has caused a stir socially and been the subject of university research as well as nationwide debate. It is truly phenomenal for a gaming product to be the subject of serious discussion on its contribution to a nation's health and is the mark of the brand's dramatic repositioning.

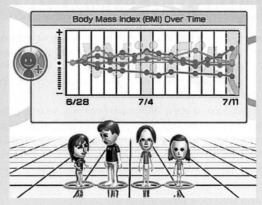

The forerunner to the *Wii*, and building on the themes of wireless interactivity and handheld portability, was the *Nintendo DS* (meaning 'Developer's System' or 'Dual Screen') released in 2004. Although tapping into the same category as *Sony's PSP*, the *DS* was marketed with the positional similarity of the *iPod* and underscored *Nintendo*'s repositioning as introducing innovative 'Touch' generation products. Both brands are targeted at an adult demographic, highlighting the social and cognitive aspects. *Nintendo*'s campaigns for the *DS* and *Wii* are centred on the multiple use of celebrities using an implicit form of endorsement (McCracken 1999) to reach the many different segments within the adult demographic: Fern Britton and Phillip Schofield; Nicole Kidman; Patrick Stewart and Julie Walters for the *DS*; Michael Owen, Ian Wright and the whole of the Rednapp family and *Girls Aloud* for the *Wii*. Hsu and McDonald (2002) found using a number of celebrities can be effective at attracting, and relating to, a number of different reference groups.

By late January 2008, outselling *Xbox* and *PlayStation* by a ratio of 2:1, *Nintendo* had sold over six million units of the *Wii* console. Although *Nintendo* changed product concepts – both *Wii* and the *DS* consoles – the marketing communications had to express a new inclusive positioning and create a new story arc for the brand. *Nintendo*'s advertising has been highly successful at repositioning the *Nintendo* brand and building equity. Whilst the motion-sensitive, wireless technology undoubtedly opened up the opportunities to take the product out of a restrictive gamers' category, breaking down the barriers between man and machine, it was the clever repositioning of the 'family-orientation' communications which changed gaming forever, being made for 'people who don't like video games' (Blakely 2007, p. 1). The console has continued to thrive and won six Bafta awards in 2008, including trophies for 'Best Gameplay', 'Most Innovative Game' and 'Best Multiplayer Title', and was hailed 'the best strategy and simulation game released in the last year' (*Daily Telegraph* 2007). *Nintendo* has managed to do what would seem to be impossible, it has made gaming available for everyone.

QUESTIONS

1. When the *WiiFit*'s 'balance board' called a 10 year old 'fat', an 'obesity expert' expressed fears that the marketing communications of the *Wii* would damage children's body image. Do you think this will detract from the positive dialogue with the target audience?

2. What elements of strategic positioning and tactical positioning have *Nintendo* employed to achieve leadership in the category?

3. Has *Nintendo* created a new category or merely extended the frame of reference of the target audience?

CHAPTER SUMMARY

In this chapter, we looked at the concept of strategic positioning. As we have seen, positioning plays a pivotal role in marketing strategy because it provides a link between what analysis is done in terms of market dynamics and internal corporate analysis. We learnt that positioning is about a brand's territorial rights, owning both product/market space in the target market segment and mind space in the consciousness of the target audience.

We looked at the difference between 'strategic' and 'tactical' positioning and demonstrated how they support one another. It was established that positioning can be considered as being a systematic approach to finding a space for dialogue with an audience. The importance of categorisation issues was outlined as being fundamental in creating and maintaining brand positioning in both new and emerging markets as well as in mature markets.

REFLECTIVE QUESTIONS

a. Can you think of examples where communications has not only helped brands to gain market share but fundamentally changed their product market categories?

b. What was Kotler (1997) suggesting when he said that the strategic task of positioning is for the brand to occupy 'a meaningful and distinctive competitive position in the target customers' minds'?

c. To achieve 'competitive positioning', both strategic and tactical considerations must be taken into account. What's the difference?

d. Why is a positioning statement important to creating and maintaining successful marketing communications?

e. Explain the difference between 'absolute' and 'relative' positioning.

f. Go to www.smirnoff.com and www.smirnoffice.com. Does the claim 'Responsible drinking is clearly original' reinforce or detract from the *Smirnoff* story?

RESEARCH PROJECTS

Look at Olof Holm's 2006 paper on 'Integrated Marketing Communication: from Tactics to Strategy' published in the *Corporate Communications International Journal* (11(1), pp. 23–33) and evaluate the difference between strategic and tactical positioning.

Research the strategic positions of several challenger brands in different product categories and compare how they aim at achieving relative and absolute positioning.

CHAPTER  7

TACTICS AND TECHNIQUES OF POSITIONING

"Creativity has no boundaries, yet in the creative industry we think of ourselves as operating in separate disciplines – design, advertising, promotion, interactive. However, today, more than ever before, our clients need work that creates a deep lasting impact. For this to happen, brands increasingly need to tell a more seamless, complete narrative . . . to operate in a more holistic manner."
Ford (2007)

We now turn to the second part of the positioning process. In the previous chapter, we learned that strategic positioning is about identifying an enduring position in the product category. The chosen strategy must then have a range of carefully selected tools and media to achieve this. This chapter therefore is about the tactics and techniques of positioning and how this helps to underpin and reinforce the brand's strategic positioning.

LEARNING OBJECTIVES

After reading this chapter, you'll be able to:

- Understand the link between positioning strategy and tactics.
- Understand how tactical elements affect the positioning of the brand and how they contribute to brand equity.
- Appreciate how marketing communications can help create 'meaning' for consumers.
- Examine the communicative aspects of different brand elements such as brand name, logotype, typeface and packaging.
- Enable tactical use (e.g. comparative advertising, advertising alliances and context effects) of other brands to strengthen the brand's positioning.
- Distinguish a number of ways to improve the current brand position.

Consumers don't understand what 'strategic' or 'tactical' positioning is. They will probably not understand what 'positioning' is either. Nor should they! That is the job of the organisation; that is the purpose of marketing communications. What consumers need to understand is: how the brand is going to be the best choice for them in the search to fulfil a need or answer a problem; why it will be the best choice between all the other alternatives; and whether they will feel that their choice has been the right one after purchase. In other words, the consumer doesn't see the process, may not see the product, but has to see the benefits of the brand.

Marketing communications has to help consumers make these product selections by careful placing of the product in the physical space of the marketplace and the psychological space of the mind. Tactical positioning is the execution of strategic positioning; it should not be seen as an alternative. The two must present a cohesive, coherent message to consumers which informs, differentiates and persuades. Often, the term 'positioning statement' acts as a critical fulcrum to help identify the category criteria, focus the purpose and design of campaigns, and help engage the target audience in explicit and implicit communications.

OPENING CASE STUDY

Diesel: Is Green the New Black? 'I care, therefore I am'

When Renzo Rosso created the Italian fashion label *Diesel* in 1975, its strategic positioning in an overpopulated fashion denim category was to set its brand in opposition to the established 'All American' brands like *Levi*, *Wrangler* and *Lee Jeans*. The name *Diesel* was chosen because it was easy to

Environment impacts on Diesel communications

understand and even had resonance of 'alternative energy'. Yet it certainly turned up the heat with its provocative 'Global Warming Ready' campaign, drawing attention to a world affected by raised water levels and temperatures, but putting their models posing in *Diesel* clothing on the most startling of catwalks: a flooded Manhattan; walking amongst tropical birds in St Mark's Square, Venice; and leaning provocatively on a desert-strewn Great Wall of China. Even the cold Nordic glaciers of Finland were dramatically turned into a desert.

Fashion is notorious for being transient: what is 'cool' today is suddenly out of favour tomorrow. How often do we hear that the latest colour is 'the new black' and often the trends of the street are born on the catwalk without any reference to the real world. The advertising for fashion brands is necessarily glamorous and creative, but equally projecting an image which is often vacuous and self-centred. Hedonism rather than conscience tends to be the main appeal and this is reflected in depictions of aspirational lifestyle. Many beauty and fashion companies are either going green or collaborating with green charities and organisations to promote awareness of what we are doing to our planet. For example, *Lancôme* collaborated with *Carbonfund.org*, a non-profit organisation which advises companies on reducing climate change impact.

So when *Diesel* announced to the world that its products were 'global warming ready' was it challenging its own long-term positioning of fashion 'for successful living' with a strategic shift to 'eco-fashion' or was this merely a short-term 'green wash' use of tactical positioning to gain attention?

Eco-fashion differs from conventional fashion in that there are environmental, ethical and social considerations in the design and production of product: fair trade supply, ethical production and sustainable fabrics. 'Vegan', animal-friendly shoes made of organic cotton products, recycled wood or cork as a substitute for leather; recycled stones, gold and other metals in jewellery brands eliminating the need for excessive mining; mass retailers like *The Gap* looking to established independent brands for inspiration and direction. Green is definitely the new black in this respect. But is it a marketing ploy and is this 'faux eco-friendliness'?

Joelle Berdugo Adler of *Diesel* claimed that the campaign was consistent with its tradition of generating attention and provoking discussion of serious societal issues in an ironic way: 'Global warming was a tremendously hot button issue, superseding things like health and poverty, and these are subtly revealed through details in the print ads depicting ordinary scenes in a surreal, post-global warming world. At first glance, this appeared to be just another fashion advertisement, and not just a swipe at the competition, but a swipe at the concerns of environmentalists. The campaign storyline continues in various promotional materials such as in

The tide is high for Diesel

'The World's Coolest Hotspots' – little red hardback books which include the full range of advertisements and simulated 'future world' maps.

The website reveals further ambiguities with various consumer materials aimed at engaging with global warming:

- A tongue-in-cheek video raises issue relating to climate change.
- A map showing the world's seaside regions completely under water.
- *Diesel* 'dune buggy tours' in Lapland and windsurfing in New York.
- Encouraging website visitors to watch Al Gore's Oscar-winning environmental documentary *An Inconvenient Truth*.

(Continued)

Diesel's site visitors were encouraged to save the planet by having sex (quietly) to cut down on heating, walking to the shops, turning off lights, insulating homes with recycled denim, never taking a shower, unplugging guitars at the wall, giving fashion magazines to grannies, friends or anyone, hanging up towels, planting trees, and getting rid of the fridge at home.

Rather more seriously *Diesel* outlines a partnership with climate change watchdog, *www.stopglobalwarming.org*. This is a direct technique for engaging consumers in a 'citizen conversation'. Some claimed that this was an example of 'cause marketing' and a brand such as *Diesel* is perfectly placed to communicate serious messages with a young audience. Critics slammed *Diesel* for being less concerned with fomenting political activism and lifestyle change than selling the *Diesel* brand.

Although these advertisements are tongue in cheek, would they be apparent to anyone other than the *Diesel* demographic who are used to provocative 'ironic' imagery such as advocating smoking 145 cigarettes a day (for that 'sexy cough'), the drinking of urine to stay young or even the sponsorship of happiness.

QUESTIONS

1. Do you think *Diesel's* approach to positioning is strategic or tactical?

2. Will the tactics of this campaign reinforce the positioning of the brand as 'irreverent and independent'?

3. Will there be a backlash to brands that appear to undermine serious environmental issues with apparently superficial attention-seeking creative platforms?

THE LINK BETWEEN POSITIONING STRATEGY AND TACTICS

Tactical positioning is often seen as short-term expediency, defending market position or fending off competitive attacks, or even as a holding operation until changes in market conditions can be fully met. Some companies are 'too embroiled in tactical issues and so fail to gain the best possible returns for their brands' (de Chernatony and McDonald 1998). However, whilst concentrating on naming, packaging or communicating may be short term and short-sighted, tactical positioning is just as important as strategic positioning: the proof of whether objectives will be met may be immediately evident in consumers' response to communications stimuli. Strategy may not be obvious to a target user; tactics are how strategy is communicated. Figure 7.1 shows the 'visible' and 'invisible' elements from a consumer's perspective. These tactics are used to convey meaning, create dialogues and differentiate our proposition from the competition. More importantly, this is how we attempt to achieve salient positioning in the minds of the target audience.

Once strategy has been agreed, the methods of how to achieve this need to be formulated. Before this can be done, an estimate of positioning objectives and the health of the brand has to be determined. Lightfoot and Gerstman (1998, p. 55) provide us with a good framework:

- an estimate of the brand's personality;
- current and future brand character;
- strength of the brand equities;
- the brand's heritage;
- existing and desired shelf or store impact;
- the level of brand recognition enjoyed by the product;
- perceived strength and weakness of competitors' brands;

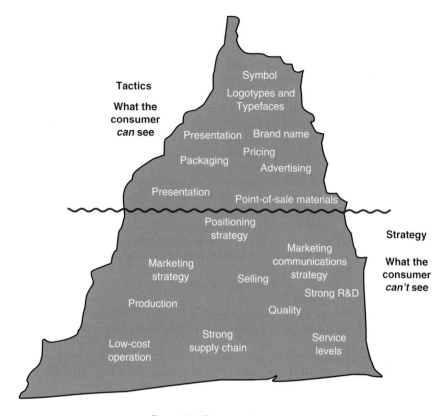

Figure 7.1: The branding iceberg

Source: adapted from Davidson (1997, p. 376) with permission.

- the sales performance of the brand; and
- the desired positioning in the marketplace.

Added to this, Hart (1998, p. 35) suggests four strategic positioning questions which need to be asked:

- Is the new product innovative or not? A distinctive brand name is an opportunity to differentiate a product from the competition either because of actual or perceived innovation.
- Is the new product likely to be an international brand in the future? Strong international brands have the same name, common pack design, similar target audiences and similar formulation.
- Is the new product likely to produce line extensions, or to be part of a range? Line extensions and ranges of products are more effective and less costly if there is a planned cohesion.
- What is the nature of the protection which the brand can be afforded? If proprietary protection is not part of the competitive shield of the brand, an inherently strong and protectable brand name may be essential.

The tools and techniques to help achieve the tactical requirements of positioning consist of aspects like brand name, logotypes, packaging, communication devices used in advertising, slogans/strap lines, selection of distribution channels and retailers, in-store placement and collaboration with other brands. Indeed all the brand encounters we have previously discussed must convey tactically the meaning we want the brand to have. We look at these in detail below. Please note that advertising is the core of positioning technique and because of its importance is given two chapters (Chapters 11 and 12).

COMMUNICATION EFFECTS REQUIRED

Whenever a current or potential user comes into contact with the brand, meaning is being created and individually negotiated. The brand is always talking! In order to ensure that the audience is listening and that the intended message is correctly received, all communication ingredients – media as well as message – must be integrated and support each other so that a unified, clear message is conveyed.

Before we examine the different tactical positioning elements, let us firstly remind ourselves of the five communication effects (Rossiter and Percy 1998) which we discussed in Chapter 4 and how they impact on positioning. These communication effects (or buyer states) which we try to achieve through strategic and tactical positioning include:

- **Category need:** a perceived discrepancy between the current motivational state and the desired motivational state has to be satisfied. Although this sometimes precedes recognition, memory can store brand information which may evoke feelings of dissatisfaction or provoke latent desire. A picture of an ice cool beer on TV late in the evening may make consumers think about planning a visit to the pub the next night or taking a trip to the supermarket to stock up. *SAAB* had no discernible positioning profile in Norway until it was positioned as 'the car for winter' and subsequently became first choice for Norwegian winters.
- **Brand awareness:** a buyer must have the ability to identify (recognise or recall) the brand, within the category, in sufficient detail to make a purchase.
- **Brand preference:** the attitude we have towards a brand and the evaluation of its ability to meet a currently relevant motivation is based on what benefits are communicated by the brand's image.
- **Brand purchase intention:** the attraction a buyer has to a brand must be enough to purchase.
- **Purchase facilitation:** the buyer's assurance that images and association projected by positional tactics (i.e. the marketing mix) will not hinder purchase.

TACTICAL POSITIONING GUIDELINES

For tactical positioning to help achieve these communication effects, the following criteria must be met: the elements should provide **awareness**, **clarity** and **liking** for the brand, as well as maintaining **flexibility** of use for the future and offering protection from competitive intrusion. Consumers should be able to easily recognise and/or recall the brand name and understand the brand's central proposition from the communication cues in elements such as: what value proposition is being offered (e.g. on packaging, point of purchase, displays); where the brand is available (e.g. exclusive outlets); why the brand will meet our needs (e.g. present in advertising, slogan, demonstrations). Some products are fairly obviously targeted and the brand name and packaging leave little doubt as to what category need is being satisfied! All elements, even when they represent only part of the story, must reinforce the desired position. For example, *Toyota* uses car stickers proclaiming 'The car in front is a *Toyota*' and 'My *Toyota* is fantastic' to reinforce the main claims in its advertising but also to continually be at the 'front of mind' of customers and, more importantly, potential customers.

Tactical positioning elements should also be used to create brand clarity in order to help consumers understand the nature of the product category and the particular attributes and features of the particular brand which will help satisfy the need. As we saw in Chapter 6, a brand has to have absolute positioning (parity and similarity to other brands in the category) and also relative positioning (difference from the competition). In other words, the brand should be given tactical descriptive meaning by sharing certain product characteristics with other brands in the category, but also convince people about the brand's superiority. Clarity is created by using visual and verbal techniques to make the marketing communications of the brand clear to the consumers. *MasterCard*'s 'Priceless' campaign has shown that 'There are some things money can't buy. For everything else there's *MasterCard*'. The campaign idea has been communicated in many different ways (advertisements, events, contests and website) and has also been played with and parodied on the Internet.

Blankson and Kalafatis (2004) offered a typology of the different positioning alternatives, illustrated in Table 7.1.

Another more recent perspective is adopted by a lot of organisations these days: **green positioning**. This type of brand identity is defined by a specific set of attributes and benefits related to the environmental impact of the brand and its perception of being environmentally friendly. (The two case studies featured in this chapter show two different aspects of green positioning. One organisation sees a tactical, short-term opportunity manifest in a 'green washing' campaign; the other has a deep-seated, long-term strategic approach to its business.)

Factor	Measurement items
1. Top of the range	Upper class Top of the range Status Prestigious Posh
2. Service	Impressive service Personal attention Consider people as important Friendly
3. Value for money	Reasonable price Value for money Affordability
4. Reliability	Durability Warranty Safety Reliability
5. Attractiveness	Good aesthetics Attractive Cool Elegant
6. Country of origin	Patriotism Country of origin
7. The brand name	The name of the offering Leaders in the market Extra features Choice Wide range
8. Selectivity	Discriminatory Non-selective High principles

Table 7.1: Typology of positioning alternatives

Source: Blankson and Kalafatis (2004).

All tactical elements need to convey the key product meaning of category need identification and attribute fit. Durgee and Stuart (1987) proposed a framework for identifying symbols (which may be used in advertising or other tactical positioning) that represent key product meanings. These are featured in the Matter of Fact box below.

MATTER OF FACT

Key Product Meanings

Research looking at establishing what the core consumption experience in a certain category was, used 'free association tests' to produce a framework for designing a symbol (i.e. a sign, a word or phrase or image) that had shared meaning with the consumption experience. The symbol was tested for congruity with the consumption experience (e.g. smoking signified masculinity, independence, outdoors, days gone by and the symbol of 'cowboy' was deemed to be strong for smoking).

Key product meanings framework

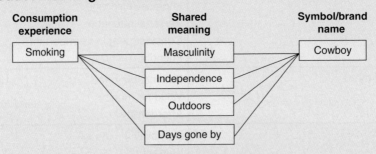

Key product meanings framework

Empirical tests in real categories show that some brands are better at communicating key product meanings than others (see Durgee and Stuart for more tests on ice tea (advertising), computers (brand name), gasoline (logotype/slogan) and casual shoes (name/logotype)). Research into the pick-up truck category showed that the symbolism of the 'ram' was much better than *Cherokee* for conveying key product meanings (tough, powerful, rugged, strong and fun). The ram symbol was a much more accessible symbol than an Indian tribe (see table below)

Consumption experience	Category	Symbol brand 1	Symbol brand 2
Adjectives	Pick-up trucks (key product meanings)	Ram (Dodge)	Cherokee (Jeep)
Tough	34%	27%	1%
Powerful	32%	28%	4%
Rugged	16%	6%	—
Strong	32%	43%	14%
Fun	13%	—	—

Fast	—	10%	—
Horns	—	25%	—
Loyal	—	—	10%
Brave	—	4%	16%
Proud	—	5%	17%
Wild	—	5%	11%

Empirical results of key product meanings

Source: Durgee and Stuart (1987). Reproduced with permission.

MATTER OF FACT

Shades of Meaning

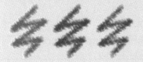

What are the colours above? Red? Green? Blue? One might think so. But the correct answers are Razzmatazz, Tropical Rain Forest and Denim. At least if you ask the marketers at *Crayola* – a brand that sell crayons and pens to children. The colours above are three of more than 120 crayon colours that *Crayola* has. *Crayola* is not unique in using creative names for concrete product attributes. Many companies are putting suggestive and communicative names on their colours, flavours or whatever may be relevant in their particular market. *Hawaiian Punch* has fruit juices with imaginary names like bodacious berry (blue berry), wild purple smash (grape and berry) and orange ocean. *Ben & Jerry's* ice cream has flavour names like Chocolate Therapy, Fossil Fuel, Peace of Cake and Dublin Mudslide.

According to researchers Elisabeth Miller and Barbara Kahn, the usage of unusual and creative product attribute (e.g. flavours) names is effective. The two core variables to consider are typicality and specificity. Product attribute name categories are *common* (typical, unspecific; dark green, light yellow), *common descriptive* (typical, specific; pine green, lemon yellow), *unexpected descriptive* (atypical, specific; Kermit green, rainslicker yellow), and *ambiguous* (atypical, unspecific; friendly green, party yellow).

Their results show convincingly that atypical names – ambiguous and unexpected descriptive - are better than typical names both in choice tests and attitude/satisfaction tests. The results on specificity are mixed (see the table overleaf for results on satisfaction). In recall situations (when name is mentioned before seeing the product), the ambiguous names are superior. The ambiguous name is likely to create curiosity and that is good before product exposure. The product flavour/colour perceptions will be guided by the previous name exposure. In recognition situations (when the name is revealed after

(Continued)

the product has been seen), the unexpected descriptive names are superior. Consumers are here making a spontaneous appraisal of the colour and an ambiguous name may be confusing and may not add explanations to the spontaneous inferences. An unexpected descriptive name may be interesting to consumers and still have high perceived fit with the flavour/colour name just tasted/seen.

	Name first	Picture first
Unexpected descriptive	4.4	6.6
Ambiguous	5.6	3.9

Mean ratings of satisfaction

Mean ratings of satisfaction (11-point scale) for unexpected descriptive and ambiguous product attribute names

This shows that the tactical manifestations of the strategic positioning are not only about advertising anymore.

Sources: Miller and Kahn (2005);

http://www.crayola.com/colorcensus/history/current_120_colors.cfm;

http://www.benjerry.com/our_products/flavorWorld.cfm; http://www.hawaiianpunch.com.

The four main techniques which are used in tactical positioning are:

1. brand name;
2. logotypes;
3. typefaces; and
4. packaging.

A brand which perfectly encapsulates category usage and audience appeal – the user-authored *YouTube* Internet site – combines name, logotype and typeface to suggest keyboard, screen, audience and the purpose of the service.

You Tube logo

BRAND NAME

According to Kapferer (2000, p. 112), 'the brand's name is often revealing of the brand's intentions'. It is a powerful source of identity and helps to project the intended image of the product against the competition and in the process of positioning a brand in the minds of the target audience (Ries and Trout 1980). In overcrowded markets with narrower segments, brand name plays a crucial role. Susannah Hart (1998, p. 34) of *Interbrand* suggests that the key attributes of a brand name are:

- allows brands to become part of everyday life by enabling consumers to specify, reject or recommend brands;
- can communicate overtly (e.g. *Rentokil*) or subconsciously; and
- can become a valuable asset as it functions as a legal device.

A name itself need not necessarily convey objectives or associations. Freestanding names like *Shell*, *Kodak* and *Sony* don't actually suggest any attribute or benefit, whereas associative names like

Pampers, *Visa* and *Comfort* do. The notion of brand name suggestiveness is discussed in the Matter of Fact box below.

MATTER OF FACT

Brand Name Suggestiveness

A research study on brand name recall showed that a brand name which was suggestive of a benefit is good for initial recall but reduces flexibility in later positioning. The study tested brand names in five different product categories: TV sets, luggage, tennis racquets, personal computers and cameras. Suggestive and non-suggestive brand names were compared in each category and consistent and unrelated benefit claims were associated to the brand names through advertising. For instance, in the luggage category the suggestive brand name and the consistent benefit were *LifeLong* and durability. The non-suggestive brand name was *Ocean* and the unrelated benefit was fashionable appearance. Note that both benefits are relevant in the category.

Respondents saw advertisements (embedded in a larger group of advertisements) in two sessions. In Session 1, the advertisement had the consistent claim and in Session 2, the advertisement had the unrelated claim. Recall of advertised claims was measured for each brand. The results are shown in the table below and clearly show the suggestive brand name to be superior in its ability to be linked to the consistent benefit claim (i.e. *LifeLong* was better in communicating luggage durability than *Ocean* with recall of 0.33 versus 0.15). Even though the unrelated benefit is communicated in the second session, the first learned association is stuck in people's minds (recall: 0.45 versus 0.23). The original association is still remembered and interferes with the new information. The unrelated benefit is more re-called for a non-suggestive brand name (recall: 0.50 versus 0.35) than for a suggestive brand name. The non-suggestive brand name is not inhibiting for new information to the same extent as a suggestive brand name.

	Consistent benefit Session 1	Consistent benefit, Session 2	Unrelated benefit, Session 2
Suggestive brand name	0.33	0.45	0.35
Non-suggestive brand name	0.15	0.23	0.50

Brand name suggestiveness and benefit claim recall

Source: Keller, Heckler and Houston (1998).

If all elements of marketing communicate, the brand name is fundamental to all marketing communications. The mere presence of a brand name may evoke positive feelings and unique associations to the brand (Keller 2003); the brand name may show what the brand is all about and what the brand can and cannot do. The name can be pivotal to the associations the brand is carrying and, as such, a highly familiar brand name evokes associations instantly. If the name is remembered, the brand may get into the consideration set more easily and the brand stands more chance of being selected, since the consumer's purchase propensity for the brand is enhanced.

The use of linguistics may affect consumers' ability to remember the brand name (Klink 2001; Robertson 1989). Beer brand names like *Weihenstephaner Hefe Weissbier* or *Budvar Budejovicky*, even *Hyundai* and *Häagen-Dazs* are difficult to pronounce in some countries. Positioning effectiveness may be enhanced for these brands as they may be easy to recognise due to unusual spelling.

How Brand Names Help Achieve Awareness

For low-involvement products, the decision-making process is short and it is important to create top-of-mind awareness. Brand names should be simple and easy to pronounce, like *Fairy* washing-up liquid, *Nike* sports shoes/clothes, *Lux* soap or *Daz* soap powder. However, some high-involvement brands sometimes get shorter nicknames to facilitate awareness as *Coke* for *Coca-Cola*, *FedEx* for *Federal Express*, *Merc* for *Mercedes-Benz*, *HOGS* for *Harley-Davidson* owner groups, and *Bud* for *Budweiser*.

There are techniques to select names so that they are easier to remember and pronounce (Keller 2003, Riezebos 2003, Robertson 1989). The marketer should look for words that have a natural rhythm and that have a pleasant sound when pronounced. One technique is alliteration (repetition of consonants, for instance *Rolls-Royce* and *Coca-Cola*). Other techniques are assonance (i.e. vowel rhymes as in the hotel chain *Ramada Inn* and biscuit brand *HobNobs*), consonance (i.e. repetition of consonants with changed vowels as in *Kit Kat* and *WeightWatchers*), and rhythm (i.e. repeated patterns with emphasis on a certain letter or syllable as in *Pedigree Pal*, *Bacardi Breezer* and *Black & Decker*).

Brand names should be familiar and meaningful and use consumers' images and associations already encoded in memory: people, geographical places, animals, events and other phenomena

may create highly familiar and meaningful connections. The brand name should therefore evoke a mental image of a relevant product attribute or an essential imagery aspect. If the primary communication objective is brand recognition, the brand name should instead be different, distinct and unusual. In this case, it is a good idea to use words from 'dead' languages like *Drambuie* (means the drink that satisfies in Scottish Gaelic) and ancient names like *Nike* (a Greek goddess symbolising victory). It is also relatively common that companies come up with their own words – or use acronyms or word play for the same purpose – that they use as brand name. Examples of this are *7-Up*, *Exxon*, *IKEA* (Ingvar Kamprad Elmtaryd Agunnaryd), *Saab* (*Saab* has used the strap line 'Very Saabish'). The main advantage is that the brand does not carry any negative linguistic associations. The main disadvantage is that the brand does not use the associative short cuts that existing languages may offer.

IKEA flies the Swedish flag

Reproduced by permission of *IKEA*

How Brand Names Help Positioning Clarity

The brand name should ideally also communicate associations effectively. Therefore, it is beneficial if the brand name is selected to evoke rich and familiar associations (Klink 2001) The name should also be separated from the category name to avoid becoming generic (e.g. *Thermos*, *Kleenex*). To associate a brand with a category, sometimes metaphors are used: 'cheetah' for speed; 'apple' for knowledge; 'Everest' for high; 'mustang' for power and strength all have connotations beyond the brand name. Acronyms or unusual spellings may be used for positioning purposes as well (e.g. French radio station *NRJ*, the soft drink *Sunkist*, and the computer company *Intel* as in intelligence). The name may connote a clear link between the brand name and its positioning without denoting a description.

Another way to create clear brand names is to use **morphemes**. According to linguistic research, morphemes are the smallest unit in the language that has a consistent meaning (Klink 2001). Examples are prefixes (pro-, pan-, bio-, super-), roots (form, quick, care) and suffixes (-ia, -ness, -ity, -al). Well-known brands that have used morphemes are *Duracell* (durable batteries), *Panasonic* (all about sound), *Lufthansa* (airlines companies in collaboration), *Volkswagen* (cars for the masses) and *Domestos* (hygiene products for the home). Even smaller language parts are **phonemes** – individual sounds and single letters. These do not carry any meaning but may be used by the marketer to create symbolic value to the brand (Klink 2001). A fundamental aspect of phonemes is that different letters and sounds have connotations. Some are round and soft (for example *s, m, n* and *f*) and others are sharp and hard (*k,*

Duracell's durable batteries

x, t and *p* among others). *Nivea* is an example of a soft phoneme and *Bahco* (tools) is an example of a hard phoneme. These are important when the brand name is a 'non-word'. In these cases the brand should not have any conflicting associations. The marketer should avoid sharp sounds for products that should be soft and gentle, and vice versa. Linguistic research has shown that different words, pronunciations and letters convey different things about size, movement, shape and light (see Robertson 1989). Furthermore, some sounds are masculine (hard, guttural sounds) as the deodorant *AXE* and other sounds are feminine (soft, whispering sounds) like the shampoo brand *Wella*.

MATTER OF FACT

Semantic (Morphemes) and Sound Symbolism (Phonemes)

Research into branding strategies for new products has tried to distinguish between 'meaningful' brand names (often referred to as 'imbed' brand names suggesting positive attributes or benefits) and non-meaningful brand names (often referred to as 'no-imbed' brand names which don't suggest positive attributes or benefits). Brand name effectiveness – in terms of 'liking' and 'positioning clarity' – has been studied by way of sound symbolism and semantics, as well as a combination of both. Both types of naming concepts add value to the brand name.

The study was conducted in three product categories: shampoo (benefit: leaves hair soft); laptop computers (benefit: lightweight); and pain relievers (benefit: fast working). The no-imbed shampoo was named *Polbee*. As the letters *s* and *i* are more associated to softness than *p* and *o*, the sound symbolism name was *Silbee*. The combination name, *Silsoft*, added the suffix *-soft* to the name. The laptop computer names were *Guxtrill*, *Vextrill* and *Vexlight* (*v* and *e* are more light than *g* and *u*) and the pain reliever names were *Bondin*, *Zindin* and *Zinfast* (*z* and *i* are more associated to rapidity than *b* and *o*).

	Liking*	Positioning clarity*
No-imbed name	3.67	3.48
Sound-symbolism	4.29	3.93
Sound-symbolism + semantics	4.61	4.68

The use of brand name techniques to improve liking and positioning

* Measured on seven-point scale.

Source: Klink (2001).

Brands can also get their names from people and human names, with associations and emotions transferred from the individual to the brand. Celebrities attach their 'name' to new products like Jennifer Lopez's *JLo* perfume or Paul Newman's *Newman's Own Sauces*. Other celebrities have allowed their names to be used as a sub-brand for established brands (e.g. Madonna and *H&M*, Scarlett Johansson and *Reebok*) or the name of the originator as brand name (e.g. *Ralph Lauren, Heinz, Yamaha*) is used which communicates a success story when the brand is growing and helps to create a personality and identity for the brand.

The brand can get a clear identity also by the use of invented personalities. Many brands have created or used existing characters or a personality association that either is conveyed in the brand name (e.g. *Uncle Ben* evokes 'tradition and trust') or is tightly connected to the brand name (e.g. *Marlboro* cowboy or the *Michelin* man). What this demonstrates is that brand names can have a symbolic value. Psychological research shows that consumers' ability to remember information is enhanced by stimuli with strong emotional signals. The name should therefore be linked to strong and positive symbols and associations that evoke pleasant and favourable thoughts (e.g. comfort, joy, warmth and excitement).

Products which use 'foreign name' branding may be perceived as being more attractive. A research study showed that American consumers perceive the same brand name differently if the brand is pronounced in French than in English (Leclerc, Schmitt and Dubé 1994). For this reason, mock brand names like *Randal, Varner* and *Rimor* have been used. French brand names were perceived as more hedonistic than English brand names. As a consequence, brand names pronounced in French were more attractive when it comes to hedonistic products (e.g. perfume, wine, fashion). Domestic (English) brand names were preferred for utilitarian products.

Foreign brand names are common in most countries. The English language is used all over the world and by many non-English companies. In addition, many brands use foreign brand names from other languages to create the right associations for the brand. *Carlsberg* has been selling a mineral water on the Swedish market with the name *Vichy Nouveau* (sounds very French), *Matsui* is a UK-based consumer electronics brand but sounds Japanese, *Häagen-Dazs* sounds more European (due to the unusual spelling) even though the brand owner is American.

How Brand Names Help Consumers to Like Brands

As we have already seen, sound symbolism and semantics, and the use of foreign-sounding brands, improve 'liking' ratings. In addition, brand names that convey a certain benefit have an instant liking advantage over other brand names for new products. They are liked more at first exposure to the brand. These brand names also have a halo effect on quality as they are perceived as higher-quality products than non-meaningful brand names. With repeated exposures, meaningful brand names gain more by repeated brand exposure (Kohli, Harich and Leuthesser 2005). Some examples are: *Black & Decker Alligator* – a chain saw with an alligator-like gap; *Powerade Arctic Shatter* – sports drink with icy-white shade; and *L'Oréal Paris Lash Architect* – mascara for the right 'design' of the eye lashes.

POSITIONING IN FOCUS

P&G. **The Relationship between Brands and the Product**

The relationship between brands and the product portfolio is dependent upon the choice between whether a brand is to have complete autonomy or total affiliation. Organisations like *P&G* have many individual brands all representing different product categories; whereas companies like *Rentokil* believe that there are enormous benefits from having a broad range of product categories under a single brand name. The dilemma is whether to aim at creating distinction between products without losing the origins of the brand. *Allure, Anthaeus, Chance, Coco, Mademoiselle, Cristalle, Egoistes, No. 19, No. 5, Precision*, are all perfume brands which are covered by the *Chanel* label. *Lexus* uses numbers for its car models: *IS, IS F, GS, LS, RX* and *SC*. *Sky* groups its products by: 'See' – all *Sky* TV programmes like *Sky Sports, Sky Movies*; 'Surf' – Sky Broadband Internet; and 'Speak' – telephone options.

Kapferer (1997, p. 211) identifies seven forms of branding strategy, each with an increasing degree of autonomy:

- The *Lacoste* brand name transcends a range of shirts, socks, jackets, sweaters, tennis rackets and eau de toilette, imbuing each product with a badge of distinction, personified by the famous crocodile logo.
- *Mercedes* names its cars Class A, C, E or S; *BMW* has a number scale: 3, 5 and 7 series.
- Brands use prefixes to link sub-brands to one main brand: the range of perfumes *Diorissimo, Miss Dior* or *Diorella* use 'Dior' to signify their collective brand parentage; the drinks *Nescafé, Nescore, Nesquik* and *Nestea* from *Nestlé* use 'Nesc' in much the same way.
- *Lancôme*, on the other hand, uses the suffix 'ome' for brands like *Niosome* and *Noctosome*, serving the main brand but still emphasising the innovating qualities of the main brand.
- *Clarins* uses 'multi' as a bridging device for products such as *Multi-Tensing Gel* and *Multi-Restoring Fluid* to emphasise its core identity and suggest 'a complete range of treatment'.
- *Volkswagen* has turned to individual brand names like the *Golf*, as *Renault* has with *Clio* and *Twingo* demonstrating the product–brand relationship is a bottom-up one.
- The final stage refers to the fully autonomous product brand that exists without any reference to the source or company.

P&G has a massive range of brands like *Secret, Wella, Pantene, Max Factor, Olay* and *Cover Girl*, but spread much further, taking in baby care, feminine care, health care, fabric/laundry, food and beverage and tissues and towels as well as beauty care. Big non-beauty brands in the *P&G* portfolio include such blockbusters as *Tide* washing powder, *Pampers* nappies, *Pringles* snacks and *Iams* pet foods, as well as *Camay, Zest, Lenor, Old Spice, Gillette, Mach 3, Oral-B*, and so on, all of which have individual brand equity.

LOGOTYPES

Whilst a familiar brand name will easily and quickly be perceived by consumers, images are perceived even faster than words. To maximise the effectiveness of brand positioning, a clear logotype is needed as it can communicate visually with consumers. Consumers may only be exposed to the sender of a message during a very short time span (e.g. walking in stores and passing aisles and store shelves, browsing through a magazine or newspaper, or driving by an outdoor billboard). A logo is a visual cue to remind consumers about brand essence: all the tangible and intangible associations they have with the brand. Therefore, companies use standardised logotypes in the form of words, images and symbols for brand identification, and to help us understand the brand's culture and personality, as a sort of brand signature. What is important about logos is that they are symbolic of something; it is 'not so much that they help identify the brand, but that the brand identifies with them' (Kapferer 1997, p. 115).

Logotypes comprise everything from stylised brand names (e.g. *IKEA* and *IBM*) to abstract symbols that do not perceptually relate to the brand name (e.g. the *Mercedes* star, the *Nike* 'swoosh', the five circles of the Olympic Games, and the *Citroën* arrows). Many logotypes combine names and symbols that are related to the brand name or the brand associations that should be linked to the brand (e.g. the *McDonald's* golden arches, the *Rolex* crown, the *Sprite* lemon and *Ferrari's* black prancing stallion). An effective logotype is easily recognised, promotes meaningful associations to the brand and the product category, and creates positive brand emotions. Our discussion on logotypes is mainly inspired by the influential research article by Henderson and Cote (1998).

Logotype Recognition

Recall and recognition are key objectives in achieving communication effects and reinforcing positioning. There are two types of logotype recognition:

- **Correct recognition:** occurs when consumers recognise a logotype they have seen before. It is essential for major brands that the logotype be designed so that it gets firmly established in people's  memory and in a way that ensures automatic associations to the brand. To achieve this, the logotype should be natural so that it represents the brand and the category in a clear way (e.g. the lemon in the *Sprite* logo). Other factors that facilitate true recognition are departures from perfect symmetry and balance (e.g. *Volvo* arrow but not *BMW* circle) and that logotype elements are repeated (e.g. the *Audi* circles) as these factors tend to enhance people's ability to memorise logos.

  Four rings spell Audi
- **False recognition:** If consumers do not recognise the logo after being exposed to it, it may be that it is too complex or unclear. False recognition, when people will think they have seen a logo, is important when consumers make choices between unfamiliar alternatives as when they are looking in the *Yellow Pages* for a carpenter or a hairdresser or when they are looking for restaurants while on vacation. Different types of design elements that tap into people's associative network may simulate typical and familiar logotypes and affect consumers subconsciously. False recognition logotypes should not be distinctive and should easily be mixed with others.

Logotype Meaning

Under the right circumstances a logotype may also evoke meaningful brand associations. To achieve this, the logotype must first and foremost be based on familiar elements that are easy to understand. Unfamiliar and anonymous signs and images will not create meaning initially. In that case, other parts of the marketing of the brand create the brand meaning and not the logotype.

The most commonly used design style (and the most familiar one) both historically and in modern times is called the **golden section** and is based on how different logotype parts relate to each other in predetermined proportions (see Matter of Fact box below). The golden section uses ratios that are appealing and meaningful to people automatically (Henderson and Cote 1998). Moreover, a meaningful logotype is unique and special but still easily interpreted. Empirical studies show that consumers perceive more meaning with natural logotypes. Organic elements should be used rather than synthetic elements. The logotype should represent the brand and the product category in a good way. The *Red Bull* logo with charging bulls is a good representation of energy drink associations. *Becel* spread has used a heart in its logotype to convey that the product is a healthy alternative that may lower cholesterol levels. *Rolex* uses a crown to express the brand's elegance.

Red Bull logo

MATTER OF FACT

The Golden Section

The golden section is based on geometry. If a line is split into two parts, the ratio of the long line (A–C) and the entire line (A–B) should be similar to the ratio of the short line (C–B) and the long line (A–C). When this rule is satisfied, the proportions are perfect. The pyramids of Egypt and Notre Dame in Paris are built on this principle.

```
A _____C_____B
0                              0.61            1
```

Golden section

The golden section is created when the point C on the line A to B is placed so that AC/AB = CB/AC. The golden ratio is always 0.61.

Source: Henderson and Cote (1998).

Logotype meaning is important for companies with large brand portfolios where each brand has a clear product category or attribute association (e.g. P&G). However, it can be restrictive if the brand owner wants to be flexible.

Logotype Liking

It has also been shown that logotypes produce positive emotions. An explanation for this is that people are attracted to art and design and that aesthetically designed logotypes appeal to people. Positive reactions to a logotype may spill over to the brand and to the company. One study showed that consumer reactions varied greatly when brands were presented with name only or with full logotype. *Nike* was more positively evaluated when the swoosh logo appeared alongside the brand name. The *Cadillac* logo also contributed to the brand image whereas *Minolta* and *Texas Instruments* had logotypes that reduced the brand image compared to the brand name only (Schechter 1993).

Nike swoosh

© Nike, Inc.

Positive emotions may be built over time – familiar things tend to be more liked – but can also be stimulated quickly by the right logotype design: **complexity**, **activity** and **depth**. These aspects may promote thoughts about the logotype that may lead to logotype liking. Two other logotype characteristics that may lead to more positive emotions are **natural aspects** (i.e. representative and organic logotypes) and **harmony** (i.e. symmetry and balance). *Jaguar, Xbox, Apple* and *Red Bull* are some logotypes that satisfy most of the conditions for positive effect. The colour of the logotype is also important for meaningfulness and positive emotions. Blue is associated with future, tranquillity and rationality and should work well for companies who want to be perceived as competent and innovative (e.g. *American Express, IBM, Ericsson*), whereas red is more emotional, warm and social and is therefore more used for fast-moving consumer goods and transformational brands (e.g. *Coca-Cola, Levi's, Red Bull*).

O2 spreads brand image

Design lies right at the heart of the O_2 brand's communication. It uses the original visual mnemonic of the droplet of water and transforms it into a highly evocative and expressive visual language: life itself.

TYPEFACES

Brand names normally use some kind of typeface design. The choice of typeface may have a great impact on the brand (product brand and corporate brand) perceptions (Childers and Jass 2002, Henderson, Giese and Cote 2004), and choice of typeface may strengthen the way a brand is communicated. A brand that wants to convey a certain image should use the right typeface in copy text and for the brand name: a casual brand should use casual fonts and an exclusive brand should use an exclusive font.

According to Henderson, Giese and Cote (2004), four design elements may be used and combined to achieve the desired impressions:

- pleasing;
- engaging;
- reassuring;
- prominent.

The typeface design dimensions that may be used to create this are elaborate (ornate, distinctive, special, meaningful, depth), harmony (balance, symmetry, smoothness, uniformity), natural (active, curved, organic, slant, handwritten), flourish (serifs, ascenders, descenders), weight (heavy, short and fat, repetition) and compressed (condensed, tall). The three last dimensions are specific to typeface.

In Table 7.2, typefaces that convey certain impressions are listed with examples, presented in order of importance. For instance, a natural typeface is most important when the typeface should be pleasing. Moreover, the relationship between dimensions and elements should be read in the following way. Less natural fonts are perceived as more prominent. Pleasing brands should have a

Element	Dimensions	Examples
Pleasing	Natural, positive (strong) Elaborate, negative Harmony, positive Flourish, positive Compressed, moderate	*Cartier* *Kleenex*
Engaging	Natural, positive (strong) Elaborate, positive (strong) Harmony, negative Compressed, positive (small) Flourish, negative (small)	*Pizza Hut* *Yahoo*
Reassuring	Harmony, positive (strong) Elaborate, negative (strong) Flourish, positive (small)	*McKinsey* *Toyota*
Prominent	Natural, negative (strong) Weight, positive Flourish, negative Harmony, negative (small)	*Pepsi* *Absolut*

Table 7.2: Typeface design

Source: Henderson, Giese and Cote. (2004).

typeface that is based mostly on natural and harmonious typeface design that is not elaborate. Engaging brands' typefaces should be natural and elaborate but not harmonious. Reassuring brands should convey a trustworthy image. Thus, harmony is helpful whereas elaboration is harmful. Finally, prominent brands should avoid being natural (straight, passive, not handwritten) and emphasise weight (fat and heavy fonts).

PACKAGING

A fourth visual positioning aspect is packaging, often the strongest image consumers have when they visualise a brand. This brand element is of course to a large extent functional as the packaging must withstand transportation and product storage and consumers expect product protection as a minimum. But packaging also helps achieve positioning objectives by projecting the brand. Think of brand packages which are not just incredibly distinctive, but have become iconic, even for consumers who don't use the brand: *Jack Daniel's, Gitanes, Heinz, Perrier, Rizla, Oxo, Kellogg's, Kit Kat* and the ubiquitous *Coca-Cola* bottle. In fact, last year *Coca-Cola* ran a series of ads which featured only the famous contoured *Coke* bottle.

MATTER OF FACT

Golden Section in Packaging Ratios

The golden section principle has also been tested for package shapes. There is strong evidence that consumer preferences and purchase intentions depend on the ratio of rectangular packages. People seem to have a preference for a range of packaging ratios rather than a particular ratio. However, the golden section ratio lies within the preferred range. In laboratory experiments, the evaluation of the package is lower when the shape is either similar to a square (1:1) or has a ratio of 2:1 than when it has a ratio between 1.38:1 and 1.62:1. The effect is strongest for relatively serious product categories and usage contexts. There is also a relationship between package ratio and market share for frequently purchased consumer goods (tested for cereal, cookies, detergent and soap). For cookies and cereal (less serious categories), packages that are close to a square have higher market share. For detergent and soap (more serious packages), packages with clear rectangular ratios have higher market share.

Source: Raghubir and Greenleaf (2006).

If branding is the dressing of the product, packaging can be seen as offering different types of 'shells' for the actual product content. PET plastic bottles for soft drinks, mobile phone shapes, yoghurt containers, containers for mints and so on are all familiar shapes in those respective categories and are an integral part of the brand appeal. At the centre of this combination is **perceived value**, a subjective (often visual) evaluation of brands of which packaging plays an important part. This can be applied to services as well, with the atmosphere and ambience in retail and restaurant chains effectively the service 'packaging'.

Ferrero Rocher: perceived value or packaging overkill?

Packaging is an important trigger in the purchase process, particularly at point of purchase as it helps consumers to identify the brand when making a purchase, receive descriptive information before purchase, and enhance brand associations evoked in communications (Keller 1991). Strong attractive packaging may stand out above the clutter of brands and communicate brand salience at point of purchase. Packaging changes may also signal a changed position in the market, or enable increases in price or product improvements. For example, when *P&G* changed the target audience for its deodorant *Old Spice* (from old men to teenagers), it changed the entire look of the brand. New products were introduced and the packaging was made younger and trendier. Another example is the fact that *Evian* uses more luxurious packaging designs for the restaurant market than for supermarkets. The *Evian Palace* (used at restaurants) bottle can be viewed on www.evian.com/us. Also, *Evian* creates each year a limited edition bottle to attract attention and evoke brand interest (see Figure 7.2).

Repackaging the brand may become more appropriate in different consumption situations (e.g. ceramic bathroom accessories, normally only available through builders' merchants can be blister-packed for the self-merchandising requirements of the DIY market). Consumer preferences for typical and atypical packages are dependent on the level of perceived risk involved in a purchase (Campbell and Goodstein 2001). When the perceived risk is high (e.g. the purchase of perfume as a gift in a socially important context), people are relatively conservative and prefer typical packages. The packaging becomes the signifier for the category. When the perceived risk is low, people are more likely to try an atypical package. When a brand has many different package solutions, it becomes more versatile. And, it is likely that the versatility leads to enhanced brand salience. Packaging variation may come from changes in size, packaging material and proportions.

Innovations in packaging may also result in the market expanding as new target groups are attracted to the product category. When *Nokia* started with replaceable mobile phone covers to individualise and enhance the product, it got additional sales from existing and new customers. *Campbell's Soup* has tried new packaging styles (e.g. paper cans for its 'good to go' microwavable soup bowls and cups) to attract new customers.

Liking may be created by aesthetical appeals in packaging and logotypes and by creative solutions for brand names and brand benefits.

Flexibility is also often needed in the tactical positioning. It is important to enable adjustments and updates to the brand associations over time so that they stay current and modern. This is particularly important when the marketer is using celebrity endorsers or is capitalising in other ways on market trends. The brand must survive an athlete's career or a musician's popularity. Moreover, it is important

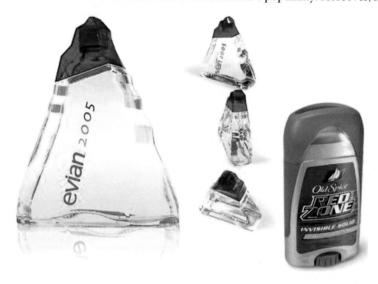

Figure 7.2: The *Evian* Holiday 2005 bottle and the new *Old Spice* deodorant

© P&G. Reproduced with permission.

to be flexible in other choices of brand elements. It is recommended to use positioning tactics that are possible to expand and adjust within the category, to other categories, geographically and culturally.

Another aspect of tactical positioning is the protection of the brand, both legally and from competitors. Brand elements that can be legally protected from intrusions help reinforce category positioning.

POSITIONING IN FOCUS

Packaging Design

One of the tactical elements which helps to reinforce strategic category positioning of new products onto the market is packaging design. Whilst the primary purpose is to protect product, its most important function is to project brand image. Packaging has to be convenient, attractive and 'talk' from the supermarket shelves. It can be through shape, texture, ergonomics and on-pack graphics: the iconic *Coca-Cola* hour-glass, contoured shape; the on-pack jokey graphics on *Innocent* drink cartons; the upside-down design on an *HP Tomato Ketchup* plastic bottle dispenser. Good packaging can infuse cultural significance, engage in brand conversation or suggest product usage.

Bottles reflect Isklar brand

When Norwegian bottled water brand *Isklar* launched in the UK in 2008, the design agency Blue Marlin had to project the category need of 'health and refreshment' by creating a bottle shape which was resonant with crisp, naturally filtered Norwegian pure mineral water. Inspired by the structure of glacial ice, the *Isklar* water bottle, an embodiment of *Isklar's* pristine glacial provenance, was designed as a 73-faceted prism. 'We'd designed it to sparkle like a faceted chunk of ice' said designer Tim Hayes. This was hugely instrumental in both differentiating the brand from the competition and suggesting heritage, quality and country-of-origin branding.

The Belgian premium beer brand *Stella Artois* needed to reclaim lost market share and reposition the brand with a superior quality image. This was to be suggested at point of purchase and in the experience of consuming the product. One of the tactics was to personify quality in a specially designed chalice-style beer glass for the brand to enhance the new upmarket target audience and brand positioning. The perceived quality of the brand on the *Stella* glass included etching on the stem and full-colour branding.

Lux's luxury look

Even soap can be remodelled to help perceptions and positioning. According to Seymour Powell design director Adrian Caroen: 'Soap communicates the values of the brand through its form. There is a tactile element. You need to pick it up, put it in your hand and roll it around your fingers'. The design for the new *Lux* soap brand had to evoke luxury whilst enhancing the soft, silky texture needed in the ritual of luxuriating cleansing.

(Continued)

How can all these elements be incorporated into tactical positioning? Take *Kellogg's Corn Flakes* as an example. The brand name is synonymous with the breakfast cereal market and has a well-recognised, readily recalled brand name. Its 'absolute positioning' in this category is enhanced by the use of the 'cockerel' which has a semiotic association with 'morning'. The distinctive logotype and consistent typefaces used help this, and the breakfast cereal in the pack is protected in 'keep-fresh' bags and projects a premium quality image. The advantage of its relative positioning is the rich associative imagery which has allowed *Kellogg's* to expand into other categories (the breakfast 'on the go' cereal bar category) and geographical areas, as well as giving sustained meaning and relevance over time. As its strapline goes: 'If it doesn't say *Kellogg's on* the pack, it isn't *Kellogg's* in the pack'.

OTHER TACTICAL ELEMENTS

Other tactical elements that also need attention in tactical positioning are slogans, tag lines, jingles, Url for web sites, characters, and spokespeople. They all should be designed to optimise awareness, clarity, and liking while at the same time avoiding conflicting associations.

Tactical Positioning of Benefits and Associations

The role of brand name, logotype, typeface and packaging is mainly to effect and support the desired strategic positioning for the brand. In addition, there is also advertising, which has a separate chapter (Chapter 13) dedicated to its impact on positioning. The application of tactical positioning decisions is affected by the maturity of the product category, how far it is developed and what competitive conditions there are. What should be the approach for emerging and mature markets and how best should marketing communications be designed? We know from the previous chapter that pioneering advantage/differentiation is desirable in emerging markets (the introductory and growth stages), and that brand salience is desirable in mature markets. See Figure 7.3.

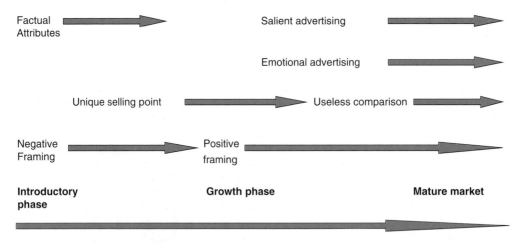

Figure 7.3: Recommended strategies for tactical positioning in advertising based on product life cycle development

Source: Dahlen and Lange (2003). *Optimal marknadskommunikation*, Liber Ekonomi. Reproduced with permission.

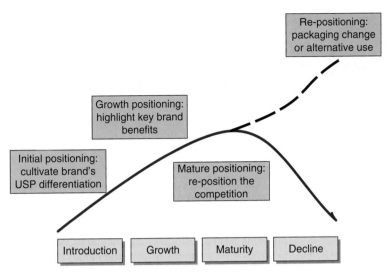

Figure 7.4: Objectives at different stages of adoption and life cycle

As we can see in Figure 7.4, different positioning tactics apply at different stages of the product life cycle, with different degrees of appropriateness and effectiveness. At various stages, and dependent upon competition, positioning tactics might: (i) strengthen the brand's current position; (ii) reposition the brand; or (iii) reposition the competition.

Tactics for Existing or Emerging Markets

Three tactical positioning options are used for existing or emerging markets:

- negative and positive framing;
- product or functional attributes;
- unique selling point.

Negative and Positive Framing

When a new category is formed, or a new competitor enters an existing market, consumer knowledge is initially low and the objective of marketing communications is usually to create awareness, recognition and recall, as well as provide information. To encourage consumers to purchase a new product, effective marketing communications will connect perceived problems which consumers can relate to. Tactical positioning is aimed at emphasising negative framing: avoiding, preventing or solving a problem (Chandy *et al*, 2001). This type of positioning is most effective in the introductory stage. Comparisons with how the market is currently served may be particularly effective when the new brand communicates how it solves an existing problem. A low-fat margarine spreads like *I Can't Believe It's Not Butter* uses packaging design to achieve absolute category positioning (it looks like a pack of butter) and the brand name to achieve relative positioning (it tastes like butter – but without the negative attribute of fat content).

Can't Believe It's Not Butter

The opposite of negative framing is of course positive framing. When a product category is developing and more and more consumers realise the value of using a product, these positive

Flora Pro Activ

benefits should be stressed. Positive framing can be appropriate either when a new brand is being introduced or towards the end of the growth stage and beyond (Chandy *et al.* 2001). The ability of the brand to problem solve and answer category need is normally established at this stage, communicating new and more positive attributes about the brand. Communications for low-fat margarine spreads like *Flora* are changing and the focus is more on ingredients (like *pro-activ* cholesterol-reducing content) to promote health rather than the potential dangers with high-fat alternatives.

Product Attributes

With regards to the problem-solving nature of the positioning objectives in the introductory stage, the focus should be on the actual product attributes. The low degree of initial knowledge implies that the brand must build associations with actual product attributes and enhance brand attitude. Pioneering advantage is built by way of emphasising product attributes and functional benefits. *Gillette* emphasised a 'closer shave' whereas *Bic* focused on economy of time and money. Playing on emotions is more effective when consumers have some product experience and may relate the experience to the emotions in the advertising. Advertising for Broadband delivery brands, for example, has focused on attributes like Mbits and speed in the introductory stage. The case study on *Sky* in Chapter 4 shows the success of *Sky* introducing a PVR based on a campaign of celebrities like Kelly Brook, Felicity Kendall and Michael Parkinson promoting the 'control your time' benefits of using the product.

Unique Selling Point

Innovative entrants or market leaders will attract attention from other competitors who will see the market potential. New (me-too and differentiated) brands may be launched into the category, and the best way to achieve this absolute positioning in the early stages of the product life cycle is to identify a relevant category characteristic and link it strongly to the brand. Each brand should identify a unique selling point (USP), a product attribute or a benefit that the brand can use in its marketing communications. A good starting point for different USP tactics is looking at 'informational' and 'transformational' purchase motivations (e.g. problem removal, incomplete satisfaction, social approval, intellectual stimulation). If the competing brands in the category are positioned based on a specific purchase motivation, a unique position could be obtained by focusing on an aspect not covered by competitors. The brand should be perceived as standing alone and communicating the attribute to be perceived as unique. The brand should also make sure that the attribute is perceived as relevant. Consumers should be convinced enough to evaluate the attribute before they make purchases in the category, otherwise it cannot be regarded as a selling point.

A related model to USP is the IDU model (Importance – Delivery – Uniqueness). According to this model, the company should select an attribute that consumers feel is important to them, that the brand may 'deliver' (the attribute should be in line with the brand associations), and that is uniquely related to the brand (Rossiter and Percy 1998). The brand should be perceived as credible when communicating the attribute and there cannot be any conflicting associations.

Nude's brand stripped bare
© Nude Skincare. Reproduced with permission.

Cosmetics brand *Nude* is a good example of a 'challenger' brand entering a mature category with an attribute which is distinctive, and with a coordinated tactical positioning approach involving name, logo, typeface, packaging and advertising. *Nude*, which is an organic, bio-dynamic skincare range, has a brand narrative which tunes into the growing eco-consciousness: an ecologically friendly offer wrapped up in a very sensual, stripped-down and highly evocative story. The brand and packaging are stripped bare to evoke a very single-minded, minimal sensuality through packaging, website and in-store display. The perfectly balanced logotype and neutral, muted colours communicate the brand's essence: 'simplicity' and 'purity'. *Naked Cosmetics* have followed into this category with a similar positioning.

Tactics for Mature Markets

As the product category matures, competition is well established, consumers are more knowledgeable, and any differences in actual benefits between brands are likely to be limited. Over time, consumers tend to demand more functional and emotional benefits from each brand. Competitors tend to follow each other and differences are negligible and perceived rather than actual. Any differences are as a result of the way the brands are positioned due to marketing communications. There are three main ways to tactically show the position of brands in mature markets:

- emotional positioning;
- salience advertising;
- meaningless differentiation.

Emotional Positioning

As categories mature and consumers become more knowledgeable, there is less need to communicate about product attributes, and it is difficult to sustain a competitive advantage as competing brands are less likely to have unique product characteristics. Marketing communications must be used to evoke positive emotions around the brand (Chandy *et al.* 2001), sometimes referred to as 'emotional selling points'. 'Emotional resonance sometimes emerges independently of an underlying function' (Ries and Trout 1986). Creating strong emotional associations with the brand may be achieved by infusing a brand with images of beauty, humour, warmth or comfort. Emotional positioning is used for both low- and high-involvement transformational products, but may also be used for informational products. Although grounded in product attributes, this offers self-expression and affiliation. If the brand is successful in getting consumers to choose the brand for emotional reasons, it is much easier to maintain brand loyalty.

Salience Advertising

Salience advertising has to do with increasing the brand's versatility and complexity (Ehrenberg *et al.* 2002). Positioning should depict the brand's flexibility in appealing to a number of different users, as well as demonstrating the ability to fulfil various category needs, and be flexible enough to compete with smaller, non-salient brands (Meyvis and Janiszewski 2004). However, salience is built on creating mind space and this requires having advertising expenditure greater than competitors.

Meaningless Differentiation

Brand parity is high in a mature market and it is difficult for consumers to identify any real meaningful differences between brands – they will all be able to fulfil the category need, with broadly the same benefits and offer similar value propositions. Meaningless differentiation (Broniarczyk and Gershoff 2003, Brown and Carpenter 2000, Carpenter, Glazer and Nakamoto 1994) refers to the communication of trivial attributes that are not fundamentally significantly different from the competition. Examples of trivial attributes might be skiing jackets with 'alpine class filling', coffee that is produced with 'the Brazilian high-altitude, roasting process', mineral water that is 'bottled during full moon', shampoo with 'natural silk', and medication 'with aloe made in White Plains'. Is *Irn Bru* really 'made in Scotland from girders'? Other examples of trivial attributes are shown in Figure 7.5: *Piz Buin* sunscreen is Sahara tested; *Llanllyr* mineral water is made of spring water drawn from beneath organic fields for over 800 years; *Signal AIR* toothbrush has the 'air cushion effect'.

Trivial attributes are more effective in situations where consumers are convinced by peripheral attributes, for example, low-involvement product categories (Carpenter, Glazer and Nakamoto 1994). In these cases, consumers try to simplify their decision process by having a simple choice heuristic. As a result, they seek any kind of information that differs between brands even though it

Figure 7.5: Some examples of real products with trivial-like attributes

may not be a meaningful difference. Trivial attributes make the brand unique (at least in the short term) and consumers perceive value due to uniqueness even though they cannot fully appraise it (Brown and Carpenter 2000). Research shows that trivial attribute effectiveness is due to consumers tending to believe claims made by advertising (Broniaczyk and Gershoff 2003). If a company invests large amounts of money in producing an attribute and communicating about it, it may indicate to the market that the attribute has value (see the Erdem and Swait (1998) model in Chapter 6). There is more on trivial attributes in the Matter of Fact box below.

MATTER OF FACT

Trivial Attributes and Price Tiers

Meaningless differentiation has a highly interesting relationship to pricing. Research studies show that consumers like brands with trivial attributes even more at high prices. This relationship holds to some degree also when consumers are informed that the attribute does not improve the functioning of the product.

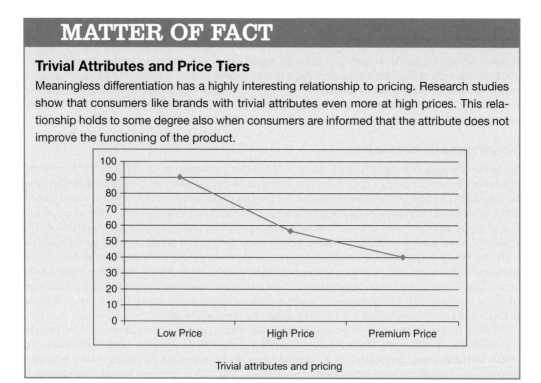

Trivial attributes and pricing

Evaluation of a brand without a trivial attribute at different prices. The brand's value is decreased when the price is increased (normal case).

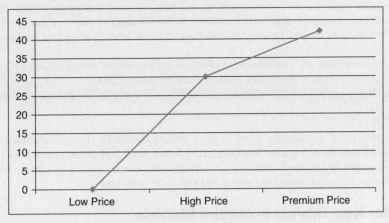

Trivial attributes and positive impact on pricing

Here, a trivial attribute is added to the product and the figure depicts the relative increase in brand value compared to the normal case at different price levels. The trivial attribute was subjectively evaluated. The relative value of the trivial attribute is highest at premium price.

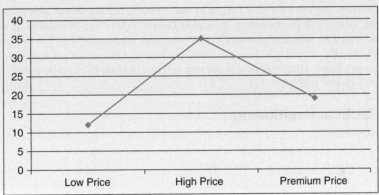

Trivial attributes and neutral impact on pricing

Here, a trivial attribute is added to the product and it is revealed to consumers that the attribute does not improve the product. The relative value of the trivial attribute is highest at high price and decreases at premium price.

Source: Carpenter, Glazer and Nakamoto (1994).

Five interesting empirical results have been presented in research on meaningless differentiation.

1. Trivial attributes are evaluated higher at high prices than at low prices. The reason is the credibility of the trivial attribute is decreased if the brand is inexpensive. For instance, if a shampoo brand contains an atypical trivial attribute or if a soda contains an exclusive aphrodisiacal herb, the brands send a signal that they have made efforts out of the ordinary to manufacture the product. Then, consumers expect that it should also cost more.

2. Trivial attributes may lead to enhanced brand equity and higher brand sales even if consumers know that the attribute has no real value. The explanation may be that the attribute in itself is associated with positive things (high-altitude coffee roasting and alpine class down jackets 'sound nice and reasonable') and that the attribute still is a differentiating factor from the competitors.

3. Trivial attributes should be positively evaluated by consumers (Broniarczyk and Gershoff 1997). In other words, they should be carefully selected and communicated so that consumer liking is ensured.

4. It has been shown that the positive effect of the trivial attribute is clearly reduced if a majority of the brands in the category start using it (Brown and Carpenter 2000).

5. Trivial attributes are more believable if a strong brand is using them (Broniarczyk and Gershoff 2003).

When this type of positioning tactic is used, efforts should be directed at maintaining 'sole rights' to the attribute by linking the attribute to the brand. *Carlsberg* humorously uses a '*Carlsberg* don't do....' to imply its assumed superiority. *Smirnoff* had a humorous 'I didn't know what . . . was until I discovered *Smirnoff* campaign which did much the same thing.

Tactics for New Brands in Mature Markets

The positioning tactics illustrated above are based on developing markets and brands launched into emerging markets. In a mature market, most brands are well known and the category knowledge is high. However, new brands can be launched in mature markets (e.g. *Ryanair* and *Flybe* in the airline industry) by following more or less the same tactics as well-established brands by using salience advertising, emotional positioning or meaningless differentiation or the tactics and techniques used in new markets.

Trivial attributes can work for new brands in mature markets if the brand uses consumer knowledge about the category (e.g. consistent packaging design, other core attributes). It may be more difficult to succeed with salience advertising and emotional positioning for new brands as they are relatively unknown. The situation is the same with brands in emerging markets as all new brands must educate consumers about what the brand is offering in terms of attributes and benefits. Therefore, the same techniques can be applied.

Relative Tactical Positioning

An essential part of a brand's tactical positioning is to strengthen the brand versus its competitors. It is possible, and sometimes very effective, to refer to the competitors – directly or indirectly – in tactical positioning. Techniques which can be used are:

- comparative advertising;
- in-store positioning;
- the attraction effect;
- using advertising alliances;
- exclusive distribution channels and analogies.

Comparative Advertising

Comparative advertising is the technique of using direct references to other brands in advertising and this can be done obliquely ('indirect' comparative advertising), where inferences are made about competition, or explicitly ('direct' comparative advertising) where at least one competitor is mentioned. *Unisys* communicated that it is more consumer oriented in its e-business solutions by indirectly referring to competitors: 'To become an e-business, some companies suggest you throw everything away. We suggest that you throw away their business cards'. In the post-credit crunch aftermath of the 2008 supermarket 'price wars', *ASDA* directly compares the amount of price cuts it has made compared to rival *Tesco*. The use of comparative advertising varies across countries to a large extent due to cultural differences and traditions in the advertising industries. It is relatively common in the USA, more common in the UK and Europe, but less so in South East Asian countries.

The effectiveness of this technique depends on market position; sometimes it is not effective for a market leader to compare with others as this may be misconstrued as undermining its own superiority (Chattopadhyay 1998). Less familiar brands and relatively weaker brands may use others as a benchmark and attempt to make consumers perceive the smaller brand as offering similar value or even be regarded as superior on the comparison attribute (Chattopadhyay 1998, Grewal *et al.* 1997). *Avis* used this technique to compare itself to market leader *Hertz* by implying that bigger companies are more complacent because, in order to compete, *Avis* had to 'try harder', thus implying better service than the competition.

Research has shown that comparative advertising makes consumers think about and cognitively reflect on the brands that are compared to a higher extent (Grewal *et al.* 1997). A smaller brand gains when emotional factors become less relevant in the category. Even if consumers do not like the comparative advertising, smaller brands may still get a positive 'delayed effect' because of the thought processes induced by the comparative advertising. When the advertising cognitions are forgotten, the comparison at brand level remains in consumers' minds where the smaller brand has communicated an advantage compared to the big competitor (Chattopadhyay 1998). By using comparative advertising, the smaller brand signals that consumers can 'count on them'. More about comparative advertising is found in the Matter of Fact box below.

MATTER OF FACT

Positive Comparisons and Alignable Differences in Comparative Advertising

One problem with comparative advertising is that it lacks believability and credibility. This problem has been attributed to the fact that comparisons are often made in a way that the referent brand is portrayed in a negative and derogatory manner (We are OK. You're not OK). A research study shows that communications showing positive comparisons (You are OK. We are better) are better received: advertised claims are more believable, the brand attitude is enhanced and the attributions towards the advertiser are more positive.

Another issue in comparative advertising is how the between-brand comparison should be made. Should the advertising communicate relative differences on the same attribute (e.g. taste, speed of service) or should it communicate that the main difference is distinctive attributes (e.g. taste or speed of service). Alignable differences (same attributes) are easier to process for consumers because the advertising contains less information. Moreover, the focus is clearly on relative differences on one salient attribute. In empirical research, the target brand evaluation is systematically increased when alignability is increased.

The car brand *SAAB* used comparative advertising against *Volvo* where it stated that 'Being in a car crash with a *Volvo* is safe. If you are sitting in a *SAAB*'. This advertisement used positive comparisons (was not *directly* derogatory towards *Volvo*) and alignability (compared the same attribute – safety).

Sources: Jain and Posavac (2004), Zhang, Kardes and Cronley (2002).

In-Store Positioning

As we have seen, in-store positioning may be problematic for manufacturer brands as there may not be full control over how the brand is presented. The retail chain (or individual retailer) often unilaterally plans displays, merchandising, POS materials, what context each brand presents and will allocate space sometimes unfairly or irrationally. Attempts must be made by brand owners to influence factors which will affect the in-store brand awareness, clarity and liking. A new chocolate bar may fail, not because of its quality or the way the brand is packaged or advertised, but because the sales-force ability or the trade incentives to achieve 'facings' (number of bars in a row of all competing chocolate bars in a confectionery stand or on-counter display unit) have not achieved these tactical objectives. A kitchen or bathroom manufacturer, supplying product to *B&Q DIY* stores, who gains only one display per store, will lose the ability to sell as many kitchen units or bathroom suites through upwards of 1000 stores in the UK. Both of these examples underline the importance of positioning tactics to achieve 'opportunities to see and sell' in retail in-store situations. Similarly, if *Macy's* presents its underwear brand *Alfani* close to *Calvin Klein* and *Polo Ralph Lauren* underwear, or *Carrefour* place its *J'Aime* healthy product line next to major manufacturer brands, this may severely affect consumer perceptions and sales.

Perceptions are critical in the positioning of different brands in a category. Some insightful research by Buchanan, Simmons and Bickart (1999) on brand perceptions is presented in the Matter of Fact box below.

MATTER OF FACT

Consumer Expectations and Beliefs

Buchanan, Simmons and Bickart (1999) found that a less familiar brand may not always gain from being displayed next to a stronger and more familiar brand (also called 'high-equity' brand). Conversely, it is not always the case that the high-equity brand loses in comparison. Certain conditions must be fulfilled.

Marketers may affect the brand perceptions of the own brand and of competitors' brands at the point of purchase. The process is based on two sequential issues on how brands should be presented in the store:

1. Where high-equity brands are presented with less familiar brands, the display may be mixed or separate. If the merchandise presentation is separate (e.g. in different departments or clearly separated within the department) the value of the high-equity brand is unaffected by the less familiar context brands, and it is a good idea for high-equity brands to be presented together with other high-equity brands. For mixed displays, perceptions may be affected.
2. Perceptions are also dependent on which brand has precedence in the mixed presentation. Research has shown that consumers believe that brands in 'prime locations' (get a lot of quality store space with maximum traffic flow) are: (i) good; (ii) important; and (iii) of good quality. If an unfamiliar brand has precedence over a high-equity brand in a mixed-store display, consumers will assume that they are similar or even that the unfamiliar brand must be better. If the high-equity brand gets precedence, consumers will expect that the unfamiliar brand is different or worse.

These findings are summarised in the following table.

Mixed in-store display	Unfamiliar brand is different	Unfamiliar brand is similar
High-equity brand has precedence	Expectations confirmed Stored judgements are used	Expectations disconfirmed Judgements are constructed
Expect differences between brands	High-equity brand reinforced	High-equity brand revised
Unfamiliar brand has precedence Expect similarities between brands	Expectations disconfirmed Judgements are constructed High-equity brand revised	Expectations confirmed Stored judgements are used High-equity brand reinforced

In-store positioning of high-equity brands and an unfamiliar context brand

Therefore, consumer expectations and beliefs may be sustained or reinforced as consumers use brand knowledge 'stored' from other marketing communications. The 'challenger' brand must attempt to get consumers to 'disconfirm' their expectations in one way or another by thinking about what they are seeing in the store environment. At that point, consumers are forced to construct new evaluative criteria at the point of purchase.

Source: Buchanan, Simmons and Bickart (1999).

The Attraction Effect

When new brands enter a market category, consumers may alter their current brand judgements. This is known as the attraction effect, which shows that the perception and sales of one brand may be enhanced when a similar brand is introduced in the category (Ratneshwar, Shocker and Stewart 1987). Table 7.3 shows the results of a research study on microwave ovens, where the low-priced ($109.99) *Emerson* brand had a 57% market share and high-priced ($179.99) *Panasonic* 43% market share, and the attraction effect of *Panasonic's* decision to introduce an even higher priced ($199.99) *Panasonic II* on market shares.

The *Panasonic Corporation* increased its market share to 73% (an increase of 30 percentage points) because *Panasonic II* changed the reference point in the category and the original *Panasonic* gained a lot of sales because it was not perceived as equally expensive (see Riezebos 2003). These types of brands

Brand	Market share before new brand introduction	Market share after new brand introduction	Market share effect
Emerson	57%	27%	−30 percentage points
Panasonic	43%	60%	+17 percentage points
Panasonic II		13 %	

Table 7.3: Market shares of microwave sales of *Emerson, Panasonic* and *Panasonic II* in 2003

Source: Riezebos (2003). Reproduced with permission.

Attribute	Brand A	Brand B	Decoy A	Decoy B
Price (US dollars)	2.60	1.80	3.00	1.80
Quality (0 = low; 100 = high)	70	50	70	40
Market shares (only A and B)	43%	57%		
Market shares (A + B + Decoy A)	63%	37%	< 2%	
Market shares (A + B + Decoy B)	25%	75%		< 2%

Table 7.4: Adding asymmetrically dominated alternatives

Source: Huber, Payne, and Puto (1982). Reproduced with permission.

are called 'decoys' and you may remember the same positioning tactic was used by *Smirnoff* against its rivals *Wolfschmidt* in the vodka category (see 'Positioning in Focus' in Chapter 6). In 1982, Huber, Payne and Puto tested this decoy phenomenon for the first time, which is illustrated in Table 7.4.

There are two brands in the 'six-pack beer' category: Brand A which is more expensive and has higher quality than Brand B. Market shares are 43% and 57%, respectively. As we can see from Table 7.4, the new brand introductions (or decoys) clearly affect the market shares of Brands A and B. When Brand A competes with Brand B and the decoy A (which has the same quality but a higher price than Brand A), the market share of Brand A increases from 43% to 63%. The market share of Brand B decreases from 57% to about 37%. When decoy B is introduced (which is the same price but lower quality than Brand B), the market share of Brand B increases from 57% to 75%, and the market share of Brand A decreases from 43% to about 25%. Few customers, less than 2%, select the decoy brand.

The attraction effect is normally greater for high-quality brands (studies show an increase of 15–25%) than for low-quality brands (studies show an increase of 2–7%) and for durable goods more than for fast-moving consumer goods (Heath and Chatterjee 1995), with consumers being drawn towards the part of the category that has the largest number of alternatives (Riezebos 2003). They also show that 'non-dominated decoys' (decoys that are similar to an existing brand but compete on a certain attribute) may affect the category structure. For non-dominated decoys, the similar brand is unaffected but the market share for the competitor is reduced (on average 17–19%).

In these instances, it is important tactically to position brand associations that are linked to salient category attributes.

MATTER OF FACT

More Context Effects

Ideal point shifts – the category ideal can shift from a leading brand to another by the introduction of a new brand in the category. By introducing a third brand that is different from other brands in the category but mostly different from the category leader, the ideal shifts from the category leader to one of the smaller brands in the category. Other attributes or attribute levels emerge as relatively more important than the original ones as a result of the new brand introduction. This is illustrated in the example of the *Flora* brand in the margarine spread category where brands with lower fat content have been introduced (Prelec, Wernerfelt and Zettelmeyer 1997).

Extremeness aversion – this context effect has to do with the notion that consumers dislike losses more than they like gains. Therefore, brands that are positioned intermediately on an attribute dimension (40–60% fat instead of 30% or 80% fat) will be chosen more often than brands on extreme positions. One can say that each attribute advantage has a perceptual cost. If a consumer sees an alternative with high levels on one particular attribute, they feel that they probably lose much on the attribute that they are 'rejecting'. For instance, high fat/good taste has a health cost; low fat/bad taste has a taste cost. Balanced attributes should therefore be preferred to more extreme alternatives since losses are higher valued than gains (Simonson and Tversky 1992).

Range and frequency effects – the similarity to another brand is strongly affected by the presence of brands in the total category set. This implies that two brands will be perceived as more or less similar to each other (i.e. as competitors or not) based on the context in which they are presented.

One study shows that the similarity of two brands is affected by new brand introductions in the following manner. If the new brand is 'placed between' the two old brands, the old brands are perceived as less similar (the frequency effect). If the new brand is 'placed outside' of the two old brands, the similarity between the old brands increases (the range effect) (Pan and Lehmann 1993).

Context variation – an experiment tested the effect of context variation on consumer loyalty to a certain product. The study tested whether consumer loyalty towards a potato chips brand increased when consumers could choose between different kinds of beverages compared to when they had to choose within a beverage sub-category. Consumers made four choices of a brand constellation consisting of potato chips and beverages. In all three scenarios, they could choose between four different potato chips for each choice. In one scenario, they had to select one of four cola brands in all four choices (no context variation). In a second scenario, they could choose between cola brands in choices 1 and 3 and choose between lemon/lime sodas in choices 2 and 4 (moderate variation). In a third scenario, lemon/lime sodas were exchanged to orange juice in choices 2 and 4 (high variation). The highest (lowest) potato chips brand loyalty was demonstrated in the third scenario where the context variation was the highest (lowest) (Menon and Kahn 1995).

Advertising Alliances

We discuss only advertising here but alliances may also comprise cross-merchandising and in-store promotions. We will come back to joint in-store promotions in a later chapter. Advertising alliances may be based on either high product complementarity or low product complementarity. An example of high complementarity is the *Kellogg's Corn Flakes* and *Tropicana* orange juice advertising alliance that aimed to link the brands strongly to the breakfast category. At high product complementarity, the connection between the two product categories is easily understood. To cooperate with a brand in a naturally related product category is appropriate when one wants to enhance brand awareness in the own product category and/or link the brand and the product category stronger to the usage situation (Samu, Krishnan and Smith 1999).

The product categories are not so clearly connected at low complementarity. This may be useful when one wants to communicate an abstract brand benefit or brand association (Samu, Krishnan and Smith 1999). The fashion brand *Fruit of the Loom* collaborated with the car brand *Dodge* to communicate the abstract association: comfort. It is important that the advertising is designed so that consumers elaborate on the advertisement content so that the message gets across. You can read more about this in Chapters 11 and 12.

Distribution Channels and Advertising Analogies

As we have seen relative positioning is about creating a better perceived brand position in comparison to the other competitors in a category. Exclusive distribution allows a brand to clarify its position by selling its products only through specially selected retailers or by accentuating perceived quality

French car under German clothing

by selling different variants of the product in different retail channels (Keller 2003). Alternatively, oblique or indirect reference may be implied by using analogies in the positioning tactics (Gregan-Paxton *et al.* 2002). This cannot be done with direct reference to the brand, other associations may be used. This was done by French car company *Citroën* who used 'German engineering' as a reference point to accentuate the quality of its *Citroën C5* brand's 'Unmistakeably German' campaign. The images in the advertisements – a traditional Bavarian bar and grill, sections

of the Autobahn and the historic Brandenburg Gate in Berlin – all played on 'teutonic' references. This positioning tactic was also used by *Ford* whose campaigns for the *Ford Focus* delivered the message 'European styling; German technology'.

IMPROVE THE POSITION

Sometimes a brand may need to adjust or revitalise its position in the market. Outside factors and market trends may pull the brand and the product category in a different direction (e.g. when computers took over from typewriters and Internet downloading challenged the music industry). As consumer habits and behaviours gradually change, consumers may also update their evaluative criteria when making purchases in the category. We have seen several times in this book how new product attributes affect the consumer decision-making process: a brand that is strongly linked to a certain attribute may become marginalised if the consumers start to evaluate other attributes when making purchases. The brand may need to be revitalised.

Based on the IDU model (Importance – Delivery – Uniqueness), there are five positioning tactics which can be used for brands that want to improve their position:

1. Increase the perceived value of an attribute for the brand (D).
2. Increase the importance (I) of an attribute that is uniquely related to the brand (i.e. where the brand is better than competitors).
3. Reduce the perceived value (D for competitor) on an attribute that the competitor is positioned on.
4. Add a new relevant (I) attribute to the category, an attribute that becomes unique (U) for the brand.
5. Change the choice rule so that it favours the own brand (IDU).

The first tactic is the simplest and the fifth is the most complicated and most difficult to use (Rossiter and Percy 1998).

THE CUMULATIVE MEMETIC EFFECTS OF POSITIONING

The concept of 'memes' dates back to the pioneering work of Richard Dawkins in 1976 and later explication in 1999. Memes are replicators of cultural meaning. They are units of association in memory that are culturally transmitted as received ideas or behaviours. The relevance of memes to marketers is that they can be mapped and used to audit how brands are positioned in the minds of consumers. For example, *Fed Ex*, as category leader, may 'own' the association 'overnight'. Challenger brands will know that their success in the category where *Fed Ex* has brand leadership will depend on positioning their brand against 'overnight'. This is because consumers have become accustomed to the association of *Fed Ex* as being synonymous with the category's chief point of salience. This can be a disadvantage as well. The cases of *Volvo* being memetically associated with 'safety', as *Hoover* was with 'vaccuum cleaning', prove that it can be a millstone for brands should circumstances change.

CLOSING CASE STUDY

Green & Black's: Is Green & Black's the New Chocolate? Telling a Complete Brand Narrative

Green and Black and White

© Green & Black's Chocolate Ltd. Reproduced with permission.

Everything in the marketing mix and marketing communications mix communicates. But the visual imagery of the brand – the name, the logotypes, the advertising, and, often most importantly, the packaging – helps to tell the complete brand story. According to Ford (2007) 'creativity has no boundaries, yet in the creative industry we think of ourselves as operating in separate disciplines – design, advertising, promotion, interactive. However, today, more than ever before, our clients need work that creates a deep lasting impact. For this to happen, brands increasingly need to tell a more seamless, complete narrative . . . to operate in a more holistic manner'.

A product has a name, a logo, unique packaging – all material markers of the brand. They are the shells of meaning which will speak to target audiences and carry the brand story. But, without a story, they are devoid of meaning and will only be informational not transformational devices. The most famous brands have 'markers': a name (*McDonald's* and *IBM*); a logo (the *Nike* swoosh); a distinctive product design feature (the *Harley's* engine sound) or any other design element which is associated with the product (Holt 2004). But they have also been filled with meaning: the brand's narrative. This is even more critical for challenger brands which enter mature markets and need to evoke a brave new story through the visual identity of the brand against the competition. Such a brand is *Green & Black's*.

(Continued)

To enter a mature market like the chocolate category, *Green & Black's* – as a challenger brand – required more than just accentuating communicated differences.

Like *Ben & Jerry's* and *Innocent Smoothies*, positioning against well-established categories cannot be based on me-too positioning. Inspiring a market with a new vision, passion and total immersion in a new narrative is required. Tactical positioning needed to project the soul of the brand in the same way that Anita Roddick's *The Body Shop* had done. It had to capture its inherent fabric and texture and all elements of the tactical positioning – name, logo, packaging, advertising, website and all other brand encounters with the target audience – had to accord with the strategic positioning inherent in the product range and the orientation of the company. This is *Green & Black's* story.

It all started back in 1991 when Craig Sams, founder of *Whole Earth* – the pioneering organic food company – was sent a sample of dark 70% chocolate made from organic cocoa beans. His wife, environment columnist for *The Times* and confirmed chocoholic, Josephine Fairley, found the half-eaten bar on Craig's desk and sampled some for herself. The intense flavour was unique and unlike anything she had tasted before. Jo was convinced other chocolate lovers would appreciate it in the same way she had and they set about making the world's first organic chocolate. The final product was a high-quality, bittersweet dark chocolate bar, packed with 70% organic cacao from Belize – enough to make chocolate fans sit up and take notice (www.greenandblacks.com).

The name *Green & Black's* at once created a linked association to the heritage of confectionery brands like *Callard & Bowser* and *Barker & Dobson* and brilliantly symbolised the true foundations of the products: *green* for organic and *black* for the deep, rich dark brown (almost black) colour of the chocolate. In 1994, the *Maya Gold* flavour was created to capture the taste of the rainforests where the cocoa is grown. When it was discovered that cocoa farmers were being penalised by larger confectionery companies who were driving cocoa prices down, they agreed to pay the farmers a fair price for their crops. This established a fundamental difference from existing competitors in the UK chocolate category and was subsequently awarded the Fairtrade Mark by the Fairtrade Foundation.

The *Green & Black's* company principles and brand ethos are encapsulated in the 'every step from bean to bar' values which are applied to all product ranges including ice cream, cereal chocolate bars and biscuits.

There is a paradox to this: the Fairtrade Foundation charges *Green & Black's* a commission of 2% on its *Maya Gold* sales and this has meant that, whilst *Maya Gold* helped *Green & Black's* forge its reputation for gourmet chocolate, it remains the only Fairtrade product in the company's 15-strong portfolio. The company prefers to reinvest in ethical supply in its own way. The remaining 14 bars are simply organic, a far more promising niche. While UK sales of Fairtrade products grew by 40% in 2005, organic chocolate bars are seeing a 60% growth year on year – and in the US, the figure is 200%.

However, some of *Green & Black's* competitors have embraced 'organic and fair' schemes such as *Kaoka* (in France) and *Rapunzel* (in Germany), and others are looking at a new ethical trademark being developed by the Soil Association. Critics of *Green & Black's* – and of its new owner *Cadbury* in particular – say spurning Fairtrade saves the multinational money by avoiding the Foundation's 2% levy and enabling it to buy at depressed market prices with no fixed minimum for growers. Still, *Green & Black's* has 30 employees and an annual turnover of £22 million, hardly a chocolate button next to *Cadbury's*, but enough to make it the biggest organic chocolate brand in the UK and now the US. It is the fastest-growing UK confectionery brand, with year-on-year growth of 69%. And it achieved this by building a brand narrative of ethical, organic quality chocolate differentiated by salience and emotion from the traditional manufacturers.

QUESTIONS

1. What tactical positioning elements allowed *Green & Black's* to build its brand narrative in order to differentiate from the existing UK manufacturers?

2. What long-term impact will not paying the Fairtrade Association for more than one brand have on *Green & Black's* positioning?

3. Do you think consumers are more interested in the tactics like product and packaging of the *Green & Black's* products or are these dependent upon the long-term brand narrative?

CHAPTER SUMMARY

In this chapter we have presented some central tools for tactical positioning. It is important for the brand to use these to create awareness, clarity and liking for the brand name, the logotype, the packaging, the attributes and so forth. The main idea is to ensure that consumers do not feel any uncertainty or hesitation with regard to what the brand stands for and what the brand can do for them. The tactical positioning is an important tool to create the right connections so that the brand gets the right amount of mind space.

We have looked at communicative tools for brand elements, different ways to communicate brand beliefs over the product life cycle, how the brand may use other brands to strengthen its position, and tactics for a brand that needs to improve its position in the market.

REFLECTIVE QUESTIONS

a. What tactical positioning techniques help a brand to obtain: (i) brand awareness (recall and/or recognition); (ii) brand clarity; and (iii) brand liking?

b. Select one relatively new product category and one mature product category. Collect at least five advertisements from each product category and compare the approaches. Are they following the guidelines presented in Table 7.1 and discussed in this chapter?

c. Trivial attributes are often based on geographical locations and cultural contexts. Use your own country as a starting point and identify country-related aspects that may be used as trivial attributes for certain products.

d. Select one of your favourite brands. Analyse how the brand has worked on its brand elements (name, typeface, logotype and so forth) and how the brand is communicating about its benefits. Is the brand clear and consistent when it comes to tactical positioning? If you find imperfections, suggest improvements.

e. When it comes to brand names, there is a conflict between brand awareness and brand clarity on one hand and brand flexibility on the other hand. Discuss this conflict.

RESEARCH PROJECTS

Brown and Carpenter (2000) argue that consumers' choice heuristics are often based on placing disproportionate importance on 'trivial attributes'. Their research shows that the value placed on minor brand features is instrumental but perceived as being integral. Look up the paper from the *Journal of Consumer Research* (26) and evaluate how this argument adds to our discussion on tactical positioning.

For a brand of your choice, critique the tactical positioning elements present in that brand's marketing communications.

PART 3

IMPLEMENTATION AND CONTROL
OF MARKETING COMMUNICATIONS

CHAPTER  8

BUILDING BRAND EQUITY

"At birth, a brand is all potential: it can develop in any possible way. With time, however, it tends to lose some degree of freedom; while gaining conviction, its facets take shape delineating the brand's legitimate territory."
Kapferer (2000, p. 106)

"A brand is a business strategy to encourage us to consume one product over its competitors and it is a sign loaded with meaning that we choose to consume because we feel we relate to it."
Williams (2000, p. 7)

This chapter discusses the concept of branding, both the corollary and driving force of segmentation and positioning. In any product category, brands differentiate the seller's promise to deliver a set of specific features, benefits and value, sometimes better than the competition, (Kapferer 1992, Aaker 1997) by creating meaningful images in the minds of targeted customers (Keller 1993, Shocker, Srivastava and Ruekert 1994). Defining a brand as 'a name, term, symbol or design (or combination of them) which is intended to signify the goods or services of one seller or groups of sellers and to differentiate them from those of the competitors' (Kotler 2000) or broadening this to include tangible features (Dibb *et al.* 1997) like verbal or physical response-producing stimuli suggests the idea of transmitting a range of explicit and implicit cues to potential customers.

After reading this chapter, you'll be able to:

- Establish the function of brands to the main stakeholders.
- Analyse how brands are an asset for organisations and a source of value for customers.
- Demonstrate the sources and concepts of brand equity.
- Provide a structure for the financial and economic outcomes of brand equity.
- Describe how the brand can be developed through different types of brand expansion.
- Understand how brand extensions are used to develop and capitalise on the brand's potential as a result of positioning.
- Analyse the market opportunities for brand portfolios and design effective market coverage through several brands.

Successful brands connect with target audiences both functionally and emotionally. Branding is about 'adding emotional meaning to a product or service, a strong layer of emotional affinity, or identification, between brand and constituent [target audience]' (Bergstrom, Blumenthal and Crothers 2002, p. 134). The creation and maintenance of brands requires the development of deep, salient associations which resonate not just in terms of short-term category need fulfilment, but also long-term meaningful symbiotic relationships from which organisations achieve lifetime loyalty and consumers acquire individual and group meaning. The relationship-building element of branding gives it prominence in marketing communications, and it is important to recognise that this is a two-way process where customer/brand interaction is a reciprocal activity (Blackston 1993). Branding is about the creation of value (perceived or actual) over and above the utilitarian function of products. We need to be sure what we are dealing with here, so let's start by distinguishing the difference between a product and a brand.

The product is part of the brand; it is not the brand. It may offer the market a unique aspect of design or function, but it is the brand which is the promise, implicit in the name, the logo and packaging and all communication encounters. However, these elements may be instrumental in achieving differentiation and even sustainable competitive advantage, but they need a history of use, a build up of dialogues and to be firmly established in the minds of consumers. As Holt (2004) points out, without a heritage, without customer experiences, 'the brand does not truly exist . . . these markers are empty . . . as they are devoid of meaning'. All the elements which we will soon examine as constituting brand equity – awareness, perceived quality, associations and loyalty – need to be cumulatively established and nurtured (Aaker 2001).

Branding, with its origins in the marking of cattle to signify ownership, has turned full circle. Now, branding is about narratives – the story arc that is negotiated for the brand and the life experience of the consumer. In order for a brand to survive, it has to be perpetually salient and the consumer permanently engaged. The consumer, in effect, owns the brand and indeed owns the brand narrative. An organisation can attempt to create a brand, but it is customers who will determine whether a brand comes alive or not (Timacheff and Rand 2001).

OPENING CASE STUDY

Isklar: Pure Glacier. Pure Branding

'I am ice. I am as cold as a Norwegian winter'. So speaks The *Isklar* Ice Woman who 'once born, dazzles briefly like the glacier from which she originates before dissolving, gradually and beautifully morphing into a bottle of natural mineral water'. This is as pure a product as you can get – *Isklar* is Norwegian for 'ice clear'. It is also pure branding. But as the mythical Ice Woman travels on her 'long journey through wilderness and Hardanger mountains', the brand had to travel all the way to the UK before it entered its home market: Norway.

Isklar bottles project product qualities

The UK campaign was aimed at 'mass-market premium consumers' through quality TV and press advertisements in upmarket publications and lifestyle magazines like *Marie Claire* and *Waitrose Food Illustrated*, and is now distributed in stores like *Waitrose* and *Morrisons*. The glacier theme

Isklar Ice Woman projects brand image

is carried through onto the packaging and point-of-sale materials. A specially designed bottle was inspired by the crystal qualities of ice, mirroring nature by reflecting and refracting light through its angular-shaped facets. The bottling of water is, in some ways, the ultimate testimony to marketing communications: the branding of a commodity which is, to all intents and purposes, free. As lifestyle becomes an increasingly relevant part of our lives, a bottle of water has been positioned as healthy, convenient, calorie-free, and now part of ritual consumption. Coffee houses were the consumer choice of the 1950s; soft drinks boomed from the 1960s on. Now, the European bottled water market is the fastest-growing drinks sector in the world and continues to outperform the overall soft drinks market.

With the European market for still water becoming increasingly competitive, and established brands such as the French *Evian*, Swedish *Volvic* and British *Buxton* dominating the category, the Norwegian company decided to build the brand initially in mainstream retailers across the UK. In the spring of 2008, with a £2.5 million communications budget, the brand positioning had three main platforms: product, personification and heritage.

The *Isklar* product is naturally filtered through glacier ice and aquifer rock, creating water that is so exceptionally low in mineral content it delivers an unmatchable crisp taste that is both pure and invigorating. The Ice Woman is the brand personification of the mystery, purity and spirit of the mythical *Isklar* brand world – an embodiment of *Isklar's* pristine glacial provenance. And then there is the Norwegian brand heritage. Captured at source from a 6000-year-old glacier in the remote Hardanger region, a breathtaking expanse of unsurpassed natural beauty with soaring mountains, cascading waterfalls and mysterious crystal-clear fjords, the bottling of *Isklar* has resonance with the Hardanger legend. As far back as 1823, ice from the same glacier from which *Isklar* water flows was regularly shipped to London.

And so, with brand equity built on foreign shores, the brand has at last been launched in Norway. In November 2008, *Isklar* was prelaunched in Oslo and Bergen, increasing the Norwegian water category by 90% and now represents a staggering 45% of the Norwegian home market. The home company *airline Norwegian* increased its sales of bottled water by 40% after switching to *Isklar* and now the plans are to expand in the rest of the Scandinavian countries and enter markets in the Middle East, China and Japan.

QUESTIONS

1. Is it ethical to bottle water and present an idealised image of a natural product?

2. Distinguish between the elements of 'product' and 'brand' in the *Isklar* case.

3. What are the key brand ingredients which will make *Isklar* succeed or not in the rest of the Scandinavian markets?

4. Was it a good marketing communications strategy to launch in another market before entering the Norwegian home market?

UNDERSTANDING WHAT BRANDING IS

In a global market characterised by overcapacity, proliferation of media and the increasing fragmentation of consumer markets, traditional channels and methods of communication are being challenged and undermined: consumer passivity has morphed into interactivity. Incredible advances in technology have compressed product life cycles; retailer brand dominance has transformed the marketplace; demarcation lines of competition have become blurred. As a result, Aufreiter, Elzinga and Gordon (2003) argue that brands are losing their distinctiveness, becoming commoditised and getting lost in the clutter of saturated categories. This is echoed in Aaker's (1991) comment about brands being mismanaged, and in later research by Clancy and Trout (2002) who reported on 40 out of 46 categories where the impact of branding was less evident.

Indeed, as a channel of communication, a brand is 'a democratic one whose audiences are free to vote against it at any time' (MacCrae 1995) and there is pressure to make sure investment in branding is correctly applied and managed. In today's devastating economic climate, some have referred to a Darwinian effect in branding (Groucutt 2006) where even famous brands like *Woolworths* have perished without a sustainable truth, narrative or category purpose.

Research shows that the reason why organisations invest in branding is that brand image and reputation does enhance differentiation and can lead to brand equity (McEnally and de Chernatony 1999). According to Lindström and Andersen (2000, p. 3): 'Huge amounts are invested in the development and maintenance of brands. The reason is that strong brands and consumer loyalty to them are the be-all and end-all for the owners of the brand'. Every organisation, in every country, in every context now has a brand-building imperative instilled into their corporate strategy and modus operandi.

The combined creative synergy of segmentation, targeting and positioning, together with the creation and management of salient brands not only achieves sustainable competitive distinction, but can act as a catalyst for category transformation and help the process of meaningful consumption. Rubinstein (1996) argues that branding goes beyond being merely another element of integrated marketing communications and should be regarded as an integral part of the overall business process, embedded in the whole company not just marketing; the essence of the brand must be present from production to communication. In an increasingly global market, brands are the only truly international language (Kapferer 1994).

From an organisation's perspective, we need to analyse the context within which the brand is created:

- Which market or markets do we want to target?
- What is the customer profile and behaviour of the target market?
- Who are or will be our main competitors?
- What do we want our brand(s) to stand for?
- How do we ensure that our target audience (or audiences) perceives our brand as the superior alternative?

- Can we ensure that we have a better position than our competitors?
- Do we use one brand or several brands to achieve effective market coverage?

From a consumer's perspective, branding should answer the questions:

- What is it?
- What's it for?
- What does it do?
- What will it do for me?
- What are the benefits for me?
- Why is it different to my regular brand?
- Will it be worth using this brand long term?

What brand is present in every country on Earth, has fierce ever-growing competition, has a red and white logo and relies on marketing communications and a rich brand heritage to help create consumer meaning and achieve its organisational objectives? No, it's not *Coca-Cola* for a change! This competitive environment describes the market dynamics of the *Red Cross*. Except for the fact that the exchange relationship is not a product or service; it is an expression of altruism or the partial relief of guilt. It's not paid for by the end user. And of course we refer to people being 'donors' not consumers. But it is consumption and whether or not the transaction is for the purpose of 'feeding the world' or consoling the conscience, as soon as we sign our direct debit forms and start a long-term relationship with the *Red Cross*, we are making a choice between forgoing expenditure on other consumables and other competition: *Oxfam*, *Feed Africa*, *Greenpeace*, or even the local church charity.

How do we make this choice? Every time we see the *Red Cross* flag, emblazoned with its distinctive logo, at the site of a disaster or relief effort; every time we see a hospital unit or listen to a *Red Cross* spokesperson, it is like 'public relations' coverage for the *Red Cross*. What happens when we see harrowing images juxtaposed with entertainment from our favourite comedian? Do we change brand allegiance and buy into *Comic Relief*? Charity brand proliferation has caused 'compassion fatigue' and these organisations must use all the power of segmentation, targeting and positioning to build and sustain their brands. To do this, there has to be mutual, sustainable benefit, and in that context, it is no different to branding products for consumption.

Branding is increasingly seen from a holistic perspective; a 'fundamental strategic process that involves all parts of the firm in its delivery' (Randall 2000, p. 3). As Hart and Murphy (1998, p. 2) put it, companies are increasingly concerned with a 'brand's Gestalt, with assembling together and maintaining a mix of values, both tangible and intangible, which are relevant to consumers and which meaningfully and appropriately distinguish one supplier's brand from that of another'. The brand is therefore a synthesis of all physical, aesthetic, rational and psychological elements manifest in the market and in the network of associations in the mind of the consumer.

From an organisation's point of view, a brand allows profitable dialogue with its most valuable asset: the customer. From a customer's perspective, 'brands are part of the fabric of life' (Dan'l 1994) and are a promise that allows the construction of identity, affiliation and meaning. It is a 'contract, albeit a virtual one, between a company and a customer' (Kapferer 1994, p. 16). Brands are the end product, the focus of marketing communications and the driving force of any market-oriented organisation. Keller (2001, p. 1) says that 'strong brands are properly positioned, stay consistent and are relevant to customers over time, delivering the benefits that customers truly desire'. In determining what constitutes a 'strong brand', he lists the following attributes which the best and most enduring brands have:

1. the brand excels at delivering the benefits customers truly desire;
2. the brand stays relevant;
3. the pricing strategy is based on consumers' perceptions of value;
4. the brand is properly positioned;
5. the brand is consistent;
6. the brand portfolio and hierarchy make sense;
7. the brand makes use of and coordinates a full repertoire of marketing activities to build equity;

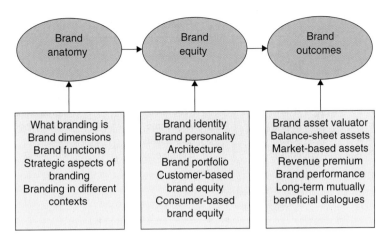

Figure 8.1: Brand anatomy, brand equity and brand outcome framework

8. the brand managers understand what the brand means to consumers;
9. the brand is given proper support, and that support is sustained over a long time; and
10. the company monitors sources of brand equity.

The first task of integrated marketing communications is to have an understanding of the equity of the brand. If branding is seen as the hub of all marketing communications (Proctor and Kitchen 2000), it will soon become clear why brand equity is the hub of branding. This chapter deals specifically with what constitutes brand equity, its applications and how it can be measured. In order to make sense of this, we need to establish what the key dimensions and functions of branding are (the brand anatomy as it were), what the key elements of brand equity are and how they can be used; and what can be achieved from managing brand equity and how we can measure it (Figure 8.1).

DIMENSIONS OF BRANDS

The American Marketing Association defines a brand as 'a name, term, sign, symbol, or design, or a combination of them, intended to identify the goods and services of one seller or a group of sellers and to differentiate them from those of competitors' (see Kotler and Keller 2006, p. 274). Plummer (1984) suggested defining a brand on three dimensions: (i) physical attributes; (ii) functional attributes or benefits associated with using the brand; and (iii) personality traits associated with the brand. Therefore, to get into 'the minds of the consumer' and create bonding relationships, brands have to be differentiated from products.

Kapferer (2004) describes the product–brand relationship where expectations are tangible and intangible (experiential ones like driving pleasure or reliability), where the 'halo effect' of branding is a major source of value created: knowing the name of the brand increases the positive perceptions of the brand beyond the visible cues and the intangible, invisible advantages (Figure 8.2). The product contains the intrinsic features and functions; the brand grows out from the basic, undifferentiated product, carrying its values and identity into new markets and categories, creating associations and connecting with consumers.

Brands like *Virgin, Calvin Klein, Disney, Ferrari* and *Moët et Chandon* transcend mere product parameters to take on a whole different aura which envelopes the company and consumer. As Randall (2000, p. 4) says, it is a 'holistic combination of product and added values'. Brands 'give product meanings and define its identity in space and time' (Kapferer 2000, p. 17). Even the word 'identity' now has more significance: brand managers used to refer to creating identity through brands as a sort of **badging exercise**; increasingly, consumers seek identity as a consumer validation and this consumer validation as a form of identity.

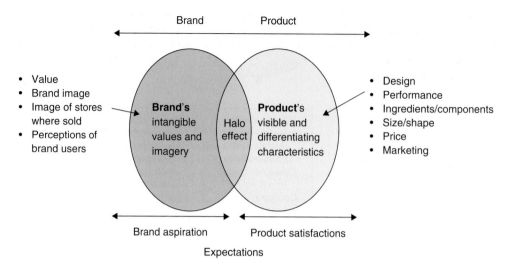

- Value
- Brand image
- Image of stores where sold
- Perceptions of brand users

Brand's intangible values and imagery

Halo effect

Product's visible and differentiating characteristics

- Design
- Performance
- Ingredients/components
- Size/shape
- Price
- Marketing

Brand aspiration

Product satisfactions

Expectations

Figure 8.2: Product/brand 'halo effect'

Source: Kapferer (2004).

Whilst an examination of common characteristics, dimensions and applications of branding will be undertaken in the following sections, it is important to remember that all brands are not the same and consumers engage with brands for different reasons. Brands like *Prada* and *Cricket* are identity-driven; *Ronseal* and the *Prudential* are valued for reliability. Brands are purchased for intrinsic reasons (because they don't contain fat, or sugar, or salt, or do contain omega fish oil or aloe vera extract) and extrinsic reasons (because they project an image of the self, help us gain identity, belong to a group).

Randall (2000, p. 7) describes a model used by advertising agency *Leo Burnett* when analysing and proposing strategies for brand building (see Figure 8.3). The centre of the model comprises four

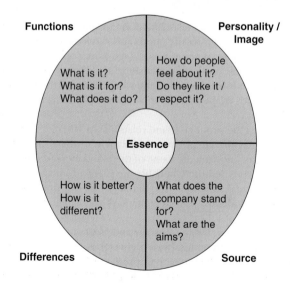

Figure 8.3: Model of brand dimensions

Source: Leo Burnett Brand Consultancy in Randall (2000, p. 7).

dimensions: **functions** (what the brand is and what it is supposed to do); **personality or image** (what user imagery the brand has in terms of people's cognitive and affective disposition to the brand); **source** (what the company stands for and what its aims are); and **differences** (how distinctive it is from the competition). It shows how these components have to be cohesive and consistent, and the aggregate is the **brand essence**.

Many expressions have been used to describe brand essence including 'brand core', 'brand DNA', 'brand soul', 'brand genetic code', and so on, but they all amount to the same thing: the quintessential aggregate 'meaning' of the brand as intended by the company and negotiated by consumers. A fuller discussion on brand dimensions below owes a lot to the research undertaken by de Chernatony and Dall'Olmo Riley (1998) into extant brand descriptions showing different interpretations about what constitutes a brand and provides a comprehensive framework for discussion.

The brand can be a logo and visual signifier which differentiates, evokes and associates in recognition and selection situations. The *Red Cross* emblem waving across the landscapes of disaster we mentioned earlier has similar objectives to the *Nike* swoosh adorning Tiger Woods' cap as he contemplates the last putt of the Masters: to differentiate, remind and shout above the competition to a target audience. Logos can gain semiotic recognition and achieve iconic status by being more than brand markers but become representative symbols. *Coca-Cola*, *Nike*, *Apple*, *Windows* and *Bentley* are all brands which have achieved this type of ubiquitous iconic recognition. Look at the *Gucci* bag illustrated. Does the logo indicate the quality of the leather and stitching, or is the bag a device to display the logo? Is the consumer involvement in this purchase really about the conspicuous consumption of displaying a desirable and highly recognised symbol rather than buying high-quality craftsmanship?

Ostentatious Gucci bag

The brand is a legal instrument which acts as protection in actual (e.g. competitors 'passing off' as original brand) and perceived brand similarity in a category. The French luxury luggage brand *Louis Vuitton* recently sued the online auction house – *eBay* – for selling copies of its products in an attempt not just to protect the brand but publicly reassert proprietary rights and therefore re-establish the brand's authenticity. *McDonalds*, a family firm in Scotland established well before the American giant was forced to change its name; *Yale*, an educational institution in Wales, came under attack from *Yale* in the USA because of the desire to protect their respective brands' 'intellectual property'.

Halifax logo

The brand as company may have a broader audience appeal in the sense that developing relationships and the projection of corporate values and ethics to all stakeholders are of paramount importance. Corporate brands may have a public face like *Virgin*, *HSBC*, *Halifax*, etc. or may focus on individual branding for category development for individual retailers as manufacturers such as *Unilever* and *P&G* do.

In amongst the media and message clutter, brands can act as a shorthand communicator, a decision-making heuristic which aids recall, evokes memory of previous communications and brand experiences. To a hungry motorway traveller, the appearance of *McDonald's* 'Golden Arches', *Marks & Spencer's* 'Simply Food' logo or *Costa Coffee's* coffee steaming cup graphic on the horizon will signify a whole business system of research and development, hygiene, quality control, reliability, quality of food, efficiency of service and previous enjoyable use.

A key element in buyer behaviour is eradicating 'perceived risk' in purchase decision making. Well-established brands, with a history of proven consumer experience, act as risk reducers and help us eliminate or diminish actual or perceived social, functional, financial, time or even psychological

Ronseal has the same message
for women

uncertainties that may accrue from use of the brand. How the brand is positioned to help reduce perceived risk is dependent upon the needs of the category: communicating a brand endorsed by a stylish celebrity, or a tradesman (e.g. *Ronseal*'s 'Does exactly what it says on the tin' man) or explaining the benefits of extended payments (e.g. '0% finance on all *DFS* sofas') will help minimise social functional or financial risks, respectively.

Brands are an integral part of the positioning process as they help to present a key attribute, benefit or aura about how the brand is to be located in the market and perceived in the consumer's mind. The example below of the *Levi's* jeans brand being deliberately limited in distribution in order to enhance its positioning and therefore its currency as a brand demonstrates this well.

Giving a brand a **personality** is a metaphorical dressing of a product with emotional qualities as well as attributes. These characteristics are projected extrinsically through packaging, brand name, communications, attachment to events or celebrities and so on, and will give the brand a life outside its category and resonate with its target audience. Researchers into consumers' perceptions often use projective techniques in focus groups to try and unearth what 'personalities' brands have. *Chrysler* took this idea directly to its audience asking the question: 'What if brands spoke to you?' The image of a car almost smiling to prospective buyers touched on the anthropomorphic elements we sometimes project into products, giving inanimate objects human qualities. The *Mini* has always been instilled with a sense of fun; *Tango* reinvented itself as a wacky orange drink; and the *WKD* alcohol brand has a 'darker side' which gives it a laddish edge. Keller (1998, p. 97) states that 'brand personality reflects how people feel about a brand rather than what they think the brand is or does'. The blind taste tests of *Coca-Cola* and *Pepsi* we mentioned earlier are testimony to this. The matching of the personality of a brand with an individual's sense of 'self' – 'individual brand congruity' (Smith 2007) – is a key issue in branding and is discussed at length below.

BRANDING IN FOCUS

Consumer Shopping Motivations

Retail brands, also known as 'store brands' or 'private labels', have enjoyed increased success in recent years. Rising disposable incomes, growth in individual purchasing power, urban expansion, increased mobility and a wider choice of goods and services have all been key factors in changing consumer attitudes towards shopping. There are 'macro' trends such as 'penny-pinching' because of the restrictions of the credit crunch and 'micro' trends which are about personal motivations.

Research has examined different shopping motivations and shown how emotional brand connections live beyond the transaction to create feelings and memories that last. Foxall and Goldsmith (1994) used a multidimensional approach:

- **Physiological needs:** allow consumers to function in day-to-day life.
- **Social needs:** the expression of group membership, or signal social relations.
- **Symbolic needs:** symbols of success, achievement, status or power.
- **Hedonistic needs:** sensory benefits, such as taste, smell, sound and visual imageries.

- **Cognitive needs:** the need to know and be knowledgeable.
- **Experiential needs:** how it makes consumers feel, producing desired emotions or moods.

Tauber's (1972) research described personal shopping motivations to be:

- **Role playing:** shopping may be a learned and expected behaviour pattern.
- **Diversion:** shopping may provide a break from the daily routine.
- **Self-gratification:** an antidote to loneliness or boredom.
- **Learning about new trends:** an opportunity to see new things and get new ideas.
- **Physical activity:** the exercise provided by shopping is an attraction to some.
- **Sensory stimulation:** through light, colours, sounds, scents and through handling products.
- **Social experiences outside the home:** social interaction or simply 'people watching'.
- **Communication with others having a similar interest:** opportunity for interaction.
- **Peer group attraction:** group affiliation.
- **Status and authority:** stores seek to serve the customer.
- **Pleasure of bargaining:** haggling or from shopping around to obtain the best bargains.

Therefore, by understanding the dynamics of the shopping experience, the store becomes a physical connection to, and expression of, the brand. It is a sensory environment which provides an opportunity to make emotional connections and influence choice. When you walk into a store, you are entering a brand and this is a primary means of consumer engagement.

Great European retail brands like *Compagnie Financière Richemont* in Switzerland; *Sephora, FNAC* and *Grand Optical* in France; *M&S* and *Topshop* in the UK; *IKEA* and *H&S* in Sweden; *Zara* and *Mango* in Spain; and *OBI* and *Kaufland* in Germany, have all succeeded by focusing on retail brand 'concepts'. They orchestrate a complete shopper journey, and stay true to the brand's promise from messaging at every touch-point, to the assortment and layout in the store, with the objective of achieving long-term customer loyalty.

Sources: Interbrand (2009), Tauber (1972), Foxall and Goldsmith (1994).

As values influence buyer behaviour, brands which are perceived as offering more than a basic proposition are highly valued. A brand that is synonymous with offering a **cluster of values** is the *Tesco* approach where store utility, excellent product range and good service are complemented by the relationship being extended through other activities and promotional schemes under the auspices of its *Clubcard*.

Imagining the pathway, a trajectory for the brand to take, is the subject of the section on 'brand narrative' where the organisation conceives a **vision** for the brand and the consumer locks into a developing story. This can see the brand vision as: ethically oriented (e.g. *Ben & Jerry's, The Body Shop*); the 'people's champion' (e.g. *Virgin, Apple, Snapple*); individual empowerment (e.g. *Nike*); or even the personification of 'real people' as hero employers (e.g. *Halifax, B&Q*).

The notion of brands **adding value** to a product is an obvious if variable one. For example, a brand which gives a bundle of extra fraternity benefits (e.g. *RAC* membership facilitating free entry into *English Heritage* stately homes; cheaper fuel and free air at supermarket petrol stations) is compatible with its image and may be perceived as offering unexpected value. Every little helps as we know! However, a brand using a database to sell extra products and services may be perceived as detracting from the original value of the brand.

The brand is manifest in all strategic and tactical brand encounters; it 'is a holistic entity' (de Chernatony 2008, p. 314). The all-pervasive nature of identity underlines vision, staff development, service levels, brochures, advertising, products and all external and internal communications. Physical evidence is extremely important in service brands where intangible products like financial services must be given a tangibility through store layout and presentation. It is what the organisation intends the market to think of the brand, although it may be different to how consumers see the brand. This is the **brand identity**. Brand identity is to brand strategy what strategic intent is to a business strategy (Aaker and Joachimsthaler 2000). Retail brands use olfactory and sensory stimuli and store ambience 'cues' to coax the narrative out of consumers at a deeper level.

The *Stella Artois* case study in Chapter 1 demonstrated the difference between a company-projected identity which is created in an advertising agency, and a consumer-negotiated image which is born out of user experience and word-of-mouth communications. Brand image is 'the perceptions and beliefs held by consumers, as reflected in the associations held in consumer memory (Kotler and Keller 2006, p. 286).

The metaphor of a **relationship** is often used to describe the emotional, financial and behavioural connection consumers have with brands. *P&G* make *Pampers*, but it is the *Pampers* brand with which mothers have an emotional connection. With a heritage of delivering 'emotion' to consumers, *Hallmark Greeting Cards* has become a symbol for 'caring and sharing'. It is based on reciprocity and symbiosis: mutual benefit in growing the brand and the individual. Because consumers engage with the brand on all levels and the management of positive brand exposures is critical, the focus on relationship has given companies a service orientation. Products involve transactions; brands involve relationships.

FUNCTIONS OF BRANDING

Branding is the driving force of marketing and as such is the central focus of marketing communications. Fill (2005, p. 405) distinguishes three strategic dimensions to brands:

- **Integration:** all brand encounters have to be consistent and coherent and the brand is the glue which binds the elements of integrated marketing communications.
- **Differentiation:** the brand acts as a way of positioning away from the competition.
- **Added value:** brands enable customers to derive extra benefits which may be functional, social or even psychological.

In a cluttered marketplace, the primary purpose of branding is the locating of the product: that is, **identification**. Guaranteeing function, utility and availability is a prerequisite of relative category positioning. 'Inherently, brands exist as soon as there is perceived risk. Once the risk perceived by the buyer disappears, the brand has no longer any benefit' (Kapferer 2000, p. 26). The notion of perceived risk is contextual and changeable because the environments in which all brands operate are dynamic and volatile, making the application of branding a constant consideration.

For consumers, brands therefore have an informational, directional or transformational function. They inform us about the use, the benefits against similar brands and they may change our behaviour in terms of consumption. Consumers have a clear picture of what familiar brands stand for (Escalas and Bettman 2005) since they have been exposed to the brands through many different communications such as advertising messages, in-store promotions, recommendations from peers, own brand usage and other consumers' brand usage. In a choice situation, where differentiation from competitors is vital, well-known brands work as a **heuristic**: consumers use previously acquired knowledge of different brands to aid decision making (Maheswaran, Mackie and Chaiken 1992). Brands are also important for the identity construction at the individual level (Fournier 1998) and for various reference points (family, community and social groups) at group level.

A brand does not have to be limited to specific product categories and the scope of brands to expand into other categories, customer segments and markets gives companies flexibility. Equally, as with organisations like *Unilever* and *P&G*, more than one product may be developed

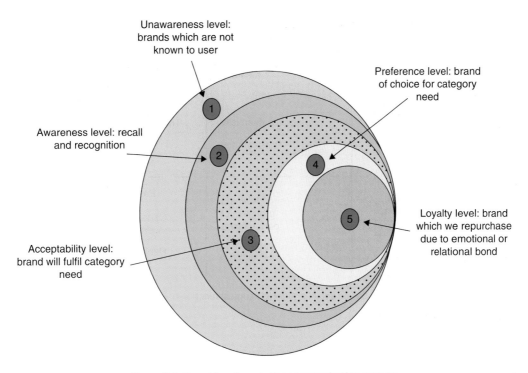

Figure 8.4: Brand functions in the communication process

Source: after Keller (2003, p. 67).

for the same category. *Kellogg's* has extended products under its positioning in the 'breakfast cereal category' (e.g. *Nutri-Grain* breakfast bars). Brands may also give companies a degree of immunity against competition by creating strong relations between the brand and its customers, which act as barriers to entry.

Developing Keller's (2003) ideas on the functions of brands, Figure 8.4 shows the levels that brands operate at. At the very basic level, there are brands which are not known by the target audience. They may exist in the marketplace but may not have entered the consumers' radar due to intense competition, poor communications or consumers' lack of need or opportunity to see. If communications work well, a brand may move to the **awareness level** where recall and recognition may place a brand hypothetically in an evoked set. If the brand is perceived as being capable of fulfilling a category need, it is placed in the **acceptability level**, mentally placing the brand in a consideration set for possible brand selection.

Preference is the level at which all brand communications resonate with the consumer and selection of that brand is made. The ultimate goal for branding is the **loyalty level** where an emotional and relational bond is made between consumer and brand and repeat purchase accrues from brand loyalty. *Burger King* has a 'means-end' approach or ladder where brand loyalty moves through the following stages: features, functions, rewards, values and personality. Figure 8.5 shows how consumers engage with brands within two realms: a basic functional realm in which simple selection and repurchase requirements are evident; and an emotional level where symbolic consumption is an important factor.

Depending upon the level of involvement a consumer has with a brand, the relationship can be at either the functional or emotional level. For low-involvement brands, providing that a brand's quality is consistent and it keeps its promise of performance, the feeling of certainty and the reassurance of repeated satisfaction will ensure continued purchase. It is the function of brand communications

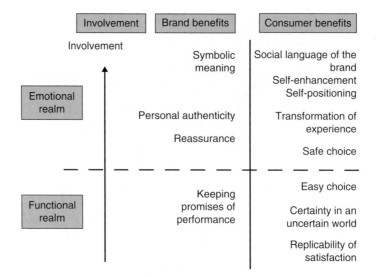

Figure 8.5: The social and psychological function of the brand

Source: Ellis (2000).

to reinforce the brand as a safe choice and make selection of the brand an easy transaction for the consumer. A brand which purports to have significance for the user in terms of enhancing self-image, affiliation, social standing or even help the user to achieve self-actualisation needs to contain and communicate some social language to the consumer by projecting symbolic meaning.

INTRODUCING BRAND EQUITY

Against the backdrop of intense competition and shifting orientation of communication, 'one industry after another has discovered that brand awareness, perceived quality, customer loyalty, and strong brand associations and personality are necessary to compete in the marketplace' (Aaker and Joachimsthaler 2000, p. ix). This requires strategic and visionary management in order to create and maintain lifetime customer value. Whenever attempts are made to understand the term 'brand value', we refer to this as **brand equity**.

Brand equity is 'the differential effect that brand knowledge has on consumer response to the marketing of that brand' (Keller 2003, p. 60). Aaker (1991, p. 15) broadens this: 'a set of assets and liabilities linked to the brand, its name and symbol, that add value or subtract from the value provided by a product or service to a firm and/or to that firm's customers'. Figure 8.6 shows that by managing the key brand equity components of brand description, brand strength and the future of the brand, brand equity assets can be developed and enhanced (Pickton and Broderick 2005, p. 254).

Management of brand equity should be considered as a formal component of corporate strategy (Shocker, Srivastava and Ruekert 1994) and, as such, is a construct of marketing effectiveness. Some brands may not have legal protection in the form of trademarks, but have associations and perceived quality which give them strength and immunity against the competition. *Intel* is an example of a brand which has safeguarded against competition by building strong brand associations and a quality image due to its manufacturers' links in co-branding. Some brands can survive on the brink of brand equity in the heritage of the brand. *M&S* withstood pressures when sales declines could have been terminal because of the customer equity for the brand; Dutch clothing giant *C&A* did not survive in the UK because there was not the same customer bond and its low pricing strategy left it vulnerable to similar brands such as *Matalan, Topshop* and the Spanish brand *Zara* as well as the supermarkets (the likes of *ASDA* with its own *George* brand).

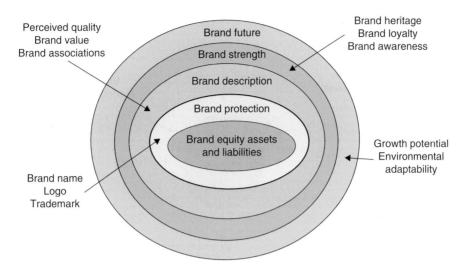

Figure 8.6: Managing brand equity

Source: Pickton and Broderick (2005, p. 256). Reproduced with permission.

Although Farquhar's (1989) definition of 'the value added to the product by the brand' has been revisited on many occasions, it is Keller (1993, p. 1) who sums it up well, describing it as 'marketing effects uniquely attributable to the brand – for example when certain outcomes result from the marketing of a product or service because of its brand name that would not occur if the same product or service did not have that name' (name means 'reputation' here not 'title'). Two factors are most important to this: how brands can simplify and facilitate purchases; and how brands contribute to consumer identity. The importance to organisations is two-fold: building equity through the brands' expected utility to consumers (Erdem and Swait 1998) achieved through brand awareness and brand image; and the development of an intangible balance-sheet asset.

Keller (2001) outlines the four key steps to building brand equity in his CBBE (Customer-Based Brand Equity) model: establishing brand identity with depth and width of brand awareness; creating the appropriate brand meaning through strong, favourable and unique brand associations; eliciting positive, unique brand responses; and forging brand relationships with customers that are characterised by intense, active loyalty. The 'six brand building blocks' which constitute this process are:

1. **Brand salience:** the relevance of the brand in meeting customers' needs.
2. **Brand performance:** the result of competitiveness.
3. **Brand imagery:** denotations and connotations of the brand.
4. **Brand judgements:** decisions made in terms of areas like brand extensions.
5. **Brand feelings:** user brand experiential assessment.
6. **Brand resonance:** all other 'building blocks' are established and customers express a high degree of loyalty, sharing brand experiences with others.

Aaker (2000, p. 15) described the five elements of the 'brand equity model' (Figure 8.7) for managing brand equity as:

- **Brand awareness:** recognition of the familiar is a key customer buying trigger and as such a valuable company asset.
- **Perceived quality** affects association in many contexts for a customer and positively affects profitability for a company.

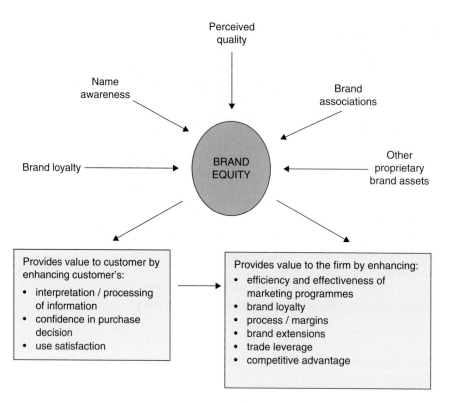

Figure 8.7: Aaker's model of brand equity

Source: Aaker (2000, p. 15). Reproduced with permission.

- **Brand associations** are any part of marketing communications which connect the customer to the brand.
- **Brand loyalty** is the qualitative customer loyalty which underpins the brand's value.
- Other **proprietary brand assets**: patents, trademarks, channel relationships.

    The key element here is the notion that a brand is a combination of elements, has a presence against the competition and in the minds of the consumer – it has individuality, uniqueness, a character. It has an **identity** and provides a link between, and offers value to, company and customer. Let's look at what we mean by a brand having an identity.

Retail Brands

Retailers have grown from being intermediaries for manufacturers to the axis of power in branding. *Wal-Mart* and *Harrods* are seen as separate brands in themselves. Interbrand (2009) describes three types of retail brand:

- **Aggregator retail brands**, such as *Wal-Mart* in the USA, *ASDA* in the UK and *Carrefour* in France, are primarily providers of manufacturer choice, environment and price to mass consumers.
- **Branded own-label retail brands**, such as Spain's *Zara* and *Mango*, Germany's *Aldi* and France's *Auchan*, are primarily providers of a private-label proposition, environment and price.
- **Product retail brands**, such as Germany's *Adidas*, the Japanese *Sony*, the UK's *Burberry* and the US *Levi's*, are primarily providers of a private-label proposition with brands distributed through third-party retailers.

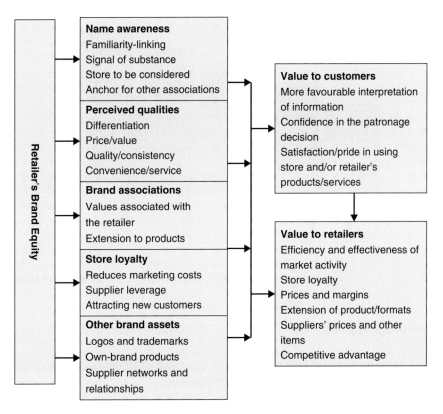

Figure 8.8: Retailer's brand equity

Source: McGoldrick (2002, p. 186). Adapted from Aaker (1991, 1994).

Figure 8.8 shows the components of a retailer's brand equity and demonstrates how this can generate value through loyalty, awareness, image, associations and other brand assets (McGoldrick 2002, p. 187) for both the customer and the retailer. A retail store with strong brand equity conveys clear, relevant values to customers which translate into process, quality, convenience, ethical stance and so on. Confidence in the patronage decision (selection of store and product) is increased and consumption experience is likely to be enhanced. A retailer will benefit from the consistency of custom that allows growth, profitability and buying power.

MATTER OF FACT

Calculating the Value of Brands

Retailers are not homogeneous; they come in all shapes and sizes. So how do we evaluate retail brands? Top brand analysts Interbrand's method for calculating the value is a proven formula that examines brands through the lens of financial strength, the importance of driving consumer selection, and the likelihood of ongoing branded revenue. This method evaluates the brands much like any other asset: on the basis of how much they are likely to earn in the future. There are three core components:

(Continued)

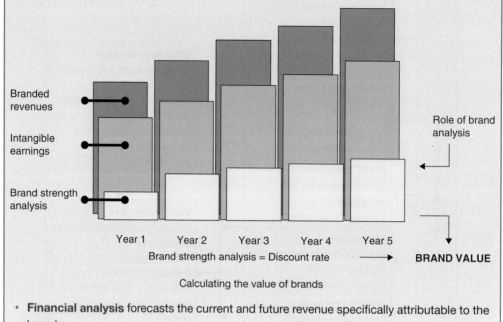

Calculating the value of brands

- **Financial analysis** forecasts the current and future revenue specifically attributable to the brand.
- **Brand analysis** measures how the brand influences customer demand, adding this to the intangible earnings and calculating 'branded earnings'.
- **Brand strength score** is a benchmark of the brand's ability to secure ongoing customer demand (loyalty, repurchase and retention) and thus sustain future earnings, translating brand earnings into net present value. This assessment looks at the specific risks to the brand, compared against market position, customer franchise, image and support.

Source: Interbrand (2009).

Branding is therefore obviously vitally important to retailers. The main drivers of own-label retailer brands are analysed in the Interbrand 2009 Retail Report illustrated in Figure 8.9.

Corporate Branding

According to Gregory (2004, p. 47), a corporate brand strategy 'provides a framework for creating a corporate branding culture' which will be consistent with audience experiences of the brand. It is what Catherine Ostheimer of CoreBrand, a leading corporate brand strategy specialist agency, calls the 'missing link of marketing communications'. A company with a healthy branding culture is one in which everybody understands what their role is in delivering the brand and what individually and collectively they are supposed to do. A corporate brand is the culmination of the many experiences and emotional feelings which employees, sellers, investors, stakeholders, communities and customers have when brand encounters with product, service, processes and company culture occur. It is therefore important to create, manage and fulfil expectations amongst many stakeholders as projection of a clear, consistent brand message is crucial to the successful delivery of the brand promise.

Corporate brands affect product brands in that a bad corporate image makes building brand equity (for products) difficult, but a good reputation does not guarantee strong product brands (Page and Fearn 2005, p. 309). The effect is stronger for high-involvement products, but a lack of corporate image does not necessarily mean product brand equity will be eroded (Berens, van Riel and van Bruggen 2005, p. 42).

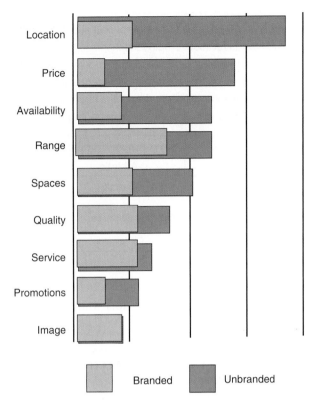

Figure 8.9: Retail own-label brand drivers/role of brand

Source: Interbrand (2009).

Internal Branding

The brand and its values must be communicated internally. The internal market is a key target audience for communications as 'living the brand' is the essence of customer service. Delivering the brand promise requires the complicity of customer-facing employees who act as **brand champions** in communications with customers. The idea is that employees do the right things when they know what the brand is supposed to deliver and that they can add value to the product brand. Ultimately, they are proud of being a part of the organisation. Bergstrom, Blumenthal and Crothers (2002, p. 139) highlight the three most important aspects of internal branding as:

1. communicating the brand effectively to employees;
2. convincing them of its relevance and its worth; and
3. successfully linking every job in the organisation to delivery of the brand.

MATTER OF FACT

Brand Mantra for Employees

Internal branding is often communicated as a brand mantra. This is the heart and soul of the brand and may guide both everyday aspects of work within the company and long-term decisions about the future. This should be short (3–5 words) and should 'screen out' marketing

(Continued)

activities that are not congruent with the brand. Moreover, it should help the company to communicate what the brand stands for to its employees.

It should consist of brand functions, a descriptive modifier and an emotional modifier. These parts describe the nature of the customer experience (brand functions), clarify the nature of the function (descriptive modifier), and express how the brand delivers its benefits (emotional modifier). The mantra should be simple, inspiring and communicative.

	Emotional modifier	**Descriptive modifier**	**Brand functions**
Nike	Authentic	Athletic	Performance
Disney	Fun	Family	Entertainment

Brand mantra for employees

Source: Keller (1999).

Branding across Cultures

According to Usunier and Lee (2005, p. 286), the factors which affect perceptions of 'product nationality' are:

1. the image of national products versus international products;
2. national images of generic products (e.g. perfume evokes France; fashion spells Italian; a pair of jeans invariably is associated with America);
3. the national image of the manufacturing company;
4. the image diffused by the brand name; and
5. the image of the 'made in' label depicting the manufacturing origin (mandatory in international trade).

BRANDING IN FOCUS

Country of Origin

The accelerated movement of globalisation, together with the purchase of large chunks of equity in localised brands such as *Snapple*, *Innocent Smoothies* and *Green & Black's*, gives rise to the issue of whether brand image appeals affect different people in different countries (Hsieh, Pan and Setiono 2004). This is exacerbated by the fact that brand origins and product manufacture are often not in the same place. Would it matter if the Irish associations of *Guinness*, the 'Born in the USA' stamp of *Budweiser* or the Italian pedigree of *Gucci*, *Prada* and *Armani* were only brand origins rather than country of manufacture? Anholt (2003) claims that country of origin is an essential part of beer branding. As there is significant product parity in this category, reliance on strong place orientation is prevalent. *Foster's* has underlined its Australian heritage with Paul Hogan endorsements and even featured a kangaroo in the logo. *Lapin Kulta* uses stark Lapland landscapes on bottle labels and other communications to reinforce its Finnish provenance.

Research by Kenny and Aron (2001) revealed an important distinction between 'country of origin' (COO) and 'culture of brand origin' (COBO). The brand name *Volkswagen* immediately calls to mind German efficiency and engineering and yet a considerable amount of *VW* manufacture takes place in Brazil. *Häagen-Dazs* has continental brand connotations but New York ice cream making connections. Early penetration of the European electronics market by Japanese manufacturers disguised the Asian origins. *Panasonic's* 2008 take-over of *Sanyo* confirmed its brand position even if the 'Western' name remained.

What of the Scandinavian countries? *Danish Bacon, Bang & Olufsen* and *Carlsberg* are synonymous with Denmark; *Heineken, Grolsch* and *Philips* from the Netherlands; *IKEA, Absolut, Volvo* and *H&M* unmistakably Swedish; *Nokia* is Finnish; and the massive potential of Norwegian and Icelandic mineral water brands trades on the 'land of the ice and snow' associations.

What part does 'national pride' play in brand loyalty? A study of over 6000 brands in Europe presented at the 'Latest Insights into Branding Symposium' organised by Young & Rubicam's *Consult Brand Strategy* and *Universiteit Nyenrode* in Amsterdam showed that national brands outperform global brands in the European brand arena, with the number one brand always being of national origin. The study based on the world's largest brand database and *BrandAsset™ Valuator* showed the following national brands holding strong positions: *IKEA* in Sweden; *Aldi* in Germany; *Bang & Olufsen* in Denmark; *C&A* and *ANWB* in Holland; *Greyerzer* and *Toblerone* in Switzerland.

Sources: Interbrand (2009), Y&R *Consult Brand Strategy* (2004), Kenny and Aron (2001), Hsieh, Pan and Setiono (2004), Anholt (2003).

BRAND IDENTITY

The distinction between **brand identity** and **brand image** is acute, and is one which is fundamental to understanding how successful brands work: brand image is usually passive and looks to the past; brand identity should be active and look to the future (Aaker 2004). Brand image tends to be tactical; brand identity should be strategic. Brand identity is to brand strategy what strategic intent is to a business strategy. Provided that an organisation understands the marketplace and is empathetic with the consumer, the intended, transmitted identity may resonate and connect with audiences. And yet, brand identity is the cumulative impressions and representations of users, potential users, opinion leaders, word of mouth, mediated meaning and 'what resides in the minds of consumers' (Ries and Trout 1980). As Aaker and Joachimsthaler (2000, p. 43) put it 'brand identity should help establish a relationship between the brand and the customer by generating a value proposition potentially involving functional, emotional or self-expressive benefits'.

As we have seen from Chapter 2, communications which are transmitted can also be distorted by 'noise' from competitors and negative PR. Image is from a receiver's point of view and depends on decoding of the sender's projected intended identity. To paraphrase what Holt (2004) has said, the image of the brand is born when the brand has been exposed in use and conversation. Kapferer (2000, p. 9) captures this well: 'Brands eventually gain their independence and their own meaning, even though they may start out as mere product names'. He argues (p. 92) that brand image and positioning are only two components of what constitutes a brand identity. This can be defined 'by addressing the issue of its difference, its permanence, its value and its personal view. Brand identity defines what must stay and what is allowed to change'. He illustrates this well by distinguishing between the parts of *Peugeot* and *Citroën* products which are identical and the distinct identities these two brands have.

An overview of brand identity (Aaker and Joachimsthaler 2000) – organised around the four perspectives of: brand as product; organisation; person; and symbol – is shown in Figure 8.10. Although there are 12 categories, this does not mean that all categories are relevant to each brand and equally

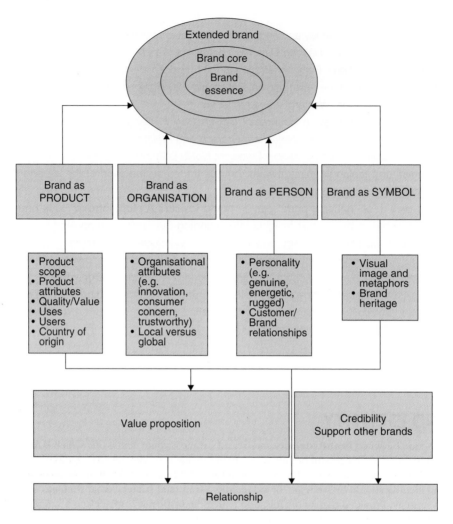

Figure 8.10: Brand identity

Source: Aaker and Joachimsthaler (2000, p. 44).

no one brand features in all 12 categories. At the centre is the brand essence which is the 'soul' of the brand and drives customer expectations and company value proposition. For example, 'excelling' is the essence of the *Nike* brand; *Avis* 'extra service'; *Innocent* 'eco-friendly' and so on.

The ability of the brand to be extended beyond its original category depends on the strength of the brand's core. This 'brand identity structure' includes a core identity – strategy and values of the organisation and that which differentiates the brand to consumers – and this should remain constant on the brand's narrative journey to other markets and meanings. This creates a focus for both company and consumer.

Kapferer develops this in a graphic representation of what he calls a 'prism of identity' (Figure 8.11). This includes the 'social facets which give the brand its outward expression: physique, relationship and reflection' (Kapferer 1992, p. 106); and those elements 'incorporated within the brand itself, within its spirit' which include personality, culture and self-image.

- Firstly, a brand must have **physical properties** (i.e. 'physique') made up of key product and brand attributes. These are evident in the tactile product/packaging elements of bottled beverages

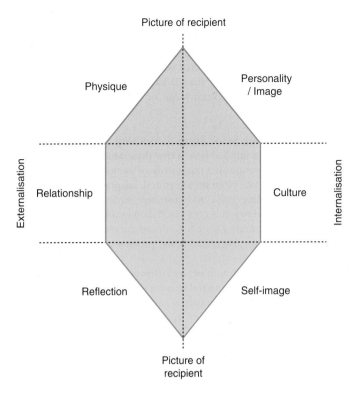

Figure 8.11: Kapferer's prism of identity

Source: Kapferer (1992, p. 38). Reproduced with permission.

(*Orangina, Coca-Cola, Corona, Budweiser, Jack Daniels, Absolut Vodka, Red Bull*); perfumes (*Chanel, Jean-Paul Gaultier, Poison*); or chocolate (*Ferrero Rocher, After Eights, Yorkie*).

- The idea of a brand having a **personality** is manifest in the actual associations (e.g. *Virgin* as Richard Branson; *The Body Shop* as Anita Roddick) and metaphorical ones (e.g. *Esso*'s Tiger, *Frostie's* Tony the Tiger, *McDonald's* Ronald) and associations used in advertising.
- The **culture** of a brand is the set of values that inform and inspire the brand's raison d'être: *Benetton*'s focus is on innovation in producing colour and communicating this; *Apple*'s Californian 'think outside the system' approach sets the organisation and brand apart from the competition; the 'spirit of order' conveyed in *Mercedes* cars; the *CO-OP Bank* has always expressed an ethical conscience; and *American Express* is infused with conspicuous capitalism.
- The **relationships** that consumers have with brands are dependent upon consumers' needs: some are transient transactional interactions, typically 'distress' purchases like repairing car exhausts; some are deep, emotional maybe irrational associations like supporting a football team. However, even irregular contact with a brand like *Kwik-Fit Tyres* may build up a relationship of repeat purchase if exposure to the brand has been positive. Some have associations with the brand which are 'guilty pleasures'. When *Pot Noodle* came under pressure from health watchdogs, it did not concentrate on the contents of the pots, but repositioned its relationship with consumers by emphasising the 'illicit' aspect of the product, giving it an almost sexual personality with its 'Slag of all Snacks' campaign.
- The brand should be a **reflection** of who consumers would like to be not who they actually are. With fashion brands like *Marks & Spencer*, image building and self-creation is crucial. They have recently corrected the way their target audience is reflected in their communications by using aspirational role models such as Twiggy and Myleene Klass to convey idealised personalities and image. In the 1980s, the use of images of realistic consumers (white, overweight, middle-class women)

was disastrous as people did not want to see themselves the way they actually are. (The irony of this is that there has now been a backlash from female *M&S* shareholders who took boss Stuart Rose to task for not recognising the 'average' *M&S* size of 'more trunky than twiggy!')
· The use of brands is also an inner dialogue that we have with ourselves. We reflect our interpretation of the creation of our **self-image**. Brands like *WeightWatchers* may reflect individuality, conscience, achievement, innovation, knowledge or conspicuous demonstration of wealth or status.

Kapferer (2000) talks of 'leaving brand image, personality and positioning behind as we enter the modern age of identity'. What is implied here is that these are only integral components, whereas brand identity, as a holistic, all-encompassing framework of identity – the brand narrative if you will – has primacy. Brand identity has to be coherent, integrated, adaptable, durable and therefore dynamic in the face of rapidly changing competitive and customer environmental factors. Looking at brand identity as the amalgam of how the brand is conceived, communicated and consumed illustrates this holistic approach to brand management. Figure 8.12 shows the overlapping components which make up brand identity: brand orientation, articulated brand promise and the brand 'in use' in the market and mind of the consumer.

Brand identity is the product of different perspectives of the brand in thought, deed and through experience. Image results from the decoding and interpretation of communications mediated through customer-facing service personnel, other employees, intermediaries, opinion formers, other brand users and even competitors. It is a 'synthesis made by all the various brand signals' (Kapferer 2000, p. 95) – intentional, unintentional and negotiated. The components which comprise identity are corporate brand image, company brand culture and customer brand image.

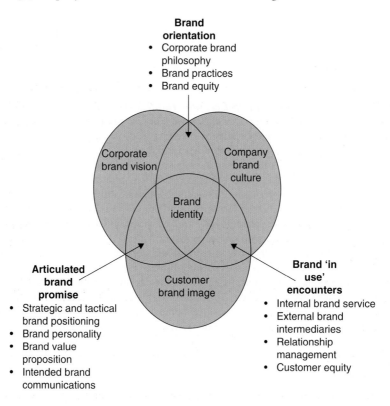

Figure 8.12: The components of brand identity

Source: after de Chernatony and McDonald (2003).

- Corporate **brand vision** is the conception of the brand in its targeted market with a customer profile which is consistent with organisational goals and operating framework.
- Company **brand culture** is the level to which an organisation is market oriented and promotes the primacy of brand communications.
- Customer **brand image** is the result of experience of brand use and qualitative feedback from others exposed to the brand and marketing communications.

How the brand vision is interpreted by the user is often referred to as the 'brand promise'. This is the articulation of what the brand is, what it is intended to do and how it will fit in with the category needs and extended expected experience of the user. This is a result of strategic and tactical positioning, the 'personality' which is initially injected into the product, the proposed value proposition and how all this is projected through marketing communications. Of course, the intended stated mission statement and vision are not always enacted. Therefore, there must be an underpinning of this throughout the organisation – employee buy-in or complicity – implicit in brand philosophy, explicit in employee practice. In addition, all investment in brand equity should add to this customer orientation. How company brand culture translates into positive customer experience is the result of internal brand service, external intermediary contact and the management of relationships which feed into customer equity.

Consumer brand judgements are highly subjective and dependent upon direct experience and individual perceptions about brand beliefs and benefits. The Matter of Fact box below illustrates how consumers are affected by beliefs.

MATTER OF FACT

Belief Crystallisation

Besides direct extensive experience, consumers are also affected by the amount of thoughts they devote to a brand and its benefits. This is called **belief crystallisation** and deals with the nature of mere mental elaboration about benefits and how this process induces decision biases. Thinking about a brand will paint a more positive picture of the brand in the minds of consumers. The combination of experience and belief crystallisation was tested in a study where a brand was under attack by another brand that was objectively superior. When experience was limited (one product trial) and belief crystallisation low (no questions about beliefs), the attacking brand was chosen by almost 90% of the consumers. In the table below we show that high belief crystallisation (questions about eight beliefs) and/or extensive experience (six product trials) lead to enhanced preferences for the focal brand as well as increased confidence in the decision.

Effects for focal brand	Low-belief crystallisation		High-belief crystallisation	
	Limited experience	Extensive experience	Limited experience	Extensive experience
Choice	14%	73%	68%	82%
Confidence	3.95	4.68	5.45	5.55

Choice share for focal brand and confidence in the decision (measured on a nine-point scale)

Sources: Hoch (2002), Muthukrishnan (1995).

A first step in the branding process, which should not be underestimated, is to create opportunities for customers to spend time with the brand and to think about the brand; in other words: brand engagement. This highlights the difference between brand equity and brand awareness: high brand awareness may not necessarily translate into brand loyalty; it does not discriminate between brands that people like and brands that people dislike. Similarly, in times of brand crisis (e.g. *Coca-Cola*'s UK *Dasani* bottled water disaster; the safety issues with the *Ford Pinto*; the *TeGenero* test patient medicine scandal; or the consumer boycott against *Shell* when the Dutch company was about to sink its oil platform in the North Atlantic Ocean in 1995), this may lead to extremely high levels of brand awareness but suffer from strongly negative associations.

Some brands have high brand awareness and a weak brand image and are associated with outdated ways of marketing. For a long time, *Polaroid*'s dominance of the instant camera category was undermined with the development of digital technology. Its repositioning was by reinventing the category with the *i-Zone* camera (an instant camera that can take a picture that is a sticker) developed for the 'tweens' and teenage girl segments.

Other brands have a 'high brand awareness–weak brand image' relationship due to nostalgia. *Heinz* allowed salad cream to fade away due to the popularity of mayonnaise until consumers complained and it was relaunched and saved. The old *VW Beetle* is another example of this. *Volkswagen* reintroduced the new *Beetle* long after it was first discontinued with a similar design but modern technology.

Brand Identity Traps

Brand identity can become an imprisoning tactical framework unless 'brand identity traps' are avoided (Aaker 2004). He describes four 'traps' (see Figure 8.13) to be avoided if the brand is not to be restricted:

- **The brand image trap** – brand image is how customers and others perceive the brand. If this is not controlled and becomes dominant, it is entirely possible for the brand image to become the brand identity rather than just one input to be considered. When a brand consumer has had a negative experience using the brand, or uncontrolled negative word-of-mouth communications is allowed to dominate, the use of the brand image as an identity statement often goes unchallenged, the customer dictating what you are. As Aaker (2004) says 'Creating a brand identity is more than finding out what customers say they want. It must also reflect the soul and vision of the brand, what it hopes to achieve'. A brand identity should not accept existing perceptions, but instead should be willing to consider creating changes.

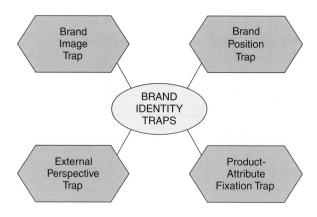

Figure 8.13: Brand identity traps

Source: Aaker (2004).

- **The brand position trap** – brand positioning is about communicating the part of the identity which tells the customer what the brand's value proposition is vis-à-vis the competition. As we have seen, positioning should drive all brand communications, but the brand position trap occurs when focus on product attributes is intensified, and there is often no room to consider brand personality, organisational associations or long-term brand building. A brand position does not usually have the texture and depth needed to guide the brand-building effort: which event to sponsor, which package is superior, or what store display supports the brand. There is a need for a richer, more complete understanding of what the brand stands for.
- **The external perspective trap** – brand identity is something that gets customers to buy the product or service because of how they perceive the brand, but there also needs to be an internal perspective which is about the role that brand identity has in internal market communications in gaining the understanding and complicity of employees of organisational values and purpose. Employees must buy into the organisation's brand vision.
- **The product-attribute fixation trap** – this is where everything is centred entirely on extolling product attributes without sufficient reference to other benefits associated with the brand.

BRAND PERSONALITY

Attempts to 'humanise' the brand are explored by Aaker (1997, p. 352) where she suggests some dimensions of brand personality (Figure 8.14), and proposes a 42-point BPS (Brand Personality Scale) for plotting possible brand personality strategies. Try and match some brands with personality types and see what target audience 'personality profile' might match these brand personalities. Examples of brands that fit a personality are for sincere brands (*Campbell's* soup), exciting brands (*MTV*), competent brands (*Wall Street Journal*), sophisticated brands (*Mercedes*) and rugged brands (*Marlboro*). Some brands score high on more than one personality like *Hallmark Greeting Cards* (sincere and sophisticated) and *Porsche* (exciting and sophisticated). Brand personalities are a good starting point for marketing communications as they are a good way of describing brands and understanding what competitors stand for, and how the brand can best be positioned.

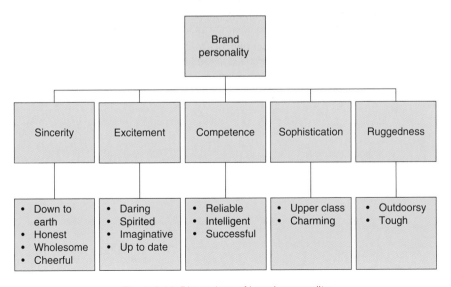

Figure 8.14: Dimensions of brand personality

Source: Aaker (1997, p. 352). Reproduced with permission.

Williams (2000, p. 8) offers some alternative personality types for brands:

- **Real things:** brands like *Coca-Cola* and *Levi's* who claim 'originality' and 'authenticity' create myths around the brand's past to reinforce their position.
- **The appliance of science:** we are given promises of security by brands like *Zanussi* and *Bosch* known for scientific development.
- **Excessories:** the so-called 'premium brands' promise indulgence and hedonistic consumption and might reflect status. Could be an expensive *Rolex* watch or a bar of *Galaxy* chocolate.
- **Get on and get up:** examples of brands that offer empowerment can be information technology products like the *Sony VAIO* lightweight notepad or *Nike* which allow us to 'Just Do It' by encouraging us to use sports attire worn by champions. Or sports footwear brands like *Adidas*, which uses celebrity sports stars to endorse its product to position it as an aspirational lifestyle brand. These essentially 'sports' brands have entered into mainstream fashion and taken on a different edge to the brand's personality. The symbolic 'conspicuous consumption' and the matching of brand and consumer personality elements of this brand is perfectly captured in the 1984 track 'My *Adidas*' by rappers *Run-DMC*. The words 'I like to flaunt 'em. That's why I bought 'em . . . We make a mean team my *Adidas* and me' leave no doubt about the connection.

High flying VAIO laptop

- **Irreverent and Independent:** Brands often employ complex codes and require consumers to decode their meaning. Whilst some brands offer straightforward value propositions, and image brands like *Levi's, Wrangler* and *Lee Jeans* all purport to represent 'All American values', brands like the Italian fashion label *Diesel* set their brand in opposition to established brand practice and mock conventions and competition. These types of brands (like *Benetton* and *Snapple*) are subversive, attacking the very promise and premise of branding. Indeed, as Williams (2000, p. 54) says: 'If brands are about promises, *Diesel* makes ludicrous comical promises'. He describes this as 'postmodern' because it espouses anti-branding through the use of ironic humour, ridiculing advertising clichés, projecting a rebellious and irreverent brand personality and appealing to free-thinkers and independent individuals. Another brand which has this approach and has an 'all value – no frills' identity is the Japanese *Muji* brand. *Muji* benefits from foreign kudos, and the seriously stylish, 'fashion statement' positioning is projected in its minimalist personality, consistent through all stores, packaging and products. One of the products – *Muji Cola* – brings these values to the soft drinks 'cola' category where brands struggle to differentiate from one another.
- **Wonderlands:** some brands offer a holistic brand experience which permeates all aspects of exposure to the brand. *Disney* is a good example of this, where the experience is present in the services, the theme parks, merchandise, films and DVDs. *Cadbury's* has tried to emulate this by creating a Willy Wonka-type 'Chocolate Factory' experience at its Midlands factory.
- **Fun and Friendly:** some brands develop standalone characters which personify the brand, become friends to the users and make it easier to form a quasi-human relationship with the organisation or product. Ronald McDonald, *Halifax's* 'Howard', *Churchill's* bulldog (insurance) are all examples of the brand projecting source credibility through fun and friendship. Tony the Tiger is the personification of *Kellogg's* breakfast cereal *Frosties* and is now 53 years old! Tony has achieved brand longevity by keeping his relevance to the target audience and sharing in their lives in various contemporary events. The anthropomorphically created characters which inhabit children's TV and films (like *Disney* for example) find an extended life in advertising campaigns, promotions and various 'inter-textual' references. The personality of the comic book or cartoon character acts as a friendly source to the consumer and helps to differentiate the brand against the competition.
- **Globally local:** brands are used as a way to define and express our identities. Global brands maintain a consistent image over the world and most are American in origin, therefore expressing Western

values. After the world-changing events of '9/11', there has been more anti-American feeling and this has sometimes manifested itself in brands such as *Mecca Cola* and *Zam Zam Cola* which are marketed to pro-Muslim and Arab consumers as alternatives to *Coca-Cola* and *Pepsi*. The brand name *Mecca Cola* contains the traditional transliteration of ﺔﻜﻠﻤﻟﺍﺮﻣﺪﻗ in Saudi Arabia – the holiest Islamic city.

Headline: Don't ignore me.
China has over 1.5 million underprivileged children.
To help, call 020 82266673.

Invisible boy a visual metaphor

The 'activist' personality projected through the name calls for Muslims to clearly place a brand as something other than a mere drink, urging cola drinkers to 'Shake Your Conscience'.

- **Guilt and anxiety:** brands which provoke feelings of fear play on our anxieties of safety or assurance. A *British Gas* advertisement promoting annual service contracts memorably showed a consumer's freezing cold home (complete with shivering Eskimos!) caused because the owner had not taken out a contract. Advertisements which make us feel guilty about social injustices or provoke compassion for our fellow citizens can be very powerful. This advertisement for *UNICEF* shows the 'invisible' street beggar boy that we do not see and provokes us to at least think about other people.

BUILDING BRANDS

As we have seen, branding is all about the management of perceptions since brands are chiefly 'in the minds' of consumers. According to Duncan and Moriarty (1997), 'perception is more important than reality'. Upon the foundations of brand positioning and brand identity, according to Aaker and Joachimsthaler (2000, p. 263), the three cornerstones of successful brand building are:

- Creating **visibility** in a crowded marketplace: share of voice, market dominance, category parity, opportunities to see and so on, all help brands to remain within sight of customers. Recognition, unaided recall and top-of-mind status are critical in successful brands.
- **Associations** are constructed through brand identity. Loyalty has to be forged in unique characteristics which differentiate and resonate with consumers. What do *Klarbrunn* waters, *Giorgio di Sant'Angelo* design wear and *Häagen-Dazs* ice cream have in common? *Klarbrunn* is not mountain-spring water from the Alps, it's bottled in Wisconsin. *Giorgio di Sant'Angelo* is not Italian fashion, it's also American. And you probably already know that *Häagen-Dazs* is not Hungarian or Danish, it is made in New York (Leclerc, Schmitt and Dubé 1994, p. 263). Associations are critical to identity.
- The development of meaningful relationships with customers is key to brand longevity and is covered in more detail below.

Interbrand, the worldwide brand consultancy, uses a brand platform model to demonstrate the symbiotic relationship between brand and individual (Figure 8.15).

This describes two parallel hierarchies of matching brand and consumer functional, expressive and central values. From a consumer's perspective, at the basic level, **functional values** refer to the economic or time utility required in order to fulfil hunger or physiological needs or ease of purchase or minimising cost. The product or service must reflect this in providing the benefit of use, cost or composition. *Ronseal* 'does exactly what it says on the tin'; *Argos* offer 'The best deals always'. The **expressive values** of a brand aim at matching what type of person the consumer wants to be or thinks she/he is. *Costa Coffee* 'helps communities grow' by extending its ethical standpoint not just to 'fair trade supply' but improving the welfare of communities where its beans are purchased through its Costa Foundation. This reflects the desired 'socially responsible' nature of the consumer. Coffee *and* conscience! What the brand and the purchaser share at a moral or philosophical level – power, stability and fulfilment – should accord in terms of the brand/consumer central values.

Brand values hierarchy   **Consumer values hierarchy**

Reflect what the purchaser and the brand share in fundamental terms: morally, behaviourally, philosophically.

Central values

What kind of life do I want? Successful, fulfilling, meaningful, stable, powerful?

Reflect the nature of the purchaser: sex, characteristics, personality, status.

Expressive values

What kind of person do I want to be? Active, contemporary, important, in control, socially responsible?

Reflect what kind of product or service the brand offers and/or what functional benefits it provides to the customer: composition, use, effect, appearance, cost.

Functional values

What kind of products do I want to have? Natural, convenient, safe, technologically advanced, effective, money-saving?

Figure 8.15: Brand platform structure 1

Source: Hart and Murphy (1998).

Ultimately, we predispose the consumer to our brand by linking brand values with consumer values – the values unique to each individual that guide consumption.

Now we need to see these values in the overall context of the model (Figure 8.16). The first step in creating a differentiated and appropriate brand platform is to create a brand vision of the

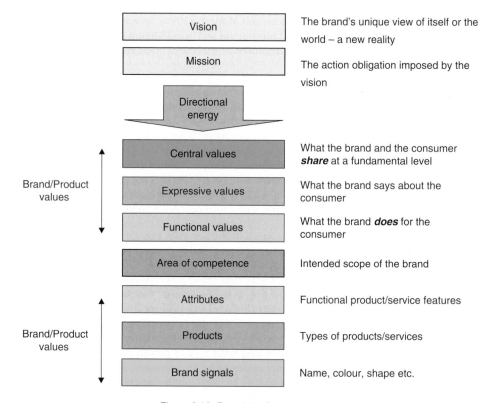

Figure 8.16: Brand platform structure 2

Source: Hart and Murphy (1998).

competitor/customer context of the category or consumer experience which is unique to the brand. The vision should be distinctive and what Andrew (1998, p. 189) calls 'an element of dislocation relative to the conventional wisdom of current category thinking'. The *Apple* narrative of being 'above systems and structures' is a good example of this. This is the brand's unique view of itself and may create a new direction for both the brand and the brand users – what Interbrand refers to as 'a new reality'. The new reality for *Lucozade* was to grow out of being associated with old-age tonics to become a 'sports' drink. How the brand intends to achieve this – the brand's direction and thrust – is what we call the **brand's mission**. This is the action obligation imposed by the vision. If *Benetton's* vision – or brand narrative – is to 'celebrate diversity and colour of product through challenging the beliefs and ethical values of consumers globally', then that must be evident in all brand encounters which carry the mission.

Together, the mission and vision give the brand **directional energy** which feeds into brand/consumer values. The overlap between values defines the scope of the brand. Some brands are restricted to one category; others can grow into other areas which might not be in the same product category but are compatible. The link between brand equity and the lifecycle concept is made in the Matter of Fact box below proposing that a brand's value will go through parallel life stages.

MATTER OF FACT

Brand Equity Life Stage Model

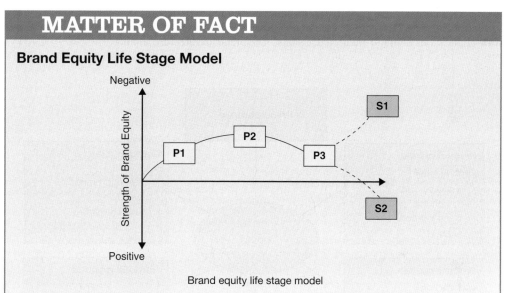

Brand equity life stage model

- **P1:** the rapidly rising brand equity of a relatively new brand. This does not apply to all new brands which quickly capture or reinvent product categories. Where a market segment is approached from a radically new angle or with an innovative product offer, often associated with entrepreneurial organisations, initial impact can often raise brand equity. Early innovators in car insurance – *Direct Line* – and in banking – *First Bank Direct* – provided a totally new way of servicing these sectors and, as a result, their respective brand equity ratings benefited hugely. *Egg, Goldfish* and *Virgin Direct* have followed and had the same sort of equity impact.
- **P2:** mature brands which enjoy market share dominance but have to fend off attack from new innovative or more market-aligned brands. *Barclays Bank* still benefits from years of brand-building marketing communications but has yet again come under attack from anti-Apartheid protesters because of its South African links.
- **P3:** perceived to be waning brands.

(*Continued*)

- **S1:** these are formerly waning brands which have reinvented themselves such as *Heinz Salad Cream*, *Brylcreem*, *Baileys*, *Durex* and *Harley-Davidson* (see Opening Case Study of Chapter 9 for a full discussion of *Harley-Davidson*'s brand equity revival).
- **S2:** brands which have no chance of recovery due to irreversible unsuitability to market or dramatically altered consumer tastes.

Source: Cooper and Simons (1997).

BRAND ARCHITECTURE

In a multi-brand organisation, a rational, structured approach to managing the totality of brands, and, at the same time, the broader organisational or brand narrative, is called the **brand architecture** (Uncles, Cocks and Macrae 1995) – see Figure 8.17. Brand architecture refers to the organising structure of the **brand portfolio**, which is the full range of brands, sub-brands and any co-brand arrangements with third parties within the organisation's market/product offer. It specifies roles, relationships and the different contexts that each market/product positioning will occupy. It's what Petromilli, Morrison and Million (2002) refer to as 'continuously emphasising the portfolio-wide thinking and business-wide implications of brand-oriented decisions'. The brand architecture should:

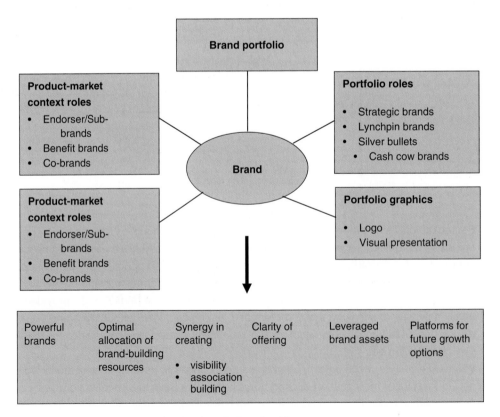

Figure 8.17: Brand architecture

Source: Aaker and Joachimsthaler (2000, p. 135).

- define the different branching hierarchies within an organisation;
- identify the specific brand roles within the portfolio;
- manage the relationships between brands;
- identify how the corporate brand and sub-brands relate to and support each other; and
- determine how the sub-brands reflect or reinforce the core purpose of the corporate brand to which they belong (Aaker and Joachimsthaler 2000, p 135).

What brand architecture can do is 'clarify linkages so that brands in a genuine family can gain from their association' (Randall 2000, p. 119). Different strategies require different architecture. The most common types are: 'branded house' architecture where a single brand spans a series of offerings with different brand names; and a 'house of brands' where each brand is standalone and the sum of the parts is greater than the whole. Davidson (2002) proposed a schematic for mapping out the different elements of brand architecture shown in Figure 8.18. There are three generic relationships between a master brand and sub-brands:

- **Monolithic or single brand** across an organisation: *Virgin, Red Cross* or the British *National Health Service,* where a single brand name is used and known to all employees, shareholders, partners, suppliers, individual and business customers and other stakeholders. *Unilever* has the Elida Institute as an umbrella for hair care products and the Pond Institute for skin care. We are now familiar with the brands from *Laboratoires Garnier* as an umbrella or pillar company brand.
- **Endorsed brands:** companies who operate in many categories need to differentiate individual products' competitive positioning and will enhance the brand by having a company endorsement which adds credibility: *Nestlé Kit Kat, Sony PlayStation, Ford Focus.*
- **House of brands:** parent brands like *P&G* and *Unilever* have individual sub-brands like *Pampers* and *Persil* which take prominence in the eyes of the consumer.

There are six 'models' of brand/product relationships: product, line, range, umbrella, source or endorsing brand. If we consider whether brand orientation (or origin) is either company or individual this extends to 10 types, as illustrated in Figure 8.19.

Types of brand		Organisational brand	Individual brands
Type 1: Single brand across organisation	Brand	IBM University Greenpeace Goldman Sachs	None
Type 2: Endorsed brands	Nestlé	Ralph Lauren Microsoft Sony McDonald's	Polo Windows PlayStation Big Mac
Type 3: House of brands	Brand	P&G Pfizer Renault	Pampers Viagra Clio

Figure 8.18: Brand relationship spectrum

Source: Davidson (2002).

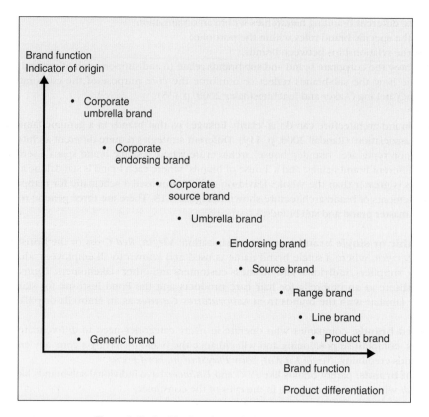

Figure 8.19: Positioning alternative brand strategies

Source: Kapferer (2000, p. 189). Reproduced with permission.

- **Product brand** strategy is a portfolio approach in which there is a range of individual products/ brands each with their own unique positioning. *P&G* and *Unilever* are companies that have a range of individual brands, some competing with each other (e.g. soap powders like *Daz, Ariel, Vizir* and *Dash*).
- **Line brand** strategy is an offer extended to products which have synergy under one brand name (e.g. different variations of hair treatments). *Nestlé* introduced a new variation to the 'countline' (a chocolate-based bar) – the *Kit Kat Chunky* – to reinvigorate its chocolate bar range when the target market saw no relevance in the original 'four-finger' bar.
- **Range brand** strategy involves offering a wide selection of products under a single area of competence, and is most prevalent in the food sector. Product names (e.g. 'fish pie', 'haddock pieces') are kept distinct but they all carry the overriding brand name (e.g. *Bird's Eye*).
- **Umbrella brand** strategy is where there is a house brand (e.g. *Canon, Honda, Mitsubishi*) but the individual products are distinctly different (e.g. cameras, photocopiers, inks etc).
- **Source brand** strategy is similar to umbrella brands where there is a house brand (e.g. *Yves St Laurent* perfumes) but the individual products carry their own distinctly different brand name (e.g. *Opium,* etc.).
- **Endorsing brand** strategy is the umbrella brand which covers all product types, product lines and individual brands.

Davidson (2002) listed six ways in which portfolio management enhances growth:

1. Clear prioritisation of future focus by major market.
2. Prioritisation by brand and product.

3. Concentration of spend on priority market, brands and products.
4. Operational cost savings through simplified business.
5. Disposal of brands which don't fit.
6. Gap filling by product development and acquisition.

Aaker (2004) discusses *Intel*'s hi-tech brand portfolio strategy which involved a clever co-branding strategy. In 1978, *Intel*'s 8086 microprocessor chip had just been approved by *IBM* to power its first personal computer. In 1991, with no patent protection on its *X86* processor, various competitive clones threatened *Intel*'s position. What did the company do? It instigated an innovative approach to branding – an ingredient-branding 'Intel inside' campaign costing $100 million based on highlighting the inclusion of its microprocessors as a key component of manufacturers' PCs. There were some doubts as to whether this was relevant for a B2B organisation. However, the 'Intel Inside' logo became ubiquitous and a controlled partnership between *Intel* and PC manufacturers was implemented. A kick-back to manufacturers for using the *Intel* logo (offering a 6% rebate) went into a marketing fund where *Intel* funded up to 50% in cooperative advertising. This massively increased the promotion of computers across the category, creating a differential which gave manufacturers who used the *Intel* logo (and chip obviously!) a 10% price premium. Branding not only provided competitive immunity, but also gave added value to the product by helping to minimise perceived risk.

MEASURING THE VALUE OF BRAND EQUITY

The chief benefits of having high brand equity are financial (e.g. profitability) and growth (see Table 8.1). A higher market share accrues in both cases. Measures such as relative price, market penetration, perceived quality/esteem, familiarity/awareness are essentially derived from a 'micro-economics framework' (Ambler 1997, p. 283) and assume a financial value orientation. However, the attitudinal and observable behavioural benefits which stem from relational aspects are increasingly seen as the main driver. Really, the essential brand equity is 'the strength, currency and value of the brand . . . the description, and assessment of the appeal, of a brand to all the target audiences who interact with it' (Cooper and Simons 1997, p. 1). Every time the various stakeholders – customers, prospects, intermediaries, media, shareholders, current and future employees, local residents and extended society – are exposed to the brand, 'equity' (both in terms of customer dialogue and company financial value) is registered.

Profitability Benefits

Customer loyalty may increase as a result of high brand equity and this translates into repeat purchase and attitudinal loyalty, which has a positive effect on sales (Chaudhuri and Holbrook, 2001). Increased market share may come from more purchases by existing customers (profitability) and by new customers converting to the brand (growth). High-equity brands have an easier task when it comes to attracting new customers (Anscheutz 2002). Strong brands are less price sensitive (Erdem, Swait and Louvière 2002) and able to attract a price premium and as a result get **higher margins**

Profitability	Growth
Increased customer loyalty	Brand expansion
Higher margins	Attract new customers
Lower price sensitivity	Competitor immunity
Increased effectiveness in the marketing communications	Crisis immunity
More power in distribution channels Higher market share	Geographical expansion

Table 8.1: Benefits of high brand equity

(Ailawadi, Lehmann and Neslin 2003). High-equity brands have established brand awareness and favourable brand associations, so marketing communications are more effective which makes the costs of reaching the customers with the brand message lower (Keller 2003). There is power in **distribution channels** of a number of manufacturer brands due to high brand equity. *Marks & Spencer* has recently had to rescind its 'own brand only' policy due to the demand for proprietary brands.

Growth Benefits

High-equity brands are also more protected against competitors' actions (Keller 2003), especially when consumer preferences are built on non-product-related attributes or user imagery. Strong relationships between the brand and consumers may stop low-priced competitors from entering the market and changing product category perceptions. A good example of a high-equity brand that has attained competitor immunity is *Harley-Davidson*. However, as we have seen in the case of *Levi Strauss*, high-equity brands may not be totally immune to low-priced competition. High-equity brands are more effective in managing crises that may emerge (Dahlén and Lange 2006). The detergent brand *Persil Power* (or *Omo Power/VIA Power* in some countries) that was launched in the early 1990s is another example of this. The detergent was so strong that the clothes were ruined during laundry. *Persil* was able to quickly recover from what could have been very damaging PR and customer backlash.

Expansion into new markets and new countries is helped by having high brand equity (Keller 2003). For example, the Spanish fashion retailer *Zara* launched its first store in Spain in 1975, outside Spain for the first time 13 years later in Portugal, and now has more than 1000 stores in over 64 countries. The risk of new product development is minimised due to the existing relationship that consumers have with the brand. And of course the potential for brand expansion is highest for high-equity brands (Czellar 2003, Simonin and Ruth 1998, Volckner and Sattler 2006).

Balance-Sheet Benefits

Brand equity is a balance-sheet asset as brands are 'wealth-generating financial assets, albeit intangible ones, so that we can actually place a financial value on them' (Batchelor 2000, p. 4). Buying the corner shop will involve premises costs, fittings, stock and so on and a payment for 'goodwill'. Goodwill is an intangible value estimated at the cost of building up brand name, recruiting and keeping customers, and the guaranteed income streams and positive word of mouth which will result. The *Nestlé* takeover of *Rowntree Mackintosh* (the price paid exceeded tangible assets by 300% – Neilsen 1993, p. 154) marked the start of the recognition of the value of the intangible balance-sheet asset of brand equity. What *Nestlé* was actually buying was the future potential of brands like *Kit Kat, Quality Street* and *After Eight*, a barrier to competition, as well as enormous brand start-up costs. *Coca-Cola's* brand equity was estimated to be $64 billion in 2002, representing 62% of the firm's capitalisation (Interbrand). It is evident that brands are an important asset to companies.

Google paid $1.65 billion for *YouTube* at a time when *YouTube* was not profitable. 'Accounting goodwill is the monetary value of the psychological goodwill which the brand has created over time through communication investment and consistent focus on products, both of which help build the reputation of the name' (Kapferer 2000, p. 24). *P&G* acquired *Gillette* for $57 billion. Besides *Gillette*, *P&G* got brands like *Duracell, Braun* and *Oral-B* in the deal. *L'Oréal* purchased *The Body Shop* for $1.4 billion. The price paid included a significant premium to the current shareholders. Srivastava, Shervani and Fahey (1998) established four types of shareholder values:

- Accelerate cash flows: faster response to marketing efforts, earlier brand trials, time-to-market acceptance.
- Enhance cash flows: new uses, cross-selling, price/market share premiums, lower sales and service costs, brand extensions.
- Reduce volatility and vulnerability of cash flows: the risk in the investment goes down with a strong brand which affects the net present value for the brand.
- Enhance residual value of cash flows: the residual value of the business is the value at the investment horizon. It is enhanced as cash flows increase during the investment period.

Originator	Factors measured
Aaker 1991	Awareness
	Brand associations and differentiations (e.g. personality, perceived value)
	Loyalty
	Market share measures
	Market behaviour measures
Cooper & Simons 1997	Brand quality reflects distinctiveness and relevance of its associations, esteem and perceived popularity
	Brand quantity covers awareness, penetration, loyalty, satisfaction ratings and sales
	Brand future reflects its potential for organic growth, fitness for changing marketplace and brand extendibility
Young & Rubicam 2000	Differentiation + Relevance = Strength
	Esteem + Knowledge = Stature
Interbrand 2003	Market (10%) structured attractiveness of market and its projected growth
	Stability (15%) brands that have been well established for a long time that constantly command customer loyalty
	Leadership (25%) ability to influence market
	Trend (10%) ability to remain contemporary
	Support (10%) quantity and quality of investments
	Internalisation/Globalisation (25%) appeal across a multiplicity of markets
	Protection (5%) legal protection, patents, trademarks

Table 8.2: Measuring brand equity

Source: adapted from Cooper and Simons (1997, p. 8).

There are different approaches to measuring brand equity. Main brand equity outcome models measure brand performance, revenue premium and market-based assets. A summary extracted from a paper on brand equity by Cooper and Simons (1997, p. 8) showing a selection of these over the years is illustrated in Table 8.2.

Differentiation is building brand equity, more so than esteem, relevance or knowledge. This is demonstrated in the Matter of Fact box below describing the Brand Asset Valuator model.

MATTER OF FACT

Brand Asset Valuator Model

The advertising agency *Young & Rubicam* developed the Brand Asset Valuator (BAV) model, the world's largest database on consumer-derived information on brands. Because of its comprehensiveness, BAV offers a great opportunity to follow how brand equity is

(Continued)

created and built (or lost), providing information on brand assets globally or country by country and within and across category comparisons. BAV is built on four pillars showing the current status, historical development and suggested future development. The pillars are:

- **Differentiation** – the degree to which a brand is seen as different from others.
- **Relevance** – the breadth of the brand's appeal but not necessarily profitability.
- **Esteem** – measures how well the brand is regarded and respected.
- **Knowledge** – measures familiarity and intimacy in the consumer–brand relationship.

Differentiation and relevance are keys to the future and determine brand strength. Esteem and knowledge are keys to past performance and determine brand stature.

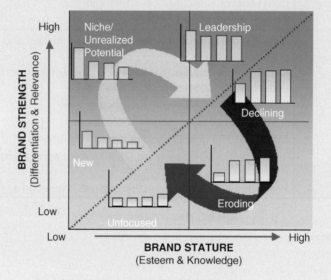

Brand Asset Valuator power grid

The figure shows the BAV power grid. The pillars are, from left to right: differentiation, relevance, esteem and knowledge. New brands begin their life in the lower left quadrant. Normally, they move upwards by increasing brand strength and become 'Niche' brands (who stay here) or brands with 'Unrealised Potential' (in mass markets with a potential to move towards the right). Brands that have high strength and stature are 'Leadership' brands (only 2% according to Young & Rubicam). These brands have a value of above 80% on all four pillars. They are differentiated from other brands, are relevant in their category, are well liked and have a strong relationship with customers. Leadership may be sustained over a long time if the brand is managed correctly. Some brands add stature but lose strength (mainly differentiation) and become 'Declining Leaders'. If this process continues, the influence of these brands will become eroded. The worst scenario is when brand stature is affected negatively and the brand turns into an unfocused brand and gradually loses its way and purpose with the target audience.

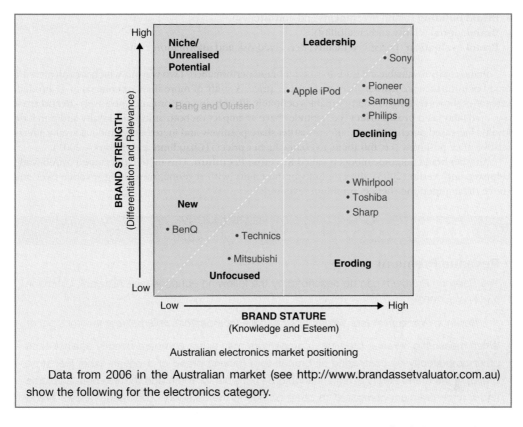

Australian electronics market positioning

Data from 2006 in the Australian market (see http://www.brandassetvaluator.com.au) show the following for the electronics category.

Erdem and Swait (1998) have developed a model (see Figure 8.20) that helps us understand consumer-based brand equity. The basis is that brands are valuable to consumers when they have high expected utility. The model has three main parts:

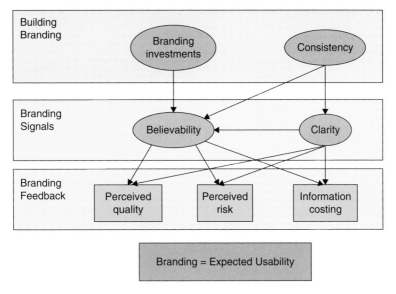

Figure 8.20: A model of consumer-based brand equity

Source: adapted from Erdem and Swait (1998).

- **Brand building** (brand investments and consistency).
- **Brand signal** (clarity and credibility).
- **Brand evaluation** (perceived quality, perceived risk and information costs).

Brand equity is valuable if it leads to a better brand performance. Two ways in which we can measure brand performance are market share and relative price. A study of more than 100 brands in 41 product categories shows that brand equity variables definitely affect brand performance positively. **Brand trust** (i.e. credibility) and **brand affect** (i.e. attitude) have an impact on both attitudinal loyalty and purchase loyalty. Increased purchase loyalty affects market share positively and increased attitudinal loyalty affects relative price positively (i.e. the ability to charge higher prices) (Chaudhuri and Holbrook 2001).

Another brand outcome model is called **Revenue Premium**. This model, developed by Ailawadi, Lehmann and Neslin (2003), directly links brand equity with revenue, measuring revenue over and above the competition (hence 'premium revenue').

MATTER OF FACT

Revenue Premium

The *Revenue Premium* can be described by the following equation (see Ailawadi, Lehmann and Neslin 2003):

Revenue Premium = (our volume) (our price) – (competitor's volume) (competitor's price)

When measuring revenue premium, competitors may either compare directly against each other or indirectly by comparing all brands to a generic brand or a private label (i.e. store brand). If the brand equity is high, it should be possible for the brand to have both a volume and a price premium compared to other brands in the category. This model allows brand equity to affect brand outcomes for volume or price or both variables simultaneously. In the figure below, we show the four possible revenue premium outcomes when a brand is compared to a private label. Our brand may have a dual premium (case A), a price premium (case B), volume premium (case C) or negative premium (case D). The revenue premium in case B and case C may be either positive or negative based on the size of the components.

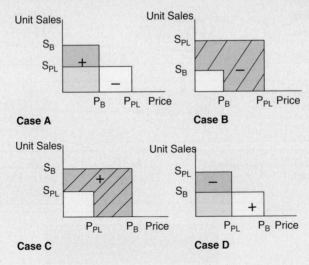

Measuring revenue premium

Source: Ailawadi, Lehmann and Neslin (2003).

CLOSING CASE STUDY

Levi's Jeans: Focusing on the Legend gives Legs to the Levi's Brand

Levi's logo worn with pride

Levi Strauss & Co is the largest and most successful brand name in the apparel business in the world. Since opening its first store in 1856, selling supplies to California Gold Rush miners, the *Levi's* name has been synonymous with the original blue jean and central to the brand's global positioning as an American icon and 'coveted symbol of the casual, unpretentious American lifestyle' (*Forbes* Magazine 1996). *Levi's* history is written into the actual fabric of each pair of jeans: the Two Horse label, the seam-strengthening rivets, and the orange thread all indicate the strength and workmanlike value for money brand ethos. By the early 1980s, this most enduring 'value-driven' (Yeshin 2007, p. 348) brand was now under severe threat from copycat, 'me-too' brands and the growing influence of powerful retailers. The challenge was to 'remain relevant to a target audience that regenerates itself every four or five years and to avoid the distractions of success' (Robert Holloway, *Levi Strauss*).

As an aspirational, inspirational brand, *Levi's* undoubted strength has been the ability to connect with the target audience of 15–19-year-old males who not only account for over 30% of all jeans sold, but provide a stimulus to all other demographic categories. Its position as the 'original American blue jean' communicates the key positioning statement: *Levi's* is the genuine article. In the minds of its target audience, *Levi's* brand stands for: rebellion, youthfulness, quality, originality, excitement and fun. In the brand's heritage, Levi's appropriated cowboy and Wild West imagery. It lived in the mythology of James Dean, Jack Kerouac's Beat Generation, rock 'n roll, and that crucial period when young consumers 'find themselves'. It had become a sort of peer group uniform which represented the ultimate consumer paradoxical positioning: mass-produced individuality.

In order to maintain this, the brand had not only to be relevant to social, cultural and consumer trends, but retain its special positioning in the minds of the target audience. However, in the late 1970s, the company made the mistake of expanding beyond the core 'blue jean' lines (even baby clothes and leisure suits) and *Levi's* jeans became available on an increasingly wide basis. Far from this being evidence of the growing dominance of the brand, the 'distraction of success' caused a loss of focus which precipitated a rapid decline and succeeded only in diluting the appeal of the brand to its key customers.

When extensive distribution became a negative factor in diluting the brand, *Levi's* decided to limit exposure in outlets which 'contaminated the brand'. Their 'Five Point Dealer' retail policy effectively 'controls its image and preserves its brand capital' (Kapferer 2000, p. 160). This actually resulted in a court case in the UK when *Tesco* not only represented the wrong customer profile but undercut the price, resulting in the perceived value of the brand being diminished. The launch of 'Original Levi's Stores' gave a perfect platform to present heritage and evolution, core values and proved to be a great test-bed for new ideas. *Levi's* was also not immune to low-priced competition, suffering profitability and market share problems due to copycats (even *Virgin* became competition) making similar jeans as its flagship 501s. Even the filing of law suits to prevent infringement has not offered protection and the brand equity has been severely damaged.

When *Levi Strauss's* top management met to discuss the crisis in the 1980s, the unanimous decision to 'get back to basics' and refocus on core strengths was taken. A brand-equity

(Continued)

measurement system (Keller 2001, p. 19) was installed and it was quickly discovered that the brand image was beginning to slip. A diversification policy of brand extensions was reversed and the key to survival was seen as 'image not volume'. With the iconic *Levi's 501®* at the centre, all marketing communications were to be concentrated on jeans as the repositioning platform. Web and cinema advertisements were abandoned because not enough of the youth market was being reached and the campaigns were TV and print-oriented (*Ad News*, April 20 2000, p. 16). Strategically, any product introductions would now be done separately, outside of the *Levi's* brand halo (the *Dockers* and *Slates* brands service different customers).

To accentuate the theme of individuality, an innovative Personal Pair Programme was introduced which helped develop one-to-one relationships with consumers, providing a huge database of customer profiling information. *Levi's* describes this as a 'truly heartland *Levi Strauss & Co.* concept for the modern age'. This is enforced in Europe by what it calls the 'acid wall test' which is a concrete statement of values, attributes and core associations of the *Levi's* brand. The equity of the *Levi's* brand was severely diminished and now it had to be protected. This equity is driven by a youth mindset and has been facilitated by the technological possibilities of the *Levi's* website. This has given an opportunity to leverage its position as a leading-edge marketer and brand builder. This allows the delivery of much deeper message content and for two-way, self-directed media experience between brand and audience.

Levi's mobile fashion

The purchase of a brand like *Levi's* owes much to its symbolism and perceived quality over the competition, allowing premium pricing against me-too inferior brands. It also has the huge advantage of competing in global markets which are largely homogeneous. Yet despite this, the brand is once again in decline. The nadir came in 2003 when a reputedly $3 million 30-second TV slot in the US Superbowl broadcast featuring an obscure 'product-oriented' advertisement for *Levi's Type One Jeans* failed dramatically (*Advertising Age*, 31 March 2003, p. 1). Even innovations like mobile phones and links with *iPods* have been instigated a little too late for the current target market. *Levi Strauss* has largely ignored contemporary fashion trends and failed to innovate or stay relevant to its customers. The *Levi Strauss* problem has been attributed to the company's failure to transcend a mere product association – and one with outdated imagery at that – and promote a lifestyle narrative.

QUESTIONS

1. Identify the strategic and tactical aspects of *Levi*'s positioning exercise.

2. How risky is limiting a product's market potential for the sake of maintaining brand integrity?

3. The *Levi's* product has not really changed since the Gold Rush days. How do you account for the phenomenal transformation to become an American icon and 'coveted symbol of the casual, unpretentious American lifestyle'?

CHAPTER SUMMARY

In this chapter, we have discussed the concept of branding, both the corollary and driving force of segmentation and positioning. We have explored the different important aspects of brands including the function of brands and the symbolic meaning projected by brands. We have presented several branding models with different focuses. All these models are useful when the marketer wants to analyse the current situation for the brand and understand its status. Brand anatomy models show what people think about the brand in absolute terms. Brand equity models show relative strengths of the brands in the product category. We have looked at customer-based brand equity and consumer-based brand equity as well as brand outcome models which show the links between brand equity and various economic and financial outcomes.

We examined how brands are an asset for organisations and a source of value for customers. We demonstrated the sources and concepts of brand equity and how a structure for the financial and economic outcomes of brand equity is provided.

We also described how the brand can be developed through different types of brand expansion through the application of brand portfolios and how this is used to develop and capitalise on the brand's potential.

REFLECTIVE QUESTIONS

a. Describe the sources and outcomes of brand equity.

b. Explain why high brand awareness is not equal to brand strength.

c. *Adidas* and *Goodyear* have a brand alliance for shoes. *Adidas* has also collaborated with *Stella McCartney* (clothes) and *Porsche* (shoes). What do you think about these alliances? In addition, can you identify partners for *Adidas* where the other company sells the products and *Adidas* contributes with its brand image?

d. Discuss the brand extension issues for *Google* and suggest three possible product categories that you think *Google* could extend the brand to.

e. What are the key functions of brands?

RESEARCH PROJECTS

Earlier in the chapter, we referred to Aaker's (2004) discussion of the ingredient-branding 'Intel Inside' campaign. Investigate further how *Intel* built brand equity through this approach.

The *Coca-Cola 'Dasani* Disaster' showed that even a brand with a proven global track record and massive market leadership can have brand equity diminished by one brand failure. Dahlén and Lange (2006) explore how brand disasters can be contagious and impact on other brands in the portfolio. Look up their paper ('A Disaster Is Contagious: How a Brand in Crisis Affects Other Brands', *Journal of Advertising Research*, 46(4), 388–97) and analyse the reasons why organisations must be wary of containing negative brand equity.

CHAPTER  9

BRAND NARRATIVE AND RELATIONAL MANAGEMENT

"Brands can turn customers into 'fans', especially when they connect with consumers' culture. That's why brand managers must evaluate, emulate and infiltrate the core culture of their customers."
Blackwell, Miniard and Engel (2006, p. 435)

"Brands are the greatest gift that commerce has brought to popular culture."
Olins (2000, p. 52)

This chapter discusses the concept of organisations and products having brand narratives, story arcs which parallel product life cycles and provide longevity for brands, reliable income streams for organisations and, more importantly, provide meaning for consumers. It takes the long view that all marketing communications – media and messages – are bonded in strategic and tactical dialogues and consumers co-create, disseminate and advocate all communications about the brand.

After reading this chapter, you'll be able to:

- Appreciate the difference between a 'brand image' approach to marketing communications and an 'experiential' perspective.
- Understand why the emphasis has shifted to creating environments conducive towards encouraging long-term brand loyalty.
- Appreciate changing levels of brand communications.
- Understand why it is necessary to have brand narratives in today's overcrowded marketplace.
- Evaluate how investing in relationships with customers is key to building and sustaining brand longevity.
- Examine the rise in brand communities.
- Evaluate the strategic significance of reward as a way of creating customer loyalty.

The creation and maintenance of brands requires the development of deep, salient associations which resonate not just in terms of short-term category need fulfilment, but long-term meaningful symbiotic relationships from which organisations achieve lifetime loyalty and consumers acquire individual and group meaning. It is this relationship-building element of branding which gives it prominence in marketing communications. As McQuail (2000, p. 363) points out, 'people in audiences do not normally have any awareness of themselves as belonging to markets, and the market discourse in relation to the audience is implicitly manipulative'. However, it is a two-way process where customer/brand interaction is a reciprocal activity (Blackston 1993) and it involves the creation of value (perceived or actual) in addition to the utilitarian function of products.

Products are made in factories, but brands are born in the many conversations which circulate culturally in the brand narratives of: the companies who send them out into the marketplace and infuse a positioning story into the strategic and tactical communications wrapped around the brand; the intermediaries who stock, display and sell the brand; the culture industries who deconstruct and evaluate meaning; and the end users who negotiate meaning from brand communication, community and complicity.

In an overcrowded marketplace the notion that brands will become the chief storytellers which both generate and articulate social values and myths is becoming more pertinent. Sherry (2005) refers to this as 'marketing mythopeia' and describes the chief function of marketing communications as being the creation and perpetuation of deep meaning through narrative. Brand narratives are about the story arc that is negotiated for the brand and the life experience of the consumer. In order for a brand to survive, it has to be perpetually salient and the consumer permanently engaged. The consumer, in effect, owns the brand and indeed owns the brand narrative. An organisation can attempt to create a brand, but it is customers who will determine whether a brand comes alive or not (Timacheff and Rand 2001).

OPENING CASE STUDY

Harley-Davidson: Born to be Wild: Zen and the Art of Brand Maintenance

A brand personality can make a brand more interesting and memorable and can even become a vehicle to express a customer's identity. The *Harley-Davidson* motorcycle is a quintessentially American brand whose value stems from the identity associated with 'outlaw' myths perpetrated by *The Harley-Davidson Company (HDC)*, *Harley* users and the populist worlds of the culture industries (Holt 2004, p. 156). Schouten and McAlexander (1995, p. 50) identified the *Harley* brand's 'DNA' as consisting of three values: American patriotism, machismo and personal freedom. Under pressure from Japanese imports and changing social landscape, the brand nearly perished; it was mechanically substandard and culturally irrelevant. Some say the revival of the *Harley-Davidson* motorcycle brand can't be explained through an analysis of marketing communications because the brand is mystical and magic; others say it celebrates marketing's 'truth' by getting closer to the customer and co-authoring an enduring brand narrative.

Early in the 1980s the *HDC* was saved from the edge of bankruptcy by a leveraged buyout of managers (including one of the original owner's grandsons). They immediately set about restoring product quality, riding with *Harley* owners and feeding back into the development of relationship communications. Getting close to the customer meant brand knowledge was transmitted through what Joanne Bischmann (Vice President of Marketing, *Harley-Davidson*) calls 'tribal knowledge'. The development of 'brand communities' had started not with company-authored stories, but with the many motorcycle clubs; they had become a 'potent populist world' (Holt 2004. p. 160) which had cultural resonance with bikers perpetuating the American ideology of the outlaw counterculture. It is widely accepted that subcultures provide influential meanings and practices that structure consumers' identities, actions and relationships (Kozinets 2001, p. 67). 'Key consumer images in the *Harley-Davidson* subculture were formed as new bikers engaged with *dramatis personae* from mass-media culture' (Schouten and McAlexander 1995, p. 57). A *Life* magazine exposé, the film *The Wild One*, and various journalist first-hand reports on Hell's Angel biker gangs (notably Hunter S. Thompson 1966) 'stitched' the outlaw myth to *Harley*. Meaning was transferred from Hell's Angel to Brando to bike to bikers, and they provided a threatening counterpoint that gave meaning and motivation to America's ideological agenda: anti-establishment, anti-conformity and authenticity. Brando's iconic figure of youth rebellion allowed men to escape the restrictions of conformist 'feminine' society and its symbols were leather, denim and motorcycles. Following events involving bikers – such as the Hell's Angels' involvement in 'policing' at a Rolling Stones' concert in Altamont; the counterculture classic *Easy Rider*; alignment with Reagan's new capitalist 'gunfighter' imagery; and a whole host of Hollywood's 'man of action' movies – the *Harley* brand had somehow repackaged the outlaw myth and still stood for a new wave of

NO. I'VE DECIDED TO OPT FOR A SMALL AND RATHER UNEVENTFUL LIFE.

An ad for the Harley lifestyle

anti-hippy America. This reincarnation of the myth was now fuelled by fighting the new enemy: the influx of Asian products undermining the American flag and destroying industry. *Harley* had become an icon for white working-class men emasculated by industrialisation and the attack of foreign manufacture. The 'stars and stripes' flags that adorned the bikers' *Harleys* now became permanently captured in a new *Harley* logo, and when a blatantly anti-Asian five-page advertisement appeared in the subversive biker magazine *Easyriders, HDC* at last held up a mirror to its target audience and started to co-author the *Harley* myth.

Informal networks of *Harley* riders grew: initially the Modified Motorcycle Association, then an action group ABATE (A Brotherhood Aimed Towards Education). What gave impetus to the brand's identity, and the subsequent creation of narrative myth and elevation to iconic status, was the harvesting of these cycle clubs as a source of popular culture material. Nowadays, buying a *Harley-Davidson*, the king of motorcycles, gives you automatic entry to another family – a membership to the one-million strong *Harley Owners Group (HOG)*. Founded in 1983 by board member Vaughan Beals, the intention was based on sound retention principles: foster customer loyalty; enhance the *Harley* lifestyle experience and deepen brand relationships. The club offers similar club benefits to joining the Automobile Association or RAC in the UK (insurance, emergency breakdown, contests, club communications), but also the opportunity to connect with other like-minded people. *Harley-Davidson's* Anniversary Reunion celebrations are comprehensive events that attract more than 100,000 *Harley* riding enthusiasts to Milwaukee in the USA with the annual 'Posse Ride' featuring a marathon 2000 mile adventure. This is what Duncan and Moriarty (1997, p. 1) refer to as a 'relationship brand' representing an affinity group.

An interesting aspect of this identity myth is the examination of the metaphors at play in the *Harley* brand narrative. Zaltman and Zaltman (2008, p. 54) refer to the part that the metaphor of 'emotional balance' plays in the relationship consumers have with the *Harley-Davidson* brand. Owners describe their riding experience as a source of emotional balance in their lives; pleasure of riding offsets the monotony of work and the stresses of responsibility. 'They become more in touch with their inner selves, feeling calm, confidence and self-esteem'. *Harley* has used this research in its marketing communications, asserting that it is a form of therapy. Another metaphor that was unearthed in research was the 'container' image: a lone motorcycle on the open road is a uniquely American symbol for freedom, and one study brought up deep-seated metaphors for containment and freedom. Consumers described how the motorcycle dissolves 'restrictive containers' of work, allowing them to express themselves: a rider 'might feel more macho and freer of a confining job and its attendant lifestyle' (Aaker and Joachimsthaler 2000). This is a brand that offers emotional, physical, environmental and even cultural roots and instils national pride. It is the epitome of customer brand engagement: a physical vehicle and also a psychological and emotional one. *Harley-Davidson* riders describe how they develop deep connections with their bikes, feeling protective, much as a parent protects a child; *HOG* members describe 'changing my bike's fluids as if I was changing diapers'.

The Harley Owners Group® is much more than just a motorcycle organization. It's one million people around the world united by a common passion: making the Harley-Davidson® dream a way of life.

The Harley-Davidson mission statement

Some brands are badges, showing that a consumer belongs to a valued user community. The *Harley Owners Group* proclaims on its website: 'Express yourself in the company of others. The *Harley Owners Group* is much more than a motorcycle organisation. It's one million people around the world united by a common passion: making the *Harley-Davidson* dream a way of life'. Really strong brands like *Harley-Davidson* have gone beyond achieving visibility and differentiation to develop deep relationships with their customers; the brand has become a meaningful part of the customer's

(Continued)

life and/or self-concept (Aaker and Joachimsthaler 2000, p. 264). *Harley* became a convincing symbol for celebrating masculine autonomy, and its myth as 'the modern-day steed of the outlaw' stemmed from its charisma, authenticity and the salient associations with key cultural turning points. Even today, the cycle is a symbol of recaptured youth and individuality: the average age of a *Harley* owner is 42 and the bike still represents autonomy and Zen-like escape. 'The *Harley* consumption experience has a spirituality derived in part from a sense of riding as a transcendental departure from the mundane' (Schouten and McAlexander 1995, p. 50), customers' brand loyalty is almost an evangelical mission. As Kunde (2002) claims: '*Harley-Davidson* is not just the most powerful motorcycle cult, it is also one of the most powerful religions – if not **the** most powerful brand religion – world-wide'.

www.harley-davidson.com/wcm/Content/Pages/HOG/HOG.jsp?locale=en_US&bmLocale=en_US

QUESTIONS

1. Part of the *HDC*'s marketing communications was aimed at customer retention. How does it do this?

2. Is it risky to associate a product with cultural meaning as part of the overarching brand story?

3. Is brand integrity really relevant against cheaper, better value motorcycle brands?

4. Can lessons be applied to other brands or is the 'magic and mystique' of the *Harley* brand only applicable to iconic brands?

EVOLVING BRAND COMMUNICATIONS

From the 1960s onwards, it has been apparent that the ability of marketing communications to stimulate sales has diminished the more saturated markets have become and the more choice consumers have. As a result, emphasis has shifted to creating environments conducive to encouraging long-term brand loyalty. And yet, even the construct of 'loyalty' is not consistent with all consumers: it means habit or passivity to one person and dedication to someone who will defer purchase until the favoured brand is found (Zaltman 2003, p. 134).

Various research has pointed to the weakness of advertising having a 'silver bullet effect' on brands (Barnard and Ehrenberg 1997), and lack of loyalty leading to 'repertoire buying' (i.e. selecting from many brands in a consideration set). Initially, this was attributed by advertising agencies, who 'blamed sales promotion for eroding the power of the brand' (Brierley 2002, p. 235). Let us re-examine what the main functions of branding are. They can be seen from different perspectives: **input-based** where branding is seen as instrumental in directing resources to affect customer response; **output-based** centring on consumers' interpretations of what brands can help them achieve; and **time-based** which recognises that brands are dynamic and, to survive, they must reflect the context they live in (de Chernatony 2002, p. 19). A cohesive integrated approach to marketing communications was required with the brand as the 'hub of the wheel' (Proctor and Kitchen 2000). The recognition of the consumer as sovereign in communications and the importance of symmetry in the process is the latest incarnation. As de Chernatony and Dall'Olmo Riley (1998, p. 428) claim, the brand exists because of this two-way, continuous process; the values imbued in the brand by the company are interpreted and redefined by consumers.

As well as being jointly created, communications must also be mutually beneficial. Kitchen (1999, p. 22) defines marketing communications as 'the process where commonness of thought and meaning is achieved or attempted between organisations and individuals' and underlines its importance by referring to it as 'the *sine qua non* underpinning all manner of exchanges in both the public and private sector' (p. 2). Although this is now a prerequisite for the achievement of company objectives, he emphasises the fact that neither partner is dominant in the process.

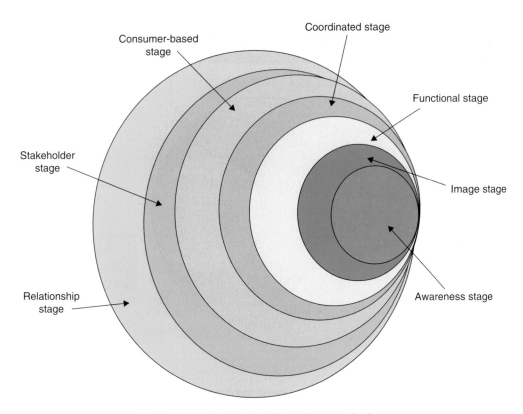

Figure 9.1: Changing levels of brand communications

In Figure 9.1 we can see this gradual gravitation from company-generated monologues to company/customer communications which are mutually constructed, the shift now having progressed to a much broader societal, relationship orientation. The inner, narrow rings in the diagram show a product-orientation (awareness, image and functional communications), where the emphasis is on category positioning vis-à-vis the competition. This leads to a coordinated (strategically integrated) perspective, through to a consumer-oriented and broader stakeholder franchise. The outer ring shows the stage where emotional, relational bonds are formed. At this point, communications are symmetrical; dialogue has replaced monologue, brand owner and brand user are co-producers of meaning.

BRAND MEANING

For consumers, a brand has different levels of meaning (Figure 9.2). At a basic level, the brand will be seen in the context of its ability to fulfil a category need as well as its relative competitiveness. The physical attributes have to be matched against assumed needs. This may change with time and will reflect competitive positioning, technological innovations and must also reflect changing consumer requirements. With the speed of technological change, product life cycles are compressed and it is incredible that a physical attribute which is seen as an innovation giving a competitive edge (e.g. the inclusion of CD units which will play MP3s in cars) can be quickly copied and the initial 'higher specification' can become the standard. In some cases, physical attributes and the functional consequences are inextricably linked. *Ronseal's Quick Finish Garden Sprayer* has the physical attributes of integral spray-gun and specially formulated paint which makes the product easy to apply and minimises time.

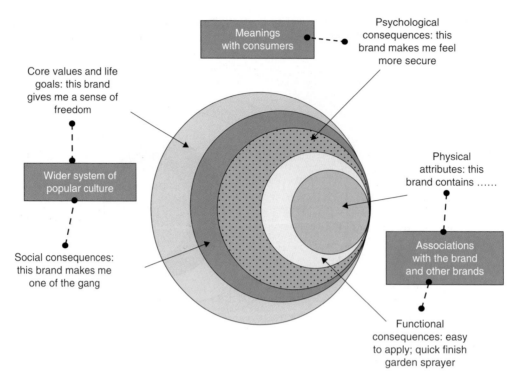

Figure 9.2: Level of brand meaning

Source: after Zaltman (2003).

At the next level, a brand will have a psychological significance for an individual: security, perceived risk, self-image, ego, status and so on. The context of the brand in the wider realm of popular culture will be measured in terms of the social consequences of the brand's ability to help affiliation and belonging, and can facilitate group identity and aspiration. Beyond this level, brands fulfil a higher order need for self-actualisation tied into core values and life goals. Therefore, branding is about attaching social meanings to products and services.

The *Dove* 'Real Beauty Campaign' was launched to 'free woman from today's beauty stereotypes and to help embrace their own beauty'. Using 'real women' in the advertisements who had been spotted on the street, the images projected in this campaign were suggested by research claiming that women preferred the natural look as opposed to 'unrealistic body perfection they are confronted with on a regular basis'. *Unilever*, who makes the *Dove* brand, has 'a commitment to breaking down stereotypes and enabling women to celebrate their beauty' and has set up the 'Self Esteem Fund' which aims at reaching five million females by 2010 conveying the brand meaning: 'every woman is beautiful and we should celebrate this'.

Dove women celebrate their beauty

This is a good example of how meaning is both instilled into the brand by brand owners and negotiated by brand users. This phenomenon happened by chance when *Unilever* contacted users of its anti-ageing cream in a routine research exercise. The response was unprecedented: women wanted to talk about their experiences – they wanted to tell their story. *Unilever* had the good sense to encourage and extend this conversation.

Brands are used to signify rites of passage and are part of the sociali-sation process. Alcoholic beverages like *Carling, WKD, John Smith's, Carlsberg,* Irish cider brands *Bul-mers* and *Magners, Smirnoff* and even drinks with associations of older target groups like *Baileys*, have added a new layer of social meaning which appeals to the need for affili-ation. Buying a pint of *Carling* may well quench thirst and refresh, but it is also a symbol of group identity. Recent *Carling* advertisements have

Carling is a symbol of group identity

used images of going out with the lads placed in the most obscure settings to emphasise the camaraderie and the security of 'belonging'.

Many communication theory analysts have been preoccupied with the 'location' of meaning. Jensen (1991) asks whether meaning resides 'with the intention of the sender, or is it embedded in the language, or is it primarily a matter of the receivers' interpretation?'. According to McCracken (1986), 'cultural meaning is located in three places: the culturally constituted world; the consum-er good; and the individual consumer, and moves in a trajectory at two points of transfer: world to good and good to individual'. As culture is the 'lens through which individuals view phenomena' (p. 72), meaning constructed in the consumer's everyday world will be created and transferred through consumption of brands to provide individuals with a framework for identity construction. Figure 9.3 illustrates how McCracken describes the transfer of meaning through 'culturally consti-tuted' conduits: marketing communications (although he uses the narrower term 'advertising' in his work), consumer rituals (such as rites of passage, weddings, exchange and possession rituals)

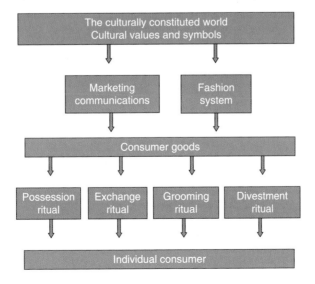

Figure 9.3: The meaning transfer model

Source: McCracken (1986). Reproduced with permission.

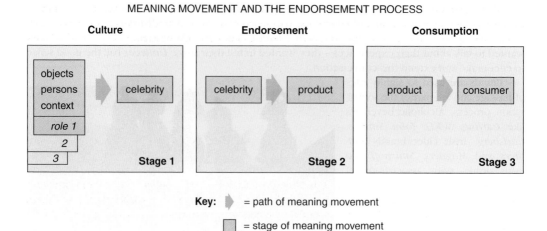

Figure 9.4: Meaning movement and the endorsement process

and the 'fashion system'. Marketing communications and the fashion system move meaning from the culturally constituted world; consumer rituals move meaning from brands to individuals. Some brands are defined more by expressive values than purely functional elements, and can transcend category boundaries because they have the ability to transfer meaning.

This movement of meaning through both marketing communications and the adoption of fashion can be illustrated with the examples of fashion retailers like *Marks & Spencer* and *Topshop* who use 'in vogue' celebrities like Myleene Klass, Twiggy, Erin O'Connor, Lily Cole, and Kate Moss to endorse their product. Here 'meaning' is transferred from the 'cultural currency' of the celebrity to the product available in *Marks & Spencer* stores to the consumer who purchases and wears the clothes: the path is 'culture', 'endorsement' to 'consumption' (Figure 9.4).

The 'meaning' that is being transferred is therefore culturally constituted and is dependent upon the context within which it is set. Hackley (1999, p. 143) refers to the signs of meaning transfer as 'culturally embedded message codes'. In an increasingly uncertain world, cues about life, role and identity are taken from brands rather than the traditional 'culturally transfusive triad' (Blackwell, Miniard and Engel 2006) of family, religion or educational institutions. In Grant's (2006) words, 'brands can now affect consumers as surrogate traditions'. Increasingly, products are used not for what they intrinsically are, but for what they represent. There is more and more emphasis on the symbolic nature of brands and with the shift in focus from tangibles to intangibles, 'the core activity of many corporations is transformed: from the production of things to the production of images' (Salzer-Morling and Strannegård 2002, p. 224).

'Our symbolic world provides a powerful "playground" for marketers to convey product attributes to consumers' (Solomon, Bambossy and Askegaard 2002, p. 53). The frame of reference for consumers comprises cultural signposts. This is what Domzal and Kernan (1992, p. 49) are referring to when they describe advertising as serving 'as a kind of culture/consumption dictionary; its entries are products, and their definitions are cultural meanings'. This occurs when consumers identify with cultural symbols such as success, affiliation, individuality or any form of self-expression.

As brands satisfy sensory, aesthetic and emotional needs in consumers, they become signs for the field of meanings consumers integrate into their personal space to enhance, complement or transform themselves into their world. As Hackley (1999, p. 137) puts it: 'Marketing messages seek to utilise signs to signify certain values to certain groups . . . the subjective world of meanings'. Research into this type of brand meaning involves analysing the semiotic components of texts and visual representation of communication images, helping to clarify the codes which shape the meaning of the brand in creative execution. The roots of semiotic analysis are in the seminal work of Roland Barthes (1967) in which he attempted to deconstruct communications as a system of signs.

Mick (1986) was an early contributor to the application of semiotics in examining the correspondence between signs and symbols. Their role in assignment of meaning provided clear evidence of the efficacy of using culturally coded communications. The beginning of modern semiotics began with Charles Sanders Peirce's (1883) account of signification, representation, reference and meaning. In his 'Sign Theory', he claimed that every message has three basic components: an object, a sign and an interpretant:

- An **icon** is a sign that resembles the product in some way (e.g. *Apple* computers).
- An **index** is connected to some sign of the product because they share some property (e.g. *Isklar* glacier 'ice'; pine trees for fresheners).
- A **symbol** is a sign related to a product because of purely conventional associations (e.g. *Mercedes Benz*).

Solomon, Bambossy and Askegaard (2002) demonstrates this by deconstructing the meaning transfer of the mythical '*Marlboro* Man' who borrows from and, at the same time, reinforces a fundamental myth of America – whilst selling cigarettes of course! Figure 9.5 illustrates this by tracing the semiotic path of image transfer from myth to man to brand to product.

- At the **basic level,** the 'object' is the product itself, the cigarettes; the 'sign' is the image which represents the intended meaning, which is the contents of the advertisement using cowboy and western imagery; and the 'interpretant' is the meaning which is derived from the semiotics of this: this man smokes this brand of cigarettes. Barthes (1967) described denotation as the 'first order of signification'

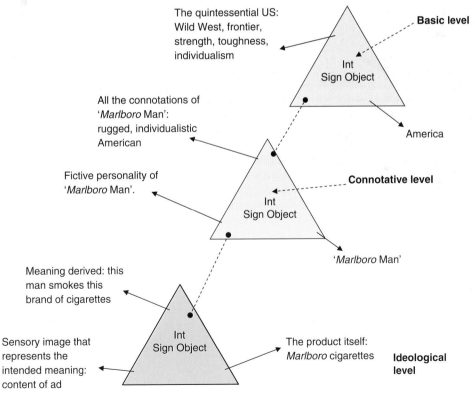

Figure 9.5: Relationship of components in semiotic analysis of meaning

Source: Solomon, Bambossy and Askegaard (2002, p. 53).

because it regards the relationship between the signifier (the cowboy in this case) and the signified (the cigarettes or product itself).

- At the **connotative level**, the 'object' is the man; the 'sign' is the fictive, mythical image of *Marlboro* Man; and the 'interpretant' element is the connotative meanings which are implied in the semiotics of the cowboy qualities: rugged, individual, cool, American. This is the 'second level of signification' as it refers to the associated meaning that may be conjured up by the object signified. All the mythical images of ruggedness, masculinity and even a contradictory association with nature are transferred to the product.

- At the **ideological level**, the 'object' is now mythical America; the 'sign' is all the connotations that are implied in the meaning transfer process; and the 'interpretant' element is the quintessential America gained from using the brand: Wild West, frontier, strength, toughness, individualism. Barthes (1977) extended this semiological discussion by referring to the notion of 'myth' which places an extra level of meaning on brand associations which have contextual or cultural significance or resonance to individuals.

Barthes's seminal textual analysis of an advertisement for an Italian pasta brand *Panzani* showed how brand communications works on a number of levels of meaning. The illustration showed a bag of groceries (invoking a domestic image) which is the physical signifier, which was meant to invoke images of freshness (the level of connotation). However the inclusion of red and green colours also signified 'Italianness' which evoked culinary tradition and excellence. Look at the advertisement for another Italian brand – *PastaVilla*. See how the clever use of sexual imagery (ingredients that look like female lingerie!) has altogether different connotations.

Sexy pasta has double meaning

Researchers in semiotic analysis often use a 'semiotic square' approach (Solomon, Bambossy and Askegaard 2002) which involves using a technique based on the principle that meanings have 'oppositions' or polarities of male/female, dark/light and so on, which can be used to mentally locate a brand. The analysis of a shopping centre, for example, yielded information on **utilitarian** values (economic and practical) and **existential** (life values and personal experience) (Hetzel 2002). This bipolar reference point approach has precedence in: the distinction by Holbrook and Hirschman (1982) suggesting the opposites of factual (tangible and verifiable) and evaluative (intangible and subjective); functional and user imagery; and the extremes of utilitarian and hedonistic (Batra and Ahtola 1990). Benoît (1998) used an innovative approach to the semiotic analysis of brand meanings when he examined the role brands play 'compared to roles played by different personalities in traditional stories or narratives such as folk tales or fairy tales'.

Meaning is contextual: physical use and social setting condition how brands are perceived, and the metaphors and images that project meaning have to be salient to the audience. It is important to understand the contemporary frame of reference of the audience within which brands will function. Zaltman (2003, p. 162) refers to this as 'consensus maps reflecting the shared frame of reference or viewing lens among those in a target market about a particular topic or issue'. They are socially shared, connected constructs most prominent in the minds of market-segment members. Maps are constructed from consumer research on central human issues: for example, examining what consumers think of 'home', may be broadened to investigating 'keeping the home clean', 'home as an area for exercise' or ' home as a place of fun'. Meaning is both in the minds of consumers and in their actual brand experiences.

There are criticisms of this fabrication of meaning through the consumption of brands. Brown (2005) claims that marketing is 'nothing more or less than the manufacture, manipulation and maintenance of **paradessences**' (taken from Shakar's (2001) *Savage Girl*). 'Paradessence' is the mutually exclusive state that brands promise and have to be simultaneously gratified (e.g. controlled danger of theme parks, sanitised air travel, ice cream melds eroticism and innocence). The 'image is the marketable entity and the product strives to represent the image' (Firat, Dholakia and Venkatesh 1995). McGuigan (2006, p. 59) asserts that post-modern culture, and in particular the role played by branding, constitutes a crisis of representation 'because it is associated with a detachment of the sign of the referent, the signifier from the signified, representation from reality, image from truth'.

THE NEED FOR BRAND NARRATIVES

Target audience experience is therefore of key importance in marketing communications and is dependent upon the relationship between source and receiver. McQuail (2000, p. 377) asserts that this can best be explained in the context of three alternative models of communicative relationships: the **transmission** model (Schramm etc.); the **expressive** or **ritual model** (Carey 1989); and the **attention model** (Elliott 1998). The transmission model assumes the audience is a target or a destination for communication and involves cognitive processing; the expressive/ritual model, which involves sharing and normative commitment, sees the audience as participants; and the attention model implies no transfer of meaning or deep ties between sender and receiver. As the development and maintenance of meaningful dialogue is the key to brand relationship building, so it is the expressive model that is the key to our discussion here.

If the brand is the full market offering that makes the product competitive, the brand narrative is the ongoing connecting dialogue between company and customer. It is where marketing communications has moved to: away from pure brand image advertising to experiential branding. This resonates with Bruner (1990, p. 45) who claims that it is a human characteristic to 'organise experience into a narrative form'. Elliott (2000) develops this idea proposing that, 'Narrative is inherently sequential in that it links together human beings, actions, events and experience into a story'. In differentiating narrative from other forms of discourse, Elliott (2000) delineates four features: its sequentiality; its 'indifference' to reality; its ability to merge the ordinary with the extraordinary; and its dramatic quality. This dramatic quality is something that the most powerful brands have: 'an emotional role that transcends their historical category usage' (Morgan 2009, p. 20).

To examine this, we need to lean on Aaker and Joachimsthaler's (2000, p. 44) explanation of the product/brand dichotomy (illustrated in Figure 9.6). We can see their explanation of the product/brand dichotomy and appreciate that these are only two dimensions in the brand framework.

Figure 9.6: Product/brand dimensions
Source: Aaker and Joachimsthaler (2000, p. 52).

Brand dimension	Explanation	Example
Scope	The range of category types that the brand is capable of spanning across. Extended possible use of product outside of the category need dimension	PCs – social networks, photographic, artwork facilities beyond word processing and number crunching *Nivea* – makes a range of 'skin protection' products
Attributes	Key ingredients or unique competitive elements relevant to a category need	*Hovis* – 'Seed Sensations' features the use of seeds in its bread *Vauxhall Astra Elite* – includes MP3 player and auxiliary *iPod* connector
Use	Suggested utility claim	*Ronseal* – 'does what it says on the tin' *Menu Masters* – time-saving meals
Quality/Value	Actual intrinsic product quality or value of attribute	*Intel Inside* – inclusion of a state-of-the-art processor enhances PC quality
Functional benefits	What the brand is What the brand offers as a proposition	*VW* – German engineering *Volvo* – safety *Curly Music* – 'Music by musicians for musicians' offers local instrument expertise

Table 9.1: Product components

Source: Aaker and Joachimsthaler (2000, p. 48).

In the original Aaker and Joachimsthaler (2000, p. 44) explanation of brand identity, the inner layer describes the intrinsic product features and capabilities of the brand as a competitive offering in a product category. The 'scope' conditions the parameters within which the brand can operate and how far it can be extended across other categories. Similarly, inclusion of special ingredients such as '*Intel* Pentium Processor Inside' in computers tells users of PCs that the brand they are buying includes the highest industry-standard components.

The functional benefits essentially say what the brand is. *BMW, Audi* and *VW* are 'German engineering'; *3M, Motorola* and *Canon* are 'innovation'; *Lexus, Gucci* and *Prada* are 'quality'. These brands try to dominate their respective categories by 'owning the relevant product attribute' most salient to that category (Aaker and Joachimsthaler 2000, p. 48). Table 9.1 expands on this, offering a more comprehensive explanation with illustrative examples of the products' components.

This can also be very limiting; if the brand becomes inextricably linked with an attribute it can become locked in its functional positioning. *Volvo* has been synonymous with 'safety' with advertisements emphasising the unique SIPS safety

Volvo's change of image

feature, to the point where it became restrictive in terms of image. Recently, a '*Volvo* for Life' platform has helped reposition the brand with less focus on product features.

The **extended brand** perspective which augments the product, gives it meaning and provides a better reinforcement of category positioning and relative competitiveness. Brand essence which transcends the mere functional benefits to offer emotional and self-expressive benefits provides a higher-order basis for relationships. Whereas functional benefits say what the brand is, emotional and self-expressive benefits say what the brand does. Whilst *Panasonic* clearly focuses on the new innovative features in its compact cameras, it also offers 'Ideas For Life'. Similarly, a PC may include an '*Intel* Pentium Processor Inside', but the appeal of the Microsoft software included is to help people realise their professional or personal potential and creative imagination, expressed in its 'Where do you want to go today?' Table 9.2 expands on this, offering a more comprehensive explanation with illustrative examples of the brands' components.

Panasonic focus on camera's brand features

Brand dimension	Explanation	Example
Brand personality	Unique character of corporate/ individual or retail brand	*The Body Shop* – caring, ethical organisation *Virgin* – 'everyman' brand taking on the traditional establishment brands
Symbols	Semiotic representation of the brand	*Coca-Cola* – contour-shaped bottle *Nike* – swoosh 'tick' *IKEA* – yellow and blue colours signify Swedish culture
Brand/customer relationships	Formal and informal links between company and customer	*Tesco* – the 'every little helps' ethos projects a caring corporation *COOP* – ethical orientation
Self-expressive benefits	What the brand says about itself and how it resonates with user's self-image	*Apple* – think and be different *Nike* – excel, succeed *Microsoft* – help people realise potential

(Continued)

Brand dimension	Explanation	Example
Emotional benefits	Affective attachment to a brand	*Harley-Davidson* – HOGS group affiliation demonstrating pride of users in using the brand
User imagery	Image projected by brand users	*Rolex* – conspicuous consumption *Carling* – affiliation *GM Saturn* – pride in manufacture *Armani* – users of the brand
Country of origin	Essence of the brand is associated with country	*Guinness* – Irish Celtic soul *California Wines* – new world wines *BMW* – German engineering
Organisational associations	Image of the organisation particularly service brands	*Innocent Smoothies* – eco-friendly health *Ben & Jerry's* – hippy, individualism *B&Q* – employ experienced trades-people *Halifax* – employees demonstrate credibility

Table 9.2: Brand components

Self-expressive and emotional benefits add richness to the product which can resonate and help build affective attachments with consumers. Organisations express strategy and values such as trust, quality and social responsibility through marketing communications by making associations which are intangible. In a situation where there is no real difference in strategy and competitive parity cancels out any degree of advantage, the communication of organisational associations is essential.

MATTER OF FACT

Most Trusted European Brands

A vital ingredient of a brand's personality is trust. Trust underpins every purchase a consumer or organisation makes, and it is implicit in all brand encounters. It is the most crucial ingredient in relationships between company and customer, and it can help to instil customer loyalty and build long-term brand equity. Research across 16 European countries for the *Reader's Digest Trusted European Brands* in 2009 was one of the widest consumer surveys ever undertaken. This annual research asks consumers to vote for the 'Most Trusted Brands' in 20 categories and rank them in terms of 'Quality', 'Image', 'Excellent Value' and 'Understanding Customer Needs'.

For the third year running, all countries voted *Nokia* as most trusted mobile phone handset and *Nivea* the most trusted skin care brand. *Barclaycard* was most trusted credit card in the UK, but *Visa* was highest in 14 other countries. For other categories, *Canon* was top camera in 10 countries; *Kellogg's* and *Nestlé* top breakfast cereals in 10; mobile phone and Internet service providers, holiday companies, financial and health services were the most diverse categories with evidence of localised trust, especially with ISPs.

CATEGORY	No. of different winning brands across Europe	Brands in more than 3 countries in this category
Skin Care	1	Nivea
Mobile Phone	1	Nokia
Breakfast Cereal	3	Kellogg's, Nestlé
Camera	3	Canon
Credit Card	3	Visa
PC	5	HP, Dell
Cosmetic	6	Avon, Nivea, Yves Rocher
Car	8	Mercedes, Toyota, VW
Soap Powder	9	Ariel, Persil
Hair Care	11	Pantene
Kitchen Appliance	11	Miele
Vitamins	12	Centrum
Cold Remedy	13	Vick
Pain Relief	13	Aspirin
Mobile Phone Service	13	-
Insurance Company	14	-
Bank/Building Society	15	-
Holiday Company	15	-
Petrol Retailer	15	-
Internet Service Provider	16	-

Most trusted European brands

A brand category which has seen the biggest erosion of trust, due to the global economic meltdown, is the banking sector. Trust has fallen by an average 39% across all countries, 44% in Western Europe and 27% in CEER (Czech Republic, Hungary and Romania) countries. The biggest fall in confidence in these institutions has been in Germany (58%), Switzerland (67%) and the UK (57%).

Source: www.rdtrustedbrands.com.

Factors which contribute to consumers' trust in brands and help communicate differentiation in saturated markets are those which suggest personal links which help dialogue and company/customer relationships (*Reader's Digest* 2009). They are:

- **The perception of high quality:** *M&S* enjoys a perceived advantage over *ALDI* for quality of food although this has been contested in blind taste tests.
- **Understanding what the customers want:** mobile phone service provider *02* had a 'Lend us a quid' scheme for users to 'borrow' a £1's worth of top-up which projects the sort of 'trusted mate' image the target audience would value.
- **A sense of humour:** *Ford*, *Lloyds TSB* and *Specsavers* all benefit from promoting a certain light-heartedness which endears users to the brand and softens the organisational image.
- **Environmental consciousness:** various examples of brands extending their values to broader societal issues are featured throughout the book. Brands include *Saab's 9-3 BioPower Convertible*, the *Bosch ActiveWater Dishwasher* and *Sainsbury's* 'Fish for now, fish for the future' sustainable supply initiative.

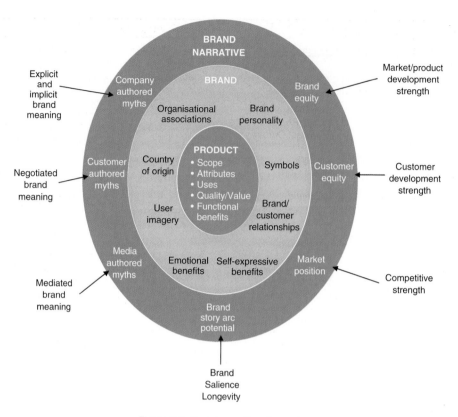

Figure 9.7: Brand narrative dimensions

- **Strength of heritage:** well-established brands like *Cadbury's* and *M&S* have been able to draw on the brand equity built up in their long history to maintain brand loyalty.
- **Perceived differentiation from the competition:** the direct *Dell*, Howard's 'human' *Halifax*, the humour of *Specsavers* all have perceptions of difference which helps engender consumer trust.

So, as the brand gives social and psychological substance and meaning to the product, enduring loyalty will not come from 'transforming the product category' (Kapferer 2000, p. 46), but must be rooted in the engagement of audiences in salient, social narratives. Zaltman and Zaltman (2008, p. 186) provide a basic framework for visualising the development of branding beyond product and service attributes and functional consequences. We need to reach to deeper levels of thinking about the emotional consequences of the brand: the social and psychological aspects of brand meaning; and how these link consumers' personal values and goals. Figure 9.7 illustrates this progression from product to brand to the broader social and psychological meaning enveloped in the brand's story or narrative. Table 9.3 expands on this, offering a more comprehensive explanation with illustrative examples of the components of the brand narrative.

This involves reaching to deeper levels of thinking about the emotional consequences of the brand: the social and psychological aspects of brand meaning; and how these link consumers' personal values and goals. Figure 9.8 illustrates this progression from product to brand to the meaning enveloped in the brand's story or narrative.

As we have seen in the previous chapter, a well-known brand may contribute to the experience of satisfaction both when the consumer buys and when (s)he uses the branded product, and our 'evaluation of a product typically is about what it means rather than what it does' (Solomon, Bambossy

Brand dimension	Explanation	Example
Company authored myths	Planned, company-controlled explicitly and implicitly projected corporate and brand communications	*Coca-Cola* – symbolises American values *Virgin* – anti-establishment *Arctic Monkeys* – music label released downloadable material before the band was established to build up word of mouth and create a buzz
Customer authored myths	User negotiated image and meaning	*Stella Artois* – user projected 'Wife Beater' image aligned to use
Media authored myths	Brand meaning mediated through channels of communication such as media, intermediaries and agency either through planned dissemination of communication or voluntary word of mouth	During the first throes of the Credit Crunch, the perception of banking and financial services in general was severely damaged by very negative press coverage which undermined trust in this sector.
Brand equity	Total positive and negative connotations communicated by and about the brand	Cumulative multiplier effect of integrated marketing communications and environmental communications
Customer equity	Total positive and negative customer experience with the brand	Assets of customer loyalty from which brand can grow
Market position	Strength of competitive market share	Power in market
Brand story arc potential	Ongoing brand narrative	Longevity of brand and ability to engage audience in ongoing dialogue

Table 9.3: Components of the brand narrative

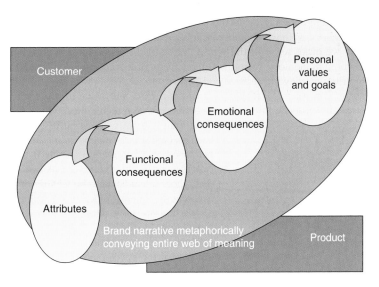

Figure 9.8: Reaching customer value and goals

Source: Zaltman and Zaltman (2008, p. 187). Reproduced with permission.

and Askegaard 2002, p. 57). As Hackley (1999, p. 143) points out: 'the symbolic content of promotional messages must, in order to be meaningful to the consumer, make use of the cultural currency of symbolic codes in contemporary use'. Cultural currency describes the salience of brands, celebrity and so on in being socially meaningful.

Brands have to not only be relevant to consumers' lives but communicate in ways that resonate. In this context, enduring narratives forge a bond with audiences allowing us to live vicariously through the characters. 'Narrative helps to provide the logic of human motive that makes sense of fragmentary observations, whether fictional or realistic' (McQuail 2000, p. 346). 'The largest activity in marketing is the provision and consumption of stories. Stories are bought and sold, they are part of the media of exchange, and they are vehicles for all other goods and services' (Levy 2003). Stories, including myths, are becoming central to branding; they are not just vehicles to carry fixed meanings, increasingly they are the meaning itself.

When a consumer tries to make sense of information from a myriad of sources and a plethora of brands, the memory bank of brand experience, emotions and linkages all come into play. The fusion of memory, metaphor and story in branding enables consumers to create meaning around, or see relevance in, a company or a specific brand' (Zaltman 2003, p. 189). Narratives are discursive spaces constituted through language practices, the telling and re-telling of stories, some fully-drawn, others 'terse' or 'fragmentary' (Foucault 1977, Boje 2001, Gabriel 1999). According to Zaltman (2003, p. 198), 'a story is an accounting of one or more experiences involving both episodic and semantic memory'. Semantic memories (the what and how of experience) and episodic memories (the actual event or experience itself) are stored in popular culture through films, TV, music, magazines and indeed the texts of marketing communications (advertisements, posters, events, PR, product placement, sponsorship etc.). The elements of the marketing communications mix are used to stimulate associations to help this process. Zaltman refers to this as 'social memory' with advertisements being 'social containers' covering norms, values, objects, sensory stimuli, icons, rituals and rites, all providing a cultural framework of meaning. The 'human universals' (like journey, punishment, reward for effort, achievement and caring) are the categories of thought found in all cultures.

Metaphors are often the common denominator between brands and consumers. Brands are shorthand for business systems, category positioning, competitive comparisons; metaphors are shorthand for associations derived from memory. Brand owners 'try to establish their products and brands as metaphors and attempt to not only attach meanings to brands but attach brands to meanings' (Brierley 2002, p. 144). So 'love and sharing' means *Rolos* instead of *Rolos* meaning 'love and sharing'.

As we have seen, associations of the product with cultural references cause a transfer of meanings and that cultural reference is transferred to the brand. The comfort of going back to favourite brands echoes the reliance we have on memory; it is a reassuring cognitive and emotional touchstone which frames how we make sense of the world. Much of the social information that an individual acquires is represented in memory. Narratives persuade people to construct a mental representation of the information they are viewing (Adaval and Wyer 1998).

Organisations such as *GlaxoSmithKline*, *Coca-Cola*, *P&G* and *General Motors* engage in 'deep dive emotions research' involving 'metaphor elicitation research techniques' which help to construct

their brand stories and narratives. For example, *P&G* used metaphor in its campaign for *Febreze*, a new product based on a patented molecule. It was the most successful new product launch in its history, tapping into metaphors of eradicating the feelings of 'disgust' caused by domestic smells (Miller 1997). Zaltman and Zaltman (2008) describe how 'deep metaphors' provide the basic foundations for the brand stories people create based on marketing communications and are fundamental building blocks for developing customer relationships. We rely on images and associations which are embedded in our subconscious, activated when the content of an

Fabreze eradicating 'disgust'

advertisement, a jingle, an evocative image, a nostalgic reference hits the right emotional trigger. The deep metaphor of the classic 'I'd Like To Teach The World To Sing' *Coca-Cola* advertisement is very similar to the *Carling* 'Belong' advertisements, both appealing to togetherness and connectivity.

Zaltman and Zaltman (2008, p. 19) list eight giant metaphors which represent about 70% of the deep images they have come across in the cognitive science research into consumer behaviour:

- **Balance or imbalance:** ideas of equilibrium, adjusting including physical, social, moral aesthetic and psychological balance.
- **Transformation:** changing state or status, emotionally, socially or psychologically.
- **Journey:** the unknown 'life' voyages of 'The road not taken' (Robert Frost) or 'A journey of a 1000 miles starts with a single step' (Confucious) are part of the meaning that brands offer consumers.
- **Container:** physical, social or psychological states for 'keeping things in' or 'keeping things out'.
- **Connection or disconnection:** feelings of belonging or exclusion.
- **Resource:** knowledge, information, the essence of brand utility.
- **Control:** the need for power over our decisions, choices, calm, order.
- **Other metaphors:** movement or motion, nature, force, system.

When a brand manager tells a story, consumers' **consensus maps** are engaged. Consensus maps are 'networks of abstract understandings that constitute part of our mental imagery' (Zaltman 2003. p. 89). But consumers don't passively receive these brand stories. As Fournier has demonstrated in her work on brand relationships and meaning, managers and consumers procreate meaning. As we have seen in the opening case study, with the dedicated commitment of a loyal customer base, *Harley-Davidson* transformed the driving experience into a mystical, spiritual event. This type of branding is **transformational** in the sense that the consumer associates the experience of product usage with some subjective sensation, but also sees the benefits of the brand in affecting a change in lifestyle, appearance, acceptance or sense of being. This is vital for brand longevity as brands which properly engage on an experiential and relational level 'can turn customers into "fans", especially when they connect with consumers' culture . . . (and) . . . brand managers must evaluate, emulate and infiltrate the core culture of their customers' (Blackwell, Miniard and Engel 2006, p. 435). Table 9.4 illustrates this in research done by Blackwell and Stephan (2003). They draw the distinction between 'customers', 'friends' (i.e. repeat purchasers) and 'fans'.

Culturally relevant brands are ones that resonate with important values of target markets. Investing in relationships with customers and their culture ultimately leads to behavioural loyalty, a finding verified in cross-cultural research in a three-country (United States, Belgium and Netherlands) comparative study (Wulf, Odekerken-Schroeder and Iacobucci 2001). This emphasises a relational approach to brand encounter management which encompasses all aspects of marketing communications.

Customers	Friends (repeat customers)	Fans
Are price driven	Are value driven	Are experience driven
Shop opportunistically	Shop purposefully	Shop for pleasure
Want you to sell them products	Want products and good service	Want personalised advice and solutions
Need a reason to buy from you	Prefer to buy from you	Are devoted to you and are yours to lose
Are surprised by good service	Have a history of good experiences	Automatically assume you will delight them

(Continued)

Customers	Friends (repeat customers)	Fans
Drop you if they are disappointed	Tell you if they're disappointed and give you a chance to respond	Tell you if they're disappointed, want you to fix it, and are anxious to forgive and forget
Are indifferent to your company	Feel a connection with you rationally and/or emotionally	Actively invest time, emotion, attention and money in their relationship with you
Don't think or talk about your firm	Recommend your firm casually	Evangelise about your firm

Table 9.4: Converting customers into fans

Source: adapted from Blackwell and Stephan (2003).

BRANDING IN FOCUS

The Heineken Experience. Relationship Branding

The Heineken brewery in Amsterdam

Brands have such a cultural significance that their meaning often extends beyond the actual functionality of the product. One way organisations can reinforce the experiential consumption of their products is by extending the brand's story into an all-encompassing brand-themed visitor attraction. '*Heineken* – Born in Amsterdam, Raised by the world . . . Cheers!' So hails the sign at the *Heineken Experience* in Amsterdam where visitors can experience a celebration of the Dutch beer's brand heritage via a variety of storytelling techniques.

Situated on Amsterdam's Stadhouderskade, the *Heineken Experience* pulls in around 450,000 guests a year, and like the hugely popular *Guinness Storehouse* in Dublin, has become one of the city's most popular tourist attractions. Originally opened in 2001, the *Heineken Experience* replaced a brewery tour that, while popular with drinkers, failed to convey much about the brand other than its intoxicating qualities.

The new-look interactive brand *Experience* is no longer part of a fully-functioning brewery tour, but guests see, smell, touch and taste everything involved in the brewing process, including of course an ice-cold beer. Various state-of-the-art technologies are employed at various stages in the tour: guests must first be 'brewed' themselves inside 'Brew U'; a stand-up simulator ride explains a trip through the bottling process; the first beer is served inside the futuristic Star Bar, where *Heineken*'s red star motif and corporate colours are exploited to their full potential.

There's a *Heineken Gallery*, where visitors can relive over 140 years of advertising, and appreciate the social significance of the brand messages throughout the years. There are the famous *Heineken* sponsorships, such as films and football, and guests can order a 330ml bottle of Heineken with their own name on as part of *Bottle Your Own Heineken*. The result is a visitor attraction that cuts through the clutter of fragmented media messages and leaves guests thirsty for more – beer and brand that is!

RELATIONSHIP MARKETING AND RELATIONSHIP BRANDING

A distinction should be made here between two (sometimes confused) interpretations of what is meant by 'relational'. The narrower concept of relationship marketing or customer relationship management (CRM) has its roots in a business-to-business orientation and often describes an extension of personal selling, account management and the management of the marketing/customer interface. Morgan and Hunt (1994) offered a broader perspective by defining it as 'all marketing activities directed towards establishing, developing and maintaining relational exchanges'.

Malthouse and Calder (2005, p. 150) draw a distinction between CRM and relationship branding: the former is an operational approach to managing customer relationships; the latter is a 'strategic approach aimed at making consumers feel a sense of relationship or personal connection with the brand'. The idea of a consumer having a relationship with a brand as opposed to an organisation is a key element of brand equity theory (Keller 2001) and is referred to as 'customer equity'.

MATTER OF FACT

Every Little Helps, Everywhere to Everybody

UK supermarket giant *Tesco* has moved strategy from an early cost leadership 'Pile it high. Sell it cheap' orientation, through an every day low pricing attack in the 1980s to one of differentiating itself from *Sainsbury's* and other discounting grocery multiples by building a relationship brand. Operationally, the company started with a CRM scheme rewarding loyalty through use of the *Clubcard*. As the strategy evolved, *Tesco* moved progressively towards a relationship brand by actively exploiting the *Clubcard* programme.

The key to success, and the difference between a CRM approach and a relationship brand approach, was allowing sub-segments of consumers to experience the brand in a more individualised way. One of *Tesco's* most successful sub-segment applications was the 'Baby and Toddler Club' programme started in 1996. This traditionally underperforming category did not try to sell product, but aimed at relating to the special needs of young mothers and toddlers. Time-dependent advice on pregnancy planning, immunisation, dietary considerations as well as suitable product promotions were directed under the 'Help and offers every little step of the way' programme. This allowed young mothers to experience the *Tesco* brand as all other customers do – '*Tesco* allows you to buy more of what you want' – but in an idiosyncratic, individualised way.

Source: Humby and Hunt (2003).

Transactional marketing	Relationship marketing
One-way communication	Two-way communication
Focus on single sale	Focus on customer retention
Orientation on product features	Orientation on product benefits
Short time scale	Long time scale
Little customer service	High customer service
Limited customer commitment	High customer commitment

Table 9.5: Comparison of transactional and relationship marketing

The key to the mass-customisation paradox of relational management is 'having a shared mass appeal that can be experienced in a more individualistic, idiosyncratic way' (Malthouse and Calder 2005, p. 150). The broader perspective is the totality of brand encounters, dialogues in a wider social and individual context seen as 'a network of value-laden relationships' (Kotler 1991), and that is the frame of reference for the development of brand narratives. Let us look at the roots of building relationships.

The traditional focus in marketing communications has been one of acquiring customers, either from the competition or converting people who had not previously purchased in the category. In an overly populated marketplace, with intense competition in almost every sphere, the need to have strategies and policies for customer retention is of paramount importance. You may recall from Chapter 4 that, as a method of segmenting our target audience, Rossiter and Bellman (2005, p. 83) proposed three major groups of customers based on category orientation:

1. our current brand customers;
2. other brands' customers who might be persuaded to convert to our brand; and
3. those who have stopped or have never used the category but might be converted using marketing communications.

The criterion for segmentation was based on brand loyalty. Some customers may only want a transactional connection with the organisation as they see the brand as fulfilling a basic 'top-up' when their regular brand is not available, or because the product is a low-involvement and possibly generic product. Some consumers are necessarily 'brand promiscuous' and will migrate from one offer to another without any loyalty at all. However, the objective is to get consumers locked into a brand and form a bond of some degree. The differences between the transactional and relational approaches are summarised in Table 9.5.

The goal for any relationship marketing strategy must be to firstly retain customers, build a mutually beneficial association, and develop customer equity with the overall objective of securing long-term income flows from lifetime customer value. The antecedents for relationship marketing are with McKinsey's call to reduce 'customer churn' and Reichheld and Sasser's (1990) now famous mantra of 'zero customer defections' (echoing the virtues of total quality management's 'zero defects'). This is important not just to maintain income flows, but loyal customers will buy more, and will help you develop and act as brand champions in the marketplace, generating cheap publicity in the form of positive word of mouth.

BRANDING IN FOCUS

The Casa *Buitoni* Club. Relationship Marketing

Buitoni were one of the few Italian pasta manufacturers to open factories outside of Italy. In 1988, *Nestlé* bought *Buitoni*, by then the biggest in Italy and number 1 brand in the UK. Whilst *Buitoni* enjoyed sales right across Europe, the British were not great pasta eaters. Sales were predominantly through retailers like *Tesco* and *Sainsbury's* who also sold their own-label brands made for them by other manufacturers. *Buitoni's* position was becoming undermined by the commoditisation of pasta ranges and increased vulnerability to more and more competition. To make matters worse, they were finding themselves increasingly cut off from the end customer – the consumer.

Buitoni pasta packs

The big retailers were becoming increasingly dominant and were reflecting this in massive advertising expenditure. *Nestlé* decided that it was time to act in order to secure the long-term future of the brand and they chose the UK as a sort of test market, an experiment in building the brand. The first decision was to extend the range into other product areas, and the second was to build a database of users and potential users through marketing communications in order to develop a meaningful brand platform.

In 1992, a direct response print campaign was aimed at women, with a media schedule which covered a wide range of women's magazines. This had the campaign objectives of changing perceptions of the brand and emphasised the Italian heritage. Recipes and promotional discounts were used as incentives and this was followed up the next year, this time broadening the appeal to a wider audience with a more mainstream media schedule. At the end of 1993, a direct response TV campaign was launched, although the spend was not enormous. In-store promotions in retailers like *Tesco* provided a great opportunity for people to experience the product first hand, and this was enhanced by money-off coupons which tied in with point-of-sale materials in store. Sponsorship followed in the shape of the Great North Run in Newcastle, the site of the *Buitoni* UK factory, and the *De Medici Kitchen* TV programme. Great PR came from this and word of mouth started to spread. The database that had been built up from all the respondents was now sizeable and *Buitoni* felt that the time was right to go to the next stage – the *Casa Buitoni Club*.

This was a community of pasta lovers and influential customers. Over 150,000 database customers were communicated to, and a careline created the first real meaningful dialogue between company and customers. A full colour newsletter was despatched every month and a promotion to encourage visits to the original villa helped engender the club spirit. They had created brand ambassadors who acted as opinion leaders. The Italian lifestyle was prominent in all *Casa Buitoni Club* activities and this helped to develop a sense of ownership. *Buitoni* were able to use this platform to reinforce their authority and Italian expert credentials. Overall the objective had been to develop a deep and strong brand loyalty; a warmth and sense of belonging which was to insulate them from the pressures of own brand. Relationship marketing principles had ensured that the *Buitoni* brand had built up a strong impenetrable force around the brand.

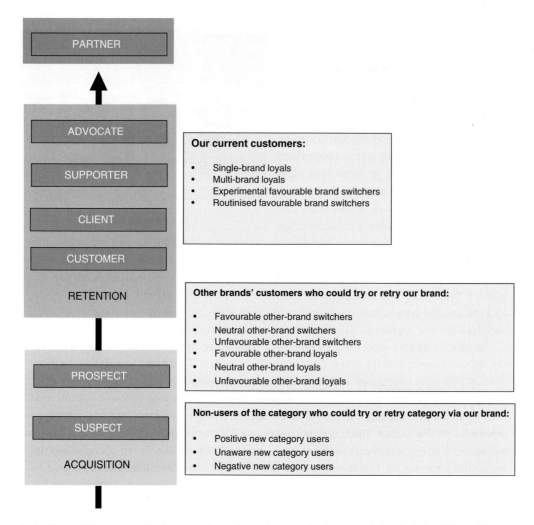

Note: Figure 9.9 combines the 'ladder of loyalty' (which is usually attributed to Peck *et al.* (1999, p. 45) but has its roots in sales management techniques of old) and the excellent categorisation of customer equity types by Rossiter and Bellman (2005, p. 83) discussed above and in great depth in Chapter 4

Figure 9.9: Customer loyalty categorisation

Source: Based on Peck *et al.* (1999) and Rossiter and Bellman (2005).

Figure 9.9 illustrates different categories of customer loyalty. In the context of business-to-business, **suspects** are possible business deals which may be generated from new building and construction work for example. Companies supplying information on advanced building work may use planning permission applications and the like to investigate even before a need or problem is determined. European database companies such as *ABI* (*Advanced Building Information*) and *Glenigan Leads* offer manufacturers and designers information on planning permission for construction, providing opportunities for products to be specified. The building of an airport may involve thousands of products, and matching organisation to client need is an involved process, requiring communication to many members of the decision making unit. These are non-users of the category who may be persuaded by marketing communications to try or retry the category.

Prospects are people or organisations that are believed to be someone that an organisation could possibly do business with or turn into a customer. They may have a need for the particular product in the category but are currently buying from another organisation. This might be through inertia (most bank loyalty is based on the fear or apathy of moving banks), or force of habit, or people who are not likely to be loyal to the brand. These are other brands' customers (who buy from us also) who are either favourably or unfavourably disposed to converting or switching back to our brand. Peck *et al.* (1999, p. 45) use the term 'purchaser' rather than 'customer', but this doesn't really help as most categories involve purchase.

Once the **acquisition stage** has been achieved the prospect becomes, or has been, someone who buys at least something from the organisation. This can be deceptive, as not only does it show little or no loyalty, but sales statistics may distort the actual relationship the company and customer have with each other. For example, the Pareto (or '80/20') rule applies to products and customers. According to *P&G*'s Jim Stengel (quoted in Jaffe 2005, p. 77), 'no *Procter & Gamble* brand is really a mass brand, not even *Tide*, whose top 18% of consumers drive 80% of sales'.

The next stage is when an infrequent customer becomes a **client**, someone who buys on a reasonably regular basis. Even this can be deceptive as repeat business may not be based on positive feelings but pragmatism. The client may actually be hostile to your brand or organisation. A **supporter** is someone who likes the product but supports passively, whereas someone who is an **advocate** will actively promote your organisation and brand and spreads positive word of mouth, acting as an unpaid sales person for the organisation. These are the *Apple* geeks, or *The Body Shop* brand ambassadors who have an almost evangelical brand affinity. If creating long-term band narratives is about building differentiated, consistent, sustainable stories, customer relationship management has to be the starting point.

Retail relationships are often engendered by a number of mainly tactical means. Store loyalty cards have become more and more prevalent since the database which is generated is a source of future business. As far back as 1983, Denison and Knox (see McGoldrick 2002) devised the 'diamond of loyalty' to help position customers on a four-grid matrix, using the axes of 'number of stores visited' and the level of 'commitment to those stores' (Figure 9.10).

Switchers who show no real commitment to a particular store but visit a number of stores have no loyalty, but have a category need which may be developed. **Habituals** may not be worth the same communication effort. Loyalty, in a retail context, can be described as 'a customer's commitment to

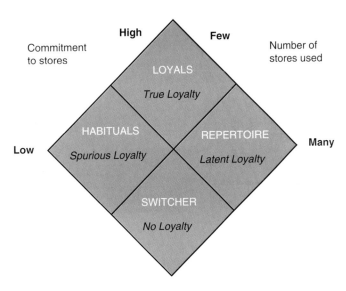

Figure 9.10: The retail diamond of loyalty

Source: Denison and Knox (1983).

do business with a particular organisation, purchasing its goods and services repeatedly, and recommending to friends and associates' (McIlroy and Barnett 2000, p. 349). Sopanen (1996) put this into a framework to describe six types of loyalty:

- **Monopoly loyalty** where there are no alternatives.
- **Inertia loyalty** where there is no active seeking of alternatives.
- **Convenience loyalty** where loyalty is conditioned by location.
- **Price loyalty** where price is the dominant factor.
- **Incentivised loyalty** where the benefits are gained from reward card schemes.
- **Emotional loyalty** where consumers engage with the brand on personal and psychological levels.

INVESTING IN RELATIONSHIPS WITH CUSTOMERS

Customer loyalty is a complex relational process that evolves, builds and develops dynamically over time: a process driven by meaningful customer-centric experiences that allow consumers to develop the necessary connections and strong bonds of satisfaction and commitment (McAlexander, Kim and Roberts 2003). According to Marcus (2008, p. 120), 'value creation is shifting from a focus on product and media efficiencies largely shaped by economies of scale to emerging means of value creation driven by economies of scope in customer relationships'. Communications is vital in all aspects of marketing, but none more so than in the personal interaction of brand service encounters where evaluations are made rationally and emotionally. Ambler (1997, p. 283) claims that 'brand equity exists in the hearts and minds of consumers and other marketplace players'. Figure 9.11 illustrates how

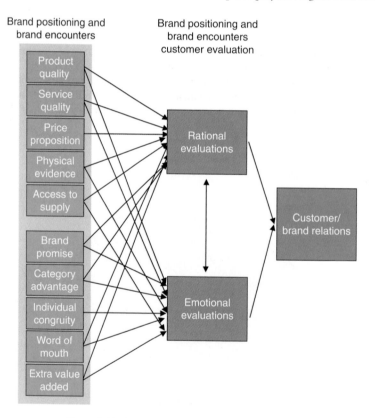

Figure 9.11: Customer-based brand equity model

Source: adapted from Martesen and Grønholdt (2004, p. 39).

a customer's perceptions of the positioning of the product and the brand encounter experience are an amalgam of rational and emotional evaluations (Martesen and Grønholdt 2004, p. 39).

A brand is like an ecosystem which links into the wider social system, and it is the connections within the system that are the heartbeat of the brand. The root of customer equity can be traced to the interactive dynamic of service marketing (Grönroos 2004, p. 238), where the customer forms a differentiating image of the service on the basis of various brand contacts to which the customer is exposed. In the previous chapter, we referred to Aaker's (2000, p. 263) model of brand building with the components of: creating visibility in order to aid product selection choice; developing associations and differentiations against the category competition; and the construction and maintenance of customer relationships. The company doesn't completely own the brand; it guides it. Relationships between customers and brands are assets through which companies can capitalise customer equity value (Lindberg-Repo and Grönroos 2004, p. 238).

Louro and Cunha (2001) identified four paradigms in brand management which relate to company/customer dialogue: product; projective; adaptive; and relational. These are represented in Figure 9.12.

The two axes show **brand centrality** – the degree to which an organisation's strategy is governed by its brands; and **customer centrality** – the level of involvement that consumers have in creating meaning and value. The continuum on the vertical dimension shows the polarities of brands as tactical instruments appended to a product (e.g. the legal values of brands), to one of brand orientation where all revolves around the creation, development and protection of brand value. The horizontal dimension of customer centrality shows the measure of passivity of recipients (i.e. a 'unilateral orientation') or the degree to which value is mutually created. The more the company/customer interface is interactive and interdependent, the more brand value will be continuously co-created, co-sustained, and co-transformed through the firm–customer interface (Louro and Cunha 2001, p. 856).

The **product paradigm** describes a situation whereby the legal protection of logos is the main pre-occupation of brand activities and there is no dialogue between organisation and customer; a metaphor of 'silence' is used. The central focus of the **projective paradigm** is the projection of company-created brand image and this assumes asymmetrical communication. This is referred to as 'monologue' communications because brand management is focused on projecting relevant brand identity to the selected target groups of the firm and communications are one way.

The **adaptive paradigm** stresses the role of consumers as central constructors of brand meaning and uses a 'listening' metaphor. And finally, the **relational paradigm** is where there is full involvement

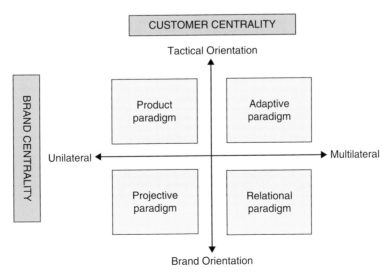

Figure 9.12: Brand dialogue metaphors

Source: Louro and Cunha (2001, p. 855). Reproduced with permission of Westbum Publishers Ltd.

of customers as co-authors of brand meaning and value and there is full two-way dialogue. In the relational paradigm, brands are anthropomorphised to the extent that people have 'relationships with them' (Ambler 1997, p. 283).

The framework of B2C communications will achieve customer complicity and lock-in if the organisation/customer relationship is a meaningful part of the consumer's life. The need for an ongoing organisational narrative is imperative. According to Brown, Humphreys and Gurney (2005, p. 313), organisational narratives are 'accounts of value-laden symbolic actions embedded in words and incorporating sequence, time and place and one discursive practice by which organisations are constituted'. They describe continuously evolving shared narratives which may be experienced in the praxis of function and in turning the brand's promise into reality.

Various attempts (Hatch and Schultz 2002) have been made at distinguishing corporate culture as a key component of overall brand image enacted internally but projected externally. Technology has facilitated the possibilities of constant 24/7 customer contact with companies which make the organisational narrative a dynamic construct. This is represented in continuing B2B, B2C and internal marketing communications, including those between employees and external stakeholders such as customers, suppliers, other users and media.

Aaker (2001) describes how the *General Motors* development of the *Saturn* car achieved long-lasting market penetration by selling the company, its values and culture, its employees and its customers – rather than the car. The initial advertising showed *Saturn* employees as people with personalities and a deep emotional commitment to both quality and the teamwork approach. The sense of community was used as a metaphor for the brand and this had a wider 'America' resonance.

Often, a relationship metaphor is used to describe what is really 'asymmetrical loyalty'. If the organisation consistently delivers what it promises, and resonates emotionally, brand loyalty may result. Lifetime customer value may be enhanced and the relationship reinforced by progressive and cumulative communication links between company and customer. This type of 'funnelling effect' of maturing relationship marketing is illustrated well in Figure 9.13 where data captured can be profiled, targeted and converted into solid long-lasting loyalty.

Parasocial relationships involve objects, symbols and other less tangible artefacts. They are impersonal communications with the firm, its products and people and the images they project of service, quality and so on.

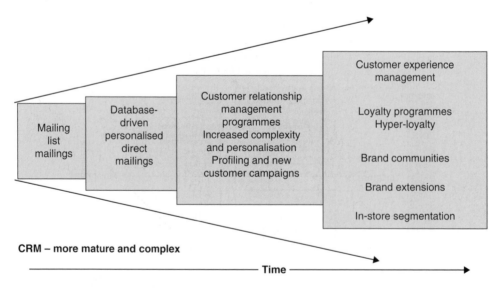

Figure 9.13: Maturing relationship marketing

Source: adapted from Katsioloudes, Grant and McKechnie (2007) by permission of Emerald Group Publishing Ltd.

One growing development has been the development of brand 'communities'. Whether it is '*Jeep* Jamborees', '*Rover* Country Affairs', '*Harley* Posse Runs' or *Apple* computer groups, these communities can deepen customer loyalty and create relationships between consumers and companies that have lasting customer value.

BUILDING RETAIL CUSTOMER RELATIONSHIPS THROUGH LOYALTY CARDS

In times of economic depression, the pressure on retailers to retain customers is the most critical factor. Although our relationships with organisations who stock thousands of branded goods are sometimes based on trust and commitment, the bonds are often not as emotional as with manufacturers' brands. Added to this, the power of the modern-day consumer to be promiscuous with purchasing behaviour, the merging of product and service dimensions, and the expanding alternative competition mean that the emphasis is moving towards customer relationship management. Loyalty cards provide a source of customer data and the ability to profile for the organisation, facilitating classically conditioned reinforced purchase behaviour. They offer the consumer a source of reward, communicate group affiliation status by allowing membership of an exclusive club and provide incremental value to the brand. The impact of these schemes typically represents about 1% of sales (Worthington 1998). However, as Woolf (1996, p. 4) points out, the emphasis is now on developing profitable loyal customers not just loyal customers: 'Greater success comes from a marketing strategy based primarily on understanding customer economics and only secondarily on customer loyalty'.

A 'Research Report on Loyalty Cards in European Retailing' by *KPMG Consulting Group* describes how advances in card technology and usage as well as the need to get closer to the customer, are all driving retailer attitudes to loyalty and management of relationships. They have devised a 'Purchaser-Purveyor Loyalty Card Model' which lists five types of loyalty card:

- **Pure loyalty card** – spending and accruing benefits with the card-issuing retailer. Quite often market leader led. These are often aimed at retaining customers. Examples are the *ICA Kundkort* and *Tesco Clubcard*.
- **Push loyalty card** – used by multiple retailers but benefits accruing from the card-issuing retailer. Often used by number 2 or 3 retailers who are keen to attract new primary customers and retain existing customers. *Sainsbury's Nectar* and *Albert Heijn* grocery stores are examples.

- **Pull loyalty card** – various Visa or MasterCard applications such as GM (General Motors) or Sainsbury's Bank Visa cards are often used by smaller players in a narrow market or bit players in a broad retail market. The SuperClub Membership card works with non-competing retail partners such as Texaco, UCI Cinemas and Atlantic Homeware. The Cofinga Carte offers an extended Air Miles (Points Ciel) scheme within non-competing retailers or members of the same group.
- **Purchase loyalty card** – spending and benefits accrue across many retailers as with American Express. These encourage spending through building transactions and are often used by payment companies.
- **Purge loyalty card** – where no loyalty card scheme exists (such as ASDA store purchases) and benefits are offered in other ways.

ICA Kundkort credit card

The *Shell SMART Card* is an amalgam of all these elements and allows the customer to decide how the loyalty card works both in terms of the places and the way the card is

Shell Smart card

used, and the benefits redeemed (including *Vision Express, Hilton Hotels, John Menzies* and *Commercial Union*).

The findings of the *KPMG Group* research into retail loyalty cards carried out in 10 European countries across 10 different retail sectors were that: 33% used pure schemes, 14% push, 31% pull, and 22% were purchase card schemes. Grocery retailers mainly used pure schemes; mixed retailers (like *Marks & Spencer*) adopted either push or pull; financial services used purchase; and retailers like petrol stations operated mainly pull card schemes.

The future of retailer loyalty card schemes as a means of engendering and building long-term customer relationships is dependent upon the economic climate, as well as the national and cultural issues impacting. For example, French customers are less inclined to surrender personal information to retailers. It is argued by *KPMG* that it is as a tactical tool rather than a strategic expansion of narrative that this approach will contribute most in the deployment of marketing communications.

BRAND COMMUNITIES

The concept of brand communities implies an experience-driven, socio-cultural relationship of aggregate consumption, shared values and an ethos of mutual respect for each other and for the brand (Muniz and Guinn 2001), usually focused on a particular consumption object. (Note: a distinction should be made between **brand communities** (e.g. HOGs) and **interpretive communities** (e.g. lesbian motorcycle riders Dykes on Bikes).) These essentially social groupings consist of consumers with a common brand enthusiasm, bonded by a well-developed social identity, whose members engage jointly in collective actions and express mutual commitment. It is where branding intersects with social networking, and can be characterised by three dimensions: consciousness of kind; evidence of rituals and traditions; and having a sense of obligation to its community and individual members (Muniz and Guinn 2001).

The *Citroën 2CV Club* in Finland still exists but has extended its loyalty to other *Citroën* products now that the *2CV* is no longer available. Group identity is shown in symbolic consumption and a quasi-religious zeal (e.g. Belk and Tumbat's 2005 study of *Apple Macintosh* users) for the brand with the intrinsic emotional connection between members often causing hatred towards competitive rival brands (Fournier, Sele and Schögel 2005, p. 16). They make the distinction between brands which are lifestyle brands (e.g. *Ralph Lauren*) and those that foster a real community spirit which only thrives at the centrality of the brand, consumption activity and strong social ties. For organisations, communities are vital for building brand equity by instilling a strong and sustainable differentiation potential against other category competitors (Aaker and Joachimsthaler 2000, p. 88).

There are four levels of community:

- between the consumer and the product;
- between the consumer and the brand;
- between the consumer and the organisation; and
- between the consumer and other consumers (McAlexander, Schouten and Koenig 2002, p. 38).

The more these relationships are 'internalised as part of the consumer's life experience, the more the customer is integrated into the brand community and the more loyal the customer is in consuming the brand' (McAlexander, Schouten and Koenig 2002, p. 48). They illustrated these four elements by applying them to the *HOGS* 'Posse Ride' event reproduced in Figure 9.14. These researchers have also applied the same model principles to *Chrysler* in their 'Camp *Jeep*', to *Starbucks* and a host of other motor companies like *General Motors Saturn* 'Homecoming' brand programme.

Manufacturers of cereal aimed at children have created websites for their young consumers, where the level of consumer to company and consumer to consumer communication is facilitated by online games interactivity. Universities attempt to extend the 'learning community' and create long-term brand loyalty by establishing alumni. McAlexander, Koenig and Schouten (2005) have examined how the nature of relationships amongst students affects their long-term loyalty to a university.

Product	Brand
The rally offers settings that enhance core brand associations such as camaraderie, freedom, adventure, discovery, irreverence, the purchase of *Harley* branded goods and that extend the brand's reach into consumers' lifestyles.	The ride fosters enthusiasm for the sport of motorcycling, supports the customers' riding habits, provides challenges and peak experiences to increase their commitment, and to deliver a lifetime experience.
The journey fosters the cultivation and development of social processes and links riders together by taking part in shared rituals, events and activities and by supporting one another in the challenges and crises that arise.	Riding side by side with consumers gives managers an incomparable opportunity to get to know them first, to find out what matters to them, and to deepen the collaboration especially regarding future product developments.
Customer	Marketer

Figure 9.14: Customer-centric model of brand community

Source: McAlexander, Schouten and Koenig (2002, p. 39). Reproduced with permission.

The quality and meaning of these relationships is predicated on reciprocity (Fournier 1998), but the paradox can be for brand owners that the term 'brand community' can be oxymoronic since the ownership of the community has to be chiefly in the hands of the brand users not owners (Muniz and Guinn 2001, p. 415). One of the other problems in managing these groups is that they are not homogeneous and have the following tensions for management to attempt to deal with:

- **Fragmentation and unity:** common interest in the product may not be shared by geography, demographics, genes, socioeconomic characteristics. Broadening the global appeal of *Harley-Davidson* may diminish the appeal of the *HOG* community.
- **Structure and chaos:** the more management tries to structure, the less of a community it becomes. The consumer-to-company bond is a key relationship principle which must be balanced.
- **Empathy versus intimacy:** meetings, online chat rooms and so on provide a good opportunity for dialogue and 'getting close to the customer'.
- **Marketing versus authenticity:** source credibility is key in good marketing communications and customers' perceptions of management being 'company champion' or 'community advocate' may be contradictory.

Fournier, Sele and Schögel (2005, p. 19) advocate the following for successful brand communities to function properly:

- Enable the social life of the brand.
- Facilitate socialisation of new members.
- Accelerate new members' acculturation into the group.
- Provide tools for identity markers and status/cultural capital in the system.
- Fuel the brand mystique that serves the foundation of the group.
- Respect brand heritage and support core brand meaning.
- Limit dilution of brand by rejecting incongruous brand extensions.
- Encourage the four main relationships.
- Adopt a close-to-customer ethos.

- Balance the tensions of community growth versus maintenance.
- Evaluate the community against relationship-relevant metrics.

Holt (2004, p. 13) underlines this culturally constituted meaning through brand narratives by what he refers to as a 'cultural branding model'. He draws the distinction (particularly with long-established iconic brands) between:

- **Mind-share branding:** a cognitive model where attempts are made to 'identify the transcendental core of the brand' and maintain competitive parity or superiority in a product category consistently over time in all brand encounters.
- **Emotional branding:** a progression from mind-share branding, emotional branding emphasises how this 'transcendental core' is communicated through emotionally charged relationships. And
- **Viral branding:** the accelerated word of mouth facilitated by the Internet has added another dimension to, and changed the dynamic of, company-to-customer communications.

The focus of mind-share branding activities is always on owning a space in the consumer's mind in which your brand is favourably positioned against other category competitors. Reiteration of distinctive benefits and associations with cultural and consumption myths (Barthes 1977) is the essence of this approach.

Soap powder imitating soaps

© *P&G*. Reproduced with permission.

In the detergent category, an FMCG, low-involvement brand like *Daz* is constrained by both position in relation to the competition (*Persil* from Unilever and *Ariel* from P&G), and also by retailers' own brands (UK own brands represent about 20% in supermarkets compared to less than 10% in the USA). *Daz* is also exposed to ecological environmental constraints, developments in washing machine technology, new soft-iron fabrics and changing consumer needs, and the fact that this type of brand purchase is based on habitual repeat purchase. The consumer myth of the detergent category is that whiteness remains a benchmark. When new upstarts like *Radion* exploded into the category in the late 1980s with its brash colours, approach and differentiation, the impact of associations with '*Daz* washes WHITER' and '*Daz* whites' was diminished. *Daz* has had to hit back with a platform that not only re-emphasises 'whiteness' but also engages with the target audience. This has been achieved by the creation of 'Cleaner Close' (a great pun on the product feature), a mythical domestic setting in which the idioms of soap opera are enacted with archetypical characters in domestic situations where cleaner laundry is the communication linkage. This has a nice historical irony as soap operas were originally invented by *P&G* to capture target audiences to sell soap! What is really interesting is that even in this habit-driven, competitive comparison category, an essentially functional mind-share branding position has had to build a narrative to engage 'the minds of the consumer'.

However, as Holt (2004, p. 21) points out: 'the problem with applying mind-share principles to identity brands is that the impulse to conceive of the brand in abstract terms, and then to focus on keeping these abstractions consistent over time, necessarily overlooks what makes identity brands valuable to their consumers'. So mind-share branding has been extended to include 'emotional, personality and sensory' ingredients in the brand essence (Gobe 2001). Brand associations should still be consistently reiterated in communications but a brand's personality and intimate connection with the consumer is critical. Sometimes this can be quasi-religious as with *Apple* and *Harley-Davidson* (as we have seen in the opening case).

A brand which transcended the mind-share mode of branding and became an exemplar of emotional branding is *Coca-Cola*. Not only is the name *Coca-Cola* the most known worldwide brand ever, it has developed an incredible emotional bond with its audience. From the Second World War, *Coke* has been symbolically associated with American identity myths of the spirit of national solidarity, new suburban nuclear life, through the global village unity of 'buying the world a *Coke*', and even racial harmony and it has done this by balancing the equity of nostalgia with contemporary relevance, by balancing mind-share and emotional branding. Images of bonding and affection are evident in polar bears, Father Christmas and the furry creatures that populate the '*Coke* side of life'. This mythical, second-life construct is exemplified in the video game advertisements viewed on TV, cinema and particularly online. These advertisements simultaneously connect with its target audience by using imagery echoing the idioms of the popular video game *Grand Theft Auto*, but subverting the gross, nihilistic violence and positioning the advertisement's hero as the antithesis of this. The hero is always *Coca-Cola*! As Holt (2004, p. 28) rightly points out: 'the emotional connections we routinely witness with iconic brands and their core customers are the result of potent identity myths spun by the brand'.

The further development of this is viral branding, which assumes that the brand narrative is spun by company and non-company stories and consumers can create potent brand identity myths. Narrative is present in the public conversations of public relations, word of mouth, 'below-the-radar' opinion formation, diffusion of innovation, meaning transfer, unplanned brand encounters and fuelled by the power and empowerment of the Internet. Communication 'seeded' in the most influential consumers and commentators helps consumers to discover the brand, as the brand narrative is spread like a virus through the social networks.

The ownership of the brand's story is partly illusion. When their record company in 2004 planted musical downloads and information about an up-and-coming British band on the Internet, the *Arctic Monkeys'* story was conceived, spread and owned by an audience accepting the source as credible. The resulting success of the band owed a lot to the initial momentum (or 'buzz') built up in the communities of youth social networks.

The *Snapple* drink brand, created and communicated with the help of Internet word of mouth, became a cult brand with a strong and loyal following, representing a sort of anti-corporation, amateurish identity. The 'covert public relations mode' (Holt 2004, p. 29) created 'buzz', underground street credibility and spawned an online brand community of loyal converts. The brand story benefited from an intertextual presence with radio shock jock advocates, 'cool' sponsorship and spoof celebrity endorsement. *Snapple* was one of those 'anti-brand brands' which purport to eschew conventional branding principles which 'championed a fantastic populist alternative . . . . . . and the buzz that *Snapple* generated was the consequence of the power of its myth' (Holt 2004, p. 35). The *Snapple* story wasn't about unusual flavours, or the extra-wide glass jars, or even the distribution policy of keeping the brand for 'mom and pop' independents, it was the brand story helping consumers to articulate their own corporate critique and connect to a sort of underground ethic because of the associations generated by the identity myth of the brand.

Snapple logo

A legendary brand is different from other brands because it projects a sense of celebrity within its customer base. It takes on a human persona; it attracts consumers in the same way that human celebrities do. Legendary brands stand for concepts, values and objects that consumers use to interpret meaning in their own lives. They represent, indeed manifest, the personality of the consumer, allowing them to order themselves in social, cultural and personal space.

Similarly, Vincent's (2002) brand mythology system comprises:

1. a worldwide view composed of a set of sacred beliefs;
2. a brand agent: person, place or thing;
3. brand narrative or story; and,
4. consumer participation through feedback activities.

Barthes (1977) introduced the concept of myth in the context of communication discourse. Myths are 'pre-existing and value-laden sets of ideas derived from the culture and transmitted by communication' (McQuail 2000, p. 313). Invocations of national identity, science or nature, society values, representations of gender, class and so on are often chiefly mediated for brand communication purposes.

CLOSING CASE STUDY

Ben & Jerry's: All We are Saying is Give Peace, Love and Ice Cream a Chance

Peace, Love and Ice Cream ad campaign

Reproduced by permission of Unilever.

In 1977, when two ex-hippies, Ben Cohen and Jerry Greenfield, had completed an ice cream making correspondence course, and opened their first ice cream parlour in downtown Burlington, Vermont, the world of ice cream – and in some ways the world – would never be the same again. To celebrate their first year of business, a great promotional tactic of free ice cream – the first of over 30 'Free Cone Days' – turned into a unique long-term strategic positioning combining ice cream making with social activism. The latest manifestation of this combines all aspects of the brand's narrative: product features, brand benefits and a wider societal relationship which is both highly relevant and participatory. The introduction of a number of products aimed at accentuating their ex-hippy, environmentally aware image – *Cherry Garcia*, *Whirled Peace* to name but two – has invigorated the brand, added to the sense of fun and reminded consumers of the 'ice cream with a conscience' ethos of the brand. But none captures this quite as well as *Baked Alaska*, a new flavour which underlines their key environmental platform to arrest climate change.

In order to establish long-term loyalty and consumer advocacy, the *Ben & Jerry's* narrative has had to be driven by the context within which the brand is consumed (literally and metaphorically). Characterisations of brands often present inconsistent dualities. How can an act of individual indulgence be allied to a shared social conscience? Brands grow even more powerful when consumers position them as resolving these sorts of conflicts in a higher order of thought. *Ben & Jerry's* do this by having authenticity and credibility, by according with salient desires, and resonating with a wide range of consumer experiences and beliefs in the way the brand is characterised (i.e. what the *Ben & Jerry's* brand is) and its *character* (what it does). But character and characterisation are only parts of the *Ben & Jerry's* narrative. Events play a huge part in projecting the brand ethos and extending the brand story arc. Even if the annual 'National Free Cone Day' promotions and Sundae in the Park Music Festivals are seen as tactical, the establishment of Fairtrade links, 'climate-neutral' production and their 'climate change college' have constructed a participatory narrative which is salient, relevant and co-produced. The controlling idea for *Ben & Jerry's* is no longer the consumption of ice cream, it is the consumption of values.

It is interesting that the UK exposure to *Ben & Jerry's* is nowhere near the levels of America and, as a consequence, not engaged to the same level with the other sides to the brand's story.

QUESTIONS

1. Do you think that the ethical, social stance taken by *Ben & Jerry's* is a superficial branding device or a strategic part of an ongoing brand narrative?

2. Brands with ethical, anti-establishment narratives like *Snapple*, *Green & Black's* and more recently *Innocent Smoothies* have had huge parts of their brand equity taken over by big corporations like *Coca-Cola* and *Cadbury*. Do you think this will alienate their original audience or will the individual brand image stay intact?

3. *Ben & Jerry's* approach to social branding has not impacted as much in Europe as it has in America. Why do you think that is?

CHAPTER SUMMARY

In this chapter, we have discussed the concept of organisations and products having brand narratives, story arcs which parallel product life cycles and provide longevity for brands, reliable income streams for organisations and, more importantly, provide meaning for consumers. We looked at the reasons why all marketing communications – media and messages – are bonded in strategic and tactical dialogues and consumers co-create, disseminate and advocate all communications about the brand.

The difference between a 'brand image' approach to marketing communications and an 'experiential' perspective was discussed and we looked at the reasons why the emphasis has shifted towards creating environments conducive to encouraging long-term brand loyalty. We looked at the changing levels of brand communications and evaluated how investing in relationships with customers is key to building and sustaining brand longevity. Consequently, the rise in brand communities was seen as a significant cultural development and this was discussed alongside the strategic significance of reward as a way of creating customer loyalty.

REFLECTIVE QUESTIONS

a. The brand narrative is a platform for creating, involving and sustaining customer engagement, with an orientation around a dominant, coherent 'big brand idea'. Research your own examples for brands which have engaged audiences in a storyline.

b. What is meant by the statement that 'brands are born in the many conversations which circulate culturally in the brand narrative?

c. What are the different levels of brand meaning?

d. McQuail (2000, p. 377) describes three alternative models of communicative relationship. What are they and how do they differ?

e. Hackley (1999, p. 143) points out that: 'the symbolic content of promotional messages must, in order to be meaningful to the consumer, make use of the cultural currency of symbolic codes in contemporary use'. What exactly does he mean?

RESEARCH PROJECTS

Visit the websites of various brands and see how they continue the brand story online, particularly in terms of engaging target audiences in the brand conversation.

Look up Adaval and Wyer's (1998) discussion on 'The Role of Narratives in Consumer Information Processing' published in the *Journal of Consumer Psychology* (7(3), 207–46) and analyse their argument for the importance of a narrative approach in consumer decision making.

CHAPTER  10

THE MARKETING COMMUNICATIONS MIX

"Each element of the marketing mix should integrate with other tools so that a unified message is consistently reinforced."
Smith and Taylor (2004)

This chapter is an introduction to the marketing communications mix, the collection of communication components which can be used to construct and maintain dialogues with target audiences. It is a type of menu subset of the marketing mix used to achieve the communication goals and objectives of marketing communications strategy and includes advertising, public relations, direct marketing, promotional activities and face-to-face sales. These are the tactical elements which must be integrated in order to provide 'one-voice' messages which help achieve communication campaign objectives and positioning for the brand.

LEARNING OBJECTIVES

After reading this chapter, you'll be able to:

- Understand how communications strategy uses the tactics of the communications mix.
- Appreciate the communications options available to achieve objectives: the 'mix' of advertising, personal selling, public relations, direct marketing and sales promotion.
- Know how the elements of the marketing communications mix can be used to build both long-term loyalty and equity and also ad hoc short-term expediencies.
- Describe the differences between the personal and impersonal communications elements of the communications mix.
- Appreciate the environmental factors which affect the marketing communications mix.
- Describe the different roles (e.g. creating awareness, reinforcing image or stimulating traffic flow) that are required from the application of communication mix components.
- Appreciate the degree to which components reinforce each other and the importance of the commonality and integration between them when communication messages are replicated across the mix and echoed through different elements.
- Know that applying a brand lens to all the decisions including the marketing communications mix can help to integrate all elements and provides a basis for control of both internal and external communications.

Part of the problem with studying marketing communications is the way marketing is communicated. Academics and practitioners alike have been locked into the '4Ps of the marketing mix' as a basic structure of tactical components which have to be blended together to present a proposition to a target audience. Once marketing strategy has been cascaded down into communications strategy, objectives are achieved by employing the communications tools that constitute the 'communications mix'. Whereas marketing strategy uses the tactics of the marketing mix, communications strategy uses the tactics of the communications mix.

But there has always been a sort of communication anomaly. Besides mixing our metaphors with a communication 'mix' which is like a 'toolbox' (!), marketers use the mnemonic of the '4Ps', where 'promotion' is a key pillar. The communications mix sometimes becomes the promotions mix, and students quite rightly get confused by the terms promotions and promotional activity. Therefore, we need to be constantly aware that all elements in the marketing mix project a message. This is echoed in Shimp's (1993) definition of marketing communication as: 'the collection of all elements in a brand's marketing mix that facilitate exchanges by establishing shared meaning with the brand's customers or clients'.

As everything in the marketing mix communicates – a premium priced, beautifully packaged perfume, displayed in an exclusive retail location communicates 'quality' positioning – it could be argued that the overriding umbrella construct should be the communications mix: everything is contingent on what positioning has to be communicated to the target audience. However, it is the purpose of this chapter to focus on the communication options available to achieve objectives – the 'mix' of advertising, personal selling, public relations, direct marketing and sales promotion. Sometimes these will be used to build long-term loyalty and equity; sometimes to meet ad hoc short-term expediencies.

OPENING CASE STUDY

MINI Cooper: A Continuing Story or a New Little MINI Adventure?

After a long history of British ownership, in which it was firmly established as an iconic car brand, the original MINI was purchased by the German company *BMW*, with-

drawn from production and relaunched in 2001 with a 130%-revised appearance and an exciting new image. Aimed specifically at the affluent 20–30 segment, the new MINI had a distinctive association of quality, reflected in an improved stylish build and premium pricing which created an air of desirability.

The marketing communications challenge was how to retain MINI's symbolic appeal (seen as fun, energetic, cheeky, stylish, self-confident, reliable and exciting), whilst at the same time emphasising the functional appeal of the product. Equally, should the focus be on the brand's heritage or should a new

The BMW MINI Cooper

Reproduced by permission of MINI.

brand narrative be created? The creative strategy adopted for the new MINI was to retain an emotional association towards the product – reflected by the 'It's a MINI adventure' storyline – whilst highlighting key functional attributes. The focus had to be on the individuality of the MINI, both in terms of distancing it from the competition and focusing on the 'personality' of the brand. The heritage narrative was retained but now had a contemporary twist. With German engineering and British character, there was now a more European character to the new MINI. When the 'It's a MINI adventure' campaign hit TV screens in 2001 – and cinemas soon after – each broadcast featured a highly dramatic escapade compressed into a short space of time. This underlined the MINI 'spirit' of: small, fun, adventurous, individual. The scope of cinema advertising augmented the 'adventure' theme with a very creative approach featuring a short movie which actually won a place in the *Guinness Book of Records* as the shortest movie ever made (lasting just 12 seconds).

Creating brand personalities can be an effective way to increase equity and facilitate achievement of communication objectives (Rajagopal 2006). Brand personalities are described as the association of human attributes with a particular named product (Aaker 1997, Milas & Mlačić 2007). MINI's brand personality formed a symbolic representation which appealed to consumers on an emotional level (Simms and Trott 2006). A subsequent study conducted by Simms and Trott (2007) identified the symbolic aspect of the MINI's appeal to be highly significant in forming the brand's image. With echoes of the iconic product placement in the 1970s' *The Italian Job* movie, a 'MINI adventure stunt show' was timed to coincide with the movie preview of the updated 1990s' version. This event further emphasised the product's characteristics by associating different personalities with the three performing cars. As a result, audience members could associate with 'who' (being the car) was their favourite. This strategy complements results from previous studies which conclude that consumers favour brands with which they have matching personalities (Aaker 1999, Govers and Schoormans 2005). MINI used this tactic by introducing a strategy that enabled owners to personalise their own MINIs, reflecting the personalities of their individual owners. A more recent example of MINI product placement was evident in The Stereophonics' song video 'Pick a Part That's New' (go to *YouTube* to view this). Viewers of song videos are inclined to watch them more than once and this proved to be a highly effective method of endorsement.

(Continued)

Small car - big packaging

Reproduced by permission of MINI.

MINI's functional repositioning centred on emphasising improved reliability, build quality and practicality (Simms and Trott 2007). These key functional attributes were expressed in publicity stunts and promotions displaying the elements of fun and compact size in crowd-stopping fashion. This showed creativity of the highest order and the media chosen were both appropriate and highly original. A series of MINIs, apparently packaged as if they were toys, could be viewed in many shopping malls ensuring high impact and generating a tremendous amount of consumer interest and word of mouth amongst potential buyers.

Another key functional appeal has always been the compact and yet spacious feature of the MINI. Many publicity stunts demonstrating 'How many people can you fit in a MINI?' have been evident over the years. None could have been as creative as the advertisement board that was placed on the entrance to a London Tube Station. This created an optical illusion which appeared to show a MINI containing a vast amount of people. This drew attention to the brand in a novel manner which provoked response about a key product feature as well as being in keeping with the cheeky image of the car.

With over 35 million people in the UK having access to the Internet, the online medium is now a vital

How many people can you get in a MINI?

Reproduced by permission of MINI.

communication component for most brands. A series of MINI online advertisements were created to catch attention and encourage website visits and help extend the MINI 'adventure' story. Flash banners (advertisements which sit on top of website pages) were a very creative way to get website visitors to interact. 'Eyeblasters' (or 'page takeovers') were used to show the MINI in motion and improve the 'stickability' of the MINI site.

Use of press and outdoor billboards and posters allowed further creativity which both highlighted features and instilled a sense of excitement about the brand. One area of outdoor promotional activities which generated much press coverage was the use of 'digital outdoor' technology. The inclusion of these electronic poster sites allowed creativity, freshness and almost continual changing posters. These were located in sites like the London Underground and other railway stations. Other interactive outdoor sites included bus shelters, video messages, ringtones and downloads as well as vouchers and video messages.

Dramatic billboard emphasises brand feature

Reproduced by permission of MINI.

BMW's decision to continue the MINI heritage by transferring specific associations from the old product gave continuity to the MINI brand narrative. Website images visually illustrating the aesthetic progressions of the product were reinforced through advertising that was appropriately entitled, 'The MINI Story: It's in the Genes'. Opinion formers – racing drivers and car magazine editors – were used to generate interest and spread word of mouth; opinion leaders, such as car enthusiasts, although not formal experts, influenced the decision of other buyers.

The MINI campaign benefited from complete integration of applied brand communications which underpinned a clearly defined market position with a well-focused and coherent brand narrative – one that has the legs to grow and allow the brand to develop within an overarching storyline or brand trajectory. It took into account additional factors such as the effects of outside influences, for example opinion leaders and opinion formers.

QUESTIONS

1. How has *BMW* achieved continuity of brand message without alienating existing customers and encouraging new MINI purchasers?

2. What elements of the marketing communications mix have been used to build and/or maintain the MINI brand narrative?

3. List the 'explicit' and 'implicit' elements of communication illustrated by the 'It's a MINI adventure' campaign.

WHAT IS THE COMMUNICATIONS MIX?

As we have seen, the marketing communications mix is a subset of the marketing mix, both being the tools which deliver respectively communications and marketing strategies. The marketing communications mix provides a menu of communication methods which can be used separately or ideally blended to achieve communication objectives and usually comprise advertising, publicity,

Sony Brava bunnies

Message placement for Drink Awareness campaign

Reproduced by permission of TBWA/London.

sales promotion, packaging and personal selling. It may involve expensive multimedia advertising like the 'bouncing bunnies' campaign for the *Sony Bravia*, or it may be something relatively inexpensive but powerful like using cocktail umbrellas as part of the 'Drink Aware' campaign.

One thing that is indisputable is that there should be one central focus in communicating to the consumer: the story of the brand. Keller (2001a, p. 819) sums this up well, referring to these communication options as being 'any marketer-initiated form of communication that is related directly or indirectly to the brand'. So let's first take a look at the components or tools which make up the communications mix and then discuss which of these are direct and indirect communications options.

Figure 10.1 shows five distinct areas:

- **Advertising** – including media, place, point of purchase and direct response/interactive advertising.
- **Direct marketing** – all types of database-driven communications.
- **Sales** – all types of face-to-face and remote selling activities.
- **Promotional activities** – including trade (B2B) and consumer (B2C) promotions.
- **Public relations** – including events management sponsorship, publicity and product placement.

According to Rowley (2001), the communications mix is 'the combination of different channels or tools that are used to communicate a message'. The component parts of the communications mix form the structure of the rest of this section and will therefore be discussed separately. Although there

Figure 10.1: Marketing mix components

Source: after Keller (2003, p. 820).

has been an expansion of tools that marketers can choose to communicate with, the fragmentation of markets, technological development such as the Internet, and the move from owner-generated communications as opposed to owner-dominated media, have all contributed to blurring the edges between what is direct and indirect, what is personal and impersonal and what has been generated by companies or customers. Figure 10.2 delineates the communications mix across the two parameters of personal and impersonal communications showing:

- **Non-personal communications:** aimed at managing image and building the brand. These have been traditionally one-way, asymmetrical communications, transmitted **indirectly** through a medium like TV for advertising, an event for sponsorship, a pack for sales promotion, or a retailer for merchandising.
- **Personal communications:** aimed at managing sales, service and customer contact. These are mainly two-way, symmetrical dialogues, transmitted **directly** through face-to-face sales contact, tele-marketing, mail, email and all the interactive electronic platforms of Internet, intranet and extranet.

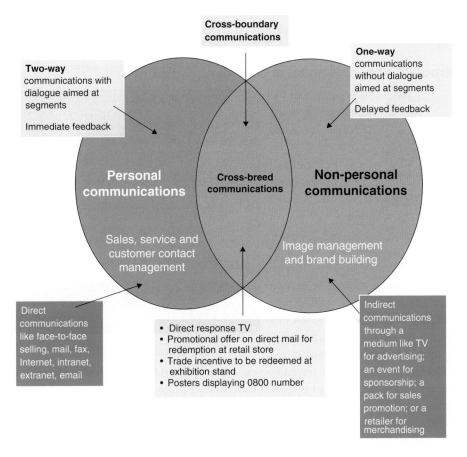

Figure 10.2: Marketing communications mix

However, some of the elements of the communications mix cross over these boundaries and are sort of cross-bred tools: direct response-based TV and magazine advertising is different to advertising which builds an image for the brand, or evokes memory of previous use or tries to tap into latent demand for a product. This type of advertising tries to build traffic flow ('footfall' into shops), generate sales leads and increase sales. Although these advertisements 'sell the dream' of the brand, a luxury bedroom in the example shown, they attempt to get consumers to ring, write into the company, fill in a coupon for a brochure, visit the website or the studio or outlet by employing the type of calls to action highlighted in the illustration of this bedroom manufacturer. The cross-boundary nature of these communication tools makes them both brand elevating and direct, asking the listener to not just engage with the brand but to act and interact directly with the organisation.

Cook (1994) spotted this trend for hybrid communications when he observed that 'discipline overlap is blurring long-standing distinctions. It's becoming increasingly difficult to categorise work as sales promotion or direct marketing . . . direct marketing is moving closer to conventional advertising'.

Direct response advertising

COMMUNICATIONS MIX IN FOCUS

Liverpool European Capital of Culture

To announce to the world the opening of the European Capital of Culture, the City of Liverpool made broadcasting history on 1 January 2008 when it took over a TV station for 24 hours. Airspace was booked on *Sky*'s Information TV Channel 167 for the whole of the day to promote just one product – Liverpool. A rolling six-minute 'teaser' programme promoting the city and all the planned celebrations ran in a continuous loop for the duration of the day.

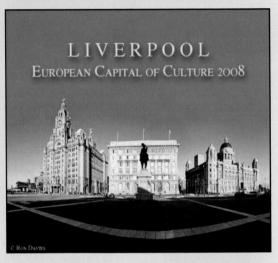

The 'Three Graces' at Liverpool's Pier Head

Although it was a paid-for advertising campaign, it was described by culture supremo Phil Redmond as 'This is not just us trying to advertise on TV, look at it as an exhibition tool and a platform. I have said it often, it is about people creating culture rather than just consuming it'.

This shows the cross-over nature of the communications mix like when someone holds a photographic exhibition, makes a programme about it, and then tells other people to tune in to watch it.

In conjunction with this one-day unique 'event', Information TV hosted a 'Capital of Culture Micro Channel' across its service, highlighting events and promoting what was essentially PR for its ongoing 'cultural conversations' agenda. The other interesting cross-over mix application here was the fact that Information TV saw this as 'product placement on a grand scale' and used the opportunity to launch its own service for other public sector use. Further underlining the use of communications mix in a creative and integrative way, key 'movers and shakers' were contacted virally by email and blogs to promote these events by word of mouth.

DESCRIPTION OF COMMUNICATIONS MIX TOOLS

The traditional tools of the marketing communications mix are usually categorised as:

- **Advertising:** traditional forms of advertising are characterised by non-personal, one-way messages paid for by an identified sponsor and transmitted to a mass and often homogeneous audience in order to influence, inform or persuade.
- **Personal selling:** face-to-face two-way communication in which a representative of the seller interprets a customer need or problem by presenting brand benefits.

- **Public relations:** the planned and sustained effort to establish and maintain goodwill and mutual understanding between an organisation and its public.
- **Direct marketing:** accurately targeted direct and personalised communications attempting to create and sustain a relationship and ongoing dialogue.

Which tools are most effective and where and how they are applicable is entirely contingent on the communication objective to be achieved and the competitive circumstance within which they must be deployed. For instance, advertising, viral marketing and direct marketing may be better employed to create awareness, especially for new products launched into a new category. Although personal selling will be important to explain a new product's features and benefits against the competitors' offers, it may be less effective in having immediate impact in the introduction of an FMCG brand. On the other hand, the slow-burn maintenance of relationships and the progression of contracts in a B2B context is where personal selling comes into its own. Public relations has an all-pervasive reputation-building role, except maybe for the actual purchase of product. As Kitchen and Proctor (2002) point out, this is a key aspect of integrated marketing communications: 'to use the strengths of one part to offset weaknesses of other parts'. Fill (2002) analyses the tools of the marketing communications mix based on (see also Table 10.1):

- The ability to achieve communication objectives. For example, if the communication objective is required to reach a wide audience, advertising, whether online or through traditional mass-market advertising, is best suited for this if one uniform message to an assumed homogeneous market is

	Advertising	Sales promotion	Public relations	Personal selling	Direct marketing
Communications					
Ability to deliver a personal message	Low	Low	Low	High	High
Ability to reach a large audience	High	Medium	Medium	Low	Medium
Level of interaction	Low	Low	Low	High	High
Credibility given by target audience	Low	Medium	High	Medium	Medium
Costs					
Absolute costs	High	Medium	Low	High	Medium
Cost per contact	Low	Medium	Low	High	High
Wastage	High	Medium	High	Low	Low
Size of investment	High	Medium	Low	High	Medium
Control					
Ability to target particular audiences	Medium	High	Low	Medium	High
Management's ability to adjust the deployment of the tool as circumstances change	Medium	High	Low	Medium	High

Table 10.1: Key characteristics of the tools of marketing communications

Source: Fill (2002). Reproduced with permission.

important. Having individual negotiations with key customers will be where personal face-to-face selling is deployed.

- Advertising is becoming very expensive relative to newer media and it may be better to use a less impactful, more cost-effective medium.
- How much control does the organisation have over the content and delivery of communication? Public relations, word of mouth and even individual selling propositions are difficult to control as two-way communication is contextual and individual and open to interpretation and variation. The instant feedback from sales promotions, on the other hand, can help change and tailor campaigns to suit audience needs and perceptions.

What this shows is that firstly each component will have some merits dependent upon the situational aspects of what marketing communication objectives have to be achieved; secondly, because objectives may be varied and audiences' requirements differ, integrated marketing communications is not and should not be planned as if these components were separate from each other. They have to be integrated and selected on their individual fit. Hughes and Fill (2007) argue that the promotional mix is no longer a viable interpretation and suggest a new marketing communications mix – MCM^2 – involving mainly message content and the media mix, an approach that 'incorporates a revised classification of direct and indirect media'.

Keller (2001, p. 831) discusses the environmental factors that affect the mix. The first criterion is **coverage** which refers to the inherent ability of the mix component to reach an audience. **Contribution** refers to the component's standalone ability to communicate without any assistance from other communications mix elements. The different roles (e.g. creating awareness, reinforcing image or stimulating traffic flow) require the skilful application of components and this is a way to assess them separately.

The degree to which components reinforce each other and the **commonality** between them is important. Burnett and Moriarty (1998) emphasise the need for integration across all mix components. When communication messages are replicated across the mix and echoed through different elements, the message is strengthened and enhanced.

The **complementarity** refers to how the components can be combined for best overall effect. If, for example, trial is key to early product adoption, sampling, package offers and merchandising may be best. The ability of a component to work on a number of levels (i.e. consumers who have already been exposed to brand messages by other components and those who haven't been exposed) describes the **robustness** of the component. Finally, it is important to evaluate how much each component costs. Table 10.2 illustrates the micro aspects and Table 10.3 the macro aspects involved in analysing and comparing the components of the communications mix.

Ability to	TV	Print	Sales promotion	Sponsorship	Interactive
Attract attention or be intrusive	Medium	Medium	Medium	Low	Low
Convey product information	Low	High	High	Low	High
Create emotional response	High	Medium	Low	Medium	Low
Link to brand	Low	Medium	Medium	High	High
Encourage or facilitate purchase	Low	Medium	High	Low	High

Table 10.2: Communications mix: micro perspectives

Source: Keller (2001, p. 836).

	TV	Print	Sales promotion	Sponsorship	Interactive
Coverage breadth	High	Low	Medium	High	Low
Coverage depth	Low	Medium	Medium	Medium	High
Contribution	High	High	High	High	High
Commonality	High	Medium	Medium	Low	High
Complementarity	High	High	High	High	High
Robustness	Low	Medium	Low	Low	High
Cost	High	High	High	High	High

Table 10.3: Communications mix: macro perspectives

Source: Keller (2001, p. 836).

MATTER OF FACT

Whirlpool's Touch Point Wheel

According to Davis (2005, p. 228), 'making the brand the central focus of the organisation helps clarify on-brand and off-brand behaviours'. He claims that applying a brand lens to all decisions including the marketing communications mix can help integrate all elements and provide a basis for control of both internal and external communications.

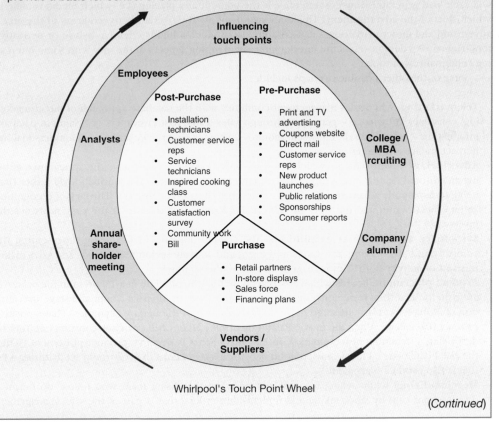

Whirlpool's Touch Point Wheel

(Continued)

He applies this to the three stages of pre-purchase, purchase and post-purchase using the *Whirlpool* organisation as a case study. The figure illustrates this, showing the various communication touch points both human and marketing communications mix components.

Source: Davis (2005).

There is a close association between the different tools in the communications mix, and a true approach to 'mixing' is to look at the different combinations of techniques as they are actually used. As we have seen, each element may combine with another to produce a cross-over application which benefits from the strengths of each component. An industry which is reliant on the generation of sales leads to provide opportunities to sell like home improvement, so-called direct selling operations or mass media brand advertising which projects imagery and associations, is not enough and relies on a cumulative, slow build up of cognitive, affective and conative stages. Direct selling requires immediate response to 'call consumers to action': ring up, write in, send in a coupon, visit our website, or even better our store and order your product. So, in this case, the imagery of brand advertising has to be combined with calls to action techniques of direct marketing. Even though the brand may be placed in, say, a Sunday newspaper magazine alongside image-building campaigns for *Calvin Klein, Porsche, Mazda* and *Omega,* if you look for the codes printed on the bottom, you will see that this advertisement will be evaluated for response. How many sales leads will be fed to the sales force? How many website hits will generate further enquiries? How many will be converted by telesales? How many appointments will be made for the sales design team? How many orders will each lead generate? How cost-effective is the content and placing (i.e. which media vehicle in which slot) of the advertisement? This demonstrates how the overlap between areas of the mix – advertising and direct marketing – can combine to produce a highly effective hybrid or derivative tool. Figure 10.3 demonstrates the interlocking, overlapping aspects of the mix with some interesting combinations of tools.

Some of the other possible overlaps include:

- **Telemarketing:** when sales management combines with the database approach of direct marketing, consumer knowledge – generated through sales leads, past customers or bought-in database information – is used to sell, cross-sell, monitor customer experience and so on in a personal but not face-to-face encounter.
- **Advertorials:** advertisements which are paid for by a company, but have the appearance of being an editorial (as they are written and presented in the idiom of the journal's style rather than being transparently advertisements), are often referred to as advertorials. The lack of recognition by an official writer and the rider of 'Advertising Content' at the top of the page is always the giveaway!
- **Sales-force attendance at exhibitions:** the age-old dilemma of balancing representing the company and 'flag-waving' at a sponsored event and actively seeking sales leads and sales makes this sort of activity both sales management and public relations.
- **Product placement:** brands which are 'placed' within the plot-line of a TV programme or movie are paid for as if they were conventional advertising. Damon Albarn's album and stage presentation of *Monkey* regularly featured in the BBC's coverage of the Beijing Olympics. That's positive product placement. When the movie Palahniuk (1996) *Fight Club* criticises consumer culture by destroying a 'feminine nest-building icon like *IKEA*', that is negative product placement. When the *IKEA* catalogue includes only computers by *Hewlett-Packard* in every room-set featuring a PC that is also product placement.
- **Merchandising:** when selling is supported by a merchandising team who follow up business development calls by stock taking and replenishing orders, that is part of the sales management

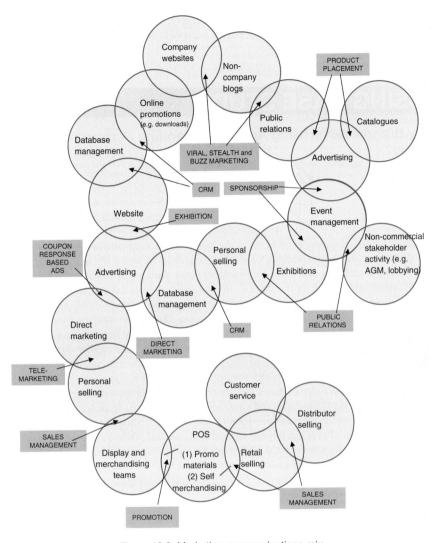

Figure 10.3: Marketing communications mix

effort; when the furnishing of displays including point-of-sale materials is the main objective, that overlaps with promotion.

- **Sponsorship:** event management overlaps with exhibitions. A flooring company may organise, sponsor and attend a trade road show which not only invites architects, quantity surveyors and various other B2B DMU members, but also anciliary manufacturers (floor adhesive, cleaning and tool companies) and is essentially the same sort of thing as the same company attending a sponsored exhibition like the *Interbuild Building Trade Exhibition* at the National Exhibition Centre (NEC) in Birmingham in the UK.
- **Direct-response advertising:** advertising which elicits sales-oriented calls to action in the form of telemarketing or coupon-response based appeals crosses over pure brand advertising and direct marketing techniques.
- **Customer relationship management:** the marriage of sales management and database management provides a very efficient approach to managing customers, both in terms of account management and customer service.

- **Viral, buzz and stealth marketing:** product placement, publicity and advertising are becoming more indistinct and demarcation lines are either purposely or inadvertently blurred (see Chapter 14 for a full description of this topic).

CLOSING CASE STUDY

Charity Brands: Advertising *Amnesty*, Branding *Barnardos:* Cause or Creativity?

AMNESTY INTERNATIONAL

Barnardos
EVERY CHILDHOOD LASTS A LIFETIME

© Barnardos. Reproduced with permission.

The Third Sector – charities, voluntary, social enterprise organisations – is a highly competitive not-for-profit market sector populated by brands which are neither goods nor services. It is odd to think of there being a category need here, in the same way as a car provides status, a deodorant social acceptability or alcohol may provide social affiliation, but charity brands like *Amnesty International* and *Barnardos* still have to compete with other NFP organisations such as the *NSPCC*, the *Ammado Foundation* and *Oxfam*. To do this they have to appeal to the hearts and minds – and consciences – of more fortunate citizens. But they have to convert that compassion into contributions. And to do this, they have to compete with other charities and good causes for every dollar or euro, rupee or rand, krone or króna.

Charity donations have become, in a way, a 'zero-sum game': one charity increasing support at the expense of others. There is evidence of what Ian Duncan Smith called the 'Tesco-isation' of the non-profit sector (i.e. larger charities squeezing out smaller organisations altogether in order to capture their market share). Even the big charities have retention issues. For example, in the UK in 2005, 30 of the 60 big national charities won repeat gifts from less than a third of the donors they had recruited during the previous 12 months. According to Dr Tom Farsides (2009), 'donors today are aware that it is a buyers' market and can walk away from a relationship with a charity at any time'. So, therefore, what sort of marketing communications mix do these types of organisations have to use in order to achieve their objectives? How do they best find their target audiences for donors? Let's look at some charities and recent campaigns.

Amnesty International's hangman promotion

Amnesty International is a worldwide movement of people who campaign for internationally recognised human rights. The purpose of its campaigns is to recruite members and subscribers (over 2.2 million in more than 150 countries and regions), and promote justice on a wide range of issues. It has used varied below-the-line mix tactics including an 'anti-censorship' poster advertising campaign in press and on sites right across Europe. This was highly effective, the simple combination of message and channel results in calls to action being diverted to the website. To raise awareness for International Human Rights Day, a novel 'hangman cookie' was used to promote the 'abolishing the death penalty' campaign and emphasise the UN resolution on abolishing the death penalty. The promotion was interactive, with a light-hearted booklet featuring cartoon alternative uses for the rope.

Barnados 'Believe in Children' campaign

Reproduced with kind permission of Kiran Master c/o Burnham Niker, and Barnardos.

Barnardos had to rebrand as its brand name was always synonymous with orphans and orphanages. The inspiration and values instilled at the brand's beginning continue as far afield as *Barnardos'* work in Australia, initiated through migration schemes for children from the UK. Although no longer associated with orphanages, and now comprising four separate charities (UK, Ireland, Aotearoa in New Zealand as well as Australia), the brand is described on its website as 'aiming to help improve the quality of life for children and their families'. *Barnardos* has formulated a number of public awareness and advocacy campaigns, mainly through powerful TV and press advertising, helping over 120,000 children each year and increasing its income by an average of 9% a year since 2001. The value of its brand has also grown with the charity and is now worth £100 million.

An emerging communication mix component which is gaining in efficacy as more people are becoming absorbed in online alternative existences is the virtual world of *Second Life*. User-generated content and social interaction of social media have provided opportunities to reach possible donors. *Amnesty* has yet to decide on whether to get involved with *Second Life*, but it's already an enthusiastic supporter of blogs, networking sites and podcasts. It used a page on *MySpace* as well as podcasts and viral video clips (on *YouTube*) to promote its annual *Sleeping Policeman's Ball*. It also recruits online: close to 60,000 were recruited to its *irrepressible.info* campaign. Bloggers are used as opinion leaders to help recruit support. Other charities such as *Christian Aid* are keen users of blogs and podcasts. *FaceBook* has raised donations through *socialvibe.com* and *Twitter* has *Twestival*. The view in the sector is that these are welcome changes from the 'bad news' culture and the usual hard-hitting 'guilt by association' appeals of direct mail campaigns. Charities have great stories that they can be pushing out there through all the media that are now available.

QUESTIONS

1. How will the rise of online 'social media charities' such as *FaceBook's socialvibe.com* and ideas such as *Twitter's Twestival* affect *Amnesty*?

2. What part does positioning play in deciding on what mix components are appropriate for charities to use in their campaigns?

3. If retention of donors is much more important than acquisition, what elements of a charity's marketing communications mix should be used to encourage donor loyalty?

CHAPTER SUMMARY

In this chapter, we were introduced to the marketing communications mix, the collection of communication components which can be used to construct and maintain dialogues with target audiences. We saw how marketing communications strategy uses this as a type of menu subset of the marketing mix to achieve the communication goals and objectives of marketing communications strategy.

We examined the component parts which included: advertising, public relations, direct marketing, promotional activities and face-to-face sales and how these can overlap to produce hybrid communication tools. These are the tactical elements which must be integrated in order to provide 'one-voice' messages which help achieve communication campaign objectives and positioning for the brand.

REFLECTIVE QUESTIONS

a. This chapter refers to the marketing communications mix as the overriding umbrella construct, everything being contingent on what positioning has to be communicated to the target audience. What does this mean?

b. What's the difference between personal and non-personal communications?

c. Keller (2001, p. 831) discusses the environmental factors which affect the mix as being coverage, contribution, commonality, and complementarity. Read back over this section and evaluate these factors.

d. The interlocking, overlapping aspect of the mix shows cross-over combinations of tools (e.g. the objectives of public relations and face-to-face selling take place when the sales force represents the organisation at a trade exhibition). Can you think of other cross-over communication tools?

e. The effectiveness of the individual communication tools is entirely contingent on the communication objective to be achieved and the competitive circumstance within which they must be deployed. Explain your understanding of this statement and illustrate with some examples.

RESEARCH PROJECTS

Visit a trade exhibition and evaluate the cross-over nature of sales personnel who are representing an organisation in a public relations capacity but also have specific sales targets.

EMAP publish a media directory and provide an online service called *BRAD* (British Rates and Data). Media planners, buyers, PR professionals, printers, advertising professionals and so on use it to compare costs for various communication tools. Visit the site or get a copy of the directory from your library and see how each component of the communications mix can be evaluated.

CHAPTER  11

ADVERTISING STRATEGY

"Advertising relies on visual imagery to connect the perceptual with the conceptual, the signifier and the signified, the product and the product benefits."
Schroeder and Borgerson (2003)

This chapter is specifically about the development and implementation of advertising strategy. Even with all the pressures on and the diminishing influence of advertising, it still represents such an important part of the marketing communications mix that a separate discussion is warranted. Furthermore, it acts as a template for other communications components in terms of its ability to create awareness, image and develop customer relationships through brand engagement.

LEARNING OBJECTIVES

After reading this chapter, you'll be able to:

- Understand the component parts of advertising strategy.
- Appreciate how the target audience's view of the product can have great influence on how advertising is perceived and help determine what objectives have to be set to elicit specific responses.
- Evaluate the relationship that target audiences have with the brand and advertising.
- Consider the vital role communication effects and objectives have in strategy.
- Examine the four frameworks within which advertising appeals may be designed.
- Understand the various appeals around which advertising can be designed.

The debate about the impact that advertising has on consumer behaviour is polarised between: the view that it works by conversion on a cognitive, rational decision-making level (the strong theory); and one where behavioural brand image is reinforced (the weak theory), which focuses on a more emotional, symbolic and intuitive view of products. The strong theory suggests that advertising can be persuasive, can generate long-run purchase behaviour, increases sales and regards consumers as passive; the weak perspective implies that purchase behaviour is based on habit, that advertising can improve knowledge and reinforce existing attitudes, and views consumers as active problem solvers. For example, the question of whether advertising is directly linked to tobacco consumption, has contributed to the rise in obesity levels through its promotion of fast food, or has conditioned young girls to pursue a 'size zero' body, juxtaposes the 'hierarchy of effects' persuasion models to one where advertising merely reflects and reinforces social and peer group behaviour.

Processing information through a central route (e.g. the Elaboration Likelihood Model of Petty and Cacioppo 1981 later extended by Rossiter, Percy and Donovan in 1991 with the Foote, Cone, Belding (FCB) framework) describes a highly motivated consumer with the ability to make rational decisions. The peripheral route places less emphasis on the cognitive process of processing and supports the view that elements such as advertising design, celebrity endorsement, music and so on, have a greater impact by reinforcing behaviour. As we have seen in Chapter 2, Barnard and Ehrenberg (1997) refer to a 'nudging' stage in the build up of the aggregate communication effects of awareness, trial and reinforcement persuading consumers to adopt product. Weilbacher (2003) supports this view, claiming that advertising 'is not a stimulus in the outmoded behavioural psychology stimulus–response model of human information processing', but is only part of the cumulative effect of everything that has been learned and remembered about the brand from all marketing communications.

OPENING CASE STUDY

Marks & Spencer: Not Just Advertising Strategy. Marks & Spencer Advertising Strategy

Changing the image of one of the UK's most famous brands required a drastic change in repositioning in terms of product offer and store configuration. However, it was the advertising strategy which changed the fortunes of *Marks & Spencer*. After images showing

YOUR M&S

popular model-cum-personality Twiggy appeared on TV, billboards and online websites, sales of a particular *M&S* blouse were higher in one week than the whole of *M&S*'s history. As Rod Whitehouse of *Deutsche Bank* claims 'this has been one of the more advertising-led recovery stories we've watched, and it's working'.

More than introducing new products, redesign and refitting of stores, or even refocusing on developing new segments, what was needed was a 'big idea', a storyline, a positioning statement which was designed to engage existing and target audiences and impact on a whole plethora of stakeholders. The execution of this advertising strategy was the 'Your M&S' campaign. As Tanya Livesey and Lucy Howard of *Marks & Spencer* claim: 'This was conceived as powerful, colloquial and symbolic of the rightful ownership of the brand to the British public. Rich in meaning and broad enough to have resonance in any product category, it also had relevance for any and every audience'. Good marketing communications depends on there being one message speaking with one voice being reinforced to different audiences, and this was a classic case of uniting disparate external customers, stakeholders and internal employees.

Like so many brands which require turning around (*Skoda*, *Mini*, the *BBC*), the key task is changing perceptions with target audiences. Reclaiming ground had to be winning over legions of loyal mature females and appealing to a younger demographic. The clarion call was to restore strength in womenswear and 'delighting the girls again'. The route to this was to use a whole stable of female celebrities who endorsed the new fashion lines. The July 2007 edition of the fashion magazine *Vogue* featured models such as Lily Cole, Elizabeth Jagger and Erin O'Connor on the front cover and they were soon to appear throughout an extensive celebrity-focused campaign along with two celebrities who appealed to both ends of the target demographic: Twiggy and Myleene Klass. *M&S* was able to benefit from the transfer of the celebrity currency and esteemed fashion tastes of the celebrities used: meaning transferred from the celebrity fashion model who is endorsing the brand to the product itself, and then from the product endorsed to the consumer. There is congruence between target audi-

Some of the M&S Girls

ence and celebrity (Till 1998) although *M&S* used the 'co-presentational mode' of endorsement ('merely appearing with the product', McCracken 1999) within all their clothes advertisements. As Kambitsis *et al.* (2002, pp.156) suggest: 'imitation or symbolic association advertisements attempt to associate attractive personal qualities with ownership'. Although Myleene Klass started with less cultural currency than her other celebrity stable mates, her exposure in celebrity-focused popular culture has caused her stock to rise and she has become the face of *M&S*.

The use of multiple celebrities helped *M&S* 'build a sense of consensus, avoid audience boredom, and appeal to multiple audiences' (Hsu and McDonald (2002, p. 25. This strategy was rolled out with male celebrities like Bryan Ferry, Jamie Rednapp, Alan Hansen and the band Take

Some of the M&S Boys

(*Continued*)

That, whose cultural currency resonated with the male target audience and changed attitudes to *M&S* positioning and product.

QUESTIONS

1. Do you think the use of celebrities to endorse brands is a sustainable tactic for *Marks & Spencer* or will it detract from long-term strategic aims?

2. Will the impact of the credit crunch undermine the creative platform adopted in *Marks & Spencer*'s advertising strategy?

3. Do you agree with *Deutsche Bank*'s claim that *Marks & Spencer*'s recovery was 'one of the more advertising-led recovery stories we've watched' or are there other contributory factors?

ADVERTISING STRATEGY

The role that advertising plays in marketing communications has gone through a number of stages. From its early informational orientation, advertising has been used to project status, moved from the product to the user with themes of family, social, and health, to a post-war era of brand image and identification which promised to transform the consumer with brands projected as emblems of group identification (Lee and Johnson 2005). Since the 1980s, the focus of most advertising has shifted away from the product (the material object and its benefits or attributes) towards the brand or more precisely the brand image – and the suggestion that the brand has the power to solve problems and bestow desired qualities (what anthropologists call a 'fetish'). The elitist, self-centred 'greed is good' mantra of the 1980s has given way to a much more conscience-led consumption with green and ethical threads running through much of today's advertising appeals. Brands like *Sainsbury's* with its 2009 'Feed a Family for a Fiver' campaign have reflected the credit crunch times of restricted spending and thrift. As Grant (2006) points out: 'the brand image approach was developed to suit the advertiser of its day: mass-produced products which required differentiation'. The 1990s saw a focus on the media, retail and services, sectors which are 'cultural, experienced in use, diverse, fluid' (Grant 2006).

Nonetheless, cognition, affect and experience are integral components of behavioural change in marketing, and the driving force of the marketing communications mix has traditionally been **media-based advertising**. Although it is only one part of the integrated marketing communications mix, advertising may initiate (and in some cases be the entire) contact with the target audience. The communicated message has to build the brand and create desirable associations to it, as well as encouraging target audience involvement and stimulating purchase. Advertising has been forced to evolve in response to changes in media, technology, culture and audience. The well-established model of repeating messages through key selected media in order to convey positioning and communication objectives has been supplemented, and often substituted, by alternative digital communications and media. We'll be discussing the impact of online marketing communications (OMC) in Chapter 17, but let's look firstly at advertising strategy (Figure 11.1). The following major factors are important to consider in determining how advertising should be designed:

1. The desired **advertising objectives** must be compatible with overall marketing communication objectives and need to be agreed prior to any creative discussions.
2. Objectives must be consistent with overarching **brand narrative development** and the **target audience**.
3. The scope of advertising must be within the **parameters of budget**.

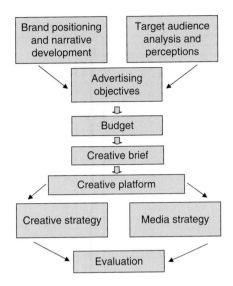

Figure 11.1: Advertising strategy formation

4. The **creative brief** must be written describing the market dynamics, brand requirements and possible positioning guidance.
5. A **creative platform** is developed providing a blueprint for creating an effective advertising campaign with possible message and media strategy, tone to be adopted, voice with which advertising will be channelled, and probably the 'big idea' or central thrust of the campaign.
6. The **creative and media strategy** proposals are the definite plans for executing the creative messages with a media schedule of where these messages will appear.
7. All marketing communications must be **evaluated** to determine whether the budget has been used effectively to achieve campaign objectives.

BRAND POSITIONING AND NARRATIVE DEVELOPMENT

Once marketing communications strategy has been established and strategic and tactical positioning has been determined, message design has to be agreed, created and implemented. As we discussed in Chapters 6 and 7, the brand positioning is formed in consumers' minds, and therefore does not exist until it has been communicated. All communications must project a coherent, single voice which reflects and reinforces an ongoing brand storyline to which target audiences can connect and help to co-create. Chapter 9 provides a comprehensive discussion on this.

TARGET AUDIENCE CHARACTERISTICS

The target audience's view of the product can have great influence on how advertising is perceived and help determine what objectives have to be set to elicit specific responses. Attitudes, perceptions and purchase intention are dependent upon the target audience's behavioural loyalty and attitude towards the product. As we have seen in Chapter 3, there are three response types which can be used to affect what consumers think, feel or do about the brand: **cognitive** which refers to the mental processing of information, problem-solving; **affective** which describes the feelings engendered towards a brand; and **conative** where behaviour or action is initiated. In Chapter 4, we looked at how target audiences can be segmented according to the state of purchase readiness towards a brand in a particular category, repeated here in Table 11.1.

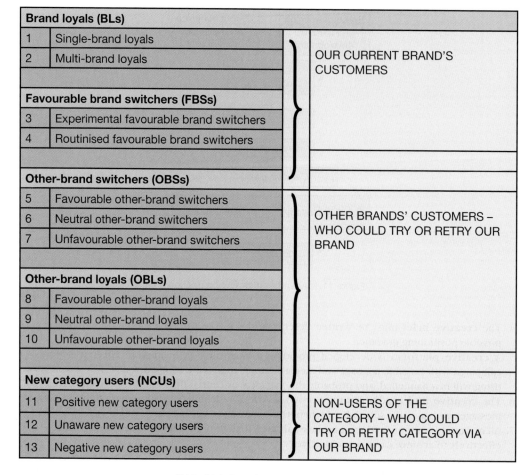

Brand loyals (BLs)		
1	Single-brand loyals	OUR CURRENT BRAND'S CUSTOMERS
2	Multi-brand loyals	
Favourable brand switchers (FBSs)		
3	Experimental favourable brand switchers	
4	Routinised favourable brand switchers	
Other-brand switchers (OBSs)		
5	Favourable other-brand switchers	OTHER BRANDS' CUSTOMERS – WHO COULD TRY OR RETRY OUR BRAND
6	Neutral other-brand switchers	
7	Unfavourable other-brand switchers	
Other-brand loyals (OBLs)		
8	Favourable other-brand loyals	
9	Neutral other-brand loyals	
10	Unfavourable other-brand loyals	
New category users (NCUs)		
11	Positive new category users	NON-USERS OF THE CATEGORY – WHO COULD TRY OR RETRY CATEGORY VIA OUR BRAND
12	Unaware new category users	
13	Negative new category users	

Table 11.1: Brand loyalty segmentation

Source: Rossiter and Bellman (2005, p. 83).

TARGET AUDIENCE RELATIONSHIP WITH THE BRAND AND ADVERTISING

A critical factor to help brands cut through the advertising clutter and avoidance of communications is target audience engagement. As Calder and Malthouse (2008) assert: 'the actual contact with the consumer is formed by both the ad and the surrounding media content', implying that engagement is a result of the experience of that content affecting the individual's interpretation of the advertising message. The buying state of users and non-users and the specific characteristics of the product have to be evaluated when determining what tactical elements of advertising will be most appropriate to ensure advertising is effectively engaging:

- **Involvement:** determines how involved the purchase is and how much information should be used, to what extent the target audience should be activated, and the amount and strength of arguments used.
- **Purchase motivation:** will also determine how much information should be used, whether argument is appropriate and what emotions the advertising should evoke.
- **Brand familiarity:** decides how much attention should be given to the product and how complex the advertising content should be.

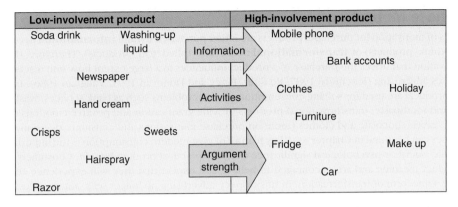

Figure 11.2: Examples of low-involvement and high-involvement products

Source: Dahlen and Lange (2003). *Optimal marknadskommunikation*, Liber Ekonomi. Reproduced with permission.

Product Involvement

Involvement refers to the individual's decision-making processes and can be divided into: **high-involvement products** (which are complex or expensive or new and need consumers to spend time in evaluating and purchasing); and **low-involvement products** (where there is low interest or complexity and consumers do not need or are not prepared to spend much time and effort in evaluating and purchasing). See Figure 11.2.

Eighty per cent of all purchases are low involvement, and because the function of advertising low-involvement products is to **remind** people about the product's existence, a lot of advertising is devoted to these products. Advertising funds are also allocated to high-involvement products (like cars and clothes), but because the purchase decision can be extended and complicated, the effectiveness of advertising depends on how involved consumers are. Advertising may appear in different media dependent upon whether it is for low- or high-involvement products. For example, advertising for high-involvement products contains, in general, more information and must be placed in media where the information can be processed, whereas advertising for low-involvement products may be placed in media where the information space possibilities are lower. What are the causes of these informational differences? Mortimer (2002) illustrated the different levels of involvement as applied to service brands (Figure 11.3).

	Think	Feel
High involvement	(Economic) Life Insurance Car Insurance Credit cards	(Psychological) Hotel Steak restaurant Holidays
Low involvement	(Responsive) Banks Photo processing	(Social) Fast food Long distance phone calls

Figure 11.3: FCB matrix applied to service brands

Source: Mortimer (2002).

Purchase Motivation

In terms of motivation for purchase, products are either purchased to fulfil **informational** needs (also called 'think' products) or **transformational** needs (also called 'feel' products). Therefore, the kind of motivation that drives the purchase of a product influences to a large extent how one reacts to and processes advertising (Ratchford 1987, Rossiter, Percy and Donovan 1991, Vaughan 1986). Informational products are used for solving consumption-related problems such as bank services, washing-up liquid and toothpaste; transformational products provide gratification and positive emotions such as holiday travel, chocolate and clothes (more on purchase motivations and consumer decision-making processes can be found in Chapter 3). A key feature of post-modern consumption is the importance of 'symbolic' social or psychological significance over any practical product benefit. Consumers search for product meaning and are encouraged to believe and expect that they will experience and even achieve some form of transformation. In this respect, advertising no longer sells: automobiles, but an image of status; beer, but the feeling of social acceptance; antiperspirant, but the aura of competence; make-up, perfume, or clothes, but an improved self-image (Rutherford 2007).

Higgins (2006) examines the relationship between engagement and positive or negative brand experience ('approach' or 'avoidance'), illustrated in Figure 11.4. The hedonistic value of the experience of the object is the pleasure or displeasure (Higgins calls this 'liking') in consuming the brand, which will affect the direction of purchase towards approach or avoidance. Engagement, on the other hand, stems from the actual desire to make something happen or NOT happen, and is thus the motivational if secondary element of the experience.

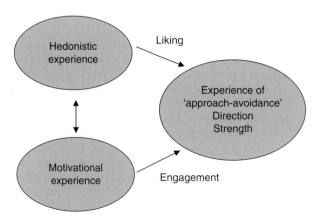

Figure 11.4: Engagement as motivational experience

Source: Calder (2008). Adapted from Higgins (2006).

MATTER OF FACT

Measuring Involvement and Motivation

To be able to classify products according to involvement and purchase motivation, Ratchford (1987) developed the questions shown in the table below. In five studies, over 2000 consumers rated more than 250 products in the two dimensions, and Ratchford was able to identify and select the questions that provided the most valid and correct answers to use in marketing research. The result was three questions that measured involvement and five questions that measured purchase motivation:

Involvement (high–low)	Purchase motivation (think/informational–feel/transformational)
Very important decision/Very unimportant decision	*Think questions:*
Very complicated decision/Very easy decision	Decision is not mainly logical or objective/ Decision is mainly logical or objective
Decision requires a lot of thought/ Decision requires little thought	Decision is based mainly on functional facts/ Decision is not based mainly on functional facts
	Feel questions:
	Decision expresses one's personality/Decision does not express one's personality
	Decision is based on a lot of feeling/Decision is not based on a lot of feeling
	Decision is based on looks, taste, touch or sound/ Decision is not based on looks, taste, touch or sound

Measuring involvement and motivation

Source: Ratchford (1987).

Brand Familiarity

It is not only the brand's positioning and associations that influence how people perceive advertising. The familiarity or unfamiliarity of a brand is also an important factor to consider in the construction of the advertising message. Let us take a closer look at the differences in how we perceive and react to advertising for familiar and unfamiliar brands. Based on knowledge about this, companies can determine the most important tactical elements in the advertising of a specific product in each group (Dahlén 2001, Ephron 1995, Tellis 1997). Some examples of the key advertising aspects for familiar and unfamiliar brands are shown in Figure 11.5.

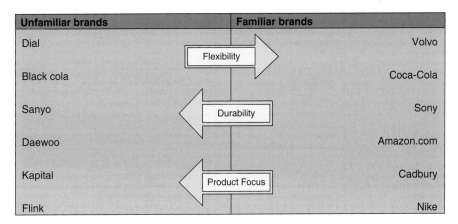

Figure 11.5: Examples of unfamiliar and familiar brands and the most important advertising aspects for these two groups

Source: Dahlen and Lange (2003). *Optimal marknadskommunikation*, Liber Ekonomi. Reproduced with permission.

Familiar brands are brands that most people in the target audience already know (i.e. they recognise the brand as soon as they see it) and have some degree of experience with the product (i.e. they have tried the product, read information about it or absorbed some information about it). **Unfamiliar brands** are brands that the target audience has no recognition of and has no previous experience of. Our selective perception makes it easier for us to notice, and to recognise, things we already are familiar with. Therefore, we see and remember advertising for familiar brands more, and it is easier for us to link advertising to the familiar brand.

COMMUNICATION OBJECTIVES

We can expand on Table 11.1 to show how advertising objectives need to be agreed and what methods can be used to change target audience perceptions and intention to purchase (Table 11.2).

Target audience characteristics and perceptions	Type of target audience response	Indicative advertising objective
Brand loyal to our brand	Cognitive	Remind and reinforce Recall Informational content
	Affective	Associate our brand with category Induce engagement
	Conative	Encourage activity and engagement Encourage repeat purchase Calls to action
Brand loyal to competitor	Cognitive	Improve salience for our brand within category Informational content Comparative statements against competition Refutational advertising
	Affective	Inspire loyal customers to spread positive word of mouth to non-users
	Conative	Facilitate sales of product
Negative towards our brand	Cognitive	Informational content Change perceptions of brand image
	Affective	Build an emotional link
	Conative	Encourage activity and engagement Increase trial usage
Negative towards competitor	Cognitive	Informational content Comparative statements against competition
	Affective	Accentuate emotional brand association
	Conative	Encourage activity and engagement

Indifferent or new to our brand	Cognitive	Create awareness of brand Informational content Educate about brand use Increase knowledge of brand
	Affective	Create positive perceptions Create or reinforce associations with brand
	Conative	Encourage activity and engagement Encourage trial of product Encourage website visit
Indifferent or new to category	Cognitive	Create awareness of category need and brand associations Educate about category use Informational content Explain how brand solves problems Increase knowledge of brand

Table 11.2: Target audience perceptions and advertising objectives

Advertising Appeals

Hall (1992) and O'Malley (1991) outline four frameworks within which advertising appeals may be designed:

- **Sales-oriented:** describes a directly measurable short-term tactical input/output model.
- **Persuasion-oriented:** a rational, accurate approach which purports to move consumers through a sequential process.
- **Involvement-oriented:** the engagement of a target audience through lifestyle resonance and individual brand congruity.
- **Salience-oriented:** where the brand and the advertising attempt to highlight a product being radically different in its category.

Table 11.3 extends this framework to include 10 different appeal approaches and links them to the desired communication objectives to be achieved.

	Appeal approach	Objectives of communication
1	Brand awareness	To elicit recall and recognition of brand following marketing communications
2	Brand salience	To differentiate a brand within a category
3	Promoting product trial	To get the target audience to start using the brand
4	Comparing our brand against the competition	To achieve relative positioning against the competition within a category
5	Changing negative brand perceptions and consumer attitudes to our brand	To get target audience to re-evaluate our brand
6	Informational content	To eliminate perceived risk from purchase decision

(Continued)

	Appeal approach	Objectives of communication
7	Activity and engagement	To seek active participation by target audience with communication message
8	Strength of argument	To apply communications relevant to the level of involvement consumers have with the brand
9	Appealing to informational and transformational needs	To tailor communications according to the level of rational or emotional requirement of target audience
10	Flexibility	To vary advertising content without affecting a consistent message

Table 11.3: Different types and objectives of advertising appeals

Brand Awareness

The two types of brand awareness – recall and recognition – require different tactical advertising approaches (Rossiter, Percy and Donovan 1991). Attaining recall is dependent upon the likelihood of advertising being remembered; recognition relies not just on remembering the advertising but also on creating positive associations with the brand and the category need.

To attain **recall**, the advertising must create strong associations which make the product memorable to the target audience. The message should thus focus on giving the product relevant and easily accessible associations. This can be achieved by:

- **Linking the brand to category need:** top-of-mind recall is desirable when consumers link a brand with a particular category need. Explicitly creating strong associations between the product and the category is important.
- **Repetition:** repetition is the most effective tool when recall is the communication objective, as recall is a form of simple learning: the more times the target audience makes the association between the product and the category, the more likely it is to be memorised. Studies show that at least four exposures of the advertisement are needed to attain the highest possible product recall. Repetition within the actual advertisements is evident too: the repetition of the message in the beginning and end of the advertisement, or by paraphrasing (i.e. repeating with other words) the headline of a newspaper advertisement further down in the text.
- **Enduring contact time:** another way to get the target audience to remember the link between the product and the category need is to maximise contact time (Singh and Cole 1993). 'Contact time' is the time spent establishing the desired product–category need link.
- **Recognition** is to a large extent about an automatic behaviour: it is less demanding to attain brand recognition as people's visual memory is highly strong and accessible. The task of advertising is to create and reinforce this automatic behaviour.
- **Clear product exposure:** the main task of the advertising is to secure product exposure. Therefore, the product must be given a lot of room in the advertising. And it must get exposure in a way that helps people to automatically react to it in a purchase situation. The product should be exposed in its packaging just as it looks when people are purchasing it in the stores. The advertising may indeed also convey an environment that relates to the purchase situation (e.g. a store or a newsstand). Likewise, the purchase situation could remind people of the advertising, for example by linking back to the advertising's theme in store displays (you can read more about this in Chapter 15).

- **Consistency:** since people's visual memory is so good, and since recognition leads to an automatic behaviour, it is extremely important to be consistent. The way that the product is depicted must not change. Many marketers have with remorse seen the negative consequences of a changed product packaging or a different advertising concept. After the initial introduction of the product, the advertising should mainly reinforce the message. It should, in other words, from time to time secure product exposure and by doing so ensure continued automatic target audience behaviour.

- **Short contact time:** because people's visual memory works fast, enduring contact time is not needed. Studies show that maximum recognition is attained after two exposures to the advertising. In contrast to recall, 15-second TV commercials have been found more appropriate than 30-second ones (Singh *et al.* 1995). The advertising could thus be short. All that is needed is time for the target audience to see the product. Therefore, the advertising should quickly present the product and not risk losing the target audience's attention. Studies of brain activity show that the likelihood that a product will be recognised increases significantly when the exposure time exceeds two seconds (Rossiter *et al.* 2001).

- **Durability:** advertising for unfamiliar brands is durable in the sense that the target audience does not know so much about the brand, the advertising has news value which should create target audience attention and curiosity. At the same time, people have some difficulty in perceiving and remembering the brand and as a result they do not link the advertisements to the brand. This makes the advertising durable. The advertising can be shown during a long period (and may gain by it), while the target audience familiarises itself with the brand and creates associations with it. Advertising for familiar brands is not as durable. The reason is that the target audience is attentive to the brand and links the brand to the advertising. Therefore, the advertising quickly loses its information and news value (i.e. the audience can quickly learn what it needs to). The risk is instead that people perceive the advertising as irritating. Each individual part of the advertising should therefore communicate its message quickly. The same advertising should not be used for a long time, it is better to have some variation.

- **High-repetition advertising:** where the audience is exposed to the same advertisement numerous times within short time intervals, allowing the audience ample opportunity to learn about an unfamiliar brand. This effect is less pronounced for familiar brands, as the audience can relate to its previous relationship with the brand and reduce the level of boredom (Campbell and Keller 2003).

  Figure 11.6 shows how these elements are used in advertising.

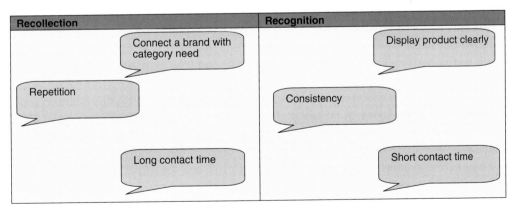

Figure 11.6: The tactical elements that are needed to get the target audience to recall and recognise the product

Source: Dahlen and Lange (2003). *Optimal marknadskommunikation*, Liber Ekonomi. Reproduced with permission.

ADVERTISING STRATEGY IN FOCUS

Adidas and Nike

Formed in the early 1920s in Herżogenaürauch by brothers Adolf and Rudolph Dassler (who went on to found rival *Puma* in 1948), German shoe company *Adidas* is now available in almost every country in the world. *Adidas* started selling in America in 1968, and with the breakthrough sponsorship of the 1972 Olympics in Munich where all officials wore *Adidas*, it quickly became market leader in both the massive American market and across Europe. However, with severe competition from *Nike* and *Reebok*, by 1990 *Adidas* was holding on to only 3% market share. Sales were down from $2 billion to nearly $1.5 billion with *Nike* going from $1.2 billion to $3.4 billion in the same period.

How have *Adidas* and *Nike* used advertising strategies to gain a foothold in the sports apparel and athletic shoes category? *Nike's* strategy has concentrated on the endorsement of individual sports stars such as Tiger Woods and Michael Jordan, creating a dominant media presence, developing flagship stores and iconic retail museums like *Nike Town*. Whilst emphasising its heritage of innovation, technological development and associations with great individual athletes like Emil Zatopek and Mohammad Ali, the approach taken by *Adidas* has been largely through celebrity endorsement, sponsorship focusing on major world sporting events, and general sports associations with teams rather than individuals.

From the late 1980s, whereas *Nike* became synonymous with sport, attitude and lifestyle, *Adidas* tried to transform itself from a shoe brand to a product which was integral to sports culture, predominantly aimed at 8–20-year-old males. The *Adidas Streetball Challenge*, a local small-team basketball tournament started in Berlin in the 1990s and soon became a huge success with over 500,000 people taking part across Europe, culminating in the finals in Germany where over 40,000 spectators attended. Sponsorship of the National Basketball Association (NBA) and formation of 'The Brotherhood', a community-based scheme for young street players linked with six top basketball stars, has helped develop credibility amongst its youth target audience. Concerning product development, both *Nike* and *Adidas* benchmark each other (*Adidas* launched *Equipment*; *Nike* introduced *Alpha*), but in broad appeal one has 'self-motivation' appeal (*Adidas* 'Compete With Yourself') and the other with everyone else.

Both advertising strategies project inclusiveness. *Nike* aims at 'bringing inspiration and innovation to every athlete in the world' (Ramaswamy 2008, p. 9). The *Adidas* phrase 'Impossible is Nothing' is both a positioning statement and a driver for all communications. *Adidas's* advertising strategy is 'standardised throughout the world with convergence of values across cultures' (La Farele and Choi 2005, p. 68) and the use of globally recognised celebrities such as David Beckham. Recently, to broaden its appeal to have more cultural currency rather than just being sports related, a new advertising strategy has been adopted for *Adidas Originals* set against the backdrop of a house party. Featuring an eclectic mix of people from the worlds of music, fashion and sport: Run DMC, Young Jeezy, Estelle, Katy Perry, The Ting Tings, Russell Simmons, David Beckham, Method Mad and Redman, *Adidas* hopes to build on its street credibility in the same way as Adi Hassler did with sports all those years ago.

View the *Adidas Originals* house party at adidas.com.

Brand Salience

If a brand is differentiated from the competition within a category, and enjoys a dominant consumer mind space (i.e. getting consumers to think about the product more often), this difference is referred to as the level of salience. Consumers have schemas or associative networks in the brain where different associations are linked to each other, and where the brand is one associative node and put in a context of other nodes. Consumers make automatic connections to certain phenomena when associations are evoked (e.g. Kate Moss linked to 'Punk Princess' linked to *Rimmel* cosmetics). The salience of a brand is the strength of these associations or links and is the key determining purchase factor (price, quality, ease of use).

Salience is desirable in mature markets where it is important to get top of mind association against established competitors. Brands that have high and stable sales, brands that are used by many consumers, and brands that get a lot of publicity and attention in media may create large mind space, a prerequisite for salience. A second basic foundation for salience is complexity in the brand associations to enable a large number of brand evocations and showing a clear link to the category or categories (for instance product categories, usage situations or goal-derived categories).

MATTER OF FACT

Brand Salience versus Brand Image

Miller and Berry (1998) show that 71% of changes in market share for rental cars over an 11-year period may be attributed to changes in awareness (company awareness, 47%, and advertising awareness, 24%). Only 29% of changes in market share may be attributed to brand image factors (advertising communications, 15%, and image, 14%). The model also takes advertising investments into account as share-of-voice differences are also accounted for. The combined effect should be interpreted as follows. Share-of-voice affects awareness more than image, and awareness has stronger impact than image on market share.

Therefore, in situations where the target audience uses other products in a category, but not our product, we must make them notice our product and make it a part of their consideration set.

Swedish ice cream company *GB*'s advertising reinforces the strength of its product in its specific category, aiming to get people thinking of (their) ice cream in more and new situations (even in the shower – or, possibly, that you can eat ice cream when it is raining – 'showering' – not only on warm summer days).

Promoting Product Trial

At the start of the adoption process, an advertising objective might be to get the target audience to start using the product. The purpose is to kick start the conative relationship a consumer has with a brand to initiate a change in behaviour: intention to purchase or not purchase. Calls to action can be explicit (like 'buy it now' or 'try it') or more implied like '1 million customers cannot be wrong – try it yourself', 'Do as David Beckham, drink Pepsi', or 'While stocks last'. These messages are psychological cues to increase consumer propensity to act, described in the Matter of Fact box below.

MATTER OF FACT

Persuasion Principles in Psychology

- **Reciprocity – a gift demands a gift in return**. When we believe that we have received something from another person, we feel a certain level of guilt. To get rid of the feeling, we feel the need to reciprocate (greater than the original gift). Start-up offers or gifts from book clubs and magazines are examples of reciprocity. In 2009, *The Times* and *The Mail* newspapers in the UK engaged in reduced price offers, encouraging take up. Similarly, a salesperson in a store that spends a lot of time on a customer may encourage a sale in exchange.
- **Scarcity – the product is unique**. As soon as something is hard to get hold of, it tends to be valued higher (the law of supply and demand). Scarcity of the *Nintendo Wii* and *Windows Xbox* created a frenzy for purchase and spread word-of-mouth publicity which boosted the respective initial launches.
- **Social proof – I do as everybody else**. We regularly observe the behaviour of others to see what they think about things – imitative or emulative behaviour. Our opinions of a brand's value may be influenced by others' experiences or opinions.
- **Commitment – actions create ties**. We want very much to act consistently and we do not want to be perceived as irrational. Therefore, we tend to adapt ourselves to our own previous actions and commitments and our brand loyalty can lock us into purchase, sometimes despite other information persuading us to the contrary.

Source: Cialdini (2001).

Comparing our Brand against the Competition

Gaining attention and recognition for our product can be achieved by using a direct competitor comparison (e.g. *I Can't Believe It's Not Butter* spread is positioned alongside actual butter brands). This has two advantages:

- Association with alternative competing products helps get attention.
- The challenger brand can gain from an advantageous comparison (Chattopadhyay 1998) of a certain feature or benefit.

This is seen most clearly with comparative advertising, where the purpose is comparison with a competitor and to achieve relative positioning. This can be a successful tactic providing the competitor who is being compared is familiar (allowing the target audience a category reference point), the focus of the advertising gives our brand prominence and our distinct competitive category advantage is emphasised. *Pepsi* has used implied depictions of main competitor *Coca-Cola* by 'debranding' the competitor's semiotic images of logo, name and some design elements, so that the focus of the advertisement is on *Pepsi*.

Debranded Coke

Changing Negative Brand Perceptions and Consumer Attitudes to our Brand

Where the target audience is loyal to competitors, or where they have a negative attitude towards our brand, emphasis has to be on awareness for the brand and encouraging trial of the product. Where the target audience has a negative attitude towards the product, the main focus is to try to change current brand perceptions and get the target audience to re-evaluate the product. See Figure 11.7.

Refutational Approach

One way of changing the target audience's attitude towards the product is to focus on the cause of the negative attitude. If our brand is seen as acceptable, but perceptions are that it is not as popular as others, this can be used to our advantage. Austrian brewer *Gösser* turned a perceived negative into a positive by projecting an exclusive beer brand for the real connoisseurs: 'Only one in ten prefers *Gösser*. We are the beer for the true beer lover'.

When using this type of refutational approach, it is important not to diminish or disregard the target audience's negative attitude and risk losing credibility. The appeal must be to the target audience's beliefs: if the belief is erroneous it should be refuted objectively; if it is not, it is better to try to turn it into something positive – without stating that their beliefs are wrong.

Influencing Attribute Evaluation

Instead of directly refuting the target audience's perceptions, advertising can try to influence how people form their opinions by concentrating on affecting evaluation of different product attributes. Sometimes emphasising the positives of using a brand ('Naughty but Nice') is a better approach: if people perceive butter as too fattening we can instead emphasise that butter tastes good, is a natural product, or that it is nutritious. In this way, the fat content is not focused on, and so we may change the target audience's perception of butter.

Repositioning the Product

A third and more drastic alternative is to address the target audience's negative attitude by repositioning the product. *McDonald's* tried to address adult consumers' attitudes that the brand was primarily aimed at families by introducing a more exclusive menu topped by the 'next generation *Big Mac Arch*

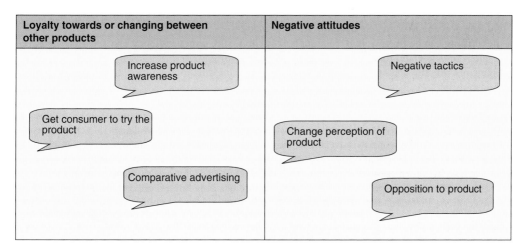

Figure 11.7: The advertising should be designed with consideration
to the target audience's view of the product

Source: Dahlen and Lange (2003). *Optimal marknadskommunikation*, Liber Ekonomi. Reproduced with permission.

Deluxe'. This emulated the *Burger King* adult-oriented approach but failed because *McDonald's* 'family' association was too strong.

The key to repositioning is to communicate entirely new product characteristics, abandoning previous associations with the product. American apparel brand *Abercrombie & Fitch* repositioned itself successfully from an outdoorsy leisure-type brand to a fashion brand by totally changing its style of communication, both in advertising and in stores, from more traditional product-focused appeals to using (sometimes controversially) trendy and attractive models and music.

Similar to the refutational approach, the key is still credibility. The target audience may only change its attitude towards the product if the new advertising is perceived as credible. All communications of the product (including design and packaging) need to be evaluated and coordinated. It is worth mentioning that repositioning may be a highly expensive strategy as it requires much time and effort to change consumers' established perceptions of a brand (Jewell and Unnava 2003).

INFORMATIONAL CONTENT

One of the most fundamental elements in advertising design is determining information content. For high-involvement products, rich information content is mainly an advantage (Celsi and Olson 1988, Zaichkowsky 1994). These products have elements of perceived risks (for instance economic risk as in they may be seen as being too expensive; psychological risk as they affect self-image; or social risk as they affect other people's views of the purchaser). People need to eliminate risk from purchase, and therefore want information to ensure that they make the right choice.

The major advantages of including a lot of information are:

- Attention span is longer: it takes time to process information, the target audience will devote more time to the advertising and, as a result, will retain and remember better.
- Advertising is more convincing: with more information content, the marketer has the space to emphasise product benefits, deal with counter-arguments, and sell the product better.
- Advertising is more flexible: it can deal with more issues and as a result attract people with different interests and knowledge levels.

The major disadvantages of including a lot of information are:

- Processing requires more effort: there is a risk that people do not have the inclination to process information and may switch attention to other matters.
- Advertising can be perceived as 'too much like selling': the target audience may feel that the advertising is tiresome and that it is too intrusive or overbearing.
- Remembering the message is more difficult: the more information included, the more difficult it is to memorise.

It may be difficult to include large amounts of information in a TV spot or on an outdoor billboard, so the selection of the appropriate media vehicles (e.g. newspapers and websites) is very important. To be effective, the appropriate advertising should focus on simplicity of message and gaining attention in order to make sure that people recognise the product and interest and curiosity is aroused, but it should also be information intensive to influence the target audience's purchase behaviour.

For low-involvement products, the target audience has only limited needs for information, there are no real risks involved, and rich information content will therefore not be effective.

ACTIVITY AND ENGAGEMENT

An issue that is relevant for all advertising is how the arguments in the advertising should be built. What is most effective? We will discuss this by looking at two topics: at what level should the argument be; and how many arguments should be used? Activity-based advertising asks us to do something or be actively involved in the message. Just as with the decision to include information, engaging advertising that demands activity has both advantages and disadvantages.

The main advantages with activity (Dahlén, Nordenstam and Murray 2004, Wang 2006) are:

- People remember the advertising more clearly. When our minds are activated, associations are created in the brain that make it easier for the information to be processed.
- The target audience may be more attracted to the advertising. By being asked to engage, the target audience feels more involved.
- The communication effects may have a greater impact. Making an effort, engaging with the message, gives a positive disposition to the product and may increase our inclination to purchase it.

The main disadvantages (Dahlén, Rasch and Rosengren 2003) are:

- People may decline to engage with the advertising. Activity demands effort and may be avoided.
- Control may be reduced. If the target audience is engaged and in control of how it interacts with the advertising it is more difficult to control how the target audience will perceive it.
- People may be disappointed and get a negative view of the product. When some effort is put into something, then we expect that there is a good reason to do so. The demands and the expectations are therefore higher and, as a result, we are more easily disappointed and may feel like we have been fooled.

Airmob.com promotion

Air France launched a campaign in which people visited *airmob.com* and registered their telephone numbers to win free travel to certain destinations. Time and again, *Air France* would call people and give them a location, and the travel was randomly distributed among the first people who showed up.

Durex campaign

Durex used billboards and TV advertisements in France asking people to sign up as 'guinea pigs' for its new condoms. Although this caused consternation amongst older people, the young target audience responded well to this direct action-inducing approach.

Activity-based advertising for high-involvement products has mainly positive effects:

- Since the products are engaging in themselves, consumers are willing to spend time and effort in learning about the product, interacting and evaluating it.
- Consumers can control marketing communications messages better and focus on the more interesting parts. Use of websites, for example, is highly appropriate for high-involvement products; it has been shown that site visitors get both an increased brand attitude and increased purchase intention.

For low-involvement products, the potential benefits of activity-based advertising are great, but so are the risks. The benefit is that the audience will take part in the advertising message to a greater extent, as the format makes the advertising more appealing than the low-involving product itself. The downside with this approach is that consumers may be reluctant to get involved with these types of products, and product-focused advertisements may alienate some people or they may be distracted by non-product-related content. Advertising for low-involvement products should offer, but not require,

Figure 11.8: Passive advertising

some sort of call to action activity. Passive advertising, quite often TV commercials and radio spots, is well suited to low-involvement products. Figure 11.8 is an example of passive advertising that promotes a brand image through projection of lifestyle and demands minimal audience activity. There are no calls to action.

STRENGTH OF ARGUMENT

The strength of an argument has to do with what the message should emphasise and call attention to. Product involvement affects how people process the information presented to them, and this is done either through learning or acceptance. This is illustrated in the Elaboration Likelihood Model (ELM) in Figure 11.9.

The ELM shows how people process and are influenced by information in two different ways, either through learning in which we react to peripheral arguments, or through acceptance which requires central arguments (the value proposition being offered). Low-involvement products require simple learning. If the advertising gets enough attention, it will be memorised.

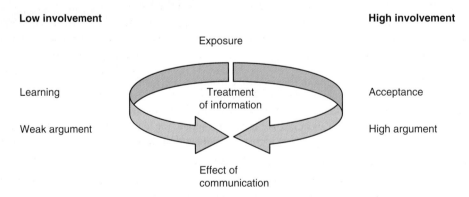

Figure 11.9: Elaboration Likelihood Model (ELM)

Sources: Petty, Cacioppo and Schumann (1983); Petty and Cacioppo (1984).

This is what we have referred to in Chapter 3 as Pavlov's 'classical conditioning', where a kind of rote learning is used by incorporating a conditioned association as with the constant repetition of the 'I'm loving it' slogan in *McDonald's* advertisments. It doesn't require evaluation, and will be automatically remembered.

MATTER OF FACT

'What you say?'

A study of 91,000 ads in 24 countries over a period of 19 years revealed that the average number of arguments, or information cues, is 2.04. The greatest number of arguments was in advertising for electronics (3.05), and the lowest for toys (1.47) and foods (1.54). The most common types of information were performance (43%), availability (37%), components (33%), price (25%), quality (19%) and special offers (13%).

Source: Abernethy and Franks (1996).

ARGUMENT LEVEL: MEANS-END CHAINS

The arguments in the advertising can be structured at different levels. The level selected will influence how the target audience perceives the advertising and it will affect the competitive arguments' which other brand sponsor (Claeys, Swinnen and Abeele 1995, Durgee 1996, Oakenfull *et al.* 2000). The different levels can be identified by way of means-end chains. These are desired goals such as when we purchase toothpaste ostensibly to avoid cavities. The real goal of the purchase is in fact less physical and more social: to get appreciation from others. This process can be done for all products. Gengler and Reynolds (1995) even applied it to dog food where 'love' and 'friendship' were the goals of the purchaser not the food!

MATTER OF FACT

'Tell me about your childhood'

In a study of the car market, American researchers Kathryn Braun-LaTour, Michael LaTour and George Zinkhan found that childhood memories of cars could be highly influential on consumers' evaluations of brand advertising. They distinguished between consumers' earliest memories (EM), which occurred on average at the age of six, and their defining memories (DM), which occurred at the age of 14. The earliest memories centred around their first experiences of cars, and were associated with, for example, comfort, family and friendliness. The defining memories centred on car experiences that were related to the expression of consumers' identity, for example 'showing off' the family's new car in front of friends. These memories were associated with, for example, styling, coolness and luxury.

Comparing consumers' brand preferences with their memories, the researchers found that consumers preferred brands that possessed the same traits as they associated with their childhood memories. The most compelling brands were those that combined both EMs and DMs. Brands corresponding strongly to EMs are more likely to appeal to families and brands with strong DM connections are more likely to attract singles.

Source: Braun-LaTour, Latour and Zinkhan (2007).

NUMBER OF ARGUMENTS

To maximise the likelihood that the message is attended to and remembered by the audience, it should be easy to process. The short-term memory, or working memory, can process 7±2 information elements (e.g., Atkinson and Hilgard 1996). This means that an average person can be expected to process and remember somewhere between five and nine pieces of information that are presented simultaneously. To make sure that everyone in the audience is able to comprehend the advertising, no more than five arguments (information points) should be used, which is the lower limit. When deciding upon the right number between one and five arguments, the following factors may be helpful, as illustrated in the Matter of Fact box below.

MATTER OF FACT

Arguments in Advertising

Factors favouring a greater number of arguments:

- Peripheral processing. The elaboration likelihood model outlined above suggests that consumers rely on peripheral cues (not rational or product-related) when involvement is low. The number of arguments in itself (rather than their content, which the audience will not remember) may be such a peripheral cue.
- Strong arguments. If the message includes a number of really strong arguments, and consumers can be expected to take an interest in them, then more should be better.
- Two-sided arguments. Persuasion research shows that messages that communicate both positive and negative (the former should of course be greater) aspects of a product can be more compelling, as they enhance credibility (reducing the audience's need to think 'What's the catch?') and inoculate against future criticism (e.g. Etgar and Goodwin, 1982).

   Factors favouring a smaller number of arguments:

- Easier to remember and connect to the brain after exposure, which could lead to the likelihood of the brand being included in future consideration sets.
- Easier to process and therefore more likely that the message will be attended to.

APPEALING TO INFORMATIONAL AND TRANSFORMATIONAL NEEDS

Advertising can either be focused on informational or transformational motivations (Ratchford 1987). Informational advertising is often more related to the product (e.g. *Clearasil*'s 'Keeps spots away'), and is often objective and rational. Transformational advertising is often more personal, more user-related (e.g. *Nike*'s classic 'Just do it'), and may include emotional, even subjective, elements.

But what are the reasons for these differences? Informational products solve consumption problems, and consumers are relatively rational when they choose amongst alternatives. The target audience therefore requires information (Dahlén, Rasch and Rosengren 2003). Informational products are sometimes called 'think products', and advertising should contain objective information that convinces the target audience that the product has the right characteristics against the competition in a product category. On the other hand, with transformational products, the target audience's need for

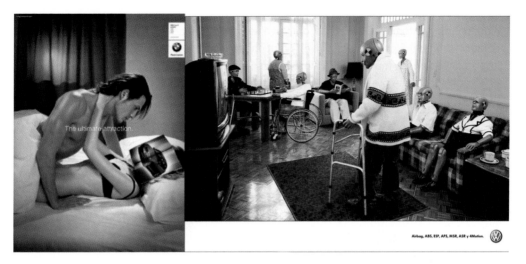

Figure 11.10: *BMW* uses transformational communication and *Volkswagen* uses informational communication

information is lower. These products are sometimes referred to as 'feel products', which is a reflection of the fact that consumers evaluate them based on affective stimulus ('Do *Pringles* really have the best taste of potato chips?' 'Will I be irresistible if I wear *Gucci*?').

Compare the two examples of informational and transformational products and the most important advertising aspects for the two types in Figure 11.10.

However, sometimes informational products are advertised with transformational motivations (e.g. a double-page spread advertisement for a *Neff* double oven had the strapline 'I Can – Icon' which cleverly juxtaposed the functional attributes of the product with the symbolic status of owning the brand).

MATTER OF FACT

Emotions as Relationship-Builders

A study of 43 advertising campaigns in the USA and England, for products ranging from toilet paper to cars, revealed that, overall, emotional content in advertising had a stronger effect on consumers' relationship with the brand (measured as how favourable their disposition towards the brand was) than the advertising's rational content. The conclusion was that, when aiming for strong consumer–brand relationships, 'emotional content should always be included'. However, the more consumers attend to and think about advertising, the less effect emotional content has.

Source: Heath, Brandt and Nairn (2006).

Emotions as 'advertising fuel'

Emotions may influence advertising effects in several ways: both positive and negative emotions may enhance attention to and processing of the advertising; and the 'last experienced

(*Continued*)

emotion' may automatically transfer onto evaluations of the advertising and the brand (this emotion should preferably be positive). Emotions may also enhance the arousal and energy levels of consumers, making them more or less inclined to take action. The valence (positive or negative) and energy-affecting directions (increase or decrease) of some common emotions are summarised in the figure below.

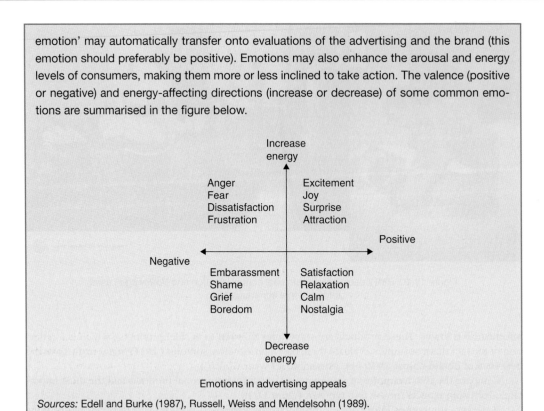

Emotions in advertising appeals

Sources: Edell and Burke (1987), Russell, Weiss and Mendelsohn (1989).

ATTITUDE TOWARDS THE COMMUNICATION

An issue that always is relevant in advertising is whether it matters if the target audience likes the communication or not. If people dislike the advertising, will it negatively affect how they evaluate the product? Studies show clearly that the response differs between the two product types (Youn *et al.* 2001, MacKenzie and Lutz 1989). Advertising for transformational products has a critical role filling the product with positive emotions and creating favourable associations that motivate people to purchase the product, and so it is very important that the target audience likes it. When people do, they remember it better, and have a more positive attitude towards the product. For informational products, it is not as important for the advertising to be liked as it is not intended to create positive emotions towards the product but merely present problem and solution convincingly.

REQUIREMENTS FOR INFORMATIONAL AND TRANSFORMATIONAL ADVERTISING APPEALS

The task of advertising for informational products is to give the customer an opportunity to rationally evaluate if the product can solve a certain problem, and it must achieve an effect quickly for informational products. To make the advertising effective, it must also communicate the solution to the negative problem credibly. It has been shown in studies that most people visit websites for informational products before they purchase them, in contrast to transformational products where visits are made after purchase.

Durability. It is very important that the advertising is durable for transformational products (Dahlén 2002, Dahlén, Rasch and Rosengren 2003). In other words, the effect doesn't decay quickly and effectiveness is not lost. It takes some time to build positive emotions. In fact, repetition in itself

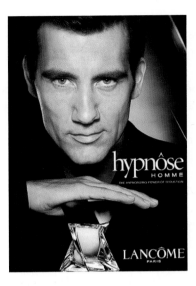

Figure 11.11: Clive Owen advertising *Hypnôse*

tends to produce a so-called **mere exposure effect**, meaning that a person's liking of a stimulus (such as an advertisement) increases the more times she/he is exposed to it. This holds for exposures both before and after purchase of a product. Thus, for transformational products the advertising has also a strengthening function after the purchase. It has been shown that website visitors for transformational products often have a positive attitude towards the product before they visit the site. Often, they have already purchased the product. The transformational advertising is an important part of the product experience, as it fills the product with the emotions that the target audience wants to have.

Identification. As transformational advertising is based on creating emotions it is also more personal (Claeys, Swinnen and Abeele 1995, Rossiter, Percy and Donovan 1991). For emotional content to appear authentic, it is important that the target audience can identify with the advertising. The more references the audience can make to themselves, the more compelling the advertising becomes. For low-involvement products the main objective is that people can recognise the emotion and relate it to an experience of their own. For high-involvement products the advertising must be adapted to the target audience's lifestyle and the emotion must correspond to their identity. The *Hypnôse* advertisement in Figure 11.11 featuring Clive Owen is a good example of this type of advertising.

Informational advertising is usually more product-oriented. The objective is to show that the product is good and to demonstrate its functionality. Therefore, it is not as important to relate to the target audience. The target audience for informational advertising does not need to identify with the advertising. It can even be a disadvantage to make informational advertising too personal if people do not want to associate themselves to negative things (for example yellow teeth or extreme obesity).

MATTER OF FACT

Informational and Transformational Message Strategies

A study of 900 American TV commercials revealed that 81% of all commercials could be classified as employing one of the following message strategies:

(Continued)

Informational advertising

- **Comparative advertising:** relates the brand to competing product(s) and compares performance.
- **Unique Selling Proposition (USP):** communicates a specific property as unique for the brand.
- **Pre-emptive:** communicates that a specific attribute is superior without any comparison with competitors.
- **Hyperbole:** exaggerates attribute's superiority.
- **Generic:** focuses on problem-solving abilities that are shared among brands in the category

Transformational advertising

- **User image:** portrays the user's personality – 'user as hero'.
- **Brand images:** portrays the brand's personality – 'brand as hero'.
- **Generic:** focuses on benefits that are shared among brands in the category.

Source: Laskey, Day and Crask (1989).

In a study comparing advertising strategies in Australia and the USA, Frazer, Sheehan and Patti (2002) found that there were significant differences in creative strategy: more Australian advertisements used brand image, resonance and affective appeals (i.e. transformational); US advertisements relied on emotion.

FLEXIBILITY

Advertising for familiar brands can have great flexibility or variation in treatment. People already have a good picture of what the brand stands for and can easily recognise it. Therefore, the risk is low that flexible advertising confuses the target audience, or that the target audience has difficulties in linking the various spots to the brand. Advertising may therefore vary; it can be done with TV and radio commercials with alternate endings or different advertising solutions can be used simultaneously. Each individual advertisement should include limited amounts of information so that people will want and be able to process the advertising. Familiar brands have an advantage as they can have more flexible advertising and consequently they may communicate multiple and more complex messages. They can, to a large extent, vary advertising between the different parts during one advertising period.

Advertising for unfamiliar brands may need to be more simple and clear without too much variation. The reason is that the target audience has not yet a clear image of what the brand stands for. Hence, it is more important that the advertising is consistent and builds strong associations with the brand. If not, people are easily confused. They may also find it more difficult to place the advertising and to link it to the brand. The risk is that flexible advertising in this case is perceived as advertising for totally different things.

MATTER OF FACT

'Me, myself and I'

Research shows that varying advertising content and using multiple expressions of the same message may have positive effects both on consumers' attention to the advertising and their memory of the message. Varying executions (environments, people, colours etc.), or *formulations* ('glad to help', 'glad to serve', 'pleased to help') across ads (or media) appeals to consumers' *differential attention*. This means that consumers are more likely to attend to advertising they perceive as new. A repeated exposure to the same advertisement may quickly be discarded as 'I have already seen this and know what it's about', whereas exposure to a somewhat different advertisement is attended to as 'I haven't seen this before, what is it about?' Different ways of expressing the same message also increase the encoding variability. That means that, rather than creating one and the same memory trace for repeated exposures to the same advertisement, consumers create a number of unique memory traces for each different one, so that the message can be recalled more easily by way of several traces.

Sources: Singh *et al.* (1995), Unnava and Burnkrant (1991).

CLOSING CASE STUDY

Red Bull: Austrian Thai Myth Creates a Global Hit with Red Bull Buzz

Take the following energy-boosting ingredients: taurine, glucoronolactone, glucose, sucrose and caffeine. Pour into a unique cylindrical metal container adorned with the image of two charging bulls, create a myth and then, as Dietrech Mateschitz, creator and founder of *Red Bull,* has said, 'bring the people to the product'.

Although it has its origins with a Thai product called *Krating Daeng*, the *Red Bull* story really begins in Austria in 1987 where the brand was created. Initially faced with a restrictive Austrian FDA who would not clear the product for distribution, the product found its way to the Austrian clubbers and snowboarders and became the energy drink of choice in ski resorts and alcohol-free raves. Soon spreading to European neighbours, Hungary, Slovenia, Germany and Switzerland, and then into the US market in 1997, the 'anti-brand brand' had proved a global success, dominating the €250 million energy drink category.

By 2004, the brand was not only popular in over 100 countries (enjoying over 40% of the US market), it was also market leader with 70% market share in a mature market which was experiencing a dramatic reduction in European growth from nearly 44% in 2000 down to just 6%. Following unsubstantiated but damaging PR in Sweden and Ireland (where people had died after drinking the brand), *Red Bull* was banned in Denmark and France. The pressure was on to continue to grow and maintain the excitement the brand was famous for. With severe competition from the industry giants such as *Pepsi* and *Coca-Cola*, and large parts of the market blocked off by own brand distribution such as *Wal-Mart*, what marketing communications strategy with what marketing communications mix could *Red Bull* deploy to do this?

Communications were a mixture of pull strategy, perpetuating Mateschitz's anti-establishment 'bring the people to the product' brand myth, and a hard-nosed push strategy through regional distributors. This was partly because the road to national retailer 'approved supplier' status would have taken too long to get the product to market. Traditional communications, such as mass-media advertising, were initially eschewed for more grass roots methods. Consumer demand was largely generated by word of mouth, peer-to-peer buzz and stealth communications, and by using the source credibility of DJs, nightclubs and trendy bars, enhanced with promotional point-of-sale materials and sales promotions, feeding into the associations of the target market culture: danger, excitement,

(Continued)

energy, youth, anti-establishment. Even stealth marketing methods like leaving empty cans in clubs helped build brand image. *Red Bull* epitomised the modern brand: using the marketing communications mix to become culturally relevant by selling style, a way of life not just product.

In terms of distribution of product, there was a policy of 'perceived exclusivity' of sales, where small, independent retailers and cash and carry wholesalers were augmented by self-styled *Red Bull* distributors. The *Red Bull* sales force, part business developers, part merchandising team, had selective territories and created a local feel for the brand. They were also highly visible brand educators, driving *Red Bull* vehicles to help category need association by taking samples to places 'needing an energy lift': offices, garages and building sites. Retailer brand loyalty was cemented in some cases by the 'tied distribution' tactic of using dedicated branded refrigerated display units. However, some regions had different distribution arrangements which were proving strategically advantageous. The Australian market, for example, was serviced by a distribution alliance with *Cadbury-Schweppes*.

Red Bull promotional vehicle

Event sponsorship of adrenaline-charged sports such as snowboarding, BMX biking, skydiving, kite-boarding, surfing and the legendary *Red Bull Flutag* were complemented by creating cultural brand experiences across the globe such as the *Red Bull Music Academy*, break dancing and art competitions, all designed to not just associate the brand with youth culture but encourage hands-on brand experience. The strength of its marketing communications was keeping a consistent, reinforcing image replicated in many different messages with multimedia exposure. Mateschitz described this as having 'the same tone of voice'.

But then came the energy drink category challenger brands: *Battery* in Finland, *Carlsberg's Shark* in Denmark and Sweden, as well as the American giants *Coca-Cola's Burn* and *KMX*, *Pepsi's Amp* and even *180* from *Anheuser-Bush*. Each mimicked some element of the *Red Bull* brand mystique: sexual virility, anti-establishment, youth culture; some used direct tactics (e.g. *Red Rhino*) and others used differentiation of packaging (e.g. *Bomba's* grenade-shaped bottle) or category positioning (e.g. *Pepsi's Gatorade* or *Coca-Cola's Powerade*). On top of this, some European countries (e.g. Norway) tried to have it classified as medicine and this only added to the changing consumer trend for the 'safer' health drink: bottled water. *Red Bull's* concentration on marketing mix tactics rather than strategic brand development in terms of new markets and products also left the brand more vulnerable to attack. The fascinating aspect to its current approach is that it is still trying to maintain the *Red Bull* buzz with the '*Red Bull* gives you wings' theme extended to airport exhibits, restaurants, air shows and controlled TV and press exposure. All designed to keep market share by preserving brand mystique.

QUESTIONS

1. The carefully cultivated 'street cred' image includes nicknames such as 'liquid cocaine', 'speed-in-a-can' and 'liquid *Viagra*'. Do you think this was responsible practice?

2. How did the initial lack of traditional advertising tactical positioning elements help to underpin *Red Bull's* strategic positioning?

3. In terms of advertising strategy, what did Mateschitz mean when he described *Red Bull* as having 'the same tone of voice'?

CHAPTER SUMMARY

This chapter focused on advertising strategy. We saw that before deciding on the execution of any communication effort, identification and definition of the factors that influence the message must be analysed correctly. We examined how, with this information, the tactical elements can be designed to enhance the likelihood that the communication objectives are achieved, and that this provides the necessary input for the creative process and execution of the communication. We then examined advertising strategy:

- the components of how target audience perceptions can be changed to affect brand loyalty and buyer behaviour;
- target audience characteristics and perceptions (how target audience views of the product can influence how advertising is perceived and help determine what objectives have to be set to elicit specific responses);
- the primary reasons for buying a product influencing what kind and timing of information is most attractive to consumers;
- target audience relationship with the brand (the extent to which the target audience is involved, purchase motivation, brand familiarity and the strength of arguments to be used);
- how advertising objectives are agreed and what methods can be used to change target audience perception; and the various advertising treatments or appeals which are discussed fully in the next chapter.

REFLECTIVE QUESTIONS

a. It is common practice to reveal the brand logo at the end of a TV commercial, as it will hopefully make the advertisement more interesting and surprising. Why would this not be a good idea? When could it actually be a good idea?

b. What arguments would you use to sell bio-fuel cars to consumers with an informational purchase motivation? To consumers with a transformational purchase motivation?

c. One could argue that consistent advertising with the same message and execution is important to make the advertising easily recognisable and memorable. Could you argue in favour of the opposite?

d. What arguments would you use to sell *Pepsi* to consumers who do not drink soft drinks? To consumers who prefer *Coca-Cola*?

e. Using means-end chains, what arguments would you use to sell organic pizza?

RESEARCH PROJECTS

Retrieve a copy of Dahlén, Nordenstam and Murray's 2004 paper published in the *Journal of Marketing Communications* (10(1), 35–47) which examines 'perceptions of implicit meanings in WWW advertisements versus print advertisements'. Compare and contrast the traditional and online strategic approaches.

There is evidence that the impact of the current financial climate has undermined TV advertising as the main component of marketing communications strategy. Research brands from one particular sector and assess where they are spending their budgets.

CHAPTER  12

ADVERTISING CREATIVITY

"Advertising relies on visual imagery to connect the perceptual with the conceptual, the signifier and the signified, the product and the product benefits."
Schroeder and Borgerson (2005)

This chapter is about all the creative elements of advertising which are used to help achieve strategy. As advertising is still the major component and in some ways the driving force of the marketing communications mix, a comprehensive account of the tactical approaches to executing strategy is given here. However, the creative principles are applied, where appropriate, to other communication tools as well.

LEARNING OBJECTIVES

After reading this chapter, you'll be able to:

- Understand what creativity is and how it can be analysed.
- Describe the advantages and pitfalls of creativity in marketing communications.
- Appreciate the 'creative toolbox' for gaining attention in the advertisements, enhancing processing of the message and making the message convincing.

Let's start with quotations from two of the advertising industry's greatest contributors: Bill Bernbach, famous for his lateral-thinking approach; and David Ogilvy, the quintessential advertising genius. Bernbach achieved legendary status, gained market domination and decades of imitators by describing *Avis*'s positioning as 'We Try Harder', and helping *Volkswagen's* entry into the gas-guzzling USA with the 'Think Small' campaign. He gave this famous quote when asked about the power of advertising: 'Good advertising builds sales. Great advertising builds factories'.

David Ogilvy, often referred to as the 'Father of Advertising', was noted for his direct advertising approach. He claimed that the purpose of advertising is to sell, although a famous example of copy was 'At 60 miles an hour the loudest noise in this new *Rolls-Royce* comes from the electric clock'. Ogilvy gave this take on advertising: 'I do not regard advertising as entertainment or as an art form, but as a medium of information. When I write an advertisement, I don't want you to tell me that it is "creative". I want you to find it so interesting that you buy the product'.

This sets the scene for our discussion on the role of creativity in advertising. Is creativity an indulgence in marketing communications? Can it be a waste of money and effort, as the message may be received without the extra creative touch? There is no doubt that creative geniuses in advertising have enhanced our lives in terms of inspiring and entertaining generations of consumers. When it works, advertising can also sell lots of product!

OPENING CASE STUDY

Skoda: 'Ha!', 'Aha!' and 'Ah!' – Creativity in Advertising is a Piece of Cake!

What is communication creativity? At its best, creativity can have a multiplier effect on sales. According to a panel from the American Association of National Advertisers, the 'selling power of a creative idea can exceed that of an ordinary idea by a multiple of 10'. Studies show that marketing professionals, the general population (and students) think of, and react to, creativity based on the same dimensions, although the dimensions may differ in perceived importance between the groups. On a general level, people's reactions to creativity can best be described as a 'Ha!', an 'Aha!' and an 'Ah!'. Studies (Ang and Low 2000, El-Murad and West 2004, Kover, Goldberg and James 1995) show that the level of creativity can enhance both people's perceptions of an advertisement and, more importantly, its actual effectiveness.

(Continued)

'Ha!' is the reaction to communication that is original. Using novel stimuli like colours or characters or arguments like the 'King of Beers'. It can help to differentiate from other competing advertising and amplify brand positioning messages. This was done brilliantly by *Skoda* in its TV campaign aimed at changing perceptions about the design and construction of its cars. This featured a surreal 'car cake' of wonderful ingredients made lovingly by *Skoda* employees. The idea had a forerunner in the virtual orchestra of the *Lexus LS 460* and

Skoda shows it's all about the right ingredients

has been replicated by the *European Ford Focus* in the recent 'Orchestra' campaign which implies that the parts of the car, like a symphony, are 'beautifully arranged'.

The Guinness message hidden in the waves

'Aha, is that what it means?' is the audience's reaction to marketing communications that is meaningful and allows people to make sense of the presented message, to interpret the creative images. For example, the use of hidden messages in *Guinness* advertisements is legendary, inviting viewers to work out the message. The image shown is a still from a famous TV advertisement where surfers wait patiently for the best wave to arrive. It apparently shows the fantastic juxtaposition of surfers negotiating a massive wave accompanied by huge white stallions. The tagline reads 'Good things come to those who wait'. Surfers call the biggest wave the white horse, and the hidden message, worked out by clever individuals is 'Aha! It's worth waiting for the perfect pint – slowly poured, perfect Guinness'.

'Ah, that's clever!' is a reaction to admiring the artistry or craftsmanship of the advertisement itself. The image features an advertisement for the *Leonard Cheshire Homes Disability Charity* aimed at showing how people with disabilities lead 'normal' lives. Featuring the genius of Nick Parks' *Ardman Productions*, famous for their 'Wallace & Gromit' animations, 'Creature Comforts' characters are used to help change perceptions of handicapped people with ability not disability. This proved to be particularly effective as the audience's attraction to the characters and appreciation for the cleverness and well-crafted production engaged the audience.

© Leonard Cheshire Disability. Reproduced with permission.

All three of these campaigns moved the viewer from 'Ha!' to 'Aha!' to 'Ah!' because they had a strong message presented in a novel, creative manner and viewers could appreciate the effort and craftsmanship that went into making them. This not only makes the advertisements highly watchable but provides signals about the effort and ability of the sender and thus adds **potency** and **credibility** to the originality and meaningfulness of the communication.

QUESTIONS

1. Do you think an advertisement should be creative? Does it sometimes get in the way of the brand's message?

2. Do you think creative approaches in advertising messages have short-term effects on an audience?

3. How original is the *Skoda* advertisement? Can you think of similar approaches?

WHAT IS ADVERTISING CREATIVITY?

The opening discussion on the role of creativity in advertising posed the question as to whether it is a tactical execution of marketing communications strategy or an indulgence which does not achieve sales but awards. Dahlén, Rosengren and Törn (2008) conducted an experiment with over 1000 consumers, exposing them to differing creative versions of the same advertisements for well-known brands. The advertisements for each brand were functionally identical – communicating the same message, using the same visual elements and the same number of words – but some were 'significantly more creative' (as verified by a number of advertising professionals).

Whilst there appeared to be no discernible difference in message communication, results showed that those consumers who had been exposed to the more creative advertisements perceived the brands to be of higher quality, believed that the company was smarter, offered a better proposition and was seen as more likely to develop valuable products in the future. Further investigations revealed that the extra creative dimension sent powerful signals about the brand and the company: signalling that the sender had put effort into the advertising indicating confidence and belief in the quality of the product; and signalling ability to think 'a little extra' – to think in new and different ways. This enhanced the brand's reputation and added to the perceptions of brand promise for the future.

This experiment shows how consumers will be affected not just by the brand or the sender of the communication but by the advertisement itself. The Cognitive Response Model (Belch and Belch 2001) illustrates this very point (Figure 12.1). Here, purchase intent is seen as a result of attitude to

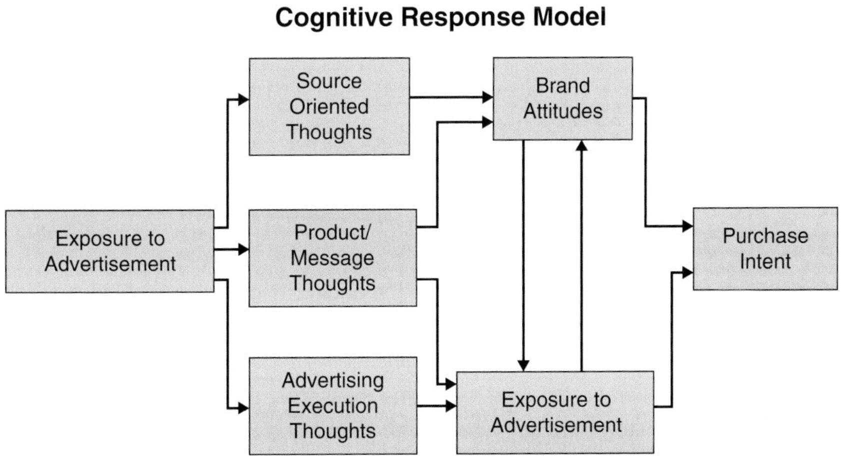

Cognitive Response Model

Figure 12.1: Cognitive response model

Source: Belch and Belch (2001).

the advertisement as well as to the brand. Thoughts that the receiver might have about the sender source and the product condition the receiver's attitude to the brand; thoughts about the product in the context of the advertisement condition the engagement and attitude to the advertisement itself.

What this demonstrates is that **engagement** is crucial in advertising as it grabs attention, forms part of the relationship that consumers have with products, distils the brand essence and value proposition and will help lock consumers into the overarching brand narrative. Once the target audience's needs have been analysed and the strategy chosen for what the proposition is and where it is to be seen (see Chapter 11), advertising creates what has been described as a 'chemical reaction'. In the creative phase, the marketer decides how the message should be expressed. The focus is on finding forms for the message that will catch the target audience's **attention**, invite them to **process** it and enhance **conviction**. This is the key focus of this chapter.

Notice how the Cognitive Response Model (Belch and Belch 2001) accords with the examples in the Opening Case Study where purchase intent is seen as a result of both attitudes to the advertisement and to the brand. In the three campaigns featured, the positive reactions to the advertisements stem from the interaction between the sender (*Guinness, Skoda* and *Leonard Cheshire Disability*), the product or focus of the advertisement (cool beer, well-made cars or the integration of all types of people) and the advertisement execution itself.

MATTER OF FACT

Enhancing Creative Output

In a study of 1011 US advertising campaigns and interviewing 357 advertising professionals, four factors were seen to have positive effects on the level of creativity in the marketing communications development process: the openness of the client (brand management) to explore new ideas yields more creative advertising; the higher the rank of the client the better the communication produced (i.e. for the communication to be really creative, top management should be involved); more time for development makes the result more creative; knowledge about the target audience enhances creativity. A study of 115 UK advertising professionals found that those who had won most awards had a higher than average risk propensity and this correlated with the size of the budget/client (the professionals were willing to take higher risks – and be more creative – with smaller clients).

Sources: Koslow, Sasser and Riordan (2006), Douglas (2003).

CREATIVITY IN FOCUS

Dirt is Good. Or is it?

Studies show that marketing professionals value the originality of the communication relatively higher than the general population does. In the worst case, this may result in a trade-off where the communication becomes 'unnecessarily' original at the expense of its marketing purposes. Creative indulgence in other words! As a result, the message may be difficult for the audience to comprehend and ultimately miss its mark (Kover, James and Sonner 1997). Alternatively, the novel meaning is comprehended, but not perceived as relevant or favourable ('OK, the "car cake" looks good enough to eat and is made of "my favourite things" but why would that make me buy a car?').

'Dirt is Good' is bad communications

Audience miscomprehension or inability to comprehend, and inability to relate to the message, are common pitfalls that we need to be aware of in the creative design process. Take the 'Dirt is Good' campaign for *Persil*. Sales of *Persil* are in decline in the UK, and *Unilever* strategically moved to tap into the social concern of over-protecting children, whilst at the same time encouraging use of its brand.

They believed that, 'The campaign was created to communicate the *Persil* brand's philosophy that children should be given the freedom to be creative – which leads to their learning and development – without worrying about getting dirty'. Unfortunately the creativity of the advertisement was at variance with marketing strategy and resulted in poor communication and poor sales. Advertising is so often the focus and 'glue' of brand communications and yet the laudable corporate social responsibility (CSR) allusions of *Persil* fall short in this execution as it lacks efficacy and does not make explicit the claim: '*Persil* will get ANY dirt out of your wash'.

Another potential pitfall is that the communication becomes overcrafted ('ah!') so that various supporting elements (images etc.) distract the audience's attention away from the sender and the core message ('ooh, what a beautiful ad that was. Hmmm, what was the product?) (see Sengupta, Goodstein and Boninger 1997).

'Tagging' is a recent development in the user-generated social networking world of the Internet. In some countries this practice has migrated to the streets where concerted 'guerrilla' action - with the objective of raising the level of consumers' awareness about the quality of outdoor advertising in cities - has seen positive and negative comments posted on various poster sites.

Consumers' creative comments

ADVERTISING TACTICS TO ACHIEVE ATTENTION – PROCESSING – CONVICTION

Therefore, the purpose of creative design is to make the communication of the intended message as effective as possible. This is done by finding a solution for three fundamental communication issues. These problems are identical for all marketing communications, regardless of sender and target audience.

All the efforts behind well thought-out positioning and message designs are useless if people do not focus on the advertisement. The creative phase – the communication platform and delivery – should make sure that the first step in the hierarchy of effects, **attention**, is activated. This is not as easy as one might imagine. With exposure to over 1500 impressions every day, the average consumer will not remember all communication messages. Exposure must be turned into attention. The media guru, Herbert E. Krugman, (1988) claimed that, 'the biggest limitation in advertising is not processing, it is attention'. If you look at the media statistics provided in Chapter 13, you can see plenty of proof that the competition for people's attention is fierce.

Once the advertising has received attention, it must also be **processed** by the target audience. In other words, people must think that the advertising is so interesting that they pay attention and actively engage with the content. This is also not easy to achieve. These days, people's attention span tends to be very short. Twenty years ago marketers talked about the 'MTV generation' who constantly zap between the plethora of TV channels, online communications and newspapers all the while simultaneously seeing and listening to different things. Development in multimedia technology has exacerbated this problem, leading to 'zap-proof' 10-second commercials now being more prevalent. As we have seen in Chapter 2, 'noise' can disrupt the intended meaning transmitted by the sender. Therefore, it is extremely important to use creative elements in advertising to maintain target audience attention and ensure that they process the advertising content. For a message to be decoded and processed, it has to break through the noise barrier of all marketing communications not just the distraction of competitive brands.

MATTER OF FACT

'More of the Same Means Less'

In a Swedish study, advertising expenditures were matched with tracking data in the bank, car, travel and TV industries over a time period of four years. The data showed a significant negative relationship between the level of advertising expenditure and the size of consumers' consideration sets. In other words, the more money spent on advertising in the category, the fewer the brands considered by consumers. The same relationship was found between the number of advertisers and the size of consideration sets – the greater number of advertisers, the smaller were consumers' consideration sets. The results were consistent over time and over categories. These findings may seem counterintuitive, more advertising and more alternatives to choose from should make people consider more, not fewer, brands. The explanation is rather simple. Further analyses revealed that consumers perceived the advertising as rather uniform and similar between competing brands. More of the same therefore decreased consumers' inclination to take interest in all of the advertising, made them perceive the brands as more similar and therefore made them less engaged in the category.

Source: Ohman (2007).

Finally, the communicated message has to be **convincing**. All efforts are wasted if the message does not reach the target audience in a compelling way. For this to occur, the target audience must learn the message and approve of the arguments. Therefore, creative elements that help people in their learning process are needed in the communication.

Research into how consumers combine information and trial (Smith 1993) shows that advertising lessens negative effects of an unfavourable trial experience on brand evaluations when the

Attention tools	Processing and conviction tools	
	Enhance learning conditions	**Ensure that the information is received correctly**
RATIONAL/COGNITIVE APPEALS: based on the provision of information		
Error	Comparative advertising	Music, mnemonics and repetition
Size and contrast	Dramatisation and slice of life	Zeigarnik effect
	Demonstration advertising	Two-fers
Semiotics and natural signals	Mystique	
Movement direction	Factual and logical appeals	Allow audience to draw conclusions
Testimonials or typical person endorsements Expert endorsement Celebrity endorsement		
AFFECTIVE APPEALS: based on emotions and feelings		
Colour and intensity	Arousal, sensory appeal and shock tactics	Rhetorical figures
Novelty	Ego, status, sense of worth	Metaphors and stereotyping
Humour	Fear	Limbic signals
Erotica	Familiar starting point	Refuge – Prospect – Hazard
Motivation	Fantasy and surrealism	Motivate attention – self-referencing
Testimonials or typical person endorsements Expert endorsement Celebrity endorsement		

Table 12.1: Creative tools

advertisement is **processed** first. This is referred to as 'effects transfer'. Essentially, the five communication effects as cited by Rossiter and Percy (1998) are category need, brand awareness, brand attitude, brand purchase intention and purchase facilitation.

So, let's examine some of the methods that can be used to design communication that gets through the noise, is processed and is convincing. All the tools and tricks are based on research into how people work and how they process information. Table 12.1 lists the creative options available to achieve the advertising objectives of attention, processing and conviction. There are two types of approaches to creating successful advertising: **cognitive** (a rational platform which purports to present a practical, factual proposition); and **affective** (emotional appeals which attempt to move the audience, convey an image and elicit feelings for the brand).

TOOLS FOR GRABBING ATTENTION

The most fundamental tools to gain people's attention and to sustain their interest originate in perceptual psychology (e.g. Atkinson and Hilgard 1996, Blackwell, Miniard and Engel 2006; Solomon, Bambossy and Askegaard 2002). **Perception ability** is a basic human trait that helps us react intuitively to outside stimuli that may be important. These outside stimuli will be environmental factors like culture, group influences, media representations and so on, but also include the marketing mix and, specifically, brand communications. Most perceptual tools used in advertising appeal to people's natural instincts and try to make the advertisements 'stand out' to get the target audience to pay attention and process the brand message. Table 12.1 lists these tools in terms of their use in gaining attention, aiding information processing or ensuring the message is correctly received and effectively decoded.

Colour and Intensity

Advertising with a lot of colour draws attention to it. Colour makes the advertisement more intense and can also make people pay attention for a longer time, as we enjoy being seduced by intense stimuli. As a result, the likelihood increases that the advertising is processed. Colour is not only a tool to gain and sustain people's attention, it affects the **perceptions of mood** in advertising. The illustrations for *Nivea Creme* in Figure 12.2 show colour can affect the mood and help to engage consumers in the benefits of the product.

Research has shown that most attention is given to advertising text, images and background when produced in red. Similarly, it has been shown that restaurant customers eat more quickly when the interior design is in red. The colour red is a long-wavelength colour evoking emotions such as love, seduction and excitement and can signal that something important is about to happen or is contained in the message. Associated with danger, heat, passion, aggression and impulsive action, when we 'see red', the pituitary gland releases adrenaline into the bloodstream, producing a quantifiable rise in our blood pressure and an increase in pulse rate and respiration – all of which prepare the body for the fight or flight survival response. Red is used effectively in the decor of high-volume restaurants to make us eat quickly and leave (thereby maximising customer turnover) because the sight of this colour raises our metabolic rate. Red denotes life and action; in contrast, green gives a sense of calm and tranquillity and has become more significant in advertising since it is redolent of the natural environment and it has significance within the Muslim community.

Green is more commonly associated in our imagination with health. Natural blues are expressive of freshness and health, something *Nivea* has used to great effect in its brand communications. The colour acts as a brand signifier and also helps campaign coordination. 'Cool' colours (blue and green) lower blood pressure, pulse rate, body temperature, respiration and promote deeper breathing, leading to a reduction in stress and anxiety. The sight of the colour blue causes the brain to release up to 11 different tranquillising hormones which, if taken to extremes, can even cause depression (hence 'feeling blue').

Figure 12.2: Engaging consumers in the benefits of *Nivea Creme*

White is also used for toiletries as it is synonymous with purity, as is the citrus colour of yellow. Black can be inappropriate in certain circumstances as it is the colour for mourning, but can also suggest elegance and sophistication. Black implies rejection of the material world as suggested by its (Western) associations with death and mourning – as well as by the vestments of priests, nuns and other orthodox sects whose members have renounced the pleasures of the material for the spiritual. Black also confers authority and blocks scepticism, and so is the traditional choice for teaching masters as well as the police and paramilitary forces of totalitarian regimes (Rutherford 2007).

Recognition can be enhanced by strong colour coordination especially when carried through on all applications of brand communication. *Cadbury's* uses purple to project an image of superior heritage, quality and elegance. *Silk Cut* cigarettes integrate a triad of images into the brand communications: silk material, the impression of a 'cut' and dominance of the colour purple, make a statement subtly and unsubtly! Both examples show how brands ensure identity and consistency.

SMOKING CAUSES FATAL DISEASES
Chief Medical   Officers' Warning
5mg Tar   0.5mg Nicotine

Image Courtesy of the Advertising Archives

As human beings, we tend to be attracted to intense stimuli. Intensity is a tool that is used to make the advertising more involved or exciting. Another aspect which facilitates intensity is the use of increased volume. This is usually done with music, which is considered to be least disturbing. It is important not to cross limits. *McDonald's* had this problem with its TV commercials in the mid-1990s. By increasing the sound level in its advertisements, it did get more attention, but at the same time, the high and surprising sound was perceived as so disturbing that *McDonald's* had to lower the sound level.

Alternatively, sound intensity can be lowered to achieve increased attention. Silent moments in TV advertisements have been used very effectively. For example, *Unilever's Via* detergent in the mid-2000s (where text about the brand's advantages rolled over the screen like end credits in a movie against a brand-signalling green background), and for donations to charities, such as for the UK's *Children in Need* and *the Red Cross's* 'Let's have a minute of silence'.

MATTER OF FACT

'Colour Me Closer'

In an experiment measuring how people approach different colours, test persons were invited to watch a film screening. At the entrance, each person grabbed a folded chair and was then allowed to sit down in front of the screen, anywhere in the room. The focus of the experiment was to see how close to or far from the wall opposite the screen people would sit down. Five screenings were arranged, and at each screening the room was painted in a different colour. The colour effects were clear. People sat closest to the wall when it was yellow, followed by red (warm colours), then blue, then green (cold colours). During the fifth screening, when there was no colour on the wall (white), people sat significantly farther from the wall. A survey of the participants revealed that they felt more relaxed and evaluated the screening more favourably when the colours were cold than when they were warm.

Source: Bellizzi, Crowley and Hasty (1983).

Size and Contrast

The importance of a visual element is suggested by both its size and its position within the frame. We have a propensity to unconsciously perceive large objects as important, and they can appear more prominent than small objects. When an object is large relative to the surrounding space, the element appears to be important, powerful and authoritative; when small compared to other elements or the surrounding space, it appears to be weak or insignificant. As a result, by determining the angle or perspective from which we perceive an object or a character in a photograph or illustration, photographers, designers and advertisers can exploit this cognitive link between size and significance to influence our attitudes towards the thing or person depicted, as well as the ideas with which they are implicitly associated.

Even the meaning of a text is determined by the 'picture' it makes on the page by the combination of **typographical design** – the style and size of the characters (the use of capitals, underlining, boldface and colour), as well as by the **layout** (the relationship created between the typographical elements) and its location and distribution on the page.

With our increasing reliance on the commercial visual media (particularly television) for our picture of the world, those who select and produce the images we see have a powerful means to exalt certain ideas and to belittle others. This is one of the reasons why outdoor billboards are so effective. A US study (Berkowitz, Allaway and D'Souza 2001) found that outdoor advertising is up to 12 times more effective than newspaper advertising. And we see a development towards advertising being expressed in larger and larger layouts, for instance covering entire building walls.

Figure 12.3 shows the power of the poster to target not only passing car traffic but also to persuade consumers to interact with the advertising poster 'exhibit' for *Nivea Cellulite Reducing Moisturiser*. The fact that this is also a great 'silent policeman' pun for passing traffic only adds to the effectiveness of the execution. Size can also be used within the press advertising format. Small advertisements can be enhanced by straplines in bold or large lettering which may 'shout out' at the target audience. Large illustrations and images can also get increased attention. Likewise, certain parts of the advertising can be enlarged to maximise impact and get attention.

Doing things differently can be very effective; people react to things that stand out from the mainstream. Therefore, **creating contrast** can be used to highlight differences or help the advertisement stand out. For instance, in a colour magazine, black-and-white advertising in between many colour advertisements can help the advertisement to stand out and thus differentiate the brand.

Figure 12.3: Poster participation for *Nivea Cellulite Reducing Moisturiser*

Figure 12.4: Brand benefits are highlighted by stripping out the colour of the meal

Size can be used in the same way. Instead of filling the advertising with large letters, images and illustrations, the content can be made very small. If all advertising is large, the empty advertisement will generate curiosity. This is what is regularly called **negative space** in advertising.

Contrast is an effective tactic in advertising. Figure 12.4 shows an advertisement for *Buffalo* tomato sauce which shows the use of contrast and negative space by making the product stand out when colour is stripped away. The juxtaposition of red on white is very striking and helps grab attention and highlight brand benefits by stripping out the colour of the meal.

Accentuating differences between competing brands or the placing of subject in contrast to the physical environment in which the advertising is presented can also help emphasise product benefits. This advertisement shows the compact design and economy of the *Smart Car*, in which we see fun and adventure encapsulated in the representation of the brand as a 'toy'. The contrast of actual brand and model car contrasts the 'small is beautiful' appeal of the brand.

Smart is small is fun

Movement and Direction

Our primitive instincts make us react very quickly to movement. Advertisements with motion get increased attention, and movement may also make the advertising much more dynamic and creates better impact.

This is important as it helps the target audience to stay focused and pay attention. We have earlier stated that people have short attention spans and movement is an effective tool to help the audience focus. The powerful effect of motion-intensive advertising explains why TV and cinema advertising is so effective. Sometimes the impression of movement can be creatively achieved photographically.

Another example of so-called 'quasi movements' is depicted in Figure 12.5. Street advertisements for the *VW R32,* the fastest *Volkswagen* ever made, showed blurred versions of the area that

Poster were placed on roadside walls around Cape Town.
Each poster was a blurred version of the area it was stuck to
This created the impression of travelling at high speeds in a
VW R32, which is Use fastest Volkswagen ever made.

Figure 12.5: Trick of the eye shows speed of the *VW R32*

Source: Volkswagen and Ogilvy Cape Town. Reproduced with permission.

the posters were stuck to. This created an illusion of speed and movement by deliberately focusing on the blurred, busy background of the street which 'suggests' movement.

Movement can be used in other media as well, like the sound effects of radio allowing the imagination of the listener to 'visualise' speed or broken glass from pictures created by sounds. This can sometimes make radio a very cost-effective communication medium as the 'pictures can be better on the radio'!

Direction is a variation of quasi movements and can also draw attention to the advertising. Direction utilises our curiosity and willingness to follow a path to see where it leads. For example, arrows, signs and other pointers can be used. Direction tools can also make use of our ability to read text. We expect that a sentence that starts in the upper, left-hand corner will finish in the lower, right-hand corner. Therefore, we will automatically follow the text to find the conclusion in the right place. Visual tricks which guide the reading of the text can ensure that the reader not only views the brand in context but against the competition. Look for the *Visa* in the *Barclaycard* advertisement! A recent campaign for the *Ford Focus* featured double-page spreads where the car is situated on the right alongside an empty end bay littered with other cars' wing mirrors. This is an effective way to get the reader to put together the information and get the message. Once our eyes move from right to left to right and back again, we are able to work out that car drivers are so impressed by the lines of the new *Focus* they have crashed into the post. This message is implied by the visual images and not made explicit in the text.

Series are another way to use direction. They can be an effective tool in the communications to target audiences that have low reading skills. But it is essential that the target audience reads the series in the intended way.

Motivation – Self-referencing

Our visual memory is much more effective than our other memory functions. Numerous advertising studies show that it takes considerably lower investments to attain **recognition** (which is about recognising something one has seen before) than to attain **recall**. Therefore, the advertising should contain pictures that stick in the minds of the target audience.

'Selling the sizzle not the steak' is an old advertising adage espousing benefits rather than features. Something which encapsulates transformation, for example recruitment for an educational

Figure 12.6: Second-hand smokers are on the worst side of the cigarette

institution might convert 'Study with us' or 'Get a good education' into 'To read this can change your future' or 'If you read the ad, there is a risk you will be a better person'.

Vividness in imagery can be a powerful tool to motivate either positively or negatively. The anti-smoking advertisement featured (Figure 12.6) inverts the image of a cigarette to draw attention to the anti-social effects of passive smoking.

Research into homeostasis (Festinger 1957) showed that when people hold opposing attitudes or opinions, they seek consonance. In advertising this can be seen in brands which have an 'ego–eco contradiction' (Smith 2007), where the desire to indulge in hedonistic, selfish purchases must be reconciled with conscience-led consumption. Many advertisements for cars are either pictured in natural surroundings or emphasise the emotional content of the brand and also the eco-friendly aspects of the product. Ironically, this Indian advert for the 4x4 *Ford Endeavour* aimed at pleasure-seeking motorists shows the presentation of hedonistic consumption above any reference to environmental concerns.

Ford's ego-eco contradiction

Novelty and Error

The novelty tool utilises uncommon and unexpected elements. It can be unusual sounds or images that do not fit the overall context. The unexpected surprise effect increases the likelihood that people will pay attention to the advertising. The advertising can also be more dynamic and attention is more easily maintained when novel elements appear at some point in a radio or TV commercial.

Novelty may also be used to make the effect of advertising more durable. In Chapter 13, we examine **advertising wear-out**, which describes the decay in communication effectiveness after a number of exposures due to the target audience becoming accustomed to, and therefore bored with, the particular communication. When the advertiser continually includes new things in the advertising, it can sustain attention and interest over a longer time period.

Volkswagen's ice cool car

Reproduced by permission of DDB London

The focal point of the launch of *Volkswagen's 'Polo Twist'*, which featured new air-conditioning, was a specially commissioned 'ice car' sculpture which was not only visually striking but gained extra attention through press coverage.

Sex, Nudity, Erotica and Provocation

What's the difference between a carton of ice cream from a brand originating in England and one from New York? One is positioned as a family brand (*Wall's*) and one (*Häagen-Dazs*) as a hedonistic, indulgent 'longer lasting pleasure', this largely achieved through associating use with sexual imagery. Sexual appeals in advertising feature a range of sexual information: nudity, behaviour, referents and physical attractiveness. The need to break through the noise in advertising has seen the use of provocative images become increasingly prevalent (Vezina and Paul 1997). The primary function of provocative advertising has been characterised as a deliberate attempt to gain attention through shock, and appears to operate through three constructs: distinctiveness, ambiguity and transgression of a social or cultural taboo (De Pelsmacker and Van Den Bergh 1996, Vezina and Paul 1997).

There is plenty of research which has made the age-old link between sex and selling in advertising. For example, fragrances are both physical products (smell) and symbolic brands, and over 49% use sex as the central positioning strategy where desirability, attractiveness and passion are key factors. Sexually explicit or mildly erotic stimuli are used to gain attention, increase recognition and recall, and improve sales. It's hard to determine which of the advertisements for *'Opium'* featuring Sophie Dahl and *Jōvan 'Sex Appeal'* (Figure 12.7) is more explicit or even which gender they are aimed at. The other key role of advertising using sex as a tactic is to enhance recall and to evoke emotional responses.

How effective are advertisements using sex as a main tactic for grabbing attention though? Is attention for the brand or the object of the advertisement? There is a considerable body of evidence to suggest that the use of nudity and sexual stimuli actually reduces consumer recall and recognition of a brand. Explicit sexual images may 'interfere with consumers' processing of message arguments and reduce message comprehension' (Severn, Belch and Belch 1990). The same is not necessarily true of

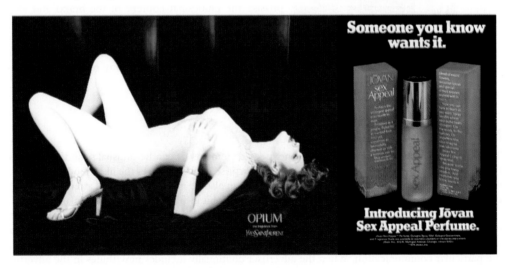

Figure 12.7: Sex sells!

provocation. Provocative appeals encompass much more than sexual appeals; for instance, they can refer to violence, drugs and political or racial issues (Vezina and Paul 1997). Where sexual appeals are appropriate to the relationship between advertising and the product, recall is improved.

Congruity plays a part in the effectiveness of advertising using nudity. Witness the recent increase in 'real beauty' campaigns where the appeal is not only from woman to woman but also the idea of normality. *Dove* has featured 'real women' in advertisements without any retouching for well over 40 years now and has sought to gain feminine credibility for the brand through its current campaign featuring on over 25 major TV channels and in more than 800 articles in opinion-leading newspapers from *El Pais* to *Le Parisien*, from *The Sun* to *The Times*, as well as in popular women's magazines. Contrast this with the idealised *L'Oréal* stable of airbrushed models and the well-oiled erotic imagery of *Calvin Klein* (see Figure 12.8). Some of the *Calvin Klein* advertisements have a bisexual as well as homoerotic appeal to both sexes and exploit sex as well as nudity.

Sex in advertising is not restricted to products and brands. Some appeals can have an ambivalence or serve a more social purpose. A US, non-profit organisation called 'Safe Campuses Now' advocates awareness about rape and sexual abuse, sexual disease prevention and sex education for students. A poster (see Figure 12.9) shows a young woman's bare back with a tattoo just visible above the top of her jeans. The copy reads: 'Just because you think she looks like she wants it doesn't mean she wants it from you.' Here, the portrayal of sex is intended to draw in the audience into the important message.

Semiotics, Motivation and Natural Signals

According to Hackley (1999), 'advertisements gain their meaning from their relation to other cultural products' and, in order to be meaningful to the target audience, 'must make use of the cultural currency of symbolic codes in contemporary use'. The study of signs, codes, conventions and myths in communications is called semiotics and describes the 'signalling' of socially derived meaning between sender and receiver, brand and consumer. It is possible to generate attention by using different kinds of signals that project a predetermined or learned meaning and are therefore shorthand for sounds or images that we acquire through learning.

Texts are created by manipulating signs, codes and symbols within the sign system to generate meaning within the communication of the advertisement and produce meanings as natural and self-evident. The advertisement for *Harvey Nichols* in Figure 12.10 uses both the speech

Figure 12.8: *Calvin Klein* signals sex but sells scent

Figure 12.9: 'Safe Campuses Now' campaign advertisement

bubble and the arrangement of subjects to convey that the clothes are a 'statement' about position and desirability.

Barthes (1988) claimed that advertising does not work within the means of denotation but through connotation. Semiotic content projects meanings that are culturally derived and directly speak to audiences through mythic significance. For example, a picture of a jar of coffee may **denote** a drink, but set in a social context may have **connotations** of something else entirely. This type of meaning is constructed in an advertisement in such a way as to appear automatic, unsurprising and perfectly natural. *Marlboro* has created a whole mythic 'cowboy' landscape that projects masculinity, strength and individualism which seems natural. This has an ideological function which allows virtual group affiliation by encouraging positive valences in the product advertised.

Figure 12.10: *Harvey Nichols* makes a statement
Photographer: Jonathan De Villiers. Reproduced by permission of DDB London.

Figure 12.11: Relax in a creamy head of Heineken beer

A good example of this is the advertisement for *Heineken* shown in Figure 12.11, which provokes connotations of relaxing and at the same time cleverly makes a product claim by illustrating the creamy 'head' of beer.

Use of fear is a negative appeal attempting to show the negative consequences of not using the product advertised or indulging in unsafe behaviour (e.g. 'Think: Don't Drink and Drive!'). In TV and radio advertising, the marketer may use sirens ('Danger! Something has happened.'), ringing telephones ('Must answer'), barking dogs ('Danger?') and crying children ('Must comfort'). The sounds do not have to be dominant – it may be enough to hear them in the background. We are programmed to react very quickly and automatically to these signals. They may affect our attention to the advertising sometimes without really thinking.

We can see evidence of when advertising tries to generate target audience motivation to encourage participation in the advertising. The Rossiter–Percy–Bellman Grid (1997) draws a distinction between informational and transformational motivations, the former with negatively originated motivations and the latter being based on positive-ending motivations. The objective of the exercise here is to activate a basic need. People strive all the time to satisfy a whole range of basic and higher needs. Examples of these are thirst, hunger, sleep, comfort and reproduction. When we get signals that activate these drives we automatically pay attention. Different kinds of temptations may be very effective in the advertising, for instance, highly appetising images that produce hunger emotions.

Intertextuality – adopting signs and meanings from other media – helps the shorthand communication aimed at specific target groups. Images with, for example, resonance in popular culture, provide a visual sign vocabulary from which meaning can be negotiated. In this situation, an understanding of micro-cultural linguistic and visual signs may help decode the mythic meanings.

Just as in the case of natural signals, motivation tools that are not related to the product may be used. There are many examples of this, especially when it comes to advertising elements that activate people's sexual drive. The advertisement in Figure 12.12 shows a comical link to sex and pasta!

The optimal solution is to link the motivation clearly to the product. By doing this, the communication effects may also get leverage. If the motivation is based on the product, it will be the focus

Figure 12.12: Pasta and passion

of the target audience attention, which is beneficial for the category need and brand awareness. In addition, the motivation is associated to the product in people's minds and may therefore contribute to enhanced brand attitude and more favourable brand associations.

'Perceived consumer risk', particularly with high-involvement brands, requires the assurance of advertising to allay our fears of functional, financial, social or psychological risk. The fear induced by an advertising appeal, however, can help to create this dissonance.

TOOLS FOR LEARNING AND CONVICTION

To be effective, the communication has to stick more or less consciously in people's minds, and they must be convinced by the message. In other words, the content of the communication must be learned, and learned the correct (intended) way. There are a number of tools that may be used based on mechanisms that control how we learn new things and how we sort information in our memory.

The tools can be classified into two categories. The first category consists of tools that enhance the conditions for learning; that is, they make people more motivated to receive and remember the information (e.g., Gail and Eves 1999, MacInnis, Moorman and Jaworski 1991, Vakratsas and Ambler 1999). The second category consists of tools that ensure that the information is received correctly and that the right elements are learned (e.g. Felton 1994, Burton 1999, MacLachlan 1984, Moore, Reardon and Durso 1986).

Enhancing Learning Conditions

The most fundamental tool that facilitates learning is **arousal**. When people in the target audience get aroused they raise their awareness and their ability to react to new stimuli. The brain automatically interprets the arousal as being something important and important things must be memorised. You can most certainly remember a number of critical events in your life indelibly imprinted in long-term memory. This has resonance in advertising design. By using powerful elements in advertising that induce arousal in the target audience, the marketer can increase receptivity to the message. A classical example is the *Benetton* advertising (see Figure 12.13).

Figure 12.13: *Benetton*'s colourful shock tactics

Benetton Group September 1991. Photographer: Olivero Toscani. Reproduced with permission.

Arousal, Sensory Appeal and Shock Tactics

Arousal can be very effective as it increases people's learning ability and may lead to the advertising being 'engraved' in memory. But it must be used with caution. The most apparent problem is of course that the arousing element is perceived as disturbing. This has certainly been the case for *Benetton*.

Another problem is that too much arousal may have the opposite effect. This is particularly likely when the advertising is about things that the brain perceives as dangerous. The brain protects itself by blocking the information instead of memorising it. A third problem with this arousal tool is that there is a risk that the arousal draws attention away from the advertising message. If marketers use an element that creates arousal but has no link to the other advertising content, there is a risk that the arousing element becomes what is processed and learned. Therefore it must be consistent with what the advertisement should convey.

The arousal effect may not necessarily come from the advertising itself. The same effects may occur if the advertising is placed in an arousing context, for instance at a commercial break during an exciting film, or on billboards at a big sporting event.

A model of how consumers may react to shock advertising appeals has been suggested by Dahlén, Rasch and Rosengren (2003) showing how the initial exposure to an advertisement, which is deliberately shocking, will at first provoke some perceived violation to the expected norm, which then is cognitively processed. Once attention has been achieved, and the message is comprehended, a further elaboration of brand intent takes place which may result in the message being retained and lead

Changing behaviour with familiar images

to some change of behaviour. This sequential process model demonstrates how the main objective of communication is to cut through the noise and grab attention.

Mystique

A clever tool to increase people's receptiveness to advertising is to make them search for information themselves. This can apply equally to informational (negatively originated motivations) or transformational (positive-ending motivations) advertising. To involve an audience in some sort of mysterious storyline is an effective way of engaging involvement and can aid brand recall. Mysterious TV commercials or radio spots where the target audience does not fully understand what is happening ensure that people stay focused on the advertising to see how it unravels, looking for clues. *Benson & Hedges* classically used the fact that advertising tobacco product and brand names was banned to great effect by making the audience look for clues in the arrangement of signs and signals (semiotics) in its advertisements. How do you advertise cigarettes without showing an actual cigarette? Draw attention to the gold pack to highlight the quality difference and make the pack the key brand trigger.

Another way of using mystique in advertising is to activate people's curiosity. Look how the advertisement for Lake Tahoe (Figure 12.14) evokes an almost mythical 'Blue World', a magical blend of nature and attitude. Notice how this mysterious illusion is given a practical twist with the image of the flying bike entering the frame of the picture.

This helps advertising to stick in the memory. An example of this was when *Virgin* launched its new cola drink. Black billboards with messages such as 'Next week we show you a topless virgin here' or 'An undressed virgin will be here next week' were used. The week after, the billboard showed a picture of the bottle with the cap (topless) or label (undressed) removed.

Fact, Logical Appeals and Demonstration

For high-involvement products or services, central processing must take place for the communication to be effective. Cognitive appeals present facts as part of the information search of the decision-making process. Abernethy and Franks (1996) list the following key information cues

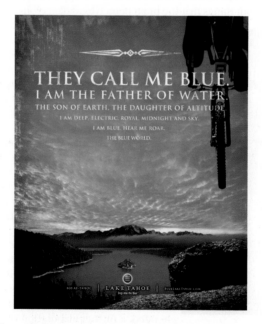

Figure 12.14: Into the mysterious blue world of Lake Tahoe

© Mering Carson. Reproduced with permission.

used in advertising: performance, availability, components, price, quality and special offers. There is higher information content in advertisements for products new to market, or durable goods, or for intangible goods (e.g. services). This hard-sell approach relies on the engagement of logically, rational argument. The use of opinion leaders in marketing helps new products to be launched and spread to new users. This is most appropriate when there is a conspicuous consumption element to the product (e.g. the launch of innovatory brands like *Sony Walkman, Apple iPods,* mobile phones). Similarly ideas which are in the *zeitgeist* benefit from demonstration. *Sainsbury's* has tapped into the UK's obsession with cookery programmes and promotes DIY recipes with 'real-time' demonstration by popular cook Jamie Oliver, a perfect, credible source who projects authority and accessibility.

Sometimes, effectiveness can be achieved by presenting unusual facts or facts in strange relationships. The idea here is to use facts that at first seem unrelated but have some sort of connection. It could be something like: 'Stand in line: 201 calories. Dance: 412 calories. Wave unsuccessfully on a cab: 112 calories. Walk home: 398 calories. Our energy drink contains 800 calories (and fits your pocket or purse). To help you manage.'

Demonstration is often used with new products in order to show how a product works and what features and benefits are most relevant to the user. This helps to educate viewers especially where the product is conceptually new. A good example of this is the campaign for *Nintendo's DS* hand-held console fronted by such prestigious British celebrities as actor Patrick Stewart who can be seen demonstrating to actress Julie Walters the best way to 'lower her Brain Age'. This type of advertising is an effective mechanism for introducing new product uses and in some ways, new ideas to a new audience.

Familiar Starting Point, Fantasy and Slice-of-Life Dramatisation

Familiarity is a powerful tool used to evoke target audience emotions, utilising people's need for **cognitive consistency**. A familiar starting point in an advertisement can help people to relate their individual knowledge and experiences of projected reality. *Carlsberg's* 'Belong' campaign uses images of affiliation displaced in unusual situations and sees a team of colleagues/friends: boarding a spaceship, climbing a mountain, joining the cowboy posse. The more associations that people can make – in *Carlsberg's* case, it is going into a nightclub and one pal being rejected, going out to celebrate a birthday – the easier it will be for them to engage with and remember the advertising.

Slice-of-life appeals present a simulated 'real-life setting' aimed at having resonance with the target audience for the product or company. Positioning a brand within a continuing storyline or narrative encourages audience engagement and allows development of character and a platform to introduce a range of products or brand features. Good examples of this are the *British Telecom* advertisements which feature a contemporary '*Oxo* family' of two divorcees living with children and coping with modern-day challenges – with the help of *BT* of course!

There may be limitations with slice-of-life platforms as the simulated real-life situations have to appear feasible and may restrict the element of extending product possibilities and scope for imagination. One way this is overcome is the use of other media to encourage audience engagement in an extended drama. Press and TV advertisements invite viewers to visit the brand's website which provides an entire universe of possibilities and an extended opportunity to discuss and demonstrate.

We like to get information that supports our views, that is in line with our established opinions. But we are highly receptive to information that supports our opinions and we are more than willing to remember such information.

One of the most powerful mechanisms of learning occurs when we can relate advertising to ourselves. This **individual brand congruity** (Smith 2007) happens when the essence of the brand accords with our own self-image, making advertising more personally relevant, and therefore much more likely to be memorised. Even simple connections like the slope of the piste suggested by the shots of the *Audi* car and character (see Figure 12.15) can help position a brand and highlight brand benefit.

Figure 12.15: Symbolic suggestion of Audi benefits

Comparative Advertising

When consumers make purchase decisions, they need information to help them make comparisons of possible products and evaluate the alternative brands within their consideration set. The use of comparative advertising allows companies to position their offer against the competition. Comparative advertising of the explicit variety was relatively unheard of in the UK until the Internet opened up the possibilities to fulfil information needs. Implicit mention of the competition (e.g. *Avis*'s classic 'We Try Harder' campaign) used to be the main way that a brand's proposition vis-à-vis the competition was outlined. Differentiation is the key objective in this instance and is now done explicitly (see Figure 12.16 – *Tesco's* 'Compare' website advertisement). The inherent danger in this approach is that brand awareness is extended to the competitors' brands and the advertising may only succeed in promoting the brand category and not the individual brand's features and benefits.

Figure 12.16: Every little helps in the evaluation of alternatives

Enhancing Intended Learning

The second category consists of tools that ensure that the information is received correctly. Message information must be organised and presented in a logical, coherent manner to ensure that the right elements are learned and processed successfully.

Often, in order to ensure that the target audience remembers the intended advertising message, information is presented in the form of a story. This has two advantages. Firstly, stories are engaging and can make it easier to maintain audience attention from beginning to end – very valuable where people's attention span is limited. Secondly, a story makes the information easier to interpret and as a consequence is easier to remember.

Using a storyline is just one example of **thematic organisation**. Here are some others.

Mnemonics and Repetition

Mnemonics are tools used to help increase brand learning and act as an aide memoire, particularly the category need/brand name association. They encourage rote learning of information by the visual or verbal, rhyming or musical repetition. This is specifically appropriate when a primary communication objective is brand recall. Repetitious use of brand logos helps depict the product category (Lutz and Lutz 1997); rhyme in advertising aids advertising processing and makes the message more memorable. A good example is *Gillette*'s famous '*Gillette*, the best a man can get'. The rhyme can feature alliteration or assonance: 'Beanz Meanz Heinz'.

Music works in the same way. By humming a melody, it is easier to remember the words of the advertisement's message: 'Maybe she's born with it – Maybe it's *Maybelline*'? Or *McDonald's* 'do-do-do-do-do . . . I'm lovin' it'. Musical jingles help the target audience to remember and are tantamount to subliminal advertising. The association of the *Intel Pentium Processor* jingle (even used in advertisements for other PC brands) or the call of the UK's *Direct Line* 'phone on wheels' alerts listeners. Psychologically, this works at the Pavlovian level of classical or respondent conditioning: consumers are taught to respond to a conditioned stimulus instilled by repetition.

Rote learning, repetition of message in this case, can help us remember brand names, prices, points of purchase, product benefits and intended message content. To ensure that advertising is convincing, it is sometimes crucial to clearly emphasise the main points of the message.

Gestalt Theory and the Zeigarnik Effect

A basic trait of our perceptual learning is that we seek harmony. We react whenever we encounter errors in stimuli. In Gestalt psychology, there is a belief that we automatically try to arrange different stimuli to find (or make) meaning. Among other things, we want to divide stimuli into a figure and a background. When this classification is difficult to do, we experience a dissonance and automatically start some sort of cognitive processing to solve the problem. We have an internal need to create entities out of stimuli and when something is missing, we try to correct the picture ourselves. Using this type of tactic in advertising helps prolong attention and instigate processing. Gestalt research into visual perception has shown that the mind looks for a unified pattern or whole ('gestalt'). From such research we know that the appearance (and therefore the meaning) of any sign or symbol is strongly influenced by its environment: and that the mind will group similar shapes together, will 'see' or 'decide' what is foreground and what is background and will even add information to make the sign or mark make sense. Gestalt psychologists have found that the mind will find the simplest explanation for the information (like the scientific principle of parsimony: that the simplest explanation which fits the facts is to be preferred). If we understand how the human mind makes connections, we will be able to design material that communicates more effectively.

An example of this is *Honda's* 'Problem playground' campaign for the hydrogen-fuelled *FCX Clarity*. With echoes of *Skoda's* 'The baking of' advertisement, *Honda*'s advertisement features a car made of jigsaw pieces and a giant sculpture of an engine constructed from thousands of Rubik's cubes. We see *Honda*'s engineers tackling a series of giant-size puzzles representing problems the engineers have to overcome to create products that are radical and to showcase the innovative nature of

Figure 12.17: When you love solving things, isn't every problem a playground?
© Wieden and Kennedy. Reproduced with permission.

the company. *Honda*'s advertisement builds on the car firm's recent online, radio and print campaign that also focused on the idea of puzzles and this is carried through to poster sites (see Figure 12.17) inviting the viewer to complete the puzzle.

The marketer can also use errors in text. When a word is spelled incorrectly, or when the words appear in the wrong order, people often unconsciously correct the text to make it right (lcuky is lucky) and read it as it should appear. But we still feel that something is wrong in the text and we devote more attention to the advertising since it is somewhat peculiar. Fashion brand *French Connection UK* has put its attention-grabbing abbreviation FCUK to great effect.

An extension of this phenomenon is the **Zeigarnik effect** named after the Russian psychologist who studied under one of the proponents of Gestalt psychology, Kurt Lewin. This demonstrates that people are motivated by incomplete information and refers to the state of tension we experience when facts or images or even truncated headlines like 'The answer to your weight problems is. . . .' instil a set-up or cliff-hanger expectation. Trying to add in information ourselves to achieve message completion often aids memory, partly because we have had to think about it, partly because we create our own picture to make it complete.

The use of this element in advertising can extend the tension of the brand's storyline to sustain engagement with the audience hooked into the progression of the brand narrative. The slice-of-life *BT* family example above allows for introductions of new characters and new products in much the same way as the *Oxo* family narrative could accommodate societal changes like vegetarianism, dysfunctional families and changing tastes. As these characters grow, we are not just witnesses but vicariously live through the brand's development because curiosity locks us in to the storyline in the same way as a TV soap opera.

Humour

A device used in many advertisements is humour. Classical conditioning links with conditioned stimuli with conditioned response. Laughter is intoxicating and the appeal generated by the positive mood created by comedy gives the brand positive associations. This helps attention, engagement, processing and comprehension, encourages recall and influences attitudes. Some people even pay more attention to and absorb the story of humorous advertisements than so-called comedy programmes.

The Zeigarnik effect is often employed here when tension is built up, attention guaranteed, and the punchline – the brand message – is delivered in an impactful way.

Decay can occur in the same way as an old joke can wear thin. Using comedians to convey a brand message (e.g. Peter Kaye projecting a funny, down-to-earth brand such as *John Smith's* beer) can be very successful if the positioning of the brand and the comedian's character and popularity are in simpatico. Once the moment has passed, the effectiveness is minimised. Similarly, the inappropriate use of comedians can have a very negative effect on a brand. *Sainsbury's* ran a campaign featuring John Cleese playing a belligerent, shouting version of his alter ego Basil Fawlty screaming about pricing. This resulted in presenting the wrong brand image and alienated current and potential customers.

The real problem with using humour is that it is subjective. However, there are several potential advantages, because humorous appeals:

- have the highest retention levels of all advertising messages;
- attract and hold consumers' attention (because we want to hear the joke);
- put consumers in a positive mood (and therefore create positive links between the consumers' mood and the product);
- distract the consumer from thinking critically (or internally arguing against) the advertisement.

But there are also several other risks in using humour:

- it is very difficult to be funny;
- the audience may not get the joke – in which case (knowing that the advertisement was intended to be funny) they will feel threatened, insulted and deprived of an experience to which they were looking forward;
- humour does not aid source credibility;
- humour is not appropriate for every product;
- the appeal of humorous messages often wears out more rapidly than serious advertisements.

All of the types of humour listed by Tom and Catanescu (2001) – comparison, personification, exaggeration, pun, sarcasm, silliness and surprise – are open to interpretation by the individual. There is some evidence that humour in advertising may be effective for gaining attention and achieving brand awareness but could actually harm comprehension and recall (Madden and Weinberger 1984).

Two-fers and Implied Conclusions

Similar to the Zeigarnik effect, two-fers require that the audience fills in the blanks. The 'fraternal twins' of good and bad have been used to great effect in advertisements for products which have a 'naughty but nice' appeal. You shouldn't really indulge it tells us, but the appeal asks you to make a judgement and come down on the side of pleasure.

The representation of a 'two sides of the argument' platform can be a strong tactic to elicit cognitive engagement. We have earlier seen how marketers can divide the advertising into two parts, for example when one wants to create mystique or curiosity. This is employed in a 'two-fer' where both parts are included in the same advertisement. Besides having the audience actively fill in the blanks, there are additional advantages. Firstly, the two-fer format attracts attention. The two parts create motion, and we saw that movement is an important perceptual tool that automatically attracts attention. Secondly, the tool makes us curious. What do the two parts have in common?

The apparent link between the two parts must not be farfetched (as we have seen in other tools as well). The message must be conveyed. At the same time, the link cannot be too trivial as the marketer may lose the curiosity effect.

Fiat's 'two-fer' advertisement projects an image of how you may look with or without a car with tinted windows. It plays a visual trick with the apparent silhouette of movie star Tom Cruise juxtaposed with a shot of the driver. The brand benefit taps right into symbolic consumption (Figure 12.18).

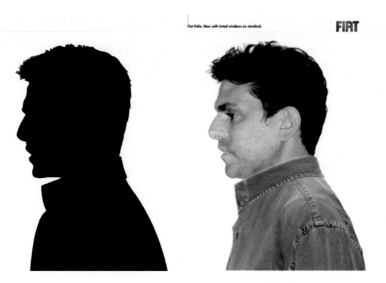

Figure 12.18: Now you see it, now you don't

Asking the target audience to draw their own conclusion from the implied advertising message – where different facts or arguments that point in one direction are presented – can be a dangerous game. Do you remember the confused messages of the *Persil* 'Dirt is good' campaign featured earlier? An advertisement for the *Jeep Cherokee* carries the bold headline: 'The end of the world is never nigh' (Figure 12.19). This calls on the target audience to eschew any conscience for the planet in place

Figure 12.19: *Jeep* – The end of the world is never nigh

of the selfish pursuit of driving a 4WD. The absence of any reference to carbon footprints may risk alienating the audience.

When the target audience is encouraged to draw its own conclusions, there are several advantages which make the message more memorable and convincing: the meaning of the message may not be explicit and therefore more interesting; the target audience is forced to process the information and think about it; the conclusion is the target audience's own. However, by handing over the responsibility for drawing the conclusion to the target audience, the company loses some control over the message.

Literary Techniques and Devices

Advertising purports to persuade as well as inform. A common way to invite the audience to draw their own conclusions is to use literary techniques or rhetorical figures. Figurative advertising language (often referred to as 'tropes') can help the message to be more memorable. According to McQuarrie and Phillips (2005), rhetorical figures (or figures of speech) can be defined as verbal or visual elements that ask the audience to 'read' the advertisement using words, phrases, expressions or images in a figurative way. One approach might be to deviate from expectations, using words in the wrong context or by combining texts and pictures that are contradictory to each other. The processing of a clever arrangement of signs can give what the semiotician Barthes called the 'pleasure of the text' and encourages engagement in the communication message.

Metaphors, Similes and Allegories

As an example of non-literal language in advertising, the metaphor deserves special mention. Using metaphor, especially in visual form (Morgan and Reichert 1999), creates associations between the brand and something different, inviting the audience to accept a link of some value or feature. An illustration depicting growth rings of a tree (Figure 12.20), a metaphor for the impact of deforestation, makes a dramatic statement, focusing our attention on damage to the ozone layer. 'Until the last breath' links the impact of environmental abuse with the commitment of the *Greenpeace* cause.

It may not denote a particular object but might suggest connotations. The use of a referent in association with the brand may eventually be inextricably linked. *Budweiser's* positioning at the top of the alcoholic product category sees it referred to as the 'King of Beers'.

Figure 12.20: The circle of life carved in wood

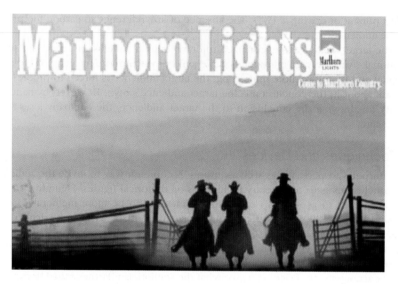

Figure 12.21: *Marlboro* Country

A weaker version of the metaphor, which has an actual comparative element, is the simile. This device makes a direct reference to another object to make the association of action or quality.

An extended metaphor, an allegory, places the brand in a narrative with meanings and connotations outside that narrative. Advertisements can use personifications of real people, brands or issues through an obscured lens projecting brand values and proposition through caricatures and parallel schemas. '*Marlboro* Country' (Figure 12.21) is a mythical, masculine, rugged landscape of almost 'natural'.

Table 12.2 lists examples of some of the most common rhetorical figures in advertising.

Rhetorical figure	Description	Example
Hyperbole	Exaggerated or extreme claim	'Experience colour so rich you can feel it' (*Cover Girl* lipstick) 'Laser beams move at the speed of light. Fortunately, our engineers move somewhat faster' (*Uniden* laser and radar detector)
Rhetorical question	Asking a question so as to make an assertion	'Don't you have something better to do?' (*Hewlett-Packard* fax)
Epanorthosis	Making an assertion so as to call it into question	'Chances are, you'll buy a Ranger for its value, economy and quality. Yeah, right' (*Ford* pickup truck)
Ellipsis	A gap or omission that has to be completed	'A lot of tires cost less than Michelin. That's because they should' (*Michelin* tyres) 'Everyday vehicles that aren't' (*Suzuki* 4WD)

Metonym	Use of an associated element to represent the object	'The imports are getting nervous' (*Buick* automobile)
Homonym	One word can be taken in two senses	'Make fun of the road' (*Ford* automobile) 'How to make a home run' (*Whirlpool* appliance)
Antanaclasis	Repeating a word in two different senses	'Today's Slims at a very slim price' (*Misty Ultralight* cigarettes) 'Nobody knows the athlete's foot like the Athletes Foot' (*The Athletes Foot* shoe store)
Syllepsis	A verb changes in sense	'It's too bad other brands don't pad their shoes as much as their prices' (*Keds* shoes) 'Built to handle the years as well as the groceries' (*Frigidaire* refrigerator)
Resonance	A phrase takes on a different meaning when coupled with a picture	'Will bite when cornered (with a picture of car splashing up water as it makes a turn' (*Goodyear* tyres) 'Success rice brings out the ham in you (with a picture of ham pieces in sauce' (*Hormel* rice)
Paradox	A self-contradictory or impossible statement	'This picture was taken by someone who didn't bring a camera' (*Kodak* film) 'Mark McGuire hit 42 home runs last year. But we held the bat' (*Franklin* batting glove)
Irony	A statement that means the opposite of what is said	'We spent years developing this incredibly comfortable contact lens, and this is how you treat it (with a picture of a finger flicking a lens away)' (*Acuvue* disposable contacts) 'Just another wholesome family sitcom (with a picture of the male lead licking cream off thighs) (*HBO* cable TV)

Table 12.2: Literary techniques and devices

Source: McQuarrie and Mick (1996). Reproduced with permission.

Rhetorical figures invite the audience to elaborate on the content of the communication, as people must make sense of the meaning themselves. Studies show that this sense-making process may be very beneficial as people construct so-called 'weak implicatures' (Phillips 1997). **Implicatures** refer to the intended explicit message and the many implicit interpretations that can be made. For instance, an advertisement for the *Franklin* batting glove could have explicitly communicated: 'Our gloves give great grip of the bat'. Instead, by using a rhetorical figure, the communication could produce a number of additional weak implicatures – the gloves are long-lasting, make you hit harder, give greater accuracy, fit nicely, etc. Another advantage of rhetorical figures is that they are likely to produce less doubt and counterarguments in the audience's mind. An explicit statement ('great grip of the bat') is easy to scrutinise ('Does it really? Don't competing brands give equally good grip?'), whereas the implied version is not. *Carlsberg* is able to assert that it is the best lager by making metaphorical arguments supporting the tagline: 'Probably the best'.

Limbic Signals – 'The Reptile Brain'

Subliminal perception (see Matter of Fact box below) is an advertising tool that has been talked about since the 1950s. However, it does not work the way most people think. The reason is that the brain cannot receive and process advanced information during such a short time – 'buy popcorn' is much too advanced to be perceived and processed in a split second (e.g. Theus 1994). But the thought of communicating to people unconsciously is still interesting.

MATTER OF FACT

Subliminal Perception

Subliminal means 'below the limit'. Subliminal perception occurs below the limit of our conscious awareness. It is usually stimuli that are shown so fast that our consciousness does not have the time to see them, but they still enter our minds and affect us.

The phenomenon was known in the 1950s when the businessman and consultant Jim Vicary published his experimental results. He reported that tests with subliminal movie advertising had strong effects. The messages 'DRINK COKE' and 'EAT POPCORN' had been shown on the movie screen so fast that nobody in the audience could perceive them consciously. However, the sales of *Coca-Cola* had increased by 18% and the sales of popcorn had increased by 52%. The results created a lot of interest and debate, even though Vicary admitted that he had falsified the results to make money on selling advertising solutions for subliminal perception. The experiment had no effect at all in reality. But the discussion and mystique involving subliminal perception still live on.

Source: Dahlén (2003).

Optimal advertising – where there is not a large cognitive effort on behalf of the audience – promotes its message directly and unambiguously. This means advertising where there is no barrier to perception and processing, and as a result, the audience will pay attention to the message and we can ensure that the message is perceived as intended.

One way of making the advertising immediately communicative and unambiguous is to use elements that do not speak to people's consciousness and cognitive side, but to their unconsciousness and emotional side. This can be done by way of limbic signals (e.g. Appleton 1966, Kroeber-Riel 1993). Limbic signals are stimuli that speak to, and are processed by, the limbic system: what we sometimes call the 'reptile brain' (the part of our brain that deals with primal instincts and makes us react instinctively to certain things without thinking about them). This is about very basic emotions and almost primal instincts like affection, warmth, comfort, anger, fear and attraction. Experiments show that people of the same culture perceive some fundamental stimuli in the same way; that is to say, the sight of a little baby promotes feelings of warmth, an image of an older couple stimulates feelings of comfort, and so forth. And it happens automatically without any cognitive effort or thought processes.

The use of limbic signals, often in the form of symbols, images, scents, sounds and colours, has two advantages: they activate *emotions* (they are in many ways emotions) and we know already that emotions enhance advertising effectiveness; these emotions are activated automatically and are linked to the advertising content. As a result, the brand is effectively associated with these emotions.

Refuge – Prospect – Hazard

A special case of limbic signals is the trinity 'refuge-prospect-hazard': our most fundamental instincts. Refuge is about our genetic need for comfort and our pursuit for a safe haven; prospect is our genetic curiosity and search for new opportunities; hazard has to do with our risk propensity and our tendency to avoid possible danger. Refuge and prospect signals can be very potent tactics to use in advertising, making advertising more recognisable and more easily linked to positive associations.

CLOSING CASE STUDY

Heineken: Heineken Know the Signs that Giving Yourself a Good Name Refreshes the Parts Others Cannot Reach

Almost 35 years after the slogan '*Heineken* refreshes the parts other beers cannot reach' had helped *Heineken* introduce foreign lager into Europe and the rest of the world, the Dutch brewery's market dominance was under threat. The market-leading beer, the most predominant beverage in Europe, Australia and the USA, had reached saturation point. Arch-rivals, Belgian *InBev,* owners of main competitor brand *Stella Artois*, had absorbed British brewers *Bass* and *Whitbread* (*Heineken's* UK partner of around 40 years), and competition was fierce from its European rivals (such as the other Dutch premium lager *Grolsch,* the Danish *Carlsberg,* Germany's *Beck's,* the Italian *Peroni* and French *Kronenbourg*), as well as a battery of American beers such as *Budweiser* and *Miller's* and late 1997 Australian entrant *Foster's.*

Heineken's global strategy of repositioning its brand by marketing a premium 5% lager beer – *Heineken Export* – had not helped falling sales (a collapse from £500 million a year to about £100 million in the UK alone). Costs of airtime, the cluttered advertising environment and the migration of viewers to other information/entertainment platforms were blamed. The decision was made to shift a major slice of its advertising budget away from TV brand image advertising to other parts of the marketing communications mix which would better reach its core target market of male 18–26 year olds. However, share of voice is critical in the premium lager category, each brand spending massive amounts on TV-led advertising campaigns. In an industry where brand image is dependent upon advertising creativity and exposure, this was seen as a huge gamble. Could it compete without a like-for-like TV presence? *Heineken* needed a new narrative: brand image is only part of the game; communications which is relevant, engaging and set in the real-world experience of consumers is where they had to be. *Heineken* knew the signs: turn the target audience into targets and engage them in a conversation in a context within which the brand is consumed!

In addition to an overcrowded beer market, research from Nugent (2005) highlighted that competition from non-alcoholic drinks, together with a surge of cross-generational

(Continued)

concerns for drink-related anti-social behaviour, was starting to have a damaging effect on consumption levels. One narrative thread which *Heineken* hit on seemed incongruous: the encouragement to drink less! In November 2008, *Heineken International* announced the launch of an Internet-based responsible drinking campaign entitled 'Know the Signs' creating greater self-awareness amongst young drinkers, encouraging more informed choices and better drinking habits. This extended the well-established narrative that had started with the 'Enjoy *Heineken* Responsibly' programme aimed at targeting those who display irresponsible behaviour and consumption patterns: *Heineken's* target audience! Its message was creatively delivered, innovatively using both Internet and mobile telephone technology and was the first campaign of its type in the alcohol communication arena.

Heineken reaches out online

Heineken had learnt through global research that, after consumption of alcohol, drinkers tend to 'transform' into one of five embarrassing characters or alter-egos: Crier, Groper (as illustrated), Exhibitionist, Fighter or Sleeper. The online 'Know The Signs' campaign incorporates a plethora of digital communication devices familiar to and used by the target audience; it educates, entertains and, most importantly, engages.

Buzz was created for the campaign via an entertaining Hollywood-style trailer introducing the campaign concept and a few of its characters. This was available in English, Spanish, Hungarian and Dutch versions and was seeded by *SocialMedia8* using a buzz toolkit and tracked for evaluation by *ViralTracker*. The campaign integrating platform www.KnowTheSigns.com asks site visitors to watch CCTV surveillance footage and use a virtual remote to pan and click on specific areas of the bar, relating to real-life experience in spotting embarrassing 'signs of transformation' in the characters. It directly encourages interaction by asking visitors to discover what character THEY are and how to spot the early signs in themselves and in others.

The 'Know the Signs' campaign is also supported by a downloadable social networking widget which allows visitors to match with friends on several popular social networks, such as *Facebook*, *MySpace*, *Netlog* and the Dutch site *Hyves*. A range of ways of connecting friends with the content is available: send an embarrassing video to a mobile phone, send a virtual glass of water (*iBoard* on the *iPhone*), assign friends to characters, and use the *Oddcast Embarrassment* tool to superimpose a friend's face onto one of the characters. A version is available on *YouTube (HD)* for non-site visitors.

Melinda Eskell, Heineken Brand Communication Manager, said: 'Consumer research tells us that our target audience is open to discuss the subject but wants to do so in a way that is relevant and appropriate to them. Our digital approach facilitates this and will allow a level of interaction and engagement vital to getting the message across. The *Heineken* brand's position as a leading premium beer is strongly supported by our quality over quantity communication.'

Other 'Enjoy *Heineken* Responsibly' elements reflect both the commitment to responsible consumption and the innovative approach to communicating the message.

On a global and local level, responsibility is now part of the core *Heineken* brand architecture, ensuring it is part of every creative internal and external brief. In 2003 *Heineken* was the first brewer to introduce a responsibility message on every can and bottle linked to an educational website outlining the impact of irresponsible consumption. This website is now customised for 40 markets and translated into 22 languages around the world. For *Heineken's* sponsorship of the 2008/09 UEFA Champions League, the most prominent and viewed pitch-side brand advertising has been changed to incorporate the Enjoy *Heineken* Responsibly message, reaching a global annual TV audience of more than four billion. Additionally, broadcast sponsorship airtime around the event has also been dedicated to this message; the *Heineken* brand is also the focus of many local partnership activities with organisations that are actively addressing responsible alcohol consumption issues.

In spring 2009 the 'Give Yourself a Good Name' 360-degree campaign extended the equity in the overarching 'responsible brand' narrative by showcasing subtle ways in which consumers can decide to 'give themselves a good name' through their actions, their words and their choices. This has helped to connect the values of the consumer to the values of the brand. This proved that, through good research, creating relevant messages which connect and locate target audiences in their domain, *Heineken* found a way to refresh the parts other marketing communications couldn't reach.

QUESTIONS

1. The online campaign can be visited on http://www.knowthesigns.com. You can download images from here: http://www.heinekeninternational.com/mediakit_gallery.aspx. More about responsible drinking can be viewed at http://www.enjoyheinekenresponsibly.com and the video on *YouTube (HD)*. Visit these sites and evaluate how effective you think this approach to communication is.

2. What is the difference in the traditional brand image mass communication approach and this sort of experiential branding adopted by *Heineken*?

3. *Heineken* has changed its brand narrative from one of social affiliation (being part of a social group) to one of being a responsible citizen. As a person within their target market, what effect do you think this has on attitudes and purchase behaviour towards the brand?

CHAPTER SUMMARY

Perceived by some to be the heart of marketing communications, creativity presents many advantages and potential pitfalls. Because creative formats enhance attention and processing to the communication they have the power both to convince and confuse the audience. Therefore, it is important to know the reasons for the creative work, and to have clear goals for the audience's reactions. This enables the marketer to choose wisely from a wide range of creative tools.

The chapter focused on the following aspects of communication creativity:

- Defining three desirable reactions from the audience that make the communication more compelling, 'ha!', 'aha!' and 'ah!'
- Avoiding pitfalls, such as failure to comprehend, irrelevance and distractions.
- Tools for gaining attention, based on perceptual psychology, ranging from colours to errors.
- Tools for enhancing processing, for example arousal and mystique.
- Tools for greater conviction, for example imagery creation and rhetorical figures.

REFLECTIVE QUESTIONS

a. When somebody reads an advertisement, the thoughts that they might have about the 'sender source' and actual product condition the receiver's attitude to the brand; thoughts about product in the context of the advertisement condition the engagement and attitude to the advertisement itself. Why is this so?

b. Krugman (1988) claimed that 'the biggest limitation in advertising is not processing, it is attention' What did he mean?

c. What part can colour and intensity play in advertising creativity?

d. The recent increase in 'real beauty' campaigns demonstrates the role that congruity plays in the effectiveness of advertising. Explain what 'congruity' means and illustrate your answer with examples of how this works in practice.

e. Hackley (1999) claims that in order to be meaningful to the target audience, 'advertising must make use of the cultural currency of symbolic codes in contemporary use'. What exactly does this mean? Illustrate with examples of brands which make reference to cultural codes.

RESEARCH PROJECTS

Visit *YouTube* to view the unconventional approach to selling *Golden Fire* beer with a mixture of ambient, website, guerrilla and buzz marketing allied to a very creative multimedia storyline.

Have a look at *Samsung*'s campaigns for the *Samsung NV100* camera ('Ultra motion capture') and *Samsung* 1300rpm washing machine. Both are product-oriented executions, and both are superbly creative advertisements.

CHAPTER  13

MEDIA CONCEPTS AND MEDIA PLANNING

"The best media plans provide the target audience with an optimum level of 'opportunities to see' the campaign whilst affording full creative scope."
Fox Media Planning

This chapter will examine the principles of media planning and the range of media tools available to assist in this process. Marketing communications requires the integration of all communication elements and a comprehensive knowledge of the media channels used to carry communication messages.

Media planning is broadly the process of finding the most cost-effective means of delivering communications to prospective and existing customers, and includes all channel brand encounters which deliver dialogue to key stakeholders in mass or specialised audiences. On a macro level, the marketer must decide upon the total amount of communication that is needed to reach the set objectives; on a micro level, the marketer must determine the allocation of communication resources over time and between media, as well as taking target groups, market situation, competitors and product and message characteristics into account.

How communication is created, managed and consumed, and equally how media, communication and culture have been, and are being, transformed is an area for critical study. But what exactly do we mean by the word 'media'? It's often used as a metaphorical message 'conduit' which holds all company communications. It also applies to all the techniques and technologies that facilitate the face and business value proposition of an organisation to its stakeholders.

In this age of network-enhanced word-of-mouth communications and interconnection of consumers through social networking, media has become a catch-all label for various activities that integrate technology, facilitate social interaction and provide channels to connect conversations to consumers. Social media has shaken up the way we communicate and send messages to each other; there have been almost 100 million videos on *YouTube*; 200 million blogs have been set up with 73% of active online users having read a blog – 45% starting their own; four million articles have been published on *Wikipedia*; there are 1.5 million *Second Life* residents; 39% subscribe to an RSS feed; 57% have joined a social network; 55% have uploaded photographs; and 83% have watched video clips.

When Alistair Darling, the UK Chancellor of the Exchequer, announced his budget plans to deal with the world's worst recession since the Second World War in April 2009, he used *YouTube* to disseminate information. When a plane crashed on the Hudson River in Manhattan, a message was sent via *iPhone* and viewed by two million *Twitter* users. As we have seen with Barack Obama, his road to the presidency was mainly through the channels of social media.

Media can be classified in a number of ways: active and passive; print and electronic. Technically speaking all marketing communications must be carried by some form of medium: advertising media such as broadcast and press; digital media like the Internet; promotional media like stationery, letterheads, giveaways, as well as sponsorships and product placements, packaging, call centres, point of sale and so on. Indeed, anything which acts as a vehicle for transmitted communications from brand to target audience can be included under the heading 'media'.

OPENING CASE STUDY

Burger King: Burger King's Crowning Glory: A Whopper of a Viral Conversation

As traditional advertising media such as TV and print lose impact, companies are looking for new ways to reach consumers. *Burger King* has earned the reputation of 'king of viral marketing' for repeatedly showing the ability to generate online buzz and create media attention for its entertaining Web campaigns. With a name for legendary interactive communications like 'Subservient Chicken' and '*Whopper* Virgins', the recent '*Whopper* Sacrifice' application on the *Facebook* social networking service has courted controversy and produced fantastic peer-to-peer word of mouth as well as widespread industry discussion. The key to this campaign's success was letting the message find its way to the audience by using the most appropriate medium.

Burger King friends dis-united on Facebook

Six years ago, *Burger King* was a product that people knew more than loved, and efforts have been made to reposition and 're-mystify' the brand and re-engage its audience. It is not positioned in the same way as its rival *McDonald's* – with its family orientation – and is squarely aimed at young adults. What *Burger King* realised is that to reach and communicate with its target audience, a viral marketing campaign which was engaging, relevant and closely aligned with the brand could be successful. The benefit of viral marketing is the willingness of consumers to pass along novel or entertaining videos, applications and websites to family, friends and co-workers, a sort of digital accelerated word-of-mouth advertising. It is a cost-effective way (origination costs aside) to spread the messages across the Internet like a virus. If it works well, it can build immediate and sustainable adoption and will get bloggers writing about it.

The *Burger King's* '*Whopper* Sacrifice' application on *Facebook* was part promotion and part word-of-mouth conversation. Users of the social networking service were asked to 'sacrifice 10 friends' to earn a free *Whopper* sandwich. Astonishingly, even for such a small reward, consumers were motivated to eliminate over a quarter of a million friendships in order to get free burgers before the application was disabled over privacy issues. Most social network brand applications have tended to rely on forcing viral word of mouth and advocacy through friend requests and gift exchanges, and users are encouraged to grow and nurture their online friendships. It is a marketing communications objective to nurture ever-increasing 'spheres of influence' and sometimes this false

Social sacrifice or media message?

(Continued)

'friendship' phenomenon can lead to an excess of casual contacts. Social networks include built-in viral tools that help share the message generated by each interaction. What *Burger King* tapped into was the excuse to offload so-called friends and have a bit of fun.

Although *Burger King* was making fun of the notion of social networking – the value of commoditising online 'friendships' – they made sure of the seriousness of participants' actions, clearly indicating that 'Each friend will be notified so choose wisely'. This bold, very controversial approach generated much media debate which made the campaign a success even based on this criterion alone.

The opportunity for extending press coverage and online debate came with the withdrawal announcement. A provocative feed story was posted on the 'landing page' for the *Facebook* application which declared that the *Whopper* Sacrifice had itself been sacrificed because 'your love for the *Whopper* sandwich proved to be stronger than 232,566 friendships'. By the time the site was closed, more than 82,000 people had participated, 'sacrificing' at least one friend.

In terms of campaign evaluation, size of audience and level of incremental sales are obvious measurements. The success of these types of campaign is judged by 'impression numbers' and one-time interactions (rather than continued use of the application). Added to this, the tracking of popular culture references, such as how often it appears in talk show monologues, entertainment shows or in the news, can increase the credibility of the brand and improve share-of-voice ratings. A parody of '*Whopper* Virgins' was featured on *Saturday Night Live* for example.

QUESTIONS

1. Do you think using an alternative digital media approach to reaching the target audience would be a long-term strategy or is it just a short-term tactic?

2. What are the main advantages of this sort of interactive medium?

3. What other 'social media' ideas could *Burger King* use to keep the conversation going with its target audience?

We live in a mediated world where projections of brand image and representations of identity proliferate more than ever before. All brand communications must be carefully targeted and systematically applied. Considering the large amounts of money spent at this stage of the marketing communications process, it is easy to understand why media planning is so important. The fundamental questions of where, when, how and price must be addressed. There has to be a balance between effectiveness, efficiency and economy.

Whilst the main objective is to achieve the strongest effect possible, it has to be accomplished with least cost and least waste. To do this systematically, modelling is used to map out the media schedules (where, when and how often the advertising is placed in media) that give the strongest effects, whereas optimisation means finding the least expensive solution for the selected schedules (Abratt and Cowan 1999, Ephron 1998). In order to describe this process, we need to first familiarise ourselves with the terminology and tools of media and media planning. And even if some objectives are qualitative – to create an aura around the brand for example – the planning of all media has to be quantified since this is where exposure of communications messages has to be costed, delivered and evaluated. Looking firstly at some media trends will help put this in context.

TRENDS IN MEDIA

From a message reception perspective, audiences have become very fragmented and migrated from single exposure media to multiple content platforms, with the growth in broadband options being the biggest driver. A full discussion of digital media can be seen in Chapter 16, but it is fair to say that the normal media measurements described below have been augmented by two core media metrics: **influence** (the ability of individuals to disseminate information and persuade other individuals) and **engagement** (the ability of the medium to get people actively involved). New voices are getting involved with peer-to-peer influence and it is now more important for the message to find the market through the correct selection of appropriate media.

From a media management perspective, there have been dramatic shifts in advertising expenditure away from traditional broadcast media like TV to newer digital platforms. Broadcasters have had to respond to better effectiveness and evaluation in order to compete. In the 1960s, 80% of consumers could be reached with three 30-second TV advertisements. That figure had increased to 117 spots by 2002 and it is estimated to be almost 300 by 2012. Convergence of media, bringing together multimedia platforms, has been a major trend which has been evolutionary rather than revolutionary. In addition to this, the fragmentation and personalisation of media has contributed to the changing media landscape.

MATTER OF FACT

New Media Trends

An extensive survey conducted by IBM's Institute for Business Value (part of its Global Business Services) with over 2800 respondents in Australia, Germany, India, Japan, the UK and the USA revealed four trends that will affect the way organisations communicate with consumers:

- **Consumer adoption of new distribution formats:** consumers are more willing to provide personal information in return for perceived value and meaningful dialogue. This confirms the acknowledgement of a new era of permission-based marketing communications.
- **A shift in brand sponsor spending:** the need by organisations to evaluate expenditure is now demanding more ROI measurability. This is likely to be exacerbated by the severe contraction of spending due to the extremely uncertain economic conditions across the world. This has increased the pressure for better use of marketing communications resources and, as a result, media schedules are evidencing a move away from traditional advertising towards more measurable, interactive digital media.
- **Digital migration of platforms:** the traditional boundaries between advertising and direct marketing forms are becoming less discrete, creating opportunities for innovative business models for content platforms.
- **Emergence of new capabilities:** as a result of technological, social and economic changes, new entrants and existing competitors are driving new types of industry innovation, challenging the way the market is served and accelerating the pace of change.

The report predicts the emergence of hybrid communications which combine the ROI measurability of direct marketing with the brand image ability of mass-market advertising. In order to survive, the report states that: 'companies must move beyond traditional advertising to combine granularity of targeting and measurement with cross-platform integration, greater insights, open collaboration and digital processes'.

(Continued)

Communication media	2002	2007	2012 (estimated)	% change in spend
Traditional advertising (e.g. TV, print, radio, outdoor)	47%	41%	32%	−15%
Traditional marketing (e.g. direct marketing, promotions)	46%	46%	42%	−4%
Alternative interactive media	7%	13%	27%	+20%

Changing advertising spend, 2002–12

Source: Veronis Suhler Stevenson (2008).

Although traditional forms of marketing communications still represent a sizeable proportion of budgets, the trend towards converging media, changing consumer needs and the demand of a new economic era for ROI-accountable metrics will see an increasing shift to media beyond traditional marketing communications.

Source: Digital Consumer Report, IBM's Institute for Business Value (March 2009).

MEDIA IN FOCUS

'Lambient' Media

If 'ambient' marketing media in advertising can be seen in messages on bus tickets, supermarket trolleys, till receipts or even temporarily projected on the sides of buildings, what might 'lambient' media be? To advertise its UK train ticket-booking service, *thetrainline.com* recruited a flock of sheep by a busy trainline to announce a 43% price reduction. Captive audience, moving media and a message with 100% reach (well at least those passengers on the left of the train!)

In commenting on the campaign, Iain Hildreth of *thetrainline.com*, said: 'Sheep are a common sight from train windows right across the country. So for us, using sheep as "billboards" felt like an interesting and attention-grabbing area to explore, especially since sheep are featured so prominently in our advertising'.

Lambient media rams home the message

As an odd-ball example of new media, 'sheepvertising' has really raised the 'baa' in ambient advertising.

This idea of using farm animals as moving media has spread further afield across Europe, an example being the use of cows for the *Dutch Environmental* campaign to protect Groene Hart , an area between Amsterdam and Utrecht. It proves one thing though: anything can be classed as media providing it can convey a message to an audience – captive or not.

MEDIA CONCEPTS

Some of the key media planning tools which are used in achieving objectives and therefore evaluation metrics are:

* frequency;
* reach;
* weight;
* opportunities to see;
* media vehicles;
* share of voice;
* ratings;
* salience;
* cost.

Frequency

One of the key roles of advertising is to build awareness through exposure to the brand. When frequency is measured, we calculate the number of possible exposures to a media 'vehicle' (e.g. the colour supplement of a Sunday newspaper) that the target audience may experience. It doesn't measure exposures to the message but exposures to the medium. For example, for a daily newspaper, the frequency could be six if the advertisement appears every day for a week and also six if it appears once a week for six weeks.

Reach

Total reach is measured by calculating the number of people expected to be exposed to the advertising over a certain time period. However, a more meaningful analysis is referred to simply as **reach** (sometimes as **useful reach**) and calculates the amount of consumers from the target group who are likely to see the advertising. The difference in the two is vitally important. One medium may have a higher total reach; another may have a more useful reach. For example, placing an advertisement on TV, where there are more possible targets exposed to a message, may be less cost-effective compared to an advertisement placed in a specialist interest magazine with more 'useful reach'.

Gross reach allows for overlapping media (e.g. TV, press and cinema) or even overlapping media vehicles (e.g. advertisements in different newspapers on different days), and measures the number of people reached regardless of whether it hits the same person repeatedly. A negative perspective on this is referred to as **duplicated reach** since the repetition of slots may dilute. Therefore, the effective reach of a message measures the number of targeted viewers, at an effective frequency level, who are expected to be exposed.

Weight

The weight of an advertising campaign's media impact is measured in gross rating points (grps) or television rating points (TVRs) for TV, which is seen as an expression of the penetration of the target audience. This can be achieved by using a mix of different media.

Opportunities to See

Opportunities to see (OTS) refers to the probability of a target audience being exposed to the message. To calculate this, we must divide gross reach by reach.

Different Types of Media and Media Vehicles

A **medium** refers to a class of message carrier such as TV, radio, newspapers or magazines. A **media vehicle** is an individual carrier within a medium like the *Sunday Times Magazine*. Traditional mass media covers wide circulation, viewing or readership such as newspapers, magazines, TV and radio.

Non-traditional media may include TV screens in surgeries, queue-line video screens, posters at public and sporting events, and the use of the Internet.

Specialised media includes special interest or 'niche' consumer magazines; trade magazines; catalogues; *Yellow Pages*.

Share, Ratings and Ratings/HUT Share

Share refers to the percentage of homes with TVs (HUT) tuned to a particular programme.

Ratings are measured by evaluating the percentage of individuals or homes exposed to a specific advertising medium, for example, TV. This can be measured by multiplying HUT by share. For magazines this is referred to as 'coverage' rather than ratings, but it means the same thing.

Share of Voice

Share of market (SOM) refers to the brand's market share in a category.

Share of voice (SOV) is the measure of how much a company should be heard (or seen) compared to its competitors, and is an indication of how much should be spent on a brand to maintain or improve market share as a percentage of all that is spent on marketing communications in that particular market category. For instance, if total advertising expenditure in the soft drinks category amounts to £100 million, and the company spends £15 million, then its SOV is $15/100 = 15\%$.

Equilibrium is where share of voice is the same as share of market.

Salience

Salience refers to how the impact of several factors (e.g. promotion frequency, distance, construction, clutter, placement) affects customer relevance and resultant media ratings.

Cost

For inter-media comparison purposes, a medium's cost is expressed by the cost of reaching 1000 people given as cost per thousand (CPT or CPM). This is achieved by calculating the cost of placement divided by the likely audience of that medium (e.g. *You Magazine* double-page spread cost £10,000 divided by circulation of 1000 = £10).

ANALYSING MARKET SITUATIONS AND CONDITIONS RESPONDING TO COMPETITORS' MEDIA EXPENDITURE

The first step of media planning is to form an overall strategy (or model) for how advertising could and should reach the target audience: what effects are required and which media schedules are appropriate? Donnelly (1996) stressed the importance of three key factors when planning media:

- **Category spending**, which is the amount spent on advertising in the product category and how it has evolved.
- **Share of voice** (SOV), which is the measure of how much a company should be heard (or seen) compared to its competitors.
- **Media mix**, which looks at the individual media mix composition of the competition.

To determine the overall media budget in order to get maximum effect compared to competitors' advertising, we need to examine the following dimensions:

- **Effective frequency**, which is about establishing the lowest number of advertising exposures needed to get the maximum effect.
- **Frequency exposure**, which attempts to ascertain when advertising is most effective.

How can we be heard in our attempts to communicate above the **media clutter** and against the competition?

To ensure efficient use of resources, media costs have to be measured: cost measures, media schedule element measures, and effect measures.

SHARE OF VOICE

Effective advertising quite often has to shout to be heard (and seen!) amidst the often saturated media and category competition. One way of achieving this is to think in terms of share of voice (SOV). As we have seen, this measures the company's share of the total advertising voice (or market expenditure) in a particular category. How do we define what advertising 'voice' is?

We could start with the total number of advertising exposures in a market. Then, we could weigh the exposures based on the expected effect in the different media that have been used. But often it is difficult to get competitor information. This can be simplified in the following way: SOV can be calculated as the company's share of the total advertising expenditure in the category. For instance, if total advertising expenditure in the car insurance category amounts to £100 million, and the company spends £15 million, then its SOV is 15/100 = 15%. The assumption here is that many companies have similar media schedules, which is a fair assumption within industries.

Many studies (e.g., Jones 1990, Miller and Berry 1998, Schroer 1990) have shown that if a brand invests in a higher share of its 'advertising voice', there is a direct correlation with increased market share. The implication here is that the marketer should attempt to have the highest SOV in the category in order to get the strongest effect of advertising and, as a consequence, attain and maintain market leadership. It is obviously expensive to dominate in most categories, so sometimes companies try to dominate a certain media vehicle (an individual carrier within a medium like a special interest magazine), creating the impression of highest SOV even if it is not the case.

This may be beneficial if the selected target audience are heavy users of that particular media vehicle, or the media vehicle has highly favourable characteristics, which may result in a larger share of the actual advertising voice. This requires careful analysis of different media vehicles' appropriateness for advertising in a category. A good example of this is the use of outdoor billboards which have limited space (and are also limited in the number of advertisers that can compete for space) and thus high impact. Figure 13.1 shows the use of billboards as part of *Nivea*'s media schedule allowing

Figure 13.1: *Nivea Cellulite Reducing Moisturiser* advertisement

'drive-by' impact, interactivity of target audience as well as the mixed media exposure which accrued from word of mouth and press reporting of this site which was seen as a media event.

How can we use SOV to increase market share? There are two well-proven methods we can follow:

- The first is relevant for new products and is called **Peckham's rule.** It describes how a company can attain the maximum market share (Peckham 1981). This assumes that there is a clear relationship between the SOV and the market share for new products (i.e. higher SOV results in higher market share).
- The second is relevant for established products and is called **Schroer's method**. It concerns strategic choice based on the company's relative market share to improve its position in the category.

MATTER OF FACT

Peckham's Rule – For New Products

As a result of an in-depth survey of over 200 brands, Peckham concluded that the company should go for an SOV that is 1.5 times the desired market share. If the desired market share is 25%, the SOV should thus be $1.5 \times 25 = 37.5\%$. All things being equal, the company is likely to reach its maximum market share within two years.

However, the relationship between these two factors can often be imperfect and this can be influenced by how many competitors exist in the category (i.e. the more established competitors there are, the lower is the ceiling for the new company's market share). There is empirical evidence from several product categories that shows how difficult it is to exceed the 'ceiling effect' and this implies that to go for a market share above the ceiling would be a waste of money.

The rule of thumb says that if the company has an SOV of 37.5%, its market share in two years will likely be 25%. But this is assuming that the ceiling of the maximum market share is not below 25%, because, if the ceiling is lower, the market share in two years' time will be identical to the ceiling for maximum market share. In that case, the company has spent money unnecessarily. Therefore, it may be valuable to first calculate what market share the company can hope for based on the competitive situation in the category. Let us see how such a calculation is conducted.

Example – Calculating the maximum market share

A simple rule of thumb for the relationship between the number of competitors and expected market share in business-to-business and business-to-consumer markets is that the competitor who entered the market just before the new company will have a 1.41 times larger market share than the new company (for grocery products, this number should be adjusted to 1.09). This builds on empirical evidence that there are 'natural' market structures; that is, distributions of market shares that are common to many markets (Buzzell 1981).

The competitor who entered the market just before the nearest competitor (and now is the third last newcomer) will in turn have a $1.41 \times 1.41 = 1.41^2$ times larger market share than the new company, and so forth. Based on this, expected market share can be calculated.

The new company's expected market share = $100/1 + 1.41 + 1.41^2 + \ldots 1.41^x$) where x is the number of established competitors in the market. The formula can be summarised as:

$y = 1/ (1 + \Sigma 1.41^x)$, where y is the newcomer's maximum market share and x is the number of existing competitors in the market.

If, for example, a hi-fi brand enters the market as number 3, it can expect a market share of $100/(1 + 1.41 + 1.41^2) = 23\%$. To reach the position in two years the company should invest in an SOV of $23 \times 1.5 = 34.5\%$.

Source: Buzzell (1981).

MATTER OF FACT

Schroer's Method – For Established Products

Schroer's method (Schroer 1990) is designed for mature categories characterised by a number of established companies. As in Peckham's rule, the method uses the empirical relationship between SOV and market share, but this time concentrates on how established companies can gain market share from each other. The method requires information regarding different competitors' SOV and market share.

To compete by increasing SOV may be very costly and result in escalating spending wars between competitors with domination derived from the highest SOV being more expensive than most companies can afford, worse if the market is large. Schroer's method focuses on getting around this problem by advocating the finding of strategic opportunities in smaller (sub) markets and by observing the competitors' market shares and SOV. Instead of working on global or continental markets, the company should concentrate its strategy on national or even regional markets.

Firstly, this lowers the costs for achieving a high or even dominant SOV. Secondly, the strategic options increase. Since we are now talking about smaller (sub) markets, the flexibility increases and the company can move more quickly. In addition, it is more difficult for competitors to defend themselves. In a large market, the market leader can normally hold its own by spending more money on advertising than the others. And the market leader may also more easily notice when someone is trying to achieve a dominant SOV as advertising spend is noticeably high. In smaller markets, companies can make investments that are not as noticeable for the market leader but still get strong effects.

Schroer's method comprises four courses of action summarised in the table below.

	Biggest competitor in the market	
	SOV < Market share	SOV > Market share
Follower	**Attack:** go for high SOV, preferably two times the competitor's SOV	**Niche:** reduce expenses and focus on small market niche
Market leader	**Maintain:** go for SOV = Market share	**Defend:** increase SOV to the same level as the competitor

Growing market share through SOV

Source: adapted from Schroer (1990).

As we can see, the company's strategy is affected by both its own position in the market (market leader or a follower) and how large the biggest competitor's SOV is in the market. The company can use this advantage (or alternatively deal with a disadvantage) by increasing or decreasing spend on SOV. Let us study the four courses of action mentioned above and examine the strategies for each cell.

- **Attack:** the objective here is to increase salience to the point where a company takes over as market leader. When the market leader has a low SOV relative to its market share, this may be possible by identifying a smaller market where the market leader is not so visible; the company may get a dominant SOV and, as a result, strongly increase its salience. The company should use its flexibility and focus in the specific market to strongly increase its SOV. By achieving a powerful SOV increase, the company can achieve huge impact in a short period of time, and before the market leader reacts. This makes it easier to defend the position later when the biggest competitor raises its SOV as a response.
- **Niche:** sometimes, however, it is too difficult to compete with an aggressive market leader who will have greater resources through economies of scale and have more cost-effective advertising. Schroer's method encourages looking for smaller parts of the market where competitors are not that active: that is, find a niche. This can be done in two ways: divide the market into several, more manageable, less general submarkets; or identify a niche in the existing market and go for a differentiated strategy (see Chapter 6 for a full explanation of this approach).
- **Defend:** if the largest competitor is aggressive in the money spent on advertising, the market leading company must react to defend its position. Although advertising effects are short term, it is important to have continued media presence to sustain a high salience. The most important measure is how large the competitor's SOV is compared to the company's. As long as the competitor's advertising expenditure is lower than the company's, it is sufficient to keep the SOV at the same level as the market share. By doing this, the company may automatically keep its market leading position without losing market share. However, if the competitor's SOV exceeds the company's SOV, the company should raise its SOV to match the competitor's (more than that is not needed since the market leader has an advantage, see above).
- **Maintain:** as long as the competitors do not invest in increased market shares through increased advertising expenditure, there is no reason for the company to extend media expenditure. The company should keep its SOV at the same level as the market share to deter competitors or potential new entrants from attacks. If a market leader in this situation invests aggressively to further increase market share, costs will be higher than benefits. As low brand awareness isn't an issue, and most customers have already decided for or against the brand, it may be difficult to gain market shares for a market leader in a mature market.

The options for effectively deploying expenditure to protect or increase market share are therefore (see Figure 13.2):

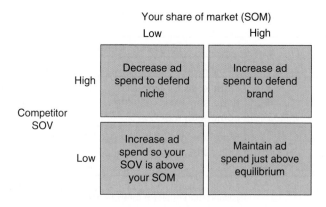

Figure 13.2: Options for effectively deploying expenditure to protect or increase market share

- Where our SOM is low, and competitor SOV is low, we could increase expenditure above our SOM to try and maintain or even increase our market share.
- Where our SOM is low, and competitor SOV is high, we could decrease expenditure to defend our niche market.
- Where our SOM is high, and competitor SOV is low, if we maintain expenditure just above equilibrium, this may maintain or increase SOM.
- Where our SOM is high, and competitor SOV is also high, we need to defend the brand and therefore an increase in our expenditure will be required.

ASYMMETRIC COMPETITION

It is important to note that Schroer's method assumes that the competition in the market is symmetric. That means that company A's advertising benefits company A and hurts company B. However, this may not always be the case. Figure 13.3 lists four different modes of competition (adapted from Yoo and Mandhachitara 2003).

Symmetric competition is most common in mature markets that are not growing, where one brand's win is another brand's loss. SOV is a simple tool to work with in these markets.

Synergy competition is common in growing markets. In these markets, all advertising (regardless of sender) may be beneficial to all brands, as they accelerate market growth. The recommendation here could be to either not outspend competitors (better to allow the competitors to sell your product as well as theirs), or to use SOV as a means to take the larger share of a growing market and secure an advantageous position that is useful when the market has stopped growing. A smaller budget would suggest the former strategy, whilst a larger budget could enable the latter.

Advertiser's advantage The advertiser gains from competitor's expenditure	**Synergy competition** Both brands gain
Symmetric competition Companies gain solely from own expenditure	**Competitor's advantage** Competitor gains from advertiser's expenditure

Figure 13.3: Effect of competitor's expenditure on advertiser

Source: adapted from Yoo and Mandhachitara (2003).

MATTER OF FACT

The Relationship between SOV and SOM

Data from 117 product categories in 23 countries, collected by Jones (1990), reveal that most brands have SOV fairly close to their market shares (SOM), but the relationships are not perfect. Typically, smaller brands have SOV that are higher than their SOM. On average, brands with market shares below 20% have SOV > SOM and brands with market shares

(Continued)

above 20% have SOV < SOM. The data show that when the SOV falls below 4 percentage points from SOM (for instance, if a company with a 23% market share has an SOV of 18.5%), market shares decline. Comparing brands with rising and declining market shares, and with high or low prices, the following patterns were found:

	% of all brands	% of brands with SOV < SOM	% of brands with SOV > SOM
Rising market share	43%	39%	49%
Static market share	26%	28%	24%
Falling market share	31%	33%	27%
Above average price	32%	28%	37%
Average price	51%	54%	46%
Below average price	17%	18%	17%

The relationship between SOV and SOM

Source: Jones (1990).

In a situation where the advertiser has advantage – gaining from competitors' advertising, but not 'leaking' its own expenditure to competitors – the company can reduce its desired SOV as per Peckham's and Schroer's rules. This situation is most common for market leading brands. When there is a competitor advantage – where the advertiser's expenditure 'leaks' to competitors, and the competitors' expenditure hurts the company – the sender's position in the market and its employed message must first be scrutinised.

MATTER OF FACT

The Relationship between SOV and Profitability

In a study of the performances of 227 consumer businesses over seven years, US researchers Paul Farris and David Reibstein found that company profits (measured as return on investment) were higher the closer the fit between SOV and price levels (a high fit means that both SOV and price are high or low, whereas a low fit means a high SOV and low price, or vice versa). This relationship was especially important for mature markets, for companies with high market shares, and in categories with high product quality. On average, the returns on investment were:

SOV–price fit	Return on investment (ROI)
Perfect	15.76%
High	12.10%
Medium	10.28%
Low	5.86%

The relationship between SOV and profitability

> The results suggest that, for example, highly priced products that are backed up by high advertising expenditure produce high pay-offs. Highly priced products at low SOV will not generate enough sales, and low product prices may not yield enough returns to justify high advertising expenditure.
>
> *Source:* Farris and Reibstein (1979).

MEDIA PLANNING OBJECTIVES

Media objectives describe the aims of planning in presenting target audiences with opportunities to see and to engage with the intended message. Reach and frequency – which indicate the depth and breadth of message parameters – are the key measures of media planning success and therefore constitute the main objectives.

The 'coverage area' of a medium refers to distribution space: the area where the medium is distributed. However, reach is a truer measure in the sense that it indicates opportunity to see rather than actual exposure to a media vehicle. It is expressed in percentage terms; whereas a magazine may be national, the circulation may indicate that it reaches a smaller percentage of a target audience. TV and radio estimates of reach are based on ratings of programmes; newspapers use circulation; special interest magazines show the likely target market; and poster sites use estimates of traffic flow. With the advent of Internet advertising, the number of website hits or 'impressions' can be used as a target although this does not really allow for duplication of multiple same-person visits.

The waste factor here is the difference between targeted reach and actual reach, which will include non-prospects. So a company expressing an objective of '50 in quarter 1 building gradually to 75 in quarter 4' will be aiming at 50% of the target audience having the opportunity to be exposed to messages and increasing to 75% over the time period of a year.

As we have seen from Chapter 12, exposure is a key element of marketing communications with brand image dependent upon advertising creativity and exposure. If campaign objectives are to create associations and instil brand essence, to explain a complex message, to aid recall or build an overarching brand narrative, then repetition of message is required.

Therefore, frequency is a key media variable. Effective frequency measures the number of times that a message has to be seen to be effective. So, for example, a frequency objective of '4 in quarter 1 building gradually to 10 in quarter 4' will be aiming at four repeats of the advertisement in a particular media vehicle (e.g. *Ideal Homes* magazine) to the target audience increasing to 10 repeats over the time period of a year. Remember that it is not exposure to the advertisement but the vehicle which is being measured here. A frequency objective can be achieved in a number of ways: 'high reach' (large numbers of the target audience being exposed only once) or 'high frequency' (a limited number of people being exposed regularly).

The weight of a media schedule is a combination of reach and frequency and is measured in gross rating points (GRPs), so the objective of 'achieving 500 GRPs within the first period' would indicate the target total exposure (OTSs).

MEDIA SELECTION CRITERIA

Once media objectives are determined, how do we evaluate the different media vehicles which may be used in placing the advertisements? Surmaneck (1995) described the criteria by which these elements could be judged:

- **Audience selectivity:** a measure of the ability of a medium to deliver an appropriate target audience with a minimum of wasted non-prospects.

- **Reach potential:** a measure of the exposure ability of a medium to prospects within the target audience (percentage of the target audience who saw the advertisement at least once during the campaign period).
- **Speed of audience accumulation:** a measure of how long it takes for the medium to accumulate its total audience.
- **Geographic flexibility:** a measure of the medium's flexibility to provide exposure potential in different geographical areas.
- **Advertising exposure control:** a measure of the medium's ability to control when an audience is exposed to advertising in that medium (often referred to as the medium's ability to be 'intrusive').
- **Lead time to buy:** addresses how far in advance advertising space has to be booked before it appears in the medium.

Fill (2002) provides a useful comparison of the various media strengths and weaknesses, shown in Table 13.1.

Type of medium	Strengths	Weaknesses
Print		
Newspapers	Wide reach	Short lifespan
	High coverage	Advertisements get little exposure
	Low costs	Relatively poor reproduction, gives poor impact
	Very flexible	Low attention-getting properties
	Short lead times	
	Speed of consumption controlled by reader	
Magazines	High-quality reproduction which allows high impact	Long lead times
	Specific and specialised target audiences	Visual dimension only
	High readership levels	Slow build-up of impact
	Longevity	Moderate costs
	High levels of information can be delivered	
Television	Flexible format, uses sight, movement and sound	High level of repetition necessary
	High prestige	Short message life
	High reach	High absolute costs
	Mass coverage	Clutter
	Low relative cost so very efficient	Increasing level of fragmentation (potentially)
Radio	Selective audience, e.g. local	Lacks impact
	Low costs (absolute, relative and production)	Audio dimension only

	Flexible	Difficult to get audience attention
	Can involve listeners	Low prestige
Outdoor	High reach	Poor image (but improving)
	High frequency	Long production time
	Low relative costs	Difficult to measure
	Good coverage as a support medium	
	Location oriented	
New media	High level of interaction	Segment specific
	Immediate response possible	Slow development of infrastructure
	Tight targeting	High user set-up costs
	Low absolute and relative costs	Transaction security issues
	Flexible and easy to update	
	Measurable	
Transport	High length of exposure	Poor coverage
	Low costs	Segment specific (travellers)
	Local orientation	Clutter
In-store POP	High attention-getting properties	Segment specific (shoppers)
	Persuasive	Prone to damage and confusion
	Low costs	Clutter
	Flexible	

Table 13.1: Comparison of media

Source: Fill (2002). Reproduced with permission.

MEDIA IN FOCUS

'There are media plans and there are media plans'

The *Campbell Soup Company* has been a major advertiser in the US market for quite some time. Trying to enhance the efficiency (reaching the same effects with smaller budgets) and effectiveness (producing greater effects with the same budgets) of its advertising efforts, it conducted a number of experiments where it shifted advertising spend between time periods, products and media. The results were clear – by changing media plans, the established brand was able to increase sales substantially in a mature market.

(Continued)

Marketing hot soup, the company had always allocated the bulk of advertising expenditure to the winter peak season, although this limited sales and marketing. In a switch of policy, 50% of advertising expenditure was reallocated to the summer 'low season'. Total media budget for the year remained unchanged, and yet sales increased significantly in the summer months and remained constant during the winter 'high season'. Fearing that marketing of new soup products would cannibalise established brands, only 'bestsellers' were marketed. But when *Campbell*'s shifted advertising expenditure from the bestsellers to a new soup product, both the *Campbell* brand and the total soup category sold more. Furthermore, advertising expenditure was reallocated between different media. One experiment moved 25% of the TV budget to outdoor advertising, resulting in increased sales during the campaign period by 8%. Similarly, budgets were alternated between different TV and radio vehicles simultaneously, increasing sales by 12%.

These advertising experiments show that thinking twice in the planning of media may yield substantially better results – because, 'there are media plans and there are media plans'.

Source: Eastlack and Rao (1989).

THE MEDIA BUDGET

The Bellwether report on UK advertising, written by research firm Markit for the IPA (the industry trade body), showed 45% of UK companies had cut media budgets in the first quarter of 2009. Although the decline was slower than the 'annus horribilis' of 2008 (when 49% of companies cut spend and just 7% increased budgets), it was the second steepest decline in its nine-year history, and just 11% of companies said that they intended to increase marketing spend by the end of 2009.

Whilst the IPA report showed that Internet advertising suffered a record reduction, traditional media budgets (for media such as TV, radio and press advertising) took the biggest hit in marketing cutbacks. The IPA report estimates that the fall will be 9.1% this year and a further 0.2% in 2010. Chris Williamson, the Chief Economist at Markit, claimed that, 'Expenditure on all types of marketing and advertising continues to fall at rates that were unprecedented prior to autumn 2008.'

There is all the more need, therefore, for effective and efficient use of expenditure. Added to the fact that, in these days of **media-neutral planning**, decisions about how much should be spent on marketing communications across a specific time period to accomplish specific objectives have taken on a more holistic perspective. The decision now requires the complete planning, coordination and appropriation of fully integrated marketing communications. The media budget is therefore only one element in this all-pervasive planning exercise, involving creative approaches, appropriation of advertising spend across a whole range of traditional and newly emerging non-traditional media, as well as the production costs, and carefully timed communication exposures.

According to Abratt and Cowan (1999), the media budget consists of three interdependent dimensions:

- **frequency:** the amount of times the advertising should be repeated;
- **continuity:** how advertising expenditure should be placed over time; and
- **reach:** how many people should be reached by the campaign.

Dependent upon objectives, the type of brand and product category and competitive dynamics, there may be differently constructed media schedules. The strengths of different schedules are summarised in Figure 13.4.

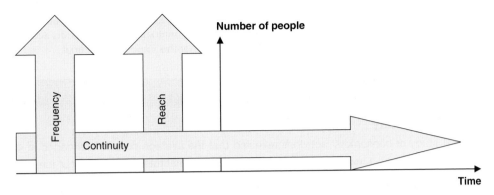

Figure 13.4: The relationships between the three dimensions of frequency, continuity and reach

Source: Dahlen and Lange (2003). *Optimal marknadskommunikation*, Liber Ekonomi. Reproduced with permission.

- The strength of **frequency schedules** lies in reaching the target audience several times and as a consequence achieving stronger target audience impact.
- **Continuity schedules** focus on advertising being spread over time with the main advantage of having a continued presence. However, frequency is relatively low and it is also difficult to reach many people in each individual campaign.
- **Reach schedules,** which are normally very short, are suitable when the company has a large target audience enabling many people to see the advertising. The downside is that a certain degree of frequency is still needed and continuity is limited.

Table 13.2 shows the range of media planning measures which can provide a basis for estimating media budgets in applying costs to achieve marketing communications objectives.

Gross rating points (GRPs) (TVRs for TV)	Gross contacts. Corresponds to the total number of exposures to the advertising
TRP – target rating points	Gross rating points in the target audience
OTS – opportunities to see	Frequency measure of number of exposures per person in a campaign. For radio, it is opportunities to hear
Net reach	The number of people reached by the campaign at least one time. Calculated as GRP/OTS
CPT – cost per thousand	Contact costs. The price for a reach of 1000 people. It is also called CPM
CPP – cost per point	Contact costs for 1% of the audience
3+	A typical measure in, for instance, TV planning. The number of people that have been exposed to the advertising at least three times
Affinity	A measure of how well the media vehicle matches the target audience
Deadweight	A measure of how many people are part of the target audience in two different media

Table 13.2: Media planning budget measures

A modern-day 'wired' consumer will have access to, and be exposed to, more opportunities to see than previous generations of target audience. An analysis of multi-tasking, multimedia activity by Yahoo and OMD (2006) dramatically illustrates the extension of this exposure potential.

MATTER OF FACT

The 43-Hour Day

A global study of consumers' activities revealed that the average person is engaged in 43 hours of activities on a normal day. Media consumption constitutes a major part of the day:

'Essentials' (47%, 20.3 hours):	Media consumption (20%, 8.7 hours):	Technology (18%, 7.9 hours):	Socialising (14%, 6 hours):
Sleep: 7.1 hours	Internet: 3.6 hours	Mobile phone, SMS,	Family: 4.5 hours
Work: 6.4 hours	TV: 2.5 hours	instant messaging,	Friends: 1.5 hours
School: 2.7 hours	Radio: 1.3 hours	email, blogs, MP3	
Chores: 2.9 hours	Newspaper: 0.7 hours	etc.	
Commuting: 1.2 hours	Magazine: 0.6 hours		

The 43-hour media day

Source: Yahoo and OMD (2006).

We have now looked at the choices for allocating the overall media budget based on what the company considers to be an appropriate SOV. A specific **media schedule** is now determined with the objective of getting the best possible returns on media expenditure: in other words, maximum efficiency and effectiveness with minimum waste and cost. Let's start with examining the three key dimensions of the media budget and how they are affected by the media schedule.

MEDIA PLANNING AND SCHEDULING

All advertising has to be placed within media in order for the message to be communicated. To do this, we need to ascertain: how many of the target audience must be reached and when; in which media the advertisements should be placed; how often the target audience should be exposed to the advertising; in which markets and regions advertisements should appear; and how much should be spent. We could spread messages (schedule the exposures) out over the course of the campaign in a number of different ways (Figure 13.5):

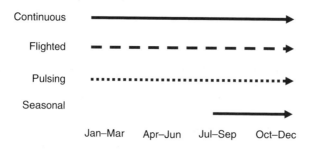

Figure 13.5: Types of media schedule

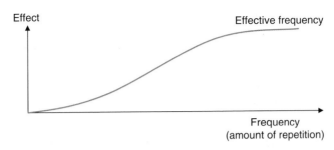

Figure 13.6: The S-curve shows that it takes repeated exposures to attain the desired effect, and after a certain number of exposures, the advertising effect is no longer increasing

Source: Dahlen and Lange (2003). *Optimal marknadskommunikation,* Liber Ekonomi. Reproduced with permission.

- **Continuous frequency schedules** aim to have high frequency (effective impact) with constant exposures in regular slots throughout the period. However, this smoothed exposure frequency may be punctuated by periods characterised by heavier expenditure.
- **Recency or 'flighted' schedules** aim at coordinating exposures just before or at the point of purchase.
- **Pulsing** schedules have an evenly spread, consistent pattern of regular but separated exposures.
- **Blitz or seasonal schedules** refer to the bombardment of the target market with concentrated advertising hits, often when products have a limited sales period (e.g. Christmas toys) or there is need to achieve exposure quickly (e.g. the launch of a new product).

Let's look closely at what these actually mean and how they achieve optimum frequency.

Frequency Schedules

Frequency schedules that have focused on effective frequency and restricted reach and continuity have dominated media schedules since the 1970s. The argument is that it is better to persuade some customers completely than to persuade all customers a little bit. In other words, the target audience is defined narrowly so that more effort is put into advertising that persuades key target prospects. These campaigns are strong and distinct and the advertising is focused on a high SOV. This assumes a spill-over effect from previous campaigns is based on customers' purchase cycle (i.e. the time between two purchases of the product such as the monthly purchase of coffee).

The main objective is **repetition** with effective frequency being the lowest number of advertisement exposures that gives maximum effect. The priority here is to have sufficiently high incidence of advertising which must be done cost effectively without wasting additional spending (Cannon, Leckenby and Abernethy 2002, Krugman 1972, Naples 1997). We can see this demonstrated in Figure 13.6 based on the well-known S-curve, which is normally used to illustrate how advertising effects vary with number of exposures.

How can we determine effective frequency? The 'three hit' decision rule (Krugman 1972) for effective frequency is sometimes called '3+', the target audience being exposed to advertising at least three times[*]:

- The first exposure evokes curiosity, a cognitive 'screening in/screening out' response – 'What is this?'
- The second exposure informs about the product and evokes an evaluative response – 'What of it? Why shall I purchase this product?'
- The third exposure is the true reminder, the reinforcement – 'I will purchase that product!'

---

[*]Additional exposures may be needed to be budgeted into the schedule for target audiences who do not pay careful attention to the advertisements. However, all subsequent exposures are a repeat of the third response.

There are several different factors that affect how many additional exposures are needed. Empirical studies have shown that the effective frequency may be stretched from three to 14 exposures (Naples 1997). This may be dependent upon customer knowledge of the product which will influence effective frequency as familiar brands are more easily recognised than unfamiliar brands. In addition, the effectiveness of different media, communication objectives and how much competitors are spending on advertising will also affect the effective frequency.

MATTER OF FACT

Calculating Effective Frequency

Rossiter and Percy (1998) claim that effective frequency results from a combination of: the impact of the media vehicle (VI); brand awareness (BA) and attitude ($BAtt$); the requirements of the target audience (TA); and the impact of word-of-mouth communications (WOM) in that target audience, described in the following formula:

$$\text{Effective frequency} = 1 + VI(BA + BAtt + TA) - WOM$$

So, if the marketer uses media with low effectiveness (for instance low-impact vehicles) the extra exposures should be doubled. The number of exposures should be increased by two if brand recall is the communication objective or the objective is to enhance brand attitude for a transformational product, since it takes time to build emotion. The less loyal the target audience, the more important it is to add extra exposures to convince them. Finally, the marketer may reduce the frequency by one exposure if the advertising is popular and creates a lot of word of mouth as the audience will act as an accelerator for communications.

In our coffee example, let us take a look at what the effective frequency might have to be for us to achieve our communication objectives. Using TV as a guide, the vehicle impact scores two 'exposures' (i.e. $VI = 2$). The communication objective is recognition, so brand awareness scores zero (i.e. $BA = 0$). We want to enhance the brand attitude and aim for a transformational purchase motivation, 'the coffee from seventh heaven', so brand attitude scores two (i.e. $BAtt = 2$). We want to target favourable brand switchers, so target audience rating is one (i.e. $TA = 1$). The advertising is not very sensational and is unlikely to create 'buzz', so word-of-mouth scores zero (i.e. $WOM = 0$). Therefore, according to Rossiter and Percy (1998), required frequency is calculated as being: $1 + 2(0 + 2 + 1) - 0 = 7$ exposures.

To obtain the highest possible effect we must repeat the coffee advertising so that the target audience is exposed to it at least seven times (but preferably not more, because each additional exposure will be unnecessarily costly) in the next month.

Now let us examine a number of typical frequency schedules. Figure 13.7 shows a basic frequency schedule, distributed evenly over the year, focused on discrete campaigns with high frequency, and shows that the intermediate purchase cycles do not have exposure. The basis for this type of schedule is to have an effective frequency during a number of evenly spread purchase cycles with no advertising in between.

When introducing a new product, the frequency schedule may look like the one in Figure 13.8. The focus here is on getting brand awareness and brand interest quickly. Therefore, a high frequency is kept initially, perhaps over multiple, sequential purchase cycles. After a while, the frequency goes down somewhat and is distributed over more purchase cycles with longer intervals.

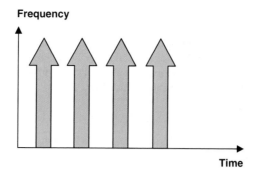

Figure 13.7: A basic frequency schedule

Source: Dahlen and Lange (2003). *Optimal marknadskommunikation,* Liber Ekonomi. Reproduced with permission.

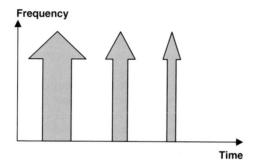

Figure 13.8: Frequency schedule for new product

Source: Dahlen and Lange (2003). *Optimal marknadskommunikation,* Liber Ekonomi. Reproduced with permission.

A frequency schedule may also follow the opposite pattern (as shown in Figure 13.9). This schedule may be used when a new product has to be introduced more slowly. For example, it could be a fashion product or a status product that should initially only be targeted at a limited audience and have exclusive or selective distribution. The objective may be to target innovators and opinion formers who hopefully will spread positive word of mouth. The media choice would have to reflect this and may be limited to more narrow, niche media.

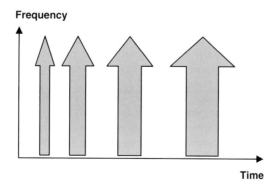

Figure 13.9: Frequency schedule for slow product launch

Source: Dahlen and Lange (2003). *Optimal marknadskommunikation,* Liber Ekonomi. Reproduced with permission.

Similarly, a product with high margins may not be aimed at mass-market distribution but targeted at a smaller, affluent audience. If wider distribution is later required, the advertising intensity increases (and media choice shifts towards broader mass media) so that the advertising covers multiple purchase cycles, more mass market targets and the distance between the discrete media expenditure decreases. In the UK, *BMW* (perhaps encouraged by its success with the populist *Mini*), has started to broaden its appeal to communicate to a bigger audience.

Recency Schedules

In Chapter 11, we described one approach to advertising as it being a 'weak force' (Ehrenberg 1974, 1988). In other words, it doesn't really persuade people to rush out and buy, but it has a primary function of reinforcement and acts as a constant reminder. In other words, it provides a continuous presence as a backdrop to the real sales triggers. This puts the focus on the consumer who filters out messages which are not of interest or relevance to them at the time. This is particularly pertinent to the FMCG packaged goods sector.

In this context, continuity schedules are fast replacing effective frequency as the key media planning model, and have superseded frequency schedules as the dominating media planning tool. The principle of recency – stressing the importance of positioning exposures close to purchase occasion – is gaining wide acceptance and is replacing the 3+ effective frequency threshold principle as a key guideline to help determine media weight levels and scheduling (Reichel and Wood 1997). Reach rather than frequency is the new media planner's mantra, but recency planning does not eliminate frequency: its focus is on providing a continuous media presence (Ephron 1995, Jones 1995, Reichel and Wood 1997), as opposed to impactful 'bursts' of exposure as with frequency schedules. Rather than be seen a lot during specific periods, here advertising is seen a little all of the time and does not have any interruptions to exposure in the schedule. The principle of recency argues powerfully for presence and, therefore, for continuity.

However, our selective perception makes us automatically more attentive and receptive to advertising when we are thinking of making a purchase in a category. The objective of recency schedules is to expose the advertising as close to the end of the purchase cycle as possible. In other words, the advertising should be as near the periods where consumers are ready to purchase. Recency is about advertising influencing the brand choice of consumers who are in the market for the product. Ephron claimed that 'recency isn't about reach and frequency. It's about how we think advertising operates in mature consumer markets. It is relevance, not repetition that makes the message work'.

So, whilst advertising influences purchase, the purpose of recency scheduling is to place the message in that window. Jones (1995) claims that 'a single exposure close to purchase can trigger a response', but what he is really referring to is the **most recent** in a series of exposures. According to Ephron (1997), 'a single exposure is reach, more exposures are frequency', and the importance of continuity instead of flighting is evident. Whilst the effects will diminish after the sales opportunity has gone (the so-called 'lag effect'), there is still a spill-over which contributes to building brand equity, creating awareness and laying the foundation for the next sale. He describes this as the 'soft and hard effects of TV advertising'.

There are two main types of continuity schedule. Figure 13.10 describes a schedule for products that are purchased regularly and when most people buy the product at the same time. When the length of the purchase cycle is known, the number of exposures can be minimised and advertisements placed just before purchase.

Obvious examples of this are wine, soft drinks, chocolates and snacks that are traditionally purchased on Fridays (before a weekend evening at home) and visits to movies, restaurants and night clubs which are likely to be concentrated on Saturdays. Variations in scheduling may be as a result of discovering regularities that may not be as apparent after closer analysis of purchase behaviour. When analysing people's workout habits it may show that a majority of consumers purchase their gym cards on Mondays, when they have a guilty conscience over the weekend's 'excess behaviour' and have therefore decided to start a new, healthy life or even when New Year resolutions are at their peak: 'New Year. New You'.

However, we cannot be sure that it is possible to place the exposure near the end of the purchase cycle for all customers; it may be difficult to get accurate customer purchase behaviour information or a regular purchase pattern may not be obvious. In this case, we cannot base the schedule on purchase

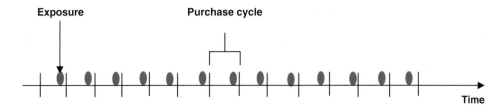

Figure 13.10: An optimal continuity schedule is based on knowledge of purchase cycle
duration and when it starts and ends

Source: Dahlen and Lange (2003). *Optimal marknadskommunikation*, Liber Ekonomi. Reproduced
with permission.

cycles and instead we have to determine a regular interval for exposures. This schedule may look like
the one in Figure 13.11.

Reach Schedules

When continuity suffers because of very expensive scheduling, it may be difficult to reach many
people during a long time period. When the product targets mass markets or when a lot of people
must be reached during a short time period, reach schedules are used (Pedrick and Zufryden 1993).
There are three main ways to attain high reach and these are often combined for maximum effect:

- The first alternative is to use very broad **mass media.** The main advantage is obviously high reach,
  but this is expensive. Both frequency and continuity will be limited and advertising must really grab
  target audience attention during the short time that it is shown.
- Alternatively, high reach may be attained by using **several different media**. Maximum exposure
  contact can be achieved: newspapers reach people in the morning; billboards during the day; TV
  covers the nights but again this may be very expensive.
- Finally, a third alternative to attain high reach is to have a very high frequency during a short period.
  This has been referred to as **blitz** or **burst schedules** and this type of scheduling is characterised
  by the target audience being bombarded with advertising. The extremely high frequency increases
  the probability that everyone in the target audience will see the advertising as the possible exposure contact points increase throughout the day.

As we have seen, with three alternative media schedules to choose from, selecting the right media
schedule is a vital part of effective advertising. Do we build up increased exposure over time (frequency
schedule)? Do we keep a low frequency but constant 'drip-drip' effect, with short bursts right before a
purchase (continuity schedule)? Or do we go for immediate target audience impact and focus on getting
as many people aware of the brand as quickly as possible (reach schedule)? How do we know which
is most appropriate? These different effects can be summarised and explained by two mechanisms that
affect our advertising receptiveness, namely **wear-in** and **wear-out** effects (Tellis 1997, Dahlén 2001).

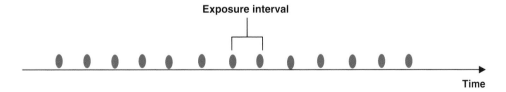

Figure 13.11: If the customers' purchase cycle cannot be mapped, there must be regular
exposure intervals that are relatively tight

Source: Dahlen and Lange (2003). *Optimal marknadskommunikation*, Liber Ekonomi. Reproduced with
permission.

Advertising Wear-In and Wear-Out – Choosing the Right Schedule

We have looked at the effect of **repetition** in advertising effectiveness in Chapter 12. The gradual, repetitive build-up in a schedule is referred to as 'wear-in' meaning that the advertising must be 'worn in' to be effective. Effectiveness increases in two ways: firstly, the advertising gets more and more attention as people see it more often (based on the fact that people's selective perception makes it easier for us to recognise things that seem familiar); and secondly, the advertising is better received and more positively accepted and favourably evaluated when it is worn in.

On the other hand, when advertisements are placed too closely together, or multiple messages compete for consumers' attention, message impact may be lost in advertising clutter. Whilst increasing the amount of advertising may increase audience penetration, there is a diminishing returns effect caused by 'advertising saturation'. Equally, this applies to the effect on sales: any linear increase in advertising exposure over threshold levels does not have a similar linear impact on demand.

Furthermore, a process of **adaptation** may take place where consumers become so familiar with an advertisement that they stop paying attention and impact is lost. Advertising effect for familiar brands may wear out quickly; consumers may become bored, uninterested or even irritated (Tellis 1997, Dahlén 2001), whilst unfamiliar brands do not suffer from diminishing advertising impact or individual consumer boredom (Tellis 1997, Machleit, Allen and Madden 1993). This phenomenon is called 'wear-out' and is the decay or 'lagged' component of advertising, diminishing the exposure effect.

Broadbent (1985) described this as 'adstock' (effects decaying), which can be mathematically modelled and is usually expressed in terms of the 'half-life' of the advertising using TV gross rating points (GRP). Academic research on wear-out phenomena describes a 'two-week half-life', meaning that it takes two weeks for the awareness effect of an advertisement to decay to half its present level, usually over 7–12 weeks. Practitioners estimate this to be within 2–5 weeks with the average for FMCG brands being 2.5 weeks.

People tend to react negatively to advertising the more times they have seen it and soon perceive old stimuli as irritating, and response to advertising dissipates rapidly. Wear-in and wear-out are two opposite effects. The former suggests a higher frequency as advertising effectiveness increases with the number of exposures. The latter suggests a lower frequency as advertising effectiveness decreases with the number of exposures. The two effects can be summarised as in Figure 13.12.

Which one of the two effects is stronger? It has been demonstrated that the effects are different for familiar and unfamiliar brands. For familiar brands, advertising has a quick wear-in period. People recognise the brand and are therefore likely to pay more attention (see Chapter 12). Moreover, they have an established view of the brand, which makes them react positively from the beginning. However, news value is limited and, as a result, consumers can become quickly bored. In other words, the advertising has a quick wear-out.

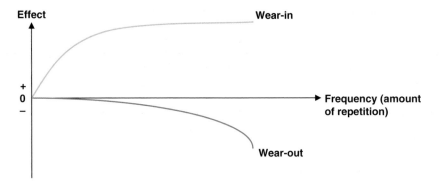

Figure 13.12: Wear-in and wear-out effects

Source: Dahlen and Lange (2003). *Optimal marknadskommunikation*, Liber Ekonomi. Reproduced with permission.

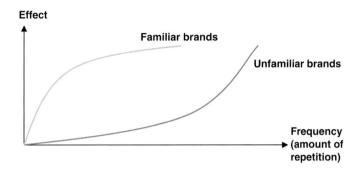

Figure 13.13: The effect of advertising on familiar and unfamiliar brands

Source: Dahlen and Lange (2003). *Optimal marknadskommunikation*, Liber Ekonomi. Reproduced with permission.

Unfamiliar brands, on the other hand, are worn in slowly. Brand familiarity takes time, thus building increasing attention and limiting wear-out effects. The differences are illustrated in Figure 13.13.

Advertising for familiar brands quickly has an effect. But the effect also declines very quickly, as the wear-out effects are strong. Advertising for unfamiliar brands needs longer time to get a strong effect. But the effect is sustained for some time and increases dramatically when the advertising starts to get the wear-in effects.

It is worth noting that **spacing** (the time interval between exposures) may yield different effects for familiar and unfamiliar brands (Campbell *et al.* 2003). When exposures are spaced closely, the message should preferably be varied between exposures (see Chapter 12), to increase differential attention and encoding variability. This is especially important when the spacing is very tight (for example, more than five times during an evening in front of the TV), as the repeated advertising for particularly unfamiliar brands generates irritation.

Besides brand familiarity, there are two additional factors that affect wear-in and wear-out effects: message complexity and news value of the message. If the message is complex, more time is needed for the cumulative wear-in effects to occur. With high involvement, complex buying decisions, more exposures have to be scheduled for message content to be received and absorbed. Equally, complex messages also take more time to wear out – there is always something new to experience and learn, whereas simple messages have the opposite effect as people perceive and understand the message quickly and soon get tired of the advertising. If a message has high news value, our selective perception automatically ensures that the advertising gets our attention, we think that advertising with news value is more exciting and we do not get tired of it as quickly.

Therefore, frequency schedules should be used for the advertising:

- When a **new brand** is created or when an existing brand is introduced to a **new target audience**, frequency should be high. The target audience must get the three fundamental exposures to become curious, well-informed and convinced to purchase the product.
- When the **message is complex**, it is also important to give the target audience enough time to process the advertising. This should be particularly relevant for complex products, for example political parties and publicity/public education messages, and technical products.
- It may be appropriate with a high frequency to wear in a **new advertising message**, for instance when a brand is repositioned.

Continuity schedules should be used for the advertising:

- When familiar brands are noticed easily and people already have some sort of relationship with them. Therefore, three fundamental exposures are not necessary for the target audience to experience. A recency schedule is best for this, using the **existing relationship to trigger brand purchase**.

- When the message is simple, repetitive exposure is not necessary. In a situation like this, the important thing is not to promote a specific message but to make the brand prominent and visible in the market. Familiar brands have **building salience** as a main communication objective (see Chapter 12).
- When the message is well established, no specific learning period is needed. It is instead more important to **avoid target audience boredom and irritation**.

Reach schedules are appropriate in two special cases:

- Products with a very short life cycle (often called fads). When a product like this is introduced, it is necessary to get maximum effect in a short time, before the fad is over. Examples of fads are the yo-yo (which comes and goes, is popular and then forgotten), unusual toys like the *Tamagotchi* (a digital pet in pocket size that was popular during the 1990s), and some fashion clothes like *Ugg Boots*. Reach schedules are highly appropriate for these products as it is important to quickly reach as many people as possible and get them to make a purchase. Sometimes, repeat purchases are very rare, and therefore it is enough to reach the target audience during one purchase cycle.
- A reach schedule may also be appropriate when the brand has no competition in a radically new product category. By using a reach schedule, high awareness of the category can quickly be attained and simultaneously brand salience can be created. In this way, the marketer may hopefully create strong demand quickly (and get large production volumes) and at the same time create a strong position in the product category. This may lead to an ideal competitive situation when the product category is expanded. Lange and Dahlén (2003) examine the use of incongruence and increased salience in advertising to extend the wear-out threshold and increase impact. Corkindale and Newall (1978) see the phenomenon of advertising wear-in and wear-out as corresponding to the budget questions of 'How little can we spend/How infrequently can we advertise?' and 'How much is too much/How infrequently is too little?'

CREATIVE MEDIA PLANNING

Media planning tends to follow certain deep-rooted heuristics:

- the choice of well-established and broad media;
- gear plans to maximising SOV and to dominate media;
- concentrate advertising spend in time periods with the greatest product demand.

However, media planning can require lateral thinking and a creative approach to the use of media in order to maximise use of resources. There are studies showing that marketers can obtain considerably stronger effects, or obtain the same effect at lower costs, by breaking the established rules and heuristics and instead be creative in the media planning process (e.g. Eastlack and Rao 1989, Law 2002).

Some creative media tools which may offer more cost-effectiveness are:

- **Using more media.** Re-appropriation of advertising funds can change the complexion of a schedule. Instead of placing the majority of the media budget in one media vehicle, for example, TV, spread expenditure on several different media. This has several advantages:
  - more contact points are established to the target audience;
  - advertising can create more associations through the distinct media used;
  - advertising durability may be increased and it is possible to get a stronger effect from each exposure;
  - instead of 'harassing' the target audience with three exposures during the same TV night, exposures could be one TV commercial at night, one billboard in the morning, and one newspaper advertisement in the afternoon.
- **Scheduling media close to physical purchase environment.** In the section on continuity schedules the use of recency planning was discussed. It builds on timing the advertising near the

purchase. But it is also possible to work with physical proximity by selecting appropriate media. It has been shown that billboards outside retail stores are much more effective than TV commercials and newspaper advertising, due to the fact that they are so close to the place where the purchase decision is made.

- **Employing 'countercyclical' advertising.** The 'normal' rule is to advertise when demand is greatest; advertising expenditure is at its highest during peak season (e.g. hot summer days for summer products; Fridays for weekend-related products). However, advertising clutter is greatest during this period and media saturation means that it is much more expensive to obtain a high SOV. There is an opportunity to get a lead over the competitors, build a dominant SOV and establish brand salience. This 'countercyclical' expenditure may be the best option for a category expansion as the overall demand increases between peak seasons.
- **Launching new products as a form of media enhancement.** The media plan can play a vital role in establishing high levels of awareness for newly launched products or services. Conversely, launching new products can stimulate media interest. Instead of wearing out advertising for the product in search of a dominant SOV, the company may launch products aimed at capturing buzz and generating media interest. *Sprite* may for instance launch *Sprite Ultra* and gain increased media attention (new product and new message) and the brand overall (*Sprite*) gets increased shelf space in stores.

An example of both countercyclical advertising and launching products for the media can be seen with Swedish ice cream giant *GB*. In 2004, *GB* wanted to increase sales during the winter season (which is quite long in Nordic Sweden and therefore not good for ice cream business). First, it advertised countercyclically, moving part of the media budget from summer to winter. This increased sales to a certain level. However, to increase the impact of advertising, a special Christmas 'seasonal' ice cream (gingerbread flavour) was launched and this was successful and quickly followed by yet another Christmas seasonal brand (with saffron flavour).

Media can be used in a variety of creative ways to enhance effectiveness. This *McDonald's* billboard shows its range of products and highlights different products throughout the course of the day. As the sun moves across the sky, the fork placed above the billboard casts a shadow pointing to the right product at the right time.

McDonalds' natural selection

MEDIA IN FOCUS

Mixed Media Schedules

Adding magazines to a media schedule instead of just more TV can have a more powerful effect on impact and effectiveness. In a 2001 econometric study by *MMA*, findings showed that the impact can be synergistic and 'nourish' the effects of TV advertising. Research on over 90 brands concluded that print advertising had a 'multiplier-media effect' which:

- improved the learning effect, leading to more intensive perception of the advertising which encouraged more response to TV appeals resulting in better recall and richer TV content;
- created a transfer of credibility and better balance between information-centred, factual print advertisements and more emotional TV advertising;

(Continued)

- led to viewing TV advertisements in a different way and supported the product claims and/or minimised any doubt about the commercial's claims;
- added extra information or messages;
- strengthened brand identification; and,
- offered scope for product-oriented messages and promoted action.

A landmark study by Millward Brown (1994) claimed that magazine advertising creates awareness levels of 13% per 100 GRPs, exactly the same as TV, but at significantly lower costs (up to three times less expensive).

A mixed media schedule delivered substantially more coverage and frequency, arguably offering support for brands above the line for longer or for a higher weight of communication. Research by Mercury Associates (2004) showed an 84% target audience coverage was enhanced to 92% by mixing women's magazines with TV (see figure below).

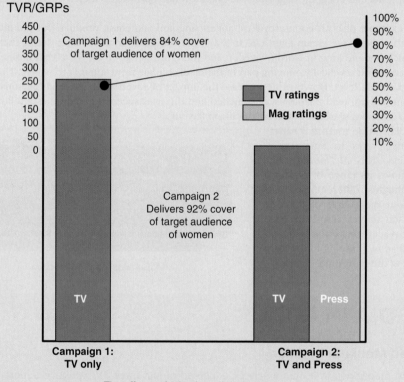

The effects of mixed media schedules

Source: Mercury Associates (2004) (adapted courtesy of PPA Marketing).

INTEGRATED MARKETING COMMUNICATIONS

Marketing communications attempts to affect an audience response either rationally or emotionally. Objectives are written as either 'hard' or 'soft' goals such as attitudinal and behavioural, which then translate into awareness, column inches, evoked and consideration sets, leads, conversations and coupon responses. Traditionally, agencies have had what Jenkinson (2006) refers to as a 'monotelic'

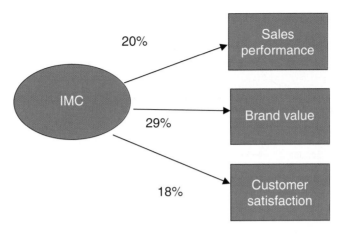

Figure 13.14: Impact of integrated marketing communications

Source: adapted from Reid (2005).

(single-goaled) approach to marketing communication objectives, matching media to message intent and outcome. Positive brand awareness is usually best achieved through TV exposure; direct mail is particularly good for disseminating information and generating sales leads. Research has shown otherwise in some cases: *VW Passat* assigned the job of building positive brand awareness to TV but actually saw a huge impact on sales; UK pharmacist *Boots* saw that direct mail in the form of a brochure was more effective than TV in building brand attitudes. So, do we use different media for different messages or adopt a multimedia approach to schedules requiring a 'politelic' approach to objectives?

As suggested above, in order to achieve multiple exposures, rather than repetitions in the same medium, it may be more effective to use a more integrated approach to planning marketing communications. The employment of several media, and indeed several elements of the marketing communications mix, is often referred to as **integrated marketing communications** (IMC). An IMC approach needs to coordinate all brand encounters, medium or message, which contribute to building the brand narrative. Therefore, by integrating all messages and all message sources, the organisation can produce powerful, comprehensive brand communications that reach the target audience in a greater number of ways and provide mutual company/customer benefits. A recent industry spin on this is the notion of media-neutral planning – or even more recently 'trans-media planning' – which attempts to view all media and creative elements from a user's perspective in order to maximise involvement and response across different media and all brand encounters. This is in accordance with the development and maintenance of an overarching brand narrative.

Figure 13.14 outlines the results from a study of IMC effects on 169 Australian consumer goods and service organisations (Reid 2005).

IMC was measured as the usage and integration of several message sources within and outside the company. On average, the effective employment of IMC was found to increase reported sales performance (in terms of market share, growth and profitability) by 20%, brand value (in terms of brand awareness, price levels and ease of distribution) by 29% and customer satisfaction by 18%.

Figure 13.15 illustrates the effects of IMC from an audience perspective (adapted from Chang and Thorson 2004). Comparing unique exposures in different media (IMC) with the same amount of (repeated) exposures in the same media, research has shown that people process the message differently.

When exposed to different media, people focus more on the message, and think more carefully and favourably about the content when forming their evaluations (similar to the central processing route in the ELM model presented in Chapter 11). When repeatedly exposed to the same medium, consumers rely more on their previous experiences of the sender and its communication, think less of the message (similar to the peripheral processing route in the ELM model) and form less favourable associations. IMC thus engages consumers more and puts the actual message across with greater impact.

Unique exposures in different media

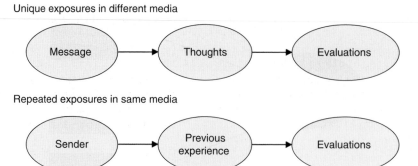

Repeated exposures in same media

Figure 13.15: Exposures in media

Source: adapted from Chang and Thorson (2004).

In Japan, many TV commercials point the audience towards a website for further interaction, by ending the commercial with a scene in which one or a few search words are typed in a search engine. The search words are supposed to be easier to remember than a website address. Furthermore, teaching the audience the search words that will list the sender first in a search engine is also a good strategy considering that search words are becoming increasingly important on the Internet, which is the fastest-growing advertising medium (see Chapter 14). Many Japanese billboards have special, coded pictures, which the audience can photograph with their mobile phones in order to automatically log onto the sender's web or wap (mobile web) site.

In the mid 2000s, the accessories retailer *Glitter* made an effort to enhance its integrated marketing communications. Realising that its stores and personnel are the retailer's main communications medium, *Glitter* developed a so-called 'brand book'. A brand book is a manual that describes what the brand stands for, how it is handled and communicated, and how everyone who is involved with the brand should act as representatives of the brand. *Glitter* developed a brand book that was a cross between comic book, scrapbook and magazine, to give everybody in the organisation a genuine feel for the brand. Being a very original and appealing way of communicating with those who actually handle the retailer's business, *Glitter*'s brand book won creative awards for business-to-business advertising.

CLOSING CASE STUDY

Barack Obama: BlackBerry and the Social Pulpit – Deconstructing Barack Obama's Use of Social Media

According to Krempasky (2009, http://issuu.com/edelman_pr), 'Barack Obama wants to be the first President to govern with BlackBerry in hand; he will certainly be the first with a legion of 13 million advocates at his fingertips'. His historic 2009 landslide victory owed much to the way his team galvanised and empowered evangelical volunteers to spread the gospel of 'Change' and engage ordinary US citizens in the biggest conversation ever witnessed. Krempasky refers to 'force multipliers' created by combining micro-targeting with the online advocacy which could only have been facilitated

The President's media presence

by the knowledge and use of technologically advanced social media. What the Obama team did was use media beyond traditional communication methods, but they also adhered to the well-established principles of customer relationship management. The combination of online media engagement and offline canvassing activity was the key.

Roosevelt's 'bully pulpit' (not as we would know the term today but meaning 'wonderful platform') has now become a 'social pulpit', allowing Obama a unique opportunity to engage and galvanise 'spheres of cross influence'. Figure 13.16 depicts Edelman's (2009, http://issuu.com/edelman_pr) 'Public Engagement Model' showing multiplicity of stakeholder audiences/participants. The traditional one-way, top down transmitted communication model has been replaced by a 360-degree conversation with which everyone has the potential to join in and create the message as well as disseminate it. For example, *Change.gov*, a website designed to keep the conversation going past the election, allows continual contact post-election. Placing speeches and announcements on sites like *YouTube* before traditional media release engenders ownership as well as mass circulation. Obama will allow a five-day feedback period before any official announcements are made and this adds to the feeling of democratic involvement. This has echoes of Clinton's 'Permanent Campaign' and Blair's 'Big Conversation' which did not differentiate between campaigning and governing. Needham (2005) describes how the seamless, continuous use of marketing communications after the one-off 'transaction' of their respective election to office was successfully augmented by media activities to retain customer loyalty right through to the next election. Obama's team acknowledge that continuous exposure in all media is a 'process seeking to manipulate sources of public approval to engage in the act of governing itself' (Heclo 2000, p. 17).

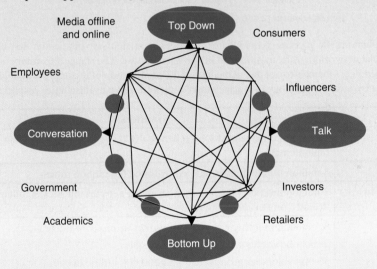

Figure 13.16: Public engagement model: spheres of cross influence

Source: Edelman (2009).

Edelman (2009) describes tiers of engagement which echo the traditional sales and relationship models used to illustrate movement of loyalty. The Obama team understood the need to offer various, flexible levels of commitment and involvement, from the casual enquirer to the hard-core advocates. As the supporter progresses metaphorically up the ladder, each level requires different commitment and service. The Obama campaign offered tailored options: *Personal*: 'befriending' Obama on a social network, signing up for SMS and email contact, donating and registering to vote; *Social*: joining or even creating groups for support and dissemination of

(Continued)

communication to others; and *Advocate*: write blogs, create UGC videos, host an offline event, ask others to start the process of registering, donating, spreading the word (Figure 13.17).

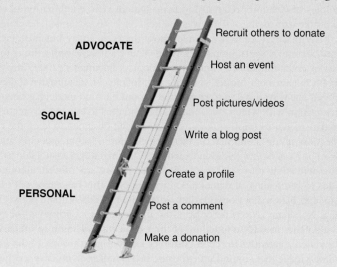

Figure 13.17: Obama's social media CRM ladder

Source: Edelman (2009).

The phenomenal success of the Obama 'Change' campaign saw him as the first BlackBerry-toting, social networking African American in the White House. The staggering numbers shown in Table 13.3 reflect Obama's use of digital media and the exploitation of the unprecedented potential of social networking technology to engage target audiences and galvanise voter potential.

Media type	Numbers
Email	13 million on email list who received 7000 variations of more than 1 billion emails
Donors	3 million online donors who contributed 6.5 million times
Social networks	5 million 'friends' on more than 15 social networking sites; 3 million 'friends' on *Facebook* alone
Website	8.5 million monthly visits to *MyBarackObama.com* (at peak) 2 million profiles with 400,000 blog posts 35,000 volunteer groups that held 200,000 offline events 700,000 fundraising hubs that raised $30 million
Video	Nearly 2000 official *YouTube* videos watched more than 80 million times with 135,000 subscribers 442,000 user-generated videos on *YouTube*
Mobile	3 million people signed up for the text-messaging programme, each receiving 5 to 20 monthly messages
Phone calls	3 million personal phone calls made in the last three days before election

Table 13.3: Obama's use of media to engage target audiences

Source: Edelman (2009).

QUESTIONS

1. What are the key integrated communication elements which reinforce the 'Change' positioning of the Obama campaign?

2. What does the Public Engagement Model have to offer as a concept for reaching audiences in consumer markets?

3. Is this successful exposition of online and offline marketing communications sustainable or do you think it was of its time and can't be repeated?

CHAPTER SUMMARY

This chapter looked at the principles of media planning and the range of media tools available to assist in this process: the basic concepts and terminology of the media planning process.

We saw that, as marketing communications requires the integration of all communication elements, there is an equal need for a comprehensive knowledge of the media channels used to carry all communication messages.

The media planning process included assessments of all brand encounters which deliver dialogue to key stakeholders in mass or specialised audiences. On a 'macro' level, the marketer must decide upon the total amount of communication that is needed to reach the set objectives; on a 'micro' level, the marketer must determine the allocation of communication resources over time and between media, as well as taking target groups, market situation, competitors, and product and message characteristics into account.

It was seen as important that we need to assess different approaches and methods of planning media, some of which may be mixed media schedules. The need for accurate media budgeting, especially in an uncertain marketplace, was of paramount importance in order to maximise effectiveness and efficiency of advertising expenditure.

Finally, a range of creative ways for enhancing the effectiveness of traditional media plans was investigated and the reasons how and why the use of multiple media could aid integrated marketing communications were discussed.

REFLECTIVE QUESTIONS

a. The market leader in the coffee category announces that it will cut advertising costs for the rest of the year (SOV significantly lower than SOM), what should the number 3 brand in the market do with its SOV? Why? What are the conditions for your recommendation?

b. Calculate what SOV you think a new regional bank should use for its launch, (i) with three existing competitors; (ii) with five existing competitors.

c. What media schedule do you think would be suitable for the launch of a new sports car? Would media schedules differ if the brand was unfamiliar or if the brand was, say, *Mercedes-Benz*?

d. What effective frequency would you use when advertising an established shampoo brand in magazines to brand switchers? On TV to other brand loyals?

e. How could creative media planning be used to increase communication effectiveness for a quit-smoking campaign?

RESEARCH PROJECTS

Look up Abratt and Cowan's 1999 paper on 'Client–Agency Perspectives of Information Needs for Media Planning' published in the *Journal of Advertising Research* (39(6), 37–52) and evaluate why the need for information is important in media planning.

Compare a mixed media campaign to a campaign using just one media vehicle.

CHAPTER 14

PUBLIC RELATIONS AND HYBRID MARKETING COMMUNICATIONS

"The findings indicate that brand positioning is perhaps the most misguided marketing idea in the last 30 years."
Advertising Research Foundation (2007)

This chapter focuses on public relations (PR) and hybrid communications. All stakeholders of an organisation can affect, or be affected by, the organisation's strategic and tactical implementation of marketing communications. Target audiences for PR are therefore wider than existing or potential customers, and the protection of the organisation's image and reputation must be applied to all stakeholders.

Hybrid communications, on the other hand, can be directed at customers and stakeholders, but may not be perceived as communications sent from the company. There is an intertextual aspect of this type of marketing communications which overlaps with other areas and may originate (or in some cases appear to originate) from different sources. Marketing communications is often not directly aimed at selling the company's product, but enhancing or maintaining corporate image and reputation.

For example, communications not explicitly sent from an organisation may include 'stealth' marketing, cross-cultural communications (such as celebrity endorsement) as well as cross-discipline communications which overlap, such as 'advertorial' hybrids of PR and advertising, product placement and sponsorship, and the combination of selling and exhibitions.

The maintenance of an organisation's reputation amongst its 'publics' is a vital corporate asset; as a result, reputation management is the core focus of public relations (PR). It is what Eisenegger (2005, p. 1) refers to as 'reputation nurturing' and describes a process of promoting and fostering all 'material and symbolic elements' (Pieckza 2006, p. 291) which may affect the organisation's well-being.

Therefore, the building of brand image and the creation positive associations is essential to the underpinning of brand equity, customer loyalty and indeed the growth of the company. PR, as a vital component of integrated marketing communications, has a strategic role to play in managing the 'intangible side of the business' through assisting in building relationships with customers and other stakeholders (Reid 2003).

The Chartered Institute of Public Relations (CIPR) defines PR as 'the discipline which looks after reputation, with the aim of earning understanding and support and influencing opinion and behaviour. It is the planned and sustained effort to establish and maintain goodwill and mutual understanding between an organisation and its publics' (sic) (2006).

This word 'publics' is an interesting one, used much by the likes of Kotler and Keller (2006, p. 593) who describe a public as 'any group that has an actual or potential interest in, or impact on, a company's ability to achieve its objectives'. Others have used stakeholder, audiences, targets and some have described these publics as 'market domains' (Christopher, Payne and Ballantyne 1991). What is important is not necessarily the labels but the fact that these 'publics' are both recipients and co-authors of the organisation's story and can be the life or death of a brand or a company if image is not promoted and protected as being mutually beneficial.

OPENING CASE STUDY

H&M: In-Store Chaos and Out-of-Store Buzz as H&M Take the Catwalk to the Sidewalk

As the most valuable European retail brand, the Stockholm-based fashion retailer *Hennes and Mauritz* (*H&M*) had been a fixture in its homeland Sweden for well over 60 years. In November 2004, it launched a special 'Karl Lagerfeld for H&M' collection consisting of clothes, accessories and a fragrance called *Liquid Karl* and the theme of 'making designer clothes affordable to the average consumer' spread rapidly throughout the world. Lagerfeld, with his high-end designer name, established with the likes of *Chanel*, *Chloé* and *Fendi*, proved to be a perfect partner. *H&M* was about to take on the American *Gap* and Spanish *Zara* and bring the catwalk to the sidewalk.

Five months prior to the launch, an intensive period of PR was used to communicate the collaboration, resulting in a frenzy of word of mouth, rumour and news leaks. The prospect of seeing

a well-known fashion designer cooperating with a mass-market clothes retailer was seen as a totally new thing in fashion and the marriage of high and low culture captured the imagination. The campaign received a lot of media attention and publicity and *H&M* achieved its campaign objectives by creating 'out-of-store buzz and in-store chaos'. Before the 12th November opening, people in 20 different countries queued in long lines for several hours outside the selected *H&M* stores. Special promotional shopping bags added to the excitement of the 'event' feel of the publicity campaign and the air of exclusivity (even though this was on a big scale!) was emphasised by the fact that the one-off

In-store buzz with H&M store opening

Liquid Karl perfume acted as a sort of promotional tactic and yet gave *H&M* the cache of a 'demi-god designer'. Shoppers went crazy, fighting over garments, stripping down to their underwear on the spot rather than miss out on the new range, provoking a spate of overpriced garments being placed on *eBay* and other Internet auction sites.

The Karl Lagerfeld PR campaign in 2004 produced fantastic publicity, an improved reputation and succeeded in repositioning *H&M* as 'a high-fashion retailer for the mass market'. *H&M* had hit on the idea of combining the opposites of haute couture and democratic fashion and the formula of marquee designer, clear brand DNA and unique high-intensity publicity was successfully repeated by other fashion designers like *Stella McCartney* (2005), the Dutch duo *Victor & Rolf* (2006), and *Roberto Cavalli* (2007). 2009 sees *Commes des Garçons* continuing the annual collaboration. It seems to be that *H&M* is able to use its publicity machine and build hype around who will be the next collaboration. The stable of celebrity models adding 'cultural currency' to the high-street brand have included Claudia Schiffer, Kate Moss, Kylie Minogue, Sophie Dahl, Anna Nicole Smith, Bridget Fonda, Izabella Scorupco and even Madonna who also designed a fashion collection for *H&M* in 2007 and featured heavily in all its promotional work.

H&M, with its biggest markets homeland Sweden, the UK and Germany, continues to expand its affordable cutting-edge fashion empire. Now in over 1738 outlets worldwide, Europe's second-largest selling apparel chain (the Spanish outfit *Zara* registered higher €4469 million sales in 2009) has expanded into the Far East in China and Hong Kong and its first Japanese store, in Tokyo's Harajuku shopping district. The designer collaboration formula has been copied but the real success for *H&M* was to create in-store chaos and out-of-store buzz by taking the 'event' excitement of the catwalk to the mass market through the power of publicity.

QUESTIONS

1. What are the main publicity issues that may contribute to the success of the Karl Lagerfeld for *H&M* collection?

2. Distinguish between the elements of 'promotion' and 'publicity' in the *H&M* case.

(Continued)

3. Have you seen similar integrated sales promotions and PR campaigns for other brands?

4. What are the broader buyer behaviour elements at play in this type of fashion brand and how do these underpin the 'brand buzz' surrounding the hype?

Public relations has a broader remit than certain other elements of marketing communications, being both **strategic** – in relating to the long-term building of brand image, and creating lasting positive associations – as well as **tactical** – in responding ad hoc to unplanned environmental threats. The establishment of status and positive linkages for a company is a continuing, coherent process involving many elements of the brand and the organisation's narrative. How a crisis is dealt with can determine whether it becomes permanent or temporary in terms of its impact on the organisation. Whilst L'Etang (2008, p. 59) describes the concepts of 'apologia' and 'reputation repair', Tilley (2005, p. 1) argues that 'transparency, consistency and responsiveness' are fundamental to handling relations with publics.

This is contextual: Sir Michael Grade's (2009) handling of ITV's 'competitions fiasco' may have rescued the corporation's reputation as a result of openness and responsiveness; Charles Ratner's *faux pas* in referring to the reason for his jewellery business's success as being 'because we sell crap' proved terminal. However, *Cadbury*'s reluctance to 'go public' with the news of the salmonella scare at its UK chocolate plants followed the same path to brand disaster. In *Cadbury*'s case, it took a gorilla and a lot of expensive marketing communications to rescue the brand (see closing case study in Chapter 1).

Grunig and Hunt (1984) highlighted the monologue and dialogue aspects of communications through public relations by describing the 'four models' which have been used as a benchmark by academics and practitioners alike (Table 14.1).

Model name	Type of communication	Model characteristics
Press agency/publicity model	One-way	After researching target audiences, uses persuasion and manipulation to influence how target audiences behave in accordance with organisational objectives
Public information model	One-way	Uses press releases and other one-way communication techniques to disseminate organisational and brand information
One-way asymmetrical model	One-way	Uses persuasion and manipulation to influence how target audiences behave in accordance with organisational objectives. Does not use research to analyse how target audiences feel about the organisation
Two-way symmetrical model	Two-way	Uses communication to negotiate with target audiences, resolve conflict and promote mutual understanding and respect between the organisation and its audiences

Table 14.1: The four models of public relations

Source: Grunig and Hunt (1984). Reproduced with permission.

PR IN FOCUS

Virgin on the Ridiculous

An example of the building of the reputation of the brand through creating positive corporate image is the 'symbiotic PR relationship' (Pickton and Broderick 2005, p. 550) between the collec-

tive *Virgin* organisation of over 200 companies and the personality of Richard Branson, its creator, chief owner and 'soul' of the *Virgin* brand. The 'brand' transcends all *Virgin* businesses and products with Branson 'meticulously cultivating the distinctive positioning of David versus Goliath' (Hatch and Schultz 2001, p. 123). Ever since the ethereal melodies of *Tubular Bells* (pre-*Exorcist*!) announced the arrival of one of the world's most innovative and customer-oriented organisations in the 1970s, the world has seen an avalanche of public relations, elevating the personality of Richard Branson and the *Virgin* name.

The face of Virgin is everywhere

In fact, the brand is the third most respected in the UK and it has achieved this by promoting the identity value (Holt 2004, p. 4) of symbolising the heroic underdog, projecting the buccaneer image of a 'freewheeling, adventurous, exciting guy... with Virgin seen to share many of those characteristics, particularly in relation to the competition' (Gregory 2004, p. 49).

Some of the most focused and well-managed corporate brands (like Anita Roddick's *The Body Shop* and Bill Gates's *Microsoft*) are inextricably linked to the personality and vision of their founder (Mottram 1998, p. 67). *Virgin*, in particular, demonstrates the advantage of well-established expressive values carrying the brand across major category barriers. The 'fame' built up by PR spreads across planes, trains and automobiles; brides and wines; money and insurance; books and phones and cola.

Virgin has used PR to position the brand against the 'big bad wolves' of the customer-hostile competition. Careful positioning of Branson as the 'people's champion', photographed alongside travellers at check-ins, phoning customers for feedback, entertaining the media and providing photo opportunities for the press, has underlined the emotional associations of 'outlook' as much as product. Branson, who reportedly sets aside 25% of his time for PR activities, claims that, 'Using yourself to get out and talk about products is a lot cheaper and more effective than a lot of advertising. In fact, if you do it correctly, it can beat advertising hands down and save tens of millions of dollars'.

The latest 'PR stunt' is to position *Virgin*'s image as the caring and ethical alternative to *BA* in championing the use of biofuels against kerosene and fossil fuel. Whether this proves to be a tactical 'moral high ground' against the competition or a pioneering long-term strategy remains to be seen. However Branson has positioned *Virgin* as eco-friendly against *BA* and done this through the effective use of PR.

PR is concerned with all the components of the communications mix and all the personnel of the company which looks after its reputation, with the aim of earning understanding and support and influencing opinion and behaviour.

L'Etang (2008, p. 36) argues that 'public relations suffers from a lack of delineation, weak boundaries and encroachment from other disciplines such as marketing and human resources'. The notion of the 'porous boundaries' that she refers to tends to be used to articulate a practitioner's argument of 'jurisdiction' (i.e. a status debate about the role of PR in the marketing communications' hierarchy). At the other end of this discussion, Kotler and Keller (2006, p. 594) advocate marketing public relations (MPR), which updates the notion of publicity to: assisting the launch or repositioning of products; building interest in a product category; influencing specific target groups; defending products exposed to public actual or perception problems; and adding to the building of the reputation of the brand through creating positive corporate image. This latter perspective better reflects the emphasis in this chapter, which focuses on target audience's negotiation of meaning, development of brand stories and integrated marketing communications.

This is particularly important as the reliance on mass advertising to 'tell the story' is becoming ineffectual, and the increasing importance of PR as a more holistic option is fast emerging. A more rounded, comprehensive approach to building awareness, knowledge and ultimately long-term customer engagement and loyalty needs to involve interactive dialogues, and MPR is right at the heart of this. As with all elements of marketing communications, the key decisions are establishing communication objectives, choosing what messages and vehicles are most appropriate to target audiences, and how these are implemented and evaluated properly; that is, how best to present the company and its products.

L'Etang (2008, p. 55) describes the framework for PR as 'impression management' and covers organisational identity and reputational zones, which equate to internal projections and external perspectives (Figure 14.1). As the name suggests, all the elements of managerial and employee

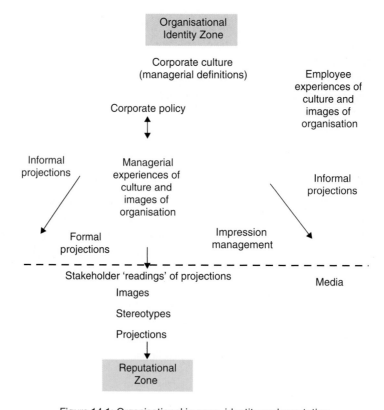

Figure 14.1: Organisational images, identity and reputation

Source: L'Etang (2008, p. 55). Reproduced by permission of SAGE Publications.

experience, culture and the images projected can be (to some degree) controlled. Staff can be trained, policies changed, structure and lines of communication can be adjusted to improve relationships in the company/customer interface. All the formal projections of image – the physical evidence of buildings, uniforms, logos, livery – together with all the informal projections – attitude, responsiveness, 'service tone' – will register an impression with customers and therefore must be managed. However, the micro-environment stretches outside the company boundaries and includes the supply chain, intermediaries and of course the customer.

TARGETS FOR PUBLIC RELATIONS

Therefore, the key task of public relations is to act as both an organisational and cultural conduit to 'negotiate competing interests' through 'adaptation and integration' (Puchan 2006, cited in L'Etang 2008, p. 11). Who are these 'competing interests' that we must target for communication? Figure 14.2 shows the various macro and micro 'publics' or audiences PR activity must be directed towards.

All these target groups are potential audiences for PR and are shown according to two criteria: the macro environment (the broader, more general environment which may apply to all organisations in an operating sector); and the micro environment (the specific environmental influences which directly affect the organisation and its brands). These market domains affect brand identity and image (which covers all the company-specific influences on the organisational and product portfolio image which are to some degree manageable) and all the targets which may affect reputation (the wider environmental influences which are not as manageable).

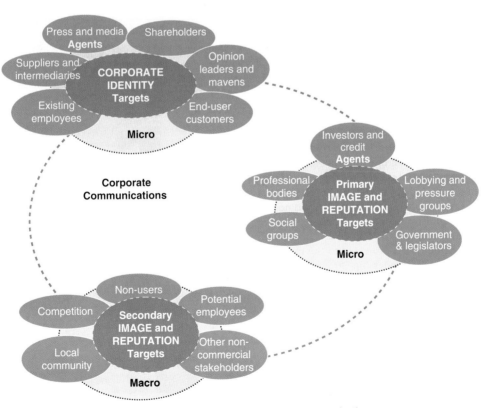

Figure 14.2: Target groups for marketing communications

Primary Image and Identity Targets

- **Press and media:** the influence of the media in presenting brand imagery and affecting consumer perceptions is huge, and needs careful managing if brand equity is to be maintained. In 2004, *Coca-Cola* handled the *Dasani* disaster in the UK very poorly when stories of the product being 'tap water', contaminated with cancer-causing bromate, leaked (excuse the pun) into the market. The bad press killed off the brand in the UK, possibly doing irreparable damage to its plans to launch another bottled water brand in the UK.
- **Suppliers and intermediaries:** those who carry the brand (agents who represent; distributors who stock; and retailers who display) are temporary 'owners' of the brand. The brand promise projected by a kitchen manufacturer's advertising may be distorted or supported dependent upon the way the product is displayed and merchandised, by its availability, or the stories of good or bad service which are generated in the trade – strong relationships with dealers are essential ingredients of any push strategy for a manufacturer. If we were to extend the value chain (Porter 1986) back into the supply chain, the partnerships with suppliers can undermine or enhance an organisation's reputation.

Retailers are keen to show their 'eco credentials' which project ethical links with Fair Trade supply. *Marks & Spencer's* 'reputational capital' diminished in the late 1970s and 1980s when its treatment of UK textile suppliers *Carrington-Viyella* and *William Baird* reflected badly on its reputation for supplier relations.

- **Opinion formers:** those who are seen as having impartial credibility because of some level of formal expertise can be targeted with a view to effecting positive publicity. Bloggers are an increasingly important medium for the dissemination of information and building of reputation.
- **Opinion leaders and mavens:** individuals who have influence over consumers from their own social group have a key role to play in the dissemination of information and creation of image. Journalists can help launch a product, release a new movie or help repair a damaged reputation. Celebrities may act as credible endorsers by transferring meaning to a product.

Making *Sainsbury's* great again - from the inside out

- **Internal market:** employees, especially in service organisations which have customer-facing personnel, are vital in building company image. Indeed customer service before and after the sale may be the most important aspect of the relationship a customer has with a company, and therefore frontline staff (drivers, receptionists, sales-force personnel, catering, credit controllers) must be trained and managed in terms of the image that is projected to the market. In the UK, *Sainsbury's* 'Leadership Programme', designed to 'culturally recapture the essence of customer value', was instrumental in regaining the ground it had lost to *Tesco* and *ASDA*, restoring customer confidence and company reputation. The poster is an example from the 'internal market' communications campaign which used notice boards, training, newsletters, incentive schemes, intranets and other elements of the internal marketing communications mix.
- **Shareholders:** *Wal-Mart,* the US supermarket giant, faced a battle with angry shareholders (including UK

Wal-mart labour works against them

pensions management company F&C), who say *Wal-Mart*'s poor business reputation is driving away customers and putting their investments at risk. A 2006 study by the US consulting firm McKinsey found that at least 2–8% of customers had stopped shopping at *Wal-Mart* as a result of the controversy surrounding the company. Investors want *Wal-Mart* to produce a report on the negative social and reputation impacts of its non-compliance with International Labour Organization (ILO) conventions (using child labour in overseas suppliers and preventing US employees from joining trades unions). The need to 'restore the corporate narrative' is evident in a quote from *Wal-Mart*'s CEO H. Lee Scott who apologised for the company's problems by citing 'a management failure for not telling its story better'.

MATTER OF FACT

Corporate Narratives through PR

The role of narrative (storytelling) in branding is now gaining more and more prominence because of its power to metaphorically connect people with brands. However, because managers are better at analytical business skills than they are at using narrative as a business communication tool, the extension of this to companies requires a change in organisational mindset. One of the most difficult things management has to do is to get stakeholder buy-in to a fundamentally different way of doing things – a new business model, a change in company culture, or a critical strategic shift. Conventional 'command and control' approaches to communication may be counter-productive.

In an article on how to use narratives in companies, Stephen Denning (2000) refers to 'springboard stories' which capture corporate vision better than business plan manuscripts and can spark transformational change. As listeners imagine the parts of the narrative that are relevant to them and set in their specific contexts, they become co-creators of the corporate story whether as internal employee or manager or linked through distribution or displaying of the product, or the dissemination of information about the brand story. Corporate complicity occurs because participants in the narrative find the stories compelling and believable and they become true brand ambassadors and create the strategic shift.

Companies are discovering that powerful narrative can give focus to managers which will make them better at directing and orchestrating the company/customer interface. *Lilly Research Laboratories* has an inspirational 'Leadership Storytelling' programme for executives, which allows managers to articulate their perspective and diffuse this notion of articulating goals and values throughout the organisation. Mark Morris of the Brand Consultancy says: 'If you're a company that understands the role of brand narrative and a company that has adopted that paradigm, then what you're really becoming is a storytelling organisation. The stories reside in your employees, customers, in your vendors . . . which will drive the value for the company. It's the stories that determine the outcome of whether customers are willing to endorse you, your product and your services'.

With the discovery of the central importance of narrative, managers must ensure that this is continually updated and relevant to what the organisation delivers. 'Taming the grapevine' refers to satirising untrue, malicious rumours or bad news through generating

(Continued)

alternative dissemination of stories. Often, formal press releases and news bulletins may be misinterpreted and misconstrued and this can be done sometimes through the generation of news stories which add to a more positive narrative. In the *Wal-Mart* story featured earlier, the company storyline of investing in small local businesses countered the negative PR over 'big business bad practice'.

Source: Denning (2005).

Perceptions of Image and Reputation

Representation is a key conceptual element of marketing communications and indeed the social sciences generally. Arguments have tended to polarise on whether the media – as 'gatekeepers' of information – act as 'organisational' or 'cultural/ ideological' agents (McQuail 2000, p. 277). In other words, do they function essentially as economic channels for companies or as meaning conduits for consumers?

L'Etang (2008, p. 54) asks whether 'contemporary developed societies are in fact image cultures'. The word 'image' is derived from the Latin *imitari* meaning 'imitation' or reproduction (Bromley 1993 cited in L'Etang 2008, p. 54), which underlines the importance of the notion of agents of communication 'representing' organisational and brand identity and image. Corporate identity is an amalgam of strategy, culture, organisational design and operations. The way corporate governance (processes, values, relationships with stakeholders, ethical orientation and so on) is presented by a company and perceived by stakeholders can build reputational capital which is a competitive advantage.

Together these elements constitute 'organisational reputation' (see Figure 14.3). Corporate image is the company's reputation with various stakeholders. Corporate identity projected from an organisation is consumed and renegotiated by target audiences who will construct alternative perspectives of the company, its products and service. The 'identity' of the organisational mission, culture and brand positionings is projected through the images and experiences of the staff and employees. This is often referred to as 'impression management' in the sense that the elements which can be 'controlled' (i.e. communication which emanates from within the organisation) are managed. However, communication outside the organisation's control (i.e. the 'readings' of the images projected by media, stakeholders and customers) cannot be so easily managed.

Primary Reputation Targets

Governments, government legislative bodies and regulators, press, media, professional bodies, investors and pressure groups are all examples of agencies which have influence over an organisation without being directly involved in any commercial relationship. These parties may not directly add value to a product or service, but they can directly influence the likelihood of purchase, or prevent an offer from even reaching the market (Peck *et al.* 1999, p. 9).

In the early 2000s, a US organisation called *Commercial Alert* filed a complaint with the Federal Trade Commission (FTC) accusing *P&G's* 'buzz marketing' division, *Tremor*, of targeting teens with deceptive advertising. This caused quite a lot of media attention, and risked both legal restraints from the FTC and negative reactions from *P&G's* potential buyers. Therefore, it became important for *P&G* to communicate with both these non-commercial stakeholders, as well as with its customers. *P&G's* objective was to deal with all macro and micro target audience stakeholders including the FTC and Commercial Alert, the teens, the teens' parents, as well as the general public. The focus was on long-term reputation rather than short-term sales.

Another example where non-commercial targets were the focus of communication concerns *Shell*'s decision to sink one of its oil platforms in the North Sea. Environmental organisation *Greenpeace* argued that this would be environmentally irresponsible, *Shell* counter-argued that the alternative of moving and dissembling the platform would pose even greater risks to the environment. *Greenpeace* was not satisfied with the response and *Shell* had to bow to its objections.

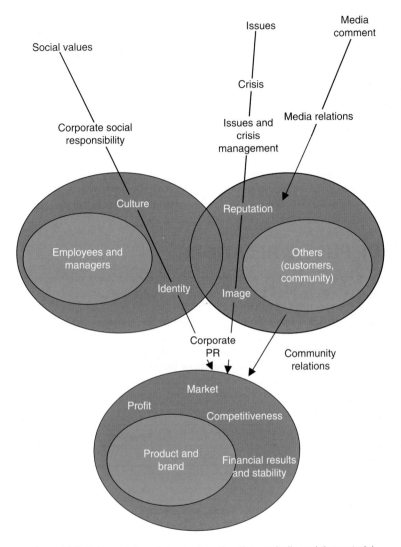

Figure 14.3: Public relations bringing together the symbolic and the material

Source: Pieckza (2006, p. 291).

As both these examples illustrate, PR includes communication to non-commercial target groups that are not the audience for product- or mission-focused marketing communications. Furthermore, it includes communication to the latter target groups as well, but the message is not focused on selling the product or mission. The examples also illustrate that the company or organisation need not be the sender of a message about itself, as *Commercial Alert* communicated a message about *P&G* and *Greenpeace* about *Shell*. While both *P&G* and *Shell* did communicate messages themselves, they were obviously not the initiators of the communication.

Secondary Reputation Targets

Secondary targets may have no direct effect on the organisation in terms of custom, but may still influence public image or ability to implement organisational strategy:

- Local community: *Everton FC*, an English Premier League football club, lost a lucrative opportunity with *Tesco* to build a new stadium when local residents complained and planning was called in by the government.
- Wider societal community.
- Potential employees.

Other Non-Commercial Stakeholders

Non-commercial targets are not the main focus of a company's immediate commercial goals, but they may be important to communicate with in order to avoid obstacles to the company's relationship with its customers.

Pieckza (2006, p. 291) demonstrates this mix of social values, issues and relations with the media which constitute the corporate narrative, as illustrated in Figure 14.3. This brings together both the symbolic and material issues of corporate social responsibility, issues and crisis management, media relations, community relations and corporate public relations.

TOOLS OF PUBLIC RELATIONS

Now that we have an appreciation of what the target audiences are, and what messages we need to convey to them, what are the tools in the PR mix at our disposal? Traditionally, PR covers strategic and tactical considerations; proactive and reactive activities; internal and external target audiences; and acts as both the driver of marketing communications and as support to other communication activities.

Table 14.2 lists the tools which are traditionally associated with PR and shows the wide range of techniques available in order to promote corporate or brand image; react to negative feedback from the marketplace or problems from the organisation; introduce a new image, product, policy or anything which encourages and maintains positive company reputation.

PR tool	Examples
Advertising	Corporate image campaigns
Publications	Annual reports, brochures, articles, company newsletters, magazines, audio-visual materials, intranets, websites
Events	Social events, news conferences, seminars, outings, factory tours, trade shows, exhibits, contests, competitions, anniversaries, annual general meetings
Sponsorships	Linkages with sports, arts and causes to gain positive association for the organisation or brand
News	Press releases and news conferences aimed at generating interest through the media or handling negative publicity
Speeches	Questions from the media, AGM feedback or promotion of ideas or products at sales conferences can help build the company image
Public service activities	Cause-related marketing is an area where companies can build goodwill with a community or audience
Identity media	Visual identity can be projected through logos, stationery, signage, literature, the physical evidence of buildings and interiors, uniforms and dress codes
Internal	Company newsletters, staff briefings, training

Table 14.2: Traditional public relations tools

With the advent of the Internet and the new Web 2.0 generation, the 'information era' has completely transformed the PR landscape: it is now characterised by the interactivity and democratisation of audiences, and a 'social media' which humanises the process of communications. PR is actually returning to its roots of two-way dialogues of connected communications rather than the broadcast monologues of company-transmitted communications. With the ability to talk to customers directly (through online forums, groups, communities, BBS etc.), companies can now communicate more effectively with target audiences and an emerging army of 'accidental influencers'.

As well as the traditional elements of the PR mix listed in Table 14.2, any PR campaign now would have to include the following new digital media electronic tools:

- **Interactive press kits:** hard copies sent to press offices and PR agents now have to be supplemented by online elements such as downloadable materials in PDF format and instant downloadable press agency photographs.
- **Viral** (e.g. *YouTube*): product and demo videos and viral campaigns to instil fun and subversive qualities guaranteeing 'word of mouse'.
- **Seeds to industry/product specific bloggers:** PR campaigns must be preceded by information sent to important industry and product-specific bloggers who act as opinion formers and credible source disseminators of information.
- **Podcasts:** both company and brand podcasts are pre-recorded downloadable messages, programmes or news designed to circulate information, enhance the original message or broadcast, and communicate directly with target audiences for the purpose of enhancing relationships. Car manufacturers like *Mercedes*, distributors and retailers like *H&M* use the podcast facility to extend the brand story and enhance communications online.
- **Website:** the Internet makes customer access permanently available (24/7 and 360 degree), instantly updatable and provides the reach (massive customer response potential) and richness (depth of information and extension to communications gives a quality of customer experience not previously available); intranets provide an internal market communication platform which is rich, instant and quickly updatable; extranets provide a lock-in key customer communication channel which helps build and sustain long-term relationships and protect business.
- **SEM/SEO:** search engine marketing or search engine optimisation.
- **Widgets:** these are electronic 'tags' which are tied in with social network sites and other sites, redirecting or recruiting viewers, the source is user credible and the action user friendly (see how *Heineken* used widgets to promote its brand and more responsible drinking in Chapter 12).
- **Email:** order confirmation, product launch and offer announcements, and the fraternity communications of being part of an online club are techniques used by the likes of *Amazon, Apple, Dell,* and all online retailers with whom we willingly open up lines of communication.
- **SMS texting:** service organisations like the *RAC* and *AA* automobile breakdown companies and couriers like *Fed Ex* and *UPS* use texting to inform and reassure users of their service (see applications for SMS texting in marketing communications in Chapter 16).
- **Social network sites:** for example, *Twitter, Jaiku, LinkedIn, Pownce, Plaxo, FriendFeed, MySpace* or *Facebook*.

In this period of interactivity and co-authorship of brand narratives, source credibility is of paramount importance. The debate about whether communication is transmitted through, or negotiated by, audiences applies just as much to PR as to any other of the general marketing communications mix. It can sometimes increase the effectiveness of PR messages if the source of the message is disguised or at least oblique – the origin of the message not distorting the message. The techniques in PR communications can therefore be described as pure PR (e.g. press releases sent out to the market from the organisation on company letterheads) and hybrid PR (attempts to obscure the associations with the company as initiator or sender of the communication).

STRATEGY AND TACTICS OF PUBLIC RELATIONS

Publics can be active, passive or latent (Grunig 1992, p. 6); organisations communicate with them either proactively or reactively. The techniques for achieving successful communication through public relations can be used to project transparency between the sender and receiver (company and customer) or obscure the source of the communication by masking who initiates and transmits the communication. Equally, recipients of communications may perceive the source to be either from the sender or not. This may be intentional from the organisation's perspective or an outside non-representative agent (e.g. an 'ad-busting anti-consumerism activist'), or it may be unintentional (due to the audience's disposition or incorrect reading of communications).

When the organisation is both the initiator and sender of the communication, it may attempt to mask the origin of the sender, the objective being for communication to appear neutral, or for it to be perceived as coming from a source more credible to the target audience. This is referred to as hybrid PR, which does not focus on direct communications with an audience but places it in different contexts (Balasubramanian 1994). Figure 14.4 places the various PR and hybrid PR techniques in a matrix describing whether the company is the sender or initiator of the communication, and whether it is perceived as having come from the company by the receiver.

The explicitly PR-oriented techniques are:

- publicity;
- lobbying;
- ad busting;
- reactive PR;
- word of mouth.

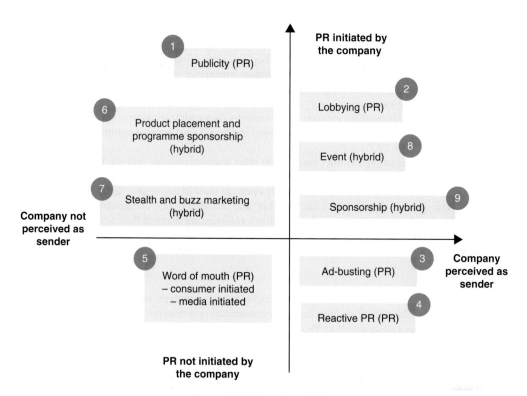

Figure 14.4: PR and hybrid PR

The more hybrid PR techniques are:

- programming;
- product placement;
- stealth marketing;
- event management;
- sponsorship.

Explicit Forms of Public Relations
Publicity

Publicity is marketing communication that is initiated by the company, but reaches the target audience through another medium and therefore is not perceived by the target audience as being generated by the sender. The *H&M* case study showed how 'buzz' can be generated by word of mouth and media discussion even though the company started the snowball effect of publicity. The message becomes part of the medium's content (often called 'editorial material' as opposed to the advertising that is separated from editorial) and has a life of its own – another narrative if you will. The buzz which preceded the introduction of the *Apple iPhone* in 2007 is a good example of this. Steve Jobs, *Apple's* CEO, 'let slip' at the Annual Macworld Conference & Expo that *Apple* was ready to launch 'some time soon' (it was actually six months later). The response was phenomenal, creating a veritable tsunami of

Apple iPhone buzz

positive publicity and hype. Approaching the launch, the *iPhone* generated 70 million *Google* hits, *Apple's* key distributor reported that it had received more than one million enquiries and the positive publicity enhanced consumer expectations to the level that a survey of consumers showed that a majority gave the *iPhone* higher marks than their own phone devices even before the *iPhone* was launched (*Electronic News*, **53**(22), 39). Table 14.3 shows the main reasons for using publicity.

Reasons	Explanation
Increasing publicity space	Fragmented media and proliferation of media vehicles means more demand for editorial
	Increased competition means smaller revenues for the media, meaning that there are fewer resources available to produce editorial material by themselves
	Demand for publicity space is increasing, and the media welcomes PR campaigns that add to the editorial material
Low costs	Cost-effective method provided it makes an interesting contribution to the editorial material and is used
	Publicity may transfer from one medium to another (repeated in different formats) which makes it an even better use of resources
Demand	Statutory legal and regulatory 'disclosure' requirements
	Stakeholders such as analysts and journalists may demand information directly from the company
	Broad reach and multiple sources that publicity can provide are important factors in disseminating information

(Continued)

Reasons	Explanation
Objectivity of message	As the message is sent by someone else, it is generally perceived as more objective than if the company or organisation were the sender itself
	Publicised information has more credibility than claims in advertising (Loda and Coleman 2005)
Integrated marketing communications	The combined effect of using other communication mix components gives a coherence and cumulative impact
	Research suggests that the effects of advertising are greater when they are preceded by publicity (Loda and Coleman 2005) and that different media for PR and advertising (Stammerjohan *et al.* 2005) and different variations of the message for PR and advertising (Wang and Nelson 2006) enhance the persuasive effect of the message

Table 14.3: Reasons for using publicity

MATTER OF FACT

'Advertising Breeds Publicity'

American newspapers write frequently about advertising campaigns. Researchers Yin, Zhao and An (2006) found that the country's four major newspapers covered more than 3000 campaigns during a year. Testing whether the publicity around the campaigns made the advertising more effective, they compared consumers' recall and recognition of advertising that was aired in the commercial breaks of the Superbowl game (sometimes called the 'world championship of advertising', because it has the highest prices in the world for its advertising spaces) in a three-year study. Analysing all 227 brands, the researchers found that recall of the advertising correlated by 56% and recognition correlated by 78% with the amount of publicity devoted to the advertising in the seven days preceding the Superbowl.

Source: Yin, Zhao and An (2006).

How can we increase the likelihood that a message will generate publicity? A study in which 12 US television editors rated 64 news stories showed that they all rated the value of the stories, and the probability that they would send them, based on the same 12 dimensions (Staab 1990). The more a story contained of each dimension, the higher they valued it (Table 4.4).

Elements	Criteria
Surprise	WOM may spread due to the 'gossip', shock or unexpected factor
Pride	Pleasure in identifying with achievement
Impact	Most salience with audience need
Fun/entertainment*	300 (84%) leading US media professionals rated entertainment before importance[a]
Threshold	Is the event big enough? Small stories may make it into small, local media, whereas major media only publish major news that affects a large group of people

Timing	The story must fit with the medium's schedule, so that it feels new and current
Meaningfulness	The more personally relevant the story is to the audience, the better
Complexity	The story must not be too complex or difficult to grasp
Composition	The story should fit the medium's or journalist's expectations and 'angle'
Continuity	If the story has a longer life-span, it becomes more interesting. This way the medium can fill more space and benefit from the 'initial investment' when it first took an interest in the story
Personalisation	People are more interesting than companies or issues. It is more interesting to read about a charismatic company leader than about a faceless company
Elite	High-status, popular people (or companies) are almost always of interest, whatever they do
Negativity	Journalists tend to favour bad news over good news, evident in reports on brands which focus more on negative than positive aspects (Dahlén and Lange 2006).

* Not mentioned in the study.
[a] *Columbia Journalism Review*, 11 June 2000.

Table 14.4: Successful elements of publicity stories

Lobbying

Lobbying is a PR form that, similar to advertising, is both initiated and sent by the company or organisation. But the overriding goal differs, as lobbying is not focused on a specific product or mission, but rather on influencing the company/organisation's macro environment. Or in the case of *Greenpeace* (as you will see from the PR in Focus box below), on representing the environment. Lobbying does not have the same consumer visibility as other elements of the communications mix because of its nature: targeting mainly governmental bodies with complex matters behind the scenes. Nevertheless, it is a highly important and widespread PR form. For instance, there were more than 3000 full-time employed lobbyists in the European Union headquarters in Brussels in 1996 (Harris and Lock 1996), and lobbying was estimated to be a \$1.5–3 billion industry in the USA in 2001 (Gabel and Boller 2003). Therefore, lobbying is sometimes also called environmental marketing or macro marketing (e.g. Zeithaml and Zeithaml 1984, Varadarajan, Bharadwaj and Thirunarayana 1991). The macro environment consists of industry structures, laws and regulations, governmental bodies and other companies and organisations.

PR IN FOCUS

Greenpeace

Greenpeace, the global pressure group and campaigning organisation, stands for 'positive change through action', and is committed to 'defending the natural world and promoting peace'. It interpreted the actions of giant chemical organisations (representing the chemical

(Continued)

industry business community) as acting against the interests of the environment, it accused them of 'corrosive lobbying' of the EU Commission, stating that this undermined the EU REACH Chemical Law Agreement.

In a report named 'Toxic Lobby: How the chemicals industry is trying to kill REACH', *Greenpeace* claimed that chemical organisations are undermining and destroying EU attempts to protect the public from hazardous chemicals.

The lobbying of the EU has been seen as scaremongering, denying problems of chemical contamination, creating fear over extensive job losses and economic costs, obstructing innovation and co-opting small and medium enterprises

Greenpeace lobbying reaches chemical industry

to their disadvantage. The series of advertisements and posters depicted Industry Commissioner Verheugen and Commission President Borosso as being complicit with the chemical companies in their flagrant abuse of the environment and future generations.

Visit the *Greenpeace* website, www.greenpeace.org.uk, and the Chemical Industries Association, www.cia.org.uk, and see how lobbying works in the real world.

The three most common goals for lobbying are (Keillor, Boller and Luke 1998):

- **Increase efficiency**. In the mid-1990s, *Microsoft* lobbied to decrease its tax liabilities to the US government on exported software, resulting in a tax break for software exporters estimated to be worth $1.7 billion. This benefited all software exporters, including (market leader) *Microsoft* (Gabel and Boller 2003).
- **Market power**. In the 1990s, *Volkswagen/Audi* lobbied for the use of a specific environmentally friendly catalytic technology for vehicle emission limitations in the European Union. Arguing that a common standard would enhance environmental control and development, the company was able to convince the legislators to adopt its technology as the standard. This gave *Volkswagen/Audi* a competitive advantage in Europe over, for example, *Ford* and *Rover* who had spent hundreds of millions on another technology that was then not accepted (Harris and Lock 1996).
- **Legitimacy**. In 1993, major British retailers, such as *Sainsbury's, Safeway and Tesco*, lobbied in a successful joint campaign to reform the Sunday Trading Laws (e.g., shorter opening hours) that limited their ability to increase business. With imaginative ways of showing politicians how beneficial it would be for everyone to have more business on Sundays, the campaign gave way to acceptance of more open Sunday trading (Harris and Lock 1996).

Several factors suggest that the use of lobbying will continue to increase:

- **Increased globalisation and competition**, creating more complex industry structures and needs for competitive advantages.
- **Increased interaction between companies and organisations**, for example mergers and acquisitions that do not fit with monopoly and competition laws.
- **Increased governmental involvement**, with new legislation and bodies, for example concerning the environment.

Figure 14.5: Who is the perceived sender of this message?

Ad Busting

Consumers who blatantly destroy or alter an advertising billboard 'to curtail rampant consumerism' can deliberately sabotage campaigns. This is called 'ad busting'. It differs from negative word of mouth in the sense that, although the company or organisation is not the initiator, it may still be perceived as the sender. 'Doppelgänger brand images' are negative WOM stories which distort the actual brand narrative and circulate in popular culture and social media by Internet-linked anti-brand activists, bloggers and legitimate news media. In recent years, several well-known brands, including *Nike, McDonald's, Apple* and *Starbucks* (who underwent a well-publicised face-off with US punk rock band *Starbucks – be my Doppelgänger*), have had attempts by people to subvert their communications message (see Figure 14.5).

Of course, the company might encourage people to use its symbols and signs, which is the case in user-generated advertising and communication. User-generated messages assist the dissemination and re-creation of communication, they may function as social proof or source credibility.

MATTER OF FACT

'Ad Busting was Beneficial'

In an experiment, researchers Henrik Sjödin and Fredrik Törn tested the effects of ad busting on people's perceptions of fashion retailer *H&M*. In Sweden, *H&M* is famous for its regular use of billboards in its lingerie campaigns. However, the blown-up advertising displays of underwear models have made *H&M* a target for the general debate on body ideals and the billboards have been ad-busted with stickers proclaiming 'may cause eating disorders'. The researchers tested the effects of these stickers by comparing brand perceptions between people who were exposed to *H&M* billboard advertising ad-busted with stickers and those who were exposed to the same billboard advertisements without stickers on them.

(Continued)

The results showed that there was a positive correlation between attitude towards *H&M* and credibility of the ad-busting message. This means that people who liked *H&M* were more prone to believe that the advertising could actually cause eating disorders, suggesting that they were so secure in their favourability towards the brand that they could cope with its potential downsides as well. Further analyses revealed that, by coping with the brand's potential downsides and realising that they still liked *H&M*, the ad-busting stickers could actually enhance people's favourability toward the brand.

The conclusion is that the ad busting could actually be beneficial to the attacked brand, as it enhanced the attitudes of consumers who were already favourable towards the brand. But what about consumers who were not already positive about *H&M*? As it turns out, they were less inclined to take part in the advertising and were therefore also less likely to attend to and think about the ad-busting message attached to it.

Source: Sjödin and Törn (2007).

Reactive PR (Ambush Marketing)

As sponsorship practice increases, so do competing activities surrounding it. Ambush marketing means that companies/organisations try to derive the same values as sponsorship out of events, without being actual sponsors. That is, companies may try to associate themselves with the event and perhaps benefit from the confusion of multiple events and sponsors so that people actually perceive that the company is a sponsor. For example, by associating with the Olympic Games, the sender can gain prestige without paying the large amounts of money that are required.

Ambush marketing has been common practice among competing brands around major events, where companies have taken turns at sponsoring or ambushing the events – for example, *Coca-Cola* vs. *Pepsi, McDonald's* vs. *Burger King, Adidas* vs. *Nike, American Express* vs. *MasterCard*. One of the more notable ambushes was *Benetton's* two-page print advertisement featuring five giant rolled-up condoms during the Barcelona Olympic Games.

Word of Mouth

Consumers may spread positive or negative WOM directly through social media such as blogs, social networks, online communities, chat rooms, special interest groups, social websites, etc. as well as offline. Finding and enabling opinion leaders, who gain the attention of many others, to initiate positive messages about the product or mission can be very fruitful. Buzz marketing can be created when consumers initiate and send positive/negative messages. Negative word of mouth is an increasingly important part of marketing communications for much the same reasons as positive publicity:

- **Publicity space** (and negative reports): is continuously increasing, as is the risk that the company or organisation will receive negative WOM.
- **Enhanced message:** media reports tend to be perceived as more credible than advertising (Dean 2004).
- **Integrated marketing communications:** just as positive publicity may enhance the effects of advertising campaigns, negative publicity may reduce effects of ongoing advertising campaigns. For example, *Firestone* had to withdraw its multimillion dollar '100 years of reliability campaign' as it was disrupted by media reports on its defective tyres (Dahlén and Lange 2006).
- **The negativity effect:** previously we discussed how media preferred negativity. There is a negativity effect at the audience end as well. Research shows that people may be more attentive to negative than positive information, as it is perceived to be more important (e.g. Ahluwalia, Burnkrant and Unnava 2002).

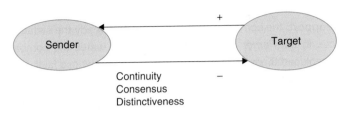

Figure 14.6: The effects of attribution

- **Diagnosticity:** people perceive a company's or organisation's actions in a crisis (which negative WOM would be associated to) to be an important sign of its actual performance, because they 'diagnose' how it is likely to act in the future (Dahlén and Lange 2006). This is because, compared to for example a planned and positive advertising campaign, the company/organisation has not been able to choose (the most favourable) setting itself and therefore its true face is revealed. An example is *Enron*'s demise in 2001 due to 'irregular accounting procedures bordering on fraud'.

Two factors are critical to the effects of negative WOM and reactive PR: **attribution** – who the audience blames for the negative reports (Laczniak, DeCarlo and Ramaswami 2001); and **expectations** – the extent to which the negative WOM and the company/organisation's response to it matches the audience's prior opinions (Dawar and Pillutla, 2000).

The effects of attribution are summarised in Figure 14.6. Attribution to the company or organisation is also affected by: the **continuity** of the negative WOM (the longer the reports continue, the greater is the chance that people will associate the negative WOM with the target); **consensus** (the more varied the media that spread the negative WOM, and the more similar their messages are, the more damaging the effects); and, finally, the more **distinctive** the negative WOM (where the company/organisation is clearly and distinctly pointed out), the stronger the effect.

Based on these findings, we can pinpoint a number of reactive PR responses for mitigating the effects of negative WOM:

- build a strong reputation and bond with the target group;
- discredit the source;
- put a quick end to the reports;
- minimise consensus;
- minimise distinctiveness;
- stonewalling;
- ambiguous support;
- unambiguous support.

MATTER OF FACT

'Consumer Expectation Causes Negative Anticipation'

The second factor that determines the effects of negative WOM is expectations. In a series of experiments, Dawar and Pillutla (2000) show that consumers tend to interpret a company's response to negative WOM in light of their previous opinions of the brand. The researchers studied three typical reactive PR responses:

- **Stonewalling:** the company does nothing to remedy the situation and refuses to take any blame. For example, in the well-known *Valdez* oil spill in 1989, oil company *Exxon* was not willing to take blame or responsibility for the consequences of the accident. *(Continued)*

- **Ambiguous support:** the company does something to remedy the situation but does not take full blame. In the *Perrier* crisis with contaminated water, the company recalled its products and replaced them, but sent mixed signals about whose fault it was.
- **Unambiguous support:** the company remedies the situation and takes full blame. In the (painkiller) *Tylenol* poisonings, owner *Johnson & Johnson* recalled products, took full blame and worked to remedy damage.

In the table below, you can see the results from Dawar and Pillutla's (2000) experiments, where they tested the effects when a number of different brands were subjected to negative publicity.

	No crisis	Unambiguous support	Ambiguous support	Stonewalling
Strong brand (positive expectations)	0	0/+	0/+	0/−
Weak brand (negative expectations)	0	−	−	−

Effects of negative publicity

As the table shows, strong (familiar and liked) brands cope better with crises than weak brands, regardless of response. Giving some support to the negative WOM may rid the strong brand of the crisis, or even enhance people's liking of the brand. This is because people expect the brand to not behave badly, and therefore read a positive behaviour and intention into the brand's response – 'of course, they did everything that was in their power to solve the problem' or even 'gee, the company took full responsibility even though it was probably not their fault'. A stonewalling behaviour may leave the brand untarnished because people do not attribute the negative WOM to it, or it may be negative if people do blame it. A weak brand is likely to be hurt by the negative WOM no matter what, but the more effort it puts in, taking blame and remedying the problem, the less negative is the effect.

Source: Dawar and Pillutla (2000).

PR IN FOCUS

'Weltklasse' or 'Vältklasse' Image for *Mercedes*?

In the 1990s, when *Mercedes-Benz* launched its new *A-Series* smaller car, the excitement of anticipation both within the company and in the marketplace was soon dissipated when news of failed pre-launch trials reached journalists in the European auto trade press. The car, on trial with one of the top Swedish motor magazines, scored very badly in a manoeuvre test when it rolled over on a sharp turn of the test track. As opinion former, the 'expert journalist' can be very influential in helping a new product to be adopted if the brand is endorsed and given a good report. The credibility that an independent expert can give is well received by the target audience. However, this was not so in this instance! The magazine's report on the new car was very negative.

At first, *Mercedes* 'stonewalled' and did not respond to the report in the magazine. However, word soon spread and gave rise to the WOM tag of 'Vältklasse' (meaning 'roll over' in Swedish), which sounds like the brand's claim to be world class – 'Weltklasse!' The German manufacturer's publicity machine initially discredited the source, insinuating that it was only a Swedish magazine and implying that in the home of competing car brands like *Volvo* and *Saab*, they had vested interests. This caused a lot of animosity in the Swedish press and even more negative publicity and WOM accrued.

When the counter WOM was spread that this test was actually referred to as the 'elk crash test', the Germans were able to play on the fact that elks run wild in Sweden and they were able to distance themselves from this 'parochial claim' and very soon perceptions started to become more positive. In addition, they physically improved the car, enabling the problem to be corrected and eventually the negative publicity subsided.

Hybrid Forms of Public Relations

As we have already stated, hybrid PR refers to all company paid-for PR activity which attempts, for commercial purposes, to influence audiences by employing PR communications which imply that they are non-commercial. Audiences are more likely to see the communication as neutral and process the content as if it has not come from the company. It is not a new phenomenon, however. It has antecedents in the attempts by cigarette manufacturers in the 1920s to influence Hollywood to encourage smoking in films by the popular movie stars of the day (Schudson 2000). The concept of product placement (the careful positioning of brands within the contextual use of a movie, TV programme or other forms of popular culture) required a distinctly hybrid orientation in the 1980s when programme or movie sponsors had progressively more control over content and product placement (Miller 1990). The script for *Rocky III* was amended to include a scene where *Rocky* eats the breakfast cereal *Wheaties* implicitly endorsing 'the breakfast of champions' (Maslin 1982). Other examples include: a scene in *Cocoon: The Return* being re-shot to feature *Quaker Instant Oatmeal* more prominently (Reed 1989, p. 103); a bidding war between *Forbes* and *Fortune* magazines over the rights to be referred to in the movie *Wall Street*; *Ford* paying the makers of the *Bond* movie *Casino Royale* a cool £1 million to feature a *Ford Focus* for 30 seconds (and as a hire car at that!). This type of hybrid communication is both sponsorship and PR and amounts to tacit endorsement, especially as there is the other factor present of celebrity endorsement.

The recent increase in the use of hybrid PR is attributed to the problems with the increasing levels of advertising noise or clutter which has diminished the effectiveness of mass-media advertising, together with the increasing opportunities to avoid conventional TV advertising due to the prevalence of digital alternatives. The increasing use of personal video recorders (PVRs), *Sky+, TiVo*, Internet advertising filters which can skip TV and Internet advertisements, as well as newer variations such as advertising-free podcasts (Russell and Stern 2006) have provoked both brand owners and advertisers to consider alternative ways of reaching audiences and maintaining revenues. The use of product placement and programming, already used heavily in the USA and almost at saturation point in movies, is an alternative approach to exposing the consumer to product and is just about to explode onto our TV screens in the UK and the rest of Europe.

Product Placement and Programme Sponsorship

Product placement and programme sponsorship are communication forms that are initiated by the company, but not perceived as being company-generated. The strategy of brands being placed or integrated into TV programmes and movies is often referred to as 'embedded marketing'. This typically comprises exposures and mentions of products in the contents of films, TV programmes, video games or music. Films and TV programmes have been the most frequent vehicles, with estimates that more

INTEGRATION

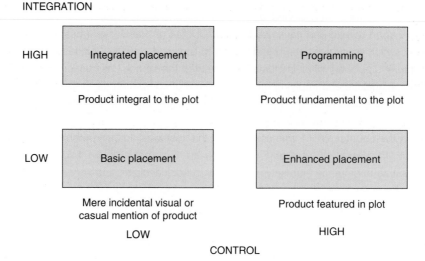

Figure 14.7: Product assimilation TV programmes
Source: adapted from: Sheehan, Bartel and Aibing (2005, pp. 79–91).

than 75% of US prime-time TV contains product placements (Russell and Stern 2006) and more than 25% of all film production is financed by product placements (Sheehan and Guo 2005). In 2002, more than half of all top-selling video games contained product placements (Nelson 2002). According to 'placement-tracking agency', PQMedia, the US product placement market for 2006 was estimated at over $2 billion which is expected to double by 2010. This may actually be as high as $7 billion rising to $10 billion by 2010 if combined with advertising, which is bundled with these elements of programme sponsorship. According to Ofcom, the UK is estimated to be about £30 million by 2012.

There are different approaches to programming and product placement. Figure 14.7 shows these approaches in two dimensions: the level of integration the brand has with the content it is placed in; and the degree of control the sender has over the placement.

- **Basic placement** is common in films and TV programmes, and may involve a planned or inadvertent shot of a brand logo or product or casual mention of the brand with only an incidental connection to the plot. For example, the characters in the film could pass by a retailer, take a bite from a well-known chocolate bar or mention a brand within the normal dialogue in order for the drama to appear more true to life. Similarly, a brand could be featured on a road-side billboard in a racing video game. Research shows that basic product placement can be especially effective when the audience is overly conscious of it (Law and Braun 2000). However, if the audience becomes aware that there is no story logic to the product placement, attempts must be made to integrate it into the plot. Research shows that mere visuals work better when they are not prominent, whereas mentions of the product work better when they are more logically part of the plot (Russell 2002). However, this is not to say that these background placements are unplanned. An alternative to conventional advertising is to buy space in video games (e.g. *EA*'s *Battlefield 2142* has featured advertisements for the *Intel Core2*). This works because it has sympathy with the target audience and may be seen as part of the landscape of the virtual scenery.

Quite often, 'prop houses' will secure brands for use in TV programmes for lucrative amounts of funding. They are able to do this in the UK because of a loophole in the broadcasting regulations which classes these sorts of placements as legitimate props. A *Sunday Times* undercover report claimed that this practice was 'blurring what is a clear distinction between television programming and advertising'. Claire Davidson, a Director of Rogers and Cowan, one of the prop firms, described a 'points system' for programme product placements. John Parker of New Media Group, a product placement company, attempts to build relationships for household names like *Heinz, Cadbury* and *Whitbread*.

This slightly 'unofficial' practice may be given a legal footing in the UK some time late in 2009 if Ofcom's 2005 research report on product placement is accepted. Its research indicated that viewers would have no objection to product placements provided 'it enhanced the realism of a programme, is relevant and is not too prominent'. Speaking at a DCMS (Department for Culture, Media and Sport) Convergence 'Think Tank', UK Culture Secretary Andy Burnham spoke out against legalising product placement on TV warning that such a move would 'contaminate programmes' (*Media Week*, 11 June 2008). The UK government, via the DCMS, is obliged by law to consult on legalising product placement on TV under the EU's Audio Visual Media Services Directive. Burnham's comments regarding the implications of technological development have shocked broadcasters and the advertising industry who are both desperate for rules on product placement to be relaxed. The Ofcom research proved that consumers are positive provided there is transparent disclosure of commercial arrangements. The significant thing, according to the report, is that they objected to 'being sold to by stealth'. Watch this space – literally!

- **Enhanced placement** means that the product is somehow featured in the plot. This gives the sender greater control. For instance, the product is a prize in a game show or reality show, and thus fills a clear and controllable role. Or it is more woven into the plot, as in the tongue-in-cheek product placements in the popular US 1990s' sitcom *Seinfeld*, where the characters could turn obsessed with certain candy brands and it was an obvious product placement that the audience could laugh at. The last *Batman* movie *The Dark Knight* featured *Armani, Bang & Olufsen, Belstaff, Bentley, Dodge, Ford, Harris Bank, Lamborghini, Mercedes, Nokia and Powerball*. Relevant for Gotham City or because they were the previous year's best brands? Examples of enhanced placements in video games are *McDonald*'s kiosks and *H&M* clothes in *The Sims* games.

- **Integrated placement** puts the product as an integral element of the plot. Tom Hanks's best friend in the film *Castaway*, the football *Wilson*, is one such example. Another is the *Sex and the City* running storyline which featured *Absolut Vodka* as central to the plot. Research shows that integrated placement works according to balance theory in the sense that that the audience's perceptions of the characters transfer onto the product (Russell and Stern 2006). Sometimes this is subverted as in *Fight Club* which attacks *IKEA* for epitomising 'the feminine nesting instincts of consumer society' (Palahniuk 1996) and *Apple* for being ubiquitous. Integrated placements are common in computer and video games, the earliest one recorded being for *KP Skips* in *Action Biker* back in 1984. The pressure to be featured in these sorts of games is increasing and becoming more akin to the hustling for TV slots. Car brands in racing games, such as *BMW* or *Toyota* in *Sony*'s popular *Gran Turismo*, are now willing to pay for the privilege. The *James Bond* movie franchise has been the driving force of product placements in the cinema, with *BMW* and *Ford* chasing *Aston Martin* for pole position. The 2006 film *Casino Royale* has an array of *Sony* products all integrated into the plot: all characters use *VAIO* laptops, *Sony Ericsson* cell phones and GPS gadgets and a character uses a *Cyber-shot* to take photographs as part of the plot. In the latest instalment, *Quantum of Solace*, our hero (*Bond* that is not *Sony*!) used a state-of-the-art *Sony Ericsson C902 Cyber-shot*.

- **Programming** puts the product at the centre of the plot. Branded examples include the British TV reality show *Airline*, showing the ups and downs of an everyday airline – a warts and all documentary on *easyJet*, video games such as *Adidas Power Soccer* and *NBA Live*. Programming may also be non-branded, for example TV shows such as *Extreme Makeover* and *Extreme Home Makeover*. The former features health and cosmetic surgery products and the latter features home repairs and interior decorating products. Non-branded programming is typically used to drive interest in an entire product category (such as home repair or cookery), and can be initiated by an industry organisation, cooperating companies, or the market leader (which is the one that would gain the most from it).

Advantages of programming and product placement are:

- **Reach.** The sender may reach a wide audience that might not be possible to reach with other marketing communications (for reasons mentioned above). The sender may also reach an audience that would otherwise not be familiar with or interested in the product, and it benefits from the interest that the surrounding content brings.

- **Image transfer.** The product may be associated with the content, for example, characters using the product, and their image may transfer onto the product. More on this in the section on sponsorship below.
- **Experience.** The audience may experience usage of the product and try it, either by watching characters or by interacting in a game. More on this in the section on events below.
- **Market testing.** In video games, the company can present virtual products and prototypes to learn about the audience's reactions and use the product placement as a market test before actually launching the products.

Potential disadvantages:

- **Distraction.** The content of the film or TV programme is naturally of greater interest to the audience than the brand. It may distract attention so that people may not even notice or remember the brand; the price for exposure may not be cost-effective. This is overcome by advance publicity in the communications campaign around the screening of the programme ('see our product in the new blockbuster movie'). Product placement and programming may actually be ways to create publicity and enhance interest in the company/organisation's advertising. This may also benefit the content that the product is placed in – for instance, whereas *Taco Bell* was placed in the US version of the film *Demolition Man* (featuring Sylvester Stallone), it was replaced by *Pizza Hut* in the international release because *Pizza Hut* agreed to promote the film heavily in its advertising.
- **Reactance.** Reactance is the psychological reaction when people feel that someone is limiting their freedom – in this case, the freedom to choose if they want to see advertising or not. If people identify the programming or product placement as being 'advertising', they may disapprove as they cannot avoid it and may feel that it ruins their enjoyment of the content.

Stealth, Buzz and Viral Marketing

As the aviator roots of the term might suggest, 'stealth marketing' refers to communications aimed at 'flying under the (consumer) radar'. The intention is to disguise the source of message so that marketing communications are not perceived by consumers as being company sponsored, even though the company might be both the initiator and sender of the communication. It is similar to viral marketing, referrals and buzz marketing in this respect, but there are fundamental differences: viral marketing does not usually hide the fact that the company has initiated the message; stealth marketing often employs people and recruits customers or members in the process of communicating.

These days, marketers are more aware of the potential of audience co-authoring and propagating brand stories. Social network sites have thrived on individuals spreading accelerated word of mouth and brand owners have witnessed the exponential growth in the power of this medium to give massive exposure and dissemination of brand messages. The digital word-of-mouth capability of the Internet, with instant messaging and rapid multiplication of images (hence its viral nature) has created the perfect conditions for viral marketing. Some say that *Microsoft's* 'Get your free email at *Hotmail*' launched the concept of viral marketing – it took only 18 months and $500,000 to recruit 12 million new subscribers, the fastest customer recruitment campaign ever. *Hotmail* subscribers willingly supply detailed demographic and psychographic profiles which is unprecedented in marketing. Without any marketing effort, *Hotmail* became the largest email provider in countries like India and Sweden.

In 2004, *Google* followed *Microsoft's* lead with its *gmail* version but this time by recruiting 1000 online opinion formers and asking them to test the unreleased service, resulting in three million users signed up in just under three months. In this era of permissive marketing, where consumers openly allow organisations to communicate with them on a one-to-one basis, the mass-marketing advertising paradigm has been challenged. An example of organisations encouraging 'authentic' reader-authored viral communications is the *Dr. Pepper/7 Up* site for *Raging Cow Milk*. Six teenage bloggers were enlisted to operate as if they were not officially linked to the company, their peer group origins appearing to give street credibility and authenticity. The hope from the organisation was that bloggers would take the endorsement of product at face value. Is this an example of buzz marketing, creating a legitimate interest in the brand or is it covert communications (i.e. stealth marketing) and somewhat underhand? The brand owners would argue that it is a legitimate attempt to create interest and build buzz for the brand.

The Internet hype for the movie *Blair Witch Project* is one of the more famous examples of a buzz campaign. This was replicated by the record company who spread the buzz about a UK band *The Arctic Monkeys*. It appeared that the word was spread within the community of fans and ostensibly from the band themselves. It was in fact initiated by the record company but accepted as authentic fan gossip. Similarly was it a buzz marketing campaign that helped singer Sandi Thom in 2007? Her single – *I Wish I Was a Punk Rocker* – apparently 'emerged from the underground', facilitated by *Streaming Tank* (a web-hosting company) and the PR agency *Quite Great*. Another example of gaining exposure in the target market context is *BMW Mini* hiring stunt drivers to drive around cities to create an expectation about the brand's launch. The trend for paying non-customers to act as customers has been noticed in the book trade, with paid 'buzz agents' phoning book retailers claiming to be customers interested in a particular title (which in fact had been sent to them by headquarters) and then writing glowing reviews of the book on *Amazon* without mentioning their relationship with its publisher. The practice of 'reverse shoplifting' or 'shop dropping' is growing in the USA, whereby merchandised book displays are rearranged on behalf of emerging authors, giving prominence in the face of competitors' offers.

STEALTH MARKETING IN FOCUS

Shiner Beer

The Global Dutch beer giant *Heineken* got a 'shiner' from small-time brewers *Shiner Beer* when it scuppered *Heineken*'s sponsorship of the Austin City Limits Music Festival, proving that creative thinking and bare-faced cheek can help spread around the smallest of budgets. *Heineken* had already secured exclusive rights to the festival and paid handsomely for the privilege of being official sponsor to an event which attracted over 65,000 visitors a day.

Using specially designed *Shiner Beer* koozies (can holders which are used to keep beer cool), into which sat the only beer available on site – namely *Heineken* – *Shiner* were able to achieve a presence at the three-day festival at minimal cost. Street merchandising teams distributed koozies to concert-goers outside the event and therefore had first impression on customers who attended. The fact that the rival beer's name and logo was obscured only added to the sense of mischief and made it appear that *Shiner Beer* was actually the official sponsor to all who attended the festival. By the time the event's organisers and the official sponsors found out what was happening, all of the 10,000 koozies had been handed out and the damage was done. Even if *Shiner* merchandisers were then ejected, the 10,000 covers were still paraded around the festival grounds and the smaller 'David' brand had succeeded in planting a 'shiner' on the Goliath from Amsterdam.

Stealth shiner for Heineken

It could be argued that these are all publicity stunts or promotional tactics and that there is a genuine attempt to engage target audiences. However, the fact that stealth marketing attempts to hide the fact that the company is the initiator and may use non-associated personnel (i.e. not employed directly by the organisation) to communicate the message, raises the question of whether this is deceptive, surreptitious marketing communications. The undercover aspect of this approach aims to create simulated peer group interest and is often used where targets are not available through conventional media. This is particularly so in situations where communications are trying to effect emulative behaviour (i.e. consumers following the lead of opinion formers), where the intention is to effect the appearance of a peer, and therefore, a trusted and credible source.

Researchers Kaikati and Kaikati (2004) provide several examples of stealth marketing activities:

- In 2002, *Sony Ericsson* launched its *T68i* camera phone by recruiting 60 novice actors and actresses in 10 major cities to play couples at popular tourist locations such as the *Seattle Space Needle*. Acting as tourists, they asked other tourists to take their picture and handed over the cell phone while they posed in front of the camera. *Sony Ericsson* used similar tactics when demonstrating the ability to play video games by placing two young recruits at opposite ends of a trendy bar playing against each other on their cell phones.
- Some companies in the music industry have placed hip-looking 'fake shoppers' in music stores talking about great new artists or songs which other shoppers are supposed to overhear in the conversation. According to the researchers, a sneaker (trainer sports shoe) brand even employed so-called 'soccer moms' (parents watching their children) to chat loudly about the brand in the audience.
- In 2001, Italian scooter brand *Piaggio* hired young, good-looking people to drive around highly visibly in Los Angeles and Houston on the scooters and park them in trendy locations.
- In 2002, the lead singer of US rock band *Heart* was hired by a weight-loss company to talk about its products when she appeared as a guest on national TV talk shows, which she did without mentioning her relation to the company.
- In the UK, a buzz marketing agency, *Sneeze*, recruited fans for a Premier football club (by using actors), ostensibly getting people to sign a petition about a sacked colleague because his boss objected to an SMS message facility available from the club.
- Musical acts *Jet, CSS, Feist* and *The Ting Tings* in 2008 got fantastic publicity when 'appearing' in the *iPod* commercials. Were they promotions for the acts, product placement or celebrity endorsement?

Sony Entertainment recently attempted a stealth campaign on the Internet to spread enthusiasm for its *PSP* console. The *alliwantforxmasisapsp.com* site appeared to be a legitimate social network blog of like-minded *Sony* gamers. When it emerged that *Zipatoni* – a marketing firm specialising in buzz marketing – was responsible for the communications, there was an immediate backlash from insulted gamers who saw through the underhand manner of the communications. Indeed, the leveraging of the potential of chat rooms and forums can be a strategy for unscrupulous organisations which use the pseudo-credibility of social media to dishonestly disseminate brand communications. Even the placement of 'plants' in a TV or radio audience can attempt to persuade people to change opinions. The audience for programmes such as BBC1's *Question Time* and Radio Four's *Any Questions?*, (whilst attempts are made to appear evenhanded) are often populated with party activists who (mis)represent political parties.

The real problem with this approach is that marketing communications which does not identify itself as such is misleading and unethical (and sometimes often illegal). The risks of being 'found out' may undermine the trust consumers have in the brand and seriously damage credibility and long-term reputation. French cigarette company *Gitanes* found this to its cost when paying Oxford University students to act as 'disguised brand ambassadors'. This is still practised by some unscrupulous tobacco manufacturers (*Freedom Tobacco* would you believe!) who seed celebrities by offering inducements to be 'bar leaners'. Kaikati and Kaikati (2004) referred to this type of covert tactic when they claimed that stealth marketing 'attempts to catch people at their most vulnerable by identifying the weak spot in their defensive shields . . . stealth marketing is seen as a viable alternative to advertising because it is perceived as softer and more personal than traditional advertising'.

But how visible does a company have to be in its marketing communications, and how transparent do intentions have to be? Detractors have referred to this underhand approach as 'roach baiting'; it is the unethical equivalent of 'simulating opinion leaders' (Evans, Jamal and Foxall 2006, p. 260). Leo Benedictus, writing in *The Guardian* (2007), takes this a stage further, describing this phase of alternative advertising as a 'new age of sponsored stooges and media manipulation'. But, trust is essential in maintaining the brand narrative, and these approaches more often than not have a negative impact. Walker (2004, p. 68) summed up the dangers to organisations who may damage the long-term equity of their brands when he referred to the *Sony Ericsson* picture phone stealth campaign as 'an act of civility [which] was converted to a brand event'. Andy Sernovitz (recent CEO of the Word of Mouth Marketing Association (WOMMA), the industry's self-regulating body) argues that disclosure of source is the only sensible choice for brand owners, saying that 'When you deceive consumers, when they find a recommendation that's supposed to be from a trusted source, a real person, but that ends up being from a marketer, they will hate your brand'.

As a rider to this, the US Federal Trade Commission (FTC) has issued an initiative 'protecting communities from commercialism' and launched an investigation into the buzz marketing industry. The agency concluded that 'the failure to disclose the relationship between the marketer and the consumer would be deceptive unless the relationship was otherwise clear from the context'. However, WOMMA makes the distinction between legitimate buzz marketing (trying to build a viral campaign that gets people talking about a product, brand or organisation without compensation) and unethical stealth marketing which is PR communications initiated and sent by the organisation, but may or may not be perceived by the target audience as having been sent by the organisation.

Event Management

Event marketing – including both events hosted by the company/organisation itself and events that the company/organisation sponsors but are hosted by someone else – are growing in importance. A survey of 200 US marketing executives revealed that they perceived event marketing to offer greater return on investment than any other form of communication (Close *et al.* 2006).This is partly due to the effects of increasing advertising clutter and the captive audience of events run counter to the trend of advertising avoidance. But the advantages of better targeting (where attendance is a specifically invited target audience) and better communications (where there is a degree of participation involved) can make events very cost-effective.

The benefit of sponsoring hosted events is not limited to the actual events and their visitors. They can generate extra advertising and publicity spent by other participating organisations. Events and sponsorships may be perfect opportunities for advertising and promotion ('come join our event', 'win tickets to the event', 'only our most loyal customers are invited') and may be a source of news value in itself, generating publicity that the company/organisation would otherwise not be able to receive. Energy drink *Red Bull* hosts 'Art of Can' events where people are invited to be artists, creating works of art with *Red Bull* cans as the only material. The works of art are used in outdoor advertising, print advertisements, websites and selected pieces are also displayed at art exhibitions. This way, both participating artists and spectators take part in the event, interacting with the product, the brand and each other. The annual *Red Bull Flugtag* events, held in several major harbour cities around the world, are where people are invited to

A drop in the ocean for Red Bull publicity

compete and see who can fly the longest when jumping off a dock with their spectacular, self-made flying devices. The events have become a tradition which gets additional local and national media coverage.

Event marketing may also be a good platform for developing new products and platforms. When *Sony Ericsson* sponsored the film *The Da Vinci Code* (featuring Tom Hanks), it sold special phone editions with a *Da Vinci Cod*e module.

The main advantages of hosted (own) events are:

- **Interaction** by target audiences with the company and its products/missions, as well as with other customers or members.
- **Loyalty** is enhanced by personal interaction and club mentality.
- **Commitment and reciprocity** increases purchase intentions.
- **Experiencing** the company and brand close up tends to increase favourable customer dispositions.
- **Emotional experiences** are essential for some brands and events create emotions because of the self-involvement of the attendees (Hoch 2002, Whelan and Wohlfeil 2006).
- Event experiences are perceived as **objective**.

Sponsorship

Sponsorship is about building long-term relationships which last and create mutual value. It differs from hosted events in the sense that the company does not host and is not responsible for the event. This means that it is usually not the sole focus in the way that dedicated events like *Red Bull*'s *Flugtag* or *Harley-Davidson*'s *Posse Run* are. However, the advantages are that it may reach a wider audience and help to achieve communication objectives on a much wider scale. Because of the potential to reach a much wider audience than sponsor-only events, sponsorship is seen as a very cost-effective use of communication funds. In 2002, global sponsorship expenditure amounted to $28 billion (Poon and Prendergast 2006). As an illustration, Table 14.5 lists some high-profile event sponsorship agreements and the money involved.

Specific marketing communications objectives are to:

- increase sales;
- develop customer loyalty;
- heighten brand awareness;
- develop new markets;

Sponsor	Event	Rights fee ($)
Nike (sports equipment, apparel)	Manchester United (English soccer team), 13 years	500 million
Hellenic Telecommunications	Athens Olympics 2004	71 million
Coors (beer)	NFL (North American Football League), 5 years	60 million
Fiat (automobiles)	Turin Winter Olympics 2006	52 million
Anheuser-Busch (beer)	Salt Lake City Winter Olympics 2002	50 million
Gillette (razors)	FIFA World Cup Football (Korea/Japan) 2002	40 million
Shell (gasoline)	Ferrari Formula 1 Grand Prix, annually	36 million
Hyundai (automobiles)	UEFA Cup 2004 (European football championship)	27 million
Foster's Brewing (beer)	Formula 1 Grand Prix, annually	14 million

Table 14.5: Event sponsorship spend

Source: Farrelly, Quester and Greyser (2005).

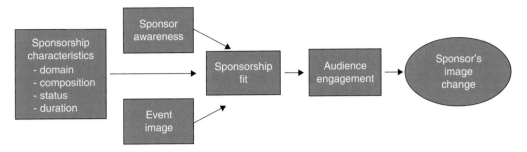

Figure 14.8: Image transfer process in sponsorship

Source: adapted from Smith (2004) and Mason and Cochetel (2006).

- develop business-to-business relationships;
- launch new products;
- broaden customer base;
- develop community relations;
- change or revitalise brand image.

The main focus of sponsorship is not just exposure of the brand to a target audience, it is **image transfer**: the sponsor ties itself to the event, organisation or team so that it becomes associated with its image in people's minds. How the image transfer process works in sponsorship is illustrated in Figure 14.8.

- **Domain** refers to the type of sponsorship, for example, sports, arts, media or charity (perceived differently from other domains, as goodwill may be high but motives and attributions become important factors).
- **Composition** refers to the exclusivity of the sponsor. The more sponsors, the weaker becomes the association to the event, and the greater is the risk that people will confuse, not notice or forget sponsors. Advertising and publicity by sponsors outside the event to differentiate brands is important (e.g. Johar and Pham 1999, Lardinoit and Quester 2001). Interestingly, sponsors of the same event may have a compatibility and transfer of image onto each other may also occur (like in a brand alliance), and therefore co-sponsorship should be taken into careful consideration (Carrillat, Lafferty and Harris 2005).
- **Status** refers to the size and prestige of the event; the bigger the event, the greater the potential boost to a sponsor's image. On the other hand, smaller events may involve a more personal customer experience (McDonald 1991).
- **Duration** refers to the length of the sponsorship. Is it a one-off or an enduring commitment? For example, for more than 50 years, the Bank *Crédit Lyonnaise* has sponsored the Tour de France cycle race and has become almost as synonymous with the race as the famous yellow leader's shirt. The longer the sponsorship, the stronger image transfer is, although research has shown that the association may still be strong even when other sponsors have taken its place (Mason and Cochetel 2006). Certainly, in the minds of English cricket supporters, the acceptance of sponsors other than *Benson & Hedges* is proving to be difficult.

Sponsor Awareness and Event Image

The *Benson & Hedges* 'problem' for sponsors of the England cricket team is also true of the England football team, whose *Green Flag* sponsorship did not work initially because of previous associations. Those people who did register the link did not know that *Green Flag* was a car recovery business and there was poor transfer of association as a result. People must be able to associate a compatibility of image and also have a clear sense of the event's image. People must understand that the *Volvo Classic* is a golf tournament for any kind of association to transfer across to the brand.

Sponsorship Fit

For people to notice and remember the sponsor, and for image to be transferred, there should be a good fit between the sponsor and the event – a sort of sponsorship simpatico if you will. There must be compatibility between the event being sponsored, the target audience and the image of the organisation itself. The fit (and the messages which are implied by this) can take several forms (Gwinner and Eaton 1999, Poon and Prendergast 2006, Smith 2004):

- **Function-based fit:** *Yamaha* pianos sponsoring a piano recital; *Air France* providing transport for the French football team's international matches; *Shell* sponsoring motor sports; or *Adidas* sponsoring athletics.
- **Image-based fit:** *Lexus* sponsoring the Los Angeles Philharmonic Orchestra; *Grand Hotêl* accommodating Luciano Pavarotti; and *Swatch* sponsoring avant-garde sports.
- **User-based fit:** financial service institute *CGNU* sponsoring national cricket games because they share the same target audience.
- **Experience-based fit:** *Heineken* sponsoring World Cup rugby because they are both part of the same experience when people socialise: drinking beer and watching the games.

Audience Engagement

The more engaged the audience is with an event, the stronger will be the perceived associations, the easier these will transfer to the sponsor, and the more enjoyable will be the audience experience which will reinforce associations with the sponsor. The degree to which an audience engages can vary from: not being at all interested in the event's 'domain' (e.g. opera); interested in the domain but does not care for the chosen entertainment (likes opera, but doesn't like the programme featured at the sponsored concert); interested in the event only (interested in the experience of being at the concert), and finally, visits the event (Poon and Prendergast 2006). The greater the engagement with the event, therefore, the better will be the experience.

MATTER OF FACT

'Sponsorship Works Both Ways'

The focus of sponsorship practice and literature is usually on the transfer of image from the sponsored event onto the sponsor, but what about transfer of image in the opposite direction? Could a sponsor's image transfer onto the sponsored event as well? Sponsors are commonly eager to publicise their sponsorship with advertisements, promotions and media coverage to amplify the fact. The more that the sponsor and the sponsored event are linked together, the more likely will be the transfer of image in both directions. Researchers Julie Ruth and Bernard Simonin tested this notion in experiments where several well-known brands, such as *Coca-Cola*, *Kodak* and *American Express*, sponsored a major US parade. Results suggested that people's attitudes towards the brands affected their attitude towards the parade: higher attitudes towards the sponsoring brands increased liking of the event and lower attitudes towards the brand decreased event liking. Furthermore, the appropriateness of the brand as a sponsor of the event had a positive effect on evaluations of the event (meaning that sponsors that were perceived as inappropriate decreased liking of the event). In England, football supporters derided the new sponsorship of the League Cup competition when it was associated with the Milk Marketing Board and yet accepted the new sponsors when it became known as the 'Coca-Cola Cup'.

Source: Ruth and Simonin (2003).

Sports sponsorship can take the form of sponsoring a tournament or event, an organisation or team, or an individual. Some examples are:

- shirt and team sponsorship: *Samsung Mobile* and *Chelsea FC*;
- squad sponsorship: *Skandia* and GB Sailing Team, *Norwich Union* and GB Athletics Team;
- athlete sponsorship: *Nike* and Tiger Woods, Mark Foster and *Speedo*;
- event sponsorship: The *Barclays* English Football Premiership;
- venue/stadium sponsorship: The *Brit* Oval;
- technology sponsorship: *Omega* and the Olympic Games;
- broadcast sponsorship: *Heineken* and ITV's Rugby World Cup.

CLOSING CASE STUDY

Beijing Olympics: One World One Dream: One Great Sponsoring Opportunity

According to the Beijing Organising Committee for the Olympic Games (BOCOG), the marketing plan for the 2008 Olympic Games was 'a partnership between  the Olympic Movement and the business community'. Whilst the International Olympic Committee (IOC) managed a series of Olympic marketing programmes to solicit support for the Olympic Movement and the Olympic Games in terms of technology and capital, the global business community found the marketing programmes an effective

One world, one dream, one voice for Beijing

communication platform for their companies. Many organisations have enjoyed an elevation of their global status due to this sort of sponsorship. For example, *Samsung* enjoyed a global breakthrough in its sales and corporate image after becoming a sponsor.

The Olympic marketing programmes are composed of four main programme areas: the TV broadcast partnership (the 2008 Olympic Games was the most-watched sporting event ever with viewing figures for the opening ceremony estimated to be 500 million); event ticketing; corporate sponsorship; and licensing (rights to use Olympic marks, imagery, themes, including emblems and mascots etc.).

There are different levels of sponsorship entitling companies to different marketing rights in various regions, category exclusivity and the use of designated Olympic images and marks. Last year's 12 Olympic 'proud partners' were predominantly US companies including *Coca-Cola, Johnson & Johnson, General Electric, McDonald's, Visa and Kodak,* but there were also local supporters such as personal computer maker, *Lenovo,* and life insurer, *Manulife.* These are referred to as TOPs (Top Olympic Partners) and will enjoy the associations of higher status – but they have to pay for it! As we have seen in the previous section, the revenues are phenomenal. According to the IOC, worldwide sponsorship generated $663 million for the 2001–4 Salt Lake City/Athens Olympics. Beijing 2008 revenues jumped 31%, with the 12 partners paying a total of $866 million, an average of roughly $72 million each. For this, they got 'sponsors' rights' only (marketing rights to the all-inclusive use of the Olympic images and logos), but this didn't include advertising costs which were estimated to be an additional $1.5 billion.

Companies can also become suppliers to the Olympic Movement providing the Olympics with the necessary support and products. Many major businesses use the Games for advertising

(Continued)

only. In 2008, there was an extensive list composed of big US names like *United Parcel Service, Anheuser-Busch, Staples, Nike* (and its German rival *Adidas*!) to name but a few, although local companies included the Chinese Internet provider *Sohu* and petroleum products company *Sinopec*. French IT firm *Atos-Origin*, timekeeper *Omega* and electronics companies like *Panasonic* and *Samsung* are also amongst the high-end marketers making 'second round' appearances at the Beijing Olympics.

General Electric (*GE*) launched a global advertising and PR campaign to publicise its sponsorship of the Beijing Olympics, designed to create awareness of *GE*'s status as one of the 12 'Proud Partners' of the International Olympic Committee. Whilst this was a global flag-waving exercise for the company, the emphasis of communications was on the *GE* products used in the construction of some of the Olympic buildings: the lighting systems used in the National Aquatic Centre; the wind turbines that powered the grid that supplied the electricity; and even the rainwater recycling systems used in the fabulous state-of-the-art 'Bird's Nest' National Stadium. Although a lot of the communications was for US TV audiences, a series of four online advertisements ran on *AOL, MSN* and *Yahoo! GE* also built an 'Imagination Centre' in the heart of the sponsor village, a specially allocated area to accommodate corporate sponsorship and entertaining. This included interactive experiences and exhibits designed to emphasise *GE*'s impressive technological input.

Global communication opportunity for the likes of GEC

How effective is sponsorship of such an event? The potential for building brand awareness is fantastic with the level of exposure on a huge scale. As it is one of only a few televised events which not only guarantees an audience but also has PR coverage in every type of media, frequency (i.e. exposures to the media vehicle of TV) and reach (i.e. the number of people expected to be exposed to the brands over the time of the event) are almost incalculable. But do organisations get a sufficient return on investment? Table 14.6 indicates that all of the Worldwide Sponsors saw a lift in their share price during the 2004 Summer Games and 60% of them saw a gain during the 2006 Winter Games. In the month leading up to the Beijing Games, 75% of the sponsors were up, with *Kodak* leading the pack.

Corporate sponsors	Symbol	Country	2004 sponsor	%Chg Summer Games '04	2006 sponsor	% Change Winter Games '06	1 month % change (as of 8/5)	YTD % change
Eastman Kodak Co	EK	US	X	7.0	X	15.0	16.2	−25.9
McDonald's Corporation	MCD	US	X	5.2	X	−2.7	9.0	5.8
General Electric Co	GE	US	X	2.8	X	−2.1	8.7	−21.1
Johnson & Johnson	JNJ	US		0.1		0.9	3.5	−11.5

The Coca-Cola Co	KO	US	X	0.8	X	2.6	6.7	−10.5
ATOS Origin	fr, ATO	France	X	7.5	X	0.2	3.6	2.7
Manulife Financial Corp	MFC	Canada		0.1		0.9	3.5	−11.5
Omega (Swatch Group)	ch, UHR.N	Swit-zerland	X	9.6	X	1.9	3.1	−30.4
Panasonic (Matsushita Electric)	MC	Japan	X	4.2	X	−0.2	1.3	7.0
Lenovo Group	hk, 992	China		2.2	X	3.2	−0.6	−23.3
Samsung	kr, 83	Korea	X	5.8	X	12.6	−1.7	−27.5
Visa Inc	V	US	X	N/A	X	N/A	−5.7	30.3*

*Visa YTD calculation based as of IPO 19 March 2008

Table 14.6: Impact of Olympic sponsorship on share price

Source: CNBC (August 2008).

QUESTIONS

1. What impact does sponsorship of the Olympic Games have on the reputation of the organisations participating and how are stakeholder perceptions affected?

2. Distinguish between the elements of 'event management' and 'event sponsorship' in the Beijing 2008 Olympics case.

3. Have environmental factors such as air pollution and human rights detracted from the impact sponsors have had with China in sponsoring this event? How will this be seen compared with the 2000 Sydney and 2004 Athens Olympics?

CHAPTER SUMMARY

This chapter focused on public relations (PR) and hybrid communications. We saw how all stakeholders of an organisation can affect, or be affected by, the organisation's strategic and tactical implementation of marketing communications. Target audiences for PR are therefore wider than potential customers or existing audiences and PR can often be marketing communications which are not directly aimed at selling the company's product, but enhancing or maintaining corporate image and reputation.

We examined how hybrid communications are directed at customers and stakeholders, but may not be perceived as communications sent from the company, and how there was an intertextual aspect of this type of marketing communications which overlaps with other areas and may originate (or in some cases appear to originate) from different sources. The chapter then centred on how communications not explicitly sent from an organisation may include stealth marketing, cross-cultural communications (such as celebrity endorsement), as well as cross-discipline communications which overlap such as 'advertorial' hybrids of PR and advertising, product placement and sponsorship, and the combination of selling and exhibitions.

REFLECTIVE QUESTIONS

a. What kind of media would you target to create publicity for a new online contact lens retailer? What news values would you focus on?

b. The *Financial Times* publishes an article about your car company's damaging effects on the environment. What reactive PR strategy would you respond with?

c. What could have been suitable PR activities during the massive negative media reports on the *Enron* scandal?

d. How would you use programming to increase demand for online banking services? Suitable TV shows or video games for product placement?

e. For the marketing of a fast food retail chain, for example *Pizza Hut*, would you prefer hosting an event or sponsoring one? Discuss pros and cons.

f. Go to www.virgin.com, www.britishairways.com and www.greenpeace.org.uk/climate and research the arguments. Is this another publicity stunt to promote the *Virgin* brand?

RESEARCH PROJECTS

Retrieve a copy of Dahlén and Lange's 2006 paper 'A Disaster is Contagious: How a Brand in Crisis Affects Other Brands' published in the *Journal of Advertising Research*. Using this as a basis, conduct your own research into how *Firestone* had to withdraw its multimillion dollar '100 years of reliability campaign' because of defective tyres and what it did to counter the negative PR.

In March 2009, Sir Michael Grade, Chairman of ITV, announced a dramatic loss of advertising revenues due to the diminishing impact of television advertising. He suggested that a different form of advertising where 'messages are contained within the format' may eventually replace traditional advertising. He was referring to content-captured product placement. Investigate the story behind this suggestion.

CHAPTER  15

SALES AND SALES PROMOTION

Selling and sales promotional activities are often seen (if at all) as the poor relations or invisible partners in marketing communications. The two are linked by the requirement for action. The beauty and cohesion of a creative advertising campaign has to be supported by frantic trade battles for stock into warehouses, commitment to push product through the supply chain, negotiating preferred supplier status with key retailers, buying category shelf-space and product facings, and supporting all activities at point of purchase. And because of the temporary nature of some sales and promotional activities, they may also be seen as, at best, supportive and at worst, tactical and ephemeral.

After reading this chapter, you'll be able to:

- Understand the nature of sales and sales promotion.
- Appreciate sales and sales promotion in the context of the marketing communications mix.
- Recognise the strategic and tactical roles played by sales and sales promotion.
- Appreciate how the two work hand in hand to achieve marketing communications objectives.
- Know how they can underpin or undermine the long-term brand narrative.
- Examine the mechanics and application of sales force face-to-face selling.
- Discuss how direct marketing underpins both sales and sales promotional activities.

It is important to recognise the strategic and tactical roles played by sales and sales promotion. Properly integrated marketing communications will need a combination of communication tactics to achieve a range of marketing objectives. The aftermath of the credit crunch in the UK supermarket sector saw an immediate rise in those retailers who had a more appropriately matched mix of marketing tactics. The likes of *ALDI, Lidl* and even *Morrisons* saw profits increase because of their low-price message. At the end of 2008, after spending so much building the brand image, *Sainsbury's* saw a dramatic fall due to the perceptions of 'quality' meaning 'expensive'. It was forced to change tack. *Sainsbury's* Chief Executive, Justin King, claimed the supermarket's focus on value accounted for the supermarket's 6.8% increase in sales at the end of the first quarter of 2009 and was 'the secret of our success'. The 'Switch and Save' and 'Feed Your Family for a Fiver' campaigns had tactically changed focus, driving a 60% year-on-year rise in sales of its cheaper 'basics' range, but had also succeeded in capturing the moment and recreating its brand positioning.

These companies have to adjust and present different images in order to retain or regain market share, and short-term tactics may take precedence in times of need. The real task is the judgement of balance between holding ground and building on those foundations. Whether objectives are short term or not, they can underpin or undermine the long-term brand narrative.

OPENING CASE STUDY

Radiohead: Somewhere Over the Rainbows, Don't Hail to the Thief as Free Downloaders become Freeloaders

When *Radiohead*, an innovative rock band who were pioneers in the digital age, released their *In Rainbows* album, they applied the same creativity to the promotion of the album as they had done to the production of the music in the studio. Tapping into the trend for viral marketing, a package of music was released as an online download, à la *iTunes*, customers being asked to decide how much they thought the album was worth. Was this daring social/promotional experiment a case

of a band getting the 'bends', repaying loyal followers with a fantastic price promotion or a cynical piece of self-promotion?

The album was released without any backing from a major record company and praised for smashing the label system, but with rival bands claiming that the free download tactic demeaned music, some have their doubts. The online promotion was pulled after only three months, and the band had to quickly revert to a conventional business model – selling CDs from retailers. Nobody other than *Radiohead* and their management company know how much money has been made or lost, but the figures that are reported (see table below) do not put this down as a successful promotion. Claims from a retail 'traffic-tracking' company *Comscore* (*NASDAQ:SCOR*), a leader in measuring digital sales, that 62% of downloaders paid nothing for the album have been rubbished by the band, but nobody is quite sure.

Radiohead 'In Rainbows' online album downloads, 1–29 October 2007			
	Worldwide	US	Non-US
Percent who paid for download	38%	40%	36%
Percent who downloaded for free	62%	60%	64%
Total downloaders	100%	100%	100%

Radiohead 'In Rainbows' online album downloads 2007

It delighted some fans and annoyed early adopters who then felt betrayed when the album got wider distribution. This is an example of how a short-term tactical promotion may have long-reaching effects. Industry insiders were astonished at the amount of people who didn't pay and this promotion, in a way, has helped to reinforce the now accepted norm of downloading free music. Some say that it is conclusive evidence that a new business model to serve the freeloader market has to be conceived, and there will be long-term damage. An additional perspective on this is echoed by Michael Laskow, CEO of *Taxi*, the world's leading Artist and Repertoire (A&R) agency: *Radiohead* have been bankrolled by their former label for the last 15 years. They've built a fan base in the millions with their label, and now they're able to cash in on that fan base with none of the income or profit going to the label this time around. That's great for the band and for fans who paid less than they would under the old school model. But at some point in the not too distant future, the music industry will run out of artists who have had major label support in helping them build a huge fan base. The question is: how will new artists be able to use this model in the future? Someone who is more optimistic is Jim Larrison of *Adify*, a provider of online network services, who stated that the percentage who paid was actually quite high and it shows that there is still perceived value in digital entertainment. He claimed that it does suggest that 'the marketplace is continuing to migrate and the music industry needs to shift with consumer behaviour. There are numerous methods to monetise the music, via shows and concerts, merchandising and box sets, commercial licensing, and even advertising; which is where the industry needs to progress towards, as the 40% paying for music might not be sustainable.'

So was it a statement, a publicity stunt, promotional tactic, or a bold move to build a relationship with an audience? According to the band's management, the material was different to CDs in that it was produced in slightly inferior 160 Kbps MP3 quality (higher fidelity than free Internet

(Continued)

radio stations, which usually stream at 128 Kbps) and was just a promotional tactic to boost the later traditional release of the full-quality CD. In addition, the effects of piracy were limited, and by giving loyal brand users a chance to allay their sense of 'guilt', they have cemented long-term credibility and underlined the relationship they have with their followers – and some new ones. Other bands have had success in using free music as a promotional tactic. *Nine Inch Nails* distributed a digital album *Ghosts-IV* in a number of ways: free samples, a low-priced version, a premium package with downloads and a merchandise offer based on the price paid. But with sales of the main *In Rainbows* CD package selling like hot cakes, *Radiohead's* promotional tactic has very definitely found them a pot of gold and helped achieve long-term strategic success.

QUESTIONS

1. Do you think *Radiohead* were wise to undervalue their product or do you think this promotion achieved its objectives?

2. Is there any difference in spending money on traditional sales promotional tactics or viral marketing?

THE NATURE OF SALES AND SALES PROMOTION

It is difficult to imagine any element of sales promotional activities not having the noun 'action' implied by verbs such as 'enquiring', 'trialling', 'sampling', 'purchasing', 'repeat purchasing', 'exchanging', or simply 'selling'. Whilst it may well add to the image of the brand, and the relationships consumers have with it, sales promotion is all about getting consumers to do things. Its spread of influence in the marketing communications mix is not limited to immediate economic response but also to long-term relationship building. Even activities which do not immediately solicit a sale (replying to a freephone number for further information) are still calls to action.

Equally, although the management of face-to-face sales operations may have long-term relationship, business-building objectives, there is a degree of tactical immediacy which is similar. Persuasion to purchase is a broad perspective which may encompass ideas and issues as well as shifting product or services. The specificity of activity, the precise nature of targeting and communication, make sales and sales promotion often the less glamorous but equally the most hard-working ingredients in the marketing communications mix. Both offer immediate value and inducement to enter into a transaction and then a loyal relationship.

SALES AND SALES PROMOTION IN THE CONTEXT OF THE MARKETING COMMUNICATIONS MIX

Egan (2007, p. 322) places the four main components of the marketing communications mix (advertising, public relations, personal selling and sales promotion) in a matrix highlighting the level of control and influence each has in terms of achieving campaign objectives (Figure 15.1). Whilst the elements of advertising (media schedule, text, visuals and consistency of message) can be controlled, personal selling is far more effective in affecting the sale, having a much more powerful personal influence on the sale. Sales promotion can be controlled better than personal selling, but both of them are more effective in the short term. This can be misleading as short term implies a sort of transient transaction. This matrix obviously is contextual, as personal selling can be at its most effective in B2B markets where the purchase is high involvement and may include many other people. Egan (2007, p. 320) puts this well: 'Personal selling is important where other communications tools are weak, particularly where instant response and complex explanations are needed and where relationship building and maintenance are major factors in the business'.

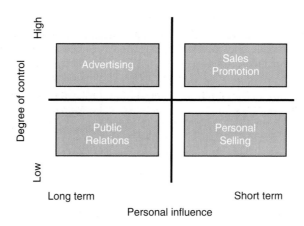

Figure 15.1: Communications mix control and influence

Source: Egan (2007, p. 322). Reproduced with permission.

SALES AND SALES PROMOTIONAL OBJECTIVES

The selling operation of any organisation may build long-term relationships but often embraces short-term objectives in terms of cash generation, competitive blocking and even survival. Sales promotional activities are generally seen as short-term tactical techniques in the marketing communications mix (although the prevalence of everyday low pricing appears to be more long term these days). Although this may add value to the product or service, and enhance the integration of other communication elements, this has to be seen in the context of specific sales and marketing objectives. The key objectives of sales promotional activities are:

- educating customers and affecting target audience awareness of the brand;
- helping the conversion of prospects;
- encouraging the early trial and eventual adoption of new products;
- attracting competitor customers;
- encouraging increased usage of the brand; and
- cross-selling and up-selling product.

Schultz, Robinson and Petrison (1998) provide an excellent framework for analysing sales tactics employed to achieve certain sales results. Table 15.1 shows the different behavioural outcomes required by different customer types dependent upon their individual needs and relationship to the brand. For example, we may wish to reinforce behaviour or increase the usage of our product with loyal customers, or conversely try to break the loyalty of a customer loyal to a competitor.

Type	Description	Desired results
Current Loyals	People who buy the 'right' product most or all of the time	Reinforce behaviour Increase usage (consumption) Change purchase timing
Competitive Loyals	People who buy a competitor's product most or all of the time	Break loyalty, persuade to switch to promoted brand
Switchers	People who buy a variety of products in the category	Persuade to buy the 'right' brand more often

(*Continued*)

Type	Description	Desired results
Price Buyers	People who consistently buy the most expensive brand	Entice with low prices or supply added value that makes price less important
Non-Users	People who don't use any product in the category	Create awareness of category and product Persuade that product is worth buying

Table 15.1: Types of consumers and sales results required

Source: Shultz, Robinson and Petrison (1998). Reproduced with permission.

SALES AND SALES PROMOTION AS PART OF STRATEGY

As we have seen in Chapter 5, message, media and audience all have to be coordinated in marketing communications strategy. The application of sales and sales promotions is dependent upon the routes to market for a manufacturer: some will deal direct with the public and have promotions based on trialling the product and repeat purchase; others will deal through retailers or through distributors who deal with retailers. See Figure 15.2; this gives the following possibilities for sales and sales promotion:

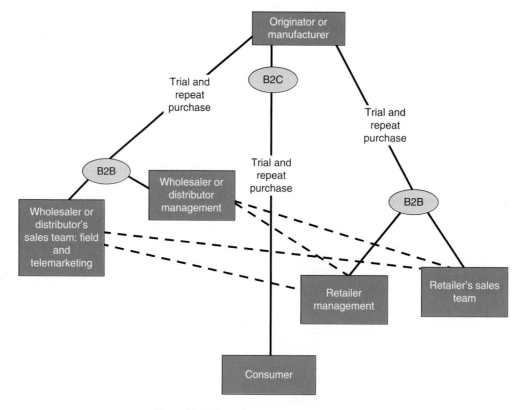

Figure 15.2: Flow of sales and sales promotion

- **B2B push strategies:** manufacturers may sell branded goods or distributor own brands or components to or through intermediaries like distributors, wholesalers and retailers, and employ a trade push strategy to assist the flow of communication from themselves as manufacturer/brand owner through to end-user consumers. The manufacturer objectives will be to prepare and service the consumer market by incentivising the trade through selling, displays, staff training, POS materials, cooperative advertising and dedicated promotional activities aimed at providing a coherent brand message through to the consumer. The retailer provides opportunities to see for the consumer and helps communicate positive messages at point of sale, particularly to counter perceived risk in purchase. This is really a linear B2B2C communication flow.
- **B2C pull strategies:** at the same time, a manufacturer will be creating consumer demand for the brand through advertising and promotional campaigns aimed at the consumer which is business-to-consumer (B2C).
- **B2C push/pull strategies:** some companies do not deal through intermediaries and have a direct link with their end customers and have a direct business-to-customer (B2C) promotional flow. They may sell through B2C communications such as a website, catalogue, mailings and online sales.
- **R2C push/pull strategies:** retailers have a dual role in promotional activity: they may act as intermediaries for manufacturers reinforcing the business-to-customer (B2C) relationship, as well a retailer-to-customer (R2C) relationship.
- **B2B push/pull strategies:** some companies supply direct to other businesses and organisations on a contract basis (e.g. *Dell Computers* has a B2B division) or sell components to other manufacturers or OEM organisations (e.g. *Michelin* tyres to *Ford Motor Company*).

Elements may be tactical and incremental, but should still be integrated appropriately into the overall long-term strategy and brand narrative. For example, if a price promotion offers a discount in order to combat competition, this may undermine the perceived quality image of the brand. If, on the other hand, the stock from a distributor is bought by a manufacturer in order to make space in the warehouse for a new product launch, this will not be seen by the consumer and will affect availability of product but not brand image.

Therefore, a manufacturer selling through a distributor, who in turn sells onto a retailer who sells direct to the public, will be involved in four types of promotional activity:

1. Direct-response promotions intended to stimulate consumer demand.
2. Sales force selling and promotional activity to aid and incentivise the selling of the brand to intermediaries.
3. Trade promotions to encourage retailers to stock, display and sell.
4. Retailer's promotions to encourage consumers to try the product and to buy again.

MATTER OF FACT

Sales Promotional Successes

The table below illustrates some exemplar examples of good practice in sales promotion as cited by the UK Institute of Sales Promotion.

Organisation	Brand	Sector	Objectives	Technique
Kellogg's Sales and Marketing	*Kellogg's Special K* Red Ball	Food	Loyalty	Self-liquidating promotion (SLP)
Ladbrokes	The Grand National	Culture, leisure and travel	Loyalty	Prize promotion

(Continued)

Organisation	Brand	Sector	Objectives	Technique
Walkers	*Walkers* Comic Relief	Food	Loyalty	Cause-related promotions (free item)
Nando's Chicken	Sandwich Mailer	Retailers and mail order	Awareness Loyalty	Price promotion
GlaxoSmith-Kline	*Ribena*: win cars that make your Dad look cool	Food	Awareness Trial	Free item prize promotion
Nikon	*Nikon Coolpix* Adventure	Culture, leisure and travel	Awareness Trial	Free item prize promotion
Diageo	*Guinness* Pocket Pundits	Alcoholic drinks	Loyalty	Free item
The Guardian newspaper	*The Guardian* Enfield Door Drop	Online and offline media	Loyalty	Price promotion
Kimberley-Clark	*Andrex* Says Thank You	FMCG products	Loyalty	On-pack promotion, free postage
P&G	*Ariel* Championship whites: free lessons at *Tesco*	FMCG products	Awareness Trial	On-pack promotion, free postage

Sales promotion successes

Source: Institute of Sales Promotion 2009.

Kellogg's Special K Red Ball promotion was successful in three ways: (i) increasing sales; (ii) covering costs of the promotion through sales of the 'Red Ball' exercise merchandise; and (iii) providing a new narrative thread for the *Special K* brand by linking consumption with a health and fitness agenda.

PROMOTION IN FOCUS

Nikon. Push and Pull Promotion

Nikon is favourably placed in the intensely competitive Compact Digital Camera category of the 'Culture, Leisure and Travel sector'. However, in order to achieve significant relative positioning amongst the 5–6 rival major manufacturers, the *Coolpix* camera was launched to help differentiate in a category which offered very similar products in terms of quality, features, range and benefits.

In order to raise awareness and interest in the *Nikon* range of *Coolpix* digital cameras within the trade, incentivise and motivate counter staff to push product through demonstration and recommendation, and to pull traffic through the stores, a *Nikon Coolpix Adventure* sales promotion was launched. This involved a clever hands-on practical promotion which required consumers to activate their memory cards to see whether they (and the sales person) had won an adventure prize. This encouraged interaction with the product. Trips such as white water rafting and flying over Ayres Rock tied in beautifully with the key benefit of the brand: capturing photo opportunities digitally.

Camera purchasers could also enter a competition to win one of 1000 *TDK* 64Mb memory cards. They did this by filling in a mail-drop questionnaire (to 500,000 households) which contained a *Nikon*-branded *CompactFlash*™ card. This also had the benefit of collecting user data for future profiling. The promotion was supported in store by point-of-sale materials, a sales trade incentive and *Nikon* 'Special Awards' for retailers whose display of POS material and support for the promotion was exceptional.

TGI was used to target digital camera users/buyers: men in the 35–44 age group, married with children and from households with incomes in excess of £35,000. A 'proximity model' was used to map specific participating retailers in geographical positions to enhance sell-in.

Average percentage sales over the promotional period increased by 30% and exceeded the target for each month of the promotional period. The overall theme *Nikon Coolpix Adventures* successfully encompassed all campaign trade and consumer sales objectives as well as strengthening *Nikon's* position in the digital camera category.

SALES FORCE SELLING

There are different approaches to selling. Newton (1969, p. 136), who regards the sales force as 'campaigners to be chosen, assigned and compensated in much the same way that creative campaigns are used for advertising', offers four types of personal selling:

- new business development and key account management;
- technical representation;
- missionary or task force selling; and
- trade selling.

Whilst the first three are just as important as trade selling, it is the purpose of this chapter to link selling to sales promotion, and therefore it is not intended to offer an in-depth discussion of sales management here.

As Smith and Taylor point out (2004, p. 295), 'winning the battle for mindshare (or share of mind) can be an important part of sales-force management'. This means that the amount of time that a distributor's sales force gives to your brand is vital as the range of other manufacturers' products has to be represented as well. There is many a time when good brands with solid marketing campaigns have fallen down because the distributor and its sales team do not properly present a manufacturer's brand. If the distributor's sales team (either in the field or in the office), do not understand your product, or don't like your company, or are not sufficiently motivated or incentivised to sell, your brand may become a 'Friday afternoon' product, barely mentioned, without enthusiasm and destined for an early withdrawal.

Often, a holistic strategic approach has to be the only way of getting a brand recommended, selected and positively sold through to end users. This will involve a long-term partnership covering product, finance, joint promotional activity and representation, merchandising, returns policy, new product development, sales methods, marketing communications materials and so on. In a protracted selling situation (e.g. the specification of flooring materials for an airport which may take years from receiving 'advanced building information' to the product being laid), a partnership is the only way.

Trade selling may be done through a manufacturer's own sales force or through commissioned agents, or through a distributor's sales force, who are paid by the distributor and may also be incentivised by the manufacturer. Consider the Matter of Fact box below which details a sanitaryware manufacturer selling bathroom suites. Figure 15.3 shows the complicated web of personal selling which may involve B2B selling between manufacturer and retailer and distributor and retailer to achieve the same objectives. Equally, a distributor may have a telemarketing team supporting the promotion of a manufacturer's brand, working in tandem.

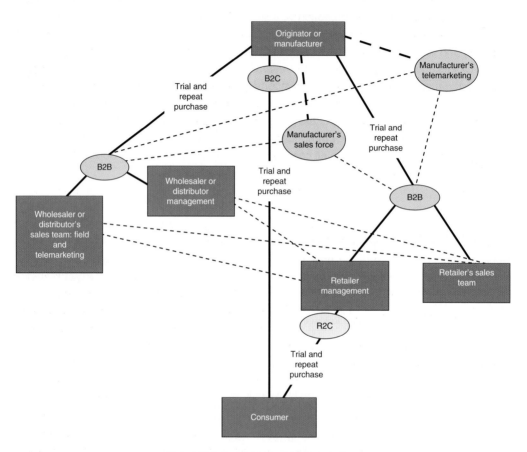

Figure 15.3: Impacts of sales-force selling

MATTER OF FACT

Making Pieces – Selling Suites

When a consumer walks into a DIY retail store or an independent local bathroom 'boutique', she may be casually looking for ideas or actively seeking out an *Ideal Standard* or *Villeroy & Boch* suite that she has seen advertised. She may be aware or unaware of any specific brands, and may have an immediate or latent need for a new or replacement bathroom suite.

Consider the position of a sanitaryware manufacturer, a company which makes vitreous china basins, pedestals, toilet pans and cisterns, as well as acrylic baths in Northern Europe, and buys in taps, wastes and ceramic tiles from Italy and Spain. Although it makes and sells components, it has to market complete bathroom suites, and its route to market is complicated. The company sells its branded products (which appear in its company sales brochures and may be displayed at trade exhibitions and product launches) through to the end user, the consumer. To do this, it has to ensure that the opportunities to see the product displayed 'as if it were in the manufacturer's own showroom' are maximised. For the retailer to properly represent the manufacturer's brand, the manufacturer's sales force must have educated the retailer about the product, secured a display space in the retailer's showroom, supplied and fitted a well-merchandised display, furnished the store with promotional literature and provided all kinds of service and relationship back-up to the retailer. The salesperson's role may also include market research feedback (being the 'eyes and ears' in the marketplace), managing display fitting and merchandising teams, as well as coordinating delivery, credit and any other support to the retailer. To some retailers, the salesperson (or 'rep') does not just represent the company, s(he) is the company.

The distributor or wholesaler who supplies the manufacturer's product may also have a sales force which sells a range of similar products to similar outlets. It is important for the manufacturer to ensure that they achieve as high a 'mindshare' of the distributor as possible, to fight for retailer opportunities to sell and secure a physical and visible presence in the marketplace. This will involve the long-term building of trust, allied to hard-nosed selling and managing of other people's sales agents and sales teams. The management of 'field' teams (business development managers, area sales managers, representatives and so on) as well as 'office' teams (telemarketing, telesales, customer service and so on) is therefore critical to this process.

Now, to complicate matters even further, the manufacturer may also supply own-brand components to the distributor (e.g. acrylic baths or 'four-piece sets of pottery') to make into distributor own brands, and also complete own-brand suites to the end retailer to sell under its own brand name. The consumer walking into the large retail outlet may be buying similar manufacturers' products but marketed under its house brand names. And equally, the retailer or builders' merchant buying a 'distributor's own-branded suite' may also buy the original manufacturer's products. The manufacturer may have got the whole demand chain going by advertising and promotional activity geared towards creating awareness and stimulating demand to 'pull' through the chain. And if the suite is displayed and dressed well, the salesperson knows the product and helps to explain what it can and can't do, and if the POS materials confirm the consumer's original expectations, then a sale may take place and the retailer will order more suites from the distributor, who in turn will place further orders from the manufacturer. Job done!

SALES PROMOTIONAL TACTICS

Sales promotions are generally predicated on the principles of operant conditioning: people will invariably respond to positive reinforcement which comes from rewards such as loyalty schemes. The fundamental downside is that often the intention is meant to be temporary and, as soon as the reward is withdrawn, the effect ceases to be effective. In other words, the results of sales promotional activity may quickly dissolve outside the promotional period. Sometimes the effect is actually to distort sales patterns and not improve them. Orders are brought forward, or delayed, in order for customers to take advantage of the lower price or the premium offer. This is not always the case. If a promotional objective is to encourage trial of a new product, or for non-users in a category to try the product, sales promotion may actually help to 'shape' consumer behaviour. The results may be to 'increase the drive for more' (de Pelsmacker, Geuens and van den Bergh 2001). And even if new users return to their regular brands after the promotion, this may change a consumer's consideration set when next evaluating alternatives; enough doubt may have been planted in their minds for them to reconsider their choice in future. In effect, trial promotions put current favoured brands under trial as much as new alternatives.

Sales promotions are often categorised as either: 'push' promotions aimed at pushing product through the chain of distribution from manufacturer through wholesale or distribution intermediaries to retailers; or 'pull' promotions aimed at creating consumer demand which will pull the brand from manufacturer through the distribution chain.

The following section highlights the different push or trade promotions used to achieve warehouse space, stock levels, in-store displays or shelf-space at the point of sale. Table 15.2 details examples of 'push B2B' promotions geared towards generating orders for the manufacturer from distributors and wholesalers. Table 15.3 gives examples of 'push B2B' promotions direct to retailers from manufacturers. Table 15.4 illustrates the type of 'push R2C' repeat purchase promotions to consumers from retailers. Table 15.5 lists examples of 'push R2C' promotions where retailers encourage trial promotions of a brand by consumers.

Product or service sampling	Free product to trial with key customers or test market to prospective segments. Product or service sampling may involve limited exposure to the manufacturer's offer to experience *in situ*
Own-brand range	Manufacturers may be forced to or willingly make 'unbranded' products which may be sold on as part of a distributor's branded range. This may undermine a manufacturer's brand or provide an entry into a market segment or a targeted customer
Rebates	Turnover related discounts or retrospective rebates (i.e. based on up-front or cumulative sales) may persuade distributors to stock and encourage them to sell
Bonus packs	Providing packaged 'bundles' of stock either of quantities of the same product or using anciliary products may be advantageous to stock and strategically useful for the manufacturer to achieve penetration of the distributor offer
Direct price-offs/ Stock cleansing	Stock cleansing involves buying a competitor's stock in order to create space in the distributor's warehouse and facilitate an initial opening stock order. Introductory lower prices or discounts will help achieve momentum and create demand
Warranties	The new distributor's perceived risk may be allayed by covering any breakages, unsold products, faulty goods, or any other element of the product in use which is not the distributor's responsibility
Premiums	Promotions may encourage loyalty and may take the form of gifts or sales-related incentives
Displays	Payments for displays at exhibitions (e.g. the *Interbuild* Building and Construction Industry exhibition at the NEC in Birmingham), or in retailers' premises

Merchandising and POS	The provision of merchandising and POS materials for use at distributor sales meetings and to distribute through retailers
Sales-force training	The education and training of the distributor's sales force is critical both for ensuring mindshare and instilling confidence in the distributor's sales people. May involve attendance at sales meetings, product launches or factory visits
Sales-force incentives	Encouragement for active involvement in selecting brand to push and sell can be in the form of sales-force competitions, incentive schemes and corporate events
Cooperative advertising	Presents a joint representation of manufacturer and distributor and involves 'marketing monies' being available either up-front or retrospectively applied
Sales conferences	Sponsorship and active support of distributor sales conferences and meetings is an integral part of relationship building and sales promotion with distributor personnel
Joint exhibitions	Exhibitions, trade evenings and PR events which link manufacturer and distributor are an integral part of relationship building and sales promotion between manufacturer, distributor and retailers

Table 15.2: Push B2B manufacturers to distributors and wholesalers

Promotion	Description
Product or service sampling	Trialling of product or service may be done by sampling, free product or extended credit facilities to encourage retailers to experience the product with a view to gaining interest and confidence in selling the manufacturer's brand
Own-brand range	Manufacturers may be forced to or willingly make 'unbranded' product which may be sold on as part of a merchant or retailer's branded range. This may undermine a manufacturer's brand or provide an entry into a market segment or a targeted customer
Rebates	Turnover related discounts or retrospective rebates (i.e. based on up-front or cumulative sales) may persuade distributors to stock and encourage them to sell
Bonus packs	Providing packaged 'bundles' of stock either of quantities of the same product or using anciliary products may be advantageous to stock and strategically useful for the manufacturer to achieve penetration of the distributor offer. Special consumer promotion kits (e.g. *PC World* offering manufacturers' computers with special software) may also be used
Direct price-offs/ Stock cleansing	In order to make space for product on display or on shelves, the cleansing of competitors' stock and displays may be involved. Introductory lower prices or discounts may be funded by the manufacturer to help achieve momentum and create demand
Warranties	Manufacturers' warranties and product guarantees and delivery service may encourage retailers to stock and display brands as they alleviate perceived risk of use

(Continued)

Promotion	Description
Premiums	Proof of purchase 'money-off' premiums are an expensive way of creating consumer demand and encouraging retailers to stock product. Free samples of the product or introductory offers also help. *McDonald's* has tie-ins with *Disney* providing free gifts in its 'Happy Meals' related to the release and promotion of a movie or DVD
Displays	Manufacturers have to 'buy' display space in retailers' showrooms either through paying for the right, the space or the cost of display
Merchandising and POS	Stores with or without displays have to be merchandised with POS materials, brochures and so on. Some companies have 'tied distribution' arrangements where display merchandising units (e.g. *Lucozade* refrigerated drinks cabinets or *Mars* counter-top confectionery pack holders) are offered free of charge in exchange for regular orders
Direct price-offs	Direct price-offs may be related to advertising campaigns which are attempting to stimulate sales or procure consumer use information
Multi-purchase sweepstakes or contests	Some retailers offer 'multi-packs' to encourage more use of the product and offer better 'value' to consumers. Incentives like sweepstakes or contests are used to encourage trial or repeat purchase
Packaging	Packaging is often used to launch new products on the back of others. *Kellogg's Special K* cereal bars were given away free on packs of *Kellogg's Special K* breakfast cereal

Table 15.3: Push B2B manufacturer's trial promotions to retailers

Promotion	Description
Store layout	The physical layout of a store can affect the shoppers' experience and encourage purchase. Stores may have a variety of layouts: 'grid systems' are typically used by supermarkets where customers are directed to categories such as 'tinned soups' or 'confectionery'
Store ambience	Sound and olfactory factors can be used to create a holistic sensory experience
Point-of-purchase displays and merchandising	In-store photographic representation and stock displays of product can act as a 'silent salesman' or provide 'self-service' of product
Product or service sampling	Some retailers will provide samples of product to test or match against customer demands. Examples are free ceramic tile samples for DIY decorating of bathrooms
Store own brands	Retailers' versions of manufacturers' product are often supplied to compete or complement with manufacturers' brands
Warranties	Retailers may reduce the perceived risk of purchase by offering guarantees or warranties to cover the product in use
Advertising	Retailers may advertise in the local press (e.g. to announce a store opening or sale to encourage footfall (i.e. customer traffic into the shop)
Loyalty card schemes	Encouragement of store patronage or increased levels of sales can often be achieved through the reward schemes of store cards

Direct price-offs	Price reductions may make the value of a brand more competitive and encourage sales (often a short-term tactic)
BOGOF	Free product promotions have the advantage of extending product use and may encourage a permanent change in behaviour. Buy One, Get One Free promotions are good examples of this
Home shopping/delivery	An extension of the store experience is the utility of a free delivery service to encourage those not able or willing to travel and collect shopping from a store
Credit facilities	One way a retailer minimises the financial risk involved in purchase is deferred payment offered by extending credit facilities

Table 15.4: Push R2C retailer's repeat purchase promotions to consumers

Promotion	Description
Product or service sampling	Some retailers will provide samples of product to test or match against customer demands. Examples are free ceramic tile samples for DIY decorating of bathrooms
Bonus packs	Promotional product 'bundles' may offer extra value without reducing price
Direct price-offs	Price reductions may make the value of a brand more competitive and encourage sales (often a short-term tactic)
Warranties	Retailers may reduce the perceived risk of purchase by offering guarantees or warranties to cover the product in use
Loyalty schemes	Encouragement of store patronage or increased levels of sales can often be achieved through the reward schemes of store cards
Relationship marketing	Sales and communications can be tailored to customers from database data to encourage the development of brand relationships

Table 15.5: Push R2C retailers' trial promotions to consumers

PROMOTION IN FOCUS

Bluewater. Retail Shopping Mall Promotion

As consumers become more and more emotionally connected with brands, experiential marketing is seen as a way of combining the short-term tactical ability of promotions to affect sales with the longer-term objectives of changing attitudes and building the brand. Even more so in a retail environment like the UK's *Bluewater* retail and leisure complex, where shopping is seen as a leisure experience. Consumer marketing specialist *iblink* is working with *Bluewater* to launch a new experiential marketing offer – *Azure*.

The package offers an opportunity for 'brand experiences that will turn the world of interactive consumer marketing in shopping malls on its head'. This includes short-term leasing of a 2700 square feet high-footfall area in the entrance hall, VIP car parking, advertising sites on the approach, space for outdoor activities, and a host of non-traditional branding opportunities within *Bluewater* itself.

(Continued)

With access being limited to so many parts of the centre, this type of interactive promotional activity provides brands with a unique opportunity to do things differently in outdoor, experiential and digital marketing in the largest retail and leisure destination in Europe. It allows brands to promote themselves for a month or more at reduced rates, and even promote their brand on *Bluewater's* centrepiece large sails, which hang from the ceiling. These can add animation to the promotion, becoming a giant, moving point of 'sale'.

DIRECT MARKETING PROMOTIONS

Direct marketing can often cut through the clutter and confusion of mass marketing and go straight to the customer (Thomas 2007). It offers an anticipated, personal and relevant 'permissive' alternative to 'interruption' marketing (Godin 1999), guaranteeing more regular engagement with marketing communication messages. It encourages 'volunteers' to participate in the brand story rather than be confronted with it. Direct and database marketing has grown from a 'junk mail' intrusive communications medium to one of being fundamentally important to engaging in interactive customer communications. The key forces which have driven the rapid rate of change have been:

- the dynamic changes in consumption and the subsequent fragmentation of lifestyle consumer categories;
- fragmentation of media;
- the phenomenal increase in consumer power;
- the undermining of transmissive marketing communications;
- increased advertising and media costs;
- increased technological facilitation of market information (database, EPOS, smart card, permissive online marketing communications).

The Institute of Direct Marketing describes direct marketing as 'The planned recording, analysis and tracking of customers' direct response behaviour over time....[...] in order to develop future marketing strategies for long-term customer loyalty'. Key objectives are to:

- build and add to a database;
- disseminate product and brand information;
- generate leads for future sales;
- encourage foot traffic, store and website visits;
- remind and reassure target audiences; and
- make sales.

Segmentation of existing and potential customers is critical in order to effectively target communications. Demographics, geodemographics (e.g. MOSAIC or CACI's 'A Classification of Residential Neighbourhoods') and psychographics (values and lifestyle; attitudes, opinions and interests) are the main methods used. The objective of segmentation is to ensure dialogues are as close to personally relevant conversations as possible. In this way, CRM and database marketing are inseparable and both inform each other. The content and quality of regular communications can depend on subject matter, brand relationships, personality types and creative execution. This can include:

- **Welcome communications:** procedural, courtesy communication encouraging permissive evaluation of needs and wants and reinforcing group membership.
- **Joining the brand and consumer conversation:** encouraging ownership of brand narrative and facilitating user-generated content where possible.
- **Up-selling and cross-selling:** moving customers 'up' to higher ticket price brands or moving customers to other product categories.

- **Renewal:** the continuation of signing up customers is key to extending communications and ensuring income streams.
- **Re-activation of customers:** lapsed customers may be worth reconnecting with.

According to Patterson (1998) direct marketing is seen to hold a number of advantages over traditional communications methods:

- It can be highly targeted, created and delivered with specific customers in mind allowing dialogue to build strong relationships.
- It can be individualised and personalised, helping to overcome the clutter inherent in traditional mass-media communications.
- It can be more cost-effective than other mass-media tactics which leads many smaller organisations to use it as a competitive tool against larger organisations with massive communications budgets.
- Through the initiation of a dialogue with customers, it can play a more useful role in building loyalty than is possible using mass-media monologues.
- The effects of direct marketing are measurable to a much greater extent than the effects of traditional communications and therefore more accountable.

Compatible techniques include telemarketing and direct response advertising:

- **Telemarketing.** This involves direct 'outbound' and 'inbound' personal contact, which provides the basis for an interactive relationship between the organisation and the customer. Telemarketing, like other components of direct marketing, has to be highly targeted and controlled in order to create and maintain customer relationships. Telemarketing can also be used for marketing research and customer service initiatives, as well as the basis for developing existing customer relationships. In addition, screening and converting sales leads, providing in-house sales support and planning, facilitating direct sales, and providing intermediary support. A debate at the moment is whether outsourcing call centre support actually benefits or undermines customer relationships, whether telemarketing is intrusive or supportive, and whether it is really integrated into the brand 'conversation' or seen as adjacent to the rest of the communications mix.
- **Direct response advertising.** This differs from standard broadcast, print and online brand or image advertising in that calls to action or response (e.g. fill in a coupon, ring up, visit website, go into store, apply for brochure) are contained within the advertising message and elicited from the target audience. More and more organisations are involving themselves in direct response advertising in order to optimise their expenditure on advertising.

CLOSING CASE STUDY

Becks: You Can Lead a Man to Culture, but Can You Make Him Drink?

At the end of 2008, *InBev* beer brand *Beck's* launched a campaign as part of an awareness drive and tied in with a promotion featuring limited edition labels designed by both well-established and up-and-coming artists. In conjunction with the Royal College of Art, the *Beck's* 'Canvas' campaign sponsored four art students to showcase their work on 27 million bottles of *Beck's*. This was backed by a fully integrated marketing communications support package which included TV and press advertising, online activities and point-of-sale materials, together with an on-pack promotion directing users to the *Beck's* website as part of a database-building exercise.

(Continued)

Beck's do have a history of supporting artistic talent. The German brand has had a long association with the world of contemporary arts and has been fostering artistic talent for nearly 27 years. And now, four students, together with artists such as Damien Hirst, The Chapman Brothers and Tracey Emin were all given this unique 'canvas': the label on a bottle of *Beck's Bier*.

Beck's bier labelled with art

This promotional campaign is consistent with *Beck's* overall positioning as a supporter of arts and music, which resonates with the predominantly male target audience. *Beck's* view is that: 'Contemporary art is a living part of our cultural heritage. Encouraging raw ability and building a broader public appreciation of the diversity and excellence of artistic accomplishment is a vision which *Beck's* has long supported'. Earlier in the year, another cultural event was held aimed at giving a memorable experiential event: *Beck's Fusions* 2008, a combination of art and music staged at Manchester's Castlefield Arena on 6 September featuring *Massive Attack* and *United Visual Artists*. *Beck's* was partnered by the Contemporary Arts Society. The initiative built on the success of the inaugural *Beck's Fusions*, held at iconic locations including London's Trafalgar Square.

Running from August to the end of 2008, the aim was to improve consumer awareness during a peak sales and social period. *InBev* UK ensured that there was a high level of participation in the event by giving consumers the chance to apply for tickets online at www.becks.co.uk. *Beck's Fusions* succeeded in raising the consumer profile of the *Beck's* family of brands and helped push the brand through retailers and pull it through pubs and other drinking venues. *InBev* supported the promotion with what it calls 'point of connection' (rather than point of sale) materials available in bars, pubs and other venues to communicate the art-linked initiative to consumers. There was a dedicated website www.becks.co.uk/canvas to continue the communications online.

A fuller supportive advertising campaign ran at the same time with the theme of 'Different By Choice' concentrating on objects, places and individuals who have achieved success 'by setting their own rules' and bucking convention. The four bottles are featured in a new vignette that has been added to the commercial – and are pictured displayed on an art gallery-style plinth with the line: 'The Artists Who Said No to Canvas'. This is both a build-up to the sales promotion and is enforced by the rewards of seeing the uniquely bottled product in pubs, clubs and off-licences or the online experience.

QUESTIONS

1. Do you think this type of promotion will limit *Beck's* future potential as the demographic of the target audience is restricted?

2. Is there a natural link between culture and brand promotions?

3. How would you measure the success of this type of promotion?

CHAPTER SUMMARY

In this chapter, we discussed the relationship between selling and sales promotional activities as being the action-based elements of the marketing communications mix. Often traditionally seen as the poor relations or invisible partners in marketing communications, the two are instrumental in providing the bedrock of a campaign: stock of product into warehouses, commitment to 'push' product through the supply chain, negotiating 'preferred supplier' status with key retailers, buying category shelf-space and product facings, and supporting all activities at point of purchase. We saw how business-to-business selling should work in tandem with all communication tools to match demand stimulated through sales and other promotional efforts.

The discussion on the supportive role played by sales and sales promotional activities illustrated how these components are often seen as tactical and ephemeral. And because of the temporary nature of some sales-oriented activities, these were often incorrectly seen as not contributing to and underpinning long-term strategy.

We also examined how the mechanics and application of sales-force face-to-face selling, together with how direct marketing underpins both sales and sales promotional activities, provides the analysis, access, communication and control elements key to campaign planning.

REFLECTIVE QUESTIONS

a. Are sales promotional activities tactical or strategic? Illustrate your answer with examples of how sales activities have been used to achieve marketing communications goals.

b. What are the key objectives of sales promotional activities? How are they different to overall communication objectives?

c. Describe the four types of personal selling and give examples of how and why they are used.

d. How does direct marketing cut through the clutter and confusion of mass marketing and go straight to the customer?

e. Evaluate the different aspects of B2B, R2C and B2C promotional activities, giving examples to show how they function both separately and in cohesion.

RESEARCH PROJECTS

Search out Thomas's 2007 paper 'The End of Mass Marketing: Or Why All Successful Marketing is now Direct Marketing' published in *Direct Marketing: an International Journal* and evaluate the arguments for a more direct communication approach.

Visit *Exhibitions.co.uk*, a UK website featuring a comprehensive listing of all the consumer, public, industrial and trade exhibitions to be held in major venues around the UK. What types of exhibition are there? What purpose do you think they serve? Why don't you visit one of the consumer shows and see for yourself?

CHAPTER  16

BEYOND TRADITIONAL MARKETING COMMUNICATIONS

"Old marketing, steeped in the archaic constructs of reach and frequency, predicates itself on the ability to whack targets over the head until they surrender helplessly. New marketing, infused by the DNA of digital innovation, upsets the imbalance of power to reveal an entirely new paradigm."
(Jaffe 2005, p. 34)

As Shultz, Tenenbaum and Lauterborn (1992) point out, the marketing communications 'catechism, written in the '60s, grew out of the US experience during and after World War II' and was predicated on a mass communications model. But just as we have witnessed the dissolution of mass marketing, we have also seen the emergence of a different marketing communications paradigm, one of convergence of communications media and interconnectivity of audience and message.

An essential ingredient to this changing landscape has been that communications in the past have been perceived as fixed and definable, whereas the post-modern marketplace emphasises the need to consider communications as dynamic, fragmented and constructed within a social context. This chapter traces the declining relationship consumers have with conventional 'interruption' advertising and the rise of interactive, user-generated social media. The discussion is based on the premise that true audience engagement is now a two-way, interactive and negotiable phenomenon.

LEARNING OBJECTIVES

After reading this chapter, you'll be able to:

- Appreciate the changing nature of marketing communications.
- Discuss the social web in the context of consumer change and communication technological development.
- Appreciate the factors affecting the transformation of marketing communications.
- Analyse the approaches that are transforming marketing communications.
- Understand the social web in the context of consumer change and communication technological development.
- Discuss the possibilities for reinventing TV advertising

Every time that a new medium has been introduced to marketing communications, some element of value has been added to offer more scope in helping to expose brands to target audiences. Magazines offered a full colour canvas to enhance newspapers; billboards exploded images to the size of a house; radio provided a musical and oral soundtrack to bring advertisements to life. Then, in the early 1950s, television arrived, provided dynamic movement and added yet another dimension. And so, the appeal of mass communications as a way of transmitting commercial messages to target audiences became the marketing communications paradigm.

This progressed to a less mediated route and offered more direct, personal communication through catalogues, direct marketing and telemarketing. All these methods of communication relied on the notion of the interruption of captive audiences. But the efficacy of 'interruptive messages' is being undermined and its impact diminishing. We are now witnessing a third incarnation for marketing: the **social web**. Jaffe (2005) describes the 'conversational marketing' of the social web as 'being at the centre of the universe. . . [where]. . .experience is the brand differentiator'. These latest developments characterise media as 'content' and communication as 'conversation'. As Morgan (2009, p. 20) claims: 'in the digital space much of the point is that people are finding their own applications for what brands are giving them'.

OPENING CASE STUDY

Volvo: 'Life is Better Lived Together'. Safety in Numbers or How Volvo Used the Net to Escape the Cage

To 'own' a category can be the ultimate objective in brand positioning. In the same way that the name *Kellogg's* is synonymous with breakfast cereal and *Hoover* stood for 'vacuuming', *Volvo* stood for SAFETY.

Associations emphasising 'protection' featured prominently in imagery used in its advertisements, classically conditioning consumers to think of the car as a huge protective cage. This ensured top-of-mind awareness for *Volvo* with the benefit of protection. And whilst features such as ABS and Side

(Continued)

445

Volvo's shark metaphor becomes a positional cage

Impact Protection System (SIPS) undoubtedly helped achieve this, it was great advertising like the 'Cages Save Lives' campaign which was mainly responsible for decades of category dominance. Its primary brand strength became a weakness. The *Volvo* car began to symbolise the safe family man and was metaphorically locked in its own safety cage.

Its main brand salience – safety – offered less distinction against the competition and the *Volvo* brand seemed dull and 'safe'. Recent changes to the *Volvo* narrative have seen its repositioning as exciting and adventurous and latterly with an affiliation appeal.

With a new stable of exciting new models to offer, *Volvo* faced two problems: the average *Volvo* buyer was now outside the more youthful '20–30 somethings' customer profile of the main car-buying target audience, and any attempts to use a traditional approach to communications were likely to miss the mark. In a fully integrated campaign which included offline and online elements, *Volvo* went to where the market was and created as many brand touch-points as possible.

Riding on the coat-tails of popular culture, *Volvo* communications targeted a much younger customer profile and created an exciting presence in media which typically fetishised cars: hip hop videos (featuring LL Cool J and Dilated Peoples) and a series of video games – *Rallisport Challenge 2* by *Xbox* and *Grand Theft Auto* for *PSP* and PC. As well as these high-profile 'street cred' media vehicles, the marketing communications campaign did not only rely on mass-communication advertising, but also embraced a whole host of multimedia components covering: a spoof viral 'mockumentary' (directed by Spike Jones); billboards; an experimental interactive cinema campaign; direct mail; and even an online media campaign. Featuring a 'For Friends For Life' promotion aimed at spreading word of mouth and embracing the theme of affiliation by offering a new *Volvo S40* and a trip for four friends, this gained maximum web exposure presence. To further ensure that the new target audience was reached, the sites used were not just automotive sites, but travel and social sites such as *Friendster* and *Match* and a host of special-interest sites like *Daily Candy, Time Out* and *Atom Films.* A DVD mailer was sent to 500,000 potential customers featuring a behind-the-scenes video of the filming of a special *Volvo* music video. Promotional tie-ups with retailers like *Virgin Megastores* extended the normal media and reach into a younger profile.

The racing video game, designed for use with *Microsoft's Xbox* system, is called 'Volvo Drive for Life' and served as a showcase for the *Volvo* nameplate, three *Volvo* models and the famous *Volvo* brand identity as the car designed for safety. It is an exciting new image, but unlike most racing video games which reward players for speed, players were taken

Volvo's new drive for brand life

through a simulated training course at the *Volvo* training grounds in Gothenberg, Sweden. Also included were a virtual tour of the *Volvo* Safety Centre and a 'greatest hits' collection of film from actual crash tests. *Volvo* dealers were asked to set up *Xbox* systems and monitors in their showrooms for visitors to play the '*Volvo* Drive for Life' game as well as offering copies of the game cartridges as a special tie-in promotion. This sort of advertising is referred to as 'adver-gaming', what Jaffe (2005, p. 155) calls 'a cultural marriage between gaming and advertising'. Karen Shulman of Electronic Arts (whose *EA Sports* games are saturated with quasi-subliminal advertising, set in the simulated game environments of real-world sports stadia) declares gaming to be 'a universal media platform as pervasive as television'. The power of this medium is that it leverages sight, sound, motion and interactivity, and its content-captured product placement reaches target audiences where and when they want to be reached, with added value and no interruptions. Indeed, because up to eight hours is spent playing these sort of games, consumers are encouraged to spend time with advertising and engage with the brand! *Volvo* has actually pioneered 'alternative media', being the first car company to have its own website, to run online banner advertisements and to sponsor a podcast with *Autoblog*.

Continuing the theme of gaming, but this time in a more social context, a special cinema game was devised for the *Volvo CX70* using 'interactive audience' motion-sensing technology from the USA. Audiences at Cineworld's Nottingham, Wandsworth, Bolton, Chesterfield, Sheffield, Brighton, Cardiff, Ipswich, Edinburgh, Stevenage, Birmingham and West India Quay cinemas competed head to head. David Polinchock, chief 'experience' officer at the Brand Experience Lab, which worked on the new gaming technology for *Volvo*, claimed that 'audience gaming is a new genre, and it creates a very social experience'.

QUESTIONS

1. What is meant by 'owning a category'? Is this a dangerous position to hold?

2. Why has *Volvo* extended beyond traditional marketing communications?

3. What do you think about this new form of hybrid communication where messages are essentially 'captured' in entertainment content?

Mass communications is rapidly becoming a contradiction in terms: audiences are diminishing; there is an over-proliferation of interruptive communications; a fragmenting media environment; and the traditional broadcaster's role is being 'disintermediated' by multi-channel television, the Internet and DVDs. Technological media developments in such consumer message-avoidance hardware as *TiVo*, *Sky+* and downloadable formats, together with the explosion and clutter in media alternatives, have made audience and media engagement and interaction the most critical concepts to become centre stage in recent business-to-consumer communications. The Advertising Research Foundation (ARF) defines engagement as 'turning on a prospect to a brand idea enhanced by the surrounding media context'.

In the immediate aftermath of the Second World War, in an age of prosperity and optimism, manufacturers of consumer durables and FMCG brands began to see the benefits of television advertising as a powerful marketing communications medium. In 1950, just under 3% of *P&G*'s media spending went on television, but as the medium expanded, and offered a powerful cost-efficient method to communicate to a mass, captive audience, over 80% of all *P&G*'s advertising expenditure was devoured by television. Just over 10 years ago, the first *P&G* worldwide online centre was established (Lindström and Andersen 2000, p. 17) with the purpose of transferring its TV advertising budget onto the net at the right time. The mass communications broadcast media paradigm is under threat and the traditional fixation with above the line (ATL) is giving way to a plethora of narrowcast alternatives which are no longer just supplements but now legitimate substitutes. These two schools of thought (described rather contentiously by Jaffe as 'Catholic and Protestant') polarise between: brand image communications (where messages are transmitted) and brand innovation (negotiated, experiential new marketing).

The return on investing in TV advertising has been under question for some time, with only 18% of US and UK companies claiming a positive ROI. Costs have risen exponentially, CPM reportedly up 265% between 1996 and 2005 in the USA. In the UK, ITV Chairman Michael Grade reported a 50% fall in advertising revenues year on year for March 2009. In an age of 'time-shifted' viewing, whether the 'I' will come to mean 'interactive' or 'interrogative' or 'independent viewing' will determine its future. Too late; *Apple iTV* is here already! Most worrying for brand owners and media though is the fact that 90% of consumers who are able to, avoid TV advertising altogether.

'Clutter, creativity, the changing consumer, and the very efficacy of the 30-second commercial are four major issues that have separately and jointly made for a complex and challenging communications landscape' (Jaffe 2005, p. 23). It is a landscape of change, and according to Schultz and Schultz (2005), 'the change is in the consumer that is driving all the new concepts, approaches, technologies and the like that a whole new age of consumers have adapted and adopted'. Jaffe (2005, p. 7) claims that *Apple*'s historic campaign against the 'Big Brother' *IBM* – defined by a self-dated TV advertisement titled '1984' – is 'the only alleged mass-media moment left'. That is not to say that brands are not still advertised in this way, but consumers no longer view in anything like the same numbers. A strategic shift from push to pull marketing communications signifies a real movement towards customer-centric communications: fragmented, user generated and co-authored, rather than mass, captive audiences with transmitted asymmetrical communications. Brands like *Google, Harley-Davidson* and *Red Bull* have not used image to build up the brand, they have achieved this 'from the street up' as it were by relationship and buzz marketing. Morgan (2009, p. 17) asserts that 'an audience isn't really an audience . . .[since]. . . an audience presupposes that they are listening'. What they are doing is engaging with relevant media and co-created communications.

Social media is about the tools of the new generation. Advertisers are no longer in control of their brands. The power has shifted from brands to consumers. Modern consumers hardly ever read a newspaper or use a landline phone, they are not 'captive' in front of a TV; instead they download their own choice of programme, trust unknown bloggers and have a communal experience online through the plethora of social media. Marketing communications has moved beyond traditional audience interruption to a new era of audience engagement.

BRAND BUILDING THROUGH MARKETING COMMUNICATIONS

The scarcity of media and the limited time available to expose audiences to messages allowed the mass communication 'one-size-fits-all' brand model to work. Owning product categories through careful and creative positioning as a result of accurate targeting and customer profiling is no longer a sustainable proposition. Brand equity is shifting away from the pure economics and psychology framework of brand essence and brand recall.

Figure 16.1 describes the long-tail brand model which demonstrates the different approaches to brand building. Traditional brand models have focused on the **single-minded brand proposition:** 'If you can't speak much of it, it is too expensive to speak'. The area in blue illustrates how this model was dependent upon a 'hit' to achieve the marketing communication objectives of impact, exposure and frequency. The curve is artificially truncated to show the concentration of campaign resources at the front end.

The dominant economics of mass media dictated that one central brand proposition must form the basis of all communications. This type of focused approach falls down because brands have to live in the real world: consumers are changing; aspirations are changing; and a whole host of macro and micro environmental factors dynamically alter perceptions. As we have seen from the opening case study, *Volvo* owned the category for 'safety' by concentrating on a core brand essence. The strength of the *Volvo* actual and metaphorical 'safe cage' soon became a weakness because it limited the brand narrative.

The more common approach – the long-tail branding model – is a much more elongated narrative of different stories and campaign elements which add value and fabric to the brand proposition and

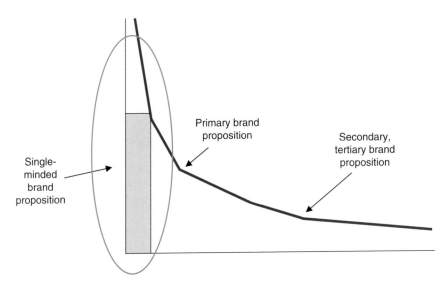

Figure 16.1: Long-tail brand model effects

Source: Iqbal (2007).

is made up of all the various communication elements and messages. And so *Volvo* has now reconstructed a story built on being fun, cool, ecologically sound and something to be shared with friends; all different stories but all consistent with the overarching brand narrative: 'Life is Better Lived Together'. This brand proposition could be a slogan for the long-tail branding model: the narrative must be organic; it must reflect consumers' real-world lives; it must be inclusive, comprising a collection of company and customer stories; and there must be open, co-authored dialogue. Great branding success stories like *Apple* and *Amazon* owe a lot, not to the replication of the initial brand proposition (the hit-driven economics of mass communications), but the business that comes from engendering retention, word of mouth and the repetition of brand loyalty.

An interesting aspect of long-tail brand building is what Mohammed Iqbal of advertising agency Ogilvy & Mather (2007, p. 5) refers to as 'building negative databases of your brand communication'. To illustrate, in the opening case, we described how *Volvo* had a core brand essence of 'safety'. If it had remained within that 'safety zone' (excuse the pun!), the brand's future would have become restricted, incarcerated by a narrow value proposition and an even narrower target audience. By focusing on what *Volvo* was not, it has rebuilt the brand and captured a whole new target market with a whole new story.

THE SOCIAL WEB IN CONTEXT

What is apparent from the success stories of *Apple* and *Volvo* is the need, and indeed the desire, to embrace what Weber (2007, p. 3) describes as 'learning to market to the social web'. Before we look at this, let us be sure what we mean by this emerging phenomenon, and let us understand the factors which have transformed marketing communications. What exactly constitutes the 'web'? Figure 16.2 shows the layers which show the social web in context.

Using the criteria suggested by Bickerton, Bickerton and Simpson-Holley (1999, p. 7), the following stages of implementation are given:

- **Presentation:** includes published information providing an image, imparting knowledge and values, gives access to information and illustrates products and services (e.g. electronic brochure, newsletter, magazine, advertising hoarding or TV commercial).

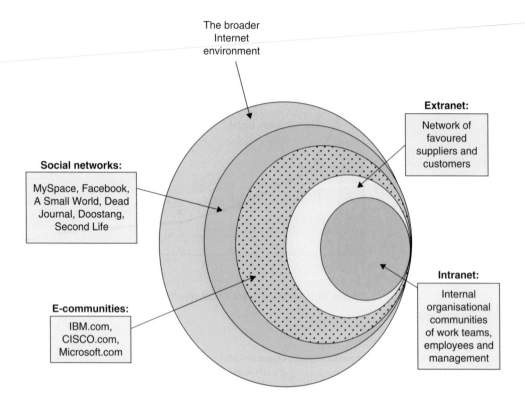

Figure 16.2: The social web in context

- **Interaction:** there is two-way communication and this goes beyond the first stage of being a mere publishing tool.
- **Representation:** the organisation replaces elements of its activities by the technology performing a business process otherwise performed by employees (e.g. stock control, data updates, producing a sales channel).

The inner circle of Figure 16.2 shows the **intranet** which uses networked or Internet technology (browser based) specifically designed to communicate within the company. A consistent corporate image and communication can be managed better by centrally controlling coherent, integrated internal communications. Employees and managers are responsible for the company/customer interface, and intranets facilitate instant, open interactive communication even with remote workers.

The next ring shows the **extranet** which uses a select audience (often suppliers, key customers, strategic alliances and other stakeholders) through networked or Internet (browser-based) connections. Cost-effective publication of materials specific to the target audience can be instant using documents in PDF form for easy and quick retrieval. Feedback from suppliers and customers helps new product development, communications and allows interaction with target audiences. Selling is more effective as even business development and field sales can be instantly supported specifically by telemarketing or routine customer services.

E-communities are 'sites where people aggregate around professionally generated content focused on a common interest area' (Weber 2007, p. 183). This phenomenon actually goes back to *Slate*, an experimental online facility devised by *Microsoft* allowing visitors to comment on professionals' articles and posts. They may be B2B sites like *IBM.com*, *Microsoft.com* or *CISCO.com* or other more public sites such as parent blogs like *Babble.com* and *MothersClick.com*. The previous generations may have had magazines rather than websites, but they were not interactive and therefore did not engender the sense of brethren that e-communities do.

Social network sites like *MySpace, Facebook, Eons, A Small World, Dead Journal, Doostang* and *Second Life* are expanding the connectivity of consumers and provide a fertile area for marketing communications. *Marks & Spencer* extended its 2007 campaign by posting TV advertisements on social network site *YouTube*. This helped it to reach a new audience who were otherwise unreachable for their specially targeted *Per Una* and *Autograph* ranges of clothes. (Do you remember the *Stella Artois* page on *Facebook* featured in the case study in Chapter 1?) The UK's Labour Party has also included *YouTube* as part of its media schedule as has the Conservative Party with 'Cameron Cam'.

THE CHANGING NATURE OF MARKETING COMMUNICATIONS

As Kitchen points out (1999, p. 2), 'marketing communications is not a static subject', but involves 'the continuous application of tried and tested techniques, it is constantly moving and dynamic, not just in terms of messages, but media, monies and changing consumer mindsets'. All communications are contingent on context, and the turbulent environment in which current marketing communications is set describes fragmented markets, compressed life cycles, intense 'hyper-competition', rapid technological developments, and the movement towards individual, cellular lifestyles. The advertising-centric, mass-market, 'transmitted' paradigm necessitated passive, captive audiences who were promoted to by brand owners. The rise of social media, the imperative of brand narratives and focus on co-authored communications is a 'natural evolution of mass-market media advertising towards targeted direct marketing' (Schultz 1999).

We are witnessing the transition from asymmetrical communications to an era of two-way dialogues. As Jaffe (2005, p. 5) puts it: 'the continued fragmentation and proliferation of media touchpoints and context alternatives makes reaching masses of audiences difficult and aggregating them even more difficult'. The new synergies of multi-vehicle integrated exposures and 'simultaneous media consumption' (Shultz 2005) have undermined the efficacy of 'interruption mass communications', and replaced it with one of permissive, communal communications.

Figure 16.3 traces the changing face of integrated marketing communications from a 'one-way message to a two-way street' (Weber 2007). Brand-owner dominated, transmitted messages are rapidly becoming brand-user generated, negotiated two-way communications. The one-to-many model of communication is moving through a one-to-one phase and might eventually become one-and-one. Non-traditional time-shifted advertising formats which allow marketing communication messages to be avoided (e.g. *TiVo, Sky+, BBC iplayer* and *Apple iTV*), are fast killing TV advertising. We will see the evolution from one of 'interruption' audience-captured advertising to one of programmes which are content-captured with product placement integrated into the plot and context as part of a broader social narrative. Consumers have lost patience with what Jaffe (2005, p. 12) describes as 'the implicit mutual agreement between commercials and content'. We have grown weary of the 'bargain' of advertisements for entertainment, even if the lines are sometimes blurred. Critics of mass-media marketing would say that 'frequency' and 'reinforcement' are really euphemisms for 'bombardment' and 'indoctrination'.

Time-shifting Apple TV
© Apple Inc. Reproduced with permission.

Consumers have 'more choices, more products, more services, more media, more messages, and more digital conversations than ever' (Weber 2007, p. 7). Cable and satellite TV offer more choice, but represent much more fragmented markets, easier to segment, but less 'mass'. Magazines have become much more specialised but reach fewer readers. Newspapers are becoming more of an online read and titles have had to resort to free DVDs to recapture readers who have been persuaded by

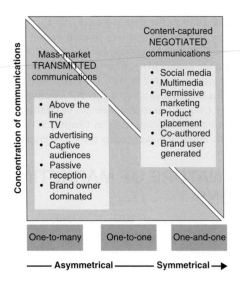

Figure 16.3: The changing face of marketing communications

eco-conscience, cost and laziness and the appeal of 'on-demand' workplace or home viewing. Even classified advertisements have migrated to online recruitment sites like *Monster.com* and *Craiglist. com*. Satellite radio stations offer commercial-free listening.

Research by In-Stat/MDR demonstrates the way consumers view TV content. Figure 16.4 pictorially represents these data and shows the consumption shifts in viewing patterns. The bars on the left represent the amount of time consumers spent watching in 2007 compared with 2006. Network or terrestrial TV (BBC, ITV etc. in the UK) shows that more than a third of people watched that medium in 2007, but the drop has been dramatic, falling to just over 5%. The other end of the spectrum sees a seven-fold increase from about 6% to just over 42% for the Internet.

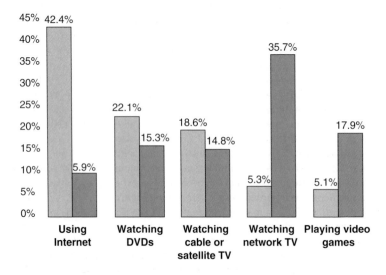

Figure 16.4: Changes in media consumption

Source: In-Stat/MDR.

FACTORS AFFECTING THE TRANSFORMATION OF MARKETING COMMUNICATIONS

All this has affected the way the 'captive' family audience has become a cellular, fragmented entity, requiring TV networks and brand sponsors to rethink media schedules. This 'joined-up media ecosystem' has been referred to as a 'Third Age' for TV where viewing is shifting in a number of exciting but challenging ways:

- Interactive media like *TiVo*, *WebTV* and *iTV* (*Interactive TV*) have changed the emphasis to viewer control. *iTV* has antecedents in direct-response advertising and elicits response and interaction.
- *Pay per View*, *Freeview*, PVR HDD hard drives, DVDs and subscriptions to rental clubs like *ilovefilm* are all examples of time-shifted viewing where 'my time has replaced prime time' (Jaffe 2005, p. 34).
- *Sony PlayStation Portable* (PSP) allows mobile 'location-shifted' viewing where there are no restrictions on location and viewing takes on a different aspect as the viewing is individually selected.
- DVDs and downloaded TV programmes which can be repeatedly shared and viewed as and when required are examples of 'device-shifted' viewing.
- High-Definition Television (HDTV), plasma screen, cinema-configured event-dedicated (i.e. *Sky Sports* or *Film*) viewing is an example of 'channel-shifting'.
- Communal experiences like *Sky Sports* in pubs and social club venues are an example of 'venue-shifting' which may give more rather than less scope for group influence.
- Alternative social network sites like *YouTube*, Room Mates on *MySpace TV* and Kate Modern on *Bebo* offer 'bite-sized chunks' of programmes, advertising campaigns and viral marketing which are examples of 'format-shifting' and expand the opportunities for accelerated word of mouth.

According to Jaffe (2005, p. 36), there are four forces which are accelerating the rate of change in the digital revolution and causing the advertising industry to rethink: broadband; wireless; search engines; and networks – demonstrated in Figure 16.5.

In homage to Malcolm Gladwell ('tipping point') Jaffe refers to a 'perfect storm brewing' in the digital world with these four ingredients a recipe for either success or disaster. With **broadband**, it is not speed which is the key but 'ubiquity'; it is almost (or soon will be) everywhere and, as such, has the power to connect and enable everyone and everything to be connected. Importantly, it 'reduces and even eliminates the lag between exposure and action' (p. 36). Broadband is not just an all-day buffet, with an open all hours mentality, it provides connectivity '24/7/365'.

Wireless (aka WiFi) is the modern-day communications paradox. It liberates consumers by the fact that it is available at all times as well as being everywhere in a variety of different ways. The fundamental difference to the mass communication model is the element of consumer choice in receiving messages; it is a kind of permissive pervasiveness! And the more applications and contexts that become 'wired' (work, home, social, shopping, public and private transportation, cities and communities), the more wire*less* we become.

The next crucial element is the concept of **search engines** as facilitators of connectivity with information, connection and knowledge. Weber (2007, p. 153) refers to these as 'reputation aggregators, the key gateway for most users to reach online content'. It underpins consumer decision making and provides real control to consumers. It is such an integral part of our lives that it took *Google* only six years to become a verb!

The last key ingredient is in some ways the most important aspect: **networks**. As Jaffe (2005, p. 39) puts it: 'Community is the only real economy of scale in today's brave new world, and the promise of community is the empowerment that comes from being informed, connected and unified'.

Technology gave us TV advertising and technology may take it away. Even if that statement is exaggerated, there is no doubt that costs, oversaturation of brands and brand messages, and an armed and dangerous consumer have undermined the primacy of TV advertising as a marketing

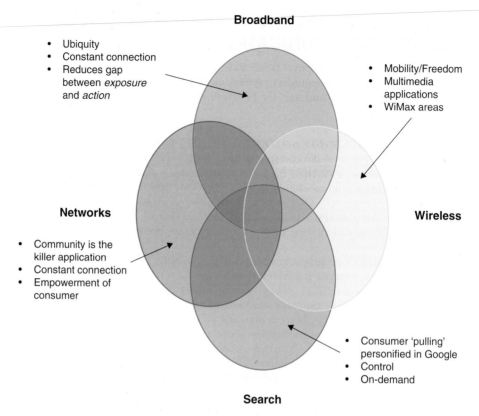

Figure 16.5: Four key ingredients in the digital revolution

Source: Jaffe (2005, p.36). Reproduced by permission of John Wiley & Sons Inc.

communications medium. Within the framework of the four cornerstones of broadband, wireless, search and networks, Jaffe (2005) lists 10 approaches that are transforming marketing communications (see also Table 16.1):

- the Internet;
- gaming;
- on-demand viewing;
- experiential marketing;
- long-form content;
- communal marketing;
- consumer-generated content;
- search;
- music and mobile phones;
- branded entertainment.

The main thread running through these essentially technological alternatives to traditional marketing communications goes right back to the source – literally! In Chapters 1 and 2 we described how all successful communication is dependent upon the message being sent coming from a 'credible source'. The more credible and trusted the source, the more likely that the message will be successfully received and accepted. Therefore, the more chance there is of achieving marketing communication objectives.

	Examples and characteristics	Features
The Internet	Mass medium Measurability Impact No prime time required Interactive Permissive Time spent viewing	*MSN* reaches more people on its home page in a day than the top seven US newspapers combined (*Source*: Audit Bureau of Circulation) *iVillage* reaches more people (15 million) than *Vogue* and *Vanity Fair*, respectively. (*Source*: Mediamatrix and Spring Mediamark Research) Audience delivery, audience interaction and ROI 50% of homes have broadband; 90% of businesses making communications are always online Not viewed linearly and can be time-shifted Two-way dialogues are facilitated Consumers consensually 'opt-in' Offers both reach and richness and stickability
Gaming	'Advergaming' Permissive Audience actively engaged Longevity of message	Commercials and content featured in realistic context within a video game (e.g. *Barclays* Premiership football games featuring 'authentic' hoardings in the stadia) Viewers choose participation Average player spends eight hours with a game Constant presence of commercial message
On-demand viewing	Time-shifted Ads 'zapped' Marketers as content and service providers Longevity of message	Viewers choose as and when viewing takes place Commercial content can be avoided Constant presence of commercial message
Experiential marketing	Synonymous with events marketing Contextual relevance Marketers as content and service providers	Creates or recreates the brand experience Use related to situational benefits Creates affinity and/or brand community
Long-form content	Creates 'content' not commercials 'Webisodes' Three-minute 'book-ends'	Creates relevant or salient items or storylines which sell experience within a framework of branding Made-for online films and videos (e.g. *BMW* Films) Made-for TV and online commercials instead of mention when company is sponsoring programme
Communal marketing	Customers are the sales force Reaching the most people by reaching the right people first CRM in action Market mavens	Viral marketing acts as 'word of mouse' and provides credible, trusted source of communication Maybe smaller numbers but highly influential opinion formers and leaders 'Palm Champions' reward scheme for referrals and creating community Individual consumers who have expertise and credibility as a source of initiating dialogue and disseminating information helping the diffusion of new products

(Continued)

	Examples and characteristics	Features
Consumer-generated content	Viral marketing Interactivity-induced consumer involvement Open-source marketing	'Word of mouse' gives undisputed credible and qualified referrals Community-driven expression of interest User-generated and co-authored
Search	Search engine marketing	User-generated and co-authored
Music, mobiles	SMS and downloads	Ubiquity and permanent access
Branded entertainment	Product placement Stealth marketing	Content-captured commercials or commercial-captured content

Table 16.1: Approaches that are transforming marketing communications

Source: Developed from Jaffe (2005).

You may recall that we said that advertising and other information sources affect how the psychological and physical aspects of a brand are perceived, and whether consumers buy-in to the image being projected of the brand. You may also recall how Grönroos and Lindberg-Repo (1998, p. 10) described planned and unplanned communications as 'What the firm SAYS', 'What the firm DOES' and 'What others SAY and DO'. The degree to which these three types of communication are trusted is in direct variance to the degree of planning and control. That is, the least trustworthy is the company's planned campaign, and the most trusted source is peers in the brand experience.

These new alternatives at best supplement and at worst substitute the use of traditional marketing communications, based on their actual or perceived credibility as sources of information. The development of less obtrusive, co-authored stories feeds right into the creation and maintenance of brand narratives. Sensible organisations will now actively encourage consumers to subvert and sometimes distort company-intended messages in order to gain their engagement and ability as peer communicators. Jaffe (2005, p. 221) refers to this as 'interactivity-induced consumer involvement' and that is the key to its power.

This era of 'open-source marketing' comes alive when the creation of online communities moves from commercial content to just content. Modern branding involves more than just turning products into brands, it involves brand experience. If consumers use products because of what they are, and buy brands because of how it makes them feel, they also need a 'contextual evaluation' of where they fit into their lives. Brands have to move consumers through functional and emotional states to experiential ones. Equally, the convergence of communications tools has called for more story-led branding. Let's look at an example of how this is successfully achieved in the In Focus box below.

INTEGRATED COMMUNICATIONS IN FOCUS

Visa builds narrative online and makes ideas happen

The *Visa* 'Ideas Happen' campaign, which included an interactive online platform, PR, special events, promotional activities, entrepreneurial and a travelling road-show, was devised to promote consumer engagement and emotional interest to 'make dreams come true'. Consumers

aged between 18 and 24 were invited to submit ideas for businesses or ventures and vote for their choices via an *MSN* custom-designed site. Online traffic was phenomenal: in just short of three months, over five million 'unique user' hits were registered. Increased brand awareness and the forging of relationships with young people who are embryonic consumers were the main objectives achieved. As well as improving *Visa's* image amongst this key target market (number who thought it the 'Best Credit Card' increased by 13% and those who thought it the 'Most Innovative Company' by 9%), the overall image of *Visa* as an ideas facilitator improved dramatically.

The logic of tapping into the 'reality TV' of 'dreams can come true' is not without irony, since communications were almost entirely online. The categories of: 'entrepreneurial', 'self-expression' and 'community' perfectly resonated with the target audience who were asked to submit entries in writing and then by video which were presented online to a panel of celebrity judges and site visitors. All were included in the vote for the lucky 12 selected for the final panel. *MSN* built the online platform and promoted it heavily through the *MSN* network of *MSN* home page, *MSN* Messenger, *MSN* Entertainment and *MSN* Hotmail. Winners were given 'seed money' and attended special '*Visa's* Young and Successful Weekend Workshops' to help kick-start their ventures. Unique 'Ideas Happen Live' road-shows were used in multiple venues as a call to action for young people to bring their ideas to life and created buzz around the central brand ethos of 'everywhere you want to be'. These days, it involves building and maintaining ongoing brand narratives: the living, organic stories which engage and construct dialogue. The stronger the dialogue, the stronger the brand. The **product** here is the credit card itself and the fact that it is accepted ubiquitously; the **brand** is the facilitation of people's dreams (using a credit card); and the **experience** is making things happen and being part of that event. Jon Raj, Director of Advertising at *Visa*, described the innovation of this campaign as being down to 'the creation of an integrated marketing communications campaign that relied less on the product that was being showcased and more on the consumers that the advertiser wanted to influence'. The *Visa* team acknowledged that a TV advertising campaign was not an option to achieve their communication objectives since the fundamental goal was to get young people to talk to each other (not the advertiser). This built credibility and affinity for the *Visa* brand.

Four variables present a powerful value proposition when combined: sight, sound, motion and interactivity. Together they represent full consumer engagement with messages being communicated. Media touch-points can be shown diagrammatically (Figure 16.6) tracing how marketing communications media have evolved, and also demonstrating the benefits and limitations of each medium: radio had sound; print had sight; television had both sight and sound but also the dramatic communications dimension of motion. It was a powerfully effective medium and for a while captivated a captive audience. The emergence of the web has added the fundamentally human dimension of interactivity. It has the additional benefit of being ubiquitous and yet is not obtrusive as users must be proactive and allow dialogue before any communication takes place. No medium has this element of permissive pervasiveness. This presents a multidimensional experience which has now added a social aspect to communications.

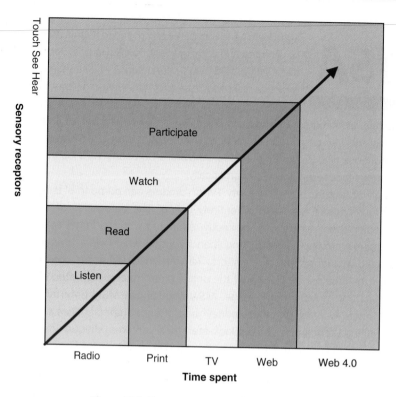

Figure 16.6: Evolution of media touch-points

Source: Jaffe (2005). Reproduced by permission of John Wiley & Sons Inc.

MATTER OF FACT

Digital Engagement

Today, there is no area of marketing communications more customer-centric and customer-driven than digital online media. New digital formats, such as social media, video, mobile, gambling, branded entertainment and advanced TV can be used for 'brands-actional' advertising (simultaneously addressing both transaction and brand requirements). There are consumers who enjoy traditional media and those who are more media-involved, with the consumer uptake in online media now greater than ever and increasing exponentially. According to a report from the *IBM Institute for Business Value* (Berman, Battino and Feldman 2009), a top media and entertainment industry executive claimed that 'consumers can no longer be considered "the audience" – they are simultaneously readers, editors and marketers, especially the young demographic'.

Engagement is evident in many varied capacities as illustrated in the figure below.

Of the categories identified by the *IBM Digital Consumer Survey*, 'Massive Passives' represent the bulk of the population (65%) who are least likely to participate in new media, with the remaining 35% comprising much more tech-savvy and typically younger consumers.

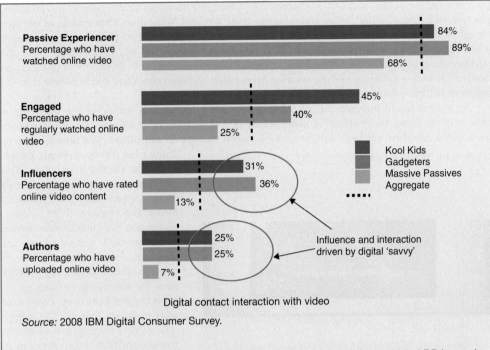

Digital contact interaction with video

Source: 2008 IBM Digital Consumer Survey.

Of this group, both want to own the new technology (such as video-enabled PDAs, multimedia), especially 'Gadgetiers' (the innovators and early adopters) representing 15% and the 'Kool Kids' (those under 24) who make up the remaining 20%. The difference appears to be the first group are 'cash rich and time poor' and the second are the opposite. Both were willing to trade information for rewards of some kind (e.g. travel discount, free content, air time minutes), 65% and 51%, respectively.

The percentage of consumers as 'Passive Experiencers' who have watched some online content is on average 80%; influence and integration are highest amongst the 'digital savvy' Gadgetiers and Kool Kids.

Source: Beyond advertising: choosing a strategic path to the digital consumer. Berman, Battino and Feldman (2009).

SOCIAL WEB

Over the last couple of decades, the web has become 'an increasingly engaging communications medium in large part because of the ability to readily tailor content to viewer, community and timely information' (Marcus 2008). The antecedents to the social web show a gradual but meaningful communal progression. In the same way that the mobile phone needed the social moment to accelerate its adoption, Web 1.0 and 2.0 prepared the ground for the expansion of the human interactive component of online communications.

Web 1.0 was a fairly static centrally managed construction which was tech-heavy and slow to change and essentially about 'commerce'. The period 1990 to 1995 saw the use of HTML and site building as the chief characteristic of Web 1.0. Browsers then facilitated transactions and interactivity with the search, pop-ups and click-throughs of Web 2.0. Web 2.0 is essentially about 'people' and concerns sharing and open communications.

Now we are in the 'social web' (Weber 2007) Web 3.0 iteration, on the cusp of the promised emotive, rich media (sound, video and even touch) of Web 4.0. What does Weber mean by the web being 'social'? It is a social digital space for consumers because it connects people with other users; it is a social web for companies because it aggregates consumers and allows discourse within the environmental context of the brand: pharmaceutical companies engage in debate about diseases; car companies discuss pollution and the need for hybrid cars; and even chocolate confectioners raise the nature of fair trade supply.

As regards brand building and narrative development, the web is becoming the most important medium. Now, the majority of other media directs viewers or readers to the host's website for a richer brand experience; *easyJet* even plasters it all over its aeroplanes. The British *Army* recruits from TV by diverting people to pick up the full story online: 'This film continues at Army.com.recruitment'. *Apple* still uses traditional media, but employs them to direct consumers to its online conversation about product enhancement and user experience. *Adidas* ran a campaign in 2008 – 'Dream Big' – which used TV advertising to open up the latest chapter in its story: connecting with grassroots football. The tagline: 'The world's biggest footballers. The world's smallest teams' sets out its appeal, but the call to the website – 'Now showing at Adidas.com/football' – pulls viewers onto its website. Competitors like *Nike* counter with

Adidas continues the conversation online

similar community events. 'Art of Speed' is a project which encourages up-and-coming filmmakers and artists to visualise 'speed'. They used Gawker, a website specialist, to facilitate the *Nike* microsite. The interesting thing from a mechanical point of view is that they distinguish it from their main site by labelling it a 'special advertising section'. (I wonder what *Adidas* thought.) They described this as 'advertainment' or 'advermovies'. These campaign weblogs allow a marketer to participate in the conversation rather than observe it as a passive sponsor. Online stories which allow visitors to choose different endings offer a similar 'bonus' to DVD extras and enhance the engagement potential.

Engagement can be achieved in many ways providing there is a human element to it; this is what user-generated content is. An excellent example of combining the involvement of viral marketing with traditional product feature advertising was the *Honda* 'It must be love' TV/online campaign. The promotion required visitors to log on to the *Honda* website (and users from the owners' database) to match themselves to a *Honda* which they most 'resembled'. Some hilarious entries were selected from the online community which was created and then featured in a user-generated website which echoed the TV and press campaign. The clever part was the user involvement and the fact that viewers were required to look at the features of individual car models in the *Honda* range in order to match their own features: function, emotional and experiential.

Other brands stimulate conversations around a moral proposition. According to Weber (2007, p. 16), the 'concept of moral purpose in branding is going to come to life in the social web'. The rise in consumer-generated content, social media and networking (Jaffe 2005) contributes to building connections. This is evident in the *Dove* 'Campaign for Real Beauty' and the *WeightWatchers* cases featured in earlier chapters. More recently, *Windows* has retaliated to *Apple*'s 'I'm a Mac' campaign with 'Windows Without Walls', with the intention of not just stating the opposite case, but aiming at generating a conversation between *Windows* users. It's a call to action and a recruitment exercise which is engaging loyal customers and appealing to new alike.

DIGITAL CONVERSATION PLATFORMS

One perspective on the new age of marketing is that communication (in its traditional context) has given way to content. James Andrews of Ketchum Interactive refers to 'Generation C' where 'C stands for content'. These are technology-savvy individuals who are using technology, websites, cell phones, digital cameras and online games to create their own 'content' and express themselves and share a more accessible and connected world. He describes the 10 'Cs' of what he refers to as the 'digital identity of Generation C':

- **Connect:** people-based social networking such as *Facebook*; mobile text messaging; *Twitter*; *Skype*.
- **Collaboration and co-creation:** mash-ups; special-interest sites such as *Wikipedia*; open-source software; creative commons; consumer-generated media.
- **Conversation:** context-based blog trackers; meme tracking; *YouTube*.
- **Collect and categorise:** tagging; social bookmarking; search engines.
- **Communicate:** photo sharing; blogs; video sharing; podcasting; video blogging.
- **Community:** customer service networks; virtual worlds such as *Second Life*.
- **Collective wisdom:** ratings sites; *Wikipedia*; social news.
- **Customisation:** one-to-one tailored communications.

Figure 16.7 shows the varied digital conversation platforms. Table 16.2 brings this together and gives some current examples of these platforms.

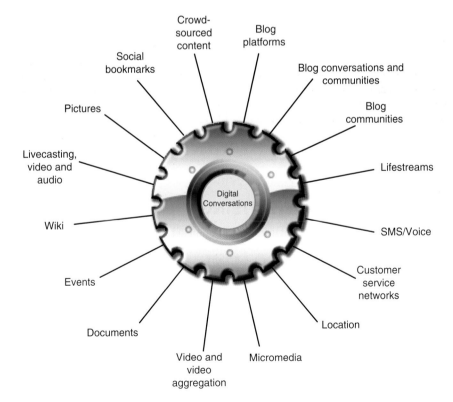

Figure 16.7: Digital conversation platforms

Source: IBM Digital Consumer Survey (2008).

Applications	Examples
Social networks	Facebook, Bebo, Hi5
Niche networks	Linkedin, Ning, Plaxo, CrowdVine
Customer service networks	Google, Yahoo!, Yelp
Location	Bright Kite, Doppur, Trip It
Video	YouTube, BlipTV, Metacafe, Rever, Vidler
Video aggregation	MagniTV
Documents	Thinkton, Scribd, Docstk
Events	Zvents, Socialzr, Madeit, Activa
Music	Lostfm, Pandora, Odeo
Wiki	Wikipedia, Twiki, Wetpaint
Livecasting, video and audio	Kite, Ustream, BlogTV, Qik, BlogTalkRadio
Pictures	Flickr, Zoooom
Social bookmarks	Diigo, Magnolia
Comment and reputation	DiscQus, Sezwho, Cocomment
Crowd-sourced content	Newsvine, Hub Dub, Mixx, Digg
Blog platforms	MovableType
Blog/Conversations	Ask, Blog Pulse, GoogleXXX, Technorati
Blog communities	Shiftr, Blogged, MyBlogLog
Micromedia	Twitter, Utterz
Lifestreams	Facebook, FriendFeed, Life21, Ping, Swurl
Specific to Twitter	twitxr, twitpic, tweetscan, summize
SMS/Voice	Jott

Table 16.2: Digital conversation platforms

REINVENTING TV ADVERTISING

The increasingly fragmented media environment, the impact of broader and greater viewer choice and TV advertising 'wear-out' through over-exposure have severely undermined the effectiveness of the traditional mass-market advertising approach. *Nike* now spends only 33% of its US advertising budget on advertising with TV networks and traditional media. Trevor Edwards, *Nike's* Vice President for Global Brands, sums up the changing priorities: 'We're not in the business of keeping the media companies alive, we're in the business of connecting with consumers'.

One-way media like TV have traditionally been used to create awareness, launch, position, reposition and ensure top-of-mind reinforcement with essentially passive recipients. In contrast, interactive media can ensure repeat purchase, build relationships and trust. It has caused major brands to rethink their media mix but also how best to use TV advertising to target audiences.

However, TV viewing is still an integral cultural phenomenon, it would be impossible to see a complete demise. Enhanced 'video advertising with the target ability of direct mail and the responsiveness of online marketing' will provide more relevant enhanced TV advertising formats (Marcus 2008). Marcus posits that, to take advantage of this 'enhanced TV advertising capability', marketers must meet the following challenges:

- **Addressability:** digital TV, *TiVo*, DVRs and VOD (video on demand) as well as online video and IPTV enhance the ability to more accurately target audiences.
- **Interactivity:** allows advertisers greater accuracy in promotional activities and calls to action techniques, although interactive video content is likely to achieve higher response rates than interactive advertisements on TV.
- **Customisation:** an 'emerging vision of video advertising that combines the storytelling power of video with the kind of targeted customisation more typically associated with direct and online marketing'.
- **Dynamism:** the ability of the medium to react and change quickly has undermined TV advertising's effectiveness, but this will undoubtedly change with video production.

Berman, Battino and Feldman (2009) suggest four distinct marketing communications models based on an acknowledgement of fragmented and rapidly expanding media choice, both the changing demands of customer engagement and the need for more accurate accountability of budget spend. The business models they describe are illustrated in Figure 16.8.

- **Traditional advertising or 'legacy' approach:** a single platform, one-way, mass communication model predicated on transactional structures and evaluating objectives such as brand impressions. This refers to the audience delivery of media vehicles usually measured in terms of CPT (cost per thousand), CPTM (cost per thousand targeted) implying that there are particular audience demographics being targeted. This evidences a 'silo' approach characteristically with lower accuracy of targeting and often lack of integration.
- **Return-on-investment (ROI) driven advertising:** the accuracy achieved by greater granularity of audience profiling leads to better communications; and greater ROI granularity refers to the minute level of detail (or 'fineness') of analysis of targets, media and so on which leads to much greater accuracy. *Google* has a level of granularity in its level of audience profiling which provides very accurate micro-level measurement to aid efficiency and effectiveness.
- **Cross-platform reach:** greater integration of communication components can enhance campaign effectiveness and improve customer engagement. This is right at the centre of the debate on what is normally (and sometimes nominally) referred to as 'integrated' marketing communications. True integration looks for synergies of message and media vehicles.
- **Consumer-centric marketing:** employing broadly contextual campaigns enabling addressability, measurement and interactivity. This is the new 'Holy Grail' of marketing communications: delivering truly customer-centric experiences where integrated messages and platforms are set and created in the frame of reference of the target audience in a powerfully holistic way.

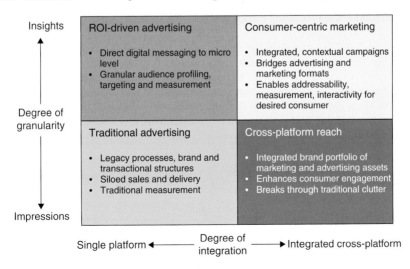

Figure 16.8: Beyond advertising: evolution of business models

Source: Berman, Battino and Feldman (2009).

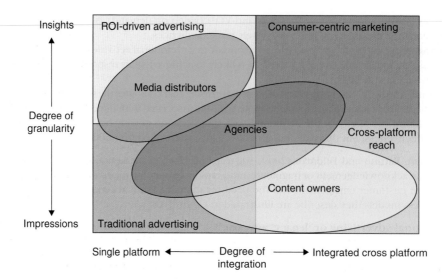

Figure 16.9: Beyond advertising: positioning of industry participants

Source: Berman, Battino and Feldman (2009).

The *IBM* report describes the key players in the music and entertainment industry – media distributors, agencies and content owners – as 'taking evolutionary divergent paths' heading towards consumer centricity dependent upon their 'legacy stronghold position'. In other words, organisations are adopting one or other of the models described above: a revised 'legacy' model of traditional impression advertising; one based on ROI being the driving force; or even a 'cross-platform' approach leading towards greater integration. However, the delivery of true customer centricity is, for the moment, elusive. Figure 16.9 shows the state of play as of today.

Content owners are using relevant placement of sponsored advertising slots within the entertainment context of their programme schedules. There is greater emphasis on premium quality content and therefore better salience between media and message. **Media distributors,** such as satellite, cable and telecommunications providers, are using their customer insight to focus on audience profiling and targeting. **Agencies** are being forced to offer measurement displaying greater granularity and integration.

Berman *et al.* (2007) reported on the demise of the legacy model of advertising in a report announcing 'the end of advertising as we know it'. Content owners, media distributors and agencies face perhaps their severest test to embrace the economic, technological and social changes which are currently dismantling the marketing communications paradigm and creating a much more customer-centric framework. What is for certain is that the future will be shaped by the increasing need for more accurate measurability and better customer engagement, and the participants who adhere to these guiding principles will be the ones who survive and thrive.

CLOSING CASE STUDY

SMS: The Joy of Text – It's Not Just Words That Count

At the start of the chapter, we described the decline of TV advertising as being due to its intrusiveness and the saturation of messages we all receive on a daily basis. TV advertisements come into our lives and invade our personal space all the time. We allow the 'permissive pervasiveness'

Gossard's texts give G-strings to the girls

of the social web, and the ubiquitous and flexible nature of WiFi technology makes it easy to receive and accept messages from brand owners. One piece of modern technology which is guaranteed to be by our side, ready to receive and respond, is the mobile phone. The modern compulsion to be 'connected' means that the use of Short Messaging Service (SMS) – 'texting' as we more commonly know it – to communicate with one another is now an integral part of our culture. We use mobile phones to connect socially and to do business. The engineer from the Gas Board, the breakdown mechanic from the *RAC*, or the *Parcel Force* delivery man will all happily send an electronic notification that 'he's on his way'. These days, you can even get an SMS prayer from the Vatican. But does texting consumers seem a bizarre way to sell lingerie?

Gossard, a *Sara Lee* lingerie company, contacted potential customers by using text messages to their mobile phones to promote a line of G-strings. This highly successful approach ran in conjunction with the TV and poster advertising campaigns which had a call to action urging viewers to send a text message to 'G4me' when they would be sent a discount on a G-string. Just over 26,000 vouchers were redeemed by SMS and had a fantastic impact on sales. *Figleaves.com*, an online retailer, reported over €75,000 worth of sales. A follow-up promotion by *Gossard* offered women the chance to win a £25,000 diamond-encrusted G-string by texting a special code given with purchase of their product. Is it sex that sells or text that tells? There is no doubting the fact that, whether in front of a TV ('Text Summer *Citroen* NOW'), in a retail cosmetic department ('*L'Oreal*: 20% off because you're worth it!) or walking past a billboard, consumers are almost always armed with the means and the inclination to respond. The *Chase Manhattan* bank in New York used the iconic yellow taxi cabs to promote its sponsorship of the American Open Tennis Tournament by 'hailing' people to text.

To promote the Australian Channel Ten reality TV programme, *Big Brother*, a unique SMS campaign was used to alert people of the show's screening by surprising them at bus stops with 'Big Brother is watching'. Bluetooth transmitters were installed at over 20 bus shelters and sent anonymous 'I'm watching you at . . ..' SMS messages to unwitting consumers, quickly followed by revealing the source of the message was from the makers of the show.

Ever since SMS was launched as a commercial facility in 1994, adoption has been rapid and use of texting has become widespread. According to the Mobile Marketing Association and the Mobile Data Association,

SMS sells sex

there are over 2.2 billion mobile phone users around the globe, with over 300 million users in Europe alone. For brands trying to reach 14–35 year olds, SMS will have to form some part of their marketing communications. With newer phones having full colour and video screens allowing

(Continued)

transmission of high-quality images (not just text), SMS marketing will become even more effective.

The use of SMS to support or use other elements of the marketing communications mix is not just restricted to promotional activities like *Sony's* pre-Christmas stock awareness campaign for the release of its new *PlayStation*, or *Coca-Cola's* continental café promotion. By using a

The language of text is the language of love as Calvin Klein gets IN2U

mobile-marketing billboard campaign, *Calvin Klein* rang up consumers asking 'What are you into?', consumers could respond by texting 'Calvin Klein CKIN2U' and seeing their message run live on the billboard. This preceded the introduction of the new *Calvin Klein IN2U* fragrance.

Because of its permissive nature, SMS marketing has been portrayed as an ethical form of communication. There is evidence of it being used for the mutual benefit of company and customer as part of a relationship which is 'opt-in'. This permissive form of advertising is used by companies like *Estée Lauder* who offer a sign-up reminder service to customers alerting them to special offers, sales and new product introductions. There are some horror stories about premium-rate service providers, some like the ITV viewer-response scandals, having tarnished the industry. The Forrester Group in the USA claimed that 75% of consumers disliked text selling and 3% actively mistrusted it. But it is early days, and the convenience and access to markets makes it such a useful tool in the marketing communica-

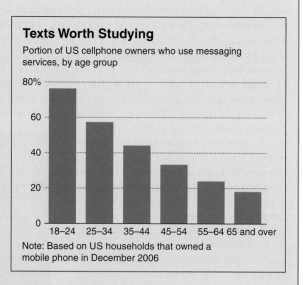

Cellphone users using messaging service by age group

tions mix. There is no doubt that customer profiling information will be used for good and bad purposes, but the sign-up, upgrade nature of mobile phones provides the ultimate database for marketers. Carriers don't just know where clients live, but where they are, who they are, the games they play, the music they like and so on.

And it is not just the 18–45 year olds that text. If US trends reflect European habits, the report from the Forrester Group shows an increasing penetration in the 45+ segments.

QUESTIONS

1. Do you think SMS marketing will be seen as an integral tactical element in the marketing communications mix once people are used to it and the novelty factor wears off?

2. Do you think it adds anything to the brand narrative?

3. Will SMS marketing become as intrusive as TV advertising, or will its social nature ensure its longevity?

CHAPTER SUMMARY

In this chapter, we examined the changing nature of marketing communications. The discussion looked at how the paradigm of asymmetrical control has shifted to one of 'permissive pervasiveness' in which the communication power has changed from transmitted to negotiated meaning.

We analysed some of the factors affecting the transformation of marketing communications: fragmenting markets; the clutter of multimedia; the sovereignty of the consumer; and the technological and social dynamics of social networking. We analysed the impacts that these elements have had and speculated on future developments. A critique of the latest marketplace and technological trends provided a fresh perspective on marketing communications.

We looked at the traditional 'interruption' model of marketing communications where advertising has primacy, and compared it with a landscape where alternative approaches such as consumer-generated content and message-capture are transforming marketing communications.

REFLECTIVE QUESTIONS

a. In 2009, Sir Michael Grade announced that ITV advertising revenues were down by a dramatic 50% year on year. What are the root causes of the demise of TV as the primary advertising medium?

b. How would you account for the rise in e-communities and online conversations as an alternative to transmitted traditional communications?

c. How have the new synergies of multi-vehicle integrated exposures and 'simultaneous media consumption' (Shultz 2005) undermined the efficacy of 'interruption mass communications'? What new model has it been replaced with?

d. What factors have transformed marketing communications?

e. What does Weber (2007) mean by the web being 'social'?

RESEARCH PROJECTS

There are a number of academic papers written about the impact of Web 2.0 on marketing communications. Look up a couple and compare the discussions outlined in the research.

Collect some examples of where SMS marketing (texting) has been used as part of a way of communicating with a target audience. Have you or your friends any experience of a retailer giving you advanced notice of a sale or announcing a new product?

Chapter

EVALUATING MARKETING COMMUNICATIONS

This chapter is about how an organisation tries to ensure that its marketing communications strategy is successfully planned, implemented and achieves its communication objectives. In order to do this, there has to be a full appreciation and analysis of the macro and micro environment before, during and after campaigns take place. Some elements are partly controllable – the effectiveness and efficiency of budgeted components of the mix – and some impact and may constrain ethical practices, regulatory restrictions and general environmental issues.

In order to ensure the most effective messages are placed in the correct media and target audiences engage with communications in a mutually beneficial manner, all mix components, and their total effects, must be evaluated. Examination of the formal and informal, planned and ad hoc metrics is discussed here, with a full contextual explanation of the relevant evaluation and measurement techniques. Measurement allows analysis of the various components of the application of marketing communications: the current dynamics of the market sector; the category need; target audience behaviour; message content; the different ways we might create communication messages; possible media channels in which to carry that communication; and a critical assessment of the suitability of the individual communication elements. Evaluation, on the other hand, allows interpretation of these measures in order to properly gauge the impacts over time. Therefore, we need to measure metrics and evaluate effectiveness.

Equally, in the most turbulent of economic, social and political conditions, it is imperative that an organisation is fully cognisant of all contemporary ethical, legal and environmental issues.

LEARNING OBJECTIVES

After reading this chapter, you'll be able to:

- Understand how and why evaluation is key to successful marketing communications.
- Appreciate what the primary purpose of evaluating marketing communications is.
- Appreciate the links between the product category, brand, media and messages.
- Consider using the CAMPAIGN planning framework as an evaluative aid to making qualitative as well as quantitative assessments of marketing communications.
- Examine the different methods and techniques for evaluating marketing communications
- Consider the evaluation of ethical, regulatory and environmental issues.

The need to measure the effectiveness and efficiency of marketing communications integration, particularly across a plethora of media options has become of paramount importance (Edell and Keller 1999). In some ways, the ability of management to reflect and reassess the application of marketing communications is the most critical factor, since although it may not have short-term impacts on an organisation and its marketing objectives, it may affect positively or negatively the growth potential of the organisation's brands.

Successful marketing communications require dialogues with carefully researched target markets, through well-executed messages placed in appropriate media. Sometimes the process is akin to driving blindfolded with someone else looking out the back window giving directions, but even retrospective analyses can help to keep the brand on the right road. The ability to accurately predict and evaluate depends upon the options and how they are deployed. Guidance and development comes from the insightful interpretation of past experiences.

In order to ensure that objectives have been achieved, the impact of marketing communications must be evaluated by carefully applied research. It is not common practice to track campaigns formally, but infer that they have worked by retrospectively observing sales. Rossiter and Bellman (2005, p. 312) refer to two different types of campaign tracking: 'aggregate' tracking which analyses sales and expenditure over time; and 'customer tracking' which assesses how the campaign is working whilst it is happening. It is important not only to have formative evaluation before the campaign is implemented, and whilst being applied, but also to have summative evaluation a long time after marketing communications has been implemented.

OPENING CASE STUDY

Ford: Evaluating the Right Vehicle for Ford's Success

In late 2003, with its leadership under challenge from fierce competition, *Ford* decided to launch a new version of its best-selling *F-150* pickup truck. This was described by CEO William Ford as 'the most important launch in the history of Ford', with an unprecedented advertising spend of $100 million. Over a period of

(Continued)

six months, the campaign aimed at creating brand awareness and differentiating against the competition, and to reach over 50% of *Ford's* target audience of truck buyers (males between 25–54 years of age) within the first two weeks and build critical sales.

Although over 90% of spend was to go on TV advertising, with a dramatic decline in effectiveness of traditional advertising media due to the increasing fragmentation of media, *Ford* was keen to evaluate all media used and was aware that post-campaign-only analyses gave only part of the picture. TV advertising still had the ability to work, especially for achieving high impact levels, but online advertising was becoming much more effective in terms of driving sales through multiple channels and at the same time having appreciable impact on building brands, therefore *Ford* was keen to incorporate a significant online element. At the time of the launch, Internet-based advertising had grown six times the rate of overall advertising and was becoming the fastest-growing section of the media (Elkin 2004).

The campaign included major spend on TV and radio, billboards and direct mail. Online content included a range of 'in-market' (i.e. the common practice of consumers using online search to look for information on motor vehicles) advertisements such as skyscrapers, rectangles and 'leader boards' plus extensive use of 'digital roadblocks' on major portals designed to extend communications. Previously, measurements of online advertising had tended to be qualitative, focusing on creativity and overall effects of campaigns.

Ford needed to examine effectiveness across all media, and dissecting the individual media contributions was critically important. *Ford* needed to evaluate the optimal mix of advertising vehicles across different media, in terms of frequency, reach and budget allocation in order to achieve its marketing communications goals. By quantifying precisely the impact of advertising, it was able to deliver productivity gains to the bottom line by analysing a number of different brand metrics.

To do this accurately, *Ford* employed the cross media optimisation study (XMOS) model devised by analysts Marketing Evolution in conjunction with the Advertising Research Foundation (see Figure 17.1). They used time series and factorial experimental design to isolate the effects of different media by translating campaign goals into survey attitudinal branding metrics questions and consumers' responses (over 16,000 'intending' individual responses) to quantify core branding metrics of aided and unaided brand awareness, brand image and intent to action. This approach had five elements of efficiency measure:

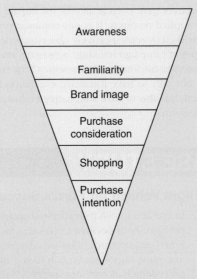

Figure 17.1: Cross media optimisation study (XMOS) model

- plotting the effectiveness of combined campaign effects;
- isolating the effects of different media in the campaign;
- examining the complementary effects and synergies of individual media;
- calculating the return on marketing objectives (ROMO) for each medium; and
- recommending budget allocation and descriptive advertisement and media suggestions if necessary.

The measurement of brand metrics covered the traditional 'purchase funnel' as illustrated above. Consistent with the sequential processes covered in previous chapters, this acknowledges the need for both brand image advertising and hard-nosed sales objectives. Study results proved that online advertising strongly contributed both to sales and branding results. Measured reach of the online campaign was huge: the comScore data showed that 49.6% of all Internet users were exposed to the online advertisements during the campaign, and 39.2% to the portal home-page 'roadblocks'. It was proved that the online campaign delivered significant sales lift (6% of new vehicle sales could be directly attributed to the online advertisements). The conversion rate for 'tracked click-through' sales was even higher.

When *Ford* wanted to look at the relative value of each medium in terms of cost efficiency, the unique return on marketing objectives (ROMO) was used. This is a 'cost per impact' metric used by a number of blue-chip organisations including *P&G*, *Colgate-Palmolive*, *Kimberley Clark*, *Johnson & Johnson*, *Nestlé*, and *McDonald's*. This model estimates the average cost it takes to influence an individual calculated by dividing the total cost of the media by the total population exhibiting that effect.

Results showed clearly that there were greater efficiencies coming from magazines and online advertisements (e.g. TV and magazines showed the same point gains) but magazines were 50% of the cost of TV. Roadblock was better value even though it had less impact.

As can be seen from Table 17.1, the return on investment (ROI) data for online advertising compared to the other traditional media showed that TV generated the greatest reach and impact on purchase intent, but it was considerably less cost effective. For every dollar spent on online advertising, it took over $21 to achieve the same increase using TV. TV was best for levels of absolute reach 'footprint' and produced high levels of purchase consideration impact but had a significantly less ROMO and was much more expensive than magazines and online advertising. Electronic roadblocks, whilst not achieving as much reach as TV, proved to be most cost efficient.

	Overall	TV	Magazine	Roadblock	Online
Ad recall	+32pts	+18pts	+13pts	+6pts	+15pts
Familiarity	+9pts	+3pts	+11pts	Not significant	+10pts
Average brand image attributes	+13pts	+2pts	+8pts	Not significant	+9pts
Purchase consideration	+17pts	+6pts	+6pts	+4pts	+6pts
Shopping	+12pts	Not significant	+4pts	+6pts	+6pts
Purchase intention	+4pts	+2pts	+3pts	+15pts	+12pts

Table 17.1: Relative cost efficiency of media vehicles used

(Continued)

Impact was measured by using pre-campaign branding levels as a baseline, and comparing post-campaign results. This showed the cost-per-person impacted index as a whole. Volume was measured as the total number of people affected by the campaign. The maximum potential volume was estimated as the total number of people that could have been affected had the reach potential been maximised for the medium. The cost per impact was the total campaign expenditure divided by the total volume of brand effect. The index was the relative cost efficiency (cost per impact) based on the campaign as a whole. See Table 17.2.

Brand metric: purchase consideration	Impact	Relative cost index
TV	6.1	1104
Magazines	6.1	456
Roadblock	3.8	100
Online	6.2	135

Table 17.2: Media vehicle relative costs

QUESTIONS

1. When *Ford* was evaluating the effectiveness of the media used in this campaign, why were they sure that post-campaign-only analyses gave only part of the picture?

2. Do you think that the cross media optimisation study (XMOS) model used by *Ford* has more universal application?

3. What were the qualitative and quantitative research elements of *Ford's* evaluation of the effectiveness of its campaign?

EVALUATING THE APPLICATION OF MARKETING COMMUNICATIONS IN A BRAND-DRIVEN ORGANISATION

For an organisation to be fully brand driven, there has to be not only complete integration of marketing communications, but also complicity and cooperation of the stakeholders who affect and are affected by marketing communications. Brand promise must start with those responsible for delivering that promise: the internal market or employees. As Davis (2005, p. 242) points out, 'the degree to which you can expect to achieve external brand success is 100% proportional to the degree to which you achieve internal brand success'. He lists the following criteria which must be met in order to ensure employees are 'on board' with the purpose of the organisation's efforts and are fully aware of their role in the process:

1. **Business understanding.** How well employees understand the philosophical and historical underpinnings of the organisation in terms of the markets that are competed in, the needs of the categories served, and who its customers are and what they require.
2. **Brand understanding.** How well key valued and differentiated elements of the brand are articulated.
3. **Brand influence.** How well the specific ways that employees have an impact on the customer experience are defined, communicated and upheld.

4. **Brand trust.** A gauge of trust and commitment level which employees have in the company leadership's ability to do the right thing relative to the values of the brand.
5. **Brand credibility.** Measurements that indicate whether employees believe that a company is capable of delivering on its promises to customers and employees.
6. **Brand delivery.** Measurements of whether employees believe that the company fulfils its promise to customers and employees.
7. **Brand preference, advocacy and satisfaction.** Measurements that show the extent to which employees prefer to work at the company rather than at its competitors and the degree to which they are comfortable referring friends and family to their employer. It is also important to track employee retention and turnover and internal satisfaction relative to the brand assimilation progress.

Schultz, Tenenbaum and Lauterborn (2004) describe a 'communications effects model' which tracks: behaviour (measured in the amount of transactions which take place before, during and after communications); commitment (the 'partial transactions' of responses to 'calls to action' such as enquiries, visits, appointments, brochure requests and so on); relationship (the affiliations which may accrue from commitment); and attitude and network outcomes (which describe the feelings, attitudes and intentions towards the brand).

MATTER OF FACT

IBM's Consumer-Centric Marketing Model

Digital communications media can provide measurable metrics in order to evaluate more accurately the effectiveness of marketing communications.

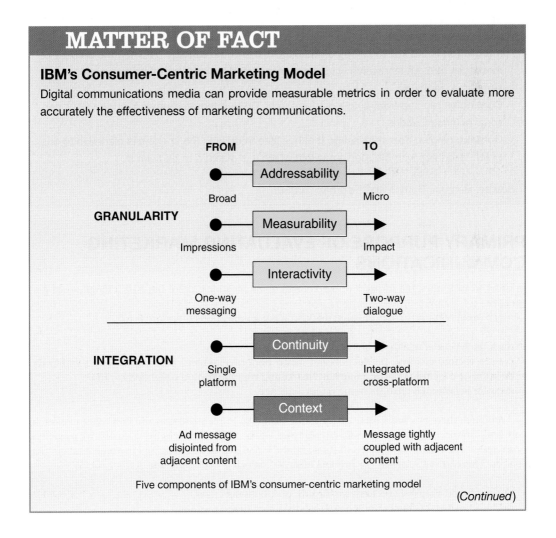

Five components of IBM's consumer-centric marketing model

(Continued)

According to a report by *IBM's Institute for Business Value*, the objectives of the two approaches of brand-oriented advertising and ROI-driven marketing can be accommodated. Because of the notions of granularity and cross-platform integration, 'awareness' and 'call to action' objectives can both be catered for, a critical factor for media scheduling and greater consumer orientation can be achieved. The figure above shows the five components of *IBM's* consumer-centric model:

Granularity allows more precise information to support ROI-driven advertising, the provision of micro data on target audiences and interaction with desired consumers whilst being able to accurately measure response and impact. This is facilitated by:

- **Addressability:** identifying a group by any number of criteria (e.g. location, demographics, affiliation, past behaviours).
- **Measurability:** links who saw the advertisement and then **what** specific action occurred in response (e.g. brand awareness, recall, purchase intention) linked back to marketing communications objectives.
- **Interactivity:** the difference in monologue, one-way communications, and dialogue which engages consumers.
- **Integration** is the key to good communications and the synergy between the delivery of messages through innovative ways across multimedia platforms offers tremendous possibilities, in terms of:
- **Continuity:** ranging from single platform (e.g. TV) to integrated cross-platform 360° personal communications.
- **Context:** ranging from a message that has little to do with the space it is placed in to one which resonates with the medium within which it is planned to be seen in.

Source: Berman, Battino and Feldman (2009).

PRIMARY PURPOSE OF EVALUATING MARKETING COMMUNICATIONS

In order to fully track the impacts of marketing communications, there must be a longitudinal perspective.

The primary purpose of evaluating marketing communications therefore is to:

- track the level and quality of brand awareness;
- pre-test (before creative, production and media performance) and post-test (assessed within the duration or conclusion of the campaign) marketing communication programmes; and
- measure behavioural changes in the target audience.

Although there is a sequential aspect to the planning, implementation and control of marketing communications, the process is really circular (see Figure 17.2). This requires a qualitative as well as quantitative assessment of objective results and the brand's fit to its changing environmental circumstances. Therefore all stages in the process must be evaluated. These include:

- Current brand status: share, heritage, health, portfolio objectives.
- Analysis: market, customer and contextual dynamics, brand meaning.

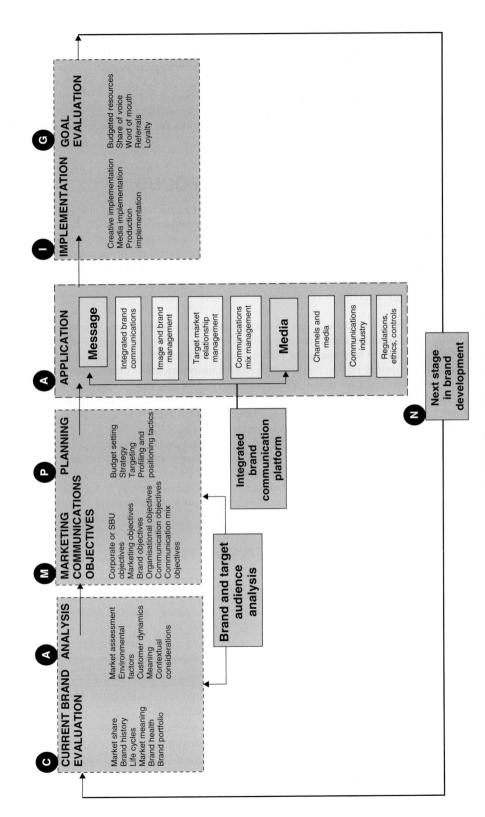

Figure 17.2: CAMPAIGN planning framework

- Marketing communications objectives: corporate, marketing, brand and communication objectives.
- Planning of marketing communications: strategy, profiling, positioning, budgeting.
- Application of marketing communications: integrated communications mix, media channel planning.
- Implementation: creative, media and production implementation.
- Goal evaluation: budgeted resources, share of voice, word of mouth, loyalty.
- Next stage in brand narrative: re-evaluation of brand's fit to market requirements and company objectives.

EVALUATION AND MEASUREMENT FOCUS

Measurement of the effectiveness of marketing communications has become a key strategic management concern and is increasingly of academic interest (Rust, Lemon and Zeithaml 2004). Kotler and Armstrong (1996) pinpoint two general areas for evaluation: the communication effect and the sales effect. To define the evaluation focus, marketing communications should not be measured only as an input/output equation. It should take a short-, medium- and long-term perspective of the impacts on target audience, organisational and brand objectives. This requires measurement and evaluation at four key stages (see Table 17.3):

- **Formative evaluation:** evaluation before the campaign begins and at the very start of implementation can gather information from market dynamics (market conditions, competition and target audience requirements) to help shape the nature of and condition the intended outcomes of the marketing communications efforts. This stage measures **communication intentions.**
- **Process evaluation:** evaluation of the implementation of marketing communications as the messages are placed (media evaluation) and received (audience perceptions), as well as the effectiveness of mix components. This stage measures **communication efforts** as opposed to effects in terms of budget, expenditure and component cost effectiveness.
- **Outcome evaluation:** evaluation of the effects on the target audience in terms of attitude or behavioural change and purchase intentions. This stage measures short- and medium-term **communication effects** of awareness, recall, saliency and so on.
- **Summative evaluation:** evaluation of the long-term impacts of brand loyalty and relationships on sales and profitability. This stage measures long-term **communication impacts** on attitude and purchase behaviour.

	Purpose	**Example questions**
FORMATIVE	Assess market dynamics, category needs, brand requirements and strengths of mix and media in meeting marketing communications objectives	What was the potential reach of the campaign? How many target users are to be reached? How much spent on each mix component? Target audience profile?
PROCESS	Measure campaign inputs and outputs during implementation of marketing communications efforts to measure what has been and is being achieved	What was the potential reach of the campaign? How many target users actually being reached? How much spent on each mix component?

OUTCOME	Measure effects and changes as a result of the campaign to target audiences	Was there any attitude change in the target audience? Has there been change in relation-ship status?
SUMMATIVE	Evaluate long-term behavioural changes in target audience in terms of permanent attitude change and purchase intentions	Has the change in behaviour resulted in intended outcomes? What impact has there been on lifetime customer value?

Table 17.3: Measurement matrix

Source: developed from Communications Consortium Media Centre, www.ccmc.org.

METHODS OF EVALUATING MARKETING COMMUNICATIONS

Measuring the overall integrated marketing communications effort has to evaluate: sales, market share, customer perceptions and attitudes and customer satisfaction. The main methods of evaluating the individual components of the marketing communications mix amount to what we referred to in Chapter 4 as the sequential 'hierarchy of effects'. Rossiter and Bellman (2005, p. 313) summarise these as providing a criterion for objectives which translate into measurable metrics:

- exposure to images and messages;
- processing of the advertisement;
- brand communication effects;
- target audience action resulting from communications;
- sales and market share; and
- brand equity.

Exposure to Images and Messages

Evaluation of the correct media vehicles must take place, and the criteria for measuring media effectiveness and efficiency tend to be by evaluating 'exposure'. Correlation between rate of media input and achievement of effects or sales can be related back to this media input measure over a given time period. Some of the methods of media evaluation are listed below (see also Table 17.4):

Adspend is very often the crudest and easiest form of evaluation: how much has been spent against return on investment (i.e. sales output from expenditure input).

Frequency is building awareness through possible **exposures** to a media 'vehicle' (e.g. ITV1 TV channel). Frequency doesn't measure exposures to the *message* but exposures to the *medium*. For example, if a daily newspaper is read, the frequency could be six if the advertisement appears every day for a week and also six if it appears once a week for six weeks.

Reach is the number of people expected to be exposed to the advertisement over a certain time period.

- **Total reach** is measured by calculating the number of people expected to be exposed to the advertisement over a certain time period.
- **Reach** (sometimes known as **useful reach**) calculates the amount of consumers from the target group who are likely to see the advertisement.

Measure	Definition
GRP – gross rating points (TVRs for TV)	Gross contacts. Corresponds to the total number of exposures to the advertising
TRP – target rating points	Gross rating points in the target audience
OTS – opportunities to see	Frequency measure of number of exposures per person in a campaign. For radio, it is opportunities to hear
Net reach	The number of people reached by the campaign at least one time. It is calculated as GRP/OTS.
CPT – cost per thousand	Contact costs. The price for a reach of 1000 people. It is also called CPM
CPP – cost per point	Contact costs for 1% of the audience
3+	A typical measure in, for instance, TV planning. The number of people that have been exposed to the advertising at least three times
Affinity	A measure of how well the media vehicle matches the target audience
Deadweight	A measure of how many people are part of the target audience in two different media

Table 17.4: Some examples of media evaluation measures

- **Gross reach** allows for overlapping media (e.g. TV, press and cinema) or even overlapping media vehicles (e.g. advertisements in *The Observer* and *Independent* on different days), and measures the number of people reached regardless of whether the advertisement hits the same person repeatedly.

The **weight** of an advertising campaign's media impact is measured in gross rating points (GRPs) or television rating points (TVRs) for TV by measuring the audience figures for all vehicles in which advertisements have been placed in a time period.

Opportunities to see (OTS) refers to the *probability* of a target audience being exposed to the message. To calculate this, we must divide gross reach by reach.

Share refers to the percentage of homes with TVs (HUT) tuned to a particular programme.

Ratings are measured by evaluating the percentage of individuals or homes exposed to a specific advertising medium, for example, TV. This can be measured by multiplying HUT by share. Magazines refer to this as 'coverage' rather than ratings, but it means the same thing.

Share of market (SOM) refers to the brand's market share in a category.

Share of voice (SOV) is the measure of how much a company should be heard (or seen) compared to its competitors, and is an indication of how much should be spent on a brand to maintain or improve market share as a percentage of all that is spent on marketing communications in that particular market category. For instance, if total advertising expenditure in the soft drink category amounts to £100 million, and the company spends £15 million, then its SOV is 15/100 = 15%.

Equilibrium is where share of voice is the same as share of market.

You may recall from Chapter 13 that we described a model which suggested possible SOV strategies. Briefly, this four-grid matrix plotted a brand's required share of SOM against competitors'

SOV. The questions for evaluating whether expenditure has been effectively deployed are therefore:

- Where our SOM is low, and competitor SOV is low, has the increase in expenditure we spent above our SOM increased our market share?
- Where our SOM is low, and competitor SOV is high, has the decrease in expenditure to defend our niche market SOM succeeded?
- Where our SOM is high, and competitor SOV is low, has maintaining expenditure just above equilibrium worked?
- Where our SOM is high, and competitor SOV is also high, has the increase in our expenditure helped to defend the brand?

For inter-media comparison purposes, a medium's **cost** is expressed by the cost of reaching 1000 people given as **cost per thousand** (CPT or CPM). This is achieved by calculating cost of placement divided by the likely audience of that medium (e.g. *You Magazine* double-page spread cost £10,000 divided by circulation of 1000 = £10).

To ensure efficient use of resources, media costs have to be measured: cost measures, media schedule element measures and effect measures.

Advertisement Processing Measures

Field testing for message impact is made for 'recognition' (respondents tested for brand awareness and key message ingredients) and 'recall' (consumers are asked to remember, for example, the contents of advertisements, images, slogans, colours). The individual consumer's response to advertising messages is dependent upon the nature of the decision-making process – whether the product is high or low involvement. Research on this tends to be retrospective and characterised by personalised indirect measures. Advertising can be measured in laboratory conditions (physiological testing: eye-movement cameras, pupilometer and voice-pitch tests) or in the field before the advertisement runs (pre-testing) or after it has run (post-testing) or on a sample of the target audience to gauge likely response. Some of the methods of advertising (indeed all communications tools) are listed below:

Recognition is often done with the brand featured, which is known as **advertisement recognition (AD),** or with pack, logo and brand name obscured, which is known as **masked advertisement recognition (MAR).** These are useful measures for testing attention and retained brand memory. **Advertisement recognition frequency (ARF)** measures how many times the advertisement has been seen, read or heard (Rossiter and Bellman 2005).

The Starch Readership Studies Test is an evaluative instrument which measures readership, reader interest and reader reactions to press advertising and editorial content. It is a post-recognition technique which estimates 'noted' (percentage who remember seeing the advertisement) 'associated' (percentage of advertisement and content recognised) and 'read most' (percentage who read more than half an advertisement). Measures are often against industry norms and like-for-like competition.

Brand-prompted recall (BPAR) measures whether brand as the memory cue or stimulus is linked correctly in advertisement processing: is the content and message of the advertisement mentally associated with the brand? In other words, it measures awareness and association.

Day after recall (DAR) tests can be used for intrusiveness and impact. It is a post-recognition technique which estimates percentage of respondents recalling the brand and those who recall key elements of the message.

Pre-test advertisement evaluation tests to gauge opinions on brand name recall, recall of key product selling points or creative themes and likelihood of purchase decision.

Category-prompted advertisement recall (CPAR) is a more precise measure which asks respondents to link a brand to a very specific category or category need.

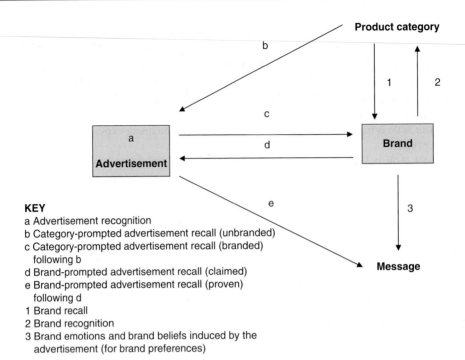

Figure 17.3: Linkages between the advertisement, product category, brand and message

Source: Rossiter and Bellman (2005, p.317).

In Figure 17.3, taken from Rossiter and Bellman (2005, p. 317), we can clearly see the linkages between the advertisement, product category, brand and the advertisement message. It shows the locations and directionality of the advertisement processing measures (letters) and brand communication effects (numbers).

EVALUATION IN FOCUS

Measuring Public Sector Effectiveness

Evaluation of marketing communications strategy is important for all organisations in order to fully assess whether the direction and tactics have been achieved effectively and within the constraints of budgeted spend. In the public sector, with a wide range of stakeholders who may not all be customers (users of services), accountability is of paramount importance. But how do you measure objectives such as 'To promote the role, purpose and effectiveness of the agency and its activities' or 'Promote regional economic strategy'? Equally how do you measure the goal of promoting good marketing and communications to internal staff or a positive image for a region? In order to comprehensively evaluate these sorts of far-ranging objectives, a range of both qualitative and quantitative metrics must be deployed. Below is a list of such measures used by the UK's North West Development Agency, one of many Regional Development Agencies (RDAs) who have the remit of promoting the economic, social and cultural development of their regions in the UK.

Activity	Qualitative measurements	Quantitative measurements
Media relations	Analysis of positive/neutral/negative coverage Types of stories covered Feedback from journalists Key messages covered	Number of articles and features Estimated advertising costs Number of media briefings Use of press releases
Public affairs	Feedback from MPs/MEPs etc. on communication methods used Independent survey of MPs	Number of briefings and presentations arranged Number of people attending
Events	Feedback from audiences at events Media coverage of events	Number of attendees at events Satisfaction ratings
Marketing campaigns and materials	Surveys of perception of the agency by target audiences Feedback from customers on usefulness of publications Feedback from partners	Outputs from campaigns Take up of agency services Response to mailings/ advertisements Number of collaborative initiatives
E-media	Feedback from users/customers Comparison with other Regional Development Agency (RDA) websites	Number of page views compared to other RDA and public sector sites Number of update news stories Average length of stay on sites
Internal communications	Feedback surveys amongst staff/board	Number of initiatives delivered Whether agency 'corporacy' is improved across the organisation
Corporate identity and branding	Feedback from users/customers on views of the logo and levels of brand recall	Usage of NWDA logo amongst partner organisations Guidelines adhered to Signage updated and maintained

Evaluating marketing communications' effectiveness in the public sector

Source: North West Regional Development Agency and at www.nwda.co.uk and www.englandsnorthwest.com.

MATTER OF FACT

ARF's New Media Model

Measurement of the effectiveness of marketing communications as discussed by Lucas and Britt (1963) covered techniques of measurement, recognition tests, opinion and aptitude tests, recall and association tests, projective methods, as well as a full range of media measurements. When Korgaonkar and Bellinger in 1984 and 1985 interviewed a wide sample of industry executives, attitude, awareness and sales were given particular practical significance. Researchers such as Jones (1990) then described the need to acknowledge the impact of competitive

(Continued)

activities (e.g. share of voice). The Advertising Research Foundation set the parameters with the original ARF model which had six levels at which media could be compared:

- **Vehicle distribution:** the physical units through which the message can flow (number of TV or radio sets tuned to the programme; copies of the magazine/ newspaper).
- **Vehicle exposure:** the number of individuals exposed to the medium vehicle.
- **Advertising exposure:** the number of individuals exposed to the advertising.
- **Advertising attentiveness and perception:** the number of individuals noticing the advertising.
- **Advertising communication:** the number of individuals receiving some kind of communication from the advertising.
- **Sales response:** the actual purchases accruing from being exposed to the advertising.

Harvey (1997) added extra stages:

- **Advertising persuasion:** the power of the medium to persuade the audience.
- **Advertising response:** the call to action responses of the medium.
- **Leads:** the ability of the medium to generate sales leads from which sales may eventually accrue.

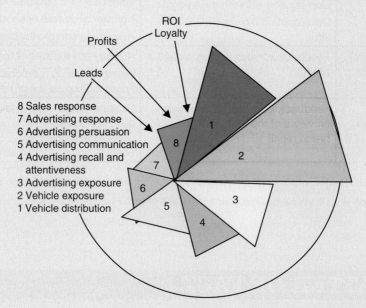

The ARF's new media model

Source: derived from original Advertising Research Foundation ARF Model (1961) and enhanced by Harvey (1997).

- **Profits:** the profits which eventually come from the income streams of sales.
- **Loyalty:** the equity generated by favourable repeat purchase in terms of brand loyalty, life-time customer value and positive word of mouth.

Source: Harvey (1997).

In order to improve the measurability of marketing communications, content owners, such as satellite, cable and telecommunications organisations, are using relevant placement of sponsored advertising slots within the entertainment context of their programme schedules. There is greater emphasis on premium quality content and therefore better salience between media and message, and, whilst this captures content rather than audience, it does lead to greater granularity of measure which facilitates better evaluation. For example, *NBC Universal* partnered with *Neilsen* in 2008 to create its TAMI (Total Audience Measurement Index) which measures effectiveness of multi-channel, multi-message communications across many platforms including TV, mobile and PC formats.

Evaluating Sales Promotions or Direct Response Advertising

Sales promotions tend to be used for short-term, incremental gain as a communication tactic as part of an overall strategy. Responses are often evaluated in terms of successful generation and fulfilment of 'calls to action', which are appeals to engage in some form of behaviour: send in a coupon, telephone a number, visit store or website, send off for a brochure and so on; and the conversion of these sales 'leads' into appointments, orders, sales. Also, we can measure the number of entries in a competition, response to mail shots or clicks or impressions on a webpage or online subscriptions, questionnaires or surveys.

Evaluating Public Relations

'Column inch' coverage tries to equate the cost of advertising for the equivalent press coverage. Sometimes, agencies will count campaign or period press clippings against the total for that period or publication. Readership and circulation or numbers of listeners or viewers may be useful measures.

Evaluating Event Marketing

Sponsorship and event management, whilst being vitally important to generating positive word of mouth and engendering good relations with stakeholders, is much more difficult to evaluate since 'goodwill' may not translate into product interest or sales. However, the ability to reach the target audience and engage in some form of dialogue, the awareness of the company or brand, the association of the event with the brand (see the 'Canvas' campaign in Chapter 15 linking emerging young artists with *Beck's Bier*), as well as enhanced brand image are all vital metrics as much as the generation of new business and actual sales are.

It is important to recognise that evaluation is not the end of a linear process but an integral and important part of the circular CAMPAIGN planning framework. It should inform, guide and correct the successful application of marketing communications and keep it relevant and meaningful, providing suitable media to convey the brand's positioning and brand narrative.

ENVIRONMENTAL ISSUES IN MARKETING COMMUNICATIONS

Whilst the issues of ethics, regulation and environmental dynamics can be examined separately, they are inextricably linked to marketing communications strategy. Unethical marketing practices may lead to greater control either within a formal framework or through industry or competitive self-regulation. Changing consumer and societal conditions will require constant monitoring, control and reassessment of how and where media and messages are delivered to target audiences.

ETHICAL CONSIDERATIONS

Moral conduct may be enforced by regulation or competitive pressure, but should start with an understanding of the target market's frame of reference of honesty, virtue and integrity. Consensus on value judgements like 'right and wrong' may be achievable, but the ethics of who can be targeted and in what manner is constantly changing. The key issues are summarised below.

Targeting Vulnerable Groups

The argument as to whether targeting is a helpful or harmful process is still raging. Presenting products and services best suited to well-researched, highly profiled consumers is surely what good marketing is all about. The ways in which brands are communicated, and whether marketing communications create wants instead of fulfilling needs, is up for scrutiny.

Communicating to children has been seen as exploitative in some instances. Because brand loyalty begins at an early age, the peer group pressure to buy brands can be manipulated from a very early stage. Exposure to advertising messages has been seen as being unethically targeted in both traditional and digital media. Children view a multiplicity of messages in many different formats – TV, Internet, *PlayStation* games, magazines – and this is largely left to the jurisdiction of the people placing the messages rather than any parental control. The scheduling of advertisements for children's toys, especially in the run up to Christmas and other key sales periods, can result in unhealthy desire for products which manifests itself in the 'pester power' pressure on parents.

The associative learning involved in, for example, using *Disney* toys to encourage consumption of food is very manipulative targeting. Children make the connections to other forms of entertainment and the habit of purchase may not be linked to nutrition but the acquisition of toys. The obesity debate, with fast-food chains accused of irresponsible practice in encouraging poor diets, has caused some organisations (and parents) to change.

The marketing of FAB (flavoured alcoholic beverages) 'alcopops' as an introduction to 'adult' drinking is another area which shows the aggressive and irresponsible nature of targeting communications. Alcohol is a 'rite of passage' product and introduces young people to the world of adults. As with all these types of products, moral or otherwise, socialisation is often tied in with consumption. There is considerable concern with regard to the way alcoholic brands are positioned with high alcoholic content being presented as desirable. Of course, the main draws are affiliation and status with the actual physical consumption almost being secondary. There are many instances where brands have been repositioned from being aimed at older people to becoming seen as fashionable, trendy drinks of choice for a younger target group. *Harvey's Bristol Cream* and *Baileys* have achieved a transformation in brand image through more youthful associations. The incidents of sampling and other promotional methods at university campuses and student pubs and clubs show how these groups may be vulnerable to aggressive marketing. The *Heineken* case study featured in Chapter 12 demonstrates how one company has responded to (either from moral or competitive pressure) the need for 'responsible drinking'.

Even the indirect encouragement of smoking and other unacceptable practices through product placement is under scrutiny. Consumers of an older persuasion will have been almost unconsciously exposed to smoking as being associated with 'sophistication', 'sexiness' and 'being grown up' by a battery of Hollywood stars and musicians. These act as opinion formers and imbue credibility into brands.

Targeting school children with 'learning' materials is often a thinly disguised way of encouraging sales of product purporting to be of educational value.

The unethical targeting of other vulnerable groups can be based on economics, ethnicity or location and usually involves gambling, drinking and aspirational consumption.

Public Relations Issues

How an organisation deals with negative publicity raises questions about the integrity and honesty of the company and will affect corporate reputation and relationships with consumers. A Gerald Ratner-type aberration (for readers too young to remember, he said the products his jewellery company sold were 'crap') may result in devastating consequences if worries about product safety are not handled with care and honesty. *Perrier* survived because faults and problems were immediately addressed and the trust of its customers was maintained. *Cadbury's* delay in dealing with a salmonella scare at its Bourneville chocolate factories in the UK could have destroyed brand equity and the company. *Coca-Cola's* failure to launch the US's top bottled water brand in the UK owed more to the way the problem of liquid contamination was dealt with than the problem itself.

Packaging Issues

The consumer, competitive and legal pressures for companies to package safely, label correctly and informatively, and dispose responsibly have dramatically changed the way products are packaged. Label information can exaggerate nutrition content or mislead (e.g. 'Contains energy-giving ingredients' might also contain high sugar content; '95% fat free!' actually might be higher than other brands and still contains 5% fat).

If a brand is packaged in a very similar way to a competitor's offer, or even a better version of the company's own brand, this may 'pass off' the product as being the same and can be misleading.

If packaging graphics misrepresent content by exaggerating the size, appearance or quality of the product, this may also be misleading.

Branding Issues

One company 'passing off' its product as being identical or similar to a competitor's is an example of misleading representation. In the case of the UK supermarket *ASDA* selling its own-brand chocolate biscuit *Puffins* in identical packaging and very similar branding to *Penguins* the market leader, this actually led to a famous court case. This is an example of unethically and illegally using the 'leveraging' power of another company without its permission and in a misleading fashion. This is evident where global brands are copied and sold under very similar names in local markets.

Unfair Competition

As we have seen in Chapter 5, the consumer pull element is dependent upon the trade push strategy being successful. This requires the buying, stocking, displaying, merchandising and selling of manufacturers' products through intermediaries. Display and shelf space in store, warehouse allocation for stocking and sales-force focus in selling to retailers may often be disguised as 'promotions, incentives and merchandising' business development. Although it is not suggested that this is unethical per se, there are accusations that this can often amount to bribery, favour bigger companies and may not present brands which consumers see as first choices. As a result, this is often seen as unethical.

Sales Promotion Problems

Misrepresentation of value in promotional activities aimed at consumers can be problematic. Promises of premium gifts which do not materialise, or points incentive schemes which encourage excessive consumption for little are notorious examples.

Ethical Issues with Online Communications

The relative lack of control and pseudo-permissive element of Internet communications raise questions over privacy invasion, data protection and the targeting of vulnerable groups. As we have seen extensively throughout this book, blogs are a growing online phenomenon, a credible source of information and opinion for consumers. 'Rating of products' in use by consumers is a common practice for brands now. Both of these marketing devices have been exploited by companies with planted bloggers or employee opinions being passed off as legitimate consumers.

Unethical and Irresponsible Advertising

Advertising has been seen as untruthful and some practitioners have been accused of employing deceptive practices. Misrepresentation of product capabilities, implied endorsement or encouragement to use by presenting false claims are unethical and may not just affect perceptions of the brand but the category and therefore unfairly affect ethical competitors.

Consumers who are not cognitively aware that they are being exposed to messages may be influenced to purchase in an unethical way. The now-illegal use of 'subliminal advertising' to brainwash cinema goers to buy *Coke* and popcorn is an extreme example of advertising being highly manipulative.

However, implicit suggestion or subtle association, even some forms of 'priming', have been cited as examples of persuasion being calculating practice.

General claims of advertising being insulting to intelligence, or tasteless, or indiscriminately aired at times when other groups are watching (e.g. children being exposed to adult ailments in advertisements scheduled in 'family' viewing periods) can be problematic. The case which ends this chapter deals with this every issue. When Australian males were targeted with a campaign aimed at changing attitudes to domestic violence, other vulnerable groups were also exposed to the images used and could have been inadvertently affected by different interpretations of those messages. Whether or not this was an example of irresponsible advertising is still being debated.

Advertising that focuses on consumers' fears, insecurities or anxieties can play on the negative aspects of life: social rejection, guilt and inadequacy. Even charities manipulate on 'compassion conscience' to make us feel guilty about not contributing to solving the world's problems.

MARKETING COMMUNICATIONS ETHICS IN FOCUS

When celebrities are used to promote brands, there is a huge element of trust involved in the meaning that is being transferred from cultural icon to product. These days, it is not unusual to see ostensibly odd connections when brands are explicitly endorsed: John Lydon (aka 'Johnny Rotten') of *Sex Pistols'* notoriety has been seen as a 'country gent' selling butter; Lemmy from *Motorhead* sells *Axa* insurance; and now we see the godfather of punk, Iggy Pop, telling us to: 'Get a Life!' and buy some car insurance. But who is this aimed at? And what message is being communicated by using such a famous hell raiser with a reputation for living life to the full? Was Iggy Pop a credible source or an incredible stooge?

Complainants to the UK Advertising Standards Authority (ASA) spotted in the fine print of the details on the *Swiftcover.com* website that musicians and people working in the entertainment business were prohibited from getting cover with the company. Even though *Swiftcover .com* has since changed its policy, the ASA recommended that the advertisement should not run as it breached the UK's TV advertising code. The ASA ruling stated: 'Because the policy was promoted by a well-known musician, which might lead some viewers to believe the policy covered those who worked in entertainment, when it did not, and because Iggy Pop did not have a policy with *Swiftcover*, we concluded the ad was misleading'.

The *Swiftcover.com* argument at the ASA hearing was that its advertisement did not refer to Pop's profession and had chosen him to front the advertisement because of his reputation for 'living life to the full'. However, the ASA pointed out that in the commercial, the 61-year-old performer said: 'I got *Swiftcovered*. I got insurance on my insurance!' and there was an implied connection between Iggy Pop as a musician and the product being offered.

By using such a punk icon, Iggy Pop and *Swiftcover.com* have certainly made motor insurance interesting for a change. The £25 million online and offline campaign – covering TV, radio, outdoor and digital advertising, along with the sponsorship of digital satellite broadcaster *Sky*'s 2009 sci-fi season, including the new series of *Battlestar Galactica* – has dramatically increased awareness for the brand and the insurance product category in general, and has sent sales soaring by almost a third. However, the advertisement's implicit suggestion of endorsing cover for musicians and the lack of specific loyalty by Iggy Pop not only undermined the message but also proved unethical.

REGULATORY CONTROLS

As we have seen, moral conduct and ethical practice may be enforced by the pressure of competitive parity, formal, legal legislation or, in the case of innovative and enlightened organisations, self-regulation. Often, the onus is on consumers to filter messages and claims and deal with marketing communications in a rational, cognitive, dare one say, adult manner. That makes a sweeping, unrealistic judgement of uniform, intelligent consumers and is a basic abrogation of manufacturers', media owners' and advertising agencies' responsibilities. It also undermines the power of the consumer to vote with their feet in response to misleading or offensive imagery and claims. It also assumes that the people taking offence are customers, or the targeted audience, or even have a need for the product.

Therefore, it is dangerous to leave content, message and delivery entirely up to the self-regulation of advertisers and schedulers. Different companies may not have the long-term interests of the market or consumer at heart. Some companies may not have the pressure of competitive parity as they may be in a monopolistic or oligopolistic market position. What if advertisers are not fully aware of the impacts on society and consumption?

Therefore, formal regulatory controls have had to be enforced in some circumstances. The general principles of practice in marketing communications in the UK for example are governed by the ASA (Advertising Standards Authority), which aims to protect consumers within 'legal, decent, honest and truthful' guidelines. 'Marketing communications that are welcome and trusted' (*Marketing Week* 2004) is a mantra across TV, radio, interactive TV and now SMS texting and covers specific areas such as guidance on advertising to vulnerable groups such as children.

GREEN AND ECO-FRIENDLY CONSIDERATIONS

Altruism, moral conscience, fear, legal regulatory restrictions and the pursuit of competitive advantage all contribute to a company adopting a 'green' stance in terms of its approach to the procurement, manufacture, selling and divestment of product. Sustainability, an appreciation of the product and process life cycles, offering sustainable and environmentally friendly product, efficiencies in production, recycling of packaging and paper, and the ethical control of a supply chain encouraging fair trade equity and protecting minorities are all part of the contemporary market dynamic.

Buzz words like 'sustainability', 'carbon footprint' and 'neutrality' have entered the vocabulary of consumers and marketers alike. There is plenty of evidence that policies such as the UK's *Marks & Spencer's* '100 Point Plan' demonstrating company ethics, supplier fairness and environmentally responsible behaviour has been received as proof of its integrity and commitment to the non-commercial cause. And this has positive impacts in terms of competitiveness and customer loyalty. But there is also a new word which accompanies these noble aims: 'green-washing'. If these policies are designed to score PR points with customers rather than saving the planet, they will be counter-productive. If company response is to fully recognise that conscience is an integral part of modern-day consumption, and it helps save the planet, that is different. All this is dependent upon consumer demand as well as manufacturer supply. The demand for an electric car or an energy-efficient light bulb is technology facilitated and customer driven.

CLOSING CASE STUDY

Australian White Ribbon Campaign: The Ethics of Hitting the Wrong Targets with Pro-Social Advertising

Marketing communications can be highly effective in disseminating information, educating, creating awareness, even indoctrinating and bringing about real changes in society. It has a power to inculcate and assist in the socialisation process (McQuail 1989), but it also has a responsibility to apply that power discriminately and control its influence on vulnerable audiences. Pro-social

(Continued)

communication campaigns (often referred to as social marketing) have environmental, social or cause-related communication objectives which often attempt to bring about behavioural change. Examples of advertising aimed at affecting children's antisocial behaviour or changing adult attitudes to smoking, exercise or conservation are more prevalent than ever. One such campaign is the *Australian White Ribbon Day*, aimed at raising awareness of vio-

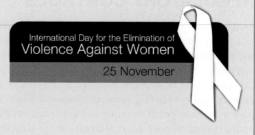

International Day for the Elimination of
Violence Against Women
25 November

©White Ribbon Day. Used with permission.

lent abuse against women. Whilst it had a positive impact on its intended target audience, it was also criticised by mental health professionals for its horrific depictions of suicide and self-harm.

White Ribbon ads embarrass Australian men to support cause

©White Ribbon Day. Used with permission.

Around the world, the emotional, psychological and quality-of-life costs for women and children exposed to domestic violence are immeasurable. According to the World Health Organisation (2002), it is a major public health problem in terms of medical and counselling costs, lost productivity, women's refuges and legal system costs. There have been many mass-media advertising campaigns to promote the ending of violence against women, often targeted at women 'breaking the silence' and seeking official support, changing the legal system or generally raising awareness levels amongst the general public. A growing trend has been the increasing involvement of men's groups advocating an end to violence against women. The *White Ribbon Day* campaign focuses each year on 25 November to coincide with United Nations International Day for the Elimination of Violence Against Women and encourages people to wear a white ribbon to publicly display their opposition to violence against women.

The agency appointed – *Saatchi & Saatchi* – used a full range of marketing mix components including TV and radio advertisements, community service announcements (CSA), simulated 'post cards', web banners as well as a viral electronic post card. The theme was based on colloquial research of what fathers would do for their daughters (e.g. 'swim through shark-infested waters'; 'give my right arm'; 'go to hell and back') and creatively represented this in shockingly graphic TV images of a young girl watching her father walking in front of a bus, swimming fully clothed with sharks, crawling over broken glass, and about to have an arm amputated. Website banners depicted mock promotions to fathers relating to features of the TV campaign such as 'Take a Trip to Hell: Special Offer for Dads'. This achieved its campaign objectives but also raised many objections; professionals in the family and domestic violence arena felt that the contradictory use of violence to help combat violence was counter-productive. Even more problematic was that the illustrations of methods of committing suicide were seen as not appropriate and a dangerous encouragement to vulnerable groups.

Because advertising involves inculcating audiences by repetition of images and messages, there is greater pressure on advertisers to use even more discretion when using images that could be misinterpreted or encourage suicide attempts by vulnerable individuals. Whilst there are plenty of legal and ethical guidelines such as 'Suicide and Mental Illness in the Media' and the Australian Commercial Television Code of Practice (CTCP), a lot of the website advertising materials were available without age restriction. Concerns were made both officially and through the media to the United Nations Development Fund for Women (UNIFEM) and the White Ribbon Day (WRD) National Leadership Group (NLG) who defended the use of images as being necessary to attract men's attention and commit them to combating violence against women.

Research into the ethical issues and communication efficacy of the campaign was conducted by Donovan, Jalleh and Fielder (2009), which seemed to suggest that not only were all target audiences not properly researched, but groups supporting the White Ribbon campaign were not consulted, leading to a campaign which was both less effective than it could have been and irresponsible in its delivery. The ethical considerations were that it was 'incumbent on the WRD NLG to pre-test the ads against [. . .] not just members of the public in general, but also against men suffering depression, children in general, children of victims of violence and suicide and women victims of violence'. In terms of the efficacy of the communication, they found that the literal concept overshadowed the intended messages about wearing a white ribbon. The use of shock tactics was clearly not relevant to the intended messages.

QUESTIONS

1. What lessons can be learned from this case in terms of the 'inculcation of audiences'?

2. Do you think that there would have been as much attention on ethical consideration if the communications objectives of raising awareness had been achieved?

3. Investigate the idea of 'social networks for social good' such as through *Facebook* and evaluate the effectiveness of marketing communications in being a source of change in society.

CHAPTER SUMMARY

In this chapter, we have discussed why it is important to understand how and why evaluation is key to successful marketing communications, and to appreciate what the primary purpose of evaluating marketing communications is. We examined the links between the product category, brand, media and messages and analysed their interrelated impacts.

The CAMPAIGN planning framework was used as an evaluative aid to illustrate the components for making qualitative as well as quantitative assessments of marketing communications.

We further examined the different methods and techniques for evaluating marketing communications and compared the relative insights these offered in assessing their effectiveness. We looked at how marketing communications is evaluated in different contexts such as the public sector, and considered the peculiar criteria for evaluating different elements of the marketing communications mix.

Lastly, we considered the evaluation of ethical, regulatory and environmental issues and discussed how these factors may impact on the effectiveness of marketing communications.

REFLECTIVE QUESTIONS

a. What is the primary purpose of evaluating marketing communications?

b. How does the CAMPAIGN planning framework relate to evaluating the impact of marketing communications?

c. How can the objectives of 'hierarchy of effects' impact on measurable metrics?

d. Are there any differences in the way that different communication tools are evaluated?

e. What do 'reach' and 'frequency' measure and how do we know that these are correct ways of evaluating the effects of marketing communications?

RESEARCH PROJECTS

Look up the academic paper by Jonathan E. Schroeder and Janet L. Borgerson entitled 'An Ethics of Representation for International Marketing' published in 2005 in the *International Marketing Review* (**22**(5), 578-600) which discusses the need for valuations of communication appropriateness to be informed by an awareness of the ethical relationship between marketing representations and identity. What are their main arguments?

Examine and comment on the contention that children are an extremely vulnerable sector of society whose innocence is being undermined by the power of marketing communications and therefore deserve special attention and must be protected from manipulation.

Marketing Communications Illustrative Glossary

The Marketing Communications Glossary is included here to help you familiarise yourself with key words and descriptions. Using the website links and examples illustrated, examine how marketing communications has been applied by the various organisations in the different contexts. Evaluate how successful you think they have been in achieving their respective brand objectives. Can you think of any examples of your own?

Feature	Description	Illustration
360° planning and control of brand communications	A holistic fully integrated approach to campaign planning management at every level scheduled throughout the whole campaign involving all media, messages and timings	See the extended case study on *BMW's Mini* in Chapter 10 www.miniadventure.com
ABC	*See* Audit Bureau of Circulation	
Absolute position	Targeted to 'market space' or category. A brand must ensure that it shares enough of the characteristics and associations with other brands in the targeted category	'*Lookers* – First for *Vauxhall* in the North West' positions this car dealership against rival suppliers *Häagen-Dazs* owns an occasion: 'A DVD at home night'. Other examples are *Gillette*'s 'The Best a Man Can Get', *Kit Kat*'s 'Have a Break, Have a Kit Kat' and *Carlsberg's* 'Probably the Best Lager in the World'
Across-category consideration	When a consumer considers brands from different product categories before a purchase	
Action-based objectives or action goals	Communication objectives aiming at affecting behaviour. Mainly sales-oriented, the generation of information and the building of customer relationships	
Actual state	How the consumer is feeling at the moment prior to purchase	Needing to remove hunger, thirst, insecurity or low self-esteem
Ad busting	Consumers who blatantly destroy or alter an advertising billboard 'to curtail rampant consumerism' can deliberately sabotage campaigns. PR communications NOT initiated by the organisation, but perceived as having been sent by the organisation	Illegal stickers of *Adobe Photoshop*'s interface panels were pasted onto Britney Spears, Leona Lewis and Christina Aguilera posters in Berlin to highlight the false airbrushing of models in advertising

Addressability	Ability to more accurately target audiences	Digital TV, *TiVo*, PVRs and video on demand
Advergaming	A cultural marriage between advertising and online gaming where brand messages are embedded in interactive, entertaining media content	Brands can be inserted into games where the relevance of the context enhances authenticity such as stadia billboards in *EASports FIFA Road to the World Cup* 2010 video game
Advertainment or advermovies	Online conversation about product enhancement and user experience where communications messages are 'captured' in the content	*Adidas'* 'Dream Big' 2008 campaign which used TV advertising to open up the latest chapter in its story: connecting with grassroots football. TV ads ('Now showing at adidas.com.football') pulled viewers onto the adidas.com website
Advertising	Non-personal, one-way mass messages paid for by an identified sponsor and disseminated to a broad audience in order to influence or change their behaviour	Corporate image or brand image campaigns
Advertising communication	The number of individuals receiving some kind of communication from the advertising	
Advertising exposure	The number of individuals exposed to the advertising	
Advertising perception	The number of individuals noticing the advertising	
Advertising spend	Usually referred to as adspend equating to the total spent on media, creativity, design and evaluation of campaign	'*Red Bull*'s total advertising spend for 2007 in the UK was £21 million covering....' www.redbull.com
Advertorials	Advertisements which are paid for by a company, but have the appearance of being an editorial (as they are written and presented in the idiom of the journal's style rather than being transparently advertisements)	Cosmetics companies *Estée Lauder* and *Clinique* place advertising in the style of an editorial or article in *Hello!* magazine
Affiliate marketing	Website that sells other websites' products (otherwise known as affiliates)	Amazon created the first large-scale affiliate programme www.amazon.com
Aggregator retail brands	Primarily providers of manufacturer choice, environment and price to mass consumers	*Wal-Mart* in the USA, *ASDA* in the UK and *Carrefour* in France
'All that you can afford' method of budget setting	Expediency may dictate priorities such as management of cash flow and even survival might condition how much the organisation can afford	
Alliteration	Words that start with the same letter used for impact and memorability	
Ambassador programme	The recruitment of key influential journalists and opinion formers to generate WOM publicity for brand	The furniture retailer *DFS* succeeded in 'seeding' positive awareness amongst an audience of over 17 million in terms of OTS/OTH

Ambiguous support	Partial agreement with claim. The company does something to remedy the situation but does not take full blame	In *Perrier*'s crisis with contaminated water the company recalled its products and replaced them
Ambush marketing	Unknowing associations with a brand or event (typically, false sponsorship) designed to derive the same values as sponsorship out of events, without being actual sponsors. Reactive PR communications NOT initiated by the organisation, AND NOT perceived as having been sent by the organisation	*Heineken* handed out hats at the Euro 2008 football tournament where rivals *Carlsberg* were an official sponsor paying $21 million for the privilege
Antanaclasis	Repeating a word in two different senses	'Today's *Slims* at a very slim price' (*Misty Ultra Light* cigarettes) 'Nobody knows the athlete's foot like the *Athletes Foot*' (*The Athletes Foot* shoe store)
Antimetabole	Repetition or reversal of clause for dramatic effect	The *Toyota* ad 'Our vehicles don't just take people to work, they put people to work!'
AOM	Academy of Marketing	
Approach–approach	Motivational conflict requiring consumers to choose between desirable alternatives	Buying a new car or funding an expensive holiday
Approach–avoidance	Motivational conflict where consumption has to be a balance between desirable and undesirable consequences	'Naughty but nice' advertising appeals try to encourage the pleasure of eating against the problem of gaining weight www.weightwatchers.com
Arbitrary method of budget setting	No predetermined set amount for expected marketing communications expenditure. Ad hoc decisions are made on the basis of market conditions, competitive activities and changing brand requirements	
ARF	The Advertising Research Foundation	
Argument strength	Degree of relationship to product/mission benefit	
Artwork	Traditionally artwork takes the form of a pasted-down bromide onto a base board. It is the final preparation before conversion into the final printed material. Digital processes can now be used to replace traditional finished artwork	
Aspirational self-image	Self-image as one would like to be	
Assonance	Words which sound the same or have the same vowel sounds used for impact and memorability	'Choose Wisely, Choose *Sony*' (an example of anaphora as the word 'choose' is repeated at the start of each sentence; 'Beanz Meanz *Heinz*', and 'You'll Never Put A Better Bit' o' Butter on your Knife'
Asymmetric competition	Imbalance of marketing communications expenditure by different competing organisations	
Atmospherics	Tools to create store design	
ATR model	Three-stage process of behaviour involving the movement from awareness to trial to repeat behaviour. *See also* Hierarchies of effects	

Attitude	Comprising three components: cognitive-affective-conative (thinking-feeling-doing), an attitude is considered to be relatively enduring and results in a consistent response to given internal or external stimuli. Katz's four functions for attitudes: utilitarian function, value expressive function, knowledge function, ego-defence function	
Attitude specificity	The level of concreteness in an attitude	
Attraction effect	A new, and inferior, brand enhances the sales of current, similar brands and reduces the sales of current, dissimilar brands	
Attribute(s)	Concrete aspects, feature(s), key ingredients or unique competitive elements of the brand relevant to the subset of needs and wants of a selected target audience in a category	Like store location, an ABS braking system, or 100% pure orange juice *Hovis* – 'Seed Sensations' features the use of seeds in its bread *Vauxhall Astra Elite* – includes MP3 player and auxiliary *iPod* connector
Attribution	Assigning responsibility to one party	
Audience actively engaged	Time spent interacting with medium. For example, the average online game player spends 8 hours with a game	
Audit Bureau of Circulation (ABC)	Organisation that certifies audited net sales of publications. Basically, the circulation figure is calculated by deducting returned copies from the number originally distributed. Audited circulation can be considered a fair reflection of the number of copies actually being read	ABC figures, which are reported in *BRAD*, indicate the actual number of copies of a publication in circulation
Automated call distributor	Electronic system by which telephone calls can be routed to appropriate departments or contacts without the need for direct human contact	
Avatar	Creation of 'cyber-identity' (alter-ego identity)	In an attempt to communicate with younger voters, the UK Labour Party has a virtual version of Peter Mandelson, the Business Secretary, as an avatar in the controversial on-line role-playing game *Second Life*
B2B	Business to business (organisational buying behaviour)	
B2B push strategies	Promotions aimed at encouraging sales between organisations for the purpose of providing stock and service to fulfil demand stimulated by the consumer as the end user	
B2B push/pull strategies	Promotions aimed at creating demand sales between organisations as well as providing stock and service to fulfil demand stimulated by the consumer as the end user	
B2B2C communication flow	Cascading communication flow from company to consumer through intermediaries	
B2C	Business to consumer (individual buying behaviour)	
B2C pull strategies	Promotions aimed at creating consumer demand	
B2C push/pull strategies	The presence and influence of opinion leaders in disseminating information requires communication to be aimed at end recipient and channelled through intermediary sources	Some e-business models work on the dialogue approach for communications and sales

Balance theory	Relationships between three attitudes	
Banded pack	Pack of products strapped or banded together	
Behavioural domains	Cognitive, affective and conative behavioural responses to communications and purchase	
Behavioural paradigm of buyer behaviour	Proponents of this paradigm generally believe that to find out what is going on in the mind of an individual is not achievable. The behaviourist approach suggests that buyer behaviour is a function of past learned experiences (behaviour) and stimuli that are predominantly found in the environment. Behavioural theorists believe that marketing communications activity should be focused on creating the correct environmental cues for the individual and on monitoring the responses to these cues as a guide to future activity	
Behavioural segmentation	Segmentation based on behavioural characteristics towards particular goods or service categories	
Behaviourist orientation	Analysis of consumer behaviour based on action orientation	
Belief crystallisation	Thinking and elaborating on a brand's beliefs	
Below-the-line communications	Marketing communications that make use of the non-commission-paying media in all their forms, i.e. all forms of promotions other than advertising. Sometimes, incorrectly, it is referred to as below-the-line advertising. Although it remains a popular term, its usefulness is limited as it encompasses such a broad range of promotional activity	
Benefits	Actual or perceived asset offering utility to user of brand	'*Radio Two*: online, on digital and on 88 to 91 FM'
Blitz schedule	Reaching audience with high frequency	
Body copy	The term given for the main text or words. Usually, body copy is brief but some creative treatments require a lot of information to be disseminated. *See also* Headlines	
BOGOF	Buy one get one free consumer promotion	Colchester-based UK online car broker Broadspeed.com offered a BOGOF promotion with its *Dodge Avenger* saloons
Bonus packs	Providing packaged 'bundles' of stock either of quantities of the same product or using ancillary products may be advantageous to stock and strategically useful for the manufacturer to achieve penetration of the distributor offer	Special consumer promotion kits (e.g. *PC World* offering manufacturers' computers with special software)
Boston Consulting Group (BCG)	Strategy matrix relating market share to category growth	
Brain scan	Measurement of a person's brain activity	
Brand/customer relationships	Formal and informal links between company and customer	The *COOP Bank*'s Ethical Policy has led to more than £1 billion in unethical business being declined
Brand added value	Brands enable customers to derive extra benefits which may be functional, social or even psychological	*The Body Shop* offers a clear conscience as well as cosmetics to its customers

Brand alliance	Two or more brands that create joint short-term or long-term products	In an alliance with the UK Government's Department of Health, *Kellogg's* launched one of its biggest on-pack promotions to date, backing both *Change4Life* and sub-brand *Breakfast4Life*
Brand anatomy	The physical and emotional characteristics of a brand	
Brand Asset Valuator	A professional brand equity model by Young & Rubicam	
Brand assimilation	New brand or new information absorbed into the category by using existing customer knowledge	The acceptance of *Apple iPods* by consumers was largely due to the path paved by *Sony Walkmans* – not transistor radios or 'ghetto blasters'
Brand associations	Awareness, image and beliefs of what the brand means	*Panasonic Lumix* cameras are linked with fun, usability and creativity www.panasonic.co.uk
Brand associations – explicit	Unequivocal, overt, intended linkages with places, personalities or even emotions	*FFI Fair Instant*: 'Coffee with a bigger heart' directly links to the ethics of Fair Trade and the Save the Children fund www.fair-instant.co.uk
Brand associations – implicit	Implied, embedded or suggested linkages with places, personalities or even emotions	*Tropicana Orange Juice*: use of iconic New York imagery to imply brand sophistication and project more than product quality
Brand awareness	Buyer's ability to identify, recognise or recall the brand within the category in sufficient detail to make a purchase	
Brand book	Employee manual for brand communications	
Brand conversations	Solicited and unsolicited communications which affect target audience and stakeholder perceptions	
Brand credibility of employees	Measurements that indicate whether employees believe that a company is capable of delivering on its promises to customers and employees	
Brand delivery	Measurements of whether employees believe that the company fulfils its promise to customer and employees	
Brand differences	How distinctive the brand is from the competition	Sandwich retailer *Pret A Manger* uses highly distinctive packaging to differentiate its quality brand against the competition
Brand differentiation	The brand acts as a way of positioning away from the competition	
Brand dominance	Market strength as primary choice in purchase decisions.	*Sainsbury*'s strategy is to be seen as first choice for food in the UK supermarket sector

Brand encounter: explicitly planned	Deliberately overtly encoded mix elements	*Singapore Airlines* offers a luxury 'cabin ambience' which includes: world-class dining from around the world; in-flight amenities, reading and rest facilities; and *KrisWorld*, its award-winning in-flight entertainment system, now offers passengers more than 500 entertainment options
Brand encounters and brand messages	All solicited and unsolicited communications situations where target audience and stakeholder are exposed to the brand. These exposure experiences are 'moments of truth'. Brand encounters are frequently the embodiment of the organisation from the customer's perspective	
Brand equity	The amalgam of brand associations (awareness, image and beliefs of what the brand means), brand dominance (market strength and financial value) and brand prospects (extension possibilities for company and customer). The value of the brand in the minds of customers. Total positive and negative connotations communicated by and about the brand	*Tesco*'s all-encompassing 'Every Little Helps' feeds into a bank of 'goodwill' positive associations and brand potential which underpins the brand's story arc and maintenance www.tesco.com
Brand essence	Comprises the aggregate of the four dimensions: functions, personality or image, source and differences. Alternative terms are: brand core, brand DNA, brand soul and brand genetic code	
Brand ethos	The essence of the brand's values	*Volvo* used to have 'safety' as its core ethos until it became restrictive. Lately a move to a more social image ('Life Is Better Lived Together') has broadened the brand's appeal www.volvocars.co.uk
Brand expansion	The ability to use the brand name for new products, either alone or with other brands	*Yamaha* (originally a Japanese manufacturer of motorbikes) into branded hi-fi equipment, pianos and sports equipment
Brand extension and brand stretching	The use of the brand for new products (alone)	
Brand function	What the brand is and what it is supposed to do	*Ronseal*: 'It does what it says on the tin'
Brand identity	How the organisation wants the brand to be perceived	
Brand image	What user imagery the brand has in terms of people's cognitive and affective disposition to the brand	
Brand inferences	Conclusions about a brand's anatomy beyond what is communicated	

Brand influence of employees	How well the specific ways that employees have an impact on the customer experience are defined, communicated and upheld	*Ford Motor Company* appealed to its employees, retirees and dealers (750,000 people) to spread the word amongst friends and family about the quality and features of *Ford* vehicles in their 'Drive one' campaign that dared consumers to drive Ford vehicles
Brand ladder	A consumer's mental arrangement of possible brands as part of the consideration set	A list of favourite restaurants, shops, clothes labels which are mentally ranked by individual
Brand map	A graphical representation of competing brands in relation to one another based on people's perceptions. Also called position maps and perceptual maps	
Brand name suggestiveness	The ability of a brand name to describe an attribute or a benefit	*Utterly Butterly*
Brand outcomes	Consequences of brand equity (e.g. monetary consequences)	
Brand parity	Situation where brands are seen as being equivalent	
Brand performance	The brand's ability to create high market share and/or high relative price	
Brand personality	Human-like characteristics of the brand	*Ben & Jerry's* 'Baked Alaska: If It's Melted It's Ruined' campaign feeds into the long-term ethos of societal concern and citizen brands *The Body Shop* – caring, ethical organisation *Virgin* – 'everyman' brand taking on the traditional establishment brands
Brand portfolios	Are used by companies who sell products under many different brand names	
Brand preference (formerly attitude)	Buyer's evaluation of the brand with respect to its perceived ability to meet a currently relevant motivation (the evaluation is based on brand benefit beliefs and the motivation-related emotional weights of the benefits and of possible freestanding emotions)	
Brand preference, advocacy and satisfaction	Measurements that show the extent to which employees prefer to work at the company rather than its competitors and the degree to which they are comfortable referring friends and family to their employer	
Brand promiscuity	Consumers who migrate to many brands and do not manifest loyalty to any one brand	
Brand prospects	Extension possibilities for company and customer	*Bosch's* 'Invented for Life' campaign reinforces the built to last functionality whilst engaging users in its developing eco-friendly brand story www.bosch.com
Brand purchase intention	Buyer's self-instruction to purchase the brand or to take purchase-related action	
Brand recall	The brand (identity) is prompted AFTER a category need arises	
Brand recognition	The consumer associates the brand (identity) with the category	

Brand source	What the company stands for and what its aims are	The *Cirque du Soleil* brand stands for an overall amazing theatrical experience
Brand story arc potential	Ongoing brand narrative. Longevity of brand and ability to engage audience in ongoing dialogue	
Brand strategy	Typically four main branding strategies are identified: corporate umbrella branding, family umbrella branding, range branding and individual branding	
Brand switching	Consumers purchase different brands in the category	
Brand touch-points	All the replications of brand image or encounters experienced by prospective and actual target audiences	
Brand trust of employees	A gauge of trust and commitment level which employees have in the company leadership's ability to do the right thing relative to the values of the brand	*See* Brand influence of employees
Brand under-standing of employees	How well key valued and differentiated elements of the brand are articulated	
Branded entertainment	Content-captured commercials or commercial-captured content such as product placement and stealth marketing	
Branded own-label retail brands	Primarily providers of a private label proposition, environment and price to mass consumers	Spain's *Zara* and *Mango*, Germany's *Aldi* and France's *Auchan*
Brandsactional advertising	Digital migration of platforms	Social media and online video are blurring the lines between advertising and marketing
Brand-specific associations	Using the brand's unique association when extending the brand. Ongoing brand loyalty which creates brand advocates and maximises 'lifetime customer value'	*Bosch*'s 'Invented for Life' campaign reinforces the built to last function-ality whilst engaging users in its developing eco-friendly brand story www.bosch.com The Harley Owner's Group (HOGS) has a lifestyle affinity with the brand www.harleydavisonowners.com
BRCs	Business reply cards	
Breadth expansion	Brand awareness is enhanced in new situations	*Pantene* combs, brushes and hair accessories, in-store communica-tions, merchandising, branded environments, sampling systems, brochures, as well as a fully interactive website www.pantene.com
Bromide	Photographic production of original artwork used as a basis in the subsequent print production process	
Bubblegram prompts	Prompts or cues provided in the form of a picture or map as guidelines to telesales operators. So called because the prompts are shown as interlinking 'bubbles' of ideas, statements or questions	

Business understanding	How well employees understand the philosophical and historical underpinnings of the organisation in terms of the markets that are competed in, the needs of the categories served, and who its customers are and what they require	
Buying centre	Different buyer roles, especially important in B2B buyer behaviour	
C2C	Consumer to consumer. Communications which go directly from individual to individual without company mediation. Peer-to-peer communications	
CAA	*See* Cinema Advertising Association	
Call centre	Central resource that groups personnel together for telemarketing, both outbound (sales calls to customers and potential customers, or relationship marketing activities) and inbound (customers, responding to direct response advertising, customers requiring service)	
Calls to action	Many promotions require that the target is encouraged to take some form of action: ring a free phone number, fill in a coupon, request more information, collect tokens, try a sample, buy a product, request a sales visit, etc. These are calls to action that should be facilitated within the promotion where they are applicable	
Capacity model of attention	Model developed by Kahneman that recognises only limited attention can be given to all the stimuli available in the environment. People have only limited information processing resources. For this reason, emphasis tends to be placed on the need for marketing communications to attract attention	
CAPI	Computer Assisted Personal Interviewing	
Captions	Captions are short descriptions of text or visuals and help to break up the body copy in layout terms	
Captive audience	Interruption communication model where audience is static and viewing occurs when scheduled and therefore can be controlled	
Carelines	Mechanisms, usually telephone but could be other facilities such as fax and email, to help facilitate easy communications between an organisation and its customers	
Category match	Alternatives are from the same category	
Category mismatch	Alternatives are from unrelated categories	
Category need	Product or service requirement or need fulfilment. Motivations (interests, concerns and needs) of target audience which are demand-creating conditions	The array of appeals for new motor cars is dependent upon demand for symbolic, functional, social or pragmatic needs
Category planning	Means that the consumer has decided on a product category but will decide on the brand in the store	Supermarkets will put crisps, sandwiches, snacks, biscuits, microwave meals etc as a 'meal replacement' category
Category space	Market/product location either in the competitive marketplace or the minds of the audience	
CATI	Computer Assisted Telephone Interviewing	
Causal or cause-related marketing	Associating an organisation with 'worthy' causes such as charities to demonstrate corporate and social responsibility.	*Tesco*'s 'Computers for Schools' is a good example of this
Cause-related promotions (free item)	Promotions aimed at raising awareness or funding for community-based activities and demonstrating corporate and social responsibility	

Celebrity endorsement	The use of a well-known person to promote a company or product brand. *See also* Ohanian's celebrity endorser credibility scale	
CEM	Customer experience management	
Centrifugal forces	Country-level forces external to an organisation 'pushing' it to adapt marketing programmes	
Centripetal forces	Internal organisational forces (e.g. policy, structure, culture, economies of scale) 'pulling' an organisation to standardise marketing programmes	
Choice rules	How consumers make choices	
CIM	Chartered Institute of Marketing	
Cinema Advertising Association (CAA)	Responsible for much of the data on cinema audiences. Information on cinema going is also collected as part of the NRS data	
CIPR	Chartered Institute of Public Relations	
Circulation	The number of copies of a publication circulated in the market. Audited circulation figures are preferable as they are certified as accurate, and represent the number of copies distributed less the number of copies returned to the publisher	
Claims	Physical or psychological brand assertion about the effects of brand use	This can be done either physically (e.g. our product gives you fresh breath when you brush with our toothpaste) or psychologically (e.g. show others how you take care of yourself)
Clarity	How clear the brand signal is to consumers	
Classical conditioning	Associating two elements with each other	*Intel Pentium Processors'* 'sound logo' and *McDonald's* use of *Disney* are examples of associative learning by classical conditioning
Classified advertising	Advertisements that appear in the classified sections of the mass media	
Click	When a visitor to a website interacts with an ad so that the visitor is directed toward the advertiser's page or website	
Click stream	A recorded path of the pages a site visitor uses when clicking on various websites in search of information	
Click-through rates (CTR)	Number of online viewers who voluntarily view flash ads or 'roadblock' online advertising	
Client brief	Usually a written document, but could be presented verbally, outlining relevant background information and the principal marketing communications task to be undertaken	
Clutter	Total amount (noise) of marketing communications the audience is exposed to	
CMYK	Cyan, magenta, yellow and black (key) are the primary inks used in printing. As these inks are used in wet proofing, they ensure a true representation of the colour to be delivered	

Co-branding	One or more brands doing joint marketing communications	The 'Intel Inside' promotion of *Intel Pentium Processor* microchips in a range of manufacturers' PCs
Cognitive consistency	The preference to fit things to existing thoughts and opinions	
Cognitive dissonance	Term coined by Leon Festinger to describe a psychological state in which there is some incongruity (dissonance) or unstable state of mind caused by the holding of two contradictory attitudes or beliefs. Post-shopping regret or uncertainty caused by guilt or poor decision-making or brand promise not being achieved by brand in use. The resulting inconsistency encourages the individual to modify his thoughts to be more compatible or harmonious	
Cognitive learning	Learning by thinking through a problem or task	
Cognitive orientation	Communication which works on appeals to processing of knowledge, facts etc. rather than emotional appeal	
Cognitive paradigm of buyer behaviour	Focuses on the individual's thought processes when making purchasing decisions. The cognitive paradigm sees consumer choice as a problem-solving and decision-making sequence of activities, the outcome of which is determined principally by the buyer's intellectual functioning, and rational, goal-directed processing of information	
Commission-earning system	System of payment in which advertising agencies are paid commission for booking media on behalf of clients	
Commission rebating	Arrangement between a client and its advertising agency (or media independent) whereby some of the media commission the agency receives is passed on to the client by way of a discount on media costs	
Commonality	The degree to which communication components reinforce each other	
Communal marketing	Customers are the sales force by acting as market mavens. CRM in action	
Communicability	Can the benefits and brand values be communicated to an audience in a coherent and effective manner?	
Communication conduit	Medium or channel such as TV or opinion leader	
Communication durability	Lifespan of the communication	
Communication effects	Desired target market behavioural response to marketing communications	
Communication objective chains	Implying a sequential process or hierarchy of effects as aims for marketing communications	
Communications loop	The two-way nature of communications from sender to receiver and back again	
Comparative advertising	Ads that compare the brand against a familiar (most often) competitor in the category	American brand *Dunkin' Donuts* tells consumers that more *'hard-working'* people prefer their coffee than the high-priced Starbucks, 'elitist' coffee

Compatibility	Does it fit in with the way a consumer currently is satisfied by a category need?	Fitted home office furniture bombed in the 1970s and has achieved rapid growth due to changing social trends and home working
Competing parity brands	Brands must strive to be similar to competing brands to be properly positioned in a category	*ASDA* ad campaign stating '2,400 items reduced by *ASDA*; only 1,200 by *Tesco*'
Competing peripheral brands	Achieves typicality whilst not directly competing	*Pot Noodle* is a 'naughty but nice' alternative meal replacement
Competitive loyals	People who buy a competitor's product most or all of the time	
Competitive parity method of budget setting	Matching spend with competitors to achieve relative positioning, share of voice or even psychological equity can often be an appropriate method of budget setting, especially for challenger brands who seek category comparison or competitive parity	
Competitive positioning	Achieving recognition by the consumer as offering a similar or better value proposition than the competition	
Competitor intensity	The number of competitors in the category and how they differ from each other	
Complementarity	Refers to how the components can be best combined for best overall effect	If, for example, trial is key to early product adoption, sampling, package offers and merchandising may be best
Complexity	Does the potential user understand the brand and can they use it?	
Compromise effect	Tendency to avoid extreme alternatives, e.g. the highest price or the lowest quality	
Concept boards	Collection of visual materials (e.g. drawings, collage, montage) to replace or complement a written description that reflects the essence of a product or its customers/consumers. *See also* Mood boards.	
Conditional value	Certain situational factors such as celebration of events (birthdays, marriage, gift giving) carry another level of significance above the functional, social and emotional levels	
Congruity	Sharing the same meaning. *See also* Consistency	
Connotative meaning	A meaning that is not shared	
Consensus	Several sources communicate same message/agree	
Consideration set	Brands which are possible alternatives to fulfil problem or need within a category	*Dell, Toshiba, Apple* as choices for a laptop purchase
Consistency	The brand is communicated in the same way over time and the brand associations share the same core meaning	
Conspicuous consumption	Desire to show purchase to others as a sign of wealth, status or knowledge	
Consumer-based brand equity	The value of the brand for consumers	

Consumer durable	Long-lasting consumer products	
Consumer engagement	User 'buy-in' to the company's brand story as being sympathetic with the individual's own values, desires and situation	The ongoing brand loyalty of *Harry Potter* fans creates brand advocates and maximises lifetime customer value
Consumer ethnocentrism	Consumer beliefs about the appropriateness and morality of buying foreign products	
Consumer-generated content	Interactivity-induced consumer involvement and open-source marketing such as viral marketing. 'Word of mouse' gives undisputed credible and qualified referrals and exhibits a community-driven expression of interest. User-generated and co-authored	
Consumption goal	End state that consumers want to achieve	*WeightWatchers* appeals to those consumers who want to lose weight
Contract proof	Proof that print buyer and printer agree shows an acceptable quality of print	
Continuity	Consistent duration of communication	
Continuum of integrated marketing communications	Concept that emphasises that integration of marketing communications occurs to different degrees, and that greater benefits accrue from greater integration. The continuum also emphasises that separation between marketing communications elements can give rise to negative consequences	
Contribution	The component's standalone ability to communicate without any assistance from other communication mix elements	
Conventional media	Traditional media such as above-the-line advertising	
Convergence	The technology-driven unification of different media channels	
Conversion (as in 'conversion ratios')	People's changes in the relationship to the marketer and/or competitor	
Cooper's creative planning cycle	Consists of six stages: familiarise, hypothesise, synthesise and inspire, optimise, evaluate and review	
Cooperative advertising	Presents a joint presentation of manufacturer and distributor; involves 'marketing monies' being available either upfront or retrospectively applied	
Copy platform	The basic verbal or written message to be conveyed	
Copywriters	Those responsible for producing creative ideas and marketing communications text or 'copy'. Typically work in partnership with art directors	
Corporate image	The impression of an organisation, created by the corporate identity, as perceived by the target audiences	
Corporate marketing public relations/product marketing public relations	Two areas of marketing public relations focused towards the corporate and product brands, respectively	
Corporate personality	The composite organisational traits, characteristics and spirit	
Corporate public relations (CPR)	Those parts of public relations not directly concerned with a marketing or brand focus but taking a broader corporate or whole business perspective	

Correct recognition	Accurate logo recognition	
Corrective advertising	The requirement for advertisers to produce promotional material to correct any previous advertising considered to be misleading or incorrect	
Cost per thousand (CPT)	Measure of media efficiency; represents the cost of achieving a given coverage	Valued impressions (VIPs) is a refinement of CPT, calculated by assigning 'weights' to the various components of the target audience. For example, all housewives might be included in the target audience. However, it may be decided that housewives with children are of greater interest. It would be possible to assign a weight of, say, 60 to housewives with children and 40 to those without children to represent their relative importance. The housewives with children would then contribute more to the resulting CPT calculation than those with no children
Countercyclical	Communicating during low season, counter to competition	
Country of origin image or positioning	Essence of the brand is usually associated with the country where product is manufactured	*Guinness* – Irish Celtic soul *California Wines* – new world wines *BMW* – German engineering
Coverage	Another term for reach	
Covert communications	Hidden or not broadcast communications may be recreated by users of the brand and the brand communications	Viral marketing, loyalty expressed by wearing clothes and using brands
CPM models	Consumer processing models referred to as being about the 'fantasies, feelings and fun' of consumption	
CPR	*See* Corporate public relations	
CPT	*See* Cost per thousand	
Creative brief	Document that provides an outline of the creative task and the basis for creatives to develop their solutions	
Creative hot shops	Agencies specialising in creative ideas and solutions, other aspects of campaigns being handled by other agencies	
Creative methods	Creatives make use of a variety of techniques to aid the creative process, these include juxtaposition, free association, convergent thinking, divergent thinking, lateral thinking, brainstorming, experimentation and the use of swipe files	
Creative platform	Communications 'big idea' which gives structure to applied brand communications	*See* Chapter 13
Creative scope	The extent of creative flexibility afforded by the medium	
Creative theme/ concept	The basic or fundamental creative idea to be conveyed	
Creatives	General term for art directors, designers and copywriters. Responsible for developing creative and design solutions	

Credentials presentation	An opportunity for selected agencies to present details of their backgrounds, history and achievements in order to convince a potential client to include them on its agency selection shortlist	
Credibility	How credible the brand signal is to consumers	
Credit facilities	Financial arrangements or promotions such as deferred payment schemes	Buy Now Pay Later promotions
Crisis management	The planned management response to potentially damaging circumstances	
CRM	*See* Customer relationship management	
Cross-category promotion scheme	Form of joint loyalty promotion involving organisations from different product categories. Frequently, customers earn points from a variety of suppliers, which are added together for later redemption	
Cross-media presence	A media-neutral approach where the message finds the target rather than fits into the medium and is placed in different media channels	
Cross-promotions	A joint sales promotion by two or more brands	
Cross-selling	Selling other products to existing customers	
CTR	*See* Click-through rates	
Cultural capital	Meaning 'currency' possessed by a celebrity which conveys significance to a target audience	*Black Eyed Peas* have a lot of credibility with *Pepsi's* target audience and this is transferred across from the celebrity to the brand www.pepsi.com
Culturally constituted world	Meaning is derived from artefacts, brands and consumption as having cultural currency	
Culturally transfusive triad	Three traditional institutional pillars of influence over values in society: family, church and education	
Culture	Hollensen has defined culture as the accumulation of shared meanings, rituals, norms and traditions among the members of an organisation or society. It is what defines a human community, its individuals, its social organisations as well as its economic and political systems. It includes abstract ideas such as values and ethics, as well as material objects and services such as clothing, food, art and sports that are produced or valued by a group of people	
Current loyals	People who buy the 'right' product most or all of the time	
Customer-authored myths	User-negotiated image and meaning	*Stella Artois* – user-projected 'Wife Beater' image aligned to use
Customer-based brand equity	The value of the brand for companies	
Customer-Based Brand Equity (CBBE) model	Comprises six components: brand salience, brand performance, brand imagery, brand judgements, brand feelings and brand resonance	
Customer contact management	The strategic and tactical tasks involved in the management of positive, personal communication between an organisation and its audiences; recognising this should be complementary to image and brand management	

Customer contact points	All positive or negative exposure to communications across ALL media and ALL messages	Uniforms, shop logos, advertising, packaging, 0800 call numbers are all examples of points of contact which may affect perceptions of a brand
Customer equity	Total positive and negative customer experience with the brand. Assets of customer loyalty from which brand can grow	
Customer relationship management	The marriage of sales management and database management provides a very efficient approach to managing customers, both in terms of account management and customer service	
Customer information and service	The systems in place to allow customers to contact the organisation quickly and easily	
Customer lifetime value	The total estimated revenue that a customer is expected to be worth to a company usually expressed as net present value (NPV) i.e. after discounting for inflation	
Customer loyalty	The degree of loyalty a customer has towards a brand or an organisation. It is something that companies endeavour to encourage but given the competitive environment frequently find that customers are not so loyal to a single brand or organisation. An alternative perspective is to reverse the consideration and think about the degree of loyalty a company has towards its customers.	
Customisation	Targeted communication typically associated with direct and online marketing	Video advertising combines the storytelling power of video with accurate, direct targeting
Cut-off points	The point that separates tolerable attribute levels from non-tolerable attribute levels	
Cyber-identity	Creation of alter-ego identity	Avatars in *Second Life*
Cyber-marketing	Term used to describe marketing activities using e-media	
DAGMAR model	In proposing DAGMAR (Define Advertising Goals for Measured Advertising Results), Russell Colley emphasised the importance of measuring advertising effectiveness against predetermined advertising objectives or goals. The same proposition is equally relevant for all forms of marketing communications. *See also* Hierarchies of effects	
Database	Collection of data, usually on computer, stored to provide useful, convenient and interactive access to information	
Database management	The interactive management and maintenance of accurate customer and prospect customer information, competitor information, market information, and internal company information	
Database marketing	The use of accurate customer and prospect customer information, competitor information, market information and internal company information stored on a computer database to focus marketing activities towards targets	
Database technology	The use of accurate customer and prospect customer information, competitor information, market information and internal company information stored on a computer database to focus marketing activities towards targets	
Deadweight	Media audience not in the target group	

Deal loyalists	Customers who purchase a brand only when it is on special promotion, and switch between brands to purchase those on 'deal'.
Deal proneness	The propensity to purchase promoted products
Decision-making process	Five- or seven-stage sequence that consumers or organisations go through when evaluating purchases
Decision-making unit (DMU)	Influential members of family or organisation involved in the purchase of a product
Decoding	The process of converting a message into meaning
Defence mechanisms	People's protection of themselves against messages that go against their current attitudes and behaviours
Deficit	Target audience members not reached by the medium
Deliberately transmitted communications or messages	Communications purposely sent from organisation TO an audience to convey a brand image
Demographic changes	Changes in basic population characteristics such as occur over time in social class constitution and age ranges
Demographic segmentation	Segmentation based on general population characteristics
Demographics	Physical audience characteristics
Denotative meaning	A meaning that is the same for everybody
Desired state	How the consumer ideally wants to feel
Diagnosticity	Information is perceived to have good predictive value, 'this is how it really is'
Dia-logos	To the Greeks this meant 'a free flowing of meaning through a group allowing the group to discover insights not available individually'
Dialogue or dialogical communications	Literally means 'thinking together' and is about the ongoing two-way communications between company and audience
Dialogues	Two-way, relational communications based on ongoing conversations between brand and key target audiences
Diffusion of innovation	Rogers's (1962) model plots the stages in the audience's adoption of the product and can also be used to gauge customer communication needs at each point in time
Digital printing	Process in which digital computer files are sent directly to the printing press, eliminating the need for intermediate stages of production
Digital technology	Range of electronic online and offline communications
Diminishing returns effect	Describes the situation where increases in marketing communications activities have a positive but reducing effect with each successive extra effort or increased spend
Direct mail	The use of postal services to deliver marketing communications materials. It may be considered an aspect of advertising in that it is used as a mass medium even though it can be used for individually targeted messages. It should not be confused with direct marketing, which is a much broader concept

Direct marketing	Promoting product directly towards consumers
Direct matching	Media choice based on actual target group reach
Direct price-offs/ stock cleansing	Stock cleansing involves buying a competitor's stock in order to create space in the distributor's warehouse and facilitate an initial opening stock order. Introductory lower prices or discounts will help achieve momentum and create demand
Direct response advertisements	Advertisements that contain the means by which a direct response may be made by the reader, viewer or listener: e.g. an email address, a coupon, or a telephone/fax number
Direct response marketing	Marketing system based on individual customer records held on a database. These records are the basis for marketing analysis, planning, implementation of programmes, and control of all this activity. This system ensures a focus on marketing to customers rather than on the marketing of products
Disintermediation	The fragmenting media environment, together with technological media developments in such consumer message-avoidance hardware as *TiVo*, *Sky+* and downloadable formats, have undermined the traditional broadcaster's role in being the primary conduit for messages
Display copy	These are the words that appear in larger or bolder type than the main text (body copy) to attract attention and allow it to flow from the headline to the body copy

Displays	Manufacturers have to 'buy' display space in retailers' showrooms either through paying for the right, the space or the cost of display	Payments for displays at exhibitions (e.g. the Interbuild Building and Construction Industry exhibition at the NEC in Birmingham), or in retailers' premises
Disposable and discretionary incomes	The sums of money available to people to spend after other committed expenditure (e.g. mortgage and tax payments) has been paid	
Distinctiveness	Communication is clearly focused on a specific company/organisation	
Divestment	Disposing of packaging or product	In Germany, consumers wouldn't use *Pampers* disposable nappies because they were not bio-degradable
DMU	*See* Decision-making unit	
Dominate	To have the greatest (perceived) share of voice	
Dynamism	Ability of a medium to react and change quickly	Whereas TV advertising's effectiveness has been undermined by its inflexibility, the flexibility of video production has been enhanced
E-communities	Online sites where consumers with special interests (e.g. young mothers) aggregate around professionally generated content	They may be B2B sites like *IBM. com, Microsoft.com* or *CISCO. com* or other more public sites such as parent blogs like *Babble. com* and *MothersClick.com* which engender a sense of brand and user e-community

Econometric modelling	The use of mathematical techniques to determine the effects of changes in marketing communications on sales and profits
Economy	When undertaking any marketing communications activity, this has to be done within resource constraints. Greatest effect is sought even within a limited budget. *See also* Efficiency and Effectiveness
Economy of scale	Increased efficiency with size
Effective frequency	The number of exposures that give the greatest attainable effect at the lowest cost
Effective reach	Refinement of the reach calculation. Effective reach is concerned with reaching target audience members with a minimum frequency, and thereby with impact. Only those target audience members who receive the marketing communication a specified number of times would be included in the effective reach measurement
Effectiveness	The magnitude of results
Efficiency	Results (output) in relation to effort (input)
Ego-defensive function	Attitudes formed to protect the person, either from external threats or internal feelings of insecurity
Ego-eco contradiction	The purchase of a car that fulfils the need for performance and social status but needs to deal with the conscience consumption element of damaging the environment
Elaboration Likelihood Model	Proposed by Petty and Cacioppo, the Elaboration Likelihood Model recognises that individuals are sometimes willing to think very carefully about a piece of marketing communication and sometimes hardly think about it at all. The degree of thoughtful consideration in these circumstances is called elaboration. It represents the amount of effort the recipients are willing to put in for themselves and, in this way, add to the communication by bringing in their own thoughts, attitudes, feelings and experiences. The nature and amount of elaboration will have an impact on the persuasiveness of the communication
Electronic data interchange (EDI)	Method of transferring data from computer to computer
Electronic inks and electronic paper	Mechanism of producing text and images by using small electronic impulses on special 'paper' that changes colour in response to electrical charge
Electronic marketing	The utilisation of the Internet to transact business; also known as e-commerce
Ellipsis	A gap or omission that has to be completed
Email	Order confirmation, product launch and offer announcements, and the fraternity communications of being part of an online club are techniques used by the like of *Amazon*, *Apple*, *Dell* and all online retailers with whom we willingly open up lines of communication
e-media	Any digital, interactive or online communication platform such as the Internet, interactive TV and electronic multimedia
Emotional attachment	Strong ties that bind a person to an object

Emotional benefits	Affective attachment to a brand	*Harley-Davidson* – HOGS group affiliation demonstrating pride of users in using the brand
Emotional level of brand	Affective connection over and above rational reasons for brand purchase.	*L'Oréal* – Because You're Worth It!
Emotional selling point	The emotional reason for choosing the brand	The 'retail therapy' of shopping at a particular shop may provide a reassuring lift in individual spirit
Emotional selling proposition	Brands which evoke unique associations over and above the functional aspects of the brand	Nostalgia of brands like *Bisto* or the magic of brands like *Disney*
Emotional value	Acquired when a brand precipitates or perpetuates specific feelings	'Retro' brands feed into our nostalgic associations which transfer us back to a different place or time in our lives through memories of family, youth or formative years
Endogenous communication process factors	Factors within the process which can distort message and meaning (e.g. placing an ad in an inappropriate medium or inappropriate creative treatment)	*Marks & Spencer* classically misinterpreted its target audience as white, obese, middle-aged females. This was factually correct, but alienated its actual and potential audience
End-user consumers	Final recipient or customer in the supply chain	
Engagement	Consumers buy in to message. Audience participation in the communication	
Environmental influences	Culture, social class, family, personal and situational influences	
Epanorthosis	Making an assertion so as to call it into question by immediate rephrasing for intensification or justification	*HP Computers* used 'It may look like a target. In fact, it's more like a vault'
Epistemic value	The 'curiosity' factor in a purchase – new adventures, different places and expanding experience	Holiday companies tap into this need for 'travel to broaden the mind'
EPOS	Electronic Point of Sale	
Ethical sourcing	Checking the provenance of product supply (e.g. *Fair Trade*)	
Ethnocentrism	The practice of assuming that others think and believe as we do	
Evaluation after purchase	The process where it is determined if the purchase was good or bad	
Evaluation of alternatives	The choice made between products selected as being suitable to fulfil needs or help solve the problem of a consumer through purchase	The *Apple Mac* case study clearly shows how its communications are geared towards demonstrating the functional and symbolic differences between *Apple Mac* and the competition www.applemac.com
Evaluative criteria	The aspects of a product that are evaluated before a purchase	

Event management	PR communications initiated by the organisation but perceived as not having been sent by the organisation	
Events	Social events, news conferences, seminars, outings, factory tours, trade shows, exhibits, contests, competitions, anniversaries, annual general meetings	
Evoked set	Brands which come to mind when purchase decision process starts	
Exchange relationships	Communication (and transactional) interactions between company and customer. Basic level trade based on financial benefits of value proposition; builds social bonds between company and customer; and customised relationships	
Exclusive distribution	Selling the brand in one store/store chain only	
Exhibitions and trade shows	Temporary events for the purpose of displaying and/or selling products; usually based around a particular theme, product category or customer grouping, They are principally designed to bring together potential buyers and sellers under one roof	
Experience-based fit	Sponsorship is congruent with social use	*Heineken* sponsoring World Cup Rugby because they are both part of the same experience when people socialise: drinking beer and watching the games
Experiential	Where experience plays a big part in brand use	Store ambience, olfactory stimuli of shopping at *Zara* rather than buying clothes online
Experiential appeals	The brand's appeals to the consumers' desire for sensory pleasure, variety and cognitive stimulation	
Experiential learning	Learning through behaviour and experience. Learning by doing	
Experiential marketing	Creates or recreates the brand experience, linking use to situational benefits, with goal of creating affinity and/or brand community	The epitome of this phenomenon is *Disney*
Experiment and test method of budget setting	Controlled experiments may prove the efficacy of campaign components within a sample market, amongst a range of communication mix elements or the space purchased in the various media	
Expert	Knowledgeable/experienced with the product/mission	
Explicitly planned	Deliberately overtly encoded mix elements	Cristiano Ronaldo and José Marinho openly endorse their homeland on the eve of Euro 2008 for *Turismo de Portugal* www.visitportugal.com
Explicitly projected marketing meaning	The intrinsic attributes of product and packaging, distribution	The ostentatious packaging of *Ferrero Rocher* chocolates projects a luxury image
Exposure (planning)	How many people are likely to be reached by the advertising	
Exposure (viewer)	Actual contact (aware or unaware) with a stimulus	
Extended marketing mix	7Ps way of classifying the marketing mix into seven categories: product, price, promotion, place, people, process and physical evidence	

Extended problem solving	Where the purchase decision is complicated and requires comprehensive information search and evaluation before the purchase decision because of the nature of the brand or as a result of limited brand loyalty	Expensive clothes, cars and brands with higher risk or innovative
Extended self	How consumers use possessions to create an identity	Cosmetics or deodorants can offer higher self-esteem; perceived improvement of status can be enhanced by the acquisition of a new car or clothing
External brand promise	Suggested by integrated marketing communications	*Carlsberg*: 'Probably the Best Lager in the World'
External search	Active, outside information search	Shopping trips and surfing the web
Extraneous communication factors	Outside environmental influences like culture, ecological considerations, competitive statements, changing values and so on which may distort the message	French energy company *EDF* used the iconic Easter Island statues, drawing on the associations of longevity, claiming that it 'develops tomorrow's energy for future generations'. The Easter Island population collapsed from deforestation and overpopulation. This has resulted in terrible PR www.ClimateDenial.org
Extranet	Website which allows controlled communications (of an intranet) between the organisation and outside agencies and intermediaries while still preventing access by the general public	
Extrinsic representational qualities	Brands help us identify real and symbolic function and meaning: emotional and psychological needs such as status, recognition, self-esteem, nostalgia, affiliation, spiritual satisfaction, companionship projected through consumption of brands	
Eye fixation	Measurement of a person's actual eye movements (watching)	
Eye movement camera	Equipment used for evaluating advertisements in print. A special camera is used to track a respondent's eye movement as an advertisement is scanned. A line tracks all movement and in this way a clear indication is given as to which parts of the advertisement are looked at	
Fad	Short-lived trend	
False recognition	False beliefs about seeing a logotype previously	
Family life cycle	Consists of stages as the partnership and family develop including bachelor stage, newly weds, full nest 1, full nest 2, full nest 3, empty nest 1, empty nest 2, solitary survivor (working), solitary survivor (retired). With the increasing incidence of single parents, separations and divorces, new categories to represent these situations could be considered	
Family umbrella branding	The organisation has a corporate brand and a separate brand for its products	*Marks and Spencer*'s St Michael brand
Fear appeals	The practice of provoking fear or shock to viewers of marketing communications	

Feature advertising	Retailer-sponsored ads with current price deals	
Fee-based remuneration	A method of charging a client for work rendered based on an agreed sum of money (a fee)	
Feedback	This occurs when there is two-way communication, so that communications flow between sender and audience and back again	
Feeling-based objectives	Changing attitudes through the development of brand identity and image, creation of shared values and associations with the brand and company	
Film	Where used, part of the print production process involving photographic reproduction	
Flash ads or flash banners	Interactive, animated online advertising	
Flexibility	The ability to vary the communication	
FMCG	Fast-moving consumer goods	Typified, for example, by such products as soap powders, cosmetics, sweets and crisps
Focus group	A group of people who discuss a particular issue together	
Foreign branding	The use of foreign pronunciation of a brand name	Two premium ice cream brands, *Häagen-Dazs*, a name which doesn't mean anything in any Scandinavian language, and *Frusen Glädjé*, which almost means 'frozen joy' in Swedish, and which includes a map of Scandinavia on the packaging, are actually manufactured in the USA
Four Cs, Four Es, Four Ps of communication	4Cs – It is proposed that integrated marketing communications should have coherence, consistency, and continuity and should be complementary 4Es – It is proposed that integrated marketing communications should be enhancing, economical, efficient and effective 4Ps – Way of classifying the marketing mix into four categories: product, price, promotion and place	
Fragmentation of media	Rapid increase in available media channels to place and view communication messages	
Free item prize promotion	Consumer promotions with a premium gift as the prize	
Frequency	The number of times the audience is exposed to the marketing communication	
Function-based fit	Sponsorship is congruent with brand use	*Yamaha* pianos sponsoring a piano recital *Air France* providing transport for the French football team's international matches *Shell* sponsoring motor sports *Adidas* sponsoring athletics

Functional benefits	What the brand is. What the brand offers as a proposition	*VW* – German engineering *Volvo* – safety *Curly Music* – 'Music by musicians for musicians', offers local instrument expertise
Functional brand	Performs basic problem solving	*Ronseal*: 'Does what it says on the tin'
Functional meaning	Ability to fulfil basic utilitarian needs and work properly	
Functional value	The capacity of the brand to fulfil 'utilitarian' or practical requirements	Soap powder brands are communicated as 'washing whiter' than alternatives and focus on very basic functional ingredients
Gatekeepers or parasocials	Communication intermediaries who disseminate and may distort communications	
GDP	*See* Gross domestic product	
Geodemographic segmentation	Method of segmenting the market based on the classification of small geographical areas (enumeration districts) according to the characteristics of their inhabitants – principally house types and house locations	
Geographical expansion	The ability to sell the brand in new geographical markets	
Geographical segmentation	Segmentation based on location measures	
Gestalt psychology	How people form an entity (*gestalt*) out of details	
Global niche strategy	Strategy for standardised marketing communications that focus on similar niche groups across countries	
Global strategy	Strategy that is based on taking advantage of cultural similarities to produce standardised, global marketing communications	
Global village	Term coined by Marshall McLuhan to describe the way in which communications appear to be making the world seem smaller and interactions more immediate	
GNP	*See* Gross national product	
Goal-derived category	The brand is instrumental in achieving higher order goals	
Golden section	Predetermined proportions used in design and architecture	
Gross domestic product (GDP)	Measure of a nation's output and wealth	
Gross national product (GNP)	Measure of a nation's output and wealth	
Gross rating points (GRPs)	Determined by multiplying reach by frequency. They may be applied to any medium. The term used in the TV industry is TVRs	
Guard book	Whenever the media refer to an organisation or its products, these may be collected and stored for reference in a guard book	
Guerrilla tactics	Communications often used by competition to spoil brand communications of a rival. Also unusual tactical communications to maximise impact	

Headlines	Main element in the creative treatment. In packaging, the product name and company name will be the equivalent concept	
Hedonistic	Emotional and experiential aspects	
Hedonistic–experiential	Consumption based on pleasure	*Cailler, Suchard, Kohler, Sprüngli* and *Maestrani* are Swiss luxury chocolate brands all offering an indulgent consumption experience
HEM model	Hedonistic, experientially-based communication model	
Heterophilous groups	Outside an individual's personal network	
Heuristics	Simplistic problem-solving rules	
Hierarchies of effects (models)	Models that describe the stages individuals are said to progress through in moving from initial unawareness to final action such as purchase and consumption	*Awareness-Interest-Desire-Action or AIDA* (Elmo Lewis): buyers move from one state to the next on the way to consumption
		Awareness-Knowledge-Liking-Preference-Conviction-Purchase (Lavidge and Steiner)
		Awareness-Comprehension-Conviction-Action (Colley): relating it to the objective to be achieved.
		DAGMAR (Defining Advertising Goals for Measured Advertising Results) associates the sequence with management objectives and an indication that results can be measured
		Exposure-Attention-Comprehension-Acceptance-Retention (McGuire)
		Attention-Interpretation-Learning-Attitudes
		Awareness-Trial-Reinforcement or ATR (Ehrenberg): approaches the question of communications effects from a behaviourist perspective. Unlike the sequential models, Ehrenberg argues that buyers are generally very aware of the range of alternative products and brands available. He argues that buyers have considerable buying experience and that they follow relatively stable buying patterns. The communications emphasis is thus shifted to the reinforcement of benefits gained from previous consumption

High-context communications	Most of the information of the communication relies on factors external to the communication itself; it relies on contextual cues to give it meaning. It requires a high level of interpretation by the receiver	
High involvement	Purchases which require in-depth decision making	The purchase of a family car or holiday or a computer system for an organisation require members of the relevant DMU
Historic basis method of budget setting	Previous levels of expenditure, cause-and-effect results and the appropriateness of the message, media and mix	
Hit rate	Term used to describe the number of times a web page or site is visited	
Home shopping/ delivery	Purchases where delivery is separated from transaction	
Homonym	One word can be taken in two senses	An ad for *Land Rover* played on the word 'spring' meaning both the season and key feature of the brand
Homophilous groups	Family and friends	
Hybrid communication	Communication that combines traits from advertising and PR	
Hyperbole (the opposite is litotes)	Exaggerated or extreme claim	'Experience colour so rich you can feel it' (*Cover Girl* lipstick)
Hypertext link	Link (a web address or graphic) on a web page, a simple computer mouse click on which moves the viewer to a new web page	
Identification	Relating the message to audience self-perceptions	
Identity media	The visual identity can be projected through logos, stationery, signage, literature, the physical evidence of buildings and interiors, uniforms and dress codes	
IDU	*See* Important, deliverable and unique benefits	
Image, brand and relational management	Describes how brands can evoke positive perceptions, differentiate and gain competitive advantage, enable faster introduction of new products, reinforce brand awareness and improve overall company and brand image and enhance trust	
Image-based fit	Sponsorship is congruent with brand image	*Lexus* sponsoring the Los Angeles Philharmonic Orchestra *Grand Hotel* accommodating Luciano Pavarotti *Swatch* sponsoring Avant
Impact	The exposures/media's ability to generate attention and stick in memory. The coverage and effectiveness of reaching target audience. One of the four most significant concepts in media planning along with reach, frequency and media cost	Measured when opportunity to see or hear has actually taken place. 'Commercial impact' is a term used in TV to represent the viewing of any commercial by a single viewer.

At a subjective level, 'impact' is a qualitative value referring to the strength of impression made by a campaign or particular piece of marketing communication. In part, impact is achieved by the creative approach adopted, such as through the use of size, colour, typography, illustration and photography. But media selection and planning also play major parts through the right choice of media, positioning and repetition

Two impacts would be equivalent to one person seeing the commercial twice or two people seeing the commercial once. The UK population is exposed to over 650 billion commercial impacts per year. Internet broadband is in 50% of UK homes and 90% of all UK businesses are connected to the Internet

Placing a food advertisement in colour in *Good Housekeeping* would have a higher impact than if it appeared in black and white (mono advertising) in the local free paper

Multiple insertions of the advertisement would further increase effective reach

Implicit brand ambassadors	Customers who 'wear the brand' and convey brand messages
Implicitly symbolic meaning	Projected through endorsement, semiotics and word of mouth
Important, deliverable and unique benefits (IDU)	The brand should focus on important, deliverable, and unique benefits
Impression management	Achieving communication goals by influencing the impressions formed by an audience through controlling or regulating information
Impression (media effectiveness)	How most web advertising is sold and the cost is quoted in terms of the cost per thousand impressions
Impulse purchases	Unplanned purchases that are motivated by intense emotions
Inbound telemarketing	Receiving telephone calls from customers
Incentives	Inducements to encourage customers to take up offers
Individual brand congruity	When communication of a brand's essence resonates with a consumer and corresponds to their individual self-image
Individual identity construction	Where an individual is a consumer of communicated messages (symbols) as much as products in creating identity
Individual meaning interpretation perspective	A view that sees communication as being symmetrical, negotiated BETWEEN company and customer
Inept set	The brands in a category that the consumer knows about and is not choosing from
Influencers	Those people who exert an influence (positive or negative) on an organisation or its public
Infomercials	TV commercials designed to convey large amounts of information

Information search	The process in which consumers gather information from marketing communications about alternatives in preparation for a purchase	
Information stream	The flow of information used in the integrated marketing communications planning process as part of the CAMPAIGN planning model	
Informational motivations	Motivations based on utilitarian needs. Positioning features solely based on helping make decisions	'Contains less fat'
Ingredient brand	A branded attribute for a host brand	
Innovation diffusion	Term given to the process whereby a new product enters and is subsequently adopted by the market. Most frequently associated with the work of Carl Rogers who has proposed that diffusion and adoption are characterised by customers falling into a range of types: innovators, early adopters, early majority, late majority and laggards	The adoption of HDTV is still in its infancy in Europe, whereas there are 141 cell phones to every UK citizen as this market is now saturated
Innovative late entrant	Brand achieving relative positioning but differentiated in some significant way	*First Direct* in banking *Direct Line* in insurance *Virgin* in all sectors
Input-based brand perspective	Where branding is seen as instrumental in directing resources to affect customer response	
Insertions	Refers to the number of times an advertisement is placed in a medium. Discounts are available for multiple insertions	
Institute of Practitioners in Advertising	One of a number of professional advertising industry bodies based in the UK	
Intangibility	Consumer benefits which can't be touched or held	Kudos of owning a *Louis Vuitton* bag
Integrated marketing communications	Coordination of all media and the full marketing communications mix wherever the customer comes into contact with the company	
Integrated marketing communications mix	In its simplest form, the process of integrating all elements of the marketing communications mix across all customer contact points to achieve greater brand coherence	
Interaction	Where there is two-way communication and online communications is not a mere publishing tool	
Interactive	Two-way dialogues are facilitated	
Interactive press kits	Online PR elements such as downloadable materials in PDF format and instant downloadable press agency photographs	
Interactivity	Allows advertisers greater accuracy in promotional activities and calls to action techniques	Interactive video content can achieve higher response rates than interactive ads on TV
Interference	Like noise, interference creates message distortion. A distinction can be made between the two by suggesting that interference is deliberately generated noise	

Inter-media	Refers to the media planners' decision of which medium to use between the media classes, i.e. the selection between TV, radio, cinema, press and posters (outdoor and transport). Some planners also include direct mail and the Internet as main media classes. Inter-media decisions are media decisions at the broadest level	
Intermediary support	Distributor, wholesaler, agent or retailer sales, logistics or promotional efforts to underpin manufacturer's brand	
Intermercial	The Internet version of a TV commercial, which appears between viewing of web pages	
Internal communications	Company newsletters, staff briefings, training	
Internal market or internal context	Employees, especially in service organisations which have customer-facing personnel, are vital in building company image, customer service before and after the sale	An 'internal market' communications campaign may use notice boards, training, newsletters, incentive schemes, intranets and other elements of the internal marketing communications mix
Internal PR	Company newsletters, staff briefings, training	
Internal search	Information search in memory	The trend for 'retro brands' plays on the fond memories of previous positive brand experiences
Internet	Collection of globally interrelated computer networks that facilitate computer communications	
Internet service providers (ISPs)	Organisations that provide access to the Internet	
Interpretivist communication process	Social definition paradigm based on social interactionism where the use of symbols and meanings communicates brand messages	
Interpretivist perspective	View that gives credence to individual, symbolic interpretation of communications	
Intra-media	Media decisions within a media class. It involves the selection of specific media vehicles	
Intranet	Electronic internal network facilitating communication with employees	
Intrinsic product qualities	The functional aspects of what the core product 'can do'	ABS braking systems and high-performing engines
Involvement	A concept that captures consumer interest and engagement in a product. It varies from low to high	
Irony	A statement that means the opposite of what is said	*Acuvue* disposable contacts: 'We spent years developing this incredibly comfortable contact lens, and this is how you treat it (with a picture of a finger flicking a lens away)'
		HBO cable TV: 'Just another wholesome family sitcom (with a picture of the male lead licking cream off thighs)'

ISO paper system	Internationally agreed system of standard paper sizes
ISP	*See* Internet service providers
itV	Interactive TV
ITV	Independent Television: UK-based commercial TV network channel
JICNARS	Joint Industry Committee for National Readership Surveys. This body is responsible for producing the National Readership Survey
JICPAR	Joint Industry Committee for Poster Audience Research. This body is now responsible for taking forward the new initiatives in poster audience research. OSCAR (Outdoor Site Classification and Audience Research) has been used in the industry for some years to classify poster sites on the basis of passers-by. This presumed that passers-by had an opportunity to see, and sites were classified according to the number of passers-by. POSTAR (Poster Audience Research), which came into force in February 1996 has now replaced OSCAR as a preferred measurement system. It covers 73,000 poster panels – the majority of all sites in the UK. It uses a measure of likelihood to see a poster panel and not just pass by it. What is now termed visibility-adjusted impact replaces the simple opportunity-to-see approach adopted by OSCAR. Transport advertising and tube advertising research are handled by other agencies
Joined-up thinking	Term used by the Institute of Practitioners in Advertising to suggest evidence of a common thread or consistency seen running throughout a marketing communications campaign
Joining the brand and consumer conversation	Encouraging ownership of brand narrative and facilitating user-generated content where possible
Joint or cooperative promotions	Promotions undertaken jointly by two or more organisations for mutual benefit e.g. two or more manufacturers or service providers or manufacturer and trade intermediaries
Joint exhibitions	Exhibitions, trade evenings and PR events which link manufacturer and distributor are an integral part of relationship building and sales promotion between manufacturer, distributor and retailers
Key account management	The process and procedures for managing key accounts
Key accounts	Usually taken to mean a major customer, but can best apply to any customer that the organisation has determined to be significant for whatever reason
Key product meanings	The core meanings of the product category
Knocking copy	Text that offers negative or disparaging comments about someone or something else
Knowledge-based objectives	Aimed at gaining attention, stimulating awareness and encouraging interest
Lag effect	Duration of effect from one exposure. Describes the situation when there may be a time delay before there is a noticeable audience response to a piece of marketing communication
Lead time	Time required prior to the distribution date to ensure all print work is completed
Leaking buckets	Spill between consecutive steps

Life stage	Segmentation based on the different stages of life that people go through, incorporating such factors as age, marital status and family size	The Family Life Cycle (FLC) is an example of life-stage segmentation
Lifestyle	People's ways of living, often defined as their actions, interests and opinions	
Limbic signal	Stimulus that forms perceptions by way of evoking instincts	
Limited problem solving	A purchase process characterised by low involvement and where there is limited information search and evaluation before the purchase decision because of the nature of the brand or as a result of long-term brand loyalty	
Lineage	Advertising space that is bought by the line and presented in classified sections of the press	
Linear brand narrative	Storyline which goes in one direction. Communication which is injected or transmitted into the target audience	
List of values (LOV)	Measurement and categorisation of values	
Listenership (readership/ viewership)	Estimate of the size of an audience determined through research. Each of the main media has bodies responsible for producing relevant data. Readership is produced by multiplying the circulation of a publication by the average number of readers per copy. *See also* CAA, JICNARS, JICPAR, MVR, RAJAR	
Lobbying	'Political marketing' to governmental bodies and other persuasive groups to favour the interests of the lobbyist. Not focused on a specific product or mission, but rather to influence the company/organisation's macro environment. PR communications initiated by the organisation, and perceived as having been sent by the organisation.	
Location-shifted	Viewing of communications not limited to static situations where audience is captive	*Sky Sports* can be experienced at home or in a social setting
Longevity of message	Constant presence of commercial message; extended brand narrative	
Long-form content	Creates relevant or salient items or storylines which sell experience within a framework of branding over an extended exposure time	*BMW* Films produce made-for on-line 'webisodes' (films and videos) Three-minute 'bookends' which are made-for TV and online commercials instead of getting a brief mention when the company is sponsoring a programme
Long-tail brand building	Elongated narrative of different stories and campaign elements which adds value and fabric to the brand proposition and is made up of all the various communication elements and messages	*Volvo* has now reconstructed a story built on being fun, cool, ecologically sound and a brand to be shared with friends; all different stories but all consistent with the overarching brand narrative: 'Life is Better Lived Together'
Long-tail demand	Audience/demand is distributed across many small media/products	
LOV	*See* List of values	
Low-context communications	The communication is largely self-contained, and does not rely on contextual cues to convey its meaning	
Low involvement	Purchases which do not require in-depth decision making	
Loyalty	Commitment to the marketer	

Loyalty card schemes	Long-term promotional reward activity in exchange for customer information and purchases
Loyalty marketing	Marketing activities intended to encourage customers to continue purchasing a particular product or purchasing from a particular supplier
Macro environment (of marketing communications)	The marketing communications macro environment is the wider environment in which the organisation operates and may affect the company/organisation. It incorporates the economics framework of macro and micro environments as well as internal organisational factors. *See also* Micro environment
Macro-level positioning	Total market segment Health and beauty market
Macro objectives	General goals relating all marketing communications to company/organisation performance
Mailshot	Promotional material sent through the post
Managerial perspective of communications	A view that sees communication as being asymmetrical, transmitted FROM the company
Market exchanges	Relationships based on transactions
Market mavens	Individual consumers who have expertise and credibility as a source of initiating dialogue and are shapers and formers in disseminating information helping the diffusion of new products. Their views are valued and they receive prestige and satisfaction from supplying information to friends and others. Play a significant role in buyer and consumer behaviour
Market position	Strength of competitive market share
Market research brief	Document or verbal instruction outlining the market research problem and task
Market research proposal	Document outlining proposals designed to fulfil the research brief
Market segmentation	The process of dividing a market into homogeneous segments using one or a range of possible alternative segmentation methods, each segment being composed of customers or consumers sharing similar characteristics. *See also* Segmentation bases and Target marketing approaches
Market share	Sales relative to other products
Market test	Trial in the marketplace before full launch
Marketing communications budget	A frequently misleading term which usually refers to the advertising and promotions budget and not, as it implies, to the marketing expenditure allocated for all marketing activities
Marketing communications mix	All the forms of message creation such as advertising, promotions, public relations and personal selling as well as 'hybrid communications' such as direct-response based advertising, sales/PR exhibitions, online ad exhibitions and so on
Mass media	Broad media reaching a majority of the (e.g. national) population
Mass medium	Ability to reach huge target audience with message
MCM^2	Different perspective on the promotional mix focusing mainly on message content and the media mix, an approach that 'incorporates a revised classification of direct and indirect media'

Meaningful brand experiences	The consumption of products or services which resonate with an individual's own experience or aspirations
Meaningful dialogue	Communications which are mutually relevant and beneficial to company and customer
Measurability	Evaluation metrics such as audience delivery, audience interaction and ROI
Mechanics of marketing communications	The underlying frameworks, strategies and tactics – both theoretical and applied – which underpin marketing communications
Media-authored myths	Brand meaning mediated through channels of communication such as media, intermediaries and agency either through planned dissemination of communication or voluntary word of mouth
Media conduits	Physical channels (press) or communication intermediaries (people) who help spread the brand message (opinion leaders) which carry and disseminate information and opinions
Media-neutral planning and trans-media	Scheduling where the message finds the market not the media
Media planning	Deciding what media to use, and when
Media schedule	Specific mix of media planning parameters
Media touch-points	Consumer engagement with messages being communicated via a combination of sight, sound, motion and interactivity
Media vehicle	An individual carrier within a medium *Sunday Times Magazine*
Media Vision Research (MVR)	In conjunction with BARB, MVR tracks, analyses and reports in-home video viewing. As the BARB panel of respondents is used, this provides single-source data, which allow video and TV viewing habits to be determined and cross-referenced
Mediascape	The array of channels available which will carry the message
Mediated environment	The communications arena within which messages are channelled
Mediated transmitted meaning	Construction of meaning by explicitly projected marketing meaning (the intrinsic attributes of product and packaging, distribution) and implicitly symbolic meaning projected through endorsement, semiotics and word of mouth
Medium	A class of message carriers such as TV, radio, newspapers or magazines
Mentometer	A device that allows people to instantaneously rate what they're watching
Merchandising	Follow-up sales team whose function is to stock take, replenish orders, furnish displays including point-of-sale materials as part of overall promotion
Merchandising and POS	Stores with or without displays have to be merchandised with POS materials, brochures and so on. Some companies have 'tied distribution' arrangements where display merchandising units are offered free of charge in exchange for regular orders *Lucozade* – refrigerated drinks cabinets *Mars* – counter-top confectionery pack holders
Mere exposure effect	Repeated exposures increase liking
Message clutter	Media saturation of communication
Message research	Part of marketing research focused on testing all aspects of creative messages

Metaphor	Assertion of an underlying resemblance of some trait or characteristic	*Philips' Sonicare* used 'The mouth is the gateway to the body' to encourage use of its oral mouthwash brand
Metonym	Use of an associated element to represent the object	*Buick*: 'The imports are getting nervous'
Micro environment (of marketing communications)	The immediate environment or surroundings in which marketing communications occur. This should not be confused with economists' views of the micro environment. *See also* Macro environment	
Micro-level positioning	Within a specific category	
Micro marketing	One-to-one marketing	Customised service of online holiday firms like holidayhypermarket.com
Micro objectives	Goals relating the specific communication to the audience	
Mind space	A consumer's mental picture of competitive offerings in a category	People carrier market sector
Minimum threshold effect	Describes the situation where a minimum has to be spent before any discernible marketing communications effect can be noticed	
Mnemonics	Elements that help rate learning by aiding memory	
Modelling	Attempt to realistically represent the processes involved in marketing communications. Maximising media usage effectiveness	
Moments of truth	Exposures to the brand experience	
Mono advertising	Black and white ads usually found in local free papers and tabloids	
Monochrome	Single colour or black and white	
Mood boards	Collection of visual materials (e.g. drawings, collage, montage) to replace or complement a written description that reflects the essence of a product or its customers/consumers. *See also* Concept boards	
MOSAIC	A commercially available geodemographic system which is obtainable for 16 countries. *GlobalMOSAIC* can analyse consumers across national markets to support the development of international strategies. In the UK there are 12 broad MOSAIC groups subdivided into 52 detailed types	
Motivation: incomplete satisfaction	Communication messages which highlight the deficiencies in current usage of brand	A campaign for the *Nationwide Building Society* plays on the dissatisfaction with other high-street finance companies who may not be meeting the requirements of existing customers
Motivation: mixed approach–avoidance	Attraction to brand attribute and repulsion of another	Customers may like the rates for *Barclay's* savings products but be put off because of the organisation's involvement in South Africa
Motivation: normal depletion	Appeals to stock up on product are normally aimed at brand loyals	
Motivation: problem avoidance	The need to avoid a negative buyer state or problem	The fear of burglary may cause a customer to anticipate a *future* problem and seek out alarms or insurance companies

Motivation: problem removal	The need to eradicate a negative buyer state or problem	A broken car exhaust or punctured tyre can be remedied by the expertise and utility of a *Kwik Fit* fitter
MPR	Marketing public relations	
Multi- or full-service agency	In contrast to an 'à la carte' agency, the full-service agency offers a complete and integrated range of marketing communications services. One-stop shop and though-the-line agency are associated terms	
Multi-purchase sweepstakes or contests	Some retailers offer 'multi-packs' to encourage more use of the product and offer better 'value' to consumers. Incentives like sweepstakes or contests are used to encourage trial or repeat purchase	
Multimedia	Using a range of media to carry message(s), usually most associated with electronic multimedia.	The *Sex and the City Movie* has had exposure in every type of media to help promote its launch www.sexandthecitymovie.com
Multimedia stations	Free-standing kiosks where computer access is facilitated either using CD-ROMs/DVDs or linked to other computers	Kiosks provided in retail stores
Multinational strategy	Strategy recognising cultural diversity to develop marketing communications adapted to suit different countries	
MVR	*See* Media Vision Research	
Narrowcast	Restricted radio, television, video and audio transmission	
National Readership Survey (NRS)	Provides information about the readership of the main newspapers and magazines. A report is produced every six months covering a period of 12 months. The survey samples over 40,000 UK individuals every day of the year	
Need recognition	The moment when consumers realise that they need to make a purchase	
Needs and wants	Needs are basic level requirements. Wants can be more aspirational symbolic purchases to acquire status, affiliation or for ego	
Needs profile	Requirement of category	Cat hygiene – 'catlit compound'
Negative framing	Showing the product as a solution to a current problem	
Negative returns effect	Describes the situation where, although marketing budgets may be increased and more effort expended, the actual effect created is negative, not positive, and further effort is counterproductive unless significant changes are made	
Negative space	Giving the background precedence over the main element in the communication	
Negative synergy	Term used to represent the negative effects of not achieving synergy between integrated marketing communications elements. Lack of integration may not merely result in no synergistic benefits, but in detrimental consequences that could be caused through confusion, lack of effectiveness and efficiency, or misunderstanding	
Negativity effect	Negative information is perceived as more important	
Negotiated meaning	Individual or group interpretation of communications	The *Stella Artois* case study in Chapter 1 is an example of a brand's meaning being subverted by actual users rather than the transmitted communications www.stella-artois.com

Neighbourhood RISC	A commercially available system that combines psychographics and geodemographics to provide an insight into why particular brands are attractive to particular consumer groups and how best to design promotional campaigns that appeal to prospective purchasers. Customers or prospects are targeted by socio-cultural type rather than by demographics – it targets by attitudes rather than behaviour. Neighbourhood RISC subdivides consumers based on three key motivational types: from self-focused to socially conscious, from conservative to explorative, from locally focused to globally aware. This results in 10 socio-cultural types; explorers, pleasure seekers, mobile networkers, avid consumers, social climbers, care givers, moral guides, traditionalists, guardians and survivors	
Net coverage/reach	Total reach less allowance for duplication	
New media	Usually most associated with new electronic media such as the Internet, interactive TV and electronic multimedia. Fast becoming an outdated term of reference	
News	Press releases and news conferences aimed at generating interest through the media or handling negative publicity	
Niche position	Have a smaller but sometimes lucrative sub-category market position	*Cricket* fashion wear
No frills	Value-only operations offering so-called 'non-brands'	The Japanese brand *Muji*
Noise	Distortions created in the encoding or decoding process that can result in inaccurate interpretation of meaning	
Non-homogeneous, fragmented marketplace	Audiences made up of dissimilar segments with different needs and media behaviour patterns	
Nonlinear brand narrative	Storyline which goes in one direction. Communication which is injected or transmitted into the target audience	
Non-personal communications	Traditionally one-way, asymmetrical communications, transmitted indirectly through a medium like TV for advertising, an event for sponsorship, a pack for sales promotion, or a retailer for merchandising	
Non-traditional media	Unusual channels other than TV advertising	TV screens in doctors' waiting rooms, airport lounges, post-offices; posters at public events or in golf clubs; combination of magazines and promotions and the use of Internet advertising
Non-users	People who don't use any product in the category	
NRS	*See* National Readership Survey	
Objective and task method	Budgeting system whereby budgets are set based on a determination of the objectives to be achieved and the means by which they are expected to be achieved	
Objectives	End results sought to be achieved	
Offers	Propositions made to customers indicating what they will receive and what they will have to give	
Off-line	Use of an e-medium/computer disconnected from a modem	
Ohanian's celebrity endorser credibility scale	Consists of attractiveness, trustworthiness, expertise	

On-demand viewing	Viewers choose as and when viewing takes place	
One message	The single 'voice' of all communication which speaks uniformly to audiences	
One-pipe convergence	The merging of multimedia platforms such as TV, Internet and SMS to facilitate integrated communications	See Microsoft's 'Without Walls' campaign
One-size-fits-all	Uniform, mass communication brand model encouraged by restricted media and limited time available to expose audiences to messages	
One-stop shop	Term used to describe agencies that claim to offer complete marketing communications solutions. Through-the-line and full-service agencies are associated terms	
One-way asymmetrical model	One-way PR model using persuasion and manipulation to influence how target audiences behave in accordance with organisational objectives	
One-way communications	Communications from a sender to a receiver with no feedback or dialogue.	
One-way media	Media used to transmit uni-directional communications messages	TV has traditionally been used to create awareness, launch, position, reposition and is good at ensuring 'top-of-mind' reinforcement with essentially passive recipients
Ongoing dialogues	Continuous communications between company and customer	
Ongoing search	External information search that is not related to a specific purchase	
Online presence	Communications which engage on the web either solely or in conjunction with other offline communications	
Online virtual communities	Social networking groups which encourage the feeling of conversational community	*Facebook* and *Bebo*
Open-source marketing	Interactivity-induced consumer involvement which enhances brand experience by allowing users to subvert message content and negotiate communication meaning	
Operant conditioning	Reinforcing behaviour	
Opinion leaders (and mavens)	Those who are seen as having impartial credibility because of some level of formal expertise (e.g. celebrities) may act as credible endorsers by transferring meaning to a product and have influence over consumers from their own social group	
Opportunities to see/hear (OTS/OTH)	A measure of frequency. It is the number of times in a specified time period (e.g. the duration of a campaign) that an average member of the target audience is exposed to the media/message. One OTS or OTH is the opportunity for a target audience member to see or hear an item of marketing communication once. It represents the potential to see or hear. It is not a guarantee of the marketing communications being seen or heard	
Optimisation	Maximising media usage efficiency	
Optimum stimulation level	The amount of information/stimuli a person prefers	
Orchestration	Graphic way of referring to the process of integrating marketing communications.	

Organisational/ audience dialogues	Any communication which 'talks' explicitly or implicitly to target audiences	
OTH	Opportunities to hear. *See* Opportunities to see/hear	
OTS	*See* Opportunities to see/hear	
Outbound telemarketing	Telephone calls to customers	
Output-based branding perspective	Centring on consumers' interpretations of what brands can help them achieve	
Outside-in approach to integrated marketing communications	Way of looking at marketing communications by adopting a perspective that starts by first looking outside the organisation for direction and understanding the task required, and then determines marketing communications by secondly considering the organisation itself	
Overstatement	Exaggerated message	
Overt communications	Open communications such as advertising, TV, word of mouth, writing or consumers signalling to each other	
Own-brand range	Manufacturers may be forced to or willingly make 'unbranded' product which may be sold on as part of a distributor's branded range. This may undermine a manufacturer's brand or provide an entry into a market segment or a targeted customer	UK department store *John Lewis* has a line of own brands designed by Italy's Guzzini and the British designer, Nick Munro Similarly, *Sainsbury's*, teamed up with big names such as Sir Terence Conran to produce an affordable own-brand designer range
Own-label brand	Product that carries the name of the resellers – wholesalers or retailers – rather than the manufacturers, and is sold exclusively through the resellers' outlets	
Packaging and packaging variation	Often used to launch new products on the back of others. The same brand in many different packages	*Kellogg's Special K* cereal bars were given away free on packs of *Kellogg's Special K* breakfast cereal
Paradessence	Taken from Alex Shakar's *Savage Girl*. 'Paradessence' is the mutually exclusive state that brands promise and have to be simultaneously gratified	Controlled danger of theme parks; sanitised air travel; ice cream melds eroticism and innocence
Paradox	A self-contradictory or impossible statement	*Kodak*: 'This picture was taken by someone who didn't bring a camera' *Franklin* batting glove: 'Mark McGuire hit 42 home runs last year. But we held the bat'
Peckham's rule	A rule of thumb for setting media budget	
Peer-to-peer communications	Communication from customer to customer (C2C) without company mediation	*Facebook* is a social network site where consumers talk to each other
Perceived fit	The connections between a brand and a product category or between two brands/two product categories	
Perceived risk	The consequences of making a purchase. May vary from low risk to high risk	

Percentage of sales method of budget setting	Fixed proportionate amount based on expected level of sales. This amounts to a formulaic approach of sorts and is often based on past experience or competitive or industry reference points	
Perceptual boundary	The brand's limitation when it comes to brand extension	Singapore Airlines has a well-established name for luxury service. If they were to try and compete with 'no frills' airlines, this would be outside the perceptual boundary of the brand. The reverse, Ryanair entering the luxury market, would also be true
Perceptual or perceptual positioning	Communicated messages which place the brand in the minds of the target audience	*Carling* has successfully positioned its brand as a young man's rite of passage drink using affiliation as the creative platform
Permissive	Consumers consensually 'opt-in'. Viewers choose participation	Signing up for a website, giving mobile phone numbers or using an 0800 number to subscribe
Personal communications	Aimed at managing sales, service and customer contact. These are mainly two-way, symmetrical dialogues, transmitted directly through face-to-face sales contact, telemarketing, mail, email, and all the interactive electronic platforms of Internet, intranet and extranet	
Personal factors or individual differences	Demographics, psychographics, values and personality; consumer resources; motivation; knowledge; and attitudes; self-image, health, beauty	
Personal selling	Two-way communication in which a seller interprets brand features in terms of brand benefits	
Personal video recorder (PVR)	Allows recording of TV programmes enabling user to watch and record simultaneously and skip advertising content	
Phonemes	Individual sounds that convey associations	*Shhhhhhh..........weppes* or *Churchill's* 'Oh Yessss!'
Planning (retail visit)	The degree of planning before a store visit	
Podcasts	Non-live broadcasting, MP3-type communications directly with target audiences for the purpose of enhancing relationships and giving user full control of content	Car manufacturers like *Mercedes*, distributors and retailers like *H&M* use the podcast facility to extend the brand story and enhance communications online
Point-of-purchase displays and merchandising	Promotional materials designed to enhance, remind or persuade consumers in campaign period announcing new product or promotional change. Merchandise materials located physically or virtually prior to sale transaction or within sale location	
Point-of-sale (POS) materials	Merchandising material communicating messages in location where purchase occurs	
Points of difference	Features of brands which have an added dimension lifting them above the competition (aka 'customer delight')	*Mercedes Benz, Sony and Harley-Davidson* all exhibit superiority over competitors, either in their superior products or their brand narrative customer linkages

Points of parity	Features and benefits shared by competing brands in a sector relevant to category need	24/7 next day delivery by *Fedex*, *UPS* and *Parcelforce*
Positioning a brand	The functional or expressive location of a product or service in the 'mind of the consumer'	*Nintendo Wii* case study demonstrates how this product has been positioned to capture the 'non-gamers' market
Positive framing	Showing the positive effects of the brand's benefits	
Post-purchase evaluation	Evaluation of satisfaction with product after the sale and possibly after consumption	
Pre-campaign 'buzz'	PR, word of mouth or advertising activities introducing concepts or characters prior to launch of brand in order to generate pre-release excitement	
Premium incentive	Promotions may encourage loyalty and may take the form of gifts or sales-related incentives	
Premiums	Proof of purchase 'money-off' premiums are an expensive way of creating consumer demand and encouraging retailers to stock product. Free samples of the product or introductory offers also help	*McDonald's* has tie-ins with *Disney* providing free gifts in its 'Happy Meals' related to the release and promotion of a movie or DVD
Press agency/ publicity model	One-way PR model using persuasion and manipulation to influence how target audiences behave in accordance with organisational objectives	
Price buyers	People who consistently buy the most expensive brand	
Price promotion	Promotion based solely on comparison of price to previous price point or to the competition	
Price sensitivity	The propensity for consumers to switch brands due to price changes in the market	
Primary reputation targets	Governments, government agencies, press, media, professional bodies, investors, and pressure groups are all examples of agencies which have influence over an organisation without being directly involved in any commercial relationship	
Product experience	Direct contact with a product	
Product factors	The physical, financial, social and psychological 'perceived risk' of use	
Product life cycle	Different stages in the market development of a product (category); is really the timeline for the life of the product, plotting the stages in the product's journey, and is used to gauge customer communication needs at each point in time	
Product/market space	Segment(s) or product categories where competitor offers and/or customer needs are located	*Renault Espace* people carrier
Product placement and programme sponsorship	Non-interrupting exposure of a product in the surrounding content. PR communications initiated by the organisation, but perceived as NOT having been sent by the organisation	When Peter Parker, as Spider-Man, snagged his webbing on a can of *Dr. Pepper*, this was a very tenuous link to the plot and an obvious example of sponsorship by product placement
Product retail brands	Primarily providers of a private label proposition with brands distributed through third party retailers	Germany's *Adidas*, Japanese *Sony*, the UK's *Burberry* and American *Levi's*

Product or service sampling	Free product or service to trial with key customers or test market to prospective segments. May be done by sampling, free product, or extended credit facilities to encourage retailers to experience the product with a view to gaining interest and confidence in selling the manufacturer's brand
Profane consumption	Unimportant consumption that fulfils everyday goals
Profitability	Profit related to money spent
Programming	Non-advertising content with a more or less obvious commercial intent
Psychological symbolic meaning	Culturally constituted significance of brand Rites of passage products which signify conformity, maturing (alcohol) or recaptured youth (retro brands which remind us of previous usage in our earlier years)
Public information model	One-way PR model using monologue communication techniques to disseminate organisational and brand information
Public relations	Communication targeted at the general public and wider stakeholders
Public service activities	Cause-related marketing is an area where companies can build goodwill with a community or audience
Publications	Annual reports, brochures, articles, company newsletters, magazines, audio-visual materials, intranets, websites
Publicity	The message becomes part of the medium's content (often called 'editorial material' as opposed to the advertising that is separated from editorial) and this has a life of its own. PR communications initiated by the organisation, but not perceived as having been sent by the organisation
Publics (aka stakeholders, targets, audiences, market domains)	Any group that has an actual or potential interest in, or impact on, a company's ability to achieve its objectives
Pun or resonance pun	The product of a context meant to imply an association (sometimes dubiously)
Purchase cycle	Time lapse between consecutive purchases
Purchase facilitation	Buyer's assurance that other marketing factors (marketing mix) will not hinder purchase
Purchase intentions	Consumer's expressed or implied stage in decision-making process
Purchase motivations	Generalised needs that may be used in the marketing communications to link to need recognition
PVR	*See* Personal video recorder
Qualitative research	An in-depth, investigative approach with discretion on the part of the interviewer to 'dig and delve' into the interviewees' responses as necessary. There are four methods of data collection commonly employed in qualitative research: depth interviews, duo interviews, focus groups and case histories. The aim of qualitative research is to find out what 'relevant others' think (e.g. target consumers about aspects of a possible TV ad), and to uncover whatever issues are important in the situation. Such an approach is only feasible on a relatively small sample, and there is deliberately no intention to measure anything, except in broad, relative terms. So, findings from such research are illustrated with 'flavoursome' quotes, rather than percentages. While the samples used may be deemed to be representative of the target market/audience, this does not mean representative in a statistical sense

Quality of Integration Assessment Profile	An approach used to assess the extent to which marketing communications are integrated across a range of dimensions. *See also* Continuum of integrated marketing communications	
Quality/Value	Actual intrinsic product quality or value of attribute	*Intel Inside* – inclusion of a state-of-the-art processor enhances PC quality
Quantitative research	Designed to explain what is happening and the frequency of occurrence. It is an approach that has measurement as its main aim, and reported findings are usually illustrated with percentages. Of necessity, samples are relatively large in size, with the intention of creating statistical validity	
Quasi-subliminal advertising	Messages which are contained in the programme ('content captured') have an almost subconscious impact on viewers	In Tom Clancy's *Splinter Cell: Pandora Tomorrow* agent Sam Fisher has to work out how to use his *Sony Ericsson P900 Smartphone* to progress
R2C push/pull strategies	Communications by retailers aimed at consumers	
RAJAR	Radio Joint Audience Research. This body is jointly owned by the BBC and the Commercial Radio Companies Association. It is responsible for conducting national and local surveys for the radio industry as a whole on a quarterly basis	
Ratchet effect	Combined effect of advertising and sales promotions	
Rating	The percentage of individuals or homes exposed to an advertising medium (magazines refer to this as 'coverage'; out-of-home media use 'showing', which means the same as gross rating points)	
Rating/HUT/share	Where Rating = HUT $\times$ Share	
Reach	Also referred to as coverage or penetration. Along with frequency, impact and media cost it is one of the four most significant concepts in media planning. It is a measure of how many members of the target audience are reached by a medium or collection of media used in a campaign. Reach may be measured as a percentage or actual number. Reach is the number of target audience members exposed to the media/message at least once during a specified time period (e.g. duration of a campaign). Related terms are exposure, GRPs, TVRs and duplication	
Reach schedule	Reaching as many people as possible with message	
Re-activation	Extending purchase arrangements on accounts which have become dormant or inactive	Online games software company *Funcom* had the first ever re-evaluation campaign for its '*MMO Age of Conan: Hyborian Adventures*' which offered a 'Come back to the game and receive 14-days' free access with no strings' promotion
Readership (viewership/listenership)	Estimate of the size of an audience determined through research. Each of the main media has bodies responsible for producing relevant data. Readership is produced by multiplying the circulation of a publication by the average number of readers per copy. *See also* CAA, JICNARS, JICPAR, MVR, RAJAR	
Rebates	Turnover-related discounts or retrospective rebates (i.e. based on upfront or cumulative sales) may persuade distributors to stock and encourage them to sell	

Recall	Evaluation of message content on the basis of aided (prompted) or unaided (unprompted) recollection of the stimulus material	
Receiver	Recipient of communication	
Recency planning	Achieving exposure of advertisements as close to the purchase occasion as possible	
Receptiveness	How easily influenced the audience is by the sender's marketing communications	
Reciprocity	A feeling that a favour should be returned	
Recognition	Visual and/or auditory memory	Visual or sound logos and jingles help a kind of rote learning where consumers remember brands
Recommendation	Suggesting a person try an offer	
Recovery	The company/organisation's satisfactory solution to a problem	
Reference groups	Other consumers that the individual consumer relates to in his or her consumption pattern	Peers, work colleagues, family, opinion leaders
Referral	Suggesting the marketer contact a person	
Refutational communication	Overcoming negative aspects of the product/mission	
Relational communications	Brand community and network sharing	*See* Chapter 9
Relationship exchanges	Value-based arrangements other than mere transactions	
Relationship marketing	View that emphasises the importance of the relationships developed between an organisation and other parties including customers, partners, suppliers and the trade	
Relative advantage	Does the 'innovation' offer a reason to change from the current brand?	The *Sinclair C5* electric car didn't; the 'greener' version of the *Peugeot 407 Coupé* does
Relative attitude	People's attitudes toward the company/organisation relative to the competitors	
Relative behaviour	People's behaviour toward the company/organisation relative to the competitors	
Relative position	A brand's unique 'label' which differentiates from the competition. Explicit and/or implicit reasons to differentiate from the competition	UK furniture manufacturer *Multiyork* has adopted its logo to imply customer ownership: 'MY Multiyork'
Renewal	The continuation of signing customers up is key to extending communications and ensuring income streams	
Re-patronage intentions	Plans to revisit a store	
Repeat purchase	Continuation of loyalty with a brand	
Repetition	One of the ironies in copywriting is that copy should be kept brief and to the point but repetition is widely used to good effect and to create emphasis and memorability	

Repositioning	Realignment of brand both in terms of its location in the marketplace and in the minds of the target audience	The *Stella Artois* case study is an example of a brand's positioning being realigned to change the perception of the brand
Representation (individual)	Mediated socialisation roles and traits	Gender, family, friends
Representation (of marketing communications)	Where the organisation replaces elements of its activities by technology performing a business process otherwise performed by employees	Stock control, data updates, producing a sales channel
Representational brand qualities	The symbolic aspects of the brand which project what the brand 'stands for'	The *Ben & Jerry's* case study shows how an organisation can represent social concerns as well as selling product
Research and decision-making cycle	The circular process of analysing, deciding and evaluating marketing communication plans and actions	
Resonance	A phrase takes on a different meaning when coupled with a picture	*Goodyear*: 'Will bite when cornered' (with a picture of car splashing up water as it makes a turn) *Hormel* rice: 'Success rice brings out the ham in you' (with a picture of ham pieces in sauce
Response latencies	The exact amount of time it takes for consumers to recognise or recall a brand	
Retailer brands	Brands for stores or store chains	
Return on assets	Profit relative to the company's total holdings	
Revenue premium	The combined premium of high volume and high price	
Rhetorical figure	Verbal or visual message that has more than one meaning	
Rhetorical question	Asking a question so as to make an assertion	*Hewlett-Packard* fax: 'Don't you have something better to do?'
Rich media	Advertising that contains perceptual or interactive elements more elaborate than the usual banner ad	
Roadblock on-line advertising	Flash ads which present online viewers with an option to view short online ads by voluntarily clicking on option	
Robustness	The ability of a component to work on a number of levels	
Roll-out	The incremental process of launching a marketing initiative into the market area by area until full market coverage is achieved	
ROP	*See* Run of paper	
Rossiter and Percy's five communications effects	Category need, brand awareness, brand attitude, brand purchase intention, purchase facilitation	
Roughs or dummies	Drawings or computer graphics indicating what the finished artwork will look like for any printed medium, e.g. packaging, posters, and press advertisements.	

Routine problem solving	Characterised by habit, this form of decision making involves little consideration of alternatives
Routinised response behaviour	A purchase process characterised by involvement and low degree of information search. The search process is mainly internal
Run of paper (ROP)	Advertisements appearing in the non-classified sections of newspapers and magazines
Sacred consumption	Consumption of products that are highly important for consumers and may include certain consumption rituals
Sales conferences	Sponsorship and active support of distributor sales conferences and meetings is an integral part of relationship building and sales promotion with distributor personnel
Sales-force incentives	Encouragement to active involvement in selecting brand to push and sell can be in the form of sales-force competitions, incentive schemes and corporate events
Sales-force training	The education and training of the distributor's sales force is critical both for ensuring mind share and instilling confidence in the distributor's sales people. May involve attendance at sales meetings, product launches or factory visits
Sales growth	The product's increase in sales
Sales promotion	Widely used term covering a myriad of promotional activities, excluding advertising, PR and personal selling. Sales promotion is associated with free offers, price deals, premium offers, and other promotions including merchandising, point-of-sale displays, leaflets and product literature.

Salience (attribute)	The most prominent and relevant evaluative criterion	Price, function, availability, colour, ingredient
Salience (effect)	The impact of several factors (e.g. promotion frequency, distance, construction, clutter, placement) on consumer relevance	
Sampling error	Inaccuracy caused through selecting a sample rather than the population as a whole	
Satisfaction/ dissatisfaction	People's approval of the offer they have been given. The post-purchase evaluation of a product	
SBU	*See* Strategic business unit	
Scamps	Drafts or 'roughs' of creative ideas that are produced cheaply to be used for pre-testing and evaluation purposes	
Scarcity	Supply smaller than demand	
Schemas	Foundations of understanding. Schemas are remembrances of experiences that allow us to make sense of our environment and determine suitable courses of action, by recognising linkages and similarities with previous experience	
Schramm's communications process	Schramm identified the communications process as consisting of four elements: sender, message, media and receivers. The IMC Process Model is a more sophisticated development from this simple model	
Schroer's method	Strategy matrix for prioritising media expenditure	
Scope	The range of category types that the brand is capable of spanning across. Extended possible use of product outside of the category need dimension	PCs – social networks, photographic, artwork facilities beyond word processing and number crunching
		Nivea makes a range of skin protection products

Screen saver	Not strictly meeting the definition as a form of advertising, screen savers have become a popular form of promotion
Script	(i) Repetition of previous behaviour
	(ii) Written description of sound and motion advertisements/promotions giving the dialogue to be used and outline of what the advertisement is to be
Search engine	Facilitator of connectivity with information, connection and knowledge. Website that maintains an index of other web pages and sites that may be searched using keywords. Access to other sites is facilitated by hypertext links – links that may be simply clicked on to move from one web page to another
Secondary media (support media)	Secondary media may also be referred to as support media. In an integrated campaign a range of media will be used, and although it is possible to use the media equally, it is more likely that emphasis will be placed on one medium – the primary medium. The other media will be used in a supporting or secondary capacity
Secondary research	Secondary research is often known as 'desk research'. A key characteristic is that it is always gathered from existing, published sources (i.e. second-hand or secondary material)
Secondary target audience	Not prioritised audience
Seeds	Industry/product specific bloggers who are targeted with information prior to PR campaigns to encourage them to act as opinion formers and credible source disseminators of information
Segment	Group of individuals who are expected to respond in a similar way to an organisation's marketing activity
Segmentation bases	Demographics, geographics, geodemographics, psychographics (lifestyle and personality), behavioural
Selective perception	The individual's inclination to see/hear what they expect or want to
Self-accountability	The own impression that one is responsible for one's behaviour and its consequences
Self-connection	The extent to which an outside object (e.g. a brand) is part of a person's identity
Self-efficacy	The own impression that one is capable of performing in a certain manner or attaining certain goals
Self-expressive benefits	What the brand says about itself and how it resonates with user's self-image	*Apple* – think and be different / *Nike* – excel, succeed / *Microsoft* – help people realise potential
Self-image	The personal perception or image of oneself
Self-liquidating offer or promotion (SLP)	Sales promotion that pays for itself
Self-regulation	Voluntary control of acceptable marketing communications agreed by the marketing communications industry itself
SEM/SEO	Search engine marketing or search engine optimisation

Semi-display advertisements	Unlike full display, semi-display advertisements have creative restrictions placed on them, with limited or no graphics and limited typeface options	
Semiotics	The scientific discipline of studying the meanings associated with signs, symbols and brands	
Sender	The root of communication being sent. Effective according to credibility, attractiveness or likeability	*Ronseal*'s 'typical tradesman' tells it like it is: 'It does what it says on the tin!'
Seven stages of personal selling (traditional)	Prospecting and evaluating, preparing, approaching the customer, making the presentation, overcoming objections, closing, follow-up	
Share of market	Brand sales represented as a percentage of total market sales for all relevant competing brands	
Share of voice	Concept that refers to how 'loud' one brand's marketing communications are compared with other competing brands. It may be measured in terms of marketing communication spends, or by subjective assessment of the relative attention created by competing marketing communications. The sender's share of the total marketing communications in the category	
Shelf display	How the products are shown on the shelf	
Shelf space allocation	The part of the store shelf given to a product	
Shopping proneness	Consumers who enjoy shopping as a leisure activity	
Sign	A sign is anything that signifies something	
Signature product	Product bearing a person's name	
Silo-based scheduling	The concentration of a narrow media or even single medium approach	
Similarity (category positioning)	Brand-to-brand comparisons (i.e. how similar two brands are)	*Dell, Compaq, Fujitsu, Toshiba, Samsung* and *Apple* have a similarity when alternative brands are being evaluated for the 'laptop' category
Similarity reference point	Proposition comparison	'Price match' money-back guarantees for cheaper quotes
Simile	Comparison of one thing with another using the words 'like' or 'as'	For example, 'He fought like a lion in battle'
Sine qua non	'Without which (there is) nothing' Here we refer to marketing communications as being indispensable to all organisational activities	
Single communication voice	Coherent communication replicated in all messages and media	
Single-minded brand proposition	Traditional models have focused on marketing communications which have short, sharp impact, exposure and frequency	
Situational (or instrumental) factors	Culturally significant events or activities such as the rituals attached to gift giving, consumption involving a shared experience or hedonistic, individual indulgence	Engagement rings, Christmas, or the purchase of wedding presents. *18–30 Holidays* or music festivals offer a shared indulgence
Skin conductance	Measurement of a person's physical response on the skin	

Slogans	Also called strap lines and tag lines. These terms essentially mean the same thing	'*BMW*: The Ultimate Driving Machine', '*Mars*: Helps You Work Rest and Play'
SLP	*See* Self-liquidating offer or promotion	
SMARRTT objectives	An acronym that represents the level of detail that objectives should aim to achieve. It is a development from 'SMART' objectives that are referred to by some other authors. SMARRTT objectives are specific, measurable, achievable, realistic, relevant, targeted and timed	
Smart-shopper feelings	Consumers perceive they have made a good purchase	
SME	Small to medium enterprise; small business employing fewer than 50 people	4.5 million UK businesses are SMEs, employing over 20 million people
SMS	Short messaging service or 'texting' via mobile phone technology	Lingerie company *Gossard* contacted potential customers by using text messages to their mobile phones to promote G-strings
		Service organisations like the *RAC* and *AA* automobile break down and couriers like *Fedex* and *UPS* use texting to inform and reassure users of their service
Social context	The presence of others	
Social contracts theory	A company cannot take actions without support from outside society	
Social mediation	Opinion leaders (sometimes called gatekeepers or parasocials) and opinion formers (sometimes known as change agents) influence other consumers by shaping opinions	
Social network sites	Ostensibly forums for social interaction rather than commercial ends	*Twitter, Jaiku, LinkedIn, Pownce, Plaxo, FriendFeed, MySpace, Facebook*
Social networking	Expanded connectivity of consumers for ostensibly social reasons, but is used for the creation and dissemination of peer-to-peer marketing communications	*MySpace, Facebook, Eons, A Small World, Dead Journal, Doostang, Second Life, YouTube*
Social norms	The system of behavioural rules and manners in society	
Social symbolic meaning	Conspicuous consumption, and status symbols	Any brand of new car
Social value	Some brands are perceived as offering value because of their ability to enable affiliation with other groups OR provide added value in terms of offering a social service	Wearing *Tommy Hilfiger* clothes can buy entry to a social group. *Vodafone* used innovation to tackle social challenges in Kenya with its *M-Pesa* mobile banking service
Socioeconomics	Acquired audience characteristics	
Socioeconomic segmentation	The classification of consumers on the basis of education, income and occupation	

Solus position	An advertisement appearing with no other advertisement around it	
Sound logo	An auditory cue which brings the brand to the attention of a listening audience	UK car insurer *Direct Line* has a prominent 'car horn' jingle which is associated with the brand
Source effects	How the sponsor of a message affects evaluations	
Sources of information	The type of information used in decision-making processes. They may be personal/non-personal and commercial/non-commercial	
Spacing	Interval between exposures	
Spam emails	Emails containing general information sent to a wider audience who have not requested the email (typically based on an email list, perhaps bought from a list broker or another company)	
Spatial competition	Product/market sector 'space' in the market or in the mind of the consumer. Market segmentation represents the demand perspective and competitive positioning represents the supply perspective	
Special display	How products are promoted in the store	
Specialised media	Special interest or niche consumer magazines, trade magazines, catalogues	*Yellow Pages*
Speeches	Questions from the media, AGM feedback or promotion of ideas or products at sales conferences can help build the company image	
Spill-over effects	The associations for one brand are transmitted to another brand	
Spill-over (process)	Effects that carry on from preceding steps	
SPIN selling	Developed by Rackham, SPIN selling is designed to draw out the customer's explicit needs through a process of investigation involving the use of situation questions, problem questions, implication questions, and need pay-off questions	
Split-run	Different versions of the same advertisement are published in the same issue, but not in the same copy of the publication. It is an approach that can be used to test advertisements	
Spokesperson	Person who speaks for the company/organisation	
Sponsorship	Contribution to an activity by an organisation. Although sponsorship may be purely altruistic, it is normally undertaken with the expectation of achieving benefit for the sponsor, e.g. in achieving corporate or marketing-related objectives	
Spot colour	Area of single or solid colour	
Stakeholders	Interest groups for brands. Term used to describe the many and various groups of people who have an interest or involvement with an organisation. Stakeholders include suppliers, customers, consumers, investors, employees and distributors	
Standardisation strategy	The use of similar or identical marketing communications across countries	
Stealth, buzz and viral marketing	PR communications initiated and sent by the organisation, but MAY or MAY NOT be perceived by the target audience as having been sent by the organisation	The *Arctic Monkeys* were 'discovered' by their fan base online and at gigs, although this is blurred by the promotional work done by their label *Domino Records*
Stock return	The shareholders' profit related to the price of the stock	

Stonewalling	Rejecting claim, refusing to take responsibility. The company does nothing to remedy negative PR situation and refuses to take any blame	The well-known *Valdez* oil spill in 1989
Store atmosphere or ambience	Selling environment created by various olfactory, auditory and tactile stimuli	Music in retail stores to evoke brand associations or create soothing environment. Bread smells piped out of supermarkets.
Store brands	Brands that are sold under the retailer's name	
Store image	The thoughts and feelings towards a store	
Store layout	The physical layout of a store can affect the shopper's experience and encourage purchase	Stores may have a variety of layouts: 'grid systems' are typically used by supermarkets where customers are directed to categories such as 'tinned soups' or 'confectionery'
Story arc	Brand narrative or brand trajectory	
Storyboard	A series of images for a proposed moving sequence (TV, video, cinema, CD-ROM/DVD, Internet) indicating the progression of images, voice over and music proposed. Visual display of selected drawings illustrating the sequence of a TV, video or cinema commercial. Indications of sound and voice over are also given	
Strap lines	*See* Slogans	
Strategic business unit (SBU)	Strategically significant and identifiable part of a larger organisation. It may be a particular section of an organisation, or even a company within a larger group of companies	
Strategic gap	The difference in position between where an organisation wants to be at a specific point in time in the future (its objectives) and where it would anticipate being at that time if it simply carried on with its current activities	
Strategic positioning	Systematic targeting of brand value proposition to a discrete market segment and/or the minds of users. Communications of the organisation's value proposition aimed at placing the brand in the correct market segment to attract target audience	
Strategy	The general means by which objectives are intended to be achieved	
Strong, favourable, and unique associations	The keys to high customer-based brand equity	The UK *Cooperative Society* has had a consistent ethical stance for many years
Sub-culture	Subdivision of a main culture with its own set of behavioural norms. A distinct cultural group that exists as an identifiable segment within a larger, more complex society. *See also* Culture	
Sub-headings	Sectional headlines that break up the text and provide focus of attention on key points	
Subjective inferences of meaning	Individual or group negotiated meaning of brand communications	When luxury fashion brand *Burberry* was adopted by label-conscious football hooligans and 'Essex Girls', the brand acquired a 'chav' connotation

Subliminal perception	Unaware exposure to and processing of something	
Substrate	Any material which is used to print on to e.g. paper, card and plastic	
Support media	*See* Secondary media	
Surplus	Same target audience members reached by different media	
Switchers	People who buy a variety of products in the category	
SWOT	Organisational analysis framework representing organisational strengths, weaknesses, opportunities and threats	
Syllepsis	A verb changes in sense	*Keds* shoes: 'It's too bad other brands don't pad their shoes as much as their prices' *Frigidaire* refrigerator: 'Built to handle the years as well as the groceries'
Symbolic appeals	The brand communications' appeal to consumers' desire for self-enhancement, group membership, affiliation and belongingness	
Symbolic brand	Brand which allows projection of consumer individual or group meaning through ownership or conspicuous consumption	*Gucci* jewellery *Armani* clothing
Symbolic consumption	Meaning derived by the connotations associated with a purchase and/or use of a brand	A *Toyota Lexus Hybrid Drive* car will project an image of success and environmental consciousness
Symbolic function and meaning	The representational associations or meaning given to or acquired by brands which have cultural significance and stand for something to users of brand	The conspicuous consumption of a *Rolex* symbolises success and power www.Rolex.com
Symbols	Things that represent, stand for, or are associated with something else. Semiotic representation (signified meaning) of the brand	*Coca-Cola* – contour-shaped bottle *Nike* – swoosh 'tick' *IKEA* – yellow and blue colours signify Swedish culture
Synergy	The effect of bringing together marketing communication elements in a mutually supportive and enhancing way so that the resulting whole is greater than the sum of its parts	
Tachistoscope	A simple device based on a photographic slide projector. Images are presented quickly and respondents are asked to report what they remember. The procedure gives an indication of the impact and quality of an ad or POS display	
Tactical positioning	Short-term application of marketing mix stimuli used to achieve and maintain strategic positioning	'No frills' branding projects a 'value positioning'
Tactics	Details of how strategies are intended to be achieved	
Tag lines	*See* Slogans	
Target audience	The people that the marketing communications are directed to. Those individuals or groups that are identified as having a direct or indirect effect on business performance, and are selected to receive marketing communications	

Target Group Index (TGI)	One of the largest continuous pieces of consumer research conducted in the UK. It involves around 24,000 respondents annually and is produced by the British Market Research Bureau. It is an example of one of a number of surveys conducted by a variety of research companies that provide consumer data. TGI provides information about buying habits across thousands of branded products (some 2500), and includes data about the media habits, attitudes and opinions of respondents. It is an extremely valuable source of consumer and media information
Target market	Market segment selected for specific targeting
Target marketing approaches	Undifferentiated marketing (mass marketing), differentiated marketing, concentrated marketing, niche marketing and mass customisation marketing. Additionally, in international contexts: global marketing and global niche marketing. *See also* Market segmentation and Segmentation bases
Targeting	The selection of one or more market segments
Telemarketing	Combines sales management, database management and direct marketing using consumer knowledge to sell, cross-sell, monitor customer experience and so on in a personal but not face-to-face encounter
Television rating points (TVRs)	Said to be the main currency in TV advertising. TVRs are an estimate of the audience for a TV advertisement, and are determined through BARB data. They are in effect index numbers that represent the proportion of the potential viewing audience
Test market	The use of a representative small geographical area of the total target market to facilitate a controlled experiment in which one or more proposed marketing actions are trialled. Test marketing assesses the viability of a new product, new market or new marketing communications before embarking on a full launch
TGI	*See* Target Group Index
Through-the-line agency	Describes agencies that claim to offer complete marketing communications solutions. Full-service and one-stop shop agencies are associated terms
Through-the-line communications	Marketing communications that span both above- and below-the-line activities
Tie-ins	Multiple products involved in a single sales promotion
Time-based branding perspective	Recognises that brands are dynamic and to survive they have to respond and change to the needs of the environment
Time-shifted	Communications not viewed linearly as no prime time required — *Delay TV*, *Sky+*, *TiVo*, DVD recorders facilitate viewing out of schedules
Tint	Process of breaking a solid colour into a series of dots or lines. Through this process, tones or tints of a colour are achieved by varying the amount or size of dots or lines for printing: the lower the concentration, the lighter the tint appears
Tipping point	Moment in time when paradigm shift occurs or change happens
TiVo	Personal video recorder which allows taping of TV programmes
Top-down budgeting	System whereby budgets are set by senior management, disaggregated and passed down to lower management
Top-of-mind awareness	Consumer's consideration set must consider our brand to get premier position in the category — 'Have a break, have a *Kit Kat*' helps Nestlé Rowntree to 'own' the category

Top-of-mind reinforcement	Brand recall for need association better than competitors in category
Total set	The complete set of alternative choices in a decision
Tracking studies	The evaluation of marketing communications at various stages during their use. In this way, effects may be monitored throughout a campaign and modifications to the marketing communications plan introduced if necessary
Trade allowances	Incentives provided to trade buyers in the form of extra allowances such as special-purchase terms
Traditional mass media	Newspaper, magazines, TV and radio
Traffic	(i) Describes the function that ensures that the development and production of agency work is completed to deadline through all the various stages from initial brief, through creative solutions, to final production. It is a crucial part of agency operations (ii) Can refer to passers-by (as in poster measurement), or to the number of viewers of web pages (also called hits)
Transactional marketing	Marketing in which the emphasis is placed on each individual purchase situation in contrast to relationship marketing. The increased focus placed on developing long-term customer relationships in today's marketing is considered to be a major shift in marketing philosophy. *See also* Relationship marketing
Transactional selling	Selling where the emphasis is simply placed on achieving the sale and following the steps proposed to a successful sale

Transformational motivations	Motivations based on hedonistic needs. Actual or perceived ability for brand use to change appearance, state or outlook of user	*Lynx* claims to instil sexual attractiveness
Trans-media and media-neutral planning .	Scheduling of communication messages based on audience requirement not media	
Transmission communications	Communications which are seen as being SENT through or injected into a communication conduit (medium) TO an audience to evoke a response	*Inland Revenue* Self-Assessment campaigns leading up to 31 January income tax deadlines www.inlandrevenue.org
Trialling the product	Used to alleviate 'perceived risk' in the buying decision process and help start brand loyalty	*Vogue* or *Elle* magazines attaching a complimentary sachet of perfume in a special edition
Trickle-across communications	Conversations from group to group. Oral communications or word of mouth as opposed to 'trickle-down' communications	
Trivial product attributes	Attributes created in the marketing communications with no real value for the product	*Alberto Natural Silk Shampoo* includes silk in the product to imply silkier hair is achievable, and using the tagline: 'We put silk in the shampoo bottle'
TVR	*See* Television rating points	
Two-way asymmetrical model	Two-way communications negotiating with target audiences, resolving conflict and promoting mutual understanding and respect between the organisation and its audiences	

Two-way conversations	Symmetrical, evenly distributed communications BETWEEN company and customer	*New Labour* has apparently been ringing dissident voters who email Gordon Brown to complain www.labourparty.com
Typicality (category positioning)	Degree to which a brand is characteristic of its product category; some brands are seen as more typical than others. Some are so typical that they are more or less synonymous with (or seen as the prototype brand for) the product category	*Kellogg's* and *Gillette* have the heritage, image and equity in their specific categories
Typicality reference point	Brand feature or category characteristic which marks either product or sector	*Kwik Fit* both positions the brand and signifies the category for quick-turn-around auto repairs
Unambiguous support	The company remedies the situation and takes full blame	In the *Tylenol* poisoning scandal, owner *Johnson & Johnson* accepted total liability
Unique associations	Special links that the brand has other than function or use	*Manchester United FC* has gained worldwide brand recognition, initially through the Munich Air Disaster and latterly through achievements
Unique selling personality	Uncommon term, used to describe a key element of a brand's personality	
Unique selling proposition or point (USP)	Single, clear and unequivocal selling proposition. The compelling reason (of a unique feature or unique benefit) for using the brand against the competition. Term coined by Rosser Reeves	*Panasonic Lumix* cameras are linked with fun, usability and creativity www.panasonic.co.uk *Duracell* batteries last longer than others *Halstead Flooring* lasts longer than other industrial floor coverings
Unitised communications	An uncommon term, used here to distinguish between marketing communications that promote the organisation as a whole (corporate communications) and those that promote parts or units of the organisation, such as its goods, services, brands, individuals or sections	
Unplanned purchases	Occur when the consumer is reminded of a purchase need or purchase motivation in the store	'Oh, that's right, I need new batteries for the remote control'
Up-selling and cross-selling	Moving customers 'up' to higher ticket price brands or moving customers to other product categories	In 2009, *BMW* resisted pressure to compete on price by offering customers a free 'trade up' to the next level in the *BMW* series
Usage complements	Products that are consumed or used together	
Usage occasions	Specific times demarcated by time, season or ritual event	Weddings, Christmas, summer holidays

Use	Suggested utility claim	The product is King *with Bang & Olufsen* hi-fi products, made from the best materials, and craftsmanship to allow customers to 'watch, listen, and be inspired'
User-based fit	Sponsorship is congruent with target audience	Financial service institute *CGNU* sponsors national cricket games because they share the same target audience
User-generated materials	Communications sometimes subverting original ads, sometimes augmenting them, created by users of social network sites to pass any marketing message to other individual consumers	*Cadbury's* 'Gorilla' was created in the style of an Internet viral ad which allowed users to reinvent the ad and post it to *YouTube* and other sites gaining extra discussion and positive reaction
User-generated website	Online space allowing consumers to 'mash up' company materials or create original contribution	
User imagery	Image projected by brand users	See *Stella Artois* case study
Utilitarian consumption	Basic product benefits which fulfil functional needs (e.g. quenching one's thirst)	
Utilities	The functional benefits of a product	
Value-added or value innovation positioning	Offer which provides enhanced bundle of benefits as part of value proposition	*British Gas* Service Contract discounts repairs and offers technical advice as well as boiler maintenance
Value expressive	Expressing consumer's central values or self-concept and highly relevant to lifestyle (activities, interests and opinions) in expressing a particular social identity	
Vehicle distribution	The physical units through which the message can flow (number of TV or radio sets tuned to the programme; copies of the magazine/newspaper)	
Vehicle exposure	The number of individuals exposed to the medium vehicle	
Vendor Relationship Management (VRM)	An advanced CRM two-way system which works on a permission principle of vendors allowing suppliers access to personal information in order to enhance customer service	
Viral marketing	A communication strategy which encourages individuals to pass any marketing message to other individual consumers, allowing for massive exposure of brand message	*Ford Sport Ka* ads showing 'the evil twin' in virals were purposely created to encourage accelerated word of mouth between regular Internet users
Visibility-adjusted impact	Replaces the simple opportunity-to-see approach adopted by OSCAR	
Visual word of mouth (word of eye)	The conspicuous consumption of proudly displaying brands generates a sort of word of mouth	
Wallet analysis	Study of the audience's expenditure	
Watershed	The time up to which TV advertising and programming are rigorously restricted. After the watershed, more adult material is considered acceptable	

Weak force	Advertising seen as a weak force suggests that advertising works through a process of reinforcing and maintaining brand values and defending market share. Its effect on sales is therefore less direct
Wear-in	Repeated exposures have positive effects
Wear-out	Repeated exposures have negative effects
Web page	A file available through the World Wide Web, typically containing text, images and links to other pages. An organisation's website is likely to contain a collection of web pages, each with its own file reference (html address)
Weighted ratings points	Rating points weighted to reflect the likely impact of a medium: the higher the weighting compared with other media, the greater the anticipated impact generated by the medium
Wilful ignorance	Reluctance to request information that makes a decision more difficult
Within category	Brands which compete solely within the parameters of a distinct market segment
WOM	*See* Word of mouth
Word of mouth (WOM)	Communications BETWEEN opinion formers/leaders, customers and other reference group members who may have a strong influence on the effectiveness of the original intended message — The movie *Cloverfield* built up a buzz by encouraging pre-release online discussion
Wordage	Advertising space that is bought by the word and presented in classified sections of the press
World Wide Web	Huge collection of documents and files available through the Internet
Xenophilia	An affinity or liking for things foreign
Young's five-step creative process	A sequential process for developing creative ideas involving immersion, digestion, incubation, illumination and verification
Zapping	Avoiding network TV ads by changing channels
Zero budgeting	Expenditure has to be justified before approval. Based on how much a specific input will cost to achieve a specific outcome and how appropriate that expenditure is likely to be

References

Aaker, D.A. (1984). *Strategic Market Management*. New York: John Wiley & Sons, Inc.

Aaker, D.A. (1991). *Managing Brand Equity*. New York: Free Press.

Aaker, D.A. (1994). The value of brand equity. *Journal of Business Strategy*, **13**(4), 27-32.

Aaker, D.A. (2000). *Building Strong Brands*. New York: Simon & Schuster.

Aaker, D.A. (2001). *Strategic Marketing Management*. New York: Simon & Schuster.

Aaker, D.A. (2004). *Brand Portfolio Strategy: Creating Relevance, Differentiation, Energy, Leverage and Clarity*. New York: Simon & Schuster.

Aaker, D.A. and Joachimsthaler, E. (2000). *Brand Leadership*. New York: Free Press.

Aaker, D.A. and McLoughlin, D. (2007). *Strategic Market Management*. Chichester: John Wiley & Sons, Ltd.

Aaker, J.L. (1997). Dimensions of brand personality. *Journal of Marketing Research*, **34**(2), 347-56.

Aaker, J.L. (1999). The malleable self: the role of self-expression in persuasion. *Journal of Marketing Research*, **36**(2), 45-57.

Aaker, J.L., Fournier, S. and Brasel, S.A. (2004). When good brands do bad. *Journal of Consumer Research*, **31**, 1-16.

Abernethy, A.M. and Franks, G.R. (1996). The information content of advertising: a meta-analysis. *Journal of Advertising*, **25**(2), 1-17.

Abratt, R. and Cowan, D. (1999). Client–agency perspectives of information needs for media planning. *Journal of Advertising Research*, **39**(6), 37-52.

Adaval, R. and Wyer Jr., R.S. (1998). The role of narratives in consumer information processing. *Journal of Consumer Psychology*, **7**(3), 207-46.

Advertising Research Foundation (1961). *Toward Better Media Comparisons*. New York: Advertising Research Foundation.

Advertising Research Foundation (2007). *On the Road to a New Effectiveness Model*. New York: Advertising Research Foundation.

Ahluwalia, R., Burnkrant, R.E. and Unnava, H.R. (2002). Consumer response to negative publicity. *Journal of Marketing Research*, **37**, 203-14.

Ahuvia, A.C. (2005). Beyond the extended self: loved objects and consumers' identity narratives. *Journal of Consumer Research*, **32**, 171-84.

Ailawadi, K.L.,Lehmann, D.R. and Neslin, S.A. (2003). Revenue premium as an outcome measure of brand equity. *Journal of Marketing*, **67**(2), 1-17.

Alba, J.W. and Chattopadhyay, A. (1985). Effects of context and part-category cues on recall of competing brands. *Journal of Marketing Research*, **22**, 340-9.

Alba, J.W. and Chattopadhyay, A. (1986). Salience effects in brand recall. *Journal of Marketing Research*, **23**, 363-9.

Ambler, T. (1995). Brand Equity as a Relational Concept. *The Journal of Brand management*, **2**(6).

Ambler, T. (1997). How much of brand equity is explained by trust? *Management Trust*, **35**(4), 283-92.

American Association of Advertising Agencies (1998). 4As standards of practice: how far does this professional association's code of ethics influence reach? *Journal of Business Ethics*, **17**(11), 1155-61.

Anders, J.C. and Narus, J.A. (1999). *Business Market Management: Understanding, Creating and Delivering Value*. Upper Saddle, NJ: Prentice Hall.

Andrew, D. (1998). Brand revitalisation and extension. In S. Hart and J. Murphy (eds) *Brands: The New Wealth Creators*. Basingstoke: Macmillan.

Ang, S.H. and Low, S.Y.M. (2000). Exploring the dimensions of ad creativity. *Psychology and Marketing*, **17**(10), 835–54.

Anholt, S. (2003). *Brand New Justice: the Upside of Global Branding*. Oxford: Butterworth-Heinemann.

Anscheutz, N. (2002). Why a brand's most valuable consumer is the next one it adds. *Journal of Advertising Research*, **42**(1), 15–21.

Appleton, J. (1966). *The Experience of Landscape*. New York: John Wiley & Sons, Inc.

Arnott, D.C. (1994). Positioning: on defining the concept. Marketing Educators' Group (MEG). Conference Proceedings, University of Ulster, Coleraine, NI, 4 July.

Assael, H. (1992). *Consumer Behaviour and Marketing Action*, 4th edition. Boston, MA: PWS-Kent.

Atkinson, R.L. and Hilgard, E.R. (1996). *Hilgard's Introduction to Psychology*. Forth Worth, TX: Harcourt Brace.

Aufreiter, N.A., Elzinga, D. and Gordon, J.W. (2003). Better branding. *McKinsey Quarterly*, **4**, 28–39.

Bagozzi, R.P. (1978). Salesforce performance and satisfaction as a function. In B. Lott and D. Maluso (eds), *The Social Psychology of Interpersonal Discrimination*. New York: Guilford Press.

Baker, M.J. and Hart, S.J. (eds) (2007). *The Marketing Book*. Oxford: Butterworth-Heinemann.

Balasubramanian, S.K. (1994). Beyond advertising and publicity: hybrid messages and public policy issues. *Journal of Advertising*, **23**(4), 29–46.

Ballantyne, D. and Varey, R.J. (2006). Introducing a dialogical orientation to the service-dominant logic of marketing. In R.F. Lusch and S.L. Vargo (eds), *The Service-Dominant Logic of Marketing: Dialogue, Debate and Directions* (pp. 224–38). New York: M.E. Sharpe.

Barnard, N. and Ehrenberg, A.S.C. (1997). Advertising: strongly persuasive or just nudging? *Journal of Advertising Research*, **37**, 21–31.

Barthes, R. (1967). *Elements of Semiology*. London: Jonathan Cape.

Barthes, R. (1977). The rhetoric of the image. In *Image, Music, Text* (pp. 32–51). London: Fontana.

Barthes, R. (1988). *The Semiotic Challenge*. Trans. Richard Howard. Oxford: Blackwell.

Batchelor, A. (1998). Brand revitalisation and extension. In S. Hart and J. Murphy (eds) *Brands: The New Wealth Creators*. Basingstoke: Macmillan.

Batra, R. and Ahtola, O.T. (1990). Measuring the hedonic and utilitarian sources of consumer attitudes. *Marketing Letters*, **2**(2), 159–70.

Belch, G.E. and Belch, M.A. (1998). *Advertising and Promotion: An Integrated Marketing Communications Perspective*, 4th edition. New York: McGraw-Hill.

Belch, G.E. and Belch, M.A. (2001). *Advertising and Promotion*. New York: McGraw-Hill.

Beldona, S. (in press). Online travel information search modes: an exploratory study. *Journal of Information Technology in Hospitality*.

Belk, R.W. (1975). Situational variables and consumer behaviour. *Journal of Consumer Research*, **2**, 157–64.

Belk, R.W. (1988). Possessions and the extended self. *Journal of Consumer Research*, **15**, 139–68.

Belk, R.W. and Tumbat, G. (2005). The cult of Macintosh. *Journal of Culture, Markets and Consumption*, **8**(3), 205–17.

Bellizzi, J.A., Crowley, A.E. and Hasty, R.W. (1983). The effects of color in store design. *Journal of Retailing*, **59**, 21–45.

Bendixen, M., Bukasa, K.A. and Abratt, R. (2004). Brand equity in the business-to-business market. *Industrial Marketing Management*, **33**, 371–80.

Benedictus, L. (2007). Psst! Have you heard? The rise of stealth and buzz marketing. *The Guardian*, 31 January.

Benoît, H. (1998). My brand the hero: a semiotic analysis of the consumer brand relationship. In S. Lambkin, F. van Raaij and B. Heibrunn (eds), *European Perspectives on Consumer Research* (pp. 370–401). London: Prentice Hall.

Berens, G., van Riel, C.B.M. and van Bruggen, G.H. (2005). Corporate associations and consumer product responses: the moderating role of corporate brand dominance. *Journal of Marketing*, **69**(3), 35–48.

Bergstrom, A., Blumenthal, D. and Crothers, S. (2002). Why internal branding matters: the case of SAAB. *Corporate Reputation Review*, **5**(2–3), 133–42.

Berkman, H., Lindquist, J. and Sirgy, J. (1997). *Consumer Behaviour*. Lincolnwood, IL: NTC Publishing Group.

Berkowitz, D., Allaway, A. and D'Souza, G. (2001). The impact of differential lag effects on the allocation of advertising budgets across media. *Journal of Advertising Research*, **41**(3), 49–58.

Berman, S.J., Battino, B. and Feldman, K. (2009). Beyond advertising: choosing a strategic path to the digital consumer. IBM Institute for Business Value.

Berman, S.J., Battino, B., Shipnuck, L. and Neus, A. (2007). The end of advertising as we know it. IBM Institute for Business Value.

Bickerton, P., Bickerton, M. and Simpson-Holley, K. (1999). *Cyberstrategy: Business Strategy for Extranets, Intranets and the Internet,* 2nd edition. Oxford: Butterworth-Heinemann.

Biehal, G. and Chakravarthi, D. (1983). Information accessibility as a moderator of consumer choice. *Journal of Consumer Research*, **10**, 1–14.

Birtwistle, G. and Freathy, P. (1998). More than just a name above the shop: a comparison of the branding strategies of two UK fashion retailers. *International Journal of Retailing and Consumer Research,* **26**(8), 318–23.

Bitner, M.J. (1992). The service encounter: diagnosing favourable and unfavourable incidents. *Journal of Marketing*, **56**, 57–71.

Blackston, M. (1993). A brand with an attitude: a suitable case for treatment. *Journal of Marketing Research Society,* **34**(3), 231–41.

Blackwell, R.D., Miniard, P.W. and Engel, J.F. (2001). *Consumer Behaviour,* 9th edition. Fort Worth, TX: Harcourt Brace.

Blackwell, R.D., Miniard, P.W. and Engel, J.F. (2006). *Consumer Behaviour*, 10th edition. Ohio: South-Western.

Blackwell, R.D. and Stephan, T. (2003). *Brands That Rock: What Business Leaders Can Learn From the World of Rock*. Chichester: John Wiley & Sons, Ltd.

Blakely, B. (2007). Can Nintendo make exercise fun with Wii Fit? *Tech Republic Website*, 7 December.

Blanco, X.R. and Salgado, J. (2004). Amancio Ortega, De Cero a Zara, La esfera de los libros, Madrid. Cited in C. Lopez and Y. Fan (2009), Internationalisation of the Spanish brand Zara. *Journal of Fashion Marketing and Management,* **13**(2), 279–96.

Blankson, C. and Kalafatis, S.P. (2004). The development and validation of a scale measuring customer/consumer-derived generic typology of positioning strategies. *Journal of Marketing Management,* **20**, 5–43.

Blythe, J. (1997). *Essence of Consumer Behaviour*. London: Prentice Hall.

Boje, B.M. (2001). Narrative methods for organisational and communication research. Cited by A.D. Brown, M. Humphreys and P.M. Gurney (2005). Narrative, identity and change: a case study of Laskarina Holidays. *Journal of Organisational Change Management*, **18**(4), 312–26.

Borcher, T. (2000). *Persuasion in the Media Age*. London: McGraw-Hill.

Brandes, D. (2004). *Bare Essentials: The Aldi Way to Do Retail Success*. London: Cyan Books.

Braun-LaTour, K., Latour, M. and Zinkhan, G.M. (2007). Using childhood memories to gain insight into brand meaning. *Journal of Marketing*, **71**, 45–60.

Brennan, R., Canning, L. and McDowell, R. (2007). *Business-to-Business Marketing*. London: Sage.

Brierley, S. (2002). *The Advertising Handbook*, 2nd edition. London: Routledge.

Broadbent, S. (1985). Modelling with Adstock. *Journal of the Market Research Society*, **26**(4).

Broniarczyk, S.M. and Gershoff, A.D. (1997). Meaningless differentiation revisited. *Advances in Consumer Research*, **24**, 223–8.

Broniarczyk, S.M. and Gershoff, A.D. (2003). The reciprocal effects of brand equity and trivial attributes. *Journal of Marketing Research*, **40**, 161–75.

Brown, A.D., Humphreys, M. and Gurney, P.M. (2005). Narrative, identity and change: a case study of Laskarina Holidays. *Journal of Organisational Change Management*, **18**(4), 312–26.

Brown, C.L. and Carpenter, G.S. (2000). Why is the trivial important? A reasons-based account for the effects of trivial attributes on choice. *Journal of Consumer Research*, **26**, 372–85.

Brown, S. (2000) Postmodern marketing: abutting for beginners. http://www.sfxbrown.com/Postmodern%20Marketing.pdf.

Brown, S. (2005). I can read you like a book! Novel thoughts on consumer behaviour. *Qualitative Market Research: An International Journal*, **8**(2), 219–37.

Bruner, G.C. and Pomazal, R.J. (1988). Problem recognition: the crucial first stage of the consumer decision process. *Journal of Consumer Marketing*, **5**(1), 53–63.

Bruner, J. (1990). *Acts of Meaning*. Cambridge, MA: Harvard University Press.

Buchanan, L., Simmons, C.J. and Bickart, B.A. (1999). Brand equity dilution: retailer display and context effects. *Journal of Marketing Research*, **36**, 345–55.

Burnett, J. and Moriarty, S. (1998). *Marketing Communications: An Integrated Approach*. Upper Saddle, NJ: Prentice Hall.

Burton, P.W. (1999). *Advertising Copywriting*. New York: NTC Business Books.

Buttle, F.A. (1995). Marketing communications theory: what do the texts teach our students? *International Journal of Advertising*, **14**, 297–313.

Buzzell, R.D. (1981). Are there natural market structures? *Journal of Marketing*, **45**(1), 42–51.

Calder, B.J. (2008). *Kellogg on Branding: the Marketing Faculty of the Kellogg School of Management*. New York: John Wiley & Sons, Inc.

Calder, B.J. and Malthouse, E. (2008). Media engagement and advertising effectiveness. In B.J. Calder (ed.), *Kellogg on Branding: the Marketing Faculty of the Kellogg School of Management*. New York: John Wiley & Sons, Inc.

Campbell, M.C. and Goodstein, R.C. (2001). The moderating effect of perceived risk on consumers' evaluation of product incongruity: preference for the norm. *Journal of Consumer Research*, **28**, 439–49.

Campbell, M.C. and Keller, K.L. (2003). Does brand meaning exist in similarity or singularity? *Journal of Consumer Research*, **30**, 292–303.

Campbell, M.C., Keller, K.L., Hoyer, M., David, G. and Hoyer, D.D. (2003). Brand familiarity and repetition effects. *Journal of Consumer Research*, **30**(2), 292–304.

Cannon, H.M., Leckenby, J.D. and Abernethy, A. (2002). Beyond effective frequency: evaluating media schedules using frequency value planning. *Journal of Advertising Research*, **42**(6), 33–47.

Carey, J.W. (1989). *Communication as Culture: Essays on Media and Society*. Winchester, MA: Unwin Hyman.

Carpenter, G.S., Glazer, R. and Nakamoto, K. (1994). Meaningful brands from meaningless differentiation: the dependence on irrelevant attributes. *Journal of Marketing Research*, **31**, 339–50.

Carrillat, F.A., Lafferty, B.A. and Harris, E.G. (2005). Investigating sponsorship effectiveness: do less familiar brands have an advantage of more familiar brands in single and multiple sponsorship arrangements? *Journal of Brand Management*, **13**(1), 50–64.

Celsi, R.L. and Olson, J.C. (1988). The role of involvement in attention and comprehension processes. *Journal of Consumer Research*, **15**, 210–24.

Chandon, P., Wansink, B. and Laurent, G. (2000). A benefit congruency framework of sales promotion effectiveness. *Journal of Marketing*, **64**, 65–81.

Chandy, R.K., Tellis, G.J., MacInnis, D.J. and Thaivanich, P. (2001). What to say when: advertising appeals in evolving markets. *Journal of Marketing Research*, **38**, 399–414.

Chang, Y. and Thorson, E. (2004). Television and web advertising synergies. *Journal of Advertising*, **33**(2), 75–84.

Chartered Institute of Public Relations (2006). www.cipr.co.uk.

Chattopadhyay, A. (1998). When does comparative advertising influence brand attitude? The role of delay and market position. *Psychology & Marketing*, **15**(5), 461–75.

Chaudhuri, A. and Holbrook, M.B. (2001). The chain of effects from brand trust and brand affect to brand performance: the role of brand loyalty. *Journal of Marketing*, **65**(1), 81–93.

Childers, T.L. (1986). Assessment of the psychometric properties of an opinion leadership scale. *Journal of Marketing Research*, **23**,184–8.

Childers, T.L. and Jass, J. (2002). All dressed up with something to say: effects of typeface semantic associations on brand perceptions and consumer memory. *Journal of Consumer Psychology*, **12**(2), 93–106.

Christensen, L.T., Firat, A.F. and Torp, S. (2008). The organisation of integrated communications. *European Journal of Marketing*, **42**(3/4), 423–52.

Christopher, M., Payne, A. and Ballantyne, D. (1991). *Relationship Marketing*. Oxford: Butterworth-Heinemann.

Cialdini, R.B. (1993). *Influence: The Power of Persuasion*. New York: Morrow.

Cialdini, R.B. (2001). *Influence. Science and Practice*. Boston, MA: Allyn & Bacon.

Cialdini, R.B. (2003). *Influence: Science and Practice*, 4th edition. Upper Saddle River, NJ: Prentice Hall.

Claeys, C., Swinnen, A. and Abeele, P.V. (1995). Consumers means-end chains for think and feel products. *International Journal of Research in Marketing*, **12**(3), 193–208.

Clancy, K. and Trout, J. (2002). Brand confusion. *Harvard Business Review*, **8**(3), 22–33.

Close, A.G., Finney, R.Z., Lacey, R.Z. and Sneath, J.Z. (2006). Engaging the consumer through event marketing: linking attendees with the sponsor, community, and brand. *Journal of Advertising Research*, **46**, 420–33.

Cobb, C.J. and Hoyer, W.D. (1986). Planned versus impulse buying behaviour. *Journal of Retailing*, **62**, 67–81.

Cobb-Walgren, C.J., Ruble, C.A. and Donthu, N. (1995). Brand equity, brand preference, and purchase intent. *Journal of Advertising*, **24**(3), 25–40.

Colonius, H. (1989). Cited in C. Grönroos (2004), The relationship marketing process: communication, interaction, dialogue, value. *Journal of Business and Industrial Marketing*, **19**(2), 99–113.

Cook, A. (1994). The end of the line, *Marketing*, **24**.

Cooper, A. and Simons, P. (1997). *Brand Equity Lifestage: An Entrepreneurial Revolution*. London: TBWA Simons Palmer.

Corkindale, D. and Newall, J. (1978). Advertising thresholds and wearout. *European Journal of Marketing*, **12**(5), 329–78.

Czellar, S. (2003). Consumer attitude toward brand extensions: an integrative model and research propositions. *International Journal of Research in Marketing*, **20**, 97–115.

Dahlén, M. (2001). Banner ads through a new lens. *Journal of Advertising Research*, **41**(4), 23–30.

Dahlén, M. (2002). Thinking and feeling on the WWW: the impact of product type and time on WWW advertising effectiveness. *Journal of Marketing Communications*, **8**(2), 115–25.

Dahlén, M. (2003). *The Marketers' New Handbook*. Malmö: Liber.

Dahlén, M. and Lange, F. (2005). Advertising weak and strong brands: who gains? *Psychology and Marketing*, **22**(6), 473–88.

Dahlén, M. and Lange, F. (2006). A disaster is contagious: how a brand in crisis affects other brands. *Journal of Advertising Research*, **46**(4), 388–97.

Dahlén, M., Nordenstam, S. and Murray, M. (2004). An empirical study of perceptions of implicit meanings in WWW advertisements versus print advertisements. *Journal of Marketing Communications*, **10**(1), 35–47.

Dahlén, M., Rasch, A. and Rosengren, S. (2003). Love at first site? A study of website advertising effectiveness, *Journal of Advertising Research*, **43**(1), 25–33.

Dahlén, M., Rosengren, S. and Törn, F. (2008). The waste in advertising creativity is the part that matters. *Journal of Advertising Research*, **48**(3), 392–403.

Dan'l, T. (1994). David Ogilvy. In E. Applegate (ed.) *The Ad Men and Women*. Westport, CT: Greenwood.

Davidson, H. (1997). *Offensive Marketing*. Harmondsworth: Penguin.

Davidson, H. (2002). *Even More Offensive Marketing*. Harmondsworth: Penguin.

Davis, S. (2005). Building brand-driven organizations. In A.M. Tybout and T. Calkins (eds), *Kellogg on Branding: the Marketing Faculty of the Kellogg School of Management*. New York: John Wiley & Sons, Inc.

Dawar, N. and Pillutla, M.M. (2000). Impact of product-harm crises on brand equity: the moderating role of consumer expectations. *Journal of Marketing Research*, **37**, 215–26.

Dawkins, R. (1976). *The Selfish Gene*. Oxford: Oxford University Press.

Dawkins, R. (1999). Foreword. In S. Blackmore, *The Meme Machine*. Oxford: Oxford University Press.

de Chernatony, L. (2002). *From Brand Vision to Brand Evaluation: Strategically Building and Sustaining Brands*. Oxford: Butterworth-Heinemann.

de Chernatony, L. (2008). Brand building. In M.J. Baker and S.J. Hart (eds), *The Marketing Book*, 6th edition (pp. 306–26). Oxford: Butterworth-Heinemann.

de Chernatony, L. and Dall'Olmo Riley, F. (1998). Defining a 'brand': beyond the literature with expert's interpretations. *Journal of Marketing Management*, **14**(5), 417–43.

de Chernatony, L. and McDonald, M. (1998). *Creating Powerful Brands*, 2nd edition. Oxford: Elsevier.

de Chernatony, L. and McDonald, M. (2003). *Creating Powerful Brands*, 3rd edition. Oxford: Elsevier.

de Pelsmacker, P., Geuens, M. and van den Bergh, J. (2001). *Marketing Communications*. London: Financial Times Management.

de Pelsmacker, P. and van den Bergh, J. (1996). The communication effects of provocation in print advertising. *International Journal of Advertising*, **15**(3), 203–21.

Dean, D.H. (2004). Consumer reaction to negative publicity. *Journal of Business Communication*, **41**(2), 192–211.

Denison, T.J. and Knox, S. (1983). Cited in P. McGoldrick (2000). *Retail Marketing*, 2nd edition. London: McGraw-Hill.

Denning, S. (2000). *The Springboard: How Storytelling Ignites Action in Knowledge-Era Organisations*. Oxford: Butterworth-Heinemann.

Denning, S. (2005). Mastering the discipline of business narrative. *Times Education Supplement*, 23 September.

Devlin, D., Birtwistle, G. and Macedo, N. (2003). Food retail positioning strategy: a means-end chain analysis. *British Food Journal*, **105**(9), 653–70.

Dibb, S., Simkin, L., Pride, W.M. and Ferrell, O.C. (1997). *Marketing: Concepts and Strategies*, 3rd edition. Boston, MA: Houghton Mifflin.

Dickson, P.R. and Sawyer, A.G. (1990). The price knowledge and search of supermarket shoppers. *Journal of Marketing*, **54**, 42–53.

Domzal, T.J. and Kernan, J.B. (1992). Reading advertising: the what and how of product meaning. *Journal of Consumer Marketing*, **9**(2), 48–64.

Donnelly, W.J. (1996). *Planning Media, Strategy and Imagination*. Upper Saddle River, NJ: Prentice Hall.

Donovan, R.J., Jalleh, G. and Fielder, L.E. (2009). Ethical issues in pro-social advertising: the Australian 2006 White Ribbon Day campaign. *Journal of Public Affairs*, **9**, 5–19.

Douglas, C. (2003). Risk and creativity in advertising. *Journal of Marketing Management*, **19**, 57–67.

Duncan, T. and Moriarty, S. (1997). *Driving Brand Value*. New York: McGraw-Hill.

Durgee, J.F. (1996). Translating values into product wants. *Journal of Advertising Research*, **36**(6), 90–100.

Durgee, J.F. and Stuart, R.W (1987). Advertising symbols and brand names that best represent key product meanings. *Journal of Consumer Marketing*, **4**(3), 15–24.

Eagly, A.H. and Chaiken, S. (1993). *The Psychology of Attitudes*. Orlando: Harcourt Brace Jovanovich.

East, R., Hammond, K., Lomax, W. and Robinson, H. (2005). What is the effect of a recommendation? *The Marketing Review*, 145–57.

Eastlack, J.O. and Rao, A.G. (1989). Advertising experiments at the Campbell Soup Company. *Marketing Science*, **8**(1), 57–71.

Edell, J.A. and Burke, M.C. (1987). The power of feelings in understanding advertising effects. *Journal of Consumer Research*, **14**, 421–33.

Edell, J.A. and Keller, K.L. (1999). Analysing media interactions: the effects of coordinated TV and print advertising campaigns. Working Paper Report No. 99-120, Marketing Science Institute.

Egan, J. (2007). *Marketing Communications*. London: Thomson Learning.

Ehrenberg, A.S.C. (1974). Repetitive advertising and the consumer. *Journal of Advertising Research,* **14**(2), 25–34.

Ehrenberg, A.S.C. (1988). *Repeat Buying: Theory and Applications*, 2nd edition. London: Charles Griffin.

Ehrenberg, A.S.C. (2000). Repetitive advertising and the consumer. *Journal of Advertising Research*, **40**(6), 39–48.

Ehrenberg, A.S.C., Barnard, N., Kennedy, R. and Bloom, H. (2002). Brand advertising as creative publicity. *Journal of Advertising Research*, **42**(40), 7–18.

Ehrenberg, A.S.C. and Goodhart, G.J. (1979). The switching constant. *Management Science*, **25**(7), 703–5.

Ehrenberg, A.S.C. and Goodhart, G. (2000). New brands: near instant loyalty. *Journal of Marketing Management*, **16**(6), 607–17.

Eisenegger, M. (2005). Reputation nurturing as a core function of PR. *Conference paper at International Communication Association*, New York.

Elkin, T. (2004). Study finding how online media lifts sales. Retrieved from www.mediapost.com/articleid=243834.

Elliott, R. (1998). A model of emotion-driven choice. *Journal of Marketing Management*, **14**(1/3), 95–108.

Elliott, R. (2000). Contra postmodernism: Machiavelli on limits to the malleability of consciousness. In P. Harris, A. Lock and P. Rees (eds), *Machiavelli, Marketing and Management*. London: Routledge.

Ellis, J. (2000). *Seeing Things: Television in an Age of Uncertainty*. London/New York: Taurus Publishers.

El-Murad, J. and West, D.C. (2003). Risk and creativity in advertising. *Journal of Marketing Management*, **19**, 657–73.

El-Murad, J. and West, D.C. (2004). The definition and measurement of creativity: what do we know? *Journal of Advertising Research*, **44**, 188–201.

Engel, J.F., Warshaw, M.R. and Kinnear, T.C. (1994). *Promotional Strategy: Managing the Marketing Communications Process*, 8th edition. Burr Ridge, IL: Irwin.

Englis, B.G. and Solomon, M.D. (1995). To be or not to be: lifestyle imagery, reference groups, and the clustering of America. *Journal of Advertising*, **24**, 13–22.

Ephron, E. (1995). More weeks, less weight: the shelf-space model of advertising. *Journal of Advertising Research*, **35**(3), 18–23.

Ephron, E. (1997). Recency planning (media planning). *Admap UK*, February.

Ephron, E. (1998). Optimizers and media planning. *Journal of Advertising Research*, **38**(4).

Erdem, T. and Swait. J. (1998). Brand equity as a signaling phenomenon. *Journal of Consumer Psychology*, **7**(2), 131–57.

Erdem, T. Swait, J. and Louvière, J. (2002). The impact of brand credibility on consumer price sensitivity. *International Journal of Research in Marketing*, **19**(1), 1–19.

Escalas, J.E. (2004). Narrative processing: building consumer connections to brands. *Journal of Consumer Psychology*, **14**, 168–80.

Escalas, J.E. (2007). Self-referencing and persuasion: narrative transportation versus analytical elaboration. *Journal of Consumer Research*, **33**(4).

Escalas, J.E. and Bettman, J.R. (2005). Self-construal, reference groups, and brand meaning. *Journal of Consumer Research*, **32**, 378–89.

Etgar, M. and Goodwin, S.A. (1982). One-sided versus two-sided comparative message appeals for new brand introductions. *Journal of Consumer Research*, **8**, 460–5.

Evans, M., Jamal, A. and Foxall, G. (2006). *Consumer Behaviour*. Chichester: John Wiley & Sons, Ltd.

Fabrega, F. (2004). Zara. El modela de negocia de Inditex. Cited in C. Lopez and Y. Fan (2005) *Internationalisation of Spanish Fashion Brand Zara*. Brunel University, UK.

Farquhar, P. (1989). Managing brand equity. *Marketing Research*, **1**, 24-33.

Farrelly, F., Quester, P. and Greyser, S.A. (2005). Defending the co-branding benefits of B2B partnerships: the case of ambush marketing. *Journal of Advertising Research*, **45**, 339-48.

Farris, P.W. and Reibstein, D.J. (1979). How prices, ad expenditures, and profits are linked. *Harvard Business Review*, Nov/Dec, 173-84.

Farsides, T. (2009). Charitable giving and donor motivation. Economic and Social Research Council (ESRC), University of Sussex.

Feick, L.F. and Price, L.L. (1987). The market maven: a diffuser of marketplace information. *Journal of Marketing*, **51**(1), 83-97.

Felton, G. (1994). *Advertising Concept and Copy*. London: Prentice-Hall.

Fennell, G. (1978). Perceptions of the product-use situation. *Journal of Marketing*, **42**, 38-47.

Festinger, L. (1957). *A Theory of Cognitive Dissonance*. Stanford, CA: Stanford University Press.

Fill, C. (2001). Essentially a matter of consistency: integrated marketing communications. *The Marketing Review*, **1**(4), 409-25.

Fill, C. (2002). *Marketing Communications: Contexts, Contents and Strategies*, 3rd edition. Upper Saddle, NJ: Prentice Hall.

Fill, C. (2005). *Marketing Communications: Engagement, Strategies and Practice*, 4th edition. London: FT Prentice Hall.

Firat, A.F., Dholakia, N. and Venkatesh, A. (1995). Marketing in a postmodern world. *European Journal of Marketing*, **29**(1), 40-56.

Fisk, R.P., Brown, S.W. and Bitner, M.J. (1993). Tracking the evolution of the services marketing literature. *Journal of Retailing*, **69**(1), 61-103.

Flynn, L.R., Goldsmith, R.E. and Eastman, J. (1996). Opinion leaders and opinion seekers: two new measurement scales. *Journal of the Academy of Marketing Science*, **24**(2), 137-47.

Ford, J. (2007). *Communication and Design: Telling a Complete Brand Narrative, Advertising, Branding Communication and Design*.

Foucault, M. (1977). *Discipline and Punish: The Birth of the Prison*. Cited by A.D. Brown, M. Humphreys and P.M. Gurney (2005). Narrative, identity and change: a case study of Laskarina Holidays. *Journal of Organisational Change Management*, **18**(4), 312-26.

Fournier, S.M. (1998). Consumers and their brands: developing relationship theory in consumer research. *Journal of Consumer Research*, **24**(4), 343-73.

Fournier, S.M., Sele, K. and Schögel, M. (2005). The paradox of brand community management. *Thexis*, **13**, 16-20.

Foxall, G. and Goldsmith, R. (1994). *Consumer Psychology for Marketing*. London: Routledge.

Frazer, C.F., Sheehan, K.B. and Patti, C.H. (2002). Advertising strategy and effective advertising: comparing the US and Australia. *Journal of Marketing Communications*, **8**(3), 149-62.

Furse, D.H., Punj, G.N. and Stewart, D.W. (1984). A typology of individual search strategies among purchasers of new automobiles. *Journal of Consumer Research*, **10**, 417-31.

Gabbott, M. and Clulow, V. (1999). The elaboration likelihood model of persuasive communication. In P. Kitchen (ed.), *Marketing Communications: Principle and Practice*. London: Thomson.

Gabel, T.G. and Boller, G.W. (2003). An introduction to politician-targeted marketing and the political customer in the United States. *Advances in Consumer Research*, **30**, 325-31.

Gabriel, Y. (1999). Cited by A.D. Brown, M. Humphreys and P.M. Gurney (2005). Narrative, identity and change: a case study of Laskarina Holidays. *Journal of Organisational Change Management*, **18**(4), 312-26.

Gail, T. and Codruta C. (2001). Types of humour in advertising. *Review of Business*, **22**(2), 92-5.

Gail, T. and Eves, A. (1999). The use of rhetorical devices in advertising. *Journal of Advertising Research*, **39**(4), 39-43.

Garfield, R. (2006). In humiliating Microsoft, Apple's so charming; Bob Garfield's ad review. *Advertising Age*, **77**(20).

Gengler, C.E. and Reynolds, T.J. (1995). Consumer understanding and advertising strategy: analysis and strategic translation of laddering data. *Journal of Advertising Research*, **53**(4), 19-33.

Gensch, D. (1987). A two-stage disaggregate attribution choice model. *Marketing Science*, **6**, 223-31.

Gil, R., Andres, E. and Salinas, E. (2007). Family as a source of consumer-based brand equity. *Journal of Product and Brand Management*, **16**, 188-99.

Ginter, J.L. (1974). An experimental investigation of attitude change and choice of a new brand. *Journal of Marketing Research*, **11**, 30-40.

Gladwell, M. (2000). *Tipping Point*. London: Little Brown.

Gobe, M. (2001). *Emotional Branding: The New Paradigm for Connecting Brands to People*. New York: Allworth Press.

Godin, S. (1999). *Permission Marketing*. New York: Simon & Shuster.

Gordon, W. (1991). Assessing the brand through research. In D. Cowley, (ed.), *Understanding Brands*. London: Kogan Page.

Govers, R.C.M. and Schoormans, J.P.L. (2005). Product personality and its influence on consumer preference. *Journal of Consumer Marketing*, **22**(4), 189.

Grant, J. (2006). *The Brand Innovation: How to Build Brands, Redefine Markets and Defy Conventions*. Chichester: John Wiley & Sons, Ltd.

Gregan-Paxton, J., Hibbard, J.D., Brunel, F.F. and Azar, P. (2002). So that's what that is? Examining the impact of analogy on consumer knowledge development for really new products. *Psychology & Marketing*, **16**(6), 533-50.

Gregory, J.R. (2004). *The Best of Branding: Best Practices Corporate Branding*. New York: McGraw-Hill.

Greve, F. (1998). Bottled water: a sign of health or wealth? *Miami Herald*.

Grewal, D., Kavanoor, S., Fern, E.F., Costley, C. and Barnes, J. (1997). Comparative versus noncomparative advertising: a meta-analysis. *Journal of Marketing*, **36**, 345-55.

Grönroos, C. (2004). The relationship marketing process: communication, interaction, dialogue, value. *Journal of Business and Industrial Marketing*, **19**(2), 99-113.

Grönroos, C. and Lindberg-Repo, K. (1998). Integrated marketing communications: the communications aspect of relationship marketing. *Integrated Communications Research Journal*, **4**(1), 10.

Groucutt, J. (2006). The life and death and resuscitation of brands. *Handbook of Business Strategy*, **1**(1), 101-6.

Grubb, E. and Hupp, G. (1968). Perception of self, generalised stereotypes and brand selection. *Journal of Marketing Research*, **5**, 58-63.

Grunig, J. (1992). Communication, public relations and effective organisations. In J. Grunig (ed.), *Excellence in Public Relations and Communications Management* (pp. 1-30). New Jersey: Hillsdale.

Grunig, J. and Hunt, T. (1984). *Managing Public Relations*. New York: Holt.

Gummesson, E. (1999). *Total Relationship Marketing: Rethinking Marketing Management – From 4Ps to 30Rs*. Oxford: Butterworth-Heinemann.

Gurău, C. (2008). Integrated online marketing communication: implementation and management. *Journal of Communication Management*, **12**(2), 169-84.

Gustafsson, A., Johnson, M.D. and Roos, I. (2005). The effects of customer satisfaction, relationship commitment, and triggers on customer retention. *Journal of Marketing*, **69**, 210-18.

Gutman, J. and Mioulis, G. (2003). Communicating a quality position in service delivery: an application in higher education. *Managing Service Quality*, **3**(2), 105-11.

Gwinner, K.P. and Eaton, J. (1999). Building brand image through event sponsorship: the role of image transfer. *Journal of Advertising*, **28**(4), 47-57.

Hackley, C. (1999). The communications process and the semiotic boundary. In P.J. Kitchen (ed.), *Marketing Communications: Principles and Practice*. London: Thomson International Business Press.

Hackley, C. and Kitchen, P. (1998). IMC: a consumer psychological perspective. *Marketing Intelligence and Planning*, **16**(3), 229-35.

Hagel, J. (1999). Net gain: expanding markets through virtual communities. *Journal of Interactive Marketing*, **13**(1), 55-65.

Hall, M. (1992). Using advertising frameworks. *Admap,* March, 17–21.

Harris, P. and Lock, A. (1996). Machiavellian marketing: the development of corporate lobbying in the UK. *Journal of Marketing Management,* **12**, 313–28.

Hart, S. (1998). Developing new brand names. In S. Hart and J. Murphy (eds), *Brands: The New Wealth Creators* (pp. 34–45). Basingstoke: Macmillan.

Hart, S. and Murphy, J. (eds) (1998). *Brands: The New Wealth Creators.* Basingstoke: Macmillan.

Harvey, B. (1997). The expanded ARF model: bridge to the accountable advertising future. *Journal of Advertising Research,* **37**, 11–20.

Hatch, M.J. and Schultz, M. (2001). Are the strategic stars aligned? *Harvard Business Review on Marketing,* 109–26.

Hatch, M.J. and Schultz, M. (2002). Scaling the Tower of Babel: relational differences between identity, image and culture in organisations. In M. Schultz, M.J. Hatch and M.H. Larsen (eds), *The Expressive Organisation: Linking Identity, Reputation and the Corporate Brand.* Oxford: Oxford University Press.

Hauser, J.R. and Wernerfelt, B. (1990). An evaluation cost model of consideration sets. *Journal of Consumer Research,* **16**, 393–408.

Heath, R., Brandt, D. and Nairn, A. (2006). Brand relationship: strengthened by emotion, weakened by attention. *Journal of Advertising Research,* **46**, 410–19.

Heath, R. and Nairn, A. (2005). Measuring affective advertising: implications of low attention processing on recall. *Journal of Advertising Research,* **45**(2), 269–81.

Heath, T.B. and Chatterjee, S. (1995). Asymmetric decoy effects on lower-quality versus higher-quality brands: meta-analytic and experimental effects. *Journal of Consumer Research,* **22**, 268–83.

Heclo, H. (2000). Campaigning and governing: a conspectus In N. Norstein and T. Mann (eds), *The Permanent Campaign and its Future* (pp. 1–37). Washington DC: American Enterprise Institute and the Brookings Institute.

Henderson, P.W. and Cote, J.A. (1998). Guidelines for selecting or modifying logos. *Journal of Marketing,* **62**, 14–30.

Henderson, P.W., Giese, J.L. and Cote, J.A. (2004). Impression management using typeface design. *Journal of Marketing,* **68**, 60–72.

Hetzel, P. (2002). When hyperreality, reality, fiction and non-fiction are brought together: a fragmented vision of the mall in America through personal interpretation. In M. Solomon, G. Bambossy and S. Askegaard (eds), *Consumer Behaviour: A European Perspective.* London: FT/Prentice Hall.

Higgins, E.T. (2006). Value for hedonic experience and engagement. *Psychological Review,* **113**, 439–60.

Hoch, S.J. (2002). Product experience is seductive. *Journal of Consumer Research,* **29**(4), 448–54.

Hoffman, D.L. and Novak, P.T. (1999). Marketing in hyper computer-mediated environments: conceptual foundations. *Journal of Marketing,* **60**, 50–68.

Holbrook, M.B. and Hirschman, E.C. (1982). The experiential aspects of consumption: consumer fantasies, feelings and fun. *Journal of Consumer Research,* **18**, 13–28.

Holden, S.J.S. and Lutz, R.J. (1992). Ask not what the brand can evoke: ask what can evoke the brand? *Advances in Consumer Research,* **19**(1), 101–7.

Holm, O. (2006). Integrated marketing communication: from tactics to strategy. *Corporate Communications: An International Journal,* **11**(1), 23–33.

Holt, D.B. (2004). *How Brands Become Icons: The Principles of Cultural Branding.* Cambridge, MA: Harvard Business School Press.

Hooley, G.J., Saunders, J. A. and Piercy, N.F. (1998). *Marketing Strategy and Competitive Positioning,* 2nd edition. Upper Saddle, NJ: Prentice Hall.

Howard, J. (1989). *Consumer Behaviour in Marketing Strategy.* Upper Saddle River, NJ: Prentice Hall.

Hoyer, W.D. (1984). An examination of consumer decision making for a common repeat purchase product. *Journal of Consumer Research,* **11**, 822–9.

Hsieh, M.H., Pan, S.L. and Setiono, R. (2004). Product-, corporate- and country-image dimensions and purchase behaviour: a multi-country analysis. *Academy of Marketing Science,* **32**(3), 251–70.

Hsu, C.K. and McDonald, D. (2002). An examination on multiple celebrity endorsers in advertising. *Journal of Product and Brand Management*, **11**(1).

Huber, J., Payne, J.W. and Puto, C. (1982). Adding asymmetrically dominated alternatives: violations of regularity and the similarity hypothesis. *Journal of Consumer Research*, **9**, 90-8.

Hughes, G. (1999). Marketing communications activities. In P.J. Kitchen (ed.), *Marketing Communications: Principles and Practice*. London: Thomson Business Press.

Hughes, G. and Fill, C. (2007). Redefining the nature and format of the marketing communications mix. *The Marketing Review*, **7**(1), 45-57.

Humby, C. and Hunt, T. (2003). *Scoring Points: How Tesco is Winning Customer Loyalty*. London: Kogan Page.

Hutt, M.D. and Speh, T.W. (1998). *Business Marketing Management: A Strategic View of Industrial and Organisational Markets*, 6th edition. London: Dryden Press.

Iddiols, D. (2000). Marketing superglue: client perceptions of IMC. *Admap*.

Interbrand (2009). Best Retail Brands 2009: global perspective on a changing marketplace.

Iqbal, M. (2007). The elongated tail of brand communication: an approach to brand building incorporating long-tail economics. Ogilvy & Mather Advertising Agency.

Jaffe, J. (2005). *Life After the 30-Second Spot: Energise Your Brand with a Bold Mix of Alternatives to Traditional Advertising*. New York: John Wiley & Sons, Inc.

Jaffe, J. (2007). *Join the Conversation: How to engage marketing weary consumers with the power of community, dialogue and partnership*. New York: John Wiley & Sons, Inc.

Jain, S.P. and Posavac, S.S. (2004). Valenced comparisons. *Journal of Marketing Research*, **16**, 46-58.

Jenkinson, A. (2006). Planning and evaluating communications in an integrated organisation. *Journal of Targeting, Measurement and Analysis of Marketing*, **15**, 47-64.

Jensen, K.B. (1991). When is meaning? Communication theory, pragmatism and mass media reception. In J. Anderson (ed.), *Communication Yearbook 14* (pp. 3-32). London: Sage.

Jensen, M.B. and Fischer, L.H. (2004). *E-Branding*. Copenhagen: Gyldendal.

Jensen, M.B. and Jepsen, A.L. (2006). Online Marketing Communications: Need for a new typology for IMC? In K. Podnar and Z. Jancic (eds), *Contemporary Issues in Corporate and Marketing Communications: Towards a socially responsible future* (pp. 133-43). Ljubljana: Pristop.

Jensen, R. (2001). *The Dream Society: How the Coming Shift from Information to Imagination Will Transform Your Business*. New York: McGraw-Hill.

Jewell, R.D. and Unnava, H.R. (2003). When competitive interference can be beneficial. *Journal of Consumer Research*, **30**, 283-91.

Joachimsthaler, E. and Aaker, D.A. (1997). Building brands without mass media. *Harvard Business Review*, **75**(1), 39-50.

Jobber, D. (2004). *Principles and Practice of Marketing*, 4th edition. London: McGraw-Hill.

Johar, G.V. and Pham, M.T. (1999). Relatedness, prominence, and constructive sponsor identification. *Journal of Marketing Research*, **36**, 299-312.

Johar, J.S. and Sirgy, J.M. (1991). Value-expressive versus utilitarian advertising appeals: when and why to use which appeal. *Journal of Advertising*, **20**, 23-33.

Johnson, M.D. (1984). Consumer choice strategies for comparing non-compatible alternatives. *Journal of Consumer Research*, **11**, 741-53.

Jones, J.P. (1990). Ad spending: maintaining market share. *Harvard Business Review*, **68**, 38-42.

Jones, J.P. (1995). Single-source begins to fulfill its promise. *Journal of Advertising Research*, **35**(3), 9-15.

Kaikati, A.M. and Kaikati, J.G. (2004). Stealth marketing: how to reach consumers surreptitiously. *California Management Review*, **46**(4), 6-22.

Kalafatis, S.P., Tsogas, M.H and Blankston, C. (2000). Positioning strategies in business markets. *Journal of Business and International Marketing*, **15**(6), 416-37.

Kambitsis, C., Harahousou, Y., Theodorakis, N. and Chatzibeis, G. (2002). Sports advertising in print media: the case of the 2000 Olympic Games. *Corporate Communications: An International Journal*, **7**(3), 155-61.

Kapferer, J.-N. (1992). *The New Strategic Brand Management: Creating and Sustaining Brand Equity Long Term*. London: Kogan Page.

Kapferer, J.-N. (1994). *Strategic Brand Management: New Approaches to Creating and Evaluating Brand Equity*. London: Kogan Page.

Kapferer, J.-N. (1997). *Strategic Brand Management*. London: Kogan Page.

Kapferer, J.-N. (2000). *Strategic Brand Management*, 2nd edition. London: Kogan Page.

Kapferer, J.-N. (2004). *The New Strategic Brand Management: Creating and Sustaining Brand Equity Long Term*. London: Kogan Page.

Katsioloudes, M., Grant, J. and McKechnie, D.S. (2007). Social marketing: strengthening company-customer bonds. *Journal of Business Strategy, 28*(3), 56–64.

Katz, E. and Laszerfeld, P.F. (1955). *Personal Influence: The Part Played by People in the Flow of Mass Communication*. Glencoe, IL: Free Press.

Keegan, W.J. and Green, M.C. (2005). *Global Marketing*, 4th edition. New Jersey: Pearson Education.

Keillor, B.D., Boller, G.W. and Luke, R.H. (1998). Firm-level political behavior and level of foreign marketing involvement: implications for international marketing strategy. *Journal of Marketing Management, 8*(1), 1–11.

Keller, K.L. (1991). Memory and evaluation effects in competitive advertising environments. *Journal of Consumer Research, 17*, 463–76.

Keller, K.L. (1993). Conceptualizing, measuring, and managing customer-based brand equity. *Journal of Marketing, 57*(1), 1–22.

Keller, K.L. (1998). *Strategic Brand Management: Building, Measuring, and Managing Brand Equity*. Upper Saddle River, NJ: Prentice Hall.

Keller, K.L. (1999). Brand mantras: rationale, criteria, and examples. *Journal of Marketing Management, 15*, 43–51.

Keller, K.L. (2000). The brand report card. *Harvard Business Review on Marketing*. Cambridge, MA: Harvard Business School Press.

Keller, K.L. (2001). Building customer-based brand equity. *Marketing Management, 10*, 14–19.

Keller, K.L. (2001a). Mastering the marketing communications mix: micro and macro perspectives on integrated marketing communication programmes. *Journal of Marketing Management, 17*, 819–947.

Keller, K.L. (2001b). Building customer-based brand equity. *Marketing Management, 10*, 14–19.

Keller, K.L. (2003). *Strategic Brand Management Building: Measuring, and Managing Brand Equity*, 2nd edition. Upper Saddle River, NJ: Pearson Education.

Keller, K.L. (2007). *Strategic Brand Management: Building, Valuing and Managing Brand Equity*, 3rd edition. London: Pearson International.

Keller, K.L., Heckler, S.E. and Houston, M.J. (1998). The effects of brand name suggestiveness on advertising recall. *Journal of Marketing, 62*, 48–57.

Kelman, H.C. (1961). Processes of opinion change. *Public Opinion Quarterly, 25*, 57–78.

Kenny, L. and Aron, O. (2001). Consumer brand classifications: an assessment of culture of origin versus country of origin. *Journal of Product and Brand Management, 10*(2), 120–36.

Kim, W.C. and Mauborgne, R. (1999). Creating new market space. *Harvard Business Review, 77*(1), 83–93.

Kitchen, P.J. (1994). The marketing communications revolution – a new Leviathan unveiled? *Marketing Intelligence and Planning, 12*(2), 19–25.

Kitchen, P.J. (1999). *Marketing Communications: Principles and Practice*. London: International Thomson Business Press.

Kitchen, P.J. (2003). Critical times: an integrated marketing communication perspective. Paper presented at the First International Conference on Business Economics, Management and Marketing, Athens.

Kitchen, P.J., Brignell, J., Li, T. and Spickett-Jones, G.J. (2004). The emergence of IMC: a theoretical perspective. *Journal of Advertising Research, 44*(1), 19–30.

Kitchen, P.J. and Proctor, T. (2002). Communications in postmodern integrated marketing campaigns. *Corporate Communications: An International Journal, 7*(3), 144-54.

Kitchen, P.J. and Schultz, D.E. (1999). A multi-country comparison of the drive for IMC. *Journal of Advertising Research*, **1**.

Kjedgaard, D. (2009). The meaning of style? Style reflexivity among Danish high school youths. *Journal of Consumer Behaviour*, **8**, 71–83.

Klapper, J.T. (1960). *The Effects of Mass Communication*. New York: Free Press.

Klein, N. (2000). *No Logo*. London: Flamingo.

Klink, R. (2001). Creating meaningful new brand names: a study of semantics and sound symbolism. *Journal of Marketing Theory and Practice*, Spring, 27–34.

Kohli, C.S., Harich, K.R. and Leuthesser, L. (2005). Creating brand identity: a study of evaluation of new brand names. *Journal of Business Research*, **58**, 1506–15.

Korgaonkar, P.K. and Bellinger, D. (1985). Correlates of successful advertising campaigns. *Journal of Advertising Research*, **24**, 34–9.

Koslow, S., Sasser, S.L. and Riordan, E.A. (2006). Do marketers get the advertising they need or the advertising they deserve? *Journal of Advertising*, **35**(3), 81–101.

Kotler, P. (1991). *Marketing Management: Analysis, Planning, Implementation and Control*. Upper Saddle, NJ: Prentice Hall.

Kotler, P. (1997). *Marketing Management*. Upper Saddle, NJ: Prentice Hall.

Kotler, P. (2000). *Marketing Management*. Upper Saddle, NJ: Prentice Hall.

Kotler, P. and Armstrong, G. (1996). *Principles of Marketing*. Upper Saddle River, NJ: Prentice Hall.

Kotler, P. and Armstrong, G. (2005). *Principles of Marketing,* 11th edition. Upper Saddle, NJ: Prentice Hall.

Kotler, P. and Keller K.L (2006). *Marketing Management*, 12th edition. Upper Saddle River, NJ: Pearson Education.

Kotler, P., Wong, V., Saunders, J. and Armstrong, G. (2004). *Principles of Marketing,* 4th edition. London: Prentice Hall.

Kover, A.J., Goldberg, S.M. and James, W.M. (1995). Creativity vs. effectiveness. An integrating classification for advertising. *Journal of Advertising Research*, **35**, 29–40.

Kover, A.J., James, W.L. and Sonner, B.S. (1997). To whom do advertising creatives write? An inferential answer. *Journal of Advertising Research*, **37**, 41–53.

Kozinets, R.V. (2001). Utopian enterprise: articulating the meanings of *Star Trek's* culture of consumption. *Journal of Consumer Research*, **28**, 67–88.

Kroeber-Riel, W. (1993). *Bild Kommunikation*. Vahlen.

Krugman, H.E. (1972). Why three exposures may be enough. *Journal of Advertising Research*, **12**(6), 11–14.

Krugman, H.E. (1988). Limits of attention to advertising. *Journal of Advertising Research*, **38**, 47–50.

Kunde, J. (2002). *Corporate Religion: Building a Strong Brand through Personality and Corporate Soul*. London: Thomson.

L'Etang, J. (2008). *Public Relations Concepts, Practice and Critique*. London: Sage.

La Farele, C. and Choi, S.M. (2005). The importance of perceived endorser credibility in South Korea. *Journal of Current Issues and Research in Advertising*, 67–72.

Laczniak, R.N., DeCarlo, T.E., and Ramaswami, S.N. (2001). Consumers' responses to negative word-of-mouth communication: an attribution theory perspective. *Journal of Consumer Psychology*, **11**(1), 57–73.

Lange, F. and Dahlén, M. (2003). Let's be strange: brand familiarity and ad-brand incongruency. *Journal of Product and Brand Management*, **12**(7), 449–61.

Lardinoit, T. and Quester, P.G (2001). Attitudinal effects of combined sponsorship and sponsors' prominence on basketball in Europe. *Journal of Advertising Research*, **41**(1), 48–58.

Laskey, H.A., Day, E. and Crask, M.R. (1989). Typology of main message strategies for television commercials. *Journal of Advertising*, **18**(1), 36–41.

Laszerfeld, P., Berelson, B. and Gaudet H. (1948). *The People's Choice*. New York: Columbia University Press.

Laszerfeld, P. and Menzel, H. (1963). Mass media and personal influence. In W. Schramm (ed.), *The Science of Human Communication* (pp. 94-115). New York: Basic Books.

Lautman, M.R. (1993). The ABC of positioning. *Marketing Research*, Winter, 12-18.

Law, S. (2002). Can repeating a brand claim lead to memory confusion? The effects of claim similarity and concurrent repetition. *Journal of Marketing Research*, **39**, 366-78.

Law, S. and Braun, K.A. (2000). I'll have what she's having: gauging the impact of product placements on viewers. *Psychology and Marketing*, **17**(12), 1059-76.

Lea-Greenwood, G. (1993). River Island clothing: a case study in changing image. *International Journal of Retail and Distribution Management*, **21**(3), 60-4.

Leclerc, F., Schmitt, B.H. and Dubé, L. (1994). Foreign branding and its effects on product perceptions and attitudes. *Journal of Marketing Research*, **31**(2), 263-70.

Lee, D.H. and Park, C.H. (2007). Conceptualisation and measurement of multidimensionality of integrated marketing communications. *Journal of Advertising Research*, 222-36.

Lee, M. and Johnson, C. (2005). *Principle of Advertising*, 2nd edition. Haworth Press.

Levy, M. and Weitz, B.A. (2007). *Retailing Management*, 6th edition. New York: McGraw-Hill.

Levy, S.J. (2003). The consumption of stories (unpublished paper). In Zaltman, G. (ed.), *How Customers Think: Essential Insights into the Mind of the Market*. Cambridge, MA: Harvard Business School Press.

Light, L. (2004). More knowledge can only lead to better ad creative. *New Media Age*, 7 October.

Lightfoot, C. and Gerstman, R. (1998). Brand packaging. In S. Hart and J. Murphy (eds), *Brands: The New Wealth Creators* (pp. 46-55). Basingstoke: Macmillan.

Lindberg-Repo, K. and Grönroos, C. (1999). Word of mouth referrals in the domain of relationship marketing. *The Australasian Marketing Journal*, **7**(1), 115.

Lindberg-Repo, K. and Grönroos, G. (2004). Conceptualising communications strategy for a relational perspective. *Industrial Marketing Management*, **33**(3), 229-38.

Lindström, M. and Andersen, T. F. (2000). *Brand Building on the Internet*. London: Kogan Page.

Linton, I. and Morley, K. (1995). *Integrated Marketing Communications*. Oxford: Butterworth-Heinemann.

Liodice, R. (2008). Essentials for integrated marketing. A speech by Bob Liodice (CEO of the Association of National Advertisers). *Advertising Age*, 16 June.

Loda, M.D. and Coleman, B.C. (2005). Sequence matters: a more effective way to use advertising and publicity. *Journal of Advertising Research*, **45**, 362-72.

Lott, B. and Maluso, D. (eds) (1995). *The Social Psychology of Interpersonal Discrimination*. New York: Guilford Press.

Louro, M. and Cunha, P. (2001). Brand management paradigms. *Journal of Marketing Management*, **17**(7-8), 849-75.

Lovelock, C.H. (1996). *Service Marketing*, 3rd edition. Upper Saddle, NJ: Prentice Hall.

Lucas, D.B. and Britt, S.H. (1963). *Measuring Advertising Effectiveness*. New York: McGraw-Hill.

Lutz, K.A. and Lutz, R.J. (1997). Effects of interactive imagery on learning: application to advertising. *Journal of Applied Psychology*, **62**(4), 493-8.

MacCrae, C. (1995). *World Class Brands*. New York: Addison-Wesley.

Machleit, K.A., Allen, C.T. and Madden, T.J. (1993). The mature brand and brand interest: an alternative consequence of ad-evoked affect. *Journal of Marketing*, **57**(4), 72-82.

MacInnis, D.J., Moorman, C. and Jaworski, B.J. (1991). Enhancing and measuring consumers' motivation, opportunity, and ability to process brand information from ads. *Journal of Marketing*, **55**, 32-53.

MacKenzie, S.B. and Lutz, R.J. (1989). An empirical examination of the structural antecedents of attitude toward the ad in an advertising pretesting context. *Journal of Marketing*, **53**, 48-65.

MacLachlan, J. (1984). Making a message memorable and persuasive. *Journal of Advertising Research*, **23**(6), 51-9.

Madden, T.J. and Weinberger, M.G. (1984). Humour in advertising: a practitioner view. *Journal of Advertising Research*, **24**(4), 23-9.

Maheswaran, D., Mackie, D.M. and Chaiken, S. (1992). Brand name as a heuristic cue: the effects of task importance and expectancy confirmation on consumer judgments. *Journal of Consumer Psychology*, **1**(4), 317–36.

Malthouse, E.C. and Calder, B.J. (2005). Relationship branding and CRM. In A.M. Tybout and T. Calkins (eds), *Kellogg on Branding: the Marketing Faculty of The Kellogg School of Management*. New York: John Wiley & Sons, Inc.

Marcus, C. (2008). Reinvention of TV advertising. In B.J. Calder (ed.), *Kellogg on Branding: the Marketing Faculty of The Kellogg School of Management*. New York: John Wiley & Sons, Inc.

Marketing Week (2004). ASA (Advertising Standards Authority). *Marketing Week*, 21 October.

Martesen, A. and Grønholdt, L. (2004). Building brand equity: a customer-based modelling approach. *Journal of Management Systems*, **16**(3), 37–51.

Maslin, B. (1982). Article in the *New York Times,* cited in Segrave, K. (2004) *Product Placement in Hollywood Films: A History*. Performing Arts.

Maslow, A.H. (1970). *Motivation and Personality*. New York: Harper Row.

Mason, R.B. and Cochetel, F. (2006). Residual brand awareness following termination of a long-term event sponsorship and the appointment of a new sponsor. *Journal of Marketing Communications*, **12**(2), 125–44.

McAlexander, J.H., Kim. S.K. and Roberts, S.D. (2003). Loyalty: the influence of satisfaction and brand community integration. *Journal of Marketing Theory and Practice*, **11**(4), 1–11.

McAlexander, J.H., Koenig, H.F. and Schouten, J.W. (2005). Building a university brand community: the long-term impact of shared experiences. *Journal of Marketing for Higher Education*, **14**(2), 61–79.

McAlexander, J.H., Schouten, J.W. and Koenig, H.F. (2002). Building brand community. *Journal of Marketing*, **27**(4), 38–54.

McCracken, G.C. (1986). Culture and consumption: a theoretical account of the structure and movement of the cultural meaning of consumer goods. *Journal of Consumer Research*, **13**, 71–84.

McCracken, G.C. (1988). *Culture and Consumption: New Approaches to the Symbolic Character of Consumer Goods and Activities*. Bloomington: Indiana University Press.

McCracken, G.C. (1999). *Culture and Consumption: New Approaches to the Symbolic Character of Consumer Goods and Activities*. Bloomington: Indiana University Press.

McCracken, G.C. (2005). *Culture and Consumption: Markets, Meaning and Brand Management*, 2nd edition. Bloomington: Indiana University Press.

McDonald, C. (1991). Sponsorship and the image of the sponsor. *European Journal of Marketing*, **25**(11), 31–8.

McEnally, M. and de Chernatony, L. (1999). The evolving nature of branding: consumer and managerial considerations. *Academy of Marketing Science Review*, **99**(2), 1–38.

McGoldrick, P. (2002). *Retail Marketing*, 2nd edition. London: McGraw-Hill.

McGuigan, J. (2006). *Modernity and Postmodern Culture*. Milton Keynes: Open University Press.

McIlroy, A. and Barnett, S. (2000). Building customer relationships: do discount cards work? *Managing Service Quality*, **10**(6), 347–55.

McQuail, D. (1989). *Mass Communication Theory: An Introduction*. Los Angeles: Sage.

McQuail, D. (2000). *Mass Communication Theory*, 4th edition. London: Sage.

McQuarrie, E.F. and Mick, D.G. (1996). Figures of rhetoric in advertising language. *Journal of Consumer Research*, **22**, 424–38.

McQuarrie, E.F. and Phillips, B.J. (2005). Indirect persuasion in advertising. *Journal of Advertising*, **34**(2), 7–20.

Menon, S. and Kahn, B.E. (1995). The impact of context on variety seeking in product choices. *Journal of Consumer Research*, **22**, 285–95.

Mercury Associates (2004). Study available at: www.mercury-assoc.com.

Meyvis, T. and Janiszewski, C. (2004). When are broader brands stronger brands? An accessibility perspective on the success of brand extensions. *Journal of Consumer Research*, **31**, 346–57.

Mick, D. (1986). Consumer research and semiotics: exploring the morphology of signs, symbols and significance. *Journal of Consumer Research*, **13**, 196–213.

Milas, G. and Mlačić, B. (2007). Brand personality and human personality: findings from ratings of familiar Croatian brands. *Journal of Business Research*, **60**, 620–6.

Miller, E.G. and Kahn, B.E. (2005). Shades of meaning: the effect of colour and flavour names on consumer choice. *Journal of Consumer Research*, **32**, 86–92.

Miller, K. (2005). *Communication Theories, Perspectives and Contexts*, 2nd edition. New York: McGraw-Hill.

Miller, M.C. (1990). Hollywood: the ad. http://www.theatlantic.com/doc/199004/hollywood. Retrieved 26 July 2008.

Miller, N.E. (1959). Liberalization of basic S-R concepts; extensions to conflict behavior motivation and social learning. In S. Koch (ed.), *Psychology: A Study of a Science*, volume 2. New York: McGraw-Hill.

Miller, S. and Berry, L. (1998). Brand salience over brand image: two theories of advertising effectiveness. *Journal of Advertising Research*, **38**(5), 78–82.

Miller, W.I. (1997). *The Anatomy of Disgust*. Cambridge, MA: Harvard University Press.

Millward Brown (1994) Study available at: www.millwardbrown.com/brandz.

Mitra, A. (1995). Price cue utilization in product evaluations: the moderating role of motivation and attribute information. *Journal of Business Research*, **33**, 187–95.

Mooij, M. (1994). *Advertising Worldwide: Concepts, Theories and Practice of International, Multinational and Global Advertising*, 2nd edition. Upper Saddle, NJ: Prentice Hall.

Moore, D.J., Reardon, R. and Durso, F.T. (1986). The generation effect in advertising appeals. *Advances in Consumer Research*, **13**(1), 117–20.

Morgan, A. (2009). *Eating the Big Fish*, 2nd edition. Chichester: John Wiley & Sons, Ltd.

Morgan, R. and Hunt, S. (1994). The commitment-trust theory of relationship marketing. *Journal of Marketing*, **58**, 20–38.

Morgan, R., Strong, C. and McGuinness, T. (2003). Product-market positioning and prospector strategy: an analysis of strategic patterns from the resource-based perspective. *European Journal of Marketing*, **10**, 1409–40.

Morgan, S.E. and Reichert, T. (1999). The message is in the metaphor: assessing the comprehension of metaphors in advertisements. *Journal of Advertising*, **28**(4), 1–12.

Mortimer, K. (2002). Integrating advertising theories with conceptual models of services advertising. *Journal of Service Marketing*, **16**(5), 460–8.

Moss, D., Warnaby, G. and Thame, L. (1996). Tactical publicity or strategic relationship management? An exploratory investigation of the role of public relations in the UK retail sector. *European Journal of Marketing*, **30**(12), 69–84.

Mottram, S. (1998). Branding the corporation. In S. Hart and J. Murphy (eds), *Brands: The New Wealth Creators*. New York: Macmillan.

Muniz, A. and Guinn, C. (2001). Brand community. *Journal of Consumer Research*, **27**(4), 412–32.

Muthukrishnan, A.V. (1995). Decision ambiguity and incumbent brand advantage. *Journal of Consumer Research*, **22**, 98–109.

Naples, M.J. (1997). *Effective Frequency*. Chichester: John Wiley & Sons, Ltd.

Needham, C. (2005). The permanent campaign. *Political Studies*, **53**, 343–61.

Negundi, P. (1990). Recall and consumer consideration sets: influencing choice without affecting brand evaluations. *Journal of Consumer Research*, **17**, 263–76.

Nelson, M.R. (2002). Recall of brand placements in computer/video games. *Journal of Advertising Research*, **42**, 80–92.

Newton, D.A. (1969). Get the most out of your sales force. *Harvard Business Review*, **47**(5), 130–43.

Normann, R. (1991). *Service Management: Strategy and Leadership in Service Businesses*. Chichester: John Wiley & Sons, Ltd.

Nugent, A. (2005). The global beer market: a world of two halves. *Euromonitor International.*

O'Malley, D. (1991). Sales without salience? *Admap,* September, 36-9.

Oakenfull, G., Blair, E., Gelb, B. and Dacin, P. (2000). Measuring brand meaning. *Journal of Advertising Research*, **40**, 43-53.

Ogilvy, D. (2007). *Ogilvy on Advertising: I Hate Rules*. London: Prion.

Ohmae, K. (1988). Getting back to strategy. *Harvard Business Review*, 149-56.

Ohman, N. (2007). Category, brand and advertising. Effects of salience. Working Paper Series, Stockholm School of Economics.

Öhman, N. and Dahlén, M. (2007). Brand salience and brand preference. Stockholm School of Economics Working Paper Series.

Olins, W. (2000). How brands are taking over the corporation. In M. Shultz, M.J. Hatch and M.H. Larsen (eds), *The Expressive Organisation*. Oxford: Oxford University Press.

Page, G. and Fearn, H. (2005). Corporate reputation: what do consumers really care about. *Journal of Advertising Research*, **45**(3), 305-12.

Pan, Y. and Lehmann, D. R. (1993). The influence of new brand entry on subjective brand judgments. *Journal of Consumer Research*, **20**, 76-86.

Patterson, M. (1998). Direct marketing in postmodernity: neo-tribes and direct communications. *Marketing Intelligence and Planning*, **16**(1), 68-74.

Patti, C.H. and Frazer, C.H. (1988). *Advertising: A Decision Making Approach*. London: Dryden Press.

Peck, H., Payne, A., Christopher, M. and Clark, M. (1999). *Relationship Marketing; Strategy and Implementation*. Oxford: Butterworth-Heinemann.

Peckham, J.O. (1981). *The Wheel of Marketing*. New York: AC Neilsen.

Pedrick, J.H. and Zufryden, F.S. (1993). Measuring the competitive effects of advertising media plans. *Journal of Advertising Research*, **33**(6), 11-20.

Peirce, C.S. (1883). In Solomon, M., Bambossy, G. and Askegaard, S. (2002) *Consumer Behaviour: A European Perspective*. Harlow: Pearson Education.

Petromilli, M., Morrison. D. and Million, M. (2002). Brand architecture: building brand portfolio value. *Strategy and Leadership*, **30**(5), 22-8.

Petty, R.E. and Cacioppo, J.T. (1979). Issue involvement can increase or decrease persuasion by enhancing message-relevant cognitive processes. *Journal of Personality and Social Psychology*, **37**, 1915-26.

Petty, R.E. and Cacioppo, J.T. (1981). *Attitudes and Persuasion: Classic and Contemporary Approaches.* Dubuque, IA: William C. Brown.

Petty, R.E. and Cacioppo, J.T. (1984). The effects of involvement on responses to argument quantity and quality: central and peripheral routes to persuasion. *Journal of Personality and Social Psychology*, **46**, 69-81.

Petty, R.E. and Cacioppo, J.T. (1986). *Communication and Persuasion: Central and Peripheral Routes to Attitude Change*. New York: Springer Verlag.

Petty, R.E., Cacioppo, J.T. and Schumann, D. (1983). Central and peripheral routes to advertising effectiveness: the moderating role of involvement. *Journal of Consumer Research*, **10**(2), 135-46.

Phillips, B.J. (1997). Thinking into it: consumer interpretation of complex advertising images. *Journal of Advertising*, **26**(2), 77-87.

Pickton, D. and Broderick, A. (2005). *Integrated Marketing Communications*, 2nd edition. London: Pearson Education.

Pieckza, M. (2006). Public relations expertise in practice. In J. L'Etang and M. Pieczka (eds), *Public Relations: Critical Debates and Contemporary Practice* (pp. 279-302). Mahwah, NJ: Lawrence Erbaum.

Plummer, J.T. (1984). How personality makes a difference. *Journal of Advertising Research,* **24**,27-31.

Poon, D.T.Y. and Prendergast, G. (2006). A new framework for evaluating sponsorship opportunities. *International Journal of Advertising*, **25**(4), 471-88.

Porter, M.E. (1986). Competition in global industries: a conceptual framework. In M.E. Porter (ed.), *Competition in Global Industries*. Cambridge, MA: Harvard Business School Press.

Porter, M. (1996). What is strategy? *Harvard Business Review*, November, 61-78.

Prelec, D., Wernerfelt, B. and Zettelmeyer, F. (1997). The role of inference in context effects: inferring what you want from what is available. *Journal of Consumer Research*, **24**, 118–25.

Proctor, T. and Kitchen, P. (2000). Communication in post-modern integrated marketing. *Corporate Communications*, **7**(3).

Pullig, C., Simmons, C.J. and Neteemyer, R.G. (2006). Brand dilution: when do new brands hurt existing brands? *Journal of Marketing*, **70**(2), 52–66.

Raghubir, P. and Greenleaf, E.A. (2006). Ratios in proportion: what should the shape of the package be? *Journal of Marketing*, **70**, 95–107.

Rajagopal, N. (2006). Measuring customer value and market dynamics for new products of a firm: an analytical construct for gaining competitive advantage. *Global Business and Economic Review*, **8**(3–4), 187–204.

Ramaswamy, V. (2008). Co-creating value through customers' experiences: the Nike case. *Strategy and Leadership*, **36**(5), 9–14.

Randall, G. (2000). *Branding: A Practical Guide to Planning Your Strategy*, 2nd edition. London: Kogan Page.

Ratchford, B.T. (1987). New insights about the FCB grid. *Journal of Advertising Research*, **27**(4), 24–38.

Ratner, R.K., Kahn, B.E. and Kahneman, D. (1999). Choosing less-preferred experiences for the sake of variety. *Journal of Consumer Research*, **26**, 1–15.

Ratneshwar, S., Barsalou, L.W., Pechmann, C. and Moore, M. (2001). Goal-derived categories: the role of personal and situational goals in category representations. *Journal of Consumer Psychology*, **10**(3), 147–57.

Ratneshwar, S., Pechmann, C. and Shocker, A.D. (1996). Goal-derived categories and the antecedents of across-category consideration. *Journal of Consumer Research*, **23**, 240–50.

Ratneshwar, S. and Shocker. A.D. (1991). Substitution in use and the role of usage context in product category structures. *Journal of Marketing Research*, **28**, 281–95.

Ratneshwar, S., Shocker, A.D. and Stewart, D.W. (1987). Toward understanding the attraction effect: the implications of product stimulus meaningfulness and familiarity. *Journal of Consumer Research*, **13**, 520–33.

Reader's Digest (2009). *Europe's most trusted brands in 2008*. Report available at: www.Rdtrusted-brands.com.

Reddy, M. (1979). The Conduit Metaphor. In A. Ortony (ed.) *Metaphor and Thought.* Cambridge: Cambridge University Press.

Reed, A., Wooten, D.B. and Bolton, L.E. (2002). The temporary construction of consumer attitudes. *Journal of Consumer Psychology*, **12**(4), 375–88.

Reed, P. (1989). Article in the *New York Times,* cited in Segrave, K. (2004) *Product Placement in Hollywood Films: A History.* Performing Arts.

Reichel, W. and Wood, L. (1997). Recency in media planning revisited. *Journal of Advertising Research*, **37**(4), 66–74.

Reichheld, F.F. and Sasser, W.E. (1990). Zero defections: quality comes to services. *Harvard Business Review*, Sept–Oct, 105–11.

Reid, M. (2003). IMC – performance relationship. Further insight and evidence from the Australian marketplace. *International Journal of Advertising*, **22**(2).

Reid, M. (2005). Performance auditing of integrated marketing communication (IMC). Actions and outcomes. *Journal of Advertising*, **34**(4), 41–54.

Reisberg, D. (2001). *Cognition: Exploring the Science of the Mind*, 2nd edition. New York: Norton.

Ries, A. and Trout, J. (1980). *Positioning: The Battle for Your Mind*. New York: McGraw-Hill.

Ries, A. and Trout, J. (1986). *Marketing Warfare*. New York: McGraw-Hill.

Riezebos, R. (2003). *Brand Management: A Theoretical and Practical Approach*. London: Prentice Hall.

Robertson, K. (1989). Strategically desirable brand name characteristics. *Journal of Consumer Marketing*, **6**, 61–71.

Rogers, E.M. (1962). *Diffusion of Innovations*. New York: Free Press.

Rogers, E.M. (1983). *Diffusion of Innovations*, 3rd edition. New York: Free Press.

Rook, D. (1987). The buying impulse. *Journal of Consumer Research*, **14**, 189-99.

Rossiter, J.R. and Bellman, S. (2005). *Marketing Communications: Theory and Applications*. London: Prentice Hall.

Rossiter, J.R. and Percy, L. (1998). *Advertising Communications and Promotion Management*, 2nd edition. Boston, MA: McGraw-Hill.

Rossiter, J.R., Percy, L. and Donovan, R.J. (1991). A better advertising planning grid. *Journal of Advertising Research*, **31**(5), 11-21.

Rossiter, J.R., Silberstein, R.B., Harris, P.G. and Neild, G. (2001). Brain imaging detection of visual scene encoding in long-term memory for TV commercials. *Journal of Advertising Research*, **41**, 13-21.

Rothschild, M.I. (1987). *Marketing Communications*. London: Heath.

Rowley, J. (2000). Product search in e-shopping: a review and research propositions. *Journal of Consumer Marketing*, **17**(1), 20-35.

Rowley, J. (2001). Remodelling marketing communications in an internet environment: electronic networking applications and policy. *Marketing Review*, **11**(3), 203-12.

Rowley, J. (2004). Partnering paradigms? Knowledge management and relational marketing. *Industrial Management and Data Systems*, **104**(2), 149-57.

Rubinstein, H. (1996). Brand first management. *Journal of Marketing Management*, **12**(4), 269-80.

Russell, C.A. (2002). Investigating the effectiveness of product placements in television shows: the role of modality and plot connection congruence on brand memory and attitude. *Journal of Consumer Research*, **29**(3), 306-18.

Russell, C.A. and Stern, B.B. (2006). Consumer characters and products: a balance model of sitcom product placement effects. *Journal of Advertising*, **35**(1), 7-21.

Russell, J.A., Weiss, A. and Mendelsohn, G.A. (1989). Affect grid: a single-item scale of pleasure and arousal. *Journal of Personality and Social Psychology*, **57**(3), 493-502.

Rust, R.T., Lemon, K.N. and Zeithaml, V.A. (2004). Return on marketing: using customer equity to focus marketing strategy. *Journal of Marketing*, **68**, 109-27.

Ruth, J.A. and Simonin, B.L. (2003). Brought to you by brand A and brand B. *Journal of Advertising*, **32**(3), 19-30.

Rutherford, D. (2007). In your right mind: a call for the integration of visual literacy in higher education curricula. Unpublished monograph.

Salzer-Morling, M. and Strannegård, L. (2002). Silence of the brands. *European Journal of Marketing*, **38**(1/2), 224-38.

Samu, S., Krishnan, S. and Smith, R.E. (1999). Using advertising alliances for new product introduction: interactions between product complementarity and promotional strategies. *Journal of Marketing*, **63**, 57-74.

Saren, M. (2006). *Marketing Graffiti: The View from the Street*. Oxford: Butterworth-Heinemann.

Sargeant, A. (2005). *Marketing Management for Non-Profit Organizations*, 2nd edition. New York: Oxford University Press.

Saunders, J. (2004). Drowning in choice: the revolution in communications planning. *Market Leader*, **24**, 34-9.

Schechter, A.H. (1993). Measuring the value of corporate and brand logos. *Design Management Journal*, **4**(1), 3-39.

Schembri, S. (2006). Rationalising service logic, or understanding services as experience? *Marketing Theory*, **6**, 381-92.

Schmitt, B.H. (2003). *Customer Experience Management*. New York: John Wiley & Sons, Inc.

Schouten, J. and McAlexander, J. (1995). Subcultures of consumption: an ethnography of the new bikers. *Journal of Consumer Research*, **22**(2), 43-61.

Schramm, W. (1971). The nature of communications between humans. In W. Schramm and D. Roberts (eds), *The Process and Effects of Mass Communications*. Urbana, IL: University of Illinois Press.

Schramm, W. (1997). *The beginnings of communication study in America: A personal memoir.* Thousand Oaks, CA: Sage.

Schroeder, J.E. and Borgerson, J.L. (2003). Dark desires: fetishism, ontology and representation in contemporary advertising. In T. Reichart and J. Lambaise (eds) *Sex in Advertising: Perspectives on the Erotic Appeal.* Manwah, NJ: Erlbaum.

Schroeder, J.E. and Borgerson, J.L. (2005). An ethics of representation for international marketing. *International Marketing Review,* **22**, 578–600.

Schroer, J.C. (1990). Ad spending: growing market share. *Harvard Business Review,* **68**(1), 44–8.

Schudson, M. (2000). Advertising as capitalist realism. *Advertising and Society Review,* **1**(1).

Shultz, D.E. (1999). Integrated marketing communications and how it relates to traditional media advertising. In J.P. Jones (ed.), *The Advertising Business: Operations, Creativity, Media Planning, Integrated Marketing Communications* (pp. 325–38). London: Sage.

Schultz, D.E. (2001). Marketing communication planning in a converging marketplace. *Journal of Integrated Communications,* 2000-2001.

Schultz, D.E., Robinson, W.E. and Petrison, L.A. (1998). *Sales Promotion Essentials: The 10 Basic Sales Promotion Techniques... and How to Use Them,* 3rd edition. Oxford: Elsevier.

Schultz, D.E. and Schultz, H. (2005). *IMC: the Next Generation: Five Steps for Delivering Value and Measuring Returns Using Marketing Communication.* New York: McGraw-Hill.

Schultz, D.E., Tenenbaum, S.I. and Lauterborn, R.F. (1992). *Integrated Marketing Communications: Putting it all Together and Making it Work.* New York: NTC Business Books.

Schultz, D.E., Tenenbaum, S.I. and Lauterborn, R.F. (2004). *The New Marketing Paradigm: Integrated Marketing Communications.* New York: McGraw-Hill.

Schultz, M. (2005). A cross-disciplinary perspective on corporate branding. In M. Schultz, Y.M. Antorini and F.F. Csaba (eds) *Corporate Branding: Purpose, People, Process.* Copenhagen: Copenhagen Business School Press.

Senge, P.M. (1990). *The Fifth Discipline.* New York: Doubleday.

Sengupta, J., Goodstein, R.C. and Boninger, D.S. (1997). All cues are not created equal: obtaining attitude persistence under low involvement conditions. *Journal of Consumer Research,* **23**, 351–61.

Sengupta, S. (2004). *Brand Positioning: Strategies for Competitive Advantage,* 2nd edition. New York: McGraw-Hill.

Severn, J., Belch, G.E. and Belch, M.A. (1990). The effects of sexual and non-sexual advertising appeals and information level on cognitive processing and communication effectiveness. *Journal of Advertising,* **19**(1), 14–22.

Shakar, A. (2001). *The Savage Girl.* London: Simon & Schuster.

Sheehan, J., Bartel, K. and Aibing, G. (2005). Leaving on a (Branded) Jet Plane: An Exploration of Audience Attitudes Towards Product Assimilation. *Journal of Current Issues and Research in Advertising,* **27**(1), 92.

Sheehan, K.B. and Guo, A. (2005). Leaving on a (branded) jet plane: an exploration of audience attitudes towards product assimilation in television content, *Journal of Current Issues and Research in Advertising,* **27**(1), 79–91.

Sherry, J.F. Jr. (2005). Brand meaning. In A.M. Tybout and T. Calkins (eds), *Kellogg on Branding: the Marketing Faculty of the Kellogg School of Management.* New York: John Wiley & Sons, Inc.

Sheth, J.N., Newman, B.I. and Gross, B.L. (1991). Why we buy what we buy: a theory of consumption values. *Journal of Business Research,* **22**, 159–70.

Sheth, J.N. and Shah, R.H. (2003). Till death do us part...but not always: six antecedents to a customer's relational preference in buyer–seller exchanges. *Industrial Marketing Management,* **32**(8), 627–31.

Shimp, T.A. (1991). Neo-Pavlovian conditioning and its implications for consumer theory and research. In T.S. Robertson and H.H. Kassarajian, (eds), *Handbook of Consumer Behaviour.* Upper Saddle, NJ: Prentice Hall.

Shimp, T.A. (1993). *Promotion Management and Marketing Communications.* London: Dryden.

Shimp, T.A. (1997). *Advertising, Promotion and Supplemental Aspects of Integrated Marketing Communications*, 4th edition. Fort Worth, TX: Harcourt Brace.

Shimp, T.A. (2000). *Advertising Promotion*. Fort Worth, TX: Harcourt Brace.

Shimp, T.A. (2008). *Advertising Promotion and Other Aspects of Integrated Marketing Communications*. London: Cengage.

Shocker, A.D., Srivastava, R.K. and Ruekert, R.W. (1994). Challenges and opportunities facing brand management: an introduction to the Special Issue. *Journal of Marketing Research*, 3(2), 149–58.

Shramm, W. (1954). How communication works. In W. Schramm and D. Roberts (eds), *The Process and Effects of Communication*. Illinois: University of Illinois Press.

Simms, C. and Trott, P. (2006). The perceptions of the BMW Mini brand: the importance of historical associations and the development of a model. *Journal of Product and Brand Management*, 15(4), 228–38.

Simms, C. and Trott, P. (2007). An analysis of the repositioning of the BMW Mini brand. *Journal of Product and Brand Management*, 16(5), 297–309.

Simonin, B.L. and Ruth, J.A. (1998). Is a company known by the company it keeps? Assessing the spillover effects of brand alliances on consumer brand attitudes. *Journal of Marketing Research*, 35, 30–42.

Simonson, I. and Tversky, A. (1992). Choice in context: trade-off contrast and extremeness aversion. *Journal of Marketing Research*, 29, 281–95.

Singh, S.N. and Cole, C.A. (1993). The effects of length, content and repetition on television commercial effectiveness. *Journal of Marketing Research*, 30(1), 91–104.

Singh, S.N., Mishra, S., Linville, D. and Sukhdial, A. (1995). Enhancing the efficacy of split thirty-second television commercials: an encoding variability application. *Journal of Advertising*, 24(3), 13–23.

Sjödin, H. and Törn, F. (2007). Ads under attack: consumer responses to activist criticism of outdoor ads. Stockholm School of Economics Working Paper Series.

Smith, G. (2004). Brand image transfer through sponsorship: a consumer learning perspective. *Journal of Marketing Management*, 20, 457–74.

Smith, P.R. and Taylor, J. (2004). *Marketing Communications: An Integrated Approach*. London: Kogan Page.

Smith, P.R., Berry, C. and Pulford, A. (1999). *Strategic Marketing Communications*. London: Kogan Page.

Smith, R.E. (1993). Integrating information from advertising and trial: processes and effects on consumer response to product information. *Journal of Marketing Research*, 30, 204–19.

Smith, T.D. (2007). The existential consumption paradox: an exploration of meaning in marketing. *The Marketing Review*, 7(4), 325–41.

Smith, W. (1956). Product differentiation and market segmentation as alternative marketing strategies. *Journal of Marketing*, 21, 3–8.

Solomon, M., Bambossy, G. and Askegaard, S. (2002). *Consumer Behaviour: A European Perspective*. Harlow: Pearson Education.

Solomon, M., Bambossy, G. and Askegaard, S. (2005). *Consumer Behaviour: A European Perspective*. Harlow: Pearson Education.

Sopanen, B. (1996). Enhancing customer loyalty. *Retail Week*, December, 21–4.

Srivastava, R.K., Shervani, T.A. and Fahey, L. (1998). Market-based assets and shareholder value: a framework for analysis. *Journal of Marketing*, 62, 2–18.

Staab, J.F. (1990). *News Value Theory: Formal Structure and Empirical Content*. Munich: Alber.

Stammerjohan, C., Wood, C.M., Chang, Y. and Thorson, E. (2005). An empirical investigation of the interaction between publicity, advertising, and previous brand attitudes and knowledge. *Journal of Advertising*, 34(4), 55–67.

Strong, E.K. (1925). Theories of selling. *Journal of Applied Psychology*, 9, 75–86.

Styles, C. and Ambler, T. (1995). Brand management. In S. Crainer (ed.), *Financial Times Handbook of Management* (pp. 581–93). London: Pitman.

Sullivan, M. and Adcock, D. (2002). *Retail Marketing*. London: Thomson.

Surmaneck, J. (1995) *Media Planning*. Lincolnwood, IL: NTC.

Szmigin, I. and Carrigan, M. (2000). Does advertising in the UK need older models? *Journal of Product and Brand Management,* **9**(2), 128-41.

Tauber, E.M. (1972). Why do people shop? *Journal of Marketing,* **36**(4), 46-9.

Tayor, R.E. (1999). A six-segment message strategy wheel. *Journal of Advertising Research,* **39**, 7-17.

Tellis, G.J. (1997). Effective frequency: one exposure or three factors? *Journal of Advertising Research,* **37**(4), 75-80.

Theus, K.T. (1994). Subliminal advertising and the psychology of processing unconscious stimuli; a review of research. *Psychology and Marketing,* **11**(3), 271-90.

Thomas, A.R. (2007). The end of mass marketing: or why all successful marketing is now direct marketing. *Direct Marketing: an International Journal,* **1**(1), 6-16.

Thomson, M., Macinnis, D.J. and Park, C.W. (2005). The ties that bind: measuring the strength of consumers' emotional attachment to brands. *Journal of Consumer Psychology,* **15**(1), 77-91.

Till, B.D. (1998). Using celebrity endorsers effectively: lessons from associative learning. *Journal of Product and Brand Management,* **7**(5), 400-7.

Tilley, E. (2005). What's in a name? Everything. The appropriateness of 'public relations' needs for further debate. web journal *Prism,* http://praxis.masseyac.nz.

Timacheff, S. and Rand, D.E. (2001). *From Bricks to Clicks: Five Steps to Creating a Durable Online Brand*. New York: McGraw-Hill.

Tom, G. and Catanescu, C. (2001). Types of Humour in advertising. *Review of Business,* **22**(2), 92-5.

Tversky, A. (1977). Features of similarity. *Psychological Review,* **84**, 327-52.

Tybout, A.M. and Calkins, T. (eds) (2005). *Kellogg on Branding: The Marketing Faculty of the Kellogg School of Management*. New York: John Wiley & Sons, Inc.

Tybout, A.M. and Sternthal, B. (2005). Brand Meaning. In A.M. Tybout and T. Calkins (eds) *Kellogg on Branding: The Marketing Faculty of the Kellogg School of Management*. New York: John Wiley & Sons, Inc.

Tynan, K. (1994). *Multi-channel Marketing: Maximizing Market Share with an Integrated Marketing Strategy*. Danvers, MA: Probus.

Uncles, M.D., Cocks, M. and Macrae, C. (1995). Brand architecture: reconfiguring organisations for effective brand management. *Journal of Brand Management,* **3**(2), 81-92.

Unnava, H.R. and Burnkrant, R.E. (1991). Effects of repeating varied ad executions on brand name memory. *Journal of Marketing Research,* **28**, 406-16.

Usunier, J.-C. and Lee, J. A. (2005). *Marketing Across Cultures*. London: Prentice Hall.

Vakratsas, D. and Ambler, T. (1999). How advertising works: what do we really know? *Journal of Marketing,* **63**(1), 26-43.

Van Raaij, W.F. (1998). Interactive communication and consumer power and initiative. *Journal of Marketing Communications,* **4**(1).

Varadarajan, P.R., Bharadwaj, S.G. and Thirunarayana, P.N. (1991). Attitudes towards marketing practices, consumerism, and government regulations: a study of managers and consumers in an industrializing country. *Journal of International Consumer Marketing,* **4**(1/2), 121-57.

Vargo, S. and Lusch, R.F. (2004). Evolution to a new dominant logic for marketing. *Journal of Marketing,* **62**(1), 12-18.

Vaughan, R. (1986). How advertising works: a planning model revisited. *Journal of Advertising Research,* **26**(1), 57-61.

Veblen, T. (1899). *The Theory of the Leisure Class*. Norwegian-American Society.

Ventkatesh, A. (1999). Postmodernism perspectives for macromarketing: an inquiry into the global information and sign economy. *Journal of Macromarketing,* **19**(12), 2-28.

Veronis Suhler Stevenson (2008) Communications Forecast; IBM analysis, March 2009.

Vezina, R. and Paul, O. (1997). Provocation in advertising: a conceptualisation and an empirical assessment. *International Journal of Research in Marketing,* **14**(2), 177-92.

Vincent, L. (2002). *Legendary Brands: Unleashing the Power of Storytelling to Create a Winning Strategy*. London: Kaplan.

Volckner, F. and Sattler, H. (2006). Drivers of brand extension success. *Journal of Marketing*, **70**, 18-34.

Voss, K.E., Spangenberg, E.R. and Grohmann, B. (2003). Measuring the hedonic and utilitarian dimension of consumer attitude. *Journal of Marketing Research*, **40**, 310-20.

Walker, R. (2004). The hidden (in plain sight) persuaders. *New York Times Magazine*, p.68.

Wang, A. (2006). Advertising engagement: a driver of message involvement on message effects. *Journal of Advertising Research*, **46**, 355-69.

Wang, S.-L.A. and Nelson, R.A. (2006). The effects of identical versus varied advertising and publicity messages on consumer response. *Journal of Marketing Communications*, **12**(2), 109-23.

Weaver, W. and Shannon, C.E. (1963). *The Mathematical Theory of Communication*. Illinois: University of Illinois Press.

Weber, L. (2007). *Marketing to the Social Web*. New York: John Wiley & Sons, Inc.

Weilbacher, W.L. (2003). How advertising affects consumers. *Journal of Advertising Research*, **43**, 230-4.

Whelan, S. and Wohlfeil, M. (2006). Communicating brands through engagement with lived experiences. *Journal of Brand Management*, **13**(4/5), 313-29.

Williams, G. (2000). *Branded? Products and Their Personalities*. London: VandA Publications.

Winchester, M., Romaniuk, J. and Bogonolova, S. (2008). Positive and negative brand beliefs and brand defection/uptake. *European Journal of Marketing*, **2**(5/6), 553-70.

Woolf, B.P. (1996). *Customer Specific Marketing*. New York: Teal Books.

World Health Organisation (2002). *World Report on Violence and Health*. Geneva: World Health Organisation.

Worthington, S. (1998). The loyalty table. *Customer Loyalty Today*, April.

Wulf, K., Odekerken-Schroeder, G. and Iacobucci, D. (2001). Investments in customer relationships: a cross-country and cross-industry exploration. *Journal of Marketing*, **65**(4), 33-50.

Yahoo and OMD (2006). It's a family affair: the media evolution of global family in the digital age. *Advertising Week*.

Yang, S., Allenby, G.M. and Fennell, G. (2002). Modelling variation in brand preference: the roles of objective environment and motivating conditions. *Marketing Science*, **21**(1), 14-31.

Yeshin, T. (2006). *Advertising*. London: Thomson.

Yeshin, T. (2007). Integrated marketing communications. In M.J. Baker and S.J. Hart (eds), *The Marketing Book*. Oxford: Butterworth-Heinemann.

Yin, H.S., Zhao, X. and An, S. (2006). Examining effects of advertising campaign publicity in a field study. *Journal of Advertising Research*, **46**, 171-82.

Yoo, B. and Mandhachitara, R. (2003). Estimating advertising effects on sales in a competitive setting. *Journal of Advertising Research*, **43**(3), 310-21.

Youn, S., Sun, T., Wells, W.D. and Zhao, X. (2001). Commercial liking and memory: moderating effects of product categories. *Journal of Advertising Research*, **41**(3), 7-14.

Zaichkowsky, J.L. (1994). The personal involvement inventory: reduction, revision, and application to advertising. *Journal of Advertising*, **23**(4), 59-70.

Zaltman, G. (2003). *How Customers Think: Essential Insights into the Mind of the Market*. Cambridge, MA: Harvard Business School Press.

Zaltman, G. and Zaltman, L. (2008). *Marketing Metaphoria: What Deep Metaphors Reveal About the Minds of Consumers*. Cambridge, MA: Harvard Business School Press.

Zeithaml, C.P. and Zeithaml, V.A. (1984). Environmental management – revising the marketing perspective. *Journal of Marketing*, **48**, 33-46.

Zhang, S., Kardes, F. R. and Cronley, M. L. (2002). Comparative advertising: effects of structural alignability on target brand evaluations. *Journal of Consumer Psychology*, **12**(40), 303-11.

Index